한 권으로 끝내는

스파르타 토익 750+

NEW EDITION

LC & RC

김수현 · 최영근 지음

English& 북스

한 권으로 끝내는

스파르타 토익 750+
LC&RC
NEW EDITION

초판 1쇄 발행 2022년 12월 7일
초판 3쇄 발행 2024년 12월 9일

지은이	김수현, 최영근
펴낸이	박성호
펴낸곳	잉글리쉬앤 (주)
편 집	박고우니, 장서원
영업마케팅	여주형, 김성윤, 방성출, 박훈효, 조민형, 이달님, 강정구, 이진희, 조병운, 조예선, 이현정, 조광민, 노희동, 김정민, 최희성, 최인태, 윤종철, 엄주아 신현수, 오지현, 최유미, 최가연, 김정호, 안혜연, 조승채
주 소	서울 특별시 관악구 쑥고개로 67-1
대표전화	(02) 878-1945
출판등록	2002년 3월 3일 제 320-2002-00045호

ISBN 978-89-6715-154-6 13740

저작권자 2024 잉글리쉬앤(주)
이 책은 잉글리쉬앤(주)에 의해 출간되었으므로
저자와 출판사의 서면에 의한 허락 없이 글과 그림의 인용, 복제, 발췌를 금합니다.

* 가격은 뒤표지에 있습니다. 파본은 바꾸어 드립니다.

www.english.co.kr

Preface

스파르타 토익 750+ LC&RC 개정판을 내면서

토익 중급서 **스파르타 토익 750+ LC&RC**가 새롭게 개정판으로 출간되었습니다.

어떻게 하면 단기간에 토익 목표 점수에 도달할 수 있을까? 토익을 공부하는 모든 수험생들의 한결같은 고민일 것입니다.

이미 많은 고득점자들이 증명한 대로, 토익은 기본기가 무엇보다 중요하고 단기간에 집중적으로 학습해서 끝내야 합니다. 또한 출제 유형이 정해져 있고 이 유형들이 반복해서 출제되기 때문에 마구잡이식 학습이 아닌, 실제로 나오는 유형만 선별하여 학습하는 것이 고득점의 관건이라고 할 수 있습니다.

스파르타 토익 750+ LC&RC 개정판은 기출 문제를 기반으로, 학습자가 효율적으로 토익 목표 점수에 도달할 수 있도록 가이드라인을 제시하는 종합 중급서입니다. 본 교재에는 저자진이 다년간 현장에서 집중 훈련을 통해 고득점자를 배출한 전략 및 노하우가 모두 응축되어 있습니다. 또한, 영어의 기본기를 다지고 효과적으로 학습할 수 있도록 토익 유형을 완벽 분석하여, 이에 맞는 문제 풀이 전략과 다양한 연습 문제들로 구성하였습니다.

토익 목표 점수가 나오지 않아 정체기를 겪는 학습자들을 위해, **스파르타 토익 750+ LC&RC 개정판**이 고득점으로 향하는 지름길을 제시하겠습니다.

Contents

토익 소개 ·· 8
파트별 유형 및 전략 ································ 10

PART 1 · 사진 묘사

| PART 1 접근법 ··· 20
| **DAY 01** | 인물 등장 사진 ···························· 21
| **DAY 02** | 사물/풍경 사진 ···························· 25

PART 2 · 질의 응답

| PART 2 접근법 ··· 34
| **DAY 03** | Who/When/Where 의문문 ········ 35
| **DAY 04** | What&Which/How/Why 의문문 ···· 40
| **DAY 05** | 일반/부정/부가 의문문 ············· 45
| **DAY 06** | 제안/요청문 ······························· 50
| **DAY 07** | 선택의문문/평서문 ···················· 54

PART 3 · 대화문

| PART 3 접근법 ··· 60
| **DAY 08** | 주제/목적, 장소/직업 ················ 61
| **DAY 09** | 이유&세부 사항/문제점 ············ 66
| **DAY 10** | 요청&제안/다음에 할 일 ·········· 71
| **DAY 11** | 의도 파악/시각 자료 ················· 76

PART 4 · 담화문

| PART 4 접근법 ··· 88
| **DAY 12** | 광고/방송 ·································· 89
| **DAY 13** | 전화 메시지 ······························· 93
| **DAY 14** | 안내/공지 ·································· 97
| **DAY 15** | 회의/소개 ·································· 101

PART 5&6 · 단문/장문 채우기

PART 5&6 접근법	116
DAY 01 명사와 대명사	118
DAY 02 형용사와 부사	126
DAY 03 전치사	134
DAY 04 부사절 접속사	142
DAY 05 동사의 5형식	150
DAY 06 수 일치와 태	158
DAY 07 동사의 시제와 가정법	166
DAY 08 to부정사와 동명사	174
DAY 09 분사	182
DAY 10 명사절과 형용사절	190

PART 7 · 독해

PART 7 접근법	200
DAY 11 주제/목적 찾기 유형	203
DAY 12 세부사항 및 추론 유형	212
DAY 13 문장 넣기 유형	222
DAY 14 의도 파악 및 유의어 유형	230
DAY 15 다중 지문 유형	244

실전 모의고사 ······ 258
(OMR 답안지 및 해설 PDF 온라인 제공 https://books.english.co.kr)

정답 및 해설 ······ 300

이 책의 구성과 특징

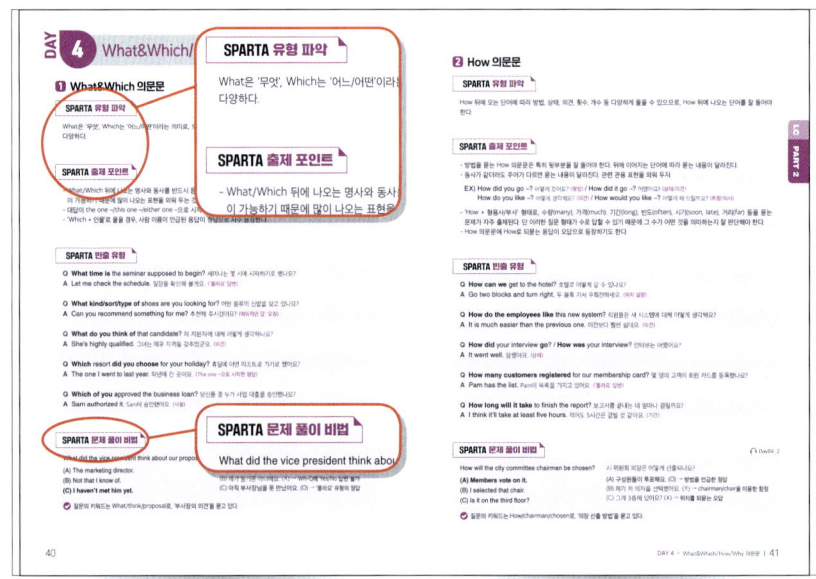

개념 및 유형 익히기
파트 별 유형 및 출제 포인트를 학습한 후, 문제 풀이 비법을 통해 유형 전략을 이해한다.

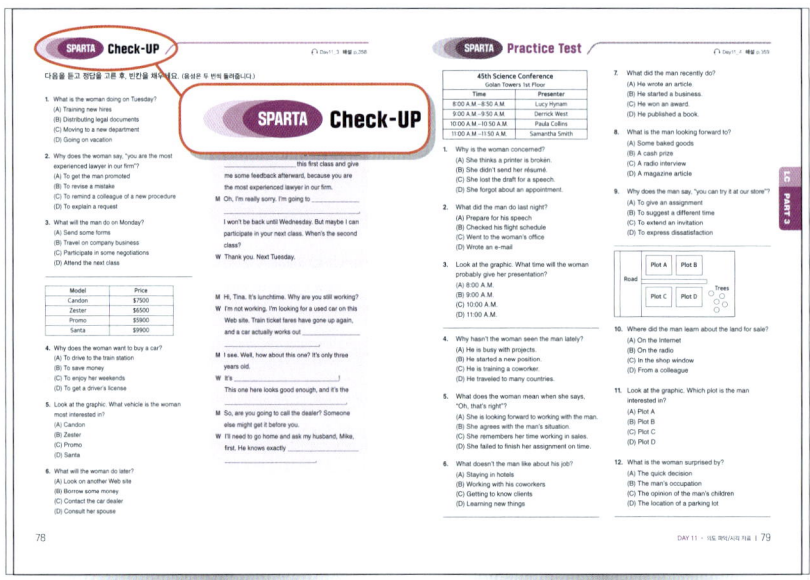

연습 문제 풀이
앞서 학습한 개념을 토대로, Check-Up 문제에 적용해 보면서 문제 풀이 접근법을 익힌다.

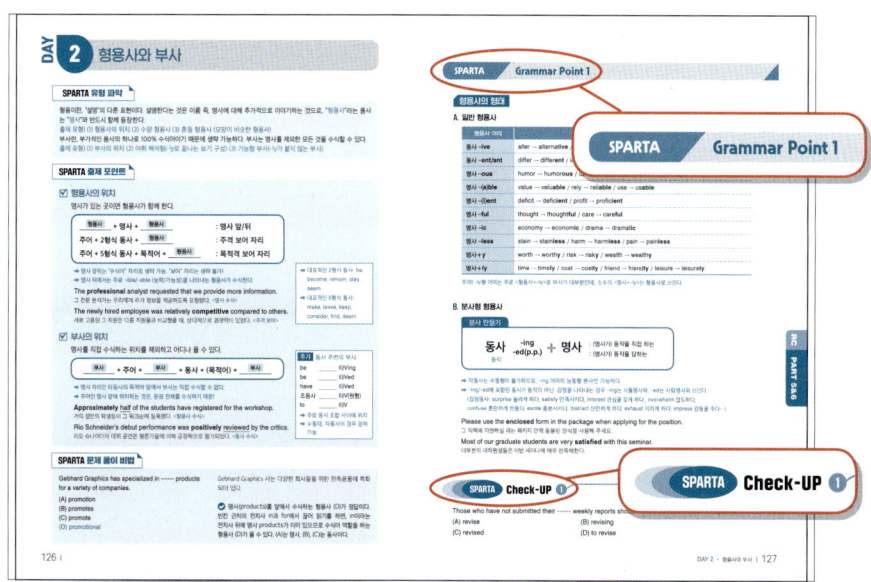

문법 개념 익히기
토익 RC와 직결되는 Grammar Point로 문법 개념을 익힌 후, Check-Up 문제를 통해 학습한 내용을 점검한다.

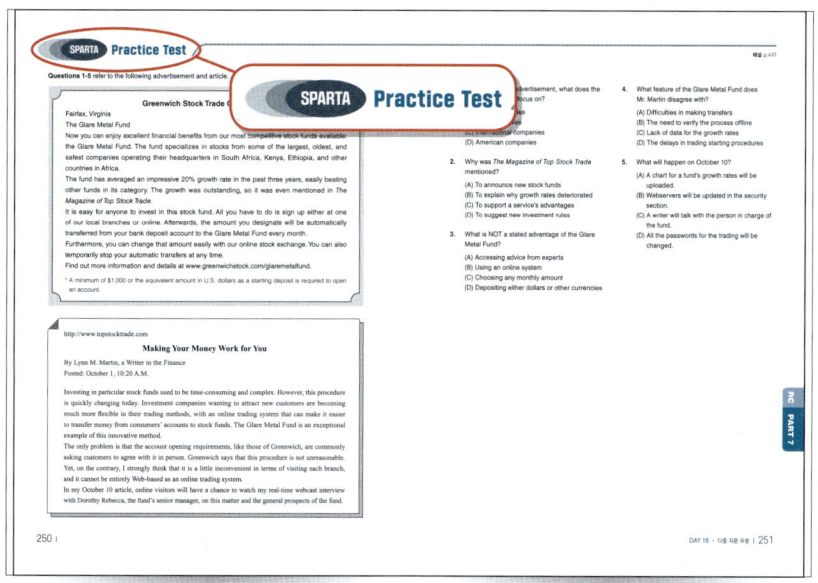

실전 감각 익히기
토익 기출을 변형한 Practice Test를 풀어 보면서 앞서 학습한 내용을 정리한다.

토익 소개

토익이란?

Test Of English for International Communication의 약자로, 영어가 모국어가 아닌 사람들의 일상생활이나 국제 업무 등에 필요한 실용 영어 능력을 평가하는 국제 평가 시험

| 시험 구성 |

구성	Part	유형		문항 수	시간	배점
듣기(LC)	1	사진 묘사		6	100	45분	495점
	2	질의 응답		25			
	3	대화문		39			
	4	담화문		30			
읽기(RC)	5	단문 공란 채우기		30	100	75분	495점
	6	장문 공란 채우기		16			
	7	지문 독해	단일 지문	29			
			복수 지문	25			
TOTAL	7 Parts			200문항	120분	990점

| 시험 내용 |

Part	유형	유형 내용
1	사진 묘사	제시된 사진을 알맞게 설명하는 보기 고르기
2	질의 응답	질문을 듣고 알맞은 대답 고르기
3	대화문	대화를 듣고 질문에 알맞은 내용 고르기
4	담화문	담화를 듣고 질문에 알맞은 내용 고르기
5	단문 공란 채우기	빈칸에 맞는 내용을 골라 단문 완성하기
6	장문 공란 채우기	빈칸에 맞는 내용을 골라 장문 완성하기
7	지문 독해	단일 지문 또는 이중·삼중 지문을 읽고 문제에 맞는 내용 고르기

접수 방법은?

▶ 한국 토익 위원회 사이트 혹은 앱으로 접수 ➜ www.toeic.co.kr
▶ 인터넷 접수할 때 시험일, 고사장, 개인 정보 등을 입력 (증명사진 필요)
　※ 접수 마감일 이후 추가 접수일에 접수 시 추가 비용 발생

응시 준비물은?

▶ 규정 신분증 (주민등록증, 운전면허증, 기간 만료 전의 여권, 공무원증, 중고등학생의 경우 국내 학생증 인정)
▶ 연필, 지우개 (볼펜이나 사인펜은 사용 금지)

시험 진행은?

▶ **시험 시간이 오전일 경우** 오전 9:20까지 입실 (오전 9:50 이후 입실 불가)
▶ **시험 시간이 오후일 경우** 오후 2:20까지 입실 (오후 2:50 이후 입실 불가)

오전 시험	오후 시험	시험 진행
오전 9:30 ~ 9:45 (15분)	오후 2:30 ~ 2:45 (15분)	답안지 작성에 관한 오리엔테이션
오전 9:45 ~ 9:50 (5분)	오후 2:45 ~ 2:50 (5분)	휴식 시간
오전 9:50 ~ 10:05 (15분)	오후 2:50 ~ 3:05 (15분)	신분증 확인
오전 10:05 ~ 10:10 (5분)	오후 3:05 ~ 3:10 (5분)	문제지 배부, 파본 확인
오전 10:10 ~ 10:55 (45분)	오후 3:10 ~ 3:55 (45분)	듣기 평가(LC)
오전 10:55 ~ 12:10 (75분)	오후 3:55 ~ 5:10 (75분)	읽기 평가(RC)

※ 읽기 평가(RC) 시간에 2차 신분 확인 실시

성적 확인은?

▶ 시험일로부터 10~11일 후에 토익 위원회 사이트(www.toeic.co.kr)와 ARS로 확인 가능
▶ 온라인 출력과 우편 수령은 1회 무료, 이후에는 유료 발급
▶ 성적은 시험일로부터 2년간 유효

파트별 유형 및 전략

 사진 묘사 | 6문제 |

파트 1은 4개의 보기 중에서 사진을 가장 잘 묘사하는 보기를 고르는 유형이다. 총 6문제가 출제되며, 인물 및 사물/풍경 사진 등 다양한 유형의 사진이 등장한다.

핵심 전략

- 사진 유형별로 자주 출제되는 어휘와 표현을 익힌다.
- 난이도가 높은 경우 주어가 사물인 보기가 자주 등장하므로 수동태, 현재완료 수동태, 수동태 진행형과 같은 문법을 완벽하게 숙지한다.
- 오답 소거법을 통해, 사진을 완벽하게 묘사한 보기가 아닌 정답에 가장 가까운 Best Answer를 고르도록 훈련한다.
- 유사 발음, 연상 어휘 등을 이용하거나, 사람과 사물의 상태 및 동작을 잘못 묘사하는 오답이 자주 등장한다.

문제 형태

1

Look at the picture marked number one in your test book.

(A) She is cleaning her desk.
(B) She is sharpening a pencil.
(C) She is filing some papers.
(D) She is holding a phone.

PART 2

질의 응답 | 25문제 |

파트 2는 3개의 보기 중에서 질문에 가장 적절한 응답을 고르는 유형이다. 문항 수는 총 25개로, 의문사 의문문, Yes/No 의문문 등이 출제된다.

핵심 전략

- 질문의 앞부분을 집중해서 듣고 질문 유형을 파악하는 연습을 한다.
- 의문사 의문문은 가장 자주 출제되는 유형으로, 답변 패턴이 정해져 있다. 의문사별로 정답 유형을 숙지해 두자.
- 평서문은 답변 패턴이 정해져 있지 않아서 어렵게 느껴질 수 있다. 오답 소거법을 이용하여 보기 중 가장 적절한 응답을 고르는 훈련이 필요하다.
- 유사 발음 어휘, 질문의 단어 반복 등을 이용한 보기가 오답으로 자주 등장하므로 이를 주의하여 정답을 골라야 한다.

문제 형태

7 Mark your answer on your answer sheet.

How much longer do you need on this project?

(A) About ten pages long.
(B) Roughly half an hour.
(C) The project was successful.

PART 3

대화문 | 39문제 |

파트 3는 2~3명이 나누는 대화를 듣고 이와 관련된 3개의 문제를 푸는 유형이다. 총 39문제가 출제되며, 3인 대화가 1~2세트 출제된다. 화자 의도 파악 문제와 시각 자료 연계 문제는 각각 2~3세트 출제된다.

핵심 전략

- 대화를 듣기 전에 문제를 먼저 읽고, 키워드를 파악한 후 그 부분을 집중적으로 듣는 훈련을 하자.
- 첫 번째 문제는 주로 주제나 장소, 신분에 관한 문제로, 정답의 단서가 대화 초반에 나오므로 처음 부분을 놓치지 않고 들어야 한다.
- 화자 의도 파악 문제는 먼저 제시된 표현을 확인하고, 음성을 들으면서 해당 표현이 나올 때까지 문맥을 정확히 파악해야 한다.
- 시각 자료 문제는 미리 도표를 읽고 지문의 내용을 예측해 본다. 또한, 시각 자료와 음성을 연계하여 정보를 파악하는 능력을 길러야 한다.
- 3인 대화에서 화자는 국적에 따라 발음이 구분되므로, 미국, 영국, 호주 등의 다양한 발음에 익숙해지도록 연습한다.

문제 형태

32 What does the woman imply when she says, "I got one for my friend"?

(A) She is inviting the man to meet her friend.
(B) Her friend is the same size with his wife.
(C) She is willing to pay for the product.
(D) She is emphasizing it's a good product.

Questions 32 through 34 refer to the following conversation.

M: Hi, I'm looking for a birthday present for my wife. I think she'd like one of these sweaters, but do you have any in a smaller size?
W: I'm pretty sure everything we have is out here on the display table. But I can check the stockroom in the back if you'd like.
M: Thanks, that'll be great. You know they look perfect for early spring. Light, but warm. You can wear them indoors or outdoors.
W: That's right. I got one for my friend who wears it a lot, so I'm sure your wife would love one. And we're selling them for 30% off this week.
M: That's good to know. I hope you have one in my wife's size.

PART 4

담화문 | 30문제 |

파트 4는 담화를 듣고 이와 관련된 3개의 문제를 푸는 유형이다. 총 30문항이 출제되며, 녹음 메시지나 공지, 뉴스 등이 주로 출제된다. 파트 3와 마찬가지로, 화자 의도 파악 문제와 시각 자료 연계 문제가 2~3세트씩 출제된다.

핵심 전략

- 담화를 듣기 전에 문제를 먼저 읽고, 키워드를 파악한 후 그 부분을 집중적으로 듣는 훈련을 하자.
- 첫 번째 문제는 주로 주제나 장소, 신분에 관한 문제로, 정답의 단서가 담화 초반에 나오므로 처음 부분을 놓치지 않고 들어야 한다.
- 화자 의도 파악 문제는 파트 3와 달리 한 사람의 담화이므로 문맥의 흐름을 더 쉽게 파악할 수 있다. 따라서 담화의 전반적인 문맥 흐름을 이해하고, 해당 문장의 앞뒤 상황을 정확히 파악하는 훈련을 하자.
- 시각 자료 문제는 미리 도표를 읽고 지문의 내용을 예측해 본다. 또한, 시각 자료와 음성을 연계하여 정보를 파악하는 능력을 길러야 한다.

문제 형태

Tour Schedule	
Garden Tour	10:00 A.M.
Lunch	Noon
Museum Visit	1:30 P.M.
Theater Performance	4:00 P.M.

98 Look at the graphic. What time is this talk most likely being given?

(A) At 10:00 A.M.
(B) At noon
(C) At 1:30 P.M.
(D) At 4:00 P.M.

Questions 98 through 100 refer to the following talk and schedule.

Can I have everyone's attention at the front of the bus? I hope you enjoyed your lunch at Restaurant Baron. As I mentioned earlier, it first opened in 1880 and has been operating longer than any other restaurants in Charlestown. Now, if you look out the window on your right, you'll see the National Museum of History and according to our schedule, we're right on time. We'll be spending about 2 hours here. I'll pass out the brochures with the information about the permanent and temporary exhibits you'll be seeing today. We'll meet again at the main entrance at 3:30 for our next schedule. Enjoy yourselves.

PART 5 단문 공란 채우기 | 30문제 |

파트 5는 문장 안에 있는 빈칸에 적절한 단어나 어구를 채워 넣는 유형이다. 총 30문항이 출제되며, 문법 문제와 어휘 문제가 등장한다. 문제 유형에 따라 풀이 방식이 다르므로 이를 가장 먼저 파악하는 것이 중요하다.

핵심 전략

- 문제를 풀기 전, 보기를 통해 문제 유형을 파악하는 연습을 한다.
- 문법 문제는 문장 구조나 빈칸 주변의 문법을 통해 문제를 풀어야 한다. 문법 문제를 단시간에 풀기 위해서 명사, 동사, 형용사 등의 기본적인 문법 규칙을 확실히 익혀 두자.
- 어휘 문제는 해석을 통해 문맥에 가장 적절한 단어를 선택해야 한다. 가능한 한 많은 어휘와 표현을 암기하고, 예문을 통해 어휘가 어떻게 사용되는지까지 익혀 두자.
- 자주 함께 쓰이는 단어 및 표현을 숙지하여 빠른 시간 내에 푸는 것이 관건이다.

문제 형태

101 Sky Motors offers a variety of training programs to help enhance ------- in the workplace.

(A) productivity
(B) produce
(C) productive
(D) productively

102 The fundraising event recorded such high ------- that the proceeds will be higher than expected.

(A) representative
(B) consultation
(C) safety
(D) attendance

PART 6

장문 공란 채우기 | 16문제 |

파트 6는 지문 안에 있는 4개의 빈칸에 알맞은 보기를 선택하는 유형이다. 문법, 어휘, 문장을 넣는 문제가 등장하며, 총 16문항이 출제된다. 문맥에 맞는 문장을 고르는 문제는 각 지문마다 1개씩 출제된다.

핵심 전략

+ 전체 문맥을 이해해야 풀 수 있는 문법 및 어휘 문제가 나오므로 지문의 흐름을 놓치지 않는 것이 중요하다.
+ 빈칸에 알맞은 문장을 넣는 문제는 빈칸 앞뒤와 전체 맥락을 파악하여 정답을 골라야 하므로 독해력을 꾸준히 길러야 한다.
+ 문장 삽입 유형은 지문을 읽으며 앞뒤 흐름상 자연스러운 내용을 예측하면 정답을 쉽게 찾을 수 있다.

문제 형태

Questions 135-138 refer to the following notice.

Important Notice about Hatter Industries

Please note that the contact information for Hatter Industries changed on March 21. Due to the closure of our Dabbley office and the ------- of our operations in Buena,
                                                              135
all correspondence concerning our products and services should now be sent to the following address: Hatter Industries, 642 Mandela Lane, Buena, CA.

Our employees' e-mail addresses, as well as our Web site's address, www.hatterindustries.com, remain -------.
                                                  136
However, we are still waiting for our new telephone and fax numbers. ------- will be
                                                                      137
updated on our Web site as soon as the new numbers are assigned as of March 25.

-------.
138

---

135 (A) decision
(B) relocation
(C) suspension
(D) result

136 (A) assigned
(B) even
(C) formal
(D) unchanged

137 (A) Yours
(B) Another
(C) These
(D) Theirs

138 (A) We apologize for any inconvenience and thank you for your understanding.
(B) Refer to the side of the packet for full details of instructions before applying.
(C) Her office location will also remain the same.
(D) For more information about the forthcoming event, visit www.lizard.org.br/events.

PART 7

지문 독해 | 54문제 |

파트 7은 지문을 읽고 지문과 관련된 문제 2~5개를 푸는 유형이다. 총 54문항이 출제되며, 편지, 문자 메시지, 광고, 공지문 등 다양한 유형의 지문이 나온다. 단일 지문 10개, 이중 지문 2개, 삼중 지문 3개의 세트가 등장한다.

핵심 전략

+ 지문의 종류와 제목, 키워드를 파악하여 내용을 미리 예측하고 정답 단서를 찾는다.
+ 지문의 정답 단서가 보기에서는 다르게 패러프레이징될 수 있으므로, 단어를 암기할 때 동의 표현을 함께 익힌다.
+ 복수 지문에서는 2개 이상의 지문을 연계하여 풀어야 하는 문제들이 출제되므로, 지문 간의 관계를 파악하는 연습을 해야 한다.

문제 형태

Questions 162-164 refer to the following advertisement.

ACCOUNT SERVICE DIRECTOR WANTED

A leading financial service bank is looking for an account services director. —[1]—. He or she will be responsible for reclassifying income payment to ensure the accurate reporting of tax payments. —[2]—. Validating tax related information, determining reclassification amounts, processing reclassifications using various internal systems, and performing quality-control checks relevant to all tax-reporting processes will be some of the other responsibilities. —[3]—. In order to qualify, the candidate must have a college degree and previous tax or brokerage experience along with strong analytical skills. —[4]—.

If you are interested, please send your résumé to:

Rosabeth Moss Kanter / Lawrence Financial, Inc.
985, Andrew Park Avenue / Houston, TX 48954

---

162 What position is being advertised?

(A) Public official
(B) Real estate agent
(C) Accountant
(D) Financial consultant

163 Which of the following is required for the position?

(A) Communication skills
(B) A license approved by a related organization
(C) Background knowledge of Lawrence Financial, Inc.
(D) A college education

164 In which of the positions marked [1], [2], [3], and [4] does the following sentence best belong?

"They must also be able to work overtime and weekends when required."

(A) [1]
(B) [2]
(C) [3]
(D) [4]

학습 플랜

2주 플랜

		Day 1	Day 2	Day 3	Day 4	Day 5
Week 1	LC	DAY 1&2	DAY 3&4	DAY 5&6	DAY 7&8	DAY 9&10
	RC	DAY 1&2	DAY 3&4	DAY 5&6	DAY 7&8	DAY 9&10
Week 2	LC	DAY 11	DAY 12	DAY 13	DAY 14	DAY 15
	RC	DAY 11	DAY 12	DAY 13	DAY 14	DAY 15

4주 플랜

		Day 1	Day 2	Day 3	Day 4	Day 5
Week 1	LC	DAY 1	DAY 2	D1~2 REVIEW	DAY 3	DAY 4
	RC	DAY 1	DAY 2	DAY 3	DAY 4	DAY 5
Week 2	LC	DAY 5	DAY 6	DAY 7	D3~7 REVIEW	DAY 8
	RC	D1~5 REVIEW	DAY 6	DAY 7	DAY 8	DAY 9
Week 3	LC	DAY 9	DAY 10	DAY 11	D8~11 REVIEW	DAY 12
	RC	DAY 10	D6~10 REVIEW	DAY 11	DAY 12	D11~12 REVIEW
Week 4	LC	DAY 13	D12~13 REVIEW	DAY 14	DAY 15	D14~15 REVIEW
	RC	DAY 13	DAY 14	D13~14 REVIEW	DAY 15	D15 REVIEW

스파르타 토익
750+
LC

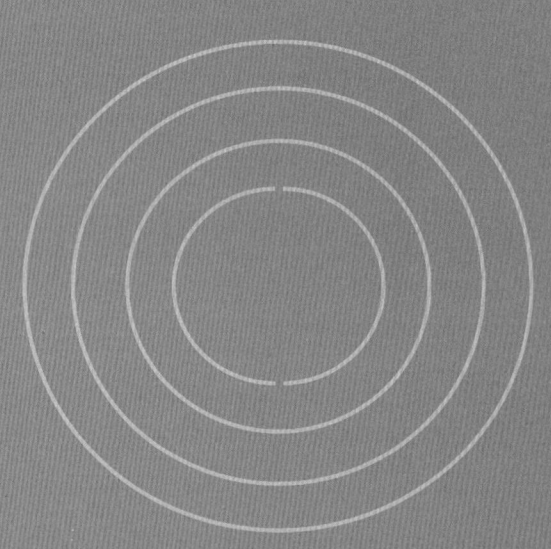

PART 1
사진 묘사

PART 1 접근법
DAY 01 | 인물 등장 사진
DAY 02 | 사물/풍경 사진

PART 1 접근법

PART 1은 (A), (B), (C), (D) 4개의 보기 중 사진을 가장 잘 묘사한 것을 고르는 문제로, 상황 분석 능력을 평가하는 파트이다.

문제 풀이 전략

1. 총 6문제 중, 난이도 높은 문제들이 1~2문제 정도 출제되므로 빈출 오답 유형에 익숙해져야 한다.
2. 음원을 듣기 전에 사진을 미리 관찰하면서 빈출 표현을 연상하는 연습을 해야 한다. 사진은 크게 두 가지 유형으로 구분되는데, 사람 중심 사진과 사물 중심 사진이 있다. 사진에 따라 자주 출제되는 표현을 외워 두면 예상 표현이 나왔을 때 정답 선택이 훨씬 쉬워진다.
3. 눈은 사진에 집중한 상태에서 음원을 들어야 한다. 혹시 보기 중 답으로 선택하기 애매한 것이 있다면 일단 보류하고 끝까지 듣자. 나머지 보기가 명확한 오답이라면 애매한 보기가 정답이 될 수 있다. 이를 소거법이라고 한다.
4. 현재형과 함께 현재 진행 수동형(be + being + p.p.)을 꼭 익히자! 인물 등장 사진에서는 사람의 동작을 표현하지만 사물 사진에서는 오답 보기에 자주 나온다.

오답 유형

- 사진 속에 보이지 않는 사물이 나온 오답
- 사람의 동작과 맞지 않는 오답
- 추상적인 표현의 오답
- 사물의 상태나 위치를 잘못 나타낸 오답
- 사물 사진에서 현재 진행 수동형(be + being + p.p.)은 대부분 오답
- 유사 발음과 혼동하기 쉬운 어휘가 포함된 오답

1.

(A) Passengers are using the ramp to board a ship. (X) 배에 타려는 승객 없음.
(B) Some people are holding the railings. (O) 난간을 잡고 있는 사람 있음.
(C) Some people are tying up a boat at the dock. (X) 배는 이미 묶여 있는 상태.
(D) A boat is sailing on the water. (X) 배는 현재 정박해 있음.

DAY 1 인물 등장 사진

SPARTA 유형 파악

인물 등장 사진은 1인 또는 2인 이상의 인물, 사람&사물 혼합 사진이 등장하며 보통 4문제 이상 출제된다. 주로 사람의 동작과 상태 중심으로 묘사되고, 2인 이상 사진은 등장인물들의 동작과 상태의 공통점과 차이점을 파악해야 한다. 사람&사물 혼합 사진은 눈에 띄는 인물 및 사물의 동작/상태를 유심히 살펴보자. 사진 유형은 과거나 미래 시제를 표현할 수 없기 때문에 현재 진행(be + V-ing), 현재 진행 수동태(be + being + p.p.) 또는 현재 완료(have + p.p.) 등의 여러 현재 시제 형태로 제시된다.

SPARTA 출제 포인트

- 사람의 동작과 상태(옷차림)를 먼저 꼼꼼히 살피고 주변의 배경을 확인하자. 오히려 사람의 모습보다 주변 배경 요소가 정답으로 나오는 경우가 많다.
- 2인 이상 사진은 사진 속 인물들의 공통점과 차이점을 정확히 파악하자.
- 사진 속 묘사 요소가 다양하기 때문에 특정 정답을 정해 놓고 기다리지 말고 오답을 소거하면서 푸는 게 유리하다.
- 인물의 동작을 나타내는 현재 진행형(be + V-ing)과 현재 진행 수동태형(be + being + p.p.)을 익혀 두자.

[예제]

✔ A man **is sweeping** the pavement. 남자가 포장도로를 쓸고 있다. (능동태)
✔ The pavement **is being swept**. (수동태)

SPARTA 문제 풀이 비법

🎧 Day01_1

(A) They're looking at a performer.
그들은 연주자를 보고 있다. (X)
→ 연주자가 아니라 발표자를 보고 있다.

(B) A woman is pointing to the chart.
여자가 차트를 가리키고 있다. (X)
→ 차트를 가리키고 있는 여자는 보이지 않는다.

(C) A man is giving a presentation.
남자는 발표를 하고 있다. (O)
→ 사진과 일치하는 정답.

(D) They're having a meeting outside.
그들은 밖에서 회의하고 있다. (X)
→ 배경은 야외가 아닌 실내.

✅ 여러 사람들이 회의하는 모습의 사진이다. 한 남자가 앞에 서서 발표하고 있고 나머지 사람들은 그의 발표를 듣고 있다. 인물 간의 차이점을 인식하고 주어/동사를 잘 포착하자.

SPARTA Check-UP

Day01_2 해설 p.300

다음을 듣고 사진을 가장 잘 묘사한 문장을 고른 후, 빈칸을 채우세요. (음성은 두 번씩 들려줍니다.)

1.

(A) He's _____ with other people.
(B) He's _____.
(C) He's _____.
(D) He's _____.

(A) (B) (C) (D)

2.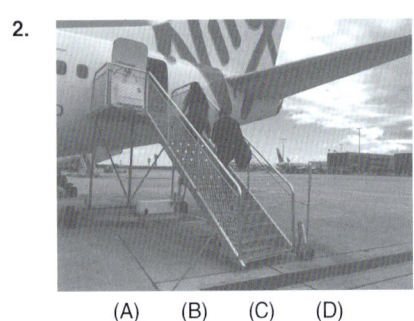

(A) They're _____ the aircraft.
(B) They're _____.
(C) They're _____ the stairs.
(D) They're _____ into the truck.

(A) (B) (C) (D)

3.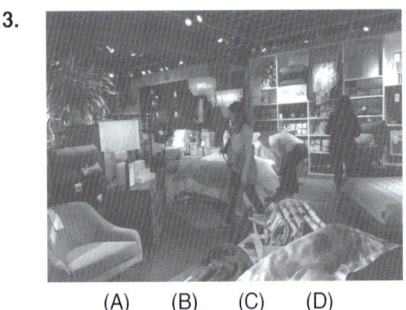

(A) _____ items.
(B) _____ on a bed.
(C) Customers are _____ at the cash register.
(D) An armchair is _____ a drawer.

(A) (B) (C) (D)

4.

(A) There are many people _____.
(B) A woman is _____ on the board.
(C) A vendor is _____.
(D) A cooking demonstration _____.

(A) (B) (C) (D)

SPARTA Practice Test

Day01_3 해설 p.301

1.

(A)   (B)   (C)   (D)

2.

(A)   (B)   (C)   (D)

3.

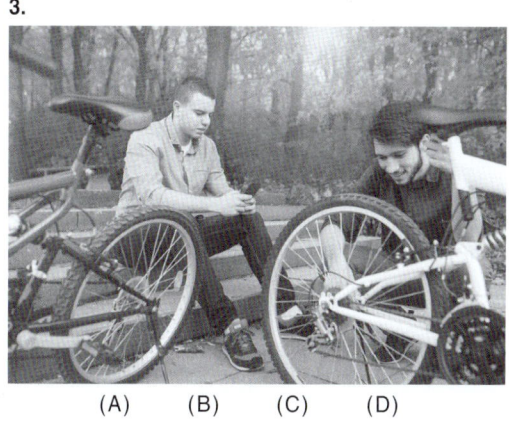

(A)   (B)   (C)   (D)

4.

(A)   (B)   (C)   (D)

5.

(A)   (B)   (C)   (D)

6.

(A)   (B)   (C)   (D)

DAY 1 • 인물 등장 사진 | 23

7.

(A)　　(B)　　(C)　　(D)

9.

(A)　　(B)　　(C)　　(D)

8.

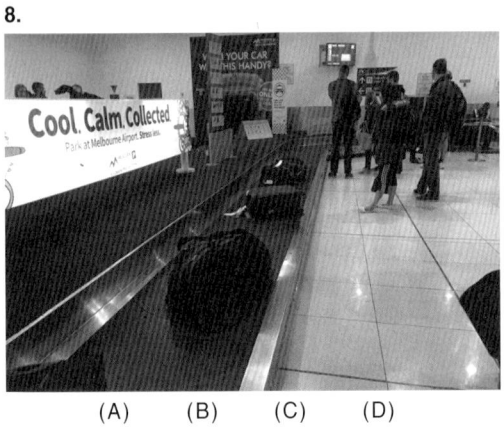

(A)　　(B)　　(C)　　(D)

10.

(A)　　(B)　　(C)　　(D)

DAY 2 사물/풍경 사진

SPARTA 유형 파악

사물/풍경 사진은 매회 1~2개 정도 출제되며, 전반적으로 난이도가 높은 편이다. 사물/풍경의 위치와 상태를 미리 파악하고 주어부터 잘 포착해야 한다. 동사 시제로는 수동태(be + p.p.)와 현재완료 수동태(have been + p.p.)가 주로 쓰이며, 사람과 관련된 표현이나 현재 진행 수동태(be + being + p.p.) 표현은 오답으로 자주 출제된다.

SPARTA 출제 포인트

- 사물의 위치나 상태를 잘못 묘사하거나 눈에 보이지 않는 인물, 사물을 언급하는 오답이 등장한다.
- 주로 진행형(be + V-ing)이나 수동형(be + p.p.) 또는 현재완료 수동태(have been + p.p.)가 쓰이고, 혹은 There is/are + 전치사구 활용 표현도 나온다.

[예제]

✔ A clock is hung[is hanging/has been hung] on the wall. 시계가 벽에 걸려 있다. (정답)
✔ A clock is being hung on the wall. 시계가 벽에 걸려지고 있다.
  (누군가 시계를 벽에 걸고 있어야 하므로 오답)

cf. be being displayed는 현재 진행 수동형임에도 상태를 나타내기 때문에 사물 묘사 유형에서 정답으로 꾸준히 등장하므로 <be + being + p.p.> 표현에 익숙해지자.

SPARTA 문제 풀이 비법

 Day02_1

(A) Pedestrians are walking on the sidewalk.
  보행자들이 인도를 걷고 있다. (X)
  → 보행자들은 보이지 않으므로 오답.

(B) The sign is being replaced.
  표지판이 교체되고 있다. (X)
  → 표지판은 있지만 교체되고 있는 상황은 아니다.

(C) Buses are lined up in rows.
  버스들이 여러 줄로 줄지어 있다. (X)
  → 버스는 한 줄로 서 있다.

(D) There are vehicles on one side of the road.
  차량들이 길 한 쪽에 있다. (O)
  → 도로 왼쪽에 차량들이 보이므로 정답.

✅ 먼저 사물들의 위치를 파악하고 관련 표현을 예상하자. 여기서 함정은 (C)이다. in a row(한 줄로)과 in rows(여러 줄로)를 구분해야 한다. 사진에서 버스는 여러 줄이 아닌 한 줄로 서 있다. 차량들이 길 한 쪽에 있으므로 정답은 이를 묘사한 (D)이다.

SPARTA Check-UP

다음을 듣고 사진을 가장 잘 묘사한 문장을 고른 후, 빈칸을 채우세요. (음성은 두 번씩 들려줍니다.)

1.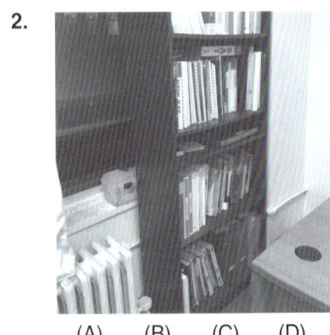

   (A) Glasses are _____ water.
   (B) _____ beside the cutlery.
   (C) _____ in the restaurant.
   (D) _____ neatly.

   (A)   (B)   (C)   (D)

2.

   (A) The bookshelf is _____.
   (B) _____ on the windowsill.
   (C) Books are _____.
   (D) Some shelves are _____.

   (A)   (B)   (C)   (D)

3.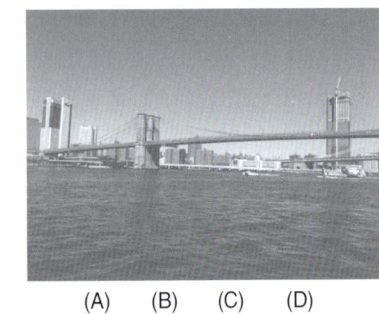

   (A) _____ behind the boxes.
   (B) _____ beside the road.
   (C) _____ onto a truck.
   (D) _____ a wheelbarrow.

   (A)   (B)   (C)   (D)

4.

   (A) _____ at the harbor.
   (B) Some people are _____.
   (C) _____ over the river.
   (D) There are some tall buildings _____.

   (A)   (B)   (C)   (D)

SPARTA Practice Test

Day02_3 해설 p.305

1.

(A)　(B)　(C)　(D)

2.

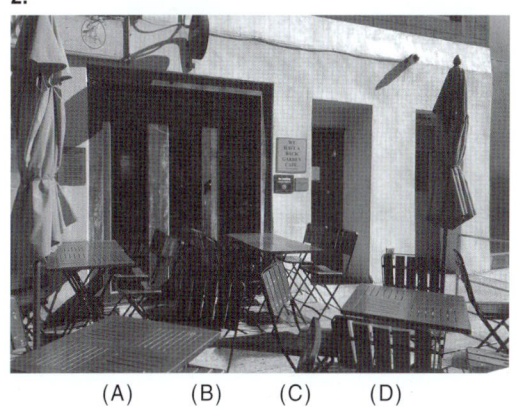

(A)　(B)　(C)　(D)

3.

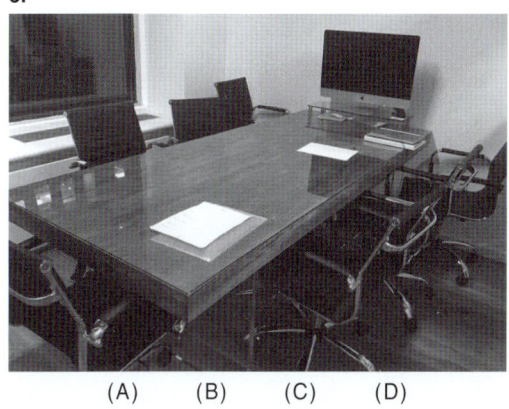

(A)　(B)　(C)　(D)

4.

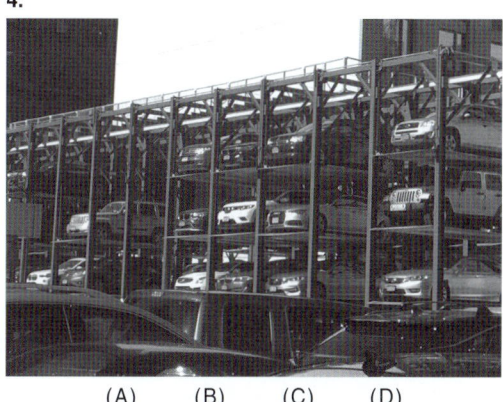

(A)　(B)　(C)　(D)

5.

(A)　(B)　(C)　(D)

6.

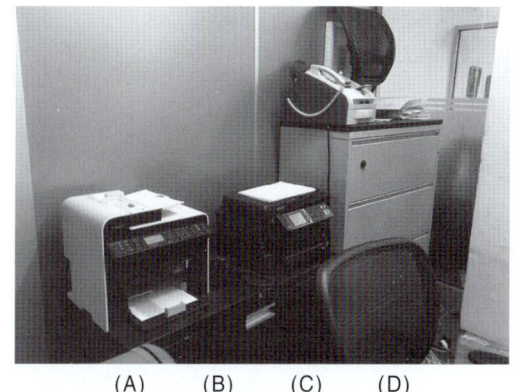

(A)　(B)　(C)　(D)

7.

(A)　　(B)　　(C)　　(D)

9.

(A)　　(B)　　(C)　　(D)

8.

(A)　　(B)　　(C)　　(D)

10.

(A)　　(B)　　(C)　　(D)

SPARTA 빈출 표현 — 혼동되는 표현

1. wear와 put on/try on을 정확히 구분하자.

사진에 나오는 인물들은 옷이나 장신구를 착용하고 있기 때문에 '입고 있는 상태'를 나타내는 wear가 정답일 확률이 높다. 하지만 '입고 있는 동작'을 나타내는 put on과 try on은 특정 행동을 보여 줘야 하기 때문에 오답으로 자주 나온다.

EX) A woman is **wearing** a coat. 여자는 코트를 입고 있다. (상태)
　　A woman is **putting on** a coat. 여자는 코트를 입으려고 하고 있다. (동작)

2. get on과 ride를 정확히 구분하자.

배경에 차량이나 배, 비행기와 같은 탈것들이 자주 등장한다. 교통 수단 안에 사람들이 타고 있는지 아니면 타려고 하는지 정확히 파악해야 한다. 교통 수단에 타려고 한다면 get on, get into 또는 enter를 동사로 쓰며, 이미 타고 있다면 ride를 쓰면 된다.

EX) A man is **getting on** a boat. 남자는 보트에 타려고 하고 있다. (동작)
　　A man is **riding** a bicycle. 남자는 자전거를 타고 있다. (상태)

3. 자주 등장하는 유사 발음 어휘나 혼동되는 어휘를 조심하자.

train 열차		training 훈련	
write 쓰다		ride 타다	
walk 걷다		work 일하다	
copy 복사		coffee 커피	
swing 그네		swim 수영	
bus stop 버스 정류장		stop sign 멈춤 표지판	
glass 유리잔		grass 잔디밭	
ladder 사다리		letter 편지	
microphone 마이크		microscope 현미경	

4. 위치를 나타내는 표현을 알아 두자.

사물/풍경 사진이나 2인 이상의 인물이 등장하는 사진은 각자의 위치를 정확하게 표현한 보기가 정답일 확률이 높다. 따라서 위치를 나타내는 빈출 표현을 익혀 두는 게 좋다.

to the right	오른쪽으로	to the left	왼쪽으로
around	~주위에	against	~에 기대어
in front of	~의 앞에	behind/at the rear of	~의 뒤에
over/above	~의 위에 (사물에 닿지 않게)	under	~의 아래에
inside/indoors	안에서	outside/outdoors	밖에서
alongside	~옆에, 나란히	at the bottom of	~의 밑에
into	~안으로	along	~을 따라
near	~의 가까이	in/into the distance	저 멀리
next to/by/beside	~의 옆에	between	사이에

SPARTA 빈출 표현 — 상황별 표현

PART 1의 표현들은 주로 be + V-ing 형태로 제시된다.

● 작업실/사무실

be		
	organizing/arranging papers	서류를 정리하고 있다
	working in the office	사무실에서 일하고 있다
	looking at a document	서류를 보고 있다
	sitting/seated at a desk	책상에 앉아 있다
	talking on the telephone	전화하고 있다
	writing down in a notebook	공책에 쓰고 있다
	copying some materials	자료를 복사하고 있다
	holding a book	책을 들고 있다
	facing a computer	컴퓨터와 마주하고 있다
	pointing at a screen	화면을 가리키고 있다
	leaning against a wall	벽에 기대어 있다
	having a meeting	회의를 하고 있다
	shaking hands	악수하고 있다
	reaching into a drawer	서랍 안으로 손을 뻗고 있다
	typing on a keyboard	키보드를 두드리고 있다
	distributing a handout	유인물을 나눠 주고 있다

● 식당/주방

be		
	wiping a table	테이블을 닦고 있다
	pouring some water	물을 따르고 있다
	preparing/cooking some food	음식을 준비하고 있다
	drinking/sipping some coffee	커피를 마시고 있다
	serving food on a plate	접시에 음식을 제공하고 있다
	examining the menu	메뉴를 보고 있다
	taking an order	주문을 받고 있다
	using a utensil	조리 기구를 이용하고 있다
	standing behind the counter	카운터 뒤에 서 있다
	setting the table	식탁을 차리고 있다
	slicing some bread	빵을 썰고 있다
	eating at a restaurant	식당에서 먹고 있다

● 정원/공원

be		
	riding a bicycle	자전거를 타고 있다
	mowing the grass/lawn	잔디를 깎고 있다
	trimming a bush	관목을 다듬고 있다
	sitting on a bench	벤치에 앉아 있다
	strolling down a path	오솔길을 거닐고 있다
	pushing a wheelbarrow	손수레를 밀고 있다
	raking the leaves	낙엽을 쓸어 모으고 있다
	planting a tree	나무를 심고 있다
	installing a ladder	사다리를 설치하고 있다
	riding in a carriage	마차를 타고 있다

● 쇼핑

be	paying for/buying/purchasing a shirt	셔츠를 구입하고 있다
	trying on glasses	안경을 써 보고 있다
	organizing some clothes	옷을 정리하고 있다
	browsing some items	물건들을 둘러보고 있다
	removing a jacket	재킷을 벗고 있다
	standing at a cash register	계산대에 서 있다
	assisting a customer	고객을 돕고 있다
	shopping for jewelry	보석을 쇼핑하고 있다
	reaching for an item	물건에 손을 뻗고 있다
	putting an item into a cart	카트에 물건을 넣고 있다
	pushing a cart	카트를 밀고 있다

● 해변/강가

be	rowing a boat	노를 젓고 있다
	swimming in the water	수영하고 있다
	getting into a boat	보트에 타고 있다
	jogging along the shore	물가를 따라 조깅하고 있다
	tying a boat to a pier	부두에 배를 묶고 있다
	folding a net at a dock	부두에서 그물을 접고 있다
	using some fishing gear	낚시 장비를 사용하고 있다
	taking a walk on the riverbank	강둑에서 산책하고 있다
	resting on a beach	해변에서 쉬고 있다
	disembarking from a ship	배에서 내리고 있다

● 연설장/공연장/강의실

be	giving a speech on a podium	연단에서 연설하고 있다
	speaking into a microphone	마이크에 대고 말하고 있다
	seated in a circle	동그랗게 앉아 있다
	performing on a stage	무대에서 공연하고 있다
	playing some instruments	악기를 연주하고 있다
	greeting an audience	청중을 맞이하고 있다
	concentrating on something	어떤 일에 집중하고 있다
	handing out some brochures	책자를 나눠주고 있다
	stepping down from a stage	무대에서 내려오고 있다
	listening to a lecturer	강연자의 강연을 듣고 있다
	sitting in rows	줄지어 앉아 있다

● 승강장/공항/정거장

be	loading the luggage into the vehicle	차량에 짐을 싣고 있다
	waiting at a platform	승강장에서 기다리고 있다
	boarding a plane	비행기에 탑승하고 있다
	showing a ticket to an attendant	승무원에게 티켓을 보여주고 있다
	sitting in a waiting area	대기실에서 기다리고 있다
	exiting a train	기차에서 내리고 있다
	descending some stairs	계단을 내려오고 있다
	packing a suitcase	여행 가방을 싸고 있다

● 실내

A rug has been rolled up.	깔개가 돌돌 말려 있다.
Some drawers have been left open.	서랍들이 열려 있다.
Some ceiling lights have been turned off.	천장에 전등들이 꺼져 있다.
All the seats are unoccupied/not occupied.	모든 좌석이 비어 있다.
The boxes are stacked on a road.	박스들이 길에 쌓여 있다.
Chairs are piled up around the table.	의자들이 테이블 주위에 쌓여 있다.
The bookcase is full of/filled with/packed with books.	책꽂이가 책으로 가득 차 있다.
A sofa is placed by/next to/beside the bed.	소파가 침대 옆에 있다.
The picture is hanging on the wall.	벽에 그림이 걸려 있다.
Potted plants have been arranged in rows.	화분들이 줄지어 배열되어 있다.
The shelves are stocked with items.	선반이 물건들로 차 있다.
There's a lamp between the beds.	침대 사이에 램프가 있다.
Documents are scattered on a desk.	책상 위에 서류들이 널려 있다.
A laptop computer is on a desk.	노트북이 책상 위에 있다.

● 실외

A ladder is propped against the wall.	사다리가 벽에 기대어 있다.
There are signs blocking a road.	길을 막고 있는 표지판들이 있다.
The cars/vehicles/automobiles are parked along the road.	차들이 길을 따라 주차되어 있다.
The boats are tied/docked to the dock/pier.	배들이 부두에 묶여 있다.
The roof is covered with snow.	지붕이 눈으로 덮여 있다.
The buildings overlook the river.	빌딩들이 강을 내려다보고 있다.
A staircase leads to a balcony.	계단이 발코니로 이어져 있다.
The bridge crosses/spans the river.	다리가 강을 가로지르고 있다.
The cars are moving in the same direction.	차들이 같은 방향으로 움직이고 있다.
A boat is passing under a bridge.	배가 다리 아래를 지나가고 있다.
There are some trees along the path.	오솔길을 따라 나무들이 있다.
The scenery is reflected in the water.	풍경이 물에 비춰져 있다.
Vehicles are parked in a construction site.	차량들이 공사장에 주차되어 있다.
A sculpture is on display outside.	야외에 조각상이 전시되어 있다.
A fountain is in the middle of a lake.	호수 중앙에 분수대가 있다.

● 빈출 오답 표현 (be + being + p.p.)

The water is being poured into a glass.	물이 유리잔에 따라지고 있다.
The railing is being installed on the deck.	난간이 갑판 위에 설치되고 있다.
The luggage/baggage is being loaded onto a truck.	짐이 트럭에 실리고 있다.
The road is being (re)paved/(re)surfaced.	도로가 (재)포장되고 있다.
The tree is being planted along the path.	나무가 오솔길을 따라 심어지고 있다.
The pavement is being swept.	포장도로가 쓸리고 있다.
The bridge is being built/constructed over the water.	다리가 물 위에 세워지고 있다.
Some cartons are being packed.	종이 상자 몇 개가 포장되고 있다.
A mug is being filled with coffee.	머그잔이 커피로 채워지고 있다.
Furniture is being removed from a room.	가구가 방에서 치워지고 있다.
Some products are being put into a cart.	물건들이 카트에 넣어지고 있다.
Lines are being painted on a crosswalk.	차선이 횡단보도에 그려지고 있다.
Some shelves are being assembled.	선반들이 조립되고 있다.

PART 2
질의 응답

PART 2 접근법
DAY 03 | Who/When/Where 의문문
DAY 04 | What&Which/How/Why 의문문
DAY 05 | 일반/부정/부가 의문문
DAY 06 | 제안/요청문
DAY 07 | 선택의문문/평서문

PART 2 접근법

PART 2는 총 25문제로 구성되어 있다. 짧은 질문을 듣고 3개의 보기 중 어울리는 응답을 고르는 유형으로, 상황 대처 능력을 보는 파트이다. 앞뒤 상황 없이 짧은 질문이 나오고 답변이 이어지므로 빠른 판단력과 집중력이 요구되며, 순간적으로 오답을 가릴 수 있는 순발력도 필요하다.

🛡 문제 풀이 전략

1. 의문사 의문문을 먼저 공략하자!(25문제 중 11~13문제 출제) 의문사와 동사를 듣는 연습을 해야 하며, 질문 유형에 따른 전형적인 답변 유형도 외워 두자. 특히 난이도 높은 How/Why 의문문의 답변 유형을 숙지하자.
2. 일반 의문문은 첫 단어를 듣고 질문의 유형을 파악할 수 있다. 앞에 나온 동사를 듣고 시제 판단을 할 수 있고, 뒤에 나오는 동사를 듣고 묻고자 하는 내용을 알 수 있다.
3. 고득점을 위해 평서문을 집중 공략하자. 대부분의 평서문은 사실 전달에 목적을 두기 때문에 전형적인 정답 패턴이 없다. 어휘를 꾸준히 습득하고 다양한 평서문 문제를 접하면서 대비해야 한다.
4. 정답인지 판단이 안 서는 보기는 우선 보류하자. 나머지 보기가 명확한 오답일 때 정답으로 처리하는 소거법이 유리하다. 전형적인 답변이 나올 수도 있지만 난이도 높은 문제는 제3의 답변, 반문 등이 정답으로 나오기 때문에 확실한 오답을 소거한 후 정답을 선택해야 한다.

🚨 오답 유형

- 질문에 나온 유사 발음 표현을 사용한 오답
- 질문에 등장한 단어를 반복한 오답(단, 선택 의문문의 경우 정답이 될 수 있다.)
- 질문과 시제 불일치로 인한 오답
- 질문의 일부 내용을 연상하게 하는 오답
- 의문사 의문문의 경우, Yes/No 답변은 오답

> 7. Why did the company cancel the product launch?
>   (A) When is the lunch break? (X) launch-lunch 유사 발음을 이용한 함정
>   (B) To release the product. (X) 질문에 나온 product를 반복한 오답
>   (C) Actually, they just moved it up a week. (O) 이유를 묻는 질문에 적절한 응답

DAY 3 Who/When/Where 의문문

1 Who 의문문

SPARTA 유형 파악

행위의 주체나 대상이 누구인지 묻는 의문문이다. 업무 담당자, 연설자, 직장 상사, 특정 부서 등 행위의 주체나 특정 대상이 정답이 된다. 하지만 보기의 특정 이름이나 직책을 듣고 무조건 정답으로 고르면 안 되고, 이름/직책 앞뒤 내용을 함께 들어 함정에 빠지지 않아야 한다.

SPARTA 출제 포인트

- 질문을 들을 때 'Who + 동사/명사'에 무게를 두고 어떤 Who를 묻는지 파악해야 한다. 난이도 높은 문제는 모든 보기에 사람 이름이나 직책이 등장한다.
- 고유 명사인 사람 이름, 회사명, 조직명, 부서명, 직책명, 직업명 등이 정답이 될 수 있다.
- 주어 자리에 나오는 어휘의 발음이 낯설다면 고유 명사로 간주하자.
- 질문에 언급되지 않은 he/she가 보기에 나온다면 오답일 가능성이 높다. (You/We/I는 예외)

SPARTA 빈출 유형

Q **Who will volunteer** for the fundraising event? 누가 기금 모금 행사에 자원할 건가요?
A I'd be happy to./ I can do it./ I'll take care of it. 제가 할게요. (1인칭)

Q **Who organized** the advertising campaign? 누가 광고 캠페인을 준비했나요?
A Let me check. 확인해 볼게요. ('몰라요' 답변)

Q **Who should I talk to** about the computer problem? 컴퓨터 문제에 대해 누구와 말해야 해요?
A Call the technician. 기술자에게 연락하세요. (직업)

Q **Who's in charge of revising** the report? 보고서 수정은 누가 담당인가요?
A Min-Hee is responsible for that. 민희가 그 일을 책임지고 있어요. (이름)

Q **Who has the copy** of the sales report? 판매 보고서 사본은 누가 가지고 있어요?
A It's on my desk. 제 책상 위에 있어요. (예외적인 답: 장소)

SPARTA 문제 풀이 비법

🎧 Day03_1

Who's organizing the company retreat?   누가 회사 야유회를 준비하나요?
(A) I heard it was Jimmy.   (A) Jimmy라고 들었어요. (O) → 사람 이름이 언급된 정답
(B) I'll accompany you.   (B) 당신과 함께 갈게요. (X) → company-accompany 유사 발음 혼동을 노린 오답
(C) At Hyde Park.   (C) Hyde 공원에서요. (X) → 장소로 혼동을 노린 오답

✓ 질문의 키워드는 Who/organizing으로, '누가 준비하는지'를 묻고 있다.

2 When 의문문

SPARTA 유형 파악

특정 행위가 발생하는 시점을 묻는 유형으로, 과거, 현재, 미래 시제를 정확히 판단해야 한다. 시작/종료 시점, 이용 가능한 시점, 업무 완료 시점 등을 많이 묻고, 과거보다 미래 시점이 더 많이 출제되고 있다.

SPARTA 출제 포인트

- 질문은 들을 때는 'When + 동사 시제'를 먼저 파악하고, 뒤에 나오는 동사를 들어야 한다.
- 자칫하면 Where로 들리기 때문에 오답으로 가장 많이 등장하는 '장소' 언급 보기를 조심해야 한다.
- 기간을 나타내는 표현이 오답으로 많이 나온다. ex) **For 2 hours.** (2시간 동안이요.) / **Since last year.** (작년부터요.)
- 답변으로 When S+V (~할 때)이 나올 수도 있다. 그 외 in, on, at, by, before, ago, after 등과 함께 시간 관련 보기가 정답으로 자주 등장한다. 또한, 언제인지 말해 줄 수 없다거나 그 이유를 설명하는 '몰라요' 유형의 답변도 자주 나온다.

SPARTA 빈출 유형

Q **When did you send** the package to the Paris office? 언제 파리에 있는 사무실로 소포를 보냈나요?
A I don't remember the exact date. 정확한 날짜가 기억 안 나요. ('몰라요' 답변)

Q **When is the deadline** of the sales report? 판매 보고서의 마감일이 언제인가요?
A By the end of the week. 이번 주말까지요. (미래)

Q **When is a** dental appointment **available**? 언제 치과 예약이 가능한가요?
A Sorry, Dr. Kim is busy this week. 죄송합니다. 김 선생님은 이번 주에 바쁩니다. (예외적인 답: 예약 불가)

Q **When should we** notify the new employees? 언제 신입 사원들에게 공지해야 하나요?
A Not until Thursday. 목요일이 되어야 해요. (시간 관용 표현: Not until 답변은 시제와 상관없이 When-Q의 응답으로 종종 등장한다.)

Q **When can I get** the reimbursement check for my business trip? 언제 출장 경비를 상환 받을 수 있나요?
A **When/Once** the manager approves it. 매니저가 승인하면요. (시간 관용 표현)

SPARTA 문제 풀이 비법

🎧 Day03_2

When will I receive my store membership card by post?

(A) Yes, you will.
(B) The receipt is given after the purchase.
(C) By the end of the month at the latest.

언제 매장 카드를 우편으로 받게 되나요?

(A) 네, 당신이 할 거예요. (X) → Yes/No 응답 불가
(B) 구매 후 영수증을 드립니다. (X) → receive-receipt
　　　　　　　　　　　　　　　　유사 발음 오답
(C) 늦어도 이달 말까지요. (O) → 미래 시점 언급 정답

✅ 질문의 키워드는 When will/receive로, '언제 받을지'를 묻고 있다.

3 Where 의문문

SPARTA 유형 파악

행사 장소, 특정 대상 등의 위치를 묻는다. 특히 Where는 미국 발음과 영국 발음이 다르기 때문에 발음 훈련이 특히 요구된다. 의문사를 통해 질문의 포인트를 잘 파악한 후 정답을 가려내자.

SPARTA 출제 포인트

- 장소(Where)와 시점(When)은 발음상 혼동하기 쉬우므로 주의가 필요하다. 특히 영국 발음 Where[웨]와 When 발음이 비슷하게 들릴 수 있다.
- 질문을 들을 때 'Where + 동사/명사'를 잘 듣고 어떤 장소를 묻는지 정확히 파악해야 한다. 난이도 있는 문제는 보기에 여러 장소가 등장하기도 한다.
- in, at, on, next to, across from 등 위치를 나타내는 표현이 정답일 확률이 높다. 하지만 종종 출처를 묻기도 하므로 사람 이름이나 직급 등이 답으로 등장할 수 있다.

SPARTA 빈출 유형

Q **Where did you leave** the agenda? 회의 안건을 어디에 두었나요?
A In the drawer. 서랍 안에요. (장소)

Q **Where can I find** a hotel nearby? 인근에 호텔이 어디에 있나요?
A I'm not familiar with this area. 저도 여기는 잘 몰라요. ('몰라요' 답변)

Q **Where did you** pick up that book? 저 책을 어디서 얻었어요?
A Marco gave it to me. Marco가 줬어요. (출처가 사람인 답변)

Q **Where is** the product specification you were working on? 당신이 작업하던 제품 설명서는 어디에 있어요?
A I'm still compiling it. 아직 편집 중이에요. (예외적인 답)

Q **Where will the orientation** be held this year? 올해 오리엔테이션이 어디서 열리나요?
A Check the company Web site. 회사 홈페이지를 확인해 보세요. (정보 출처)

SPARTA 문제 풀이 비법

🎧 Day03_3

Where can I see the list of performances? | 공연 목록을 어디서 볼 수 있어요?
(A) It's posted on the homepage. | (A) 그건 홈페이지에 게시되어 있어요. (O) → 위치 언급 정답
(B) Probably around 3 P.M. | (B) 아마도 3시 정도요. (X) → 시간 언급 오답 함정
(C) I didn't see anyone. | (C) 아무도 못 봤어요. (X) → 질문의 see를 반복한 오답 함정

● 질문의 키워드는 Where/the list of performances로, '공연 목록이 있는 위치'를 묻고 있다.

SPARTA Check-UP

Day03_4 해설 p.308

다음을 듣고 적절한 응답을 고른 후, 빈칸을 채우세요. (음성은 두 번씩 들려줍니다.)

1. Mark your answer.   (A)   (B)   (C)

   _____ with the annual fundraiser?

   (A) It's on Friday.
   (B) Louise _____ it.
   (C) Lucy is the _____.

2. Mark your answer.   (A)   (B)   (C)

   _____ you played tennis?

   (A) For a long time.
   (B) _____.
   (C) I _____ last week.

3. Mark your answer.   (A)   (B)   (C)

   _____ for the copier?

   (A) We've _____.
   (B) _____.
   (C) It's not mine.

4. Mark your answer.   (A)   (B)   (C)

   _____?

   (A) _____.
   (B) It was a nice _____.
   (C) To the _____.

5. Mark your answer.   (A)   (B)   (C)

   _____ Ms. Suzuki _____ she first started here?

   (A) For almost _____.
   (B) Is it near the lobby?
   (C) In the _____.

SPARTA Practice Test

Day03_5 해설 p.308

1. Mark your answer.   (A)   (B)   (C)
2. Mark your answer.   (A)   (B)   (C)
3. Mark your answer.   (A)   (B)   (C)
4. Mark your answer.   (A)   (B)   (C)
5. Mark your answer.   (A)   (B)   (C)
6. Mark your answer.   (A)   (B)   (C)
7. Mark your answer.   (A)   (B)   (C)
8. Mark your answer.   (A)   (B)   (C)
9. Mark your answer.   (A)   (B)   (C)
10. Mark your answer.   (A)   (B)   (C)
11. Mark your answer.   (A)   (B)   (C)
12. Mark your answer.   (A)   (B)   (C)
13. Mark your answer.   (A)   (B)   (C)
14. Mark your answer.   (A)   (B)   (C)
15. Mark your answer.   (A)   (B)   (C)
16. Mark your answer.   (A)   (B)   (C)
17. Mark your answer.   (A)   (B)   (C)
18. Mark your answer.   (A)   (B)   (C)
19. Mark your answer.   (A)   (B)   (C)
20. Mark your answer.   (A)   (B)   (C)
21. Mark your answer.   (A)   (B)   (C)
22. Mark your answer.   (A)   (B)   (C)
23. Mark your answer.   (A)   (B)   (C)
24. Mark your answer.   (A)   (B)   (C)
25. Mark your answer.   (A)   (B)   (C)

DAY 4 What&Which/How/Why 의문문

1 What&Which 의문문

SPARTA 유형 파악

What은 '무엇', Which는 '어느/어떤'이라는 의미로, 의문사 중에서 가장 다양하게 묻는 질문 유형에 속하며 답변 유형 또한 다양하다.

SPARTA 출제 포인트

- What/Which 뒤에 나오는 명사와 동사를 반드시 듣자. 대상, 직업, 행위, 의견, 시간, 날씨, 비용, 상태, 이유 등 다양한 질문이 가능하기 때문에 많이 나오는 표현을 외워 두는 것이 좋다.
- 대답이 the one ~/this one ~/either one ~으로 시작한다면 정답이 될 확률이 높다.
- 'Which + 인물'로 물을 경우, 사람 이름이 언급된 응답이 정답으로 자주 등장한다.

SPARTA 빈출 유형

Q **What time is** the seminar supposed to begin? 세미나는 몇 시에 시작하기로 했나요?
A Let me check the schedule. 일정을 확인해 볼게요. ('몰라요' 답변)

Q **What kind/sort/type of** shoes are you looking for? 어떤 종류의 신발을 찾고 있나요?
A Can you recommend something for me? 추천해 주시겠어요? (예외적인 답: 요청)

Q **What do you think of** that candidate? 저 지원자에 대해 어떻게 생각하나요?
A She's highly qualified. 그녀는 매우 자격을 갖추었군요. (의견)

Q **Which** resort **did you choose** for your holiday? 휴일에 어떤 리조트로 가기로 했어요?
A The one I went to last year. 작년에 간 곳이요. (The one ~으로 시작한 정답)

Q **Which of you** approved the business loan? 당신들 중 누가 사업 대출을 승인했나요?
A Sam authorized it. Sam이 승인했어요. (사람)

SPARTA 문제 풀이 비법

🎧 Day04_1

What did the vice president think about our proposal?

(A) The marketing director.
(B) Not that I know of.
(C) I haven't met him yet.

제안서에 대해 부사장은 어떻게 생각했어요?

(A) 마케팅 부장이요. (X) → Who 의문에 어울리는 응답
(B) 제가 알기론 아니에요. (X) → Wh-Q에 Yes/No 답변 불가
(C) 아직 부사장님을 못 만났어요. (O) → '몰라요' 유형의 정답

✅ 질문의 키워드는 What/think/proposal로, '부사장의 의견'을 묻고 있다.

2 How 의문문

SPARTA 유형 파악

How 뒤에 오는 단어에 따라 방법, 상태, 의견, 횟수, 개수 등 다양하게 물을 수 있으므로, How 뒤에 나오는 단어를 잘 들어야 한다.

SPARTA 출제 포인트

- 방법을 묻는 How 의문문은 특히 뒷부분을 잘 들어야 한다. 뒤에 이어지는 단어에 따라 묻는 내용이 달라진다.
- 동사가 같더라도 주어가 다르면 묻는 내용이 달라진다. 관련 관용 표현을 외워 두자.

    EX) How did you go ~? 어떻게 갔어요? (방법) / How did it go ~? 어땠어요? (상태/의견)
    How do you like ~? 어떻게 생각해요? (의견) / How would you like ~? 어떻게 해 드릴까요? (취향/의사)

- 'How + 형용사/부사' 형태로, 수량(many), 가격(much), 기간(long), 빈도(often), 시기(soon, late), 거리(far) 등을 묻는 문제가 자주 출제된다. 단 이러한 질문 형태가 수로 답할 수 있기 때문에 그 수가 어떤 것을 의미하는지 잘 판단해야 한다.
- How 의문문에 How로 되묻는 응답이 오답으로 등장하기도 한다.

SPARTA 빈출 유형

Q **How can we** get to the hotel? 호텔로 어떻게 갈 수 있나요?
A Go two blocks and turn right. 두 블록 가서 우회전하세요. (위치 설명)

Q **How do the employees like** this new system? 직원들은 새 시스템에 대해 어떻게 생각해요?
A It is much easier than the previous one. 이전보다 훨씬 쉽대요. (의견)

Q **How did** your interview **go**? / **How was** your interview? 인터뷰는 어땠어요?
A It went well. 잘했어요. (상태)

Q **How many customers registered** for our membership card? 몇 명의 고객이 회원 카드를 등록했나요?
A Pam has the list. Pam이 목록을 가지고 있어요. ('몰라요' 답변)

Q **How long will it take** to finish the report? 보고서를 끝내는 데 얼마나 걸릴까요?
A I think it'll take at least five hours. 적어도 5시간은 걸릴 것 같아요. (기간)

SPARTA 문제 풀이 비법

🎧 Day04_2

How will the city committee chairman be chosen? | 시 위원회 의장은 어떻게 선출되나요?
(A) Members vote on it. | (A) 구성원들이 투표해요. (O) → 방법을 언급한 정답
(B) I selected that chair. | (B) 제가 저 의자를 선택했어요. (X) → chairman/chair를 이용한 함정
(C) Is it on the third floor? | (C) 그게 3층에 있어요? (X) → 위치를 되묻는 오답

✔ 질문의 키워드는 How/chairman/chosen로, '의장 선출 방법'을 묻고 있다.

3 Why 의문문

SPARTA 유형 파악

Why 의문문은 이유를 묻는 유형으로, 지연 이유, 기기 고장 등의 이유들이 자주 언급되지만 이유를 설명할 수 없다는 응답이나, 되묻는 응답도 종종 나온다.

SPARTA 출제 포인트

- Why로 시작한다고 다 이유를 묻는 것은 아니다. 제안을 뜻하는 "Why don't you ~?(~이 어때요?)"도 자주 등장하므로 정확히 구분해야 한다.
- Because가 생략된 이유 언급 응답에 익숙해지자.
- Because로 시작하는 답변이라도 뒤에 나오는 내용이 질문과 연관이 되는지 파악해야 한다.
- 그 외 'To/In order to + 동사(~하기 위해)', 'For + 명사(~ 위해)', 'Because of/due to + 명사(~ 때문에)' 등의 표현을 익혀 두고, 뒤에 나오는 동사/명사를 잘 들어서 질문과 연계되는 답을 찾아야 한다.

SPARTA 빈출 유형

Q **Why has** the meeting **been canceled**? 왜 회의가 취소됐나요?
A Mr. Kim couldn't come. Kim 씨가 올 수 없었어요. (이유: 특정 인물의 부재)

Q **Why are you leaving** the office early today? 오늘 왜 일찍 퇴근하나요?
A **To** meet with clients. 고객을 만나려고요. (이유: To + 동사)

Q **Why has** this display case **been** left unlocked? 왜 진열대가 잠기지 않은 채로 있나요?
A I'm sorry, that's my fault. 죄송해요, 제 잘못이에요. (예외적인 답: 본인이 잠그지 않았다)

Q **Why didn't you submit** the annual report this morning? 왜 오늘 아침에 연례 보고서를 제출하지 않았나요?
A Is today the deadline? 오늘이 마감이에요? (예외적인 답: '몰라요' 답변)

Q **Why isn't** the copier **working**? 왜 복사기가 작동하지 않나요?
A Have you pressed the start button? 시작 버튼을 눌렀나요? (예외적인 답: 작동 방법 아는지 확인)

SPARTA 문제 풀이 비법

🎧 Day04_3

Why did Michael leave early today? | 왜 Michael은 오늘 일찍 나갔나요?
(A) From ten to noon. | (A) 10시부터 정오까지요. (X) → 시간을 언급한 오답
(B) To pick overseas clients up from the airport. | (B) 공항에 해외 고객들을 마중 나가려고요. (O) → 이유를 언급한 정답
(C) Because I have a dentist appointment. | (C) 제가 치과 예약이 있어서요. (X) → Because 뒤의 설명이 질문과 무관

✅ 키워드는 Why/leave early로, '일찍 나가는 이유'를 묻고 있다.

SPARTA Check-UP

다음을 듣고 적절한 응답을 고른 후, 빈칸을 채우세요. (음성은 두 번씩 들려줍니다.)

1. Mark your answer. (A) (B) (C)

   What _____ for my article?
   (A) He's a photographer.
   (B) _____ on the phone.
   (C) _____.

2. Mark your answer. (A) (B) (C)

   Which movie star _____ on the news today?
   (A) I enjoy _____.
   (B) After the business news.
   (C) _____ the Best Actor award.

3. Mark your answer. (A) (B) (C)

   _____ at Canton Electronics Store?
   (A) Please _____.
   (B) Do you think so?
   (C) _____.

4. Mark your answer. (A) (B) (C)

   Excuse me. _____ my watch?
   (A) _____?
   (B) _____ an hour.
   (C) I can repair it.

5. Mark your answer. (A) (B) (C)

   _____ the self-assessment _____?
   (A) Help yourself.
   (B) Because _____ the annual report.
   (C) _____?

SPARTA Practice Test

🎧 Day04_5 해설 p.313

1. Mark your answer. (A) (B) (C)
2. Mark your answer. (A) (B) (C)
3. Mark your answer. (A) (B) (C)
4. Mark your answer. (A) (B) (C)
5. Mark your answer. (A) (B) (C)
6. Mark your answer. (A) (B) (C)
7. Mark your answer. (A) (B) (C)
8. Mark your answer. (A) (B) (C)
9. Mark your answer. (A) (B) (C)
10. Mark your answer. (A) (B) (C)
11. Mark your answer. (A) (B) (C)
12. Mark your answer. (A) (B) (C)
13. Mark your answer. (A) (B) (C)
14. Mark your answer. (A) (B) (C)
15. Mark your answer. (A) (B) (C)
16. Mark your answer. (A) (B) (C)
17. Mark your answer. (A) (B) (C)
18. Mark your answer. (A) (B) (C)
19. Mark your answer. (A) (B) (C)
20. Mark your answer. (A) (B) (C)
21. Mark your answer. (A) (B) (C)
22. Mark your answer. (A) (B) (C)
23. Mark your answer. (A) (B) (C)
24. Mark your answer. (A) (B) (C)
25. Mark your answer. (A) (B) (C)

DAY 5 일반/부정/부가 의문문

1 일반 의문문

SPARTA 유형 파악

출제 빈도가 가장 높은 유형으로, Yes/No로 주로 답하지만 생략 가능하므로 Yes/No가 생략된 정답도 골라낼 수 있는 훈련이 필요하다. 또한 'Yes, 긍정적 표현'과 'No, 부정적 표현'이 질문과 연결되는지 파악해야 한다.

SPARTA 출제 포인트

- 처음으로 들리는 동사의 시제를 먼저 판단하자. 질문과 답변의 시제 불일치가 함정으로 이용된 오답이 자주 나온다.
  • 형태: Do/Does ~?, Did ~?, Is/Are ~?, Was/Were ~?
- <Have + p.p.>형태는 과거부터 현재까지 있었던 경험과 완료된 일을 묻는다.
- 종종 출제되는 간접의문문은 동사 뒤에 이어지는 부분이 핵심이다. 난이도 있는 문제는 'if/whether S + V'로 나오기도 한다.

SPARTA 빈출 유형

Q **Were there a lot of people** at the product demonstration? 제품 시연회에 사람들이 많았어요?
A I didn't attend. 참석하지 않았어요. ('몰라요' 유형의 정답)

Q **Is the printer working** now? 지금 프린터가 작동돼요?
A The technician is coming soon. 기술자가 곧 올 거예요. (No 생략 답변)

Q **Did you apply** for the editor position? 편집자 직책에 지원했어요?
A1 I did it 2 days ago. 이틀 전에 했어요. (Yes 생략 답변)
A2 I'm still considering it. 여전히 고려 중이에요. (No 생략 답변)

Q **Have you completed** the report I asked you to revise? 제가 수정하라고 요청한 보고서를 끝냈나요?
A I'm almost done. 거의 다했어요. (Yes 생략 답변)

Q **Can you tell me who's coming** to the party tonight? 오늘밤 누가 파티에 오는지 알려주시겠어요? (간접-Q)
A Everyone in our department except James. James를 제외한 우리 부서 모든 사람이요. (Yes 생략 답변)

Q **Do you think we should** purchase more chairs for the workshop?
워크숍용 의자를 더 구매해야 한다고 생각해요? (간접-Q)
A Have you checked the budget? 예산을 확인했어요? (예외적인 정답 유형: 반문)

SPARTA 문제 풀이 비법

🎧 Day05_1

Are you available for an interview next Monday? 다음주 월요일에 인터뷰 가능해요?

(A) Let me check my schedule.
(B) A bit earlier next time.
(C) I think that candidate is highly qualified.

(A) 제가 일정을 확인해 볼게요. (O) → '몰라요' 유형의 정답
(B) 다음 번에 좀 더 일찍요. (X) → 질문의 next 반복 함정
(C) 내 생각에 저 지원자는 능력이 뛰어나요. (X)
→ interview-candidate의 연상 어휘 함정

✓ 질문의 키워드는 available/interview/next Monday로, '다음 주 월요일에 인터뷰가 가능한지'를 묻는 일반 의문문이다.

2 부정 의문문

SPARTA 유형 파악

주로 특정 사실을 확인하거나 의견을 물을 때 또는 자신의 의견에 동의를 구할 때 쓴다. 영어에서 부정 의문문과 긍정 의문문의 대답은 동일하기 때문에 처음 들리는 부정 표현에 신경 쓰지 말고 긍정의문문과 같이 답변 내용에 포인트를 둬야 한다.

SPARTA 출제 포인트

- 처음으로 들리는 동사로 먼저 시제를 판단하자. 시제 불일치가 함정인 오답이 많이 나온다.
- '현재 완료(Haven't+주어+p.p.)로 시작하는 질문은 과거분사(p.p.)를 잘 들어야 한다.
- 긍정적인 답변은 <Yes+긍정적 부연 설명>, 부정적인 답변은 <No+부정적 부연 설명> 형태로 제시되며, Yes/No가 생략된 답변도 자주 나오므로 질문의 의도를 정확히 파악해야 한다.

SPARTA 빈출 유형

Q **Isn't Mark coming** to the farewell party tonight? Mark는 오늘밤 송별회에 안 오나요?
A Why don't you ask him? 그에게 물어보는 게 어때요? ('몰라요' 유형의 답변)

Q **Weren't** the office chairs **delivered** last week? 사무실 의자가 지난주에 배달되지 않았어요?
A The shipment has been delayed. 배송이 지연됐어요. (예외적인 답: Yes, but ~ 생략 답변)

Q **Didn't you fill out** the reimbursement request form? 상환 신청서 작성 안 했어요?
A Do you have a pen? 펜 있어요? (예외적인 답)

Q **Haven't you sent** the parcels to the clients yet? 고객에게 아직 소포를 안 보냈나요?
A No, because they said they might change the order. 아니요, 그들이 주문을 바꿀 수도 있다고 해서요. (No+부연 설명)

Q **Don't you think** Steve's presentation was really persuasive?
   Steve의 발표가 정말로 설득력 있다고 생각하지 않아요?
A Yeah, he explained the complicated concept well. 네, 그는 복잡한 개념을 잘 설명했어요. (Yes+부연 설명)

SPARTA 문제 풀이 비법

🎧 Day05_2

Weren't the room carpets cleaned over the weekend? 주말에 방 카펫을 청소하지 않았나요?

(A) Yes, I wiped the floor.
(B) Saturday would be good.
(C) There are a few stains left.

(A) 네, 제가 바닥을 닦았어요. (X) → 질문과 맞지 않는 응답
(B) 토요일이 좋아요. (X) → weekend-Saturday 연상 어휘 함정
(C) 약간의 얼룩이 남아 있네요. (O) → Yes, but이 생략된 답변

✅ 질문의 키워드는 carpets/cleaned로, '카펫을 청소했는지'를 확인하는 부정 의문문이다.

3 부가 의문문

SPARTA 유형 파악

상대방의 동의나 확인을 구할 때 쓰이는 유형으로, 평서문이 먼저 오고 그 뒤에 확인하기 위해 추가로 묻는 형태이다.

SPARTA 출제 포인트

- 처음 들리는 표현이 평서문이기 때문에 앞부분을 이해하는 것이 중요하다.
- 부가 의문문은 부정이든 긍정이든 대답은 같다. 앞에 나온 평서문 내용에 긍정하면 Yes로, 부정하면 No로 답한다. 하지만 뒤에 나오는 부연 설명도 잘 들어야 한다. Yes/No 생략 후 부연 설명이 나오는 보기도 등장한다.
- 평서문이 나온 후 뒤에 right?, okay?로 묻는 구어체 부가의문문 형태도 자주 출제된다.

SPARTA 빈출 유형

Q You went to the employment fair last month, **didn't you**? 지난달 채용 박람회에 갔었죠, 그렇죠?
A Yes, it was very informative. 네, 매우 유익했어요. (Yes+긍정 답변)

Q You haven't been to the new branch in Paris, **have you**? 파리에 있는 새 지점에 가 본 적 없죠, 그렇죠?
A I'm going there next week. 다음 주에 갈 거예요. (No, but 생략 답변)

Q Jordan transferred to the sales department, **right**? Jordan은 판매 부서로 전근 갔죠, 그렇죠?
A I haven't heard about it. 그것에 대해 못 들었어요. ('몰라요' 유형의 답변)

Q The conference room is too hot, **isn't it**? 회의장이 너무 덥죠, 그렇죠?
A Let's open the window. 창문을 엽시다. (Yes 생략 답변)

Q You didn't apply for the position, **did you**? 구직 신청을 안 했죠, 그렇죠?
A Yes, I'm waiting for the interview. 네, 인터뷰를 기다리고 있어요. (Yes+긍정 답변)

SPARTA 문제 풀이 비법

🎧 Day05_3

The power at your company has been restored, hasn't it? 당신 회사의 전력이 복구됐죠, 그렇죠?

(A) Actually, we're still having issues.
(B) I like that store.
(C) The electricity went out.

(A) 사실은, 여전히 문제예요. (O) → No가 생략된 답변
(B) 저 가게를 좋아해요. (X) → restored-store 유사 발음 함정
(C) 전기가 나갔어요. (X) → power-electricity 연상 어휘 함정

✓ 키워드는 power/ restored로, '전력이 복구됐는지'를 확인하는 부가 의문문이다.

SPARTA Check-UP

Day05_4 해설 p.318

다음을 듣고 적절한 응답을 고른 후, 빈칸을 채우세요. (음성은 두 번씩 들려줍니다.)

1. Mark your answer.   (A)   (B)   (C)

   Has Ms. Han _____?
   (A) No, her _____.
   (B) Thanks, I'm feeling much better.
   (C) Please _____.

2. Mark your answer.   (A)   (B)   (C)

   Do you know _____ in this building?
   (A) The courthouse is _____.
   (B) It's _____.
   (C) Let's meet at noon.

3. Mark your answer.   (A)   (B)   (C)

   Hasn't the _____ yet?
   (A) Delivery is _____.
   (B) Sure, they'll download that program.
   (C) Some maintenance work _____.

4. Mark your answer.   (A)   (B)   (C)

   The _____, isn't it?
   (A) Yes, but Tom _____.
   (B) I _____ all the items in there.
   (C) Please close it.

5. Mark your answer.   (A)   (B)   (C)

   Melissa _____, doesn't she?
   (A) A yearly _____.
   (B) Let's _____.
   (C) It was a great success.

48

SPARTA Practice Test

Day05_5 해설 p.318

1. Mark your answer.   (A)   (B)   (C)
2. Mark your answer.   (A)   (B)   (C)
3. Mark your answer.   (A)   (B)   (C)
4. Mark your answer.   (A)   (B)   (C)
5. Mark your answer.   (A)   (B)   (C)
6. Mark your answer.   (A)   (B)   (C)
7. Mark your answer.   (A)   (B)   (C)
8. Mark your answer.   (A)   (B)   (C)
9. Mark your answer.   (A)   (B)   (C)
10. Mark your answer.   (A)   (B)   (C)
11. Mark your answer.   (A)   (B)   (C)
12. Mark your answer.   (A)   (B)   (C)
13. Mark your answer.   (A)   (B)   (C)
14. Mark your answer.   (A)   (B)   (C)
15. Mark your answer.   (A)   (B)   (C)
16. Mark your answer.   (A)   (B)   (C)
17. Mark your answer.   (A)   (B)   (C)
18. Mark your answer.   (A)   (B)   (C)
19. Mark your answer.   (A)   (B)   (C)
20. Mark your answer.   (A)   (B)   (C)
21. Mark your answer.   (A)   (B)   (C)
22. Mark your answer.   (A)   (B)   (C)
23. Mark your answer.   (A)   (B)   (C)
24. Mark your answer.   (A)   (B)   (C)
25. Mark your answer.   (A)   (B)   (C)

DAY 6 제안/요청문

1 제안문

SPARTA 유형 파악

제안문은 질문 유형의 패턴을 익혀야 한다. 의문문뿐만 아니라 평서문과 명령문, 부정 의문문으로도 출제된다. 직접적으로 수락/동의, 거절/반대하는 응답이나, 수락할 수 없는 이유를 말하는 등 우회적인 답변이 나온다.

SPARTA 출제 포인트

- 질문의 핵심은 주어 뒤에 나오는 동사에 있다.
  - 제안: Why don't you[we] ~?, How[What] about ~?, Let's~, Would you like ~?, Shall[Should] we ~?
  - 제공: Would[Do] you like me to ~?, Don't you want me to ~?, Can[Should] I ~?

- 전형적인 수락과 거절 답변을 외우자.

수락/동의	거절/부정
Sure. 그럼요. (= Of course. / No problem.)	I've never considered that. 전혀 고려해 보지 않았어요.
Go ahead. 그렇게 하세요.	Let me think about it. 생각해 볼게요.
That's a good idea. 좋은 생각이네요.	I'm afraid I won't have time. 죄송하지만, 시간이 없을 것 같아요.
That would be great. 그거 좋겠네요.	Sorry, I have an appointment. 죄송하지만, 약속이 있어요.
It's my pleasure. 제가 좋아서 한 거예요.	I'm sorry, I am busy today. 죄송하지만, 오늘 바빠요.
If you're not busy. 바쁘지 않으시면요.	I'm not sure I can help you. 제가 도와줄 수 있을지 모르겠어요.
I'd appreciate it. 감사합니다.	No, thanks. 고맙지만 사양할게요.
I think we'd better. 그게 더 낫겠네요.	Thanks, anyway. 어쨌든 감사해요.

SPARTA 빈출 유형

Q **Why don't you** order more sandwiches for the guests? 손님들을 위해 샌드위치를 더 주문하는 게 어때요?
A How many do we need? 얼마나 필요할까요? (예외적인 답: 추가 질문)

Q **Would you like me to** drive you to the seminar? 제가 세미나까지 운전해서 데려다 줄까요?
A I'd really appreciate it. 정말 고마워요. (수락)

Q **Would you like** some cake for dessert? 디저트로 케이크 좀 먹을래요?
A What kind of cake do you have? 어떤 종류의 케이크가 있어요? (예외적인 답: 추가 질문)

Q **Should I** take the subway to the museum? 박물관에 지하철을 타고 가야 할까요?
A It's better to go by bus. 버스를 타는 게 더 나아요. (다른 제안)

SPARTA 문제 풀이 비법

🎧 Day06_1

Why don't you take a short break? 　　잠깐 쉬는 게 어때요?

(A) Because I'm so tired. 　　　　　　(A) 너무 피곤해서요. (X) → because 오답 함정
(B) He can fix anything. 　　　　　　　(B) 그는 뭐든지 고칠 수 있어요. (X) → break-fix 연상 어휘 함정
(C) I'm almost done. 　　　　　　　　(C) 거의 다했어요. (O) → 정답(우회적 거절)

✅ 질문의 키워드인 Why don't you ~?는 대표적인 제안 형태이다.

2 요청문

SPARTA 유형 파악

요청문은 Can you ~?, Would you ~?, Please~ 형태로 자주 출제된다. 답으로도 수락/거절을 하는 기본 형태의 답변도 나오지만 때로는 거절하는 이유를 말하는 우회적인 답변도 등장한다.

SPARTA 출제 포인트

- 주어와 동사를 잘 듣고 요청의 주/객체, 요청 사항이 무엇인지 판단하자.
  - 요청: Could/Can/Would you ~?, Would/Do you mind ~?, Can/May I ~?, I'd like you to ~.
- 행동의 주체를 잘 판단하자. ex) Would you like ~? (당신이) ~하겠어요?, Would you like me to ~? (제가) ~해드릴까요?
- 전형적인 수락과 거절 답변 표현을 외우자.
- 정중한 요청 표현 Would[Do] you mind ~?의 답변 형태에 유의하자. Yes는 거절, No는 수락하는 답변이 된다. 하지만 최근에는 Sure(수락), Sorry(거절)를 이용한 답변도 나온다.

SPARTA 빈출 유형

Q **Could you give me a hand** moving these boxes? 이 박스 옮기는 것 좀 도와줄래요?
A Sure, I'll be there. 물론이죠, 거기로 갈게요. **(수락)**

Q **Would you type** this report for the staff meeting? 직원 회의를 위해 이 보고서 좀 타이핑해 주실래요?
A Sorry, I have a lot of work to do. 죄송한데 제가 일이 많아서요. **(거절)**

Q **Would you mind trading** my shift tomorrow? 내일 저랑 근무조 좀 바꿔주지 않을래요?
A1 **Not at all.** 전혀 아니에요. **(수락)**
   Of course not. 물론 아니죠. **(수락)**
   Go ahead. 그렇게 하세요. **(수락)**
A2 Actually, I have an important appointment then. 사실, 저는 그때 중요한 약속이 있어요. **(거절)**

SPARTA 문제 풀이 비법

🎧 Day06_2

Could I borrow the novel after you're finished with it? 당신이 다 읽으면 제가 그 소설을 빌려도 될까요?

(A) Lucy asked me first.   (A) Lucy가 먼저 요청했어요. (O) → 거절 답변
(B) At the public library.   (B) 공공 도서관에서요. (X) → novel-library의 연상 어휘 함정
(C) To check out the book.   (C) 책을 대출받으려고요. (X) → borrow-check out 연상 어휘 함정

✅ 질문의 키워드는 Could I borrow로, 책을 빌릴 수 있는지를 묻는 요청문이다.

SPARTA Check-UP

Day06_3 해설 p.323

다음을 듣고 적절한 응답을 고른 후, 빈칸을 채우세요. (음성은 두 번씩 들려줍니다.)

1. Mark your answer.　　(A)　　(B)　　(C)

   Why don't we _____ and just go out for lunch?

   (A) Because we've _____.

   (B) I agree. Let's _____.

   (C) Good idea!

2. Mark your answer.　　(A)　　(B)　　(C)

   Could you _____ document?

   (A) I'm afraid _____.

   (B) On my desk.

   (C) I think it has a _____.

3. Mark your answer.　　(A)　　(B)　　(C)

   Should we _____ in the new Italian restaurant?

   (A) Sorry, _____.

   (B) You're right. It was _____.

   (C) Our new product is _____.

4. Mark your answer.　　(A)　　(B)　　(C)

   Would you _____?

   (A) Office supplies will _____.

   (B) The banquet room is _____.

   (C) No, _____ for me, too.

5. Mark your answer.　　(A)　　(B)　　(C)

   Why don't we _____ by the end of the day?

   (A) _____.

   (B) It was _____.

   (C) Sure, we did.

52

SPARTA Practice Test

Day06_4 해설 p.323

1. Mark your answer. (A) (B) (C)
2. Mark your answer. (A) (B) (C)
3. Mark your answer. (A) (B) (C)
4. Mark your answer. (A) (B) (C)
5. Mark your answer. (A) (B) (C)
6. Mark your answer. (A) (B) (C)
7. Mark your answer. (A) (B) (C)
8. Mark your answer. (A) (B) (C)
9. Mark your answer. (A) (B) (C)
10. Mark your answer. (A) (B) (C)
11. Mark your answer. (A) (B) (C)
12. Mark your answer. (A) (B) (C)
13. Mark your answer. (A) (B) (C)
14. Mark your answer. (A) (B) (C)
15. Mark your answer. (A) (B) (C)
16. Mark your answer. (A) (B) (C)
17. Mark your answer. (A) (B) (C)
18. Mark your answer. (A) (B) (C)
19. Mark your answer. (A) (B) (C)
20. Mark your answer. (A) (B) (C)
21. Mark your answer. (A) (B) (C)
22. Mark your answer. (A) (B) (C)
23. Mark your answer. (A) (B) (C)
24. Mark your answer. (A) (B) (C)
25. Mark your answer. (A) (B) (C)

DAY 7 선택 의문문/평서문

1 선택 의문문

SPARTA 유형 파악

<A or B> 형태로 둘 중에 하나를 어느 것이 맞는지 확인하거나 선택하라는 유형이다. 수단, 시간, 장소 등을 선택하라는 내용 등이 자주 나오므로 A와 B의 선택 사항을 정확히 파악하는 것이 중요하다.

SPARTA 출제 포인트

- <A or B> 형태로 단어와 단어, 구와 구, 절과 절 형태로 출제되며, A와 B가 무엇을 나타내는지 정확히 파악해야 한다.
- A와 B 둘 중에 하나를 선택했을 때 동일한 어휘가 그대로 정답으로 나올 수 있다. 하지만 패러프레이징(paraphrasing) 즉, 어휘 교체 표현도 자주 등장하므로 다양한 표현을 익혀 두자.
- A와 B 둘 다 부정하거나, 제3의 선택 사항 C가 등장하기도 하며, 때로는 선택을 피하거나 되묻는 응답도 나올 수 있다.
- 선택 의문문에서 자주 나오는 빈출 답변 표현을 외워 두자.

아무거나 좋아요.	
Either will be fine.	I have no preference.
I don't care[mind].	It doesn't matter.
It doesn't make any difference.	Whichever you recommend[want/like].
A, B 둘 다 좋아요.	
I use[like] both.	Can I have both?
A, B 둘 다 싫어요.	
Neither[None] of them.	I don't like either of them.
C가 좋아요.	
I want something else.	Do you have something else?

SPARTA 빈출 유형

Q Would you like some help, **or** will you do it alone? 도와드릴까요? 아니면 혼자 하실래요?
A1 I'd appreciate some help. 도와주시면 고맙죠. (A 선택)
A2 I can do it myself. 혼자 할 수 있어요. (B 선택)

Q Shall we go to a concert **or** a movie tonight? 오늘밤에 콘서트 갈래요? 아니면 영화 볼래요?
A Neither, I will stay at home. 둘 다 별로요, 집에 있을게요. (C 선택)

Q Are you going to stay here **or** come with us? 여기에 머물 거예요, 아니면 저희랑 갈 거예요?
A That's a very difficult question. 너무 어려운 질문이네요. (답변 회피)

SPARTA 문제 풀이 비법

🎧 Day07_1

Do you work in marketing or research and development? 마케팅 분야에서 일하세요, 아니면 연구개발 분야에서 일하세요?

(A) I'd like to go to the market. (A) 시장에 가고 싶어요. (X) → marketing/market 유사 발음 함정
(B) I don't like the new policies. (B) 새로운 정책을 안 좋아해요. (X) → 질문과 관련 없는 오답
(C) Actually, in the sales department. (C) 사실, 판매 부서에서요. (O) → C 선택

✅ 질문의 키워드는 work in marketing or research and development로, 'A와 B 중 어느 부서에서 일하는지'를 묻고 있다.

2 평서문

SPARTA 유형 파악

평서문은 문장 전체의 의미를 파악해야 하는 난이도 높은 유형이다. 주로 사실/의견/문제를 전달하거나 어떤 일을 요청/ 제안 하는 내용으로 출제된다. 답변으로는 정보 제공, 동의/반대, 수락/거절하는 내용이 나온다.

SPARTA 출제 포인트

- 평서문은 문장 전체 맥락을 이해해야 한다. 문장의 키워드를 파악한 후 보기를 들어야 하고 오답을 제거하면서 답을 찾는 소거법이 유리하다.
- 평서문에 대한 답변으로 Yes/No 형태의 부정/긍정 답변이 나오기도 한다.

SPARTA 빈출 유형

Q   The air conditioner on this floor isn't working properly. 이 층 에어컨이 잘 작동되지 않아요. (문제 상황)
A1 I have already called a repairperson. 이미 수리공을 불렀어요. (해결책 제시)
A2 Oh, no. This is the third time. 아, 안 돼요. 이번이 세 번째예요. (감정 표현)

Q   Nancy will be promoted to branch manager. Nancy가 지점장으로 곧 승진될 거예요. (사실 전달)
A1 Who told you that? 누가 말했어요? (반문)
A2 Really? She deserves it. 정말요? 그녀는 승진할 만해요. (동의)

Q   Please join us for a discussion after the presentation. 발표 후 토론을 같이 하죠. (요청)
A1 Thanks for inviting me. 초대해 주셔서 고맙습니다. (수락)
A2 Sorry, I'm meeting with some important clients. 죄송하지만, 중요한 고객들을 만나야 해요. (거절)

Q   Let's get together tomorrow morning. 내일 아침에 만나요. (제안)
A1 Okay, see you then. 좋아요, 그때 만나요. (수락)
A2 I'm afraid I have a dental appointment. 죄송하지만 치과 예약이 있어요. (거절)

Q   I think that show was very great. 쇼가 정말 멋졌던 것 같아요. (의견)
A1 Yes, I'd like to see it again later. 네, 나중에 또 보고 싶어요. (동의)
A2 But some parts were a little bit boring. 하지만 어떤 부분은 약간 지루했어요. (반대)

Q   I can replace the damaged part at no charge. 손된 부품을 무료로 교체해 드릴게요. (제안)
A1 That's good to hear. 반가운 소식이네요. (감정 표현)
A2 I really appreciate it. 정말 감사해요. (감사)

SPARTA 문제 풀이 비법

🎧 Day07_2

We need to hire experienced technicians to upgrade this equipment.   이 장비를 개선하기 위해 경험 있는 기술자들을 고용해야 해요.

(A) Okay, I will post a job opening on the Web site.   (A) 좋아요, 제가 웹사이트에 채용 공고를 낼게요. (O) → 동의+부연 설명
(B) It is working fine.   (B) 작동이 잘 돼요. (X) → equipment-working 연상 어휘 함정
(C) It'll pass the inspection, no problem.   (C) 점검을 통과할 거예요, 문제 없어요. (X) → 질문과 무관한 응답

✅ '경험 있는 기술자들을 고용해야 한다'는 의견을 표현한 평서문이다.

SPARTA Check-UP

다음을 듣고 적절한 응답을 고른 후, 빈칸을 채우세요. (음성은 두 번씩 들려줍니다.)

1. Mark your answer. (A) (B) (C)

   Should we _____ to the presentation or _____?
   (A) The room is _____.
   (B) _____ in the lobby.
   (C) The revised agenda topics.

2. Mark your answer. (A) (B) (C)

   _____ more raspberry pie or apple pie?
   (A) About the _____.
   (B) I'll _____.
   (C) With milk.

3. Mark your answer. (A) (B) (C)

   The office _____.
   (A) I _____.
   (B) _____ the air conditioner.
   (C) I have a jacket _____.

4. Mark your answer. (A) (B) (C)

   Would you like to _____?
   (A) It's a very _____.
   (B) Isn't it too _____?
   (C) Table for three, please.

5. Mark your answer. (A) (B) (C)

   _____ Mr. Martin's address yesterday.
   (A) Please _____ to him.
   (B) Here's _____.
   (C) I think he was _____.

SPARTA Practice Test

Day07_4 해설 p.328

1. Mark your answer. (A) (B) (C)
2. Mark your answer. (A) (B) (C)
3. Mark your answer. (A) (B) (C)
4. Mark your answer. (A) (B) (C)
5. Mark your answer. (A) (B) (C)
6. Mark your answer. (A) (B) (C)
7. Mark your answer. (A) (B) (C)
8. Mark your answer. (A) (B) (C)
9. Mark your answer. (A) (B) (C)
10. Mark your answer. (A) (B) (C)
11. Mark your answer. (A) (B) (C)
12. Mark your answer. (A) (B) (C)
13. Mark your answer. (A) (B) (C)
14. Mark your answer. (A) (B) (C)
15. Mark your answer. (A) (B) (C)
16. Mark your answer. (A) (B) (C)
17. Mark your answer. (A) (B) (C)
18. Mark your answer. (A) (B) (C)
19. Mark your answer. (A) (B) (C)
20. Mark your answer. (A) (B) (C)
21. Mark your answer. (A) (B) (C)
22. Mark your answer. (A) (B) (C)
23. Mark your answer. (A) (B) (C)
24. Mark your answer. (A) (B) (C)
25. Mark your answer. (A) (B) (C)

DAY 7 · 선택 의문문/평서문

SPARTA 빈출 표현 — 회피성 답변

몰라요.	아직 결정되지 않았어요.
I don't know./I have no idea.	I haven't decided yet. = I'm still deciding.
I'm not sure/certain.	I haven't made up my mind.
I wish I knew./I could tell you.	They haven't decided yet. = They're still deciding.
I haven't checked.	It hasn't been decided (yet). = It's still being decided.
Nobody knows.	Let me think about it.
Who knows?	It hasn't been confirmed yet.
	It hasn't been announced yet.

~가 알아요.	전혀 못 들었어요.
Why don't you ask ~?	I haven't heard about it.
~ knows it better than I do.	I haven't been told yet.
~ might/should know.	That's news to me.
It depends on ~.	I wasn't notified. = I wasn't informed.
Go to the reception desk.	He/She/They didn't tell me.
It's not my decision.	
Ask someone else.	

확인해 볼게요.	기억나지 않아요.
Let me check./I'll check it again.	I forgot.
Let me ask someone/I'll find out.	I can't remember.
I'll let you know later./I'll ask and let you know.	It slipped my mind.
I'll get back to you.	It's on the tip of my tongue.

저는 책임자가 아니에요.
I'm not in charge.
I can't decide.
It's up to the board.
It's not up to me.

PART 3
대화문

DAY 08 | 주제/목적, 장소/직업
DAY 09 | 이유&세부 사항/문제점
DAY 10 | 요청&제안/다음에 할 일
DAY 11 | 의도 파악/시각 자료

PART 3 접근법

PART 3는 두세 사람의 남녀가 주고 받는 짧은 대화문으로, 각 대화당 3문제씩 총 39문제가 나오기 때문에 가장 높은 비중을 차지한다. 대화를 잘 듣고 필요한 정보를 잘 잡아내는 능력을 판별한다.

🛡️ 문제 풀이 전략

1. 대화를 듣기 전에 반드시 문제를 먼저 파악한다. 주어진 시간은 30초 이내로 질문과 보기를 키워드 중심으로 확인한다. 시각 자료가 있는 경우, 항상 문제를 먼저 보고 문제에 따라 시각 자료를 파악해야 한다.

2. 대화의 초반을 놓치지 않고 들어야 한다. 보통 대화 초반에 문제의 단서가 집중적으로 등장한다.

3. 문제에 명시된 성별을 확인하고 그에 맞는 성별이 나올 때 집중해서 들어야 한다.

4. 담화를 들으면서, 미리 파악한 문제의 키워드 중심으로 3문제에 대한 답을 바로 선택해야 한다. 대부분 문제 순서대로 단서가 나오지만, 종종 순서가 바뀌는 경우도 있다.

5. 문제를 읽어줄 때 그 다음 문제를 파악하면서 준비한다. 명심할 것은 한 번 흐름이 끊기면 풀 수 있는 문제도 자칫 놓칠 수 있기 때문에 순발력과 판단력이 무엇보다 중요하다.

6. 화자 의도 파악 문제는 화자들의 상황에 따라 그 말을 하는 의도를 묻기 때문에 대화의 앞뒤 내용이 중요하다. 사전적인 의미보다 대화 상황에 맞는 맥락을 찾는 훈련을 해야 한다.

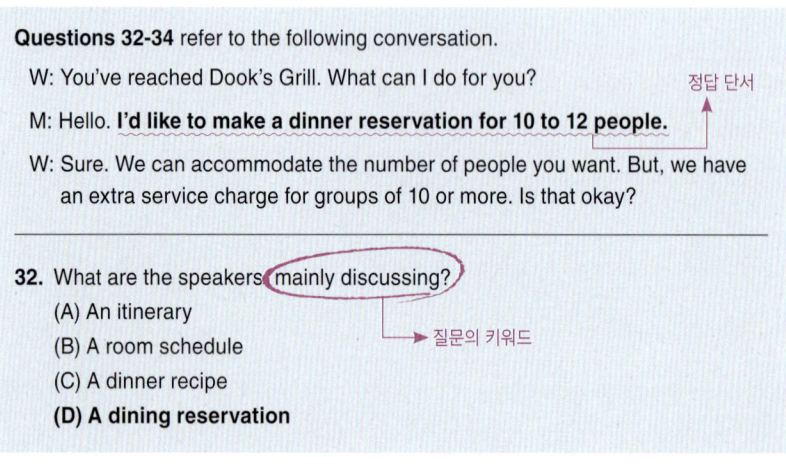

DAY 8 주제/목적, 장소/직업

1 주제/목적

SPARTA 유형 파악

주제/목적을 묻는 유형은 3문제 중 주로 앞부분에 출제되며 단서도 주로 대화 첫부분에 나온다. 하지만 난이도 있는 문제는 대화 초반에 국한되지 않고 전체 내용을 듣고 판단해야 한다. 전형적인 형태로 "화자들은 무엇을 이야기하는가?"라고 묻기도 하지만, 때로는 "여자는 무엇을 준비하고 있는가?"와 같은 내용으로 주제를 묻기도 한다.

SPARTA 출제 포인트

- 대화 초반부에 나오는 키워드를 잡아내자. 보통 첫 번째 질문은 대화의 주제/목적에 대해 묻는다.
- 대화 초반에 주제/목적의 단서가 등장하지 않는 경우 대화 중반 혹은 끝까지 듣고 풀어야 하는 경우도 있다.
- 주제를 파악하고 나면 나머지 문제를 푸는 흐름도 잡아낼 수 있다.

SPARTA 빈출 유형

What are the speakers discussing? 화자들은 무엇을 논의 중인가?
What are the speakers talking about? 화자들은 무엇에 대해 이야기하는가?
What is the conversation mainly about? 대화는 주로 무엇에 관한 것인가?
What is the purpose of the conversation? 대화의 목적은 무엇인가?
What is the purpose of the man's call? 남자가 전화한 목적은 무엇인가?
Why is the man calling the woman? 남자는 왜 여자에게 전화하는가?
Why is the woman calling? 여자는 왜 전화하는가?

SPARTA 문제 풀이 비법

🎧 Day08_1

W: Hey, Jin-Su. I just heard that the features department is looking for a new editor, and I'm interested in applying for the job.
→ 대화 주제 제시
M: It's a really good opportunity for you. Actually, you always wanted that position. Also, the article you wrote last month about the improvement of the workplace environment received praise from our readers.

W: 진수, 특집 기사 부서에서 새로운 편집자를 찾고 있다고 방금 들었는데, 저 거기에 지원하려고요.
M: 당신한테 정말 좋은 기회네요. 사실, 그 자리를 항상 원했잖아요. 그리고 지난달에 당신이 쓴 직장 환경 개선에 관한 기사가 독자들한테 좋은 평가도 받았고요.

What are the speakers mainly **talking about**?
(A) A new position
(B) A company policy
(C) A candidate
(D) A feature article

화자들은 주로 무엇에 대해 이야기 나누고 있는가?
(A) 새로운 자리
(B) 회사 방침
(C) 지원자
(D) 특집 기사

✔ 여자의 첫 대사에서 새로운 자리에 관심이 있음을 언급하고 있으므로 정답은 (A). 주제/목적을 묻는 문제는 대화 초반에 단서가 제시된다.

2 장소/직업

SPARTA 유형 파악

대화의 장소와 인물의 직업은 주로 앞부분에 나오며, 대화 초반부에 힌트가 제시된다. 직접적으로 장소나 직업을 언급하기도 하지만 대부분 대화에 나오는 키워드를 중심으로 풀어야 한다.

SPARTA 출제 포인트

- 초반부에 나오는 대화 키워드를 중심으로 판단하자. 보통 첫 대사에 장소/직업의 힌트가 나온다.
- 특정 성별의 직업을 물을 때 모든 등장 인물의 직업이 보기에 나오는 경우가 있으므로 정확히 누구의 직업을 묻고 있는지 파악해야 한다.

SPARTA 빈출 유형

Where is the conversation taking place? 대화는 어디에서 일어나는가?
Where most likely are the speakers? 화자들은 어디에 있는 것 같은가?
Where are the speakers? 화자들은 어디에 있는가?
Who is the woman? 여자는 누구인가?
Who most likely is the man? 남자는 누구일 것 같은가?
Who is the woman talking to? 여자는 누구와 말하고 있는가?
What is the man's occupation/job/profession? 남자의 직업은 무엇인가?
What type of business does the man work for? 남자는 어떤 종류의 업체에서 일하는가?

SPARTA 문제 풀이 비법

🎧 Day08_2

M: Are the minutes for the meeting ready yet, Sarah? I need to go over them as soon as possible before I meet Benjamin Smith in finance. → 직업 제시

W: I'm almost done, yes. Right now, I'm making copies for all the department heads. Could you wait a moment?

Who most likely is the **woman**?
(A) A shareholder
(B) A new hire
(C) An office assistant
(D) A department head

M: 회의록이 준비됐나요, Sarah? 재무부의 Benjamin Smith를 만나기 전에 가능한 한 빨리 검토해야 해서요.

W: 거의 다했어요. 모든 부서장님들께 드리려고 지금 복사하고 있어요. 조금만 기다려 주시겠어요?

여자는 누구인 것 같은가?
(A) 주주
(B) 신입사원
(C) 비서
(D) 부서장

✅ 첫 대사에서 남자가 여자에게 회의록 준비가 됐는지를 묻고 있다. 따라서 여자는 남자의 비서임을 알 수 있다.

SPARTA Check-UP

다음을 듣고 정답을 고른 후, 빈칸을 채우세요. (음성은 두 번씩 들려줍니다.)

1. Who most likely is the man?
   (A) A dancer
   (B) A musician
   (C) A stage director
   (D) An audience member

2. What does the woman ask about?
   (A) An instrument arrangement
   (B) A guest list
   (C) Some seating assignments
   (D) Some lights

3. What will the woman do next?
   (A) Conclude a task
   (B) Have lunch
   (C) Adjust the lighting
   (D) Start the rehearsal

M Ms. Larson, _____ _____ the instrument arrangement on the stage? Is everything _____?
W Yes, it looks good. However, can you make sure _____?
   I want all the members of my band to be visible.
M No problem. Let me know when the rehearsal starts with your band _____ _____ to be certain.
W All right. _____ and then we're coming back to the stage to rehearse.

---

4. Why is the woman calling the man?
   (A) To remind him about an appointment
   (B) To tell him about an exclusive deal
   (C) To inform him that some photographs are ready
   (D) To notify him about a cancellation

5. What problem does the man mention?
   (A) His photos are not ready.
   (B) He plans to return later.
   (C) He has difficulty arranging a schedule.
   (D) He will be a little late.

6. What does the woman say about MD Studio?
   (A) It is far from the man's workplace.
   (B) It does not require any reservations.
   (C) It has a good location.
   (D) It has longer hours.

W Hi, Mr. Collins. This is Lucy calling from Watson's Photography Studio. Unfortunately, _____ _____ with us this afternoon to have your picture taken. Our ceiling is leaking after heavy rain this morning. So, _____, as we're working on fixing it. I'm really sorry.
M Actually, _____ _____ because I'm really busy nowadays. It was hard to make this appointment. So, _____ that could take me today?
W Give me a second. Yes, I know a studio that _____ at all MD Studio nearby. If you go there now, you might have to wait a bit, but it shouldn't _____ _____.

SPARTA Practice Test

1. Why is the woman calling?
   - (A) To request a service
   - (B) To offer a job
   - (C) To reschedule an interview
   - (D) To change a position

2. What is the man concerned about?
   - (A) He is interested in a job at another company.
   - (B) He would have to relocate to an overseas country.
   - (C) He is concerned that he is not qualified.
   - (D) He would have to take many trips.

3. What part of the job is the woman willing to negotiate?
   - (A) The amount of paid time off
   - (B) The location
   - (C) The salary
   - (D) The job title

4. What is the main topic of the conversation?
   - (A) A new manager
   - (B) A sales document
   - (C) An office atmosphere
   - (D) A project deadline

5. What does the man request?
   - (A) Some opinions
   - (B) Sales tax
   - (C) Customers' feedback
   - (D) A sample document

6. What does the woman suggest the man do?
   - (A) Speak with a coworker
   - (B) Organize some files
   - (C) Record the information
   - (D) Send a memo

7. Why is the woman calling?
   - (A) To order a mobile phone
   - (B) To confirm a registration
   - (C) To close an account
   - (D) To complain about a bill

8. What did the woman do last month?
   - (A) She went on a business trip.
   - (B) She traveled abroad.
   - (C) She entered a photo contest.
   - (D) She purchased a device.

9. According to the man, what was the woman asked to do?
   - (A) Switch off a device feature
   - (B) Take many pictures
   - (C) Rewrite a policy
   - (D) Sign some documents

10. Where do the speakers most likely work?
    - (A) At a local hotel
    - (B) At a recruiting agency
    - (C) At a clothing manufacturer
    - (D) At a laundry service

11. What problem does the man mention?
    - (A) A machine is malfunctioning.
    - (B) A completion date is not realistic.
    - (C) An item is poorly made.
    - (D) A supplier went out of business.

12. How will the speakers address the problem?
    - (A) By hiring more staff
    - (B) By working extra hours
    - (C) By updating the Web site
    - (D) By negotiating with a business

13. Where does the man most likely work?
    (A) At a paint store
    (B) At a moving company
    (C) At a dental clinic
    (D) At a construction company

14. Why is the woman unavailable on Friday?
    (A) She will go to a medical office.
    (B) She will paint her house.
    (C) She will have a lot of work.
    (D) She will have an appointment with her friend.

15. What does the woman recommend for the man?
    (A) What to bring
    (B) Where to park
    (C) When to deliver
    (D) Where to paint

16. What type of business does the man work for?
    (A) A beauty parlor
    (B) A real estate agency
    (C) An advertising agency
    (D) An equipment rental service

17. What is the man worried about?
    (A) Customers' complaints
    (B) An expensive location
    (C) An increase in competition
    (D) A shortage of funds

18. What does the man emphasize about the company?
    (A) The affordable prices
    (B) The number of branch offices
    (C) The user-friendly Web site
    (D) The trendy fashion styles

19. Where are the speakers?
    (A) On a flight
    (B) In an airport
    (C) In an office
    (D) At a train station

20. What does the man offer to do?
    (A) Cancel her flight
    (B) Give her money back
    (C) Upgrade her plane seat
    (D) Check the possible flights

21. Why should the woman go to New York in a hurry?
    (A) To see her cousin
    (B) To tour the city
    (C) To meet some clients
    (D) To attend an important workshop

22. Who most likely is the woman?
    (A) A journalist
    (B) A restaurant manager
    (C) A potential applicant
    (D) A chef

23. What is the main topic of the conversation?
    (A) New restaurant menus
    (B) The expansion of a business
    (C) An increase in sales
    (D) An article about food

24. According to the man, what will happen next year?
    (A) New menus will be available.
    (B) An advertising campaign will start.
    (C) Many branches will be opened nationwide.
    (D) Business will start in the European market.

DAY 9 이유&세부 사항/문제점

1 이유&세부 사항

SPARTA 유형 파악

이유 등의 세부 사항을 묻는 문제는 일정이나 시간의 변경, 연기, 취소 관련 내용을 주로 묻는다. 그 외 특정 인물/장소/시기 등을 묻기도 한다. 보통 특정 세부 사항에 관련된 사실을 묻는 질문에는 화자 중 한 명이 자주 언급한 것을 묻는다. 그리고 이러한 유형은 문제 속에 힌트가 제시되므로 대화를 듣기 전에 문제 및 보기를 통해 미리 어떤 내용이 나올지 파악할 수 있다.

SPARTA 출제 포인트

- Why, How, What 등 다양한 의문사를 이용해 묻는 질문으로, 세 문제 중 보통 두 번째나 세 번째에 위치한다. 따라서 단서는 대화 중 세부적인 상황이 나오는 중후반부에 제시된다.
- 이유 문제의 키워드는 보기에서 to부정사, because/since, due to, so 등과 함께 언급된다.
- 특정 인물이나 장소와 관련해서 묻는 질문은 발음에 유의해야 한다. 보통 고유명사 뒤에 단서가 나오며 항상 보기를 동시에 보면서 풀어야 한다. 특정 인물의 직업은 그 인물에 관한 내용 앞뒤에 단서가 나온다.

SPARTA 빈출 유형

Why was the woman late? 왜 여자는 늦었는가?
Why is the woman concerned[worried]? 왜 여자는 걱정하는가?
Why did the man miss the workshop last week? 왜 남자는 지난주에 워크숍을 놓쳤는가?
Why is the woman unable to help the man? 왜 여자는 남자를 도와줄 수 없는가?
What caused the delay? 무엇이 지연을 야기했는가?
What can the woman receive if she spends over 500 dollars? 여자가 500달러 이상 쓴다면 무엇을 받을 수 있는가?
What does the man say about the new office? 남자는 새 사무실에 대해 뭐라고 말하는가?
According to the woman, what happened this morning? 여자에 따르면, 오늘 아침에 무슨 일이 일어났는가?

SPARTA 문제 풀이 비법

🎧 Day09_1

M: Hey, Lucia. Can you work for me this Friday? I need someone for the second half of my shift.
W: Sorry, Pete. They've scheduled me for training on the new machines then. I had to give concert tickets away because of it. Anyway, ask Sherry. She may be able to trade shifts.
M: Ah! I've never had any luck trading shifts with her. Last time she agreed to do it, but she changed her mind a day later. And the time before, she didn't make up her mind until the last minute.

What does the **man say** about **Sherry**?
(A) She is not reliable.
(B) She forgets things she promises.
(C) She complains about work.
(D) She already works too much.

M: Lucia, 이번 주 금요일에 저 대신 일할 수 있어요? 제 근무 시간대 후반에 일할 누군가가 필요해요.
W: 미안해요, Pete. 그때는 회사에서 새 기계와 관련해 교육하는 일정이 있어요. 그거 때문에 콘서트 티켓도 다른 사람한테 줘야 했어요. 어쨌든, Sherry한테 물어 봐요. 그녀가 근무 시간을 바꿔 줄 수 있을지도 몰라요.
M: 아! 그녀와 근무를 바꾸는 운은 없었어요. 지난번에 그녀가 하기로 했었는데 다음 날 마음을 바꾸더라고요. 그 전에도 마지막 순간까지 결정을 못 하더라고요.

남자는 Sherry에 대해 뭐라고 말하는가?
(A) 그녀는 믿을 수 없다.
(B) 그녀는 약속한 것을 잊어버린다.
(C) 그녀는 일에 대해 불평한다.
(D) 그녀는 이미 너무 많이 일한다.

✅ 키워드는 "Sherry"이다. 남자의 대사 "I've never had any luck trading shifts with her. ~"에서 남자는 그녀에 대해 이미 신뢰가 없는 상태임을 알 수 있다. 따라서 정답은 (A)이다.

2 문제점

SPARTA 유형 파악

문제점을 묻는 문제는 대화 전반부에 단서가 등장하는 경우가 많다. 하지만 문제 순서에 따라 중후반부에 나올 수도 있으므로 유의한다. 초반에 나오는 문제점은 대화의 주제일 가능성이 높지만 중후반부에 나온 내용이라면 세부적인 사항을 묻는 것이며, 주로 화자가 겪고 있는 문제점을 묻는다.

SPARTA 출제 포인트

- 부정적인 표현에 집중하자. 대화에서 trouble/problem/issue, I'm afraid[sorry] ~, unfortunately 등 부정적인 뉘앙스의 어휘가 문제 상황에서 자주 등장한다.
- 화자의 걱정거리를 묻는 질문도 많이 출제된다. I'm concerned[worried] about ~ 뒤의 내용이 정답 단서로 제시된다는 것도 알아 두자.
- 질문에 나온 화자의 성별을 미리 파악하고, 그 성별의 화자가 해당 내용을 말할 때를 포착한다.

SPARTA 빈출 유형

What is the woman's problem? 여자의 문제점은 무엇인가?
What problem are the speakers discussing? 화자들은 무슨 문제점을 논의하고 있는가?
What is the man concerned[worried] about? 남자는 무엇에 대해 걱정하는가?
What is the problem with the car? 차에 무슨 문제가 있는가?
What is the woman having trouble with? 여자는 무슨 문제를 겪고 있는가?
What problem does the man mention? 남자는 무슨 문제를 언급하는가?
What is the woman disappointed with? 여자는 무엇에 실망하는가?

SPARTA 문제 풀이 비법

🎧 Day09_2

M: Hello, I'd like to book a table for ten next Friday at 7 P.M. Actually, I want a private room for the company dinner. Is it possible?
W: I'm really sorry, sir. We've already reserved all the rooms that day. How about the dining hall? There are just a few tables left. Otherwise, we do have vacancies on Saturday.
M: Okay, I'll have to talk to my coworkers, and then I'll call you soon.
W: All right, but remember, we are usually fully booked every Saturday so get back to me as soon as possible.

M: 안녕하세요, 다음 주 금요일 저녁 7시에 10명 좌석을 예약하려고 하는데요. 사실 회사 회식이라서 전용 룸을 원하는데 가능한가요?
W: 정말 죄송합니다. 이미 그날은 다 예약됐어요. 큰 식당은 어떠세요? 현재 몇 테이블만 남았거든요. 아니면 토요일에 빈 방들이 몇 개 있어요.
M: 알겠습니다, 동료들과 이야기하고 나서 연락 드릴게요.
W: 네, 하지만 토요일마다 예약이 다 차기 때문에 가능한 한 빨리 연락 주세요.

What **problem** does the **woman mention**?
(A) There aren't any rooms on that day.
(B) The meeting was canceled.
(C) The restaurant is too small.
(D) The menu is limited.

여자는 무슨 문제를 언급하는가?
(A) 그날 방이 없다.
(B) 회의가 취소됐다.
(C) 레스토랑이 너무 작다.
(D) 메뉴가 한정적이다.

✅ 여자가 언급한 문제를 묻고 있으므로 여자의 대사에 집중한다. 여자가 "We've already reserved all the rooms that day."라며 이미 다 예약이 찼다고 했으므로 정답은 (A)이다.

SPARTA Check-UP

Day09_3 해설 p.341

다음을 듣고 정답을 고른 후, 빈칸을 채우세요. (음성은 두 번씩 들려줍니다.)

1. Why did the woman miss a meeting?
   (A) She was not feeling well.
   (B) She forgot the meeting time.
   (C) She was talking to a client.
   (D) She did not receive the invitation.

2. What is the woman confused about?
   (A) The details of an assignment
   (B) A reimbursement process
   (C) The terms of a contract
   (D) A travel itinerary

3. According to the man, what should the woman do?
   (A) Restart a computer
   (B) Talk to the manager about the meeting
   (C) Refer to the electronic version of the data
   (D) Upgrade the Web site

---

4. What problem does the woman mention?
   (A) A painting is blurry.
   (B) A restroom is dirty.
   (C) A job is incomplete.
   (D) A ceiling is damaged.

5. What does the man ask the woman about?
   (A) A crew member's name
   (B) A start time
   (C) A completion date
   (D) Inexperienced workers

6. What does the man say he will do right away?
   (A) Reduce the working hours
   (B) Contact the supplier
   (C) Finish some works
   (D) Adjust a schedule

W Diego, were you at the sales meeting yesterday? I couldn't make it because I was on the phone _____. Can you fill me in?

M Okay, you got a copy of the meeting materials, right?

W Yeah, but the part about _____ _____ for travel expenses was really complicated. Do you know if there's more documents on that?

M Oh, you can look at them electronically. You'll see... _____ where you can find more details on reimbursement procedures.

W Thanks for visiting, Mr. Flynn. Your work crew did a good job painting the hallway of our building. _____ our other rooms. So could I ask you a favor? As you can see, the restroom on the 10th floor _____ _____ because of leaking from the ceiling.
I know you are so busy.

M Hmm... Actually, my team is fully scheduled this week. Is it urgent? _____ _____?

W To be honest, I hope you'll be able to take care of this soon.

M All right. _____ again and let you know by the end of the day.

68

SPARTA Practice Test

1. What is the man unable to find?
   (A) Some furniture
   (B) A hand tool
   (C) A protective device
   (D) Some cleaning supplies

2. What did the man do last weekend?
   (A) He purchased a small vehicle.
   (B) He visited an art gallery.
   (C) He obtained an old object.
   (D) He worked in the garden.

3. Why most likely is the woman surprised?
   (A) She has met the man before.
   (B) She thinks the work is too hard.
   (C) She was not aware of the sale.
   (D) She knows the place the man said.

4. What do the two speakers have in common?
   (A) Both are hungry.
   (B) Both are tired.
   (C) Both want to go to Spicoli's.
   (D) Both prefer home-style pancakes.

5. Why does the woman want to go to the Breakfast Nook?
   (A) It opens at 7 A.M.
   (B) She knows the owner.
   (C) She likes the food there.
   (D) It is cheaper than Spicoli's.

6. What are the speakers going to do next?
   (A) Continue reading the pages
   (B) Get a bite to eat
   (C) Continue their discussion
   (D) Get some rest

7. What problem does the man mention?
   (A) Some defective items
   (B) The shortage of a product
   (C) A broken truck
   (D) A delivery error

8. What does the woman say is planned in three days?
   (A) A product launch
   (B) An inspection
   (C) A cooking class
   (D) A product demonstration

9. What does the man say he will do?
   (A) Call a supervisor
   (B) Install a device
   (C) Extend a warranty
   (D) Contact the woman's manager

10. What is the woman's problem?
    (A) There is a scheduling conflict.
    (B) There are no projectors available.
    (C) A contract is incorrect.
    (D) A deadline has been moved up to Friday.

11. What does the woman inquire about?
    (A) Negotiating the prices
    (B) Winning the contract
    (C) Putting off a training session
    (D) Arranging a teleconference

12. What does the man say he will do?
    (A) Forward some documents
    (B) Review the materials
    (C) Speak with a supervisor
    (D) Contact a client

13. Where do the speakers most likely work?

    (A) At a furniture warehouse
    (B) At a retail store
    (C) At a laundry
    (D) At a law firm

14. What is the problem?

    (A) Some merchandise is broken.
    (B) A receipt is missing.
    (C) The information on some labels is incorrect.
    (D) An order has not arrived.

15. What will the speakers probably do next?

    (A) Mail a discount voucher
    (B) Inspect some products
    (C) Talk to a store owner
    (D) Check the inventory

16. What kind of business do the speakers work for?

    (A) A catering company
    (B) A café
    (C) A university
    (D) A clothing manufacturer

17. What did the woman forget to bring?

    (A) A mobile phone
    (B) An apron
    (C) Some medicine
    (D) A wallet

18. What does the man mention about the event?

    (A) It is a charity fundraiser.
    (B) It has been catered several times before.
    (C) It will be able to lead to more business.
    (D) Its attendees are well known.

19. What does the man want the woman to do?

    (A) Change a camera
    (B) Recommend a product
    (C) Explain a feature
    (D) Plan a backpacking trip

20. What does the man say he will do with the camera?

    (A) Document his trips
    (B) Teach a class
    (C) Record music
    (D) Make a commercial

21. What is the feature of the Dixcon 90?

    (A) It has a long battery life.
    (B) It is for experts.
    (C) It is a new model.
    (D) It is easy to operate.

22. What problem does the woman mention?

    (A) A meal is cold.
    (B) A bill is incorrect.
    (C) An order is not processed.
    (D) A receipt is missing.

23. What does the woman say she wants to do?

    (A) Speak to the chef
    (B) Fill out a comment card
    (C) Get some details about a service
    (D) Upgrade the catering order

24. Why is the woman asked to wait?

    (A) A special dish takes time to cook.
    (B) Some food is being packaged.
    (C) There are so many customers.
    (D) A staff member is busy.

DAY 10 요청&제안/다음에 할 일

1 요청&제안

SPARTA 유형 파악

요청&제안 사항을 묻는 문제의 정답 단서는 주로 대화 중후반부에 나오며, 보통 2~3번째 순서로 많이 나온다. 요청 및 제안할 때 자주 쓰이는 표현을 미리 익혀 두면 답을 찾는 데 유리하다.

SPARTA 출제 포인트

- 질문에 나온 화자의 성별을 통해 요청의 주/객체를 파악하자.
- 요청&제안은 대화에서 명령문/요청&권유문의 형태로 나온다. 아래의 관련 표현을 외워 두자.
  - 요청: Can[Could/Would] you ~?, I'd like you to ~, Please ~, Would you mind ~?
  - 제안: Why don't you[we] ~?, How[What] about ~?, I suggest[recommend] ~, You could ~, You'd better ~, You might want to ~, I will[can] ~, Would you like me to ~?, Do you want me to ~?, Let me ~, I'd be happy[glad/honored/pleased] to ~, Why don't I ~?(주로 1인칭 중심)
  - 상기하도록 요구: Don't forget ~, Remember ~, Keep in mind ~, I'd like to remind you ~.

SPARTA 빈출 유형

What does the woman suggest[recommend/encourage]? 여자는 무엇을 제안하는가?
What does the woman ask for[about]? 여자는 무엇을 요청하는가?
What does the woman ask the man to do? 여자는 남자에게 무엇을 하라고 요청하는가?
What is the man asked to do? 남자는 무엇을 하도록 요청 받는가?
What does the man want the woman to do? 남자는 여자가 무엇을 하기를 원하는가?
What does the woman offer to do? 여자는 무엇을 해주겠다고 하는가?
What information does the man request? 남자는 무슨 정보를 요청하는가?

SPARTA 문제 풀이 비법

🎧 Day10_1

W: Sam, remember when we discussed contracting with a phone service? Well, I found a company that will provide health care information for our patients who call when the office is closed.
M: Great! But, do you think we can afford it? We can't go beyond the amount we've budgeted this year.
W: Don't worry. Their price is reasonable, and it sounds like the service we're looking for. They hire trained nurses to answer our patients' medical questions over the phone.

What does the **man ask about**?
(A) The date of an appointment
(B) The cost of a service
(C) The experience of a coworker
(D) The location of a business

W: Sam, 전화 서비스 계약에 대해 논의했던 거 기억해요? 음, 사무실이 문을 닫았을 때 전화한 환자들에게 건강 관리 정보를 제공할 회사를 찾았어요.
M: 좋네요! 근데 우리가 그럴 만한 여유가 있다고 생각해요? 올해 예산을 초과할 수는 없어요.
W: 걱정 마요. 가격이 합리적이고 우리가 찾던 서비스 같아요. 그들은 전화로 환자들의 의학 관련 질문에 답하기 위해 잘 숙련된 간호사들을 고용해요.

남자는 무엇에 대해 묻는가?
(A) 약속 날짜
(B) 서비스 비용
(C) 동료의 경험
(D) 업체의 위치

✔ 남자가 묻고 있는 것을 물었으므로 남자의 대사에 집중한다. 남자가 "do you think we can afford it?"라며 예산을 언급했으므로 재정적으로 여유가 있는지를 묻고 있음을 알 수 있다. 따라서 정답은 (B)이다.

2 다음에 할 일

SPARTA 유형 파악

미래에 할 일을 묻는 문제는 3문제 중 주로 마지막에 위치한다. 따라서 대화 후반에 정답 단서가 나온다. 지문을 듣기 전에 문제를 먼저 파악한 후 대화에서 미래 등의 특정 시점을 나타내는 키워드를 잘 포착해야 한다.

SPARTA 출제 포인트

- 대화 후반에 제안&요청(I'll ~, Let me ~, Why don't you ~?, I'm going[planning] to ~, Let's ~ 등) 표현이 나오면 뒤이어 미래에 할 일을 언급할 가능성이 높다.
- 미래를 나타내는 표현 tomorrow, next week, later, right now 등의 키워드에 집중하자.
- What will the man probably do next?처럼 화자가 다음에 무엇을 할 것인지를 묻는 문제는 남자에게 특정 행동을 요청하는 여자의 대사에도 귀 기울여야 한다.

SPARTA 빈출 유형

What will the man probably do next? 남자는 아마도 다음에 무엇을 할 것인가?
What does the woman say she will do next? 여자는 다음에 무엇을 할 거라고 하는가?
What does the woman plan to do this afternoon? 여자는 오늘 오후에 무엇을 할 계획인가?
What will happen this summer? 이번 여름에 무슨 일이 일어날 것인가?
What are the speakers going to do later? 화자들은 나중에 무엇을 할 계획인가?
What is the marketing department planning to do? 마케팅 부서는 무엇을 계획하는가?
What will take place next week? 다음 주에 무슨 일이 일어날 것인가?
What will the man do when they meet? 그들이 만나면 남자는 무엇을 할 것인가?
What does the woman expect to happen? 여자는 무슨 일이 일어날 것을 예상하는가?

SPARTA 문제 풀이 비법

🎧 Day10_2

W: Hi, Mr. Collins, I'm calling from Bright Dentistry. Your appointment with Dr. Erickson is at 2 P.M. this Friday. But, on that day, he has to attend a medical conference. I was wondering if you'd be able to move your appointment forward to Thursday. Is it alright?
M: Well, I have a sales meeting scheduled that morning, but I think that afternoon would be alright.
W: Great. Thank you so much. Would you like me to make an appointment at 2 P.M., or do you want another time?
M: I think 3 P.M. would be better.
W: Okay, I'll mark down your appointment in the schedule right now.

W: 안녕하세요, Collins 씨. 브라이트 치과에서 연락 드립니다. Erickson 박사님과 금요일 오후 2시에 예약하셨네요. 그런데 그날, 의학 학회에 참석하셔야 해서요. 혹시 예약을 목요일로 당길 수 있는지 해서요. 괜찮으실까요?
M: 음, 제가 그날 아침에는 영업 회의가 있지만 오후에는 괜찮을 것 같아요.
W: 좋아요. 정말 감사합니다. 오후 2시로 잡아 드릴까요, 아니면 다른 시간을 원하세요?
M: 제 생각에는 오후 3시가 더 좋을 것 같아요.
W: 알겠어요, 지금 바로 일정에 표시해 둘게요.

What will the **woman do next**?
(A) Update the schedule
(B) Submit her medical records
(C) Go to the market
(D) Prepare for a sales meeting

여자는 다음에 무엇을 할 것인가?
(A) 일정을 갱신한다
(B) 의료 기록을 제출한다
(C) 시장에 간다
(D) 영업 회의를 준비한다

✅ 여자가 다음에 할 일을 묻는 문제로, 대화 후반에 여자가 "I'll mark down your appointment in the schedule right now."라며 예약을 일정에 표시하겠다고 했으므로 (A)가 정답이다.

SPARTA Check-UP

Day10_3 해설 p.349

다음을 듣고 정답을 고른 후, 빈칸을 채우세요. (음성은 두 번씩 들려줍니다.)

1. Where does the man most likely work?
   (A) At an electronics store
   (B) At a clothing distributor
   (C) At a manufacturing plant
   (D) At a computer manufacturer

2. What does the woman ask about?
   (A) The size of an order
   (B) The price quote
   (C) Customer survey results
   (D) Testers' feedback

3. What does the man recommend regarding the order?
   (A) Changing the pattern
   (B) Limiting pattern options
   (C) Calling a different supplier
   (D) Completing the form first

M Hi, Ms. Rartez. I'm calling about your laptop computer case design _____. I wanted to let you know that _____ _____ here at our plastics factory next week.

W Okay, I'm glad to hear that. To begin, we'd like to start with 1,000 cases and then _____ _____ to get their feedback. Can you tell me how much it would cost for that?

M If you make them all the same pattern, _____. Also we'll be able to complete them faster.

---

4. Where do the speakers work?
   (A) At a hotel
   (B) At a concert hall
   (C) At a phone company
   (D) At a playhouse

5. What is the man concerned about?
   (A) No rooms are available at the hotel.
   (B) Tickets are sold out.
   (C) Ticket agents didn't answer the phone.
   (D) Guests canceled their reservations.

6. What will the man do after lunch?
   (A) Stop by the ticket office
   (B) Send the pamphlet
   (C) Buy some tickets
   (D) Visit the woman's office

M Jenny, some of our _____ _____ if we could get tickets for the opera performance tomorrow night. So, I've contacted the ticket office several times, but _____. I just got a recording.

W Well, I've got a pamphlet about another musical performance happening tomorrow night _____. You could ask them _____ that show instead. It also received good reviews.

M Great! I'll ask them. If they want to go there, I'll _____ to get more information.

SPARTA Practice Test

1. What does the woman say about the man's job performance?
   (A) He is a competent employee.
   (B) He always meets his deadlines.
   (C) He has creative ideas for new projects.
   (D) He has increased company profits.

2. What does the woman ask the man to do?
   (A) Attend a trade show
   (B) Join a leadership council
   (C) Meet the client in Tokyo
   (D) Accept a new position

3. What is the company planning to do next year?
   (A) Open a new overseas office
   (B) Extend the business hours
   (C) Meet the staff's family
   (D) Get feedback from employees

4. What does the man recommend?
   (A) Advertising on television
   (B) Switching the day of an event
   (C) Conducting a survey
   (D) Entertaining people in the area

5. What does the woman ask the man to do?
   (A) Communicate with employees
   (B) Reduce expenses
   (C) Attend a board meeting
   (D) Send a plan

6. What does the man say will start on Monday?
   (A) A clearance sale
   (B) An important project
   (C) A special offer
   (D) A television show

7. Why is the man calling?
   (A) To inquire about a product
   (B) To cancel an appointment
   (C) To confirm a client's schedule
   (D) To book a repair service

8. What does the woman offer to do?
   (A) Schedule a repair
   (B) Provide a replacement
   (C) Waive a service fee
   (D) Place an advertisement online

9. What will the man most likely do next?
   (A) Print a receipt
   (B) Purchase a magazine
   (C) Make a telephone call
   (D) Visit a store

10. What are the speakers mainly discussing?
    (A) An itinerary
    (B) A room schedule
    (C) A dinner recipe
    (D) A dining reservation

11. What does the woman notify the man about?
    (A) An extra fee
    (B) A long wait
    (C) A lack of space
    (D) A limited menu

12. According to the woman, what is scheduled for Friday evening?
    (A) A play
    (B) A musical performance
    (C) A movie screening
    (D) A cooking demonstration

13. What are the speakers talking about?
    (A) A performance time
    (B) A seat assignment
    (C) A ticket price
    (D) A theater location

14. What is the man's problem?
    (A) He was confused about the seat area.
    (B) He had the wrong ticket.
    (C) He doesn't know the woman well.
    (D) He lost his bags.

15. What does the man say he will do?
    (A) Arrange the chairs
    (B) Collect his possessions
    (C) Refund the ticket
    (D) Speak with an organizer

16. What type of business is the woman calling?
    (A) An Internet provider
    (B) A computer store
    (C) An accounting firm
    (D) A phone company

17. What does the man mention about the company?
    (A) They replaced their ID cards.
    (B) They had some system problems.
    (C) They moved last month.
    (D) They updated their Web site.

18. What will the man probably do next?
    (A) Change the phone number
    (B) Update the account
    (C) Give contact information
    (D) Go to the convenience store

19. Who is the woman?
    (A) A delivery person
    (B) A new employee
    (C) A warehouse supervisor
    (D) A truck driver

20. What does the woman ask about?
    (A) Some delivery processes
    (B) A training schedule
    (C) Some manufacturing equipment
    (D) An inventory process

21. According to the man, how can the woman find additional information?
    (A) By contacting a supervisor
    (B) By checking a training manual
    (C) By visiting a Web site
    (D) By posting questions on a bulletin board

22. Who is the woman?
    (A) A Web designer
    (B) A salesperson
    (C) A personnel manager
    (D) The head of the sales department

23. What has the woman been assigned to do?
    (A) Develop more efficient processes
    (B) Review online materials
    (C) Upgrade the computers
    (D) Reach financial goals

24. What does the man want the woman to do?
    (A) Share her comments
    (B) Select a group
    (C) Change the meeting time
    (D) Get familiar with other people

DAY 11 의도 파악/시각 자료

1 의도 파악

SPARTA 유형 파악

화자의 숨은 의도를 묻는 문제로, 단순히 특정 표현의 의미가 아니라 앞뒤 맥락에 따른 화자의 의도를 묻기 때문에 대화의 전체 흐름을 잘 파악해야 한다.

SPARTA 출제 포인트

- 맥락에 따른 화자의 의도를 묻기 때문에 제시된 표현만 보고 고른다면 오답을 고를 확률이 높다.
- 다른 문제에 비해 보기가 길기 때문에 키워드 중심으로 문제를 풀어야 한다.
- 문제 풀이 단서는 해당 표현 앞뒤에서 언급된다는 점에 유의하자.

SPARTA 빈출 유형

What does the man mean when he says, "Look at all these cars on the road"?
남자가 "길에 있는 모든 차들을 보세요"라고 말할 때 의도하는 것은 무엇인가?

What does the woman imply when she says, "I was just about to call you"?
여자가 "제가 막 당신에게 전화하려던 참이었어요"라고 말할 때 의도하는 것은 무엇인가?

Why does the man say, "you can try it at other stores"?
남자는 왜 "당신은 다른 가게에서 그것을 해볼 수 있어요"라고 말하는가?

SPARTA 문제 풀이 비법

🎧 Day11_1

W: Hi, there. I'm planning a reception at my office, and I want your company to handle the catering for the event. I think there are 20 in our group. We would like Italian cuisine.
M: Excellent choice. We have a group special for 40 dollars per person, and it includes a full meal, a nice glass of wine, and a chocolate dessert.
W: Hmm… I'll have to check with my supervisor on that.
M: Okay. How about this? If you can pay in cash, I can offer a 10 percent discount on your total order.
W: Much better. Thanks!

W: 안녕하세요. 제 사무실에서 환영회를 계획하고 있는데요, 이벤트를 위한 음식 공급을 귀사가 맡아 주었으면 합니다. 20명 정도 될 것 같아요. 이탈리아 요리를 원합니다.
M: 좋은 선택입니다. 저희는 인당 40달러로 특별 단체 요금이 있어요. 거기에 풀 코스 요리와 근사한 와인 한 잔 그리고 초콜릿 디저트가 포함되죠.
W: 음… 상사에게 확인해 봐야 할 것 같아요.
M: 좋아요. 이건 어때요? 만약에 현금으로 내시면 전체 주문에 10퍼센트 할인을 제공해 드릴 수 있어요.
W: 훨씬 좋네요. 고마워요!

What does the woman mean when she says, "I'll have to check with my supervisor on that"?
(A) A task is difficult to finish.
(B) She decided to prepare the food herself.
(C) She cannot make a quick decision.
(D) More employees will need to be hired.

여자가 "상사에게 확인해 봐야 할 것 같아요"라고 말할 때 의도하는 것은 무엇인가?
(A) 업무를 끝내기 어렵다.
(B) 그녀는 음식을 직접 준비하기로 결정했다.
(C) 그녀는 빠른 결정을 내릴 수 없다.
(D) 더 많은 직원들을 고용할 필요가 있다.

✓ 대화에서 남자가 가격과 메뉴에 대해 언급한 후 여자가 상사에게 확인해 본다고 한 것은 결정을 망설이고 있음을 알 수 있다. 따라서 정답은 (C)이다.

2 시각 자료

SPARTA 유형 파악

시각 자료를 대화 내용과 연계해서 푸는 문제로, 표, 그래프, 지도, 티켓, 쿠폰 등 다양한 형태의 표가 나온다. 시각 자료에서 보기와 상응하는 부분이 대화에서 단서로 나올 가능성이 높다.

SPARTA 출제 포인트

- Look at the graphic.이 먼저 나온 후 세부 사항을 묻는다. 다양한 형태의 표를 파악하는 훈련이 필요하다.
- 질문과 보기를 먼저 읽은 후 보기에 제시되지 않은 내용을 시각 자료에서 미리 파악해야 한다.
  • 그래프/차트/표: 분기 매출 실적, 회의/세미나/공연 일정표, 가격이나 건물 안내도 등
  • 지도: 상점이나 행사장으로 가는 약도, 버스/지하철 노선, 거리 약도 등
  • 그 외: 티켓, 영수증, 쿠폰, 주문서 등
- 그래프나 차트는 비중이 가장 큰 순서대로 미리 정리해 놓고 푼다. the highest(가장 높은), the lowest(가장 낮은), the second(두 번째) 등의 표현을 알아 두자.
- 시각 자료만 보고 정답을 고르면 안 된다. switch, trade, change, reverse 표현 주변에 바뀐 내용이 언급되므로 주의해서 듣자.
- 지도, 약도 문제는 위치를 나타내는 전치사 between(~사이에), across(~건너편), in front of(~앞에), by/next to/beside(~옆에), toward(~쪽으로), on the corner of(~의 모퉁이에) 등의 표현이 언급된다.

SPARTA 빈출 유형

Look at the graphic. ~? 도표를 보시오. (질문 내용) (세부 사항에 대한 질문)

SPARTA 문제 풀이 비법

🎧 Day11_2

Reservation - Room 105	
Monday, July 2	GDI Company
Tuesday, July 3	M&M Association
Wednesday, July 4	Alpha Moto
Thursday, July 5	Sam Brothers

예약 - 105호	
월요일, 7월 2일	GDI Company
화요일, 7월 3일	M&M Association
수요일, 7월 4일	Alpha Moto
목요일, 7월 5일	Sam Brothers

M: Excuse me. I'd like to change my reservation date to July 4 instead of July 2, which we booked. Also, more people registered than we expected. I want a larger room.
W: Let me check. The only room I have left is Room 110. It seats over 50 people.
M: That should be enough. Thank you.

M: 실례합니다. 예약한 7월 2일 대신 7월 4일로 날짜를 바꾸고 싶은데요. 그리고 예상보다 더 많은 사람들이 등록해서 더 큰 룸을 원합니다.
W: 확인해 볼게요. 110호만 남아 있네요. 50명 이상 앉을 수 있어요.
M: 충분해요. 감사합니다.

Look at the graphic. **Which company** does **the man work for**?
(A) GDI Company
(B) M&M Association
(C) Alpha Moto
(D) Sam Brothers

도표를 보시오. 남자는 어느 회사에서 일하는가?
(A) GDI 사
(B) M&M 협회
(C) Alpha Moto
(D) Sam Brothers

✅ 질문과 보기를 먼저 확인 후 표를 보자. 보기에는 회사명이 있고 표에는 요일, 날짜가 표기되어 있다. 회사와 날짜를 중심으로 들으면 남자가 일하는 회사를 알 수 있다. 첫 대사에서 남자가 원래 예약한 날짜인 7월 2일을 4일로 바꾸고 싶다고 했으므로 해당 날짜에 예약한 회사는 (A)임을 알 수 있다.

다음을 듣고 정답을 고른 후, 빈칸을 채우세요. (음성은 두 번씩 들려줍니다.)

1. What is the woman doing on Tuesday?
   (A) Training new hires
   (B) Distributing legal documents
   (C) Moving to a new department
   (D) Going on vacation

2. Why does the woman say, "you are the most experienced lawyer in our firm"?
   (A) To get the man promoted
   (B) To revise a mistake
   (C) To remind a colleague of a new procedure
   (D) To explain a request

3. What will the man do on Monday?
   (A) Send some forms
   (B) Travel on company business
   (C) Participate in some negotiations
   (D) Attend the next class

Model	Price
Candon	$7500
Zester	$6500
Promo	$5900
Santa	$9900

4. Why does the woman want to buy a car?
   (A) To drive to the train station
   (B) To save money
   (C) To enjoy her weekends
   (D) To get a driver's license

5. Look at the graphic. What vehicle is the woman most interested in?
   (A) Candon
   (B) Zester
   (C) Promo
   (D) Santa

6. What will the woman do later?
   (A) Look on another Web site
   (B) Borrow some money
   (C) Contact the car dealer
   (D) Consult her spouse

M Alice, I just heard that _____ _____ for new employees in the legal department. It's a good opportunity for you.

W It is. I'm doing it Tuesday after lunchtime. Can I ask a favor? I was wondering _____ _____ this first class and give me some feedback afterward, because you are the most experienced lawyer in our firm.

M Oh, I'm really sorry. I'm going to _____ _____.
I won't be back until Wednesday. But maybe I can participate in your next class. When's the second class?

W Thank you. Next Tuesday.

M Hi, Tina. It's lunchtime. Why are you still working?

W I'm not working. I'm looking for a used car on this Web site. Train ticket fares have gone up again, and a car actually works out _____ _____.

M I see. Well, how about this one? It's only three years old.

W It's _____!
This one here looks good enough, and it's the _____.

M So, are you going to call the dealer? Someone else might get it before you.

W I'll need to go home and ask my husband, Mike, first. He knows exactly _____ _____.

SPARTA Practice Test

45th Science Conference	
Golan Towers 1st Floor	
Time	Presenter
8:00 A.M.–8:50 A.M.	Lucy Hynam
9:00 A.M.–9:50 A.M.	Derrick West
10:00 A.M.–10:50 A.M.	Paula Collins
11:00 A.M.–11:50 A.M.	Samantha Smith

1. Why is the woman concerned?
   (A) She thinks a printer is broken.
   (B) She didn't send her résumé.
   (C) She lost the draft for a speech.
   (D) She forgot about an appointment.

2. What did the man do last night?
   (A) Prepare for his speech
   (B) Checked his flight schedule
   (C) Went to the woman's office
   (D) Wrote an e-mail

3. Look at the graphic. What time will the woman probably give her presentation?
   (A) 8:00 A.M.
   (B) 9:00 A.M.
   (C) 10:00 A.M.
   (D) 11:00 A.M.

4. Why hasn't the woman seen the man lately?
   (A) He is busy with projects.
   (B) He started a new position.
   (C) He is training a coworker.
   (D) He traveled to many countries.

5. What does the woman mean when she says, "Oh, that's right"?
   (A) She is looking forward to working with the man.
   (B) She agrees with the man's situation.
   (C) She remembers her time working in sales.
   (D) She failed to finish her assignment on time.

6. What doesn't the man like about his job?
   (A) Staying in hotels
   (B) Working with his coworkers
   (C) Getting to know clients
   (D) Learning new things

7. What did the man recently do?
   (A) He wrote an article.
   (B) He started a business.
   (C) He won an award.
   (D) He published a book.

8. What is the man looking forward to?
   (A) Some baked goods
   (B) A cash prize
   (C) A radio interview
   (D) A magazine article

9. Why does the man say, "you can try it at our store"?
   (A) To give an assignment
   (B) To suggest a different time
   (C) To extend an invitation
   (D) To express dissatisfaction

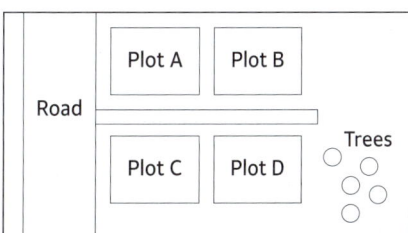

10. Where did the man learn about the land for sale?
    (A) On the Internet
    (B) On the radio
    (C) In the shop window
    (D) From a colleague

11. Look at the graphic. Which plot is the man interested in?
    (A) Plot A
    (B) Plot B
    (C) Plot C
    (D) Plot D

12. What is the woman surprised by?
    (A) The quick decision
    (B) The man's occupation
    (C) The opinion of the man's children
    (D) The location of a parking lot

13. Where do the speakers most likely work?

    (A) At an architecture firm
    (B) At a catering company
    (C) At a supermarket
    (D) At a medical clinic

14. Why does the man say, "This is the third time this has happened"?

    (A) He is very disappointed with a vendor.
    (B) He does not agree with an idea.
    (C) He knows when the items are delivered.
    (D) He is satisfied with a supplier.

15. What will the man most likely do next?

    (A) Call the architecture firm
    (B) Speak with a manager
    (C) Stop by the store
    (D) Call off the order

---

16. What are the speakers talking about?

    (A) Training materials
    (B) A job interview
    (C) New employees
    (D) Sales figures

17. What does the man imply when he says, "I've already completed my work"?

    (A) He wants comments on an assignment.
    (B) He wants to offer assistance.
    (C) He would like to leave for the day.
    (D) He wants to train new hires.

18. What will the man most likely do next?

    (A) Call the security office
    (B) Take care of the request
    (C) Contact the new hires
    (D) Make name tags

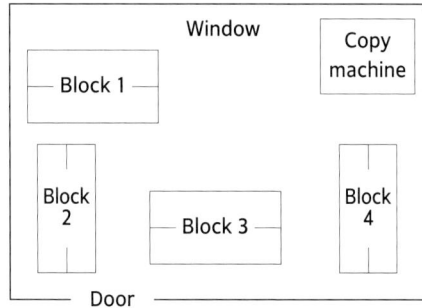

19. What has the man been asked to do?

    (A) Assign new projects
    (B) Schedule a window cleaning
    (C) Research new computers
    (D) Rearrange the office layout

20. What is the B Team's problem with their current desk location?

    (A) They dislike the breeze.
    (B) They are bored with it.
    (C) The sunlight bothers them.
    (D) The view outside is distracting.

21. Look at the graphic. Where does the woman finally think the B Team should be put?

    (A) In Block 1
    (B) In Block 2
    (C) In Block 3
    (D) In Block 4

22. What are the speakers mainly discussing?
    (A) A job opening
    (B) A new product
    (C) A medical clinic location
    (D) Some survey results

23. According to the man, what is the problem?
    (A) Patients are not satisfied with the meeting times with doctors.
    (B) Doctors need to have more experience.
    (C) Patients wait for a long time to see the doctors.
    (D) It is hard to make an appointment.

24. What does the woman imply when she says, "That would require important changes to our scheduling process"?
    (A) She doubts a change will be implemented.
    (B) She thinks more employees should be hired.
    (C) She needs more time to decide.
    (D) She believes some data is incorrect.

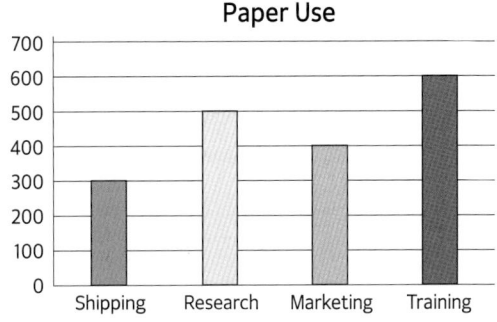

25. What are the speakers talking about?
    (A) A waste of stationery items
    (B) A billing problem
    (C) Moving to another department
    (D) A staff training event

26. Look at the graphic. Which department does the woman suggest giving the tablet computers to?
    (A) Shipping
    (B) Research
    (C) Marketing
    (D) Training

27. What is the man asked to do?
    (A) Check a price
    (B) Explain a process
    (C) Purchase the tablets computers
    (D) Contact a colleague

SPARTA 빈출 표현 — 상황별 어휘

● 회사, 조직

company/firm/corporation	회사	CEO (Chief Executive Officer)	최고경영자
board of directors	이사회	vice president	부사장
president	사장	executive	중역, 간부
director	이사, 중역	headquarters/main office/head office	본사
shareholder	주주	branch manager	지점(지사)장
branch/office	지사, 지점	department head	부서장
supervisor	감독자, 상사	clerk	점원
staff/employee/personnel	직원	secretary	비서
colleague/coworker	직장 동료	personnel department / human resources (HR)	인사과
assistant	조수		
new hire, new employee	신입 사원	marketing department	마케팅부서
sales department	영업부서	maintenance department	관리부서
accounting department	회계부서	security office	보안(경비)부서
planning department	기획부서	R&D (research and development)	연구개발
audit	(회계)감사	public relations/publicity	홍보(부)
technical support team	기술지원부서	cafeteria	구내식당
payroll division	경리부서	wing	별관
management	경영진	staff lounge	직원 휴게실

● 인사 및 급여

applicant/candidate	지원자	application	지원서
job	일, 직무	post/position	지위
job opening/job vacancy	일자리	qualified	자격 있는
job seeker	구직자	résumé	이력서
degree	학위	hire	고용하다
recruit	모집하다	transfer	전근 가다
promotion	승진; 홍보	lay off	(일시) 해고하다
retire	은퇴하다	retiree	은퇴자
work overtime/work late/ work extra hours	시간외 근무하다	pay raise	임금 인상
		dedication	헌신
paycheck	급여	payroll	급여 지급 명부
pension	연금	replacement	교체물, 후임자
in charge of/responsible for	~을 책임지는	reputation	명성
reference	추천서	career	경력
evaluate/assess	평가하다	experienced	경험이 많은
incentive	장려금; 자극책	resign	사임하다
go on strike	파업하다	supervisor	관리자, 상사

● 업무, 회의

재정, 금융	계좌, 거래처(client)	shipment	선적, 발송
ship	선적(발송)하다	deliver	배달(전달)하다
budget	예산	profit	이익; 수익
revenue/earnings	수입, 수익	client	고객(customer), 거래처
expense	경비, 비용	invest	투자하다
investment	투자	appointment	약속; 예약
reschedule	일정을 변경하다	renovate/remodel	보수하다, 개조하다
copier/photocopier/copy machine	복사기	maintenance	보수, 관리(유지)
warehouse	창고	transport	운송하다
equipment	장비; 기계	fund	자금
office supplies	사무용품	consult	상담하다
take ~ off	휴가를 내다, 근무를 쉬다	customer survey	고객 설문조사
duty	직무(임무)	performance	실적, 성과
competitor	경쟁자(업체)	merger	합병
acquisition	인수	deal	거래, 협정
law firm	법률 회사	presentation	발표, 설명
training session	교육	launch	출시하다, 착수하다
business trip	출장	strike	파업
operation	운영, 경영	oversee/supervise/superintend	감독하다
finance	재정, 금융	market share	시장 점유율
reward	보상; 보상하다	advertisement(=ad)	광고
advertising campaign	광고 캠페인	response	반응
out of the office	사무실에 없는	form	용지, 양식
fill out a form	양식을 기입(작성)하다	ID/identification	신분증
bulletin board/notice board	게시판	approval/permission/authorization	승인, 허가
estimate/quote	견적	compensate	보상하다
finish/complete/conclude/finalize	마치다, 마무리 짓다	regulation	규정
employee handbook	직원 안내서	projector	영사기
disturb/bother	방해하다	terms	조항
priority	우선 사항	survey	설문조사
questionnaire	설문지	improve	개선하다
satisfaction	만족	dissatisfaction	불만족
share	공유하다	results	결과
feedback/comment/idea/opinion	의견	sufficient/enough	충분한
insufficient	불충분한	sales figure	판매 수치
profit	수익	statistics	통계
task	일	workshop	워크숍
vendor	판매사	issue/problem	문제
conference	회의	submit/hand in/turn in	제출하다
urgent business	급한 업무	address	처리하다
understaffed/short-staffed	인원이 부족한	shortage/lack	부족
training session	교육 연수	expense/expenditure	지출
reimbursement	상환	time sheet/timecard	근무 시간표

● 병원, 건강

gain weight	체중이 늘다	lose weight	체중을 줄이다
work out/exercise	운동하다	gym	체육관
prescribe	약을 처방하다	prescription	처방(전)
medical test(exam)/physical check-up	검사, 검진	run a test	검사를 실시하다
		patient	환자
make an appointment	예약하다	pain	통증
feel well	컨디션이 좋다	feel better	증상이 호전되다
headache	두통	stomachache	위통
allergy	알레르기	wrist	손목
ankle	발목	medicine	의학, 의약품
medical conference	의학 학회	operation/surgery	수술
physician	(내과) 의사	surgeon	외과 의사
vet	수의사	eye doctor	안과 의사
vision test	시력 검사	reduce stress	스트레스를 줄이다
side effect	부작용	hurt	아프다, 아프게 하다
illness/disease	질병	high blood pressure	고혈압
pregnant	임신한	dentist	치과 의사
health insurance	건강 보험	pharmacy	약국
pharmacist	약사	pharmaceutical company	제약 회사
injury	부상	nutrition	영양
emergency room	응급실	sick leave	병가

● 문화 생활

theater/playhouse	극장	movie theater/cinema	영화관
movie/film	영화	ticket	입장권
box office/ticket booth	매표소	balcony seat	발코니 좌석
aisle seat	통로 쪽 좌석	play	연극
concert	콘서트	live performance	라이브 공연
part/role	배역(역할)	switch seats	자리를 바꾸다
audience	관객	performer	공연자, 연주자
perform	공연(연주)하다	curtain	(연극) 막
stage	무대	intermission	중간 휴식
opera	오페라	refreshments	다과
museum	박물관	art gallery	미술관
artwork	공예품(미술품)	painting	그림
sculpture/statue	조각(품)	unique	독특한
player	연주자	solo	독주, 독창
(musical) instrument	악기	critic	평론가
clap/applaud	박수 치다	conductor	지휘자
favorable review	호평	exhibit/exhibition	전시회

● 행사

welcoming party	환영회	farewell party	송별회
award ceremony	시상식	race	경기
reception dinner	환영 만찬	banquet	연회
company retreat/picnic/outing	회사 야유회	opening ceremony	개막식
caterer	출장 연회업자	host	진행자
recipient/winner	수상자	turnout	참가자 수
present an award	상을 수여하다	employee of the year	올해의 직원상
nominate	후보자로 지명하다	famous/well-known	유명한
outstanding	뛰어난	contribute to	~에 기여하다
honor	영예를 주다	win/receive an award	상을 받다
educational background	학력	give a prize	상품을 주다
giveaway	경품	raffle prize	추첨 경품
prestigious	명망 높은	recognize/acknowledge	인정하다
dedicated	헌신적인	rule	규칙
cancel/call off	취소하다	crowd	군중

● 여행, 교통

land	착륙하다(↔ take off 이륙하다)	overhead compartment	(좌석 위의) 짐 넣는 선반
cabin	객실	pillow	베개
blanket	담요	fasten seat belts	안전벨트를 매다
captain	기장	pilot	조종사
passenger	승객	flight attendant	비행기 승무원
turbulence	난기류	fare	운임
direct flight	직항편	flight	항공편
processing	탑승 수속	check the luggage/bag/suitcase	가방을 화물칸에 싣다
check-in	탑승 수속하다	seat assignment	좌석 배정
boarding gate	탑승구	board	탑승하다
connecting flight	연결 항공편	carousel	수하물 컨베이어 벨트
miss the flight	비행기를 놓치다	inclement weather	악천후
boarding pass	탑승권	abroad	해외에(서), 해외로
disembark	(기차, 배, 비행기 등에서) 내리다	departure	출발
arrival	도착	destination	목적지
stopover/layover	경유지	exit	출구
travel agency	여행사	travel agent	여행사 직원
itinerary/travel plan/schedule	여행 일정	confirm	확인하다
book	예약하다(=reserve)	resort	휴양지
rent a car	차를 빌리다	ferry	여객선
dock	부두(=pier)	harbor	항구(=port)
on board	(배, 비행기, 기차 등의) 탑승하여	gas station	주유소
highway/expressway	고속도로	downtown	시내
vehicle	차량	fix/repair	수리하다
part	부품	brake	브레이크
flat tire	펑크 난 타이어	behind schedule	예정보다 늦은

on schedule	예정대로	transfer	환승하다
public transportation	대중 교통	platform	역, 승강장
train conductor	(열차) 차장	block	막다
souvenir	기념품	sightseeing	관광
lighthouse	등대	scenery/landscape/view	경치
accommodations	숙박 시설	spectator	관중
pedestrian/walker	보행자	traffic jam	교통체증
shortcut	지름길	collision	충돌
fuel efficiency	연비	mechanic	수리공
parking lot/garage	주차장	tow	견인하다
van	승합차	waiting list	대기자 명단
convenience	편리 (↔ inconvenience 불편)	on time	제시간에
accident	사고	commuter	통근자
driver/motorist	운전자	lane	차선
intersection	교차로	sidewalk/walkway	보도

● 쇼핑, 호텔

무료로	비싼	loose	헐렁한, 느슨한
sleeve	소매	suit	정장, 옷
attire/dress/clothes	복장, 의상	dry cleaner	세탁소
fit/suit	꼭 맞다	grocery store/supermarket	식료품점
suitcase	서류 가방	bargain	흥정(하다)
negotiate	협상하다	courier	배달원, 택배회사
import	수입하다	export	수출하다
department store	백화점	reasonable/affordable price	저렴한 가격
display	진열(하다)	front window	앞쪽 진열창
shelf	진열대, 선반	rack	(옷, 모자 등의) 걸이, 선반
check-out/register counter	계산대	warranty	보증(서)
guarantee	보증(보장)하다; 보증	exchange the defective product	불량품을 교환하다
refund	환불; 환불하다	full refund	전액 환불
free of charge	무료로	be out of stock/be sold out	재고가 떨어지다
take inventory	재고 조사하다	on sale	세일 중인
for sale	판매 중인	try on/put on	입어(신어) 보다
a pair	한 벌(켤레)	aisle	통로
suite	특실	double bedroom	2인용 객실
single bedroom	1인용 객실	lobby	로비
receptionist	접수원	conference room	회의실
check-in	입실 수속하다	check-out	퇴실 수속하다
stay	숙박하다	book/reserve	예약하다
accommodate	수용하다	bill/check	계산서
facility	시설(=establishment), 설비	patron	단골 고객(=customer)
business hours	영업 시간	hours of operation	운영 시간
refund	환불하다	bill statement	대금 청구서
cashier	출납원	label	라벨
price tag	가격표	overcharge	과잉 청구하다

PART 4
담화문

DAY 12 | 광고/방송
DAY 13 | 전화 메시지
DAY 14 | 안내/공지
DAY 15 | 회의/소개

PART 4 접근법

PART 4는 한 사람이 말하는 담화문을 듣고 푸는 유형으로, 총 30문제가 출제된다. 담화를 잘 듣고 PART 3와 동일한 방법으로 필요한 정보를 잡아내는 능력을 판별한다. PART 3보다 흐름을 파악하기 쉽지만 한 사람이 쉬지 않고 이어서 말하기 때문에 무엇보다 집중력을 요한다.

문제 풀이 전략

1. 담화를 듣기 전에 반드시 문제를 완벽히 파악한다. PART 3와 같이 키워드 중심으로 문제를 확인한다. 시각 자료 유형의 경우, 해당 문제와 시각 자료를 연계해서 파악해야 한다.
2. 담화의 흐름을 파악하기 위해 담화의 초반을 반드시 집중해서 듣는다. 보통 담화 초반에서 단서의 70% 이상이 제시된다.
3. 담화를 들으면서, 미리 파악한 문제의 키워드 중심으로 3문제에 대한 답을 바로 선택해야 한다. 대부분 문제 순서대로 단서가 나오지만, 종종 순서가 바뀌는 경우도 있다.
4. 문제를 읽어줄 때 그 다음 문제를 파악하면서 준비한다. 명심할 것은 한 번 흐름이 끊기면 풀 수 있는 문제도 자칫 놓칠 수 있기 때문에 순발력과 판단력이 무엇보다 중요하다.
5. 담화는 전화 메시지를 제외하고 다수의 청자를 대상으로 한다. 장소에 따라 내용은 다르지만 내용의 순서는 [인사말 - 소개 - 주제/목적 - 내용 언급 - 요청/당부 - 미래] 순으로 진행된다. 이 순서를 파악한다면 어디쯤에서 정답 단서가 나올지 미리 감을 잡을 수 있다.
6. 화자 의도 파악 문제는 화자들의 상황에 따라 그 말을 하는 의도를 묻기 때문에 대화의 앞뒤 내용이 중요하다. 사전적인 의미보다 대화 상황에 맞는 맥락을 찾는 훈련을 해야 한다. 대화 형태인 PART 3보다 의도를 파악하기가 더 까다로운 경우가 많다.

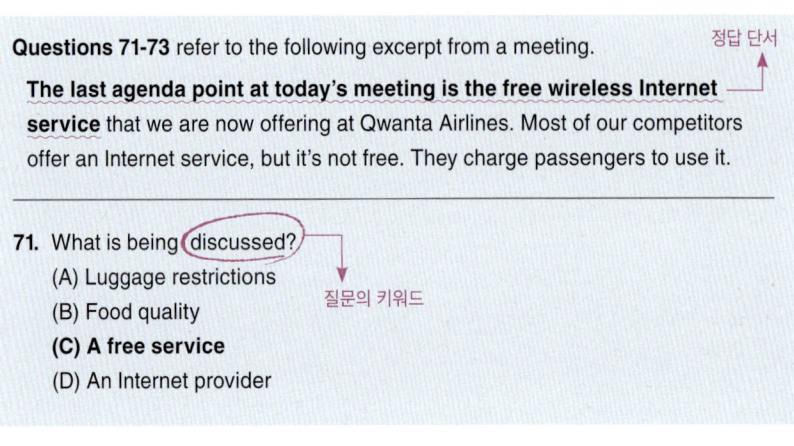

DAY 12 광고/방송

SPARTA 유형 파악

광고/방송은 평균적으로 각 1~2개의 지문이 출제되며 특정 상품이나 서비스 광고, 뉴스나 토크쇼 같은 라디오 프로그램, 지역 뉴스, 비즈니스 뉴스, 일기예보, 교통 방송 등이 출제된다.

SPARTA 출제 포인트

- 광고는 주로 광고 대상 소개 > 특징과 장점 > 특별 혜택(할인) > 추가 정보 > 이용 방법 순으로 나온다.
- 광고는 제품/서비스/회사 광고가 주로 나오며 때로 구인 광고도 나온다. 주로 광고 대상, 특징이나 장점 그 외 추가로 관련 있는 질문들이 자주 출제된다.
- 방송은 프로그램 소개 > 주제/목적 > 세부사항 > 요청/당부(일기예보/교통방송) > 다음 방송 안내 순으로 나오며 객관적인 정보 전달이 주를 이루고 토크쇼 같은 경우 청취자들의 참여를 권장하기도 한다.

SPARTA 빈출 유형

What is being advertising? 광고되고 있는 것은 무엇인가?
What feature of the product does the speaker emphasize? 화자는 제품의 어떤 특징을 강조하고 있는가?
How can the listeners get more information? 청자들은 어떻게 추가 정보를 얻을 수 있는가?
According to the advertisement, what special option is available? 광고에 따르면, 어떤 특별 옵션이 가능한가?
What event is being announced? 어떤 행사가 안내되고 있는가?
What caused the delay? 무엇이 지연을 야기했는가?
What will listeners hear next? 청취자들은 다음에 무엇을 들을 것인가?
How long has this business been operated? 얼마나 오랫동안 이 사업을 운영했는가?

SPARTA 문제 풀이 비법

🎧 Day12_1

Would you like to look great and not have to spend a lot of money? At Rainbow Planet, we've got some exciting new offers — just in time for summer. Our stylish cotton jeans are now marked down ten percent. Why not pair them with a pretty blouse? There's also 25 percent off a variety of swimwear from leading brands. Our top fashion item this season is the ladies' summer pantsuit. Pick one up for half price! Rainbow Planet members can get an additional five percent off each purchase. You should hurry because these offers are only available for another seven days!

많은 돈을 쓰지 않고 멋있게 보이고 싶으신가요? 저희 Rainbow Planet에서 오직 여름을 위한 흥미로운 새 할인 품목들을 제공합니다. 멋진 면바지를 10퍼센트 할인합니다. 그 바지와 어울리는 예쁜 블라우스는 어떤가요? 대표 브랜드들에서 만든 다양한 수영복도 25퍼센트 할인합니다. 이번 시즌의 톱 패션 아이템은 여성용 여름 바지 정장입니다. 반 가격에 가져가세요! Rainbow Planet 회원들은 각 구매에 5퍼센트 추가 할인을 받을 수 있습니다. 이 할인은 7일 동안만 가능하니 서두르세요!

According to the speaker, **how long** will the offers **last**?
(A) For five days
(B) For six days
(C) For one week
(D) For two weeks

화자에 따르면, 할인이 얼마 동안 지속되는가?
(A) 5일 동안
(B) 6일 동안
(C) 일주일 동안
(D) 2주 동안

✅ 할인이 지속되는 기간을 묻는 질문으로, 광고 후반부에 "You should hurry because these offers are only available for another seven days!"라며 7일 동안 할인한다고 했으므로 정답은 (C)이다.

SPARTA Check-UP

다음을 듣고 정답을 고른 후, 빈칸을 채우세요. (음성은 두 번씩 들려줍니다.)

1. What is being advertised?
   (A) A medical clinic
   (B) A bookstore
   (C) A bed
   (D) A sports center

2. According to the speaker, what special option is available?
   (A) An online cancelation system
   (B) Complimentary training
   (C) Daytime appointments
   (D) Reduced fees

3. How can the listeners get more information?
   (A) By attending the training
   (B) By visiting the homepage
   (C) By contacting the service center
   (D) By looking at the manual

Are you having trouble sleeping? Then come to the renowned Cypress Sleeping Center _____ _____.
You'll spend the night at our clinic, and our medical staff will monitor your sleep patterns _____ _____ in the sleep laboratory. The data we collect from these sessions can help improve your sleep. However, if you don't want to stay overnight in a sleep lab, don't worry. We have _____ that can perform the studies during the day. All you need is an appointment for four hours. For more information, look at our Web site, www.cypresssleepcenter.or.kr. _____ sleep again. To make an appointment, please call our center at 777-9191 or visit our Web site. Thank you.

4. What product is the reporter discussing?
   (A) A laptop computer
   (B) A mobile phone
   (C) A DVD player
   (D) An automobile

5. What is unique about the product?
   (A) Its logo design
   (B) Its reasonable price
   (C) Its material
   (D) Its size

6. What does the speaker suggest some listeners do?
   (A) Call a customer service number
   (B) Replace older parts
   (C) Stop by the booth
   (D) Visit a Web site

This is Naomi Leslie, your reporter for KMD News, _____ the Global Motor Show. Throughout the week, I'll be showing you some of the _____ _____ here. Right now, I'm standing in front of the latest car from Ambiquest, the Speedo 30. _____ is its revolutionary design. Ambiquest has developed an _____ for the inside and outside of the car. If you're coming to the motor show this week, be sure to _____ _____ at the Ambiquest booth in aisle one.

SPARTA Practice Test

1. What event took place last weekend?
   (A) An art exhibit
   (B) An opening ceremony
   (C) An outdoor flea market
   (D) A live performance

2. Why is the city raising money?
   (A) To construct a library
   (B) To build a new city hall
   (C) To reopen a museum
   (D) To create a monument

3. Why was the event rescheduled?
   (A) Expensive tickets
   (B) An inconvenient location
   (C) Inclement weather
   (D) Low attendance

4. What is the topic of the workshop?
   (A) Interview strategies
   (B) Speaking techniques
   (C) Leadership skills
   (D) Writing practice

5. What can participants do after the workshop?
   (A) Receive a free meal coupon
   (B) Speak with lecturers
   (C) Register for another workshop
   (D) Attend an awards banquet

6. What does the speaker encourage the listeners to do?
   (A) Refer a friend
   (B) Call the radio station
   (C) Register ahead of time
   (D) Process a payment

7. What will the speaker do?
   (A) Introduce a weekend event
   (B) Interview writers
   (C) Review best-selling books
   (D) Provide book rankings

8. What did Vince Rathbone do this year?
   (A) Won an award
   (B) Founded an organization
   (C) Organized a festival
   (D) Published a book

9. What will listeners hear next?
   (A) A traffic update
   (B) An advertisement
   (C) An author interview
   (D) A poetry reading

10. What type of business is being discussed?
    (A) A repair shop
    (B) An auto parts manufacturer
    (C) A car manufacturer
    (D) An advertising agency

11. According to the speaker, what is special about a new product?
    (A) It is made of recycled materials.
    (B) It has various models.
    (C) It was introduced a decade ago.
    (D) It is made to last longer.

12. According to the speaker, what will take place in September?
    (A) A trade show
    (B) An advertising campaign
    (C) An opening ceremony
    (D) An anniversary party

13. What is the Health Monitor?

    (A) A television program
    (B) A wearable device
    (C) A medical Web site
    (D) A fitness center

14. What does the speaker mean when she says, "Who wants to do that"?

    (A) A task is inconvenient.
    (B) A project requires more volunteers.
    (C) An event is no longer popular.
    (D) An application period has begun.

15. Why are listeners encouraged to order now?

    (A) Some stores are closing.
    (B) Tickets are almost sold out.
    (C) A product is temporarily discounted.
    (D) A deadline has been changed.

---

16. Who is the advertisement aimed at?

    (A) People who dislike treadmill exercises
    (B) People who cannot train too hard
    (C) Professional body builders
    (D) Judges of sports game

17. What does the woman mean when she says, "Here's how it works"?

    (A) She will explain her job.
    (B) She has found what she was looking for.
    (C) She has bad knees.
    (D) She will demonstrate a product.

18. What does the woman emphasize about this product?

    (A) It can help with weight loss.
    (B) It can be used anywhere.
    (C) It can gain the user body fat.
    (D) It can be made from a variety of materials.

---

19. What is the main topic of the report?

    (A) The opening of a new assembly plant
    (B) Production cuts at a local factory
    (C) An increase in the number of jobs
    (D) A merger of two corporations

20. When was the plant built?

    (A) Three years ago
    (B) Five years ago
    (C) Seven years ago
    (D) Ten years ago

21. How many units are now produced each day at the factory?

    (A) 10
    (B) 15
    (C) 20
    (D) 40

---

22. Who most likely is the speaker?

    (A) A health trainer
    (B) A research assistant
    (C) A renowned nutritionist
    (D) A radio show host

23. What is Dr. Collins's specialty?

    (A) Workouts
    (B) Sports broadcasting
    (C) Health food
    (D) Food distribution

24. What is the advantage of the exercise mentioned?

    (A) It is easy to follow.
    (B) It can help your diet.
    (C) It can make you sleep well.
    (D) It can build muscle.

DAY 13 전화 메시지

SPARTA 유형 파악

전화 메시지는 2문제 이상 꾸준히 출제된다. 발신자가 남기는 음성 메시지가 주로 나오며, 회사/공공기관 등의 자동 안내/녹음 메시지도 종종 출제된다. 메시지의 주제는 다양하지만, 정보를 전달하거나 문의 및 요청하는 내용이 주를 이룬다. 화자의 신분/근무지, 전화의 목적, 화자의 요청/제안 사항을 묻는 문제가 자주 등장한다.

SPARTA 출제 포인트

- 전화 메시지는 발신자 소개 및 인사 - 전화 건 목적 - 세부 사항 - 요청 사항(연락 당부) 순으로 전개되며, 녹음 메시지는 공공기관/회사 소개 - 전화 건 목적(서비스/운영에 관련 공지) - 세부 사항 - 요청 사항 - 추가 안내로 전개된다.
- 주문 확인이나 변경, 일정 확인/변경, 감사 전달, 회사 상사나 동료가 업무의 관련된 요청 등이 자주 출제되며, 운영 시간 알림, 주요 행사나 문제 발생 전달, 서비스 등을 알리는 내용도 자주 나온다.
- 전체 내용을 묻는 문제는 주제나 전화 건 목적, 담화 장소, 화자 및 청자의 신분을, 세부 내용을 묻는 문제는 화자의 요청/제안 사항, 화자의 의도 파악, 청자가 다음에 할 일, 앞으로 일어날 일 등을 묻는다.

SPARTA 빈출 유형

What type of business has the listener called? 청자는 어떤 종류의 업체에 연락했는가?
Why does the speaker call Ms. Larson? 왜 화자는 Larson 씨에게 전화하는가?
According to the speaker, what is the problem? 화자에 따르면, 문제점이 무엇인가?
What is the main purpose of this message? 이 메시지의 주된 목적은 무엇인가?
How can the listener get information on prices? 청자는 어떻게 가격 정보를 얻을 수 있는가?
Why does the speaker ask Ms. Deby to return the call? 화자는 왜 Deby 씨에게 연락을 달라고 요청하는가?
What is Susan asked to do? Susan 씨는 무엇을 하도록 요청 받는가?

SPARTA 문제 풀이 비법

🎧 Day13_1

Hi, Mr. Smith. This is Melanie. I know we were supposed to meet in the conference room at ten in the morning to discuss the renovation to the lobby. However, I'm calling to let you know that I'm having a problem with the public transportation. When I was on the subway, it suddenly stopped due to some mechanical problem. So, I got off the subway and took a taxi. I'm on my way to the office, but it may take a while. I won't make it on time. Why don't we meet at two after lunch instead? I hope this will work for you because I want to share some ideas for the project. I'm sorry about that.

안녕하세요, Smith 씨. Melanie입니다. 우리가 로비 보수 건을 논의하기 위해 오전 10시에 회의실에서 만나기로 했던 것으로 알고 있습니다. 하지만 제가 이용하는 대중 교통에 문제가 있어서 연락 드립니다. 지하철을 타고 있는데 갑자기 기계적인 문제로 멈췄어요. 그래서 지하철에서 내려서 택시를 탔습니다. 지금 사무실로 가고 있는데 시간이 좀 걸릴 것 같네요. 제시간에 못 갈 것 같아요. 대신 점심 이후 2시에 만나는 게 어때요? 제가 프로젝트에 대한 아이디어를 공유하고 싶기 때문에 당신도 이때 시간이 되면 좋겠네요. 죄송합니다.

What problem does the speaker **mention**?
(A) A road is being constructed.
(B) A bridge is closed.
(C) A transportation service is unavailable.
(D) A subway station is crowded.

화자는 무슨 문제를 언급하는가?
(A) 도로가 공사 중이다.
(B) 다리가 차단되었다.
(C) 교통 서비스를 이용할 수 없다.
(D) 지하철 역이 붐빈다.

✔ 초반에 화자가 "I'm having a problem with the public transportation."라며 회의에 가는 중 대중 교통 문제로 제때 못 갈 것 같다고 언급했으므로 정답은 (C)이다.

SPARTA Check-UP

다음을 듣고 정답을 고른 후, 빈칸을 채우세요. (음성은 두 번씩 들려줍니다.)

1. What is the main purpose of the message?
   (A) To get a schedule
   (B) To receive an update
   (C) To request a visit
   (D) To ask about a product

2. What is Sofia asked to do?
   (A) Provide a signature
   (B) Call a delivery person
   (C) Meet Stephen Wong
   (D) E-mail Sun Talk Corporation

3. According to the speaker, how long will James remain at the front desk?
   (A) For 10 minutes
   (B) For 15 minutes
   (C) For 30 minutes
   (D) For 35 minutes

Hi, Sofia, this is Daniel from reception downstairs. Could you _____ _____, please? I have a package addressed to you. The sender's name is Stephen Wong from Sun Talk Corporation, and the package is _____. The delivery person, James, has it at the desk, but unfortunately, _____; otherwise, it can't be received. It's 10:35 now. If you can't _____, James will have to take it with him and come back later. I hope to hear from you soon. Thanks.

---

4. What type of business has the listener called?
   (A) A news organization
   (B) A transportation company
   (C) A recruitment agency
   (D) A utilities center

5. How can the listener get information on prices?
   (A) By dialing another number
   (B) By pressing two
   (C) By pressing four
   (D) By visiting a Web site

6. Why is the message being heard?
   (A) Customer service representatives are busy.
   (B) The Web site address has changed.
   (C) The office is currently closed.
   (D) Office hours have been extended.

_____ RT Transportation Corporation. Please choose one of the following options. If you are _____ _____ a rail line, please hang up and dial 983-555-5561. For train schedules and a list of stations, please press 1. For information _____ _____, please press 2. For ticket refunds, please press 3. For information about employment opportunities, please press 4. _____ _____ about the services we offer at www.rtcorporationonline.co.ca. If you wish to speak to a customer service representative, _____.
Thank you.

SPARTA Practice Test

1. Why does the speaker congratulate Ms. Matsuda?
   (A) She started a publishing company.
   (B) She finished the research project.
   (C) She won the Best Author prize.
   (D) Her novel is very popular.

2. What does the speaker want to have happen at the end of this year?
   (A) A television show will begin.
   (B) A book signing will take place.
   (C) A new film will be introduced.
   (D) A new edition will be published.

3. Why is the listener asked to return the call?
   (A) To discuss more particulars
   (B) To talk about the grand opening
   (C) To schedule an interview
   (D) To confirm an itinerary

4. Why does the speaker call Ms. Denby?
   (A) She has applied for a job.
   (B) Her proposal has been approved.
   (C) Her interview was successful.
   (D) The position has already been filled.

5. Who is Milton Reynolds?
   (A) A newspaper writer
   (B) A personnel director
   (C) A candidate
   (D) A vice president

6. Why does the speaker ask Ms. Denby to return the call?
   (A) To correct some information
   (B) To schedule an interview
   (C) To conduct a survey
   (D) To give some directions

7. Why does the speaker call Ms. Larson?
   (A) To offer her a membership card
   (B) To ask her to return some reading materials
   (C) To invite her to a book club
   (D) To notify her that a book is available

8. What can Ms. Larson request?
   (A) A free voucher
   (B) A receipt
   (C) A discounted price
   (D) An extra time

9. What does the speaker remind the listener about?
   (A) An e-mail address
   (B) A late fee
   (C) Reduced operating hours
   (D) Parking permission

10. What type of facility is the message about?
    (A) A shipping company
    (B) A law firm
    (C) A university
    (D) A travel agency

11. What will the company do beginning on September 1st?
    (A) Win the contract
    (B) Provide service to a new country
    (C) Offer free shipping
    (D) Hire more employees

12. What does the speaker indicate about the call?
    (A) It will be transferred to a different department.
    (B) It will be recorded for future use.
    (C) It will take several minutes until a representative answers.
    (D) It will be answered promptly.

13. Who is the speaker?

    (A) A landlord
    (B) A tenant
    (C) A building manager
    (D) A hotel receptionist

14. Why does the speaker prefer to work with Cindy Guard?

    (A) She is a celebrity.
    (B) She wants to have a longer contract.
    (C) She does not want to reduce the rent.
    (D) She is familiar with the area.

15. When is the deadline for Cindy Guard to make a decision?

    (A) This morning
    (B) This evening
    (C) Tomorrow morning
    (D) Tomorrow evening

16. Where does the speaker probably work?

    (A) At a retail store
    (B) At a bed factory
    (C) At an Internet provider
    (D) At a shipping company

17. What problem is mentioned about the order?

    (A) The Web site is currently unavailable.
    (B) The payment has not been completed.
    (C) An item is out of stock.
    (D) A table was damaged in transit.

18. Why does the speaker ask the listener to call him later?

    (A) To talk about the shipping method
    (B) To renew the contract
    (C) To cancel the order
    (D) To inform him of her preference

Medicine	Dosage
Aspirin	2
Tydol	3
Vitamin B12	4
Fantex	6

19. Who most likely is the caller?

    (A) A doctor
    (B) A patient
    (C) A clinic receptionist
    (D) A pharmaceutical sales representative

20. Look at the graphic. Which quantity is no longer accurate?

    (A) 2
    (B) 3
    (C) 4
    (D) 6

21. What is the listener asked to do?

    (A) Contact the caller
    (B) Wait at home
    (C) Visit a clinic
    (D) Send some medicine

DAY 14 안내/공지

SPARTA 유형 파악

연설회, 공연장, 도서관, 회사, 기차역, 공항 등 공공장소에서 안내 사항이 있을 때 나오는 방송으로, 거의 매번 나오는 유형이다. 관광지에서 관광객 대상으로 안내하는 내용도 종종 나온다.

SPARTA 출제 포인트

- 주로 인사말/소개 - 주제/목적 - 세부사항 - 요청/당부 - 미래 할 일 순으로 나오며, 장소에 따라 다양한 내용이 출제된다.
- 시설 관련 안내나 공지는 운영 시간, 특별 행사 소개, 서비스 변경사항 등이 자주 출제되며, 사내 공지는 정책 변경이나 회사 행사 참여 요청, 보수 작업 공지 등이 출제된다.
- 교통 관련 안내는 연착, 수리 등으로 인한 지연이나 취소, 운행 시간, 주의사항을 알리는 내용이 주로 출제된다.
- 연설회나 공연장에서는 행사 지연이나 변경 사항을 주로 다룬다.

SPARTA 빈출 유형

Where is the announcement most likely being made? 안내방송이 나오는 장소는 어디인 것 같은가?
What does the speaker say about the gift shop? 화자는 선물 가게에 대해 뭐라고 하는가?
What problem does the speaker mention? 화자가 언급한 문제가 무엇인가?
What does the speaker suggest[recommend]? 화자는 무엇을 제안[추천]하는가?
What are the employees asked to do? 직원들은 무엇을 하도록 요청 받는가?
What does the speaker remind the listener about? 화자는 청자에게 무엇에 대해 상기시키는가?
What does the speaker offer to do? 화자는 무엇을 해주겠다고 하는가?
What have the attendees received? 참석자들은 무엇을 받았는가?
Why was the flight delayed? 왜 비행기가 지연됐는가?
Why was the workshop rescheduled? 왜 워크숍 일정이 변경됐는가?

SPARTA 문제 풀이 비법

🎧 Day14_1

Hello, everyone. I'm happy to announce that the Annual Healthcare Convention has more participants this year than last year. There are currently many exciting medical developments to discuss. For example, new types of equipment can quickly and painlessly test eyes, blood, and skin. Also, computers are helping doctors and others in the field make accurate decisions about patients' conditions. Later on today, Professor Rhonda Collins from Gordon University will talk about how such technology is affecting surgery. To begin with, I will show you a video that explains the various seminars and exhibitions you'll have the opportunity to attend.

안녕하세요, 여러분. 이번 연례 의료 컨벤션에 작년보다 더 많은 참석자들이 왔다는 것을 알리게 되어 기쁩니다. 현재 논의할 만한 흥미로운 의학적 성과들이 있습니다. 예를 들어, 새로운 형태의 장비는 빠르고 고통 없이 눈, 혈액, 피부를 검사할 수 있습니다. 또한 환자의 상태를 정확히 진단해야 하는 이 분야의 의사들과 관계자들을 컴퓨터가 도와주고 있습니다. 오늘 Gordon 대학의 Rhonda Collins 교수가 어떻게 그런 기술이 수술에 영향을 미치는지에 대해 얘기할 겁니다. 우선, 여러분들이 참석할 기회가 있는 다양한 세미나와 전시회를 설명하는 비디오를 보여 드리겠습니다.

What is the **main topic** of the talk?
(A) Technology sales
(B) Business results
(C) Medical subjects
(D) Insurance regulations

담화의 주제는 무엇인가?
(A) 기술 판매
(B) 사업 결과
(C) 의학 주제
(D) 보험 규정

✅ 주제는 대화 도입부에 주로 언급된다. "I'm happy to announce that the Annual Healthcare Convention ~."에서 '의료 컨벤션'에 관한 내용임을 알 수 있으므로 정답은 (C)이다.

SPARTA Check-UP

다음을 듣고 정답을 고른 후, 빈칸을 채우세요. (음성은 두 번씩 들려줍니다.)

1. Who is the speaker?
   (A) A Delft businessman
   (B) A potter
   (C) A tour guide
   (D) A tourist visiting Delft

2. What did the visitors see yesterday?
   (A) A work of art
   (B) New church
   (C) A shopping center
   (D) A pottery shop

3. At the end of the talk, what will the speaker distribute?
   (A) A map of Delft
   (B) Shopping information
   (C) A small piece of pottery
   (D) Discount coupons for pottery

_____ of Delft. Where we stand now is where the original town center _____ _____ a gunpowder explosion in 1654. You may recognize this area from the Vermeer painting we saw yesterday. _____ _____. First of all, we're going to visit the place where William of Orange is buried, which is in the New Church. After that, _____ _____ the Museum Lambert van Meerten to have a look at what Delft is famous for — its pottery. After lunch, feel free to go shopping on your own. _____ _____ that we recommend for purchasing the best in Delft pottery. Just remember to be back here by 4 30 P.M.

---

4. At what event is the announcement being made?
   (A) A book signing
   (B) A product launch
   (C) A professional conference
   (D) A charity fundraiser

5. What does the speaker suggest that some listeners do tomorrow?
   (A) Go on a tour
   (B) Attend an opening ceremony
   (C) Participate in a presentation
   (D) Make a list

6. What are the listeners instructed to do?
   (A) Use a different entrance
   (B) Sign up early
   (C) Complete a questionnaire
   (D) Sit in a designated seat

Good morning, everyone. We hope _____ _____ on medical science this week. Tomorrow, in addition to our workshops and presentations, you can go to _____ after leaving the convention center. There is a list of the medical centers in the area. You can tour one of the _____. These tours are free, and we expect them to be very popular. But we have limited seats on the buses, so please be sure to _____ _____ at the front desk by the entrance.

SPARTA Practice Test

1. Who most likely is the speaker?
   (A) A city official
   (B) A school founder
   (C) A salesperson
   (D) A hotel staff member

2. What is mentioned about the management seminar?
   (A) It serves complimentary beverages.
   (B) It will last for one day.
   (C) It has some speakers invited from overseas.
   (D) It will start tomorrow afternoon.

3. What does the speaker suggest the listeners do?
   (A) Arrive at the academy early
   (B) Submit a form
   (C) Review a schedule for an event
   (D) Access a company's Web site

4. What problem does the speaker mention?
   (A) A renovation will be delayed.
   (B) The shipment has not arrived.
   (C) The elevator is broken again.
   (D) The elevator isn't set up.

5. What does the speaker say about the gift shop?
   (A) It is on the 6th floor.
   (B) It is completed.
   (C) It is not stocked with items.
   (D) It is having an opening event.

6. Who does the speaker welcome as special guests?
   (A) Athletes
   (B) Sports magazine reporters
   (C) Stadium architects
   (D) Financial experts

7. Who most likely is the speaker?
   (A) A customer
   (B) A waiter
   (C) A food critic
   (D) A restaurant manager

8. According to the speaker, what will happen next week?
   (A) A new oven will be installed.
   (B) The headquarters will be relocated.
   (C) New menu items will be added.
   (D) Seasonal dishes will be removed.

9. What does the speaker instruct listeners about?
   (A) Taking orders carefully
   (B) Cleaning the dining hall
   (C) Setting the table neatly
   (D) Taking inventory daily

10. What product will listeners learn about on the tour?
    (A) Mobile phones
    (B) Batteries
    (C) Cameras
    (D) Computers

11. Who is Jamal Megumi?
    (A) A tour guide
    (B) A news reporter
    (C) A scientist
    (D) A plant supervisor

12. What is mentioned about the tour?
    (A) Oversized bags are prohibited.
    (B) The group size is limited.
    (C) Pre-registration is required.
    (D) Taking pictures is not allowed.

13. Why is the announcement being made?
    (A) To distribute a program to the audience
    (B) To award a prize to some speakers
    (C) To close the presentation session
    (D) To notify the audience of some schedule changes

14. What have the attendees received?
    (A) Postcards
    (B) Business cards
    (C) Printed invitations
    (D) Meal vouchers

15. What will the listeners probably do next?
    (A) Ask questions about the presentation
    (B) Get some refreshments
    (C) Sign their names on a sheet
    (D) Make some tea

16. What does the speaker thank organizers for?
    (A) Publicizing a product launch
    (B) Obtaining corporate sponsorship
    (C) Evaluating a performance
    (D) Reviewing a proposal

17. What kind of event will be provided next year?
    (A) A boat competition
    (B) A theatrical production
    (C) A clearance sale
    (D) A marathon race

18. What does the speaker mean when she says, "we won't have another opportunity next time"?
    (A) They should request a policy change.
    (B) Another team will be in charge next year.
    (C) The project's budget is limited.
    (D) The event's success is very important.

Session 1	Sam Black
Session 2	Greta Grimes
Session 3	Olly Whitfield
Session 4	Helen Chang

19. Who most likely is the audience of this event?
    (A) Photojournalists
    (B) Mobile phone sellers
    (C) Graphic designers
    (D) Mobile game developers

20. Look at the graphic. Which session has been changed?
    (A) Session 1
    (B) Session 2
    (C) Session 3
    (D) Session 4

21. How can listeners enter a contest?
    (A) By submitting a work sample
    (B) By giving some feedback
    (C) By making a deposit
    (D) By attending a Q&A session

DAY 15 회의/소개

SPARTA 유형 파악

회의 안건, 회사 업무와 관련된 공지 사항, 세미나, 기자회견, 워크숍 등 각종 행사에서 제품 발표를 하거나 특정 인물/제품을 소개하는 유형이다.

SPARTA 출제 포인트

- 회의는 주제/목적 - 세부 사항 - 제안/요청 - 추가 내용 순으로 주로 전개되며, 소개는 인사 - 소개 대상 언급 - 소개하는 사람 이력 및 업적 - 요청/당부 - 미래 할 일 순으로 전개된다.
- 회의 업무 관련 공지는 회사 매출, 인사 이동, 새 프로젝트 등에 대한 회의 안건으로 주로 출제되며, 때로 회사의 인수 합병과 정책 변경 등과 같은 소식을 회의에서 알려주는 내용으로 구성된다. 단, 회의 도입부를 생략하고 바로 본론으로 시작하는 난이도 높은 유형도 나오므로 초반부터 집중하도록 한다.
- 소개의 경우, 인물 소개는 해당 인물의 이력 및 업적에 관한 내용이, 제품 소개는 제품의 특징에 관한 내용이 주로 나온다.

SPARTA 빈출 유형

What is the speaker mainly talking about[discussing]? 화자는 주로 무엇에 대해 말하고 있는가?
Who is Vincent Butterfield? Vincent Butterfield는 누구인가?
According to the speaker, what is special about a new product? 화자에 따르면, 신제품은 무엇이 특별한가?
What does the speaker imply when she says, "I have an important project this month"?
화자가 "이번 달에 중요한 프로젝트가 있어요"라고 말할 때 의도하는 것은 무엇인가?
Why does the speaker say, "Let me say"? 왜 화자는 "제가 말할게요"라고 말하는가?
Why was the change made? 왜 변화가 생겼는가?
Why is the construction behind schedule? 왜 공사가 예정보다 늦어지는가?
Why was the project rejected? 왜 프로젝트가 거절되었는가?
Look at the graphic. What quarter will the speaker talk about first?
도표를 보시오. 화자는 어떤 분기를 먼저 말할 것인가?

SPARTA 문제 풀이 비법

🎧 Day15_1

The last agenda today relates to our weekly Lunch Talk. These talks are an excellent opportunity for employees to expand their professional knowledge. Experts from various departments give lectures on their area of specialization during lunchtime. In past months, they have been very popular with 50 or more participants every week. Unfortunately, this month is lower with only 30 people. From now, I'll forward an e-mail to all staff. Please be sure to mention Lunch Talk to your team members. Thank you.

오늘의 마지막 회의 안건은 주간 런치 토크에 관한 겁니다. 이 강연은 직원들이 전문적인 지식을 확장할 수 있는 훌륭한 기회입니다. 다양한 부서에서 온 전문가들이 점심시간 동안 그들의 전문 분야에 대해 강의합니다. 지난 몇 달 동안 매주 50명 이상이 참석하며 매우 인기 있었어요. 불행히도, 이번 달은 그보다 적은 30명이었습니다. 지금부터 모든 직원들에게 이메일을 보낼 것입니다. 여러분의 팀원들에게 런치 토크에 대해 반드시 알려 주세요. 감사합니다.

What are the **listeners asked to do**?
(A) Send an e-mail to colleagues
(B) Volunteer to give a free talk
(C) Suggest lecture topics
(D) Notify team members of an event

청자들은 무엇을 하도록 요청 받는가?
(A) 동료들에게 이메일 보내기
(B) 자유 토론에 지원하기
(C) 강의 주제 제안하기
(D) 팀원들에게 이벤트 알리기

✓ 담화 후반에 "Please be sure to mention Lunch Talk to your team members."라며 팀원들에게 런치 토크에 대해 알려 주라고 했으므로 정답은 (D)이다.

SPARTA Check-UP

Day15_2 해설 p.391

다음을 듣고 정답을 고른 후, 빈칸을 채우세요. (음성은 두 번씩 들려줍니다.)

1. What field does Sophie Moore work in?
   (A) Event planning
   (B) Accounting
   (C) Tourism
   (D) Financial loans

2. What has Sophie Moore recently done?
   (A) Started her own business
   (B) Worked from home
   (C) Wrote a book
   (D) Published an article

3. What does the speaker request the listeners do?
   (A) Take a handout before they leave
   (B) Submit their questions in writing
   (C) Put their hands up for inquiries
   (D) Divide into small discussion groups

Thank you for attending the Local Business Seminar. I'm happy _____ _____, Sophie Moore. She's _____ Moore Accounting Firm. Her company specializes in tax preparation and has many branches nationwide. Recently, _____ _____ How to Manage Your Tax Wisely, which is a best-seller. Today she'll share some tips _____ _____ when she started her firm ten years ago working from her home. As you know, if you have questions for our speaker, you should _____. She'll answer any questions you have. Without further delay, please help me welcome Sophie Moore.

4. Where is the talk most likely taking place?
   (A) In a school
   (B) In a conference room
   (C) In a newspaper
   (D) In a department store

5. What does the speaker plan to do?
   (A) Organize an event
   (B) Hire employees
   (C) Make a manual
   (D) Conduct a survey

6. What does the speaker ask the listeners to do?
   (A) Apply for a job
   (B) Register for a seminar
   (C) Share their suggestions
   (D) Leave the office early

Good morning to all board members, and thank you for _____. As you know, our residential project has been delayed, but we need to _____. To speed up the process, we're thinking of recruiting a team of temporary workers. We will post an advertisement online and in the newspapers _____. Construction experience, willingness to work in a team, and customer service skills are the qualifications we need. _____ _____ that are essential for our job, please share them with the group.

SPARTA Practice Test

1. What kind of product does Mojo produce?
   (A) Jewelry
   (B) Clothing
   (C) Art supplies
   (D) Shoes

2. Why does the speaker say, "Please look at the color selection in these samples"?
   (A) To support a decision
   (B) To assign a task
   (C) To describe a design
   (D) To introduce a new skill

3. What will You-Jin do?
   (A) Present competitor data
   (B) Conduct a survey
   (C) Introduce an advertising technique
   (D) Check financial information

4. What is the speaker talking about?
   (A) Refurbishing an office
   (B) Designing a company logo
   (C) Delaying a construction schedule
   (D) Remodeling a cafeteria

5. Why does the speaker say, "but I've had a lot of assignments this week"?
   (A) To complain about his project
   (B) To ask for help
   (C) To make an excuse
   (D) To thank colleagues

6. What does the speaker think the marketing staff will like?
   (A) The design of a work area
   (B) The type of lighting
   (C) The variety of computer programs
   (D) The size of an office

7. Where do the listeners most likely work?
   (A) At a magazine publisher
   (B) At a culinary school
   (C) At a restaurant
   (D) At a hotel

8. What does Steve Suh specialize in?
   (A) Hosting cooking demonstrations
   (B) Excellent customer service
   (C) Publishing many recipes
   (D) Innovative cooking skills

9. What will Steve Suh do from today?
   (A) Open another restaurant
   (B) Finalize a certificate program
   (C) Write an article
   (D) Train for a position

10. How long will the training program last?
    (A) One day
    (B) Two days
    (C) Four days
    (D) Seven days

11. Who will the speaker give training to?
    (A) Travel agents
    (B) Personnel executives
    (C) Visitors
    (D) Office clerks

12. What will happen next?
    (A) The listeners will tour the office.
    (B) Handouts will be distributed.
    (C) A slide show will be presented.
    (D) The listeners will visit a Web site.

13. Who is the speaker congratulating?

    (A) Advertisers
    (B) A new business partner
    (C) Marketing personnel
    (D) Food critics

14. According to the speaker, what do customers like about the commercial?

    (A) The scene with families
    (B) The various flavors
    (C) The celebrities
    (D) The background music

15. What will listeners most likely do by Friday?

    (A) Meet candidates
    (B) Send the products
    (C) Check some sales figures
    (D) Forward some ideas

---

16. Why is the event being held?

    (A) To show gratitude to an executive
    (B) To introduce a new president
    (C) To attract more customers
    (D) To launch a new product

17. What did Jane Kennedy achieve?

    (A) She developed a product.
    (B) She won a big contract.
    (C) She created more efficient processes.
    (D) She expanded a company internationally.

18. What will most likely happen next?

    (A) A plaque will be presented.
    (B) A short video will play.
    (C) A speech will be given.
    (D) Refreshments will be served.

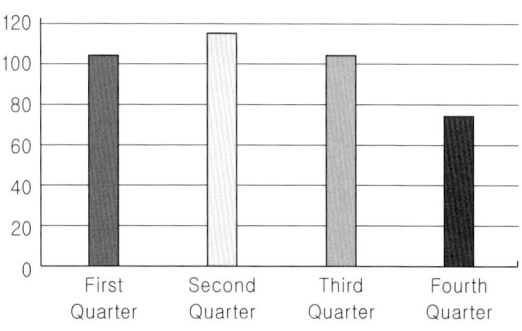

19. What is the purpose of the meeting?

    (A) To introduce a new accountant
    (B) To arrange a meeting date
    (C) To review financial data
    (D) To prepare for a merger

20. Look at the graphic. What quarter will the speaker talk about first?

    (A) First quarter
    (B) Second quarter
    (C) Third quarter
    (D) Fourth quarter

21. What will the speaker most likely do next?

    (A) Leave the office
    (B) Share customers' opinions
    (C) Ask questions
    (D) Give her ideas

SPARTA 빈출 표현 — 패러프레이징 표현

delay/postpone/put off/push back the meeting 회의를 연기하다	→ reschedule the meeting 회의 일정을 다시 잡다
take a look at a copy of my report 보고서를 보다	→ view a document 서류를 보다
extend the deadline 마감일을 연장하다	→ extend the due date 예정일을 연장하다
set up the new computers 새로운 컴퓨터를 설치하다	→ install the new equipment 새로운 장비를 설치하다
adjust my own working hours 자신의 근무 시간을 조절하다	→ work flexible hours 자유 근무 시간으로 일하다
bring it right away 바로 갖다주다	→ be back in a second 곧 돌아오다
mop the floor 바닥을 대걸레로 닦다	→ wipe the floor 바닥을 닦다
chop the vegetables 야채를 썰다	→ cut the ingredients 재료를 썰다
stop by to get the packet 소포를 가지러 들르다	→ collect the packet in person 직접 소포를 가져가다
stop/drop/come by your desk 책상(자리)에 들르다	→ visit the office 사무실을 방문하다
go over/look over the annual report 연례 보고서를 검토하다	→ review a document 서류를 검토하다
finalize the design 디자인을 마무리하다	→ complete the design 디자인을 끝내다
finish the construction 공사를 끝내다	→ complete the project 프로젝트를 끝내다
teach the new assistant 새로운 보조들을 가르치다	→ train a new staff member 신입 사원들을 교육하다
repave the pavement 도로를 재포장하다	→ perform the maintenance work 보수 공사를 하다
move the cabinet 책상을 옮기다	→ carry furniture 가구를 옮기다
participate in the jazz festival 재즈 페스티벌에 참석하다	→ go to the music event 음악 행사에 가다
get high ratings from our patrons 고객들에게 높은 평가를 받다	→ get a good reputation 좋은 평판을 얻다
a small tear, cracked 약간 찢어짐, 금이 간	→ a damaged/defective item 손상된/결함이 있는 물건

highlight the value 가치를 강조하다	→ emphasize the value 가치를 강조하다
reorganize the merchandise on the shelves 선반 위에 상품을 새로 진열하다	→ rearrange the items 물건들을 다시 진열하다
pass out/hand out/give out many flyers 전단을 나눠주다	→ distribute the leaflets 전단을 배포하다
the accounting training next month 다음 달 회계 교육	→ a training session the following month 다가오는 달에 있을 교육
sign up for the seminar 세미나에 등록하다	→ register for/enroll in the seminar 세미나에 등록하다
upgrade a membership 멤버쉽을 업그레이드하다	→ change the plan 요금제를 변경하다
move to a new location 새로운 장소로 옮기다	→ change to a new venue 새로운 장소로 바꾸다
help oneself to coffee, tea, and snacks 커피, 차, 스낵들을 마음껏 먹다	→ enjoy refreshments 다과를 즐기다
wash a car 세차하다	→ clean a vehicle 차량을 청소하다
give an address and phone number 주소와 전화번호를 주다	→ provide contact information 연락 정보를 제공하다
by cash or credit card 현금 또는 신용카드로	→ payment method 지불 방법
construct a factory 공장을 건설하다	→ build a plant 공장을 짓다
go on sale 판매하다	→ be available 구매 가능하다
bring the drill 드릴을 가져오다	→ get the equipment/tool 장비/도구를 가져오다
search for a place to live 거주할 장소를 찾다	→ find a house 집을 찾다
select blue or red 파란색을 아니면 빨간색을 선택하다	→ choose a color 색깔을 고르다
cost of purchase 구매 비용	→ total amount/the sum total 총액
enjoy a fascinating movie 흥미진진한 영화를 즐기다	→ like an interesting film 흥미로운 영화를 좋아하다
what you like the most 가장 좋아하는 것	→ preference 선호도
show the clients how to use the printer 프린터 사용하는 방법을 고객에게 보여주다	→ product demonstration 제품 시연회
remodel the restaurant 레스토랑을 보수 공사하다	→ renovate/refurbish the eating establishment 식당을 보수 공사하다

English	→	Synonym
by express mail 특급 우편으로	→	expedited delivery 특급 배송
work from home 재택 근무하다	→	telecommute 재택근무를 하다
revise some mistakes 실수를 수정하다	→	correct some errors 오류를 수정하다
modify the manuscript 원고를 수정하다	→	proofread the document 문서를 교정하다
not easy to understand/figure out 이해하기 쉽지 않은	→	confusing/complicated/difficult 혼란스러운, 복잡한, 어려운
take a different road/an alternate route 우회하다	→	take a detour 우회하다
at no charge/cost 무료로	→	for free 무료로
be stuck in traffic 차가 막히다	→	traffic congestion/jam/delay 교통 혼잡/체증/지연
transfer to the personnel division 인사과로 전근 가다	→	move to the human resources(HR) department 인사과로 옮기다
join the book club 북 클럽에 가입하다	→	become a member 회원이 되다
get together at 3 P.M. 오후 3시에 모이다	→	meet in the afternoon 오후에 만나다
deal with a matter 문제를 처리하다	→	solve/handle a problem 문제를 해결하다
take place in the banquet hall 연회장에서 열리다	→	be held in the ballroom 대연회장에서 개최되다
get off work before 6 P.M. 오후 6시 전에 퇴근하다	→	leave work early 일찍 퇴근하다
offer a deal 저렴하게 제공하다	→	reduce a price 할인하다
will not be valid 유효하지 않을 것이다	→	will expire 만료될 것이다
be not enough room 충분한 공간이 없다	→	limited space, small 제한된 공간, 작은
put together a bookshelf 책장을 조립하다	→	assemble a bookcase 책장을 조립하다
take time off 휴가를 내다	→	go on holiday/vacation 휴가를 가다
customer reviews 고객 후기	→	customer feedback 고객 의견
The schedule is pretty full. 일정이 가득 찼다.	→	a busy/hectic schedule 바쁜 일정

conduct it department by department 부서별로 실시하다	→ take turns 교대로 하다
find out about pricing information 가격 정보를 알아보다	→ research some prices 가격을 조사하다
ask how much it would cost 얼마나 많은 비용이 드는지 묻다	→ request for an estimate 견적 요청
not a permanent position 정규직이 아닌	→ a temporary worker 임시직
cut the budget 예산을 삭감하다	→ reduce the funding 자금을 줄이다
want to find out when I'll receive payment 언제 지불을 받을 수 있는지 알고 싶다	→ ask about a payment date 지불 날짜를 문의하다
The meeting room/table is already booked. 회의실/테이블이 예약되었다.	→ It's not available/unavailable. 그것을 이용할 수 없다.
The table you ordered stopped being produced. 주문한 테이블 생산이 중단됐다.	→ The item was discontinued. 그 물건이 중단됐다.
Books are sold out. 책이 다 팔렸다.	→ out of stock 품절
How many people will be attending ~? 몇 명의 사람들이 ~에 참석할 것인가?	→ the number of attendees 참석자 수
attract/increase/bring in more customers 더 많은 고객들을 끌다	→ expand the customer base 고객층을 확장하다
energy-saving feature 에너지 절약 기능	→ save energy 에너지를 절약하다
relocate the headquarters 본사를 이전하다	→ move the main/head office 본사를 옮기다
thunderstorm, storm, heavy rain, foggy 폭풍우, 폭우, 안개가 낀	→ inclement/severe/bad/poor weather 나쁜 날씨
collect one's belongings 소지품을 챙기다	→ pack personal items 개인 물품을 챙기다
give an address 연설하다	→ make a speech 연설하다
less expensive/inexpensive 저렴한	→ affordable/reasonable prices 합리적인 가격
collaborative effort 공동 노력	→ work together 함께 일하다
put up a sign on the wall 벽에 간판을 게시하다	→ hang a sign 간판을 걸다
run out of paper 종이가 떨어지다	→ Office supplies are not available. 사무용품을 이용할 수 없다.
mayor 시장	→ a city official/a local politician 시 공무원/지역 정치가

complimentary coffee 무료 커피	→ free drink/beverage 무료 음료
do not go too far 너무 멀리 가지 않다	→ stay in the area 그 지역에 머무르다
waterproof coating 방수 코팅	→ water resistance 내수성
a lot less noisy 훨씬 소음이 적은	→ quiet 조용한
medical clinic/center 의료 센터	→ hospital 병원
e-mail you a brochure and application 브로셔와 신청서를 이메일로 보내다	→ send the information electronically 컴퓨터로 정보를 보내다
mail a package 소포를 우편으로 보내다	→ forward/send a parcel by post/mail 우편으로 소포를 보내다
a corporate luncheon 회사 오찬	→ a company lunch 회사 점심
be short on chairs 의자가 부족하다	→ will not be enough seats 좌석이 충분하지 않다
gas and electric company/water company 가스 전기 공사/상수도 회사	→ utility company (가스, 전기, 수도 등의) 공익기업
open a new office abroad 해외에 지점을 열다	→ expand the business 사업을 확장하다
hold a trade show in New York 뉴욕에서 무역 박람회를 열다	→ open an international trade fair 국제 무역 박람회를 열다
stay for an extra day 하루 더 머물다	→ extend my stay 숙박을 연장하다
can't make it 참석할 수 없다	→ be unable to attend 참석할 수 없다
not accept one's offer 제안을 받아들이지 않다	→ turn down the offer 제안을 거절하다
good for the environment/non-polluting 환경에 좋은/오염되지 않은	→ environmentally friendly 친환경적인
use the rear/back doors of the building 건물 후문을 이용하다	→ use a different entrance 다른 출입구를 이용하다
take a look at the notice board 게시판을 보다	→ check a bulletin board 게시판을 확인하다
go up nearly 30% in sales 거의 30퍼센트 매출이 올랐다	→ increase/grow sales 매출이 증가하다
get in touch with a boss 상사와 연락하다	→ contact a supervisor 상사에게 연락하다
prohibit taking pictures 사진 촬영을 금하다	→ refrain from photography 사진 촬영을 삼가다/피하다

English	Korean	→	Paraphrase	Korean
send to the wrong address	잘못된 주소로 보내다	→	send incorrectly	잘못 보내다
fill out a form	양식을 작성하다	→	complete the paperwork	문서를 작성하다
run 24 hours a day, 7 days a week	하루 24시간, 1주일 내내 작동되다	→	operate continuously	계속 작동되다
someone to take care of the problem	문제를 해결할 사람	→	a repairperson/technician	수리기사/기술자
power/electricity went out	전기가 나갔다	→	a power outage/failure, blackout	정전
make your workplace more efficient	작업장을 효율적으로 만들다	→	organize a workspace	작업 공간을 정리하다
computer is not working	컴퓨터가 작동하지 않는다	→	it's out of order/broken	고장 나다
work overtime	시간 외로 일하다	→	work extra hours	잔업을 하다
extend hours of operation	영업 시간을 연장하다	→	stay open longer	더 오래 열다
need to hire more employees	더 많은 직원들을 고용해야 한다	→	understaffed/short-staffed	직원이 부족한
leave the company	회사를 떠나다	→	retire, quit a job	은퇴하다, 직장을 그만두다
The product development is behind schedule.	제품 개발이 예정보다 늦어지고 있다.	→	It is delayed.	지연되다.
book a flight and a hotel	비행기와 호텔을 예약하다	→	make travel arrangements	여행 준비를 하다
share a ride to work	직장으로 같이 타고 가다	→	carpool to work	출근 시 카풀하다
The unit has already been leased to another party.	그 집이 다른 사람에게 임대되었다.	→	It is no longer available.	더 이상 이용할 수 없다.
provide food and drink for the company events	회사 이벤트를 위해 음식과 음료를 제공하다	→	catering service	출장 연회 서비스
go to a concert this Saturday	이번 토요일에 콘서트에 가다	→	enjoy a live performance on the weekend	주말에 라이브 공연을 즐기다
duplicate the report	보고서를 복사하다	→	make a copy	복사하다
need a reference from your current manager	현재 매니저로부터 추천서가 필요하다	→	ask for a recommendation	추천서를 요청하다
order a lot	많이 주문하다	→	order in bulk	대량으로 주문하다
be reimbursed	비용을 상환 받다	→	get the money back/get a refund	돈을 돌려받다, 환불 받다

books.english.co.kr

books.english.co.kr

books.english.co.kr

스파르타 토익
750+
RC

PART 5&6
단문/장문 채우기

DAY 01 | 명사와 대명사
DAY 02 | 형용사와 부사
DAY 03 | 전치사
DAY 04 | 부사절 접속사
DAY 05 | 동사의 5형식
DAY 06 | 수 일치와 태
DAY 07 | 동사의 시제와 가정법
DAY 08 | to부정사와 동명사
DAY 09 | 분사
DAY 10 | 명사절과 형용사절

PART 5 접근법

문법과 어휘에 대한 문장 안에서의 빈칸 넣기 유형인 PART 5는 주어부터 읽기보다는, 빈칸 근처에서 구조적-문맥적으로 접근하는 것이 관건이다.
가장 중요한 1순위인 문장 구조 분석법은 빈칸 근처에서 수식어를 제거하는 것이다.
(문장 끊어 읽기 연습 → 전치사구, 접속사절, to부정사, 부사 등)

문제 풀이 전략

The report indicates that the wide use of the Internet will result in an increase / in _____ growth.

(A) economy
(B) economics
(C) economic
(D) economically

(1) 문장 구조 분석
 (끊어 읽기)
 → 빈칸 근처 수식어

(2) 빈칸의 품사 확인
 (주변 단어)
 → 명사 앞 형용사 자리

(3) 보기 확인
 (어형 변화 vs. 어휘)
 → 동일 단어로의 어형

Step 1. 문장 구조 분석 (끊어 읽기)
→ 빈칸 앞 전치사 in에서 문장을 끊어 준다.

Step 2. 빈칸의 품사 확인
→ growth(성장)이라는 명사 앞이므로 빈칸은 형용사 자리이다.

Step 3. 보기 확인
→ 한 단어의 파생어(품사 어형)로 구성된 각 보기의 품사를 확인한다. 빈칸은 형용사 자리이므로 (C)가 답이 된다.
→ (A) 명사(경제) (B) 명사(경제학) (C) 형용사(경제의) (D) 부사(경제적으로)

> **Tip**
> 어휘 문제도 문장 구조 분석(끊어 읽기)을 바탕으로 빈칸에 들어갈 품사 어휘와, 함께 쓰이는 연어(collocation)와의 의미적 관계를 매칭시켜 주는 것이 필요하다.

PART 6 접근법

PART 6는 글의 형태(passage)라는 측면에서 PART 7과, 빈칸 넣기(sentence completion) 유형의 측면에서 PART 5와 유사하다. 대부분의 문제 유형은 PART 5와 유사하지만 문장 넣기 유형을 포함한 일부 유형은 앞뒤 문장의 문맥을 통해 문제를 풀도록 연습한다.

Questions 1-4 refer to the following memo.

This is a reminder that all employees should make use of our new online scheduling software. Each member has a personal time-table page, so please record all of your scheduled events on yours and ---1.--- it regularly. ---2.---. However, if you face any troubles, contact the IT Support center for assistance.

The heads of all divisions have access to individual time-sheets for their departments, which will help to facilitate effective arrangement of meeting and workshops. ---3.---, it is possible for the executives to add all company's events and conferences to all individual pages. The software also automatically sends users e-mail notifications ---4.--- there are some conflicts between their personal schedules and any upcoming company issues.

문제 풀이 전략

1. 어형 변화

(A) to check
(B) checking
(C) checks
(D) check

(1) 보기 확인
→ PART 5 풀이와 동일

해설 등위접속사 and 뒤에 it이라는 목적격 대명사를 목적어로 취하는 동사 필요. 등위접속사는 동일 속성을 대등하게 연결하는 역할을 한다. please record ~라는 동사원형으로 시작하는 명령문이 왔으므로 and 뒤도 동일한 명령문으로 동사원형 (D) check가 답이 된다.

2. 문장 넣기

(A) This will be held on December 8 before the event.
(B) These pages are very user-friendly in many ways.
(C) The schedule is frequently changed by the board of directors.
(D) Each staff's page is completely confidential to others.

(1) 앞뒤 문장 확인
(2) 빈칸 뒤 지시어와 연결어 확인
(3) 문제 보기 해석

(1) 지시어 (대명사 / 정관사 the)
→ 앞 문장의 명사를 대신하는 "대명사"와 중복 언급 시 사용되는 "the"를 주의하라!
→ 특히, this/these는 앞 문장 전체에 대한 내용을 요약 또는 이어서 기술하는 역할을 한다.

DAY 1 명사와 대명사

SPARTA 유형 파악

명사란, 사람, 사물, 추상적인 개념을 "이름"으로 만든 것이다. 문장 안에서 주어, 목적어, 보어로 쓰이는 명사는, 명사의 자리를 물어보는 어형 변화 문제, 형용사 또는 동사와의 의미 관계를 묻는 명사 어휘 문제, 가산 명사와 불가산 명사 구분 문제, 사람 명사와 사물 명사 구분 문제, 그리고 마지막으로 두 명사가 하나의 의미 덩어리를 형성하는 복합 명사 문제로 유형을 구분할 수 있다. 그리고 대명사의 경우 명사와 달리 수식과 한정을 받을 수 없으며, 사람(인칭), 사물(인칭), 수량(부정) 대명사로 나눌 수 있다.

SPARTA 출제 포인트

☑ 명사와 대명사의 자리

[_____ 동사 _____ 전치사 _____]
　　주어　　　　목적어/보어　　　　목적어

A <u>sales manager</u> announced the <u>results</u> of the <u>sales promotion</u>.
　　주어　　　　　　　　　　목적어　　　　　　　목적어

영업부장은 판매 홍보의 결과를 발표했다.

☑ 명사구

[관사 + 부사 + 형용사 + 명사]

We offer customers our products at <u>a highly reasonable price</u>.
　　　　　　　　　　　　　　　　　관사 부사　형용사　　명사

우리는 고객들에게 매우 합리적인 가격으로 제품을 제공한다.

주의! 대명사는 형용사의 수식이나 관사 등에 한정 받을 수 없다!

SPARTA 문제 풀이 비법

The protective gear has been provided to ensure the ----- of our building construction workers.

(A) safe
(B) safely
(C) safety
(D) save

건물 공사 노동자들의 안전을 보장하기 위해 보호 장비가 제공되었다.

✅ 관사 (the) 뒤에는 적합한 것은 명사 (C)이다.
보기가 하나의 단어에서 파생된 어형 변형 문제는 자리에 알맞은 품사를 넣어야 한다. 빈칸 주변의 수식어(부사, 전치사, 접속사 등)를 제거하면서 빈칸이 문장 전체에서 어떤 역할을 하는지 확인하자.

SPARTA Grammar Point 1

명사의 형태

A. 일반 명사
주로 불가산 명사로, 동사에서 파생된 것들이 대부분이다. 추상 명사로 분류되기도 한다.

동사 + tion/sion	compete ⓥ 경쟁하다	competition ⓝ 경쟁, 경연
동사 + ment	develop ⓥ 개발하다	development ⓝ 개발
동사 + ance	rely ⓥ 의존하다	reliance ⓝ 의존
동사 + ation	modify ⓥ 수정하다	modification ⓝ 수정
동사 + al	approve ⓥ 승인하다	approval ⓝ 승인
동사 + ure	expose ⓥ 노출시키다	exposure ⓝ 노출
동사 + sis	emphasize ⓥ 강조하다	emphasis ⓝ 강조
형용사 + ness	aware ⓐ 인식하는	awareness ⓝ 인식
형용사 + ity	productive ⓐ 생산적인	productivity ⓝ 생산성
명사 + hood/ship	neighbor ⓝ 이웃, 동료	neighborhood ⓝ 주변, 근처

B. 사람 명사
주로 동사에 다양한 접미사를 붙여 사람의 의미(가산 명사)를 만들어낸다.

동사 + ant	apply ⓥ 지원하다	applicant ⓝ 지원자
동사 + ee	employ ⓥ 채용하다	employee ⓝ 직원
동사 + er	manage ⓥ 관리하다	manager ⓝ 관리자
동사 + or	supervise ⓥ 감독하다	supervisor ⓝ 감독관
명사 + ist	economy ⓝ 경제	economist ⓝ 경제학자
명사 + ian	music ⓝ 음악	musician ⓝ 음악가

그 밖의 규칙이 따로 없는 사람 명사들을 기억해 두자.

architect (건축가), representative (대표, 판매사원), relative (친척), rival (경쟁자)
expert (전문가), professional (전문가), delegate (대표), critic (비평가)

SPARTA Check-UP

정답 및 해설 p. 399

The CEO has encouraged ------- to attend the workshop for self-improvement.
(A) employees   (B) employers
(C) employment   (D) employing

SPARTA Grammar Point 2

명사의 수

A. 가산 명사

가산 명사는 반드시 앞에 한정사(관사, 소유격)가 오거나 복수형으로 써야 한다.

	단독 사용 X	a(an) 결합	the 결합	한정사 결합	a/-s와 결합 X
가산 명사	product 단독 사용 불가	a product	the product	our product	a products a/-s 동시 사용 불가

You can get ⏐a⏐ refund if you return the item with the original receipt.
영수증 원본과 제품을 함께 반품하시면 환불 받을 수 있습니다.

TOEIC 빈출 가산 명사

사람	customer, employee, client, consumer, attendant ...
돈/제품	price, refund, fund, product, item ... (주의! money와 merchandise는 불가산)
규칙	rule, regulation, requirement, qualification, standard, contract ...
절차	procedure, process, conclusion, decision, delay ...

B. 불가산 명사

불가산 명사는 부정관사(a, an)나 복수형과 쓸 수 없다.

For more **information** about this test, please visit our Web site at www.uptest.com.
이번 시험에 대한 더 많은 정보를 원하시면, www.uptest.com으로 저희 웹사이트를 방문해 주세요.

TOEIC 빈출 불가산 명사

furniture 가구	baggage 짐	luggage 짐
information 정보	equipment 장비	advice 충고
clothing 의류	jewelry 보석류	machinery 기계류
research 연구	money 돈	merchandise 상품

➡ 집합/총칭 명사는 셀 수 없는 불가산 명사!

SPARTA Check-UP

정답 및 해설 p. 399

------- made by Bradley&Joy Wood has been very popular in the European market.
(A) Items   (B) Merchandise
(C) Desk   (D) Employer

SPARTA Grammar Point 3

사람을 대신하는 대명사

A. 인칭대명사 (사람): 격에 따라 모양이 바뀐다.

인칭	수·성		주격	소유격	목적격	소유대명사	재귀대명사
1인칭	단수		I	my	me	mine	myself
	복수		we	our	us	ours	ourselves
2인칭	단·복수		you	your	you	yours	yourself/selves
3인칭	단수	남자	he	his	him	his	himself
		여자	she	her	her	hers	herself
		사물	it	its	it	–	itself
	복수		they	their	them	theirs	themselves

* 소유대명사는 주로 사물을 지칭 (= 소유격 + 명사). 사람의 경우 친구/동료 지칭 가능

ex) a friend of mine / a colleague of mine

- **주격**: People complain **when they receive** poor service.
  (접속사 when은 절을 이끌기 때문에 when 다음에 '주어+동사'가 차례로 와야 한다)

- **소유격**: Ms. Thompson lost **her assembly manual**, so she is using **mine** [my assembly manual].
  (동사 lost 뒤에 목적어로 명사가 와야 하는데 그 명사 앞에 올 수 있는 것은 소유격, mine은 소유대명사)

- **목적격**: We must package **the items**, and then we can **deliver them**.
  (동사 deliver 다음에 목적어가 와야 하므로 목적격, 복수 형태의 대명사가 온다)

B. 재귀대명사

[1] 대명사 역할 (재귀 용법)

주어가 중복되어 목적어 자리에 다시 쓰일 때 -self/selves를 붙여 표현한다. <생략 불가>

➡ 재귀대명사는 주어 자리, 명사 앞 소유격 자리에 올 수 없음에 주의!

He introduced **himself** to the audience at the start of session.
그는 세션이 시작할 때 청중들에게 자신을 소개했다.

[2] 부사 역할 (강조 용법)

재귀대명사는 대명사임에도 불구하고 생략 가능한 '부사 자리'에 위치하여 행위자를 강조한다. <생략 가능>

➡ 주어보다 앞에 올 수 없음에 주의!

The president welcomed new employees on the first day of their attendance **himself**.
사장은 신입사원들의 첫 출근날에 그들을 직접 맞이했다.

[3] 관용 표현

by oneself (= on one's own) 혼자	for oneself 혼자 힘으로
of itself 저절로	in itself 본질적으로

SPARTA Check-UP 3

정답 및 해설 p. 399

The design team was informed that the CEO ------ had approved their proposals for new items.

(A) he
(B) his
(C) him
(D) himself

SPARTA Grammar Point 4

사물을 대신하고 수량만큼 선택하는 대명사

A. 지시대명사 (사물 지칭)

지시사는 "이것", "저것"을 지칭할 때 쓰이는데, 지시하는 명사 앞에서 한정사 역할을 한다.

	this/these	that/those
지시사	이것	저것
대명사	앞 문장의 내용	한 문장에서 앞의 명사

➡ 대명사로서 this/these는 앞 문장의 내용을 지칭하므로 "한 문장"으로 구성된 파트 5에서는 정답 확률이 낮다.
➡ 파트 5에서는 that(앞 부분의 사물 단수 명사)이나 those(앞 부분의 사물 복수 명사)가 주로 답이 된다.

The SG-300 **model** of Kane Motors is more expensive than **that** of other manufacturers.
Kane Motors의 SG-300 모델은 다른 제조업체들의 모델보다 더 비싸다.

➡ that이나 those가 앞의 사물 명사를 대신 받을 때는 주로 "비교 표현"이나, "비교급"이 나오는 문장에서 답으로 등장한다.

주의! those는 "~하는 사람들"이라는 의미로, 복수 사람 명사를 나타낼 수 있다. 이때, those 뒤에는 이를 수식하는 관계대명사 who, 전치사 with, 분사(-ing/p.p.)가 나온다.

B. 수량 표현

수량의 의미를 나타내는 대명사가 전체 중 일부의 의미를 나타낼 때 등장한다. 특히, 수량 표현들은 of 뒤의 명사와 동사가 **수 일치**한다는 점에 주의할 필요가 있다. 그리고 of 뒤의 명사는 '정해져 있는 명사의 일부'를 의미하므로 반드시 the나 소유격 같은 한정사가 필요하다.

```
all / most / some / any
many / several / both /      + of + the/소유격 + 명사 + 동사
(a) few / much / (a) little
                                              ↑ 수 일치
```

단, one, each, either, neither는 주어를 무조건 단수로 만드는 표현임에 유의!

Most of the workers **are reminded** that the safety regulations have been recently updated.
대부분의 노동자들은 안전 규정이 최근에 업데이트되었다는 것을 들었다.

C. Some과 Any

일부를 나타내는 some과 전부를 나타내는 any가 보기에 등장할 때, 긍정문에서 some을, 부정문/조건문에서는 any를 쓴다.
(not ~ any / if ~ any)

D. other(나머지)의 활용

기본적으로 other는 단독으로 사용하지 않는다. other 앞에 an-/the/-s가 붙어서 another, the other, others로 쓰이거나, other 뒤에 명사(가산복수/불가산)가 위치해야 한다.

➡ 정관사 the는 범위가 정해졌는지 정해지지 않았는지를 알려주는 역할을 한다. 범위가 정해진 경우 the를 사용하는데, 문장에서 범위는 숫자로 표시된다.
➡ 관용 표현으로 "서로"를 의미하는 each other와 one another는 주어 자리에 올 수 없다.

SPARTA Check-UP ④

정답 및 해설 p. 399

Of the five candidates for the position, two need a certified license in this field, but ------- are highly qualified for the task.

(A) other (B) others
(C) the other (D) the others

SPARTA Practice Test

101. Knowing the number of visitors who are planning to attend the festival is of great ------- to the planning committee.

(A) important
(B) importance
(C) importantly
(D) more importantly

102. Travelers are reminded to check their itinerary document to verify that the airline tickets are actually -------.

(A) they
(B) them
(C) theirs
(D) themselves

103. Department heads who want to hire new staff members based on recommendations should first get ------- from the personnel division.

(A) permitting
(B) permission
(C) permissive
(D) to permit

104. Ms. Rachel asked team members to help ------- with arranging applications for the position.

(A) she
(B) her
(C) hers
(D) of her

105. JBM Software announced that the issue about the merger with ARB Ltd. is under -------.

(A) negotiates
(B) negotiating
(C) negotiation
(D) negotiator

106. Mr. Eric fixed the copy machine ------- yesterday because there is an absence of maintenance staff in the company.

(A) his
(B) his own
(C) himself
(D) him

107. Although all of his paintings are based on reality, Mr. McGrady sometimes depends on his ------- to complete the work.

(A) imaginary
(B) imaginative
(C) imagine
(D) imagination

108. ------- social clubs on campus welcome new students and accept most of their enrollment.

(A) We
(B) Our
(C) Ours
(D) Us

109. The marketing director carefully reviewed the terms of the contracts with a huge ------- company.

(A) distribute
(B) is distributed
(C) distribution
(D) distributes

110. ------- in Mr. Terry's division has been dedicated to improving the lines of electronic products.

(A) Each other
(B) Whichever
(C) One another
(D) Everyone

111. Warren Finance has sent its newest group of ------- to the factory in Bangkok for them to learn the production procedures.
    (A) recruit
    (B) recruits
    (C) recruiting
    (D) recruitment

112. A colleague of ------- will represent the Department of English Literature at the annual scholarship forum.
    (A) my
    (B) me
    (C) mine
    (D) I

113. The board of directors converted the company's unusual regulations into general ------- for all employees.
    (A) specifically
    (B) specify
    (C) specific
    (D) specifics

114. One of the four software programs has been accepted, but ------- have been rejected due to some logical errors.
    (A) other
    (B) another
    (C) others
    (D) the others

115. The tight budget for the upcoming festival was just one of the ------- faced by the hosts of the event.
    (A) problem
    (B) problematic
    (C) problems
    (D) problematically

116. ------- of the club members expect that the CEO is in favor of the proposal.
    (A) All
    (B) One
    (C) Either
    (D) Each

117. You need to present this e-mail as ------- that you have submitted the refund request on our Web site.
    (A) confirmation
    (B) confirmable
    (C) confirm
    (D) confirmed

118. ------- of the machine parts is guaranteed if you have an original receipt of purchase.
    (A) All
    (B) Many
    (C) Each
    (D) Every

119. According to the guidelines, your ------- in the seminar is required in order to get promoted.
    (A) participation
    (B) participant
    (C) participate
    (D) participated

120. Now that Ms. Rhys has been awarded several scholarships, ------- department has been granted many external research projects.
    (A) she
    (B) her
    (C) hers
    (D) herself

Questions 121-124 refer to the following advertisement.

Alpha Corp. is proud to introduce the new Bubble DX200. The DX200 has four different wash setting modes, from delicate to heavy-duty, and has special -------. This convenient and easy-to-use
121.
washing machine is also extremely energy efficient — it consumes two thirds of the electricity used by typical models. Furthermore, the unit is designed with a compact size. -------. We are so
122.
sure that you will like this ------- that we support it
123.
with a buy-back guarantee. If you are dissatisfied with the DX200, you can return ------- at any time
124.
within 45 days from the date of purchase for a full refund. For more information, please visit our Web site at www.alphaco.com.

121. (A) function
(B) functions
(C) to function
(D) functioning

122. (A) You can easily put in extra items during the wash cycle.
(B) It will be suitable for even the smallest space in your house.
(C) They have the capacity to handle some bulky laundry.
(D) You can save time washing a lot of laundry.

123. (A) appliance
(B) invention
(C) clothing
(D) residence

124. (A) it
(B) us
(C) yourself
(D) their own

SPARTA Grammar Review

(1) 명사 자리: 주어 / 목적어 / 보어, 한정사 뒤, 전치사 뒤 자리 확인

(2) 가산 vs 불가산: 셀 수 있는 가산 명사는 단독 사용 불가, 집합(총칭) 의미의 명사는 대부분 셀 수 없는 불가산명사

(3) 사람 vs 사물: 동작을 하는 사람 명사, 동작을 당하는 사물 명사는 동사와의 관계 확인

(4) 빈칸 위치에 따라 인칭대명사의 격을 맞추어 답을 고른다. < __ V __ 전 __ / __ N >

(5) 재귀대명사(-self/selves)는 부사 자리에도 가능하다.

(6) 비교 표현, 비교급 문장에서는 사물을 지칭하는 that (단수), those(복수) 중에 알맞은 것을 답으로 한다.

(7) "~하는 사람들"을 의미하는 those는 뒤에서 관계사 (who) / 전치사(with) / 분사(-ing/p.p.)로부터 수식 받는다.

(8) 수량 표현은 of 뒤의 명사와 수 일치하는 것이 원칙이다.

(9) 숫자 표현의 범위가 정해져 있으면 나머지를 나타내는 other/others는 정관사 the와 쓰인다.

DAY 2 형용사와 부사

SPARTA 유형 파악

형용이란, "설명"의 다른 표현이다. 설명한다는 것은 이름 즉, 명사에 대해 추가적으로 이야기하는 것으로, "형용사"라는 품사는 "명사"와 반드시 함께 등장한다.
출제 유형) (1) 형용사의 위치 (2) 수량 형용사 (3) 혼동 형용사 (모양이 비슷한 형용사)

부사란, 부가적인 품사의 하나로 100% 수식어이기 때문에 생략 가능하다. 부사는 명사를 제외한 모든 것을 수식할 수 있다.
출제 유형) (1) 부사의 위치 (2) 어휘 해석형(-ly로 끝나는 보기 구성) (3) 기능형 부사(-ly가 붙지 않는 부사)

SPARTA 출제 포인트

☑ 형용사의 위치

명사가 있는 곳이면 형용사가 함께 한다.

형용사 + 명사 + 형용사	: 명사 앞/뒤
주어 + 2형식 동사 + 형용사	: 주격 보어 자리
주어 + 5형식 동사 + 목적어 + 형용사	: 목적격 보어 자리

➡ 명사 앞뒤는 "수식어" 자리로 생략 가능, "보어" 자리는 생략 불가!
➡ 명사 뒤에서는 주로 -ible/-able (능력/가능성)을 나타내는 형용사가 수식한다.

The **professional** analyst requested that we provide more information.
그 전문 분석가는 우리에게 추가 정보를 제공하도록 요청했다. <명사 수식>

The newly hired employee was relatively **competitive** compared to others.
새로 고용된 그 직원은 다른 직원들과 비교했을 때, 상대적으로 경쟁력이 있었다. <주격 보어>

> ➡ 대표적인 2형식 동사: be, become, remain, stay, seem
> ➡ 대표적인 5형식 동사: make, leave, keep, consider, find, deem

☑ 부사의 위치

명사를 직접 수식하는 위치를 제외하고 어디나 올 수 있다.

| 부사 + 주어 + 부사 + 동사 + (목적어) + 부사 |

➡ 명사 자리인 타동사의 목적어 앞에서 부사는 직접 수식할 수 없다.
➡ 주어인 명사 앞에 위치하는 것은, 문장 전체를 수식하기 때문!

Approximately half of the students have registered for the workshop.
거의 절반의 학생들이 그 워크숍에 등록했다. <형용사 수식>

Rio Schneider's debut performance was **positively** reviewed by the critics.
리오 슈나이더의 데뷔 공연은 평론가들에 의해 긍정적으로 평가되었다. <동사 수식>

> **추가** 동사 주변의 부사
> be ____ 타Ving
> be ____ 타Ved
> have ____ 타Ved
> 조동사 ____ 타V(원형)
> to ____ 타V
> ➡ 주로 동사 조합 사이에 위치
> ➡ 수동태, 자동사의 경우 앞뒤 가능

SPARTA 문제 풀이 비법

Gebhard Graphics has specialized in ------ products for a variety of companies.

(A) promotion
(B) promotes
(C) promote
(D) promotional

Gebhard Graphics 사는 다양한 회사들을 위한 판촉용품에 특화되어 있다.

✓ 명사(products)를 앞에서 수식하는 형용사 (D)가 정답이다. 빈칸 근처의 전치사 in과 for에서 끊어 읽기를 하면, in이라는 전치사 뒤에 명사 products가 이미 있으므로 수식어 역할을 하는 형용사 (D)가 올 수 있다. (A)는 명사, (B), (C)는 동사이다.

SPARTA Grammar Point 1

형용사의 형태

A. 일반 형용사

형용사 어미	어휘
동사 -ive	alter → alter**nive** / describe → descript**ive**
동사 -ent/ant	differ → differ**ent** / import → import**ant**
명사 -ous	humor → humor**ous** / danger → danger**ous**
명사 -(a)ble	value → valu**able** / rely → reli**able** / use → us**able**
명사 -(i)ent	deficit → defic**ient** / profit → profic**ient**
명사 -ful	thought → thought**ful** / care → care**ful**
명사 -ic	economy → econom**ic** / drama → dramat**ic**
명사 -less	stain → stain**less** / harm → harm**less** / pain → pain**less**
명사 +y	worth → worth**y** / risk → risk**y** / wealth → wealth**y**
명사 +ly	time → time**ly** / cost → cost**ly** / friend → friend**ly** / leisure → leisure**ly**

주의! -ly형 어미는 주로 <형용사+-ly>로 부사가 대부분인데, 소수의 <명사+-ly>는 형용사로 쓰인다.

B. 분사형 형용사

분사 만들기

동사 (동작) + -ing / -ed(p.p.) + 명사
: (명사가) 동작을 직접 하는
: (명사가) 동작을 당하는

➡ 자동사는 수동형이 불가하므로, -ing 어미의 능동형 분사만 가능하다.
➡ -ing/-ed에 포함된 동사가 동작이 아닌, 감정을 나타내는 경우 -ing는 사물명사와, -ed는 사람명사와 쓰인다.
(감정동사: surprise 놀라게 하다, satisfy 만족시키다, interest 관심을 갖게 하다., overwhelm 압도하다,
confuse 혼란하게 만들다, excite 흥분시키다, distract 산만하게 하다, exhaust 지치게 하다, impress 감동을 주다…)

Please use the **enclosed** form in the package when applying for the position.
그 직책에 지원하실 때는 패키지 안에 동봉된 양식을 사용해 주세요.

Most of our graduate students are very **satisfied** with this seminar.
대부분의 대학원생들은 이번 세미나에 매우 만족해한다.

SPARTA Check-UP

정답 및 해설 p. 402

Those who have not submitted their ------ weekly reports should do so before the end of today.

(A) revise (B) revising
(C) revised (D) to revise

SPARTA Grammar Point 2

수량 형용사와 혼동 형용사

A. 수량 형용사

수량 형용사는 일반 형용사와 달리 **명사 앞**에만 위치하며 뒤따르는 명사를 **수식**하고 **한정**한다.
뒤따르는 명사의 속성(셀 수 있는지 없는지)과 형태(복수로 -s가 붙었는지 안 붙었는지)를 확인한다.

[1] 가산 명사와 수량 형용사

one / another / each / either / every	+ 단수 명사
(a) few / several / many / both	+ 복수 명사
a number of / a variety of / a range of / an array of	+ 복수 명사
a selection of / a range of / a series of / a collection of	+ 복수 명사

[2] 불가산 명사와 수량 형용사

(a) little / much / less	
a great deal of / amount of	+ 불가산 명사
a (great / good) amount / quantity of	

[3] 가산/불가산 명사 모두 가능한 수량 형용사

no / some / any	+ 단수 명사/복수 명사/불가산 명사
all / most / other / more	+ 복수 명사/불가산 명사
a lot of / lots of / plenty of	+ 복수 명사/불가산 명사

Each employee should attend the training session if they do not have any certificate.
각 직원들은 인증서가 없다면 그 교육 훈련을 참여해야 한다.

Many factories in Indiana are well equipped with the latest machines.
인디애나에 있는 많은 공장들은 최신 기계를 잘 갖추고 있다.

B. 혼동 형용사

형용사의 어근이 동일하여 모양상 비슷하게 보이는 형용사들이 있다. 명확하게 의미를 구분하여 암기하도록 한다.

consider**able** 상당한	success**ful** 성공적인	desir**ous** 바라는	respect**ive** 각각의
consider**ate** 사려 깊은	success**ive** 연속하는	desir**able** 바람직한	respect**ful** 존경하는
benefi**cial** 유용한, 이로운	reli**ant** 의지하는	profit**able** 이익이 되는	information**al** 정보의
benefi**cent** 자비심이 많은	reli**able** 믿을 만한	profici**ent** 능숙한	inform**ative** 유익한

Mr. McNab is regarded as a **successful** artist in the Modern City Design.
McNab 씨는 현대 도시 디자인의 성공적인 예술가로 간주된다.

Mr. McNab was absent from work for three **successive** days. McNab 씨는 3일 연속으로 결근했다.

SPARTA Check-UP

정답 및 해설 p. 402

Every ------ was embarrassed by the frequent changes to the company's policies for their reimbursement of business travel.

(A) employ (B) employee
(C) employees (D) employers

SPARTA Grammar Point 3

시간/빈도 부사

A. 시간 부사

시간 부사는 **동사의 시제** 또는 **문장의 구조**를 보고 결정하는 대표적인 기능형 부사이다.

already	이미, 벌써	과거나 완료(현재완료/과거완료)시제에 사용 (미래시제나 to부정사 불가) 부정어(not)와 함께 사용하지 않음
still	여전히	긍정문, 부정문, 의문문에 사용 부정문의 경우 〈still ~ not〉으로 부정어가 뒤에 위치
yet	아직	부정문에 사용. 〈not ~ yet〉 형태로 쓰임 부정어가 없다면 〈~ yet ~ to V〉 형태로 가능
ever	언제나, 항상	함께 쓰는 어구 확인 → hardly ever, if ever, ever since, 비교급/최상급 ever
ago	전에	항상 과거 시제와 쓰임 → 과거완료나 현재완료 시제에는 사용할 수 없음
once	한번 한때	"한번"의 의미일 때는 시간 단위 명사와 쓰임 〈once a + 시간 단위 명사〉 "한때"의 의미일 때는 과거시제와 쓰임
finally	마침내, 결국	오랫동안 기다린 일이 일어났을 때 사용: 현재 완료시제와 자주 등장 문맥상 "~이후"라는 의미로 after나 following이 자주 등장
soon	곧 (= shortly)	얼마 지나지 않아 일어날 일 또는 다가올 예정에 대한 문맥에서 쓰임 미래시제나 "예정"의 동사와 주로 쓰임
recently	최근에 (= lately)	과거나 현재완료 시제에 사용 *cf.* since는 현재완료와 쓰이는 부사

The board of directors has **not yet** decided whether to acquire Z-Motors.
이사회는 Z-Motors 사를 인수할 것인가에 대해 아직 결정하지 못했다.

B. 빈도부사

반복되거나 **규칙적인** 행동을 나타내는 빈도부사는 주로 **현재시제**와 쓰인다.

[빈도순]   always 〉 often, frequently 〉 usually 〉 sometimes 〉 never
[그 외]   regularly, periodically, hardly, seldom, rarely, barely…

→ 빈도부사는 조동사/be동사 뒤, 일반동사 앞에 온다.

Sales representatives **always** send their customers text messages about new items.
판매원들은 고객들에게 새로운 제품에 대해 문자메시지를 항상 보낸다.

SPARTA Check-UP

정답 및 해설 p. 402

We have ------ joined the public bidding for the construction of the new apartment complex in the area of Fairfax, Virginia.

(A) recently   (B) ago
(C) shortly   (D) yet

SPARTA Grammar Point 4

강조 부사

A. 시간 강조 부사

"즉시", "바로" 의 의미를 지닌 부사들은 주로 시간 표현, 또는 대상과 함께 쓰인다.

| right, just, immediately
soon, shortly, directly
instantly, promptly | **+** | 시간 표현
before/after
when/at + 시간 | / | 대상
to + 사람
장소
to + 장소 |

Emily Bronte began to receive a reputation in literature **just** before her death.
Emily Bronte는 죽기 바로 전에 문학계에서 명성을 얻기 시작했다.

B. 숫자 강조 부사

"숫자"나 "수량(형용사)"을 수식하는 부사들이 따로 있다.

거의/대략	almost, approximately, roughly, about, around, nearly
이상/미만	over, above, more than / under, below, less than
최대 ~까지	up to
적어도	at least
오직/단지	only / just

➡ about, around, over, above, under, below는 전치사로도 쓰이니 주의하자.
➡ 숫자/수량 대신 "완료/충족"을 나타내는 complete, finished, fulfilled, done 등과도 쓰일 수 있다.

During the period of Korea Festa Sale, most of our items will be offered **up to** 80% off the regular price.
코리아 페스타 세일 기간 동안, 우리 제품의 대부분은 정가에서 최대 80퍼센트 할인된 가격으로 제공될 것이다.

C. 비교급/최상급 강조 부사

"매우", "훨씬"이라는 의미의 부사 중에서, 비교급 또는 최상급과 쓰이는 부사가 정해져 있다.

비교급 강조 부사	far, a lot, still, even, much
최상급 강조 부사	much, by far, quite, the very

➡ 비교급(more/-er), 최상급(most/-est) 앞에서 위 부사들은 원래의 의미 대신, "강조"의 역할로 쓰인다.
➡ 최상급 강조 부사는 일반적으로 정관사(the)나 소유격 앞에 위치한다. 단, the very는 뒤에 바로 최상급이 위치.

Our service is not **much more** expensive than other competitors.
우리의 서비스는 다른 경쟁사들보다 엄청 비싸지 않습니다.

SPARTA Check-UP

정답 및 해설 p. 402

DG Holdings is giving ------ more opportunities to build up skills to its employees by providing them with in-company's extracurricular activities.

(A) very
(B) almost
(C) directly
(D) much

SPARTA Practice Test

정답 및 해설 p. 402

101. Among newly launched vehicles at this motor show, the Hoax-3 model has the most ------- engine.
 (A) efficiency
 (B) efficient
 (C) efficiently
 (D) efficiencies

102. In case of canceling the event without any notice, the cost of your ticket will be refunded ------- to your credit card.
 (A) directly
 (B) direct
 (C) direction
 (D) directing

103. Ashely's Travel Agency is offering ------- deals on last-minute hotel reservations until the end of this winter.
 (A) special
 (B) specially
 (C) specialize
 (D) specializing

104. The city of Fiorentina is ------- known as "the Center of the Medieval Culture," and it attracts visitors from all other countries.
 (A) widen
 (B) wider
 (C) widely
 (D) wide

105. ------- full-time employee at Office Depot will be provided with a security pass for the intra-web system.
 (A) Just
 (B) Many
 (C) Other
 (D) Every

106. Due to various issues, new promotional strategies ------- have not been confirmed as to how we will meet our sales goals.
 (A) ever
 (B) still
 (C) soon
 (D) almost

107. Schmidt Trans's drivers have ------- influence on rules relating to fare increases for passengers.
 (A) few
 (B) many
 (C) little
 (D) any

108. According to the market research, sales figures of TerraPower's new solar panels will increase by ------- 30 percent for the next three years.
 (A) roughly
 (B) rough
 (C) roughed
 (D) rougher

109. All worldwide companies tend to be more and more ------- on foreign workers to run their international branches.
 (A) relied
 (B) reliance
 (C) reliable
 (D) reliant

110. During tough times and in many ways, Jerry's team has ------- demonstrated their efforts and passion to others to overcome the company's crisis.
 (A) consistent
 (B) consistently
 (C) more consistent
 (D) most consistent

DAY 2 · 형용사와 부사 | 131

111. When constructing new buildings in that area, please be sure the surface of the foundation is completely -------.
    (A) flat
    (B) flatly
    (C) flatter
    (D) flatten

112. Since John Anthony restructured the sales department, profits from the quarterly sales have risen -------.
    (A) considerably
    (B) considerable
    (C) consider
    (D) considering

113. Before applying for the position, you should check ------- responsibilities of the job, posted on the company's Web site.
    (A) anyone
    (B) others
    (C) several
    (D) each

114. Many economic professionals strongly believe that Vietnam's unstable policy will ------- have to be improved to prevent the country from causing inflation.
    (A) soon
    (B) such
    (C) ever
    (D) like

115. The graduate program at the University of Seattle asked the applicants to submit three ------- recommendation letters from their academic advisors.
    (A) impress
    (B) impresses
    (C) impressed
    (D) impressive

116. Scott's article for the dissertation has been ------- evaluated by the paper examiners in the Department of Economics.
    (A) favor
    (B) favorably
    (C) favorable
    (D) favored

117. Employees who have the RED-permit can park their cars in the designated area at no ------- charge.
    (A) addition
    (B) additional
    (C) additionally
    (D) adds

118. Compiling a meaningful database is now ------- complete through interviewing the citizen and transcribing it for the file.
    (A) almost
    (B) nearby
    (C) anytime
    (D) yet

119. Improving and updating our facilities can make them more ------- to our potential customers frequently visiting here and touring the site.
    (A) attracted
    (B) attractive
    (C) attractively
    (D) attraction

120. Although the renovation of Heinle Sports Stadium Complex is not ------- finished, some of the stores are already open and attracting customers.
    (A) yet
    (B) often
    (C) quite
    (D) seldom

Questions 121-124 refer to the following letter.

Global Charity Fund
843 Lincoln Boulevard
Nashville, Tennessee

June 20
Nelson Kim
370 Central Street
Busan, Republic of Korea

Dear Mr. Kim,

I am writing to ask you to support the Global Charity Fund. There are millions of people living on less than one dollar a day around the world. -------. Therefore, even a small amount of assistance can make a considerable difference to -------.
We are all ------- about the impacts of starvation, especially among children all over the world. To stop it, please enclose your check and send it to us — in any amount you can donate — using the ------- envelope. We would be very delighted with any contribution you can make.

Sincerely,

Ezekiel Nikomo
Global Hunger Fund

---

121. (A) In contrast, people who want to be in a partnership need your help urgently.
(B) Despite this situation, living conditions have become poorer.
(C) For example, we provide them with an excellent elementary education.
(D) Furthermore, they sometimes are not given even basic healthcare.

122. (A) every
(B) much
(C) others
(D) both

123. (A) worry
(B) worries
(C) worried
(D) worriedly

124. (A) prepay
(B) prepaying
(C) prepaid
(D) to prepay

SPARTA Grammar Review

(1) 형용사 자리: 명사 앞뒤(수식어), 2형식/5형식 동사 뒤 (보어)

(2) 분사: 동작을 하는 Ving는 주로 사람 명사와, 동작을 당하는 Ved는 주로 사물 명사 (감정은 반대)

(3) 수량 형용사: 전체를 나타내는 every는 가산 단수 명사와, all은 가산 복수 또는 불가산 명사와 쓰인다.

(4) 혼동 형용사: dependent(reliant)는 전치사 on, responsible은 전치사 for가 쓰인다.

(5) be likely to V(~할 것 같은)에서 likely는 형용사로 쓰였다. (-ly로 끝나는 형용사에 주의!)

(6) 부사는 명사를 제외한 모든 구성 요소와 문장 전체까지 수식할 수도 있다.

(7) 규칙/반복의 빈도부사는 주로 현재 시제와 함께 쓰인다.

(8) "즉시, 바로"를 뜻하는 부사 just, right, directly, immediately는 시간 표현을 강조한다.

(9) "거의, 대략"을 뜻하는 부사 approximately, roughly, about, around는 숫자 표현을 수식한다.

(10) 비교급 강조 부사로 far, a lot, still, even, much가 있다.

DAY 3 전치사

> **SPARTA 유형 파악**

전치사는 명사 앞에 위치하는 품사로, 명사와 구를 형성하여 문장에서 수식어 역할을 한다. 전치사 문제는 뒤의 명사 또는 앞의 동사와의 의미 관계를 형성하는 기능형 전치사와, 2단어 이상이 하나의 의미를 만드는 전치사의 경우 조합과 의미의 이해가 요구되는 어휘형 전치사로 나뉜다. 특히, 기능형 전치사는 뒤따르는 명사의 속성을 확인한 후 푸는 연습을 해야 한다.

> **SPARTA 출제 포인트**

☑ 전치사의 위치

부사와 마찬가지로 수식어 역할을 하기 때문에, 완전한 문장 구조를 제외하고 어디에나 올 수 있다.

→ 위치 제한 없이 문장 필수 요소들을 제외한 모든 위치에서 수식할 수 있다.
→ 전치사 뒤에는 명사를 대신해, 대명사, 동명사, 명사절 등이 올 수 있다. (단, to부정사는 불가)

Jackson Theater has been temporarily closed **for** 2 months **because of** a construction project.
Jackson 극장은 공사 때문에 2개월 동안 임시로 문을 닫았다.

☑ 전치사 문제 풀이 순서

명사 앞에 위치하는 것이 전치사의 기본인 것처럼, 뒤에 나온 명사의 속성을 확인하고 동사와의 의미 관계를 확인한다. 그 다음에는, 앞의 명사나 형용사의 관계를 참조한다.

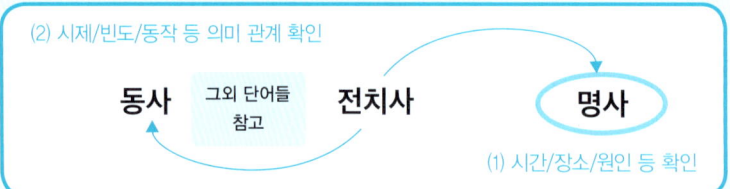

Sanctum Appliances **has offered** various discounts to customers **since** September 9.
Sanctum 가전은 9월 9일 이래로 다양한 할인을 고객들에게 제공하고 있습니다.

→ 전치사 since 뒤에 9월 9일이라는 "시점"이 나오고, 과거부터 현재까지의 시간차를 나타내기 때문에 동사의 시제로 현재완료(have Ved)가 온다.

> **SPARTA 문제 풀이 비법**

In-company server updates will be implemented ----- all our branches from Monday to Wednesday.

(A) between
(B) throughout
(C) until
(D) during

월요일부터 수요일까지 우리 전 지점에 걸쳐 사내 서버 업데이트가 실시될 예정입니다.

✅ 빈칸 뒤에 "모든 지점(all ~ branches)"이라는 장소 명사가 왔다. (A) between은 "(지점) 둘 사이에", (B) throughout은 "(공간) ~도처에", (C) until은 "(시점) ~까지", (D) during은 "(기간) ~동안"으로, "전 지점에 걸쳐"라는 의미를 이루는 (B)가 적절하다.

SPARTA Grammar Point 1

시간 전치사

A. 시점 전치사
"언제"(when)에 해당하는 시점의 속성과 함께하는 전치사의 특징을 확인한다.

전치사	의미	명사 속성	특징	사용 예시
at	~에	(점) 시각	응용] "수치 정보(가격, 비율)"에 사용	at 7 P.M. 오후 7시에
on	~에	(선/면) 날짜/요일	응용] "주제, 내용"에 사용	on March 17 3월 17일에
in	~에	(공간) 월/연도/계절	응용] "방법, 분야"에 사용	in 2018 2018년에
until	~까지	끝 시점	해당 시점까지 "동작"이 "유지"	last until 9 P.M. 9시까지 지속하다
by	~까지	끝 시점	해당 시점까지 "동작"이 "한번"	arrive by Friday 금요일까지 도착하다
from	~부터	시작 시점	시작 시점, 출발지 모두 사용 가능	from 10 to 11 10시부터 11시까지
since	~이래로	시작 시점	현재완료(have Ved)에 사용	have risen since 2011 2011년 이래로 증가하고 있다
as of	~부터	시작 시점	미래(will V) 사용 = starting, beginning	will start it as of next week 다음주부터 그것을 시작할 것이다
before	~전에	시점 (순서)	= prior to, ahead of, in advance of	before the test 시험 전에
after	~후에	시점 (순서)	= following, past, subsequent to	after the speech 연설 후에

The employees have to work **until** 9 P.M. tonight. 직원들은 오늘밤 9시까지 일해야 한다. ➡ 9시까지 "계속" 일한다.
The employees have to submit the report **by** 9 P.M. 직원들은 9시까지 보고서를 제출해야 한다. ➡ 9시까지 제출을 "완료"한다.

B. 기간 전치사
"얼마나 오래"(how long)에 해당하는 기간의 속성과 함께하는 전치사들을 구조의 특징과 함께 확인한다.

전치사	의미	명사 속성	특징	사용 예시
for	~동안	기간	주로 숫자 기간과 사용	for 2 months 2개월 동안
during	~동안	기간	주로 일반명사 기간과 사용, 동명사 사용 불가	during the vacation 방학 동안
over	~동안	기간	주로 현재완료 시제와 사용	over the last 2 years 지난 2년 동안
in	~동안, 이후	기간		in the past 4 weeks 지난 4주 동안
through(out)	~동안, 내내	기간	가장 구체적이고 연속적인 기간을 의미함	throughout the class 수업 내내
within	~이내에	기간	한정 기간 내에 동작이 한 번 발생	within 7 days 7일 이내에

The researchers have made efforts to develop a new medicine **for** 2 years.
연구원들은 2년동안 새로운 약을 개발하려는 노력을 기울이고 있다.

SPARTA Check-UP

정답 및 해설 p. 405

If you want to speak to a particular employee in our facility, please press the button 4, followed by that person's extension ------- the beep sound.

(A) during (B) after
(C) until (D) throughout

SPARTA Grammar Point 2

장소/위치/방향 전치사

A. 장소 전치사

전치사	의미	사용 예시
at (좁은 장소)	~에	at the corner 구석에서
on (길, 표면)	~에, 위에	on 1st Street 1번가에서 on the bridge 다리 위에서
in (넓은 공간)	~안에	in Korea 한국에서 in the company 회사에서
throughout	곳곳에	throughout the country 전국 곳곳에
within	이내에	within walking distance 걸어갈 수 있는 거리 내에

B. 위치 전치사

전치사	의미	사용 예시
above / over	(허공) 위에	above the clouds 구름 위에 all over the world 전세계에
below / under	(공간) 아래에	below the line 선 아래로 under construction 공사 중
beneath / underneath	(밀착) 아래에	beneath a pile of documents 문서 더미 아래
beside / next to	(지점) 옆에	next to the column 기둥 옆에
by / alongside	(지점) 옆에	alongside my car 내 차 옆에 나란히 (by는 수단으로도 사용)
opposite	(지점) 반대편에	opposite the bank 그 은행 반대편에
between	(2지점) 사이	between the U.S and Korea 미국과 한국 사이에
among	(3이상) 사이	among the leaders 리더들 사이에
behind	(지점) 뒤에	just behind X-1 model X-1 모델 바로 뒤에
beyond	(지점) 넘어서	beyond the campus 캠퍼스 너머로 beyond expectation 뜻밖에
past	(지점) 지나서	slightly past the library 도서관을 살짝 지나쳐서

C. 방향 전치사

전치사	의미	사용 예시
to	~로(끝 지점)	to the address 그 주소로 (주로 이동, 보냄 동사와 사용)
from	~에서(시작점)	from Manchester 맨체스터로부터 (주로 획득, 제거 동사와 사용)
into	안으로	into the office 사무실 안으로
out of	밖으로	out of the office 부재중 out of order 고장 난 (주로 정지 상태를 표현)
across	가로질러	across the industry 산업 전반에 걸쳐 (분야 전반을 의미)
toward	~쯤, 쪽으로	toward Busan 부산 쪽으로

SPARTA Check-UP

정답 및 해설 p. 405

Additional materials and supplies for the office are kept in room 912, ------- the data storage room on the 9th floor.

(A) among
(B) on
(C) next to
(D) beneath

SPARTA Grammar Point 3

의미형 전치사

A. 원인/결과/목적/양보

의미	전치사	사용 예시
원인	because of, due to, owing to on account of, thanks to	due to the increasing costs of raw materials 원자재 가격의 상승 때문에
결과	as a result of	as a result of the customer survey 그 고객 설문조사의 결과로
목적	for ("용도"로도 쓰임)	for the event of the 20th anniversary 20주년 행사를 위해
양보	despite, in spite of, notwithstanding	despite some errors in the article 그 기사의 몇 가지 오류에도 불구하고

B. 추가/제외/연관/가정

의미	전치사	사용 예시
추가	in addition to, as well as aside from, apart from, besides	in addition to expanding its branch 지점을 확장하는 것에 더하여
제외	except (for), but, aside from, apart from, other than	except the authorized staff members 인가된 직원을 제외하고
연관	about, as for, as to, regarding, concerning, pertaining to, on	problems regarding the service attitude 서비스 태도에 대한 문제점들
가정	without, barring, but for	without any notice 아무런 공지가 없었다면

C. 자격/구성/비교/수단

의미	전치사	사용 예시
자격	as	work as a manager 매니저로 일하다
구성	of	the head of the accounting department 회계부서의 부장
비교	like ↔ unlike	like the old model 이전 모델과 같이
수단	through(통신/절차), with(도구), by(교통/통신/지불 수단)	through the Internet 인터넷을 통해 by bus 버스를 이용하여

D. -ing형 전치사

regarding ~에 관하여	concerning ~에 관하여	barring ~이 없다면
including ~을 포함하여	excluding ~을 제외하고	following ~ 이후
starting ~부터(미래)	beginning ~부터(미래)	considering ~을 고려하면

SPARTA Check-UP 3

정답 및 해설 p. 405

No one ------ graduate students understands Dr. Jacob's presentation on effective writing in a second language.

(A) except
(B) following
(C) through
(D) as a result of

SPARTA — Grammar Point 4

연결어 구분하기

접속사 vs 전치사 vs 접속부사

```
    전치사    명사           , 주어 + 동사 ~
    접속사    주어 + 동사 ~   , 주어 + 동사 ~
    주어 + 동사 ~.  접속부사   , 주어 + 동사 ~
```

➡ 구성 요소를 연결하는 것은 전치사와 접속사이다. (하나의 문장 안에서 명사 또는 문장을 추가로 연결해 줄 때 사용)
➡ 접속부사는 앞 문장과의 의미적인 연결만 하는 "부사"의 한 종류이다. (앞 문장이 있어야 사용할 수 있다.)
➡ 접속사나 문장 부호인 세미콜론(;)이 나오면 접속부사가 하나의 문장 안에 올 수 있다.

연결어 구분하기

의미	부사절 접속사	전치사	접속부사
시간	while ~하는 동안 before / after ~하기 전에 / 후에 until ~할 때까지 as soon as ~하자 마자 since ~한 이래로	during ~동안 before = prior to after = following, subsequent to until ~까지 on(upon) +(동)명사 ~하자마자 since ~ 이래로	in addition, besides 게다가 moreover 게다가 furthermore 게다가 also 또한 meanwhile 그 동안에 afterwards 이후에 beforehand 그 전에
조건	if, providing (that), provided (that), assuming (that), considering (that) ~라면 in case (that) ~의 경우에 대비하여 unless ~가 아니라면	given, considering ~을 고려하면 in case of ~의 경우에 without ~가 아니라면	since then 그 때 이후로 otherwise 그렇지 않으면, 달리 if so 그렇다면 however 그러나
양보 (반전)	although, though, even if, even though 비록 ~일지라도	despite, in spite of, notwithstanding ~에도 불구하고	nevertheless 그럼에도 불구하고 on the contrary 그와 반대로 or else 그렇지 않으면
이유 결과	because, as, since, now that, in that ~ 때문에	because of, due to thanks to, owing to, on account of ~때문에	therefore 그러므로 consequently 그 결과 thereby 그 때문에
제외	except that ~를 제외하고는	except (for), aside from, apart from ~을 제외하고	instead 그 대신에 likewise 마찬가지로 in short 한 마디로, 요컨대
기타	as if, as though 마치~인 것처럼	according to ~에 따르면 unlike ~와 다르게 given, considering, assuming ~를 고려할 때	
	given that considering (that) ~를 고려할 때	regardless of ~와는 상관없이 instead of ~대신에 concerning/regarding/as to/as for/ pertaining to ~에 관해	

SPARTA Check-UP

정답 및 해설 p. 405

Those who would like to attend the annual conference cannot get admittance to the event hall ------- their photo identification cards.

(A) unless
(B) otherwise
(C) without
(D) although

SPARTA Practice Test

101. The item newly listed on the stock exchange is expected to rise by thirty percent ------- just two years.
(A) about
(B) within
(C) toward
(D) following

102. Lohbson Apparel will make an effort to reduce its redundant stocks by 20 percent ------- the end of the year.
(A) among
(B) under
(C) up
(D) by

103. Ian Schmitt has been nominated as the Employee of the Year ------- he has shown outstanding job performance.
(A) because
(B) due to
(C) because of
(D) owing to

104. We are delighted to hear that Ms. Monica has finally been nominated ------- the Best Employee of the Year Award, the most honorable in our company.
(A) about
(B) for
(C) when
(D) since

105. Overall, Europe's stock market has struggled for four consecutive weeks, ------- of increasing individual trading.
(A) regardless
(B) regarded
(C) regarding
(D) regard

106. ------- the last ten years, the number of students at Lafayette's elementary school has increased by 3,000.
(A) As
(B) Again
(C) Over
(D) Below

107. A copy of the company's employee manual will be provided to new recruits ------- commencing the training program.
(A) upon
(B) about
(C) through
(D) despite

108. These Web pages respond to the questions as to how far to be ------- a starting point and your destination or how to drive and use the appropriate routes.
(A) along
(B) against
(C) between
(D) near

109. Although she was promoted to accounting manager last month, her previous duties ------- a deputy still remain the same.
(A) as
(B) as though
(C) although
(D) pertaining

110. The quarterly results showed the company's outstanding ability in the global advertising market ------- strong price competition.
(A) except
(B) despite
(C) behind
(D) in spite

111. An array of panels set up throughout the state of California will generate more electricity ------- the sunlight.
    (A) up
    (B) from
    (C) upon
    (D) between

112. Ms. Hannah will soon be appointed laboratory leader ------- her educational and academic backgrounds.
    (A) in front of
    (B) across from
    (C) as a result
    (D) because of

113. All the account numbers are generally established at 12:00 P.M. ------- the director of the IT Support Department.
    (A) as
    (B) in
    (C) to
    (D) by

114. ------- the popularity of last summer's festival, the organization expects that the number of visitors will sharply increase this year.
    (A) Provided
    (B) Given
    (C) Namely
    (D) Regardless

115. If you want to place additional orders, you should refer to the following list ------- suppliers partnered with our company.
    (A) of
    (B) despite
    (C) owing to
    (D) in front of

116. Plus Technology, producer of well-made hardware and personal computers, is expanding ------- the software industry.
    (A) at
    (B) around
    (C) into
    (D) of

117. As the new version of a tablet PC is ------- sale as of Monday, CREBIZ will face the toughest competition in the mobile device market.
    (A) on
    (B) there
    (C) going
    (D) over

118. ------- completion of all coursework, Ms. Yenjing has a chance to get a Ph.D. program admission from Hong Kong University.
    (A) When
    (B) Because
    (C) After
    (D) Already

119. C&T Broadband provides its subscribers with a variety of services ------- the high-speed Internet connection and unlimited download capacity.
    (A) inside
    (B) about
    (C) regarding
    (D) including

120. All of our products can be discounted at 20%-off prices if you purchase more than 100 items ------- bulk.
    (A) at
    (B) to
    (C) for
    (D) in

Questions 121-124 refer to the following advertisement.

Ever PET World
Welcome All Animal Lovers!

If you are looking for companion pets, then come visit us. We have hundreds of animals to choose ------- here at Ever PET World.
     121.
There are popular customer choices such as dogs, cats, rabbits, and hamsters. Our experts in the store can explain in detail the level of care your pet would normally -------.
                                   122.
They can also recommend to you which pets would best ------- your house or apartment.
           123.
They'll be happy to answer any questions you may have. -------.
                           124.
Come and see us as soon as possible!

SPARTA Grammar Review

(1) 전치사는 명사와 함께 "구"를 만들어 "부사"(수식어) 자리에 위치한다.

(2) 동사(동작)와의 의미 관계를 확인하라.

(3) 2단어 이상이 하나의 전치사를 만들면, 단어들의 조합과 의미를 확인하라.

(4) **since**는 시점, **for**는 기간을 의미한다.

(5) **by**는 동작이 한번, **until**은 동작이 유지된다.

(6) **between**은 "둘" 사이에, **among**은 "셋 이상" 사이에 쓴다.

(7) 부사는 단독 수식어, 전치사는 명사와 연결된 수식어구, 부사절 접속사는 절(주어+동사) 덩어리와 연결된 수식어이므로 품사 구별이 제1순위다.

---

121. (A) from
     (B) at
     (C) on
     (D) in

122. (A) need
     (B) needs
     (C) needing
     (D) will need

123. (A) suitable
     (B) suit
     (C) suitably
     (D) suitor

124. (A) You should also make an appointment in advance.
     (B) These prices will only last until December 30.
     (C) This apartment is far from our local stores.
     (D) All of our stores are open 6 days a week from 10 A.M. to 10 P.M.

DAY 4 부사절 접속사

SPARTA 유형 파악

접속사는 앞 문장 및 내용과 대등한 것을 나열하는 등위 접속사와, 문장 전체에서 명사 역할(명사절), 형용사 역할(관계사절), 부사 역할(부사절)을 하는 종속 접속사로 나눌 수 있다. 이 중에서, 문장에서 수식어 역할을 하는 부사절 접속사는 문맥상 어울리는 접속사를 찾고, 유사 의미의 전치사와 접속사를 구분하는 문제가 등장한다. 접속사의 경우, 단순히 의미뿐만 아니라, 각 접속사가 지닌 구조적 특징을 학습하여, 정확하고 신속하게 문제 푸는 방법을 터득해야 한다.

SPARTA 출제 포인트

☑ 부사절 접속사의 위치

부사와 마찬가지로 수식어 역할을 하기 때문에, 완전한 문장 구조를 제외한 나머지 어느 자리나 위치한다.

> ___접속사 + S V O___, S 타V O ___접속사 + S V O___.

➡ <접속사+주어+동사 ~> 구조는 문장 전체를 수식하는 부사 자리에 온다.
➡ 수식어인 부사, 전치사(부사구) 같이 "시간, 조건, 원인, 양보(반전), 목적" 의미의 접속사가 등장한다.

Investors experienced a great loss of money **because** a broker made a big mistake.
중개인이 큰 실수를 저질렀기 때문에, 투자자들은 큰 손해를 봤다.

☑ 부사절 접속사 문제 풀이 순서

각 접속사가 가지고 있는 구조적 특징을 가장 먼저 살펴보고, 해석이 필요한 경우 "동작" 중심의 연결 관계를 해석으로 해결하는 연습을 한다.

➡ 두 동사 간의 시제 연결 또는 문장에서의 위치 확인!
➡ <무엇을 했는가?>에 대한 동작 중심의 연결 관계를 통해 의미 확인!
➡ 대부분의 부사절 접속사는 종속절의 동작이 먼저 일어난다.(등위 접속사, until, so that, in that 예외)

I did not receive any discount coupon **when** I registered for the membership of this gym.
제가 이 체육관에 회원 등록을 했을 때, 저는 그 어떤 할인 쿠폰도 받지 못했습니다.

➡ 두 동사의 시제가 일치한다. 이 경우, "등록"이 먼저 그리고 "받지 못한" 것이 다음에 일어난 순서로 문맥이 형성된다.

SPARTA 문제 풀이 비법

Our members kept walking along the road ------ they were too exhausted physically.

(A) even if
(B) so that
(C) only if
(D) even as

비록 우리 회원들은 육체적으로 매우 지쳤지만, 길을 따라 계속 걸었다.

✅ 너무 지쳤지만 계속 걸어갔다는 문맥으로, 양보(반전)을 나타내는 (A) even if가 가장 적절하다.
(A) 비록~일지라도[양보], (B) ~하기 위해[목적], (C) 오직~인 경우(조건), (D) 마침~할 때[시간]의 접속사 중에서, 두 동작의 반전을 연결하는 (A)가 정답이다.

SPARTA   Grammar Point 1

등위/상관 접속사

A. 등위 접속사
앞에 나온 것과 대등한 내용 또는 품사들이 연결된다.

but	or	yet	and	nor	rather than
그러나	또는	그러나	그리고	~도 아닌	~보다
[역접]	[선택]	[역접]	[인과]	[부정 선택]	[비교]

➡ 등위 접속사는 중복된 부분을 생략하기 때문에 앞뒤에 동일한 품사가 올 수 있다. (비교의 rather than은 불완전한 구조와 연결)
➡ 앞에 나온 것과 대등한 품사 또는 내용이 와야 하기 때문에 주로 주절보다 뒤에 등장한다.
➡ 동사가 연결될 때, 동사의 시제가 일치하거나 시간 순으로 나열된다.

Please be sure that the ticket is non-refundable **and** non-transferable to any others.
그 티켓은 환불도 안 되고 타인에게 양도될 수도 없다는 것을 명심하세요.

B. 상관 접속사
상관 접속사는 등위 접속사(and, or, but)와 부사(both, either, neither, not, not only)가 한 쌍을 이루어 서로 하나의 의미를 만들어낸다.

both	A and B	: A와 B 모두
either	A or B	: A 또는 B
neither	A nor B	: A도 B도 아닌
not only	A but (also) B	: A뿐만 아니라 B도
not	A but B	: A가 아니라 B

[부사]   +   [등위 접속사] → A와 B에는 어떤 단어/구/절이라도 올 수 있다.

➡ A와 B 자리에 명사가 나와서 문장 맨 앞에 오면, 뒤따르는 동사와 수 일치를 시켜야 한다.
    이때, both A and B(복수 취급)를 제외하고 나머지는 동사에 가까운 B에 수 일치를 시킨다.

Either our nurses **or** the doctor is coming to the site soon.
우리 간호사들 또는 의사 선생님이 그 현장에 곧 도착할 것이다.

SPARTA   Check-UP

정답 및 해설 p. 408

Because of heavy work on the holiday season, both the sales manager ------ her team have felt exhausted.

(A) nor   (B) or
(C) and   (D) but

SPARTA Grammar Point 2

시간/조건 부사절 접속사 1

A. 시간 부사절 접속사

접속사	의미	사용 예시	
after	~후에	After he was given the award, 그가 상을 받은 후	전치사와 접속사 둘 다 가능 * since는 부사도 가능
before	~전에	Before we load the products, 제품들을 선적하기 전에	
until	~까지	Until it causes a crisis, 위기를 초래할 때까지	
since	~이래로	Since it was unstable, 그것이 불안정해진 이래로	
when = at the time	~할 때	When they handled chemicals, 그들이 화학물질을 처리했을 때	
by the time	~할 때쯤	By the time you learn it, 당신이 그것을 배울 때쯤	시간차 표현
as soon as	~하자 마자	As soon as the order is placed, 주문되자 마자	= once
while	~하는 동안	While you are on duty, 당신이 근무하는 동안	동시 동작

➡ since가 시간(~이래로) 의미로 쓰일 때 주절에 현재완료(have Ved)가 온다.
➡ by the time(~할 때쯤)은 시간차의 접속사이므로, 주절에 주로 완료시제가 온다.
➡ while(~동안)은 동시 동작을 나타내므로 시제가 일치되어야 하고, 시간차의 완료시제는 불가능하다.
➡ as soon as/once(~하자 마자)는 다음 순서를 나타내므로 진행시제(be+Ving)와 쓰이지 않는다.

B. 조건 부사절 접속사

접속사	의미	사용 예시
if	~라면	If you renew the contract, 계약을 갱신하신다면
unless	~하지 않는다면	Unless you are otherwise directed, 다르게 지시 받지 않았다면
provided/providing (that)	~라면	Provided that the price is reasonable, 가격이 합리적이었다면
considering (that)	~을 고려하면	Considering that traffic is congested, 교통혼잡을 고려하면
given that	~을 고려하면	Given that the test is postponed, 그 시험이 연기된 것을 고려하면
in case (that)	~을 대비하여	In case the storm is coming, 태풍이 올 것을 대비하여
as long as	~하는 한	As long as you pay regularly, 정기적으로 납부하시는 한
once	일단 ~하면	Once you submit the application, 일단 지원서를 제출하고 나면
only if	오직 ~라면	Only if you attach the original receipt, 영수증 원본을 첨부한 경우에만
on condition that	~라는 조건으로	On condition that you register for it, 그것을 등록한다는 조건으로

➡ 주의! that과 반드시 조합되어야 접속사인 것들과, that 없이도 접속사로 쓰이는 것에 주의한다.

SPARTA Check-UP

정답 및 해설 p. 408

The city council has launched a public bid about constructing the new multiplex building ------- it announced a new development plan for 2019.

(A) when (B) only if
(C) since (D) while

SPARTA Grammar Point 3

양보/원인/목적 부사절 접속사

A. 양보(반전) 부사절 접속사

"비록 ~일지라도", 또는 "~에도 불구하고"라는 뜻으로, "반전"의 의미를 나타낸다.

비록 ~일지라도	although, even though, even if, though, while, whereas
~인지 아닌지	whether ~ or not
얼마든지 간에	however + 형용사/부사

➡ whether는 명사절의 경우 or not이 생략 가능하나, 부사절의 경우 or와 반드시 함께 쓰인다.
➡ however가 접속사로 쓰이려면 <주어+동사>보다 앞쪽에 형용사나 부사가 반드시 함께 등장한다.

Whether you like doing it **or not**, you have to pass the test with a grade above B+.
하고 싶든 하기 싫든 간에, 반드시 B+ 학점 이상으로 시험을 통과하셔야 합니다.

B. 원인(이유) 부사절 접속사

"~때문에", "~이니까"라는 뜻으로, 문맥상 "원인"의 의미를 나타낸다.

~때문에	because, as, since, now that, in that

➡ now that은 주로 주절 앞에, in that은 주절 뒤에 온다.

Because it is much more expensive than other similar items, our sales of the new product have not been so good.
그것은 다른 유사 제품들보다 훨씬 비싸기 때문에, 그 신제품에 대한 우리 판매량은 별로 좋지 않다.

C. 목적 부사절 접속사

"~하기 위해"라는 뜻으로, 앞으로 이루어 낼 "목적"에 대한 의미를 나타낸다.

~하기 위해	in order that, so that
너무 ~해서 ...하다	so + 형용사/부사 + that, such + 명사구 + that

➡ so that은 주로 주절 뒤에 온다.
➡ in order to + V(동사원형), so as to + V(동사원형)의 형태에 주의하자.

In order that we meet the deadline from now on, we have to hurry up.
이제부터 마감시한을 맞추기 위해, 우리는 서둘러야 한다.

SPARTA Check-UP 3

정답 및 해설 p. 408

Ms. Emily has an advantage over other candidates ------ she can speak both English and French fluently.

(A) so that
(B) in that
(C) although
(D) except that

SPARTA — Grammar Point 4

시간/조건 부사절 접속사 2

시간/조건 부사절 접속사는 시제 일치 예외가 존재하는 접속사일 뿐만 아니라, 분사구문을 연결할 수 있는 기능을 가지고 있다.

시간/조건 접속사

시간 : when, after, before, as soon as, by the time, once
조건 : if, once, unless, in case, in the event, as long as

A. 시제 일치 예외

시간/조건 부사절 접속사	S Ved (과거),	S Ved (과거)	[시제 일치]
시간/조건 부사절 접속사	S Ves (현재),	S Ves (현재)	[시제 일치]
시간/조건 부사절 접속사	S Ves (현재),	S will V (미래)	[시제 불일치]

➡ 시간/조건 부사절 접속사들은 "미래 시점"이 내포되어 있다.
➡ 미래형 조동사 will과 함께 쓰일 수 없다.

Unless you [pay] the money to use by this week, extra fees [will be] charged.
이번 주까지 결제하지 않으신다면, 추가 비용이 부과될 것입니다.

B. 분사구문과 시간-조건 부사절 접속사

문맥의 연결 관계를 보다 명확하게 하기 위해, 분사구문을 만드는 절차에 있어서 첫 단계인 접속사 생략은, 시간/조건 부사절 접속사의 경우 그대로 남겨 둘 수 있다. 즉, 중복되는 <주어+동사(be)>가 생략되면서 시간/조건 부사절 접속사에 보어 역할을 하던 요소들이 남게 된다.

| 시간/조건 부사절 접속사 + | (1) 분사 (타Ving + O / 타Ved (수식어))
(2) 형용사, S V ~
(3) 전치사구 |

➡ until/unless/as/than은 수동형 분사(타Ved)를 선호한다.
➡ if/whenever는 형용사를 선호한다.
➡ when/while은 능동형 분사(타Ving) 또는 전치사구를 선호한다.

When [preparing for the job interview], you make sure to review your application package again.
면접을 준비할 때, 당신의 지원 패키지를 재검토해야 함을 명심하세요.

SPARTA Check-UP

정답 및 해설 p. 408

------- installing the latest version of the security software on the company's main server, our Web sites temporarily shut down from 10 A.M. to 11 A.M.

(A) Because (B) During
(C) While   (D) Meanwhile

SPARTA Practice Test

101. We cannot refund the full amount ------- your item with the original receipt is delivered to the seller.
    (A) until
    (B) whether
    (C) in case of
    (D) given

102. ------- the sales of the BTA-300 model are lower than the previous season, the total revenue is well above the average.
    (A) Despite
    (B) Furthermore
    (C) Even though
    (D) Compared to

103. Establishing a new task force helps the government to not only enhance its strategies ------- escape its current economic recession.
    (A) but also
    (B) also when
    (C) just as
    (D) but for

104. ------- carefully reviewing various requirements, the committee has decided to approve Mr. Graham's admission.
    (A) If
    (B) Beside
    (C) After
    (D) Nevertheless

105. Employees who want to get reimbursement for their travel expenses can pick up a check in person ------- choose automatic transfer.
    (A) so
    (B) or
    (C) but
    (D) if

106. Mr. Luis will have been waiting for you in the airport parking area, in Section Yellow B-2, ------- you arrive at the Sydney Airport.
    (A) by the time
    (B) as soon as
    (C) except when
    (D) in the same way

107. ------- the newly developed software, Hack-Security 45, is more expensive than previous models, it is nevertheless much better in safety and quality.
    (A) Yet
    (B) Unless
    (C) Whereas
    (D) Whenever

108. ------- new recruits are hired, please let them go to Room 302 for their on-the-job training.
    (A) Other than
    (B) As soon as
    (C) In addition to
    (D) So that

109. All the investors should carefully check the company's financial statements ------- deciding to purchase stocks.
    (A) now that
    (B) since
    (C) before
    (D) forward

110. The board of directors has insisted upon the investment in new business ------- unstable the current market situation might be.
    (A) while
    (B) whereas
    (C) however
    (D) whenever

111. Culpepper's new web-order system will be available as of tomorrow morning ------- they finish the arrangement of source codes.
    (A) how
    (B) once
    (C) so too
    (D) not only

112. ------- our job openings are limited, we are ready to hire more staff if they have outstanding qualifications.
    (A) Both
    (B) So that
    (C) Whether
    (D) Even though

113. ------- applying for a driver's license, you should submit at least two forms of identification such as a passport, ID card, social security card, and so on.
    (A) When
    (B) Because
    (C) In order that
    (D) Although

114. Please log on to the Web site and provide your information ------- we can process your order quickly.
    (A) so that
    (B) in order to
    (C) because of
    (D) as well as

115. I have had a chance to meet various people around the world ------- I was employed at Belkin Airlines.
    (A) instead
    (B) while
    (C) however
    (D) since

116. The information should be released only in certain situations ------- everything contained in this report is confidential under both federal and state laws.
    (A) as for
    (B) meanwhile
    (C) for example
    (D) because

117. ------- the company in Vietnam has an advantage in labor costs, the automobile industry in Europe has strengths in technology and quality.
    (A) Although
    (B) That
    (C) Until
    (D) Whether

118. ------- the server inspection is conducted regularly, our online service will be more reliable and of higher quality to our customers.
    (A) Along with
    (B) As long as
    (C) So that
    (D) Except for

119. ------- you return the item within 10 days of the date of purchase, we are willing to refund it in full.
    (A) Unless
    (B) As long as
    (C) As if
    (D) Even if

120. Almost 2,000 more houses will be provided to Shippensburgh County ------- the construction of the new town is completed.
    (A) when
    (B) which
    (C) according to
    (D) rather than

Questions 121-124 refer to the following letter.

August 10
Q-Main Electronics
130 Jayhawk Boulevard
Lawrence, KS 66045

Dear Customer Service:

After much consideration, I bought your Power Fly Microwave RS-2 last week ------- your online store. According to the manual, the product should have automatically turned off if it ------- a designated temperature. However, the microwave I purchased stayed on, ------- I had to switch it off manually. Something is obviously wrong with the temperature controller in the device, and I would like to return it for a full refund. -------. Especially this was the first time for me to order your product, and I wanted to use it. Please tell me how I can return the microwave. I look forward to hearing from you.

Regards,

Robert Joshua

121. (A) although
 (B) through
 (C) even as
 (D) only if

122. (A) reach
 (B) reaching
 (C) reached
 (D) to reach

123. (A) wherever
 (B) as though
 (C) until
 (D) either

124. (A) Compared to other brands, your item is twice as expensive in price.
 (B) Anyway, it was too dangerous for me to use it continuously.
 (C) I would like to be informed of any information about your new products.
 (D) In addition, the safety procedures should be followed in the workstation.

SPARTA Grammar Review

(1) 등위 접속사는 중복 부분이 생략되어 동일한 품사가 올 수 있다.

(2) 부사절(접속사+주어+동사)은 문장에서 수식어인 부사 역할을 한다.

(3) 시간/조건 부사절 접속사는 현재시제와 주절의 미래시제를 일치시킬 수 있다.

(4) 시간/조건 부사절 접속사는 뒤에 분사(Ving/Ved), 형용사, 전치사구가 올 수 있다.

(5) 등위 접속사, so that(목적), in that(원인) 접속사는 주절 뒤에 온다.

(6) since는 주절의 시제가 현재완료(have Ved)일 때 접속사절의 시제가 과거(Ved)가 된다.

DAY 5 동사의 5형식

SPARTA 유형 파악

동사는 문장의 구조를 결정하는 핵심적인 역할을 한다. 동사 문제의 경우, 빈칸이 동사 자리인지를 묻는 문제, 자동사와 타동사를 구분하는 문제, 그리고 보기 4개를 모두 동사로 구성해서 문장의 의미를 해석하는 문제 등이 등장한다. 여기서 주의할 점은, 동사 어휘 문제의 대다수가 해석보다 문장의 구조(형식)를 통해 풀리는 경우가 많으므로, 각 동사의 의미에 따른 문장 구조를 반드시 함께 학습해야 한다.

SPARTA 출제 포인트

☑ 동사의 자리 확인

동사 자리에 올 수 있는 것을 묻는 문제의 경우, 아래의 수식어를 제거한 후 동사 자리에 올 수 없는 to부정사(to V)나, 동명사(V-ing)를 보기에서 제거한다.

수식어 제거: 전치사 / 접속사 / to부정사 / 부사

➡ 빈칸 근처의 (1) 전치사구(전+명), (2) 종속절(접속사+S V ~) (3) to부정사, (4) 부사(-ly)를 문장에서 우선 제거한다.

You should not ------ the storage room (without a permit). ➡ 수식어인 전치사구 제거 / 동사 필요
(A) access   (B) to access ➡ to부정사나 동명사는 동사 자리 불가

☑ 동사 문제 풀이 순서

동사 관련 문제임을 확인했다면, 문법을 적용하여 오답 소거법으로 다음 절차에 따라 문제를 풀도록 한다.

본동사 ➡ 수 일치 ➡ 태 ➡ 시제

➡ (1) 본동사 자리인지 확인하기
   (2) 주어와 동사의 수 일치시키기
   (3) 목적어 유무를 따진 후 수동/능동태 판단하기
   (4) 시간 수식어를 확인한 후 시제 확정하기

SPARTA 문제 풀이 비법

Nixon Company ----- to you that your application had been approved.

(A) announce
(B) announced
(C) to announce
(D) announcing

Nixon 사는 귀하의 지원이 승인되었음을 알려드립니다.

✅ 주어 뒤의 본동사 자리이다. 보기 중에 본동사로 쓸 수 있는 것은 (A)와 (B)인데, 주어가 단수이므로 복수동사인 (A)는 오답, 과거시제인 (B)가 정답이다.
수식어인 to you를 제거하고 that이라는 명사절 접속사 앞에서 끊어 읽기를 하면 본동사가 필요하고, that절의 동사시제가 과거완료이므로 주절은 과거시제가 되어야 한다.

SPARTA Grammar Point 1

자동사

전체 동사의 10% 정도를 차지하는 자동사는 목적어를 취하지 않으므로, (1) 수동태가 될 수 없고, (2) 능동형 분사 형태인 V-ing로만 분사 표현이 가능하다.

A. 1형식 자동사

1형식 자동사는 완전 자동사로, 생략 가능한 수식어인 전치사, 부사절 접속사, to부정사, 부사 등이 뒤에 올 수 있다. 특히, 자동사와 짝을 이루는 전치사와 묶어서 암기하도록 한다.

"증가/감소" 류	increase 증가하다 grow 성장하다 climb 오르다 dwindle 줄어들다	rise 증가하다 culminate 정점에 이르다 decrease 감소하다 decline 감소하다	soar 급등하다 peak 정점에 이르다 fall 떨어지다
"이동/발생" 류	arrive at ~에 도착하다 come to ~로 오다 happen to 발생하다	proceed to/with ~로 가다/진행하다 transfer to ~로 옮기다 occur to 발생하다	go to ~로 가다 move to ~로 이동하다 wait for ~를 기다리다
"말하다" 류	speak to/with ~에게/와 말하다 respond to ~에 대응/응답하다 agree with/on/upon ~에 동의하다	talk to/about ~에게/~관해 말하다 reply to/with ~에 대답하다 account for ~을 설명하다	
그 외	deal with 다루다 act on/upon 시행하다 register for 등록하다 look through 검토하다	comply with 준수하다 apply for/to 신청하다/적용하다 sign up for 등록하다 look into 조사하다	conform to 일치하다 enroll in 등록하다 attend to 돌보다 look after 돌보다

The committee members made a decision to **act on** the new policy about the in-company dress code.
위원회 멤버들은 사내 복장 규정에 관한 새로운 정책을 시행하기로 결정하였다.

B. 2형식 자동사

2형식 자동사는 주어의 상태를 설명하는 보어를 취하는 불완전 자동사 중 하나이다. 2형식 동사는 "상태"와 "상태 변화"를 알려준다.

"상태/변화"	be ~이다 seem ~처럼 보이다 prove ~한(상태로) 판명되다	become ~이 되다 remain 여전히 ~한(상태)이다 turn out ~한(상태로) 판명되다	stay ~(상태로) 머무르다

2형식의 경우, 주어의 상태 시점에 따라서 보어가 달라진다.
- 주어의 **현재** 상태 : 형용사, 분사, 명사 (명사의 경우 주어와 동격)
- 주어의 **미래** 상태 : to부정사 (to부정사는 "~할 것"을 나타내는 미래 시점)
- 주어의 **진행** 상태 : 전치사구 (on이나 under는 "~하는 중", out of는 "진행 중단" 상태)

To increase the number of classrooms, the building **is** currently **under construction**.
강의실 수를 늘리기 위해 그 건물은 현재 공사 중이다.

SPARTA Check-UP

정답 및 해설 p. 411

The newly developed vacuum cleaner X-10 has gradually ------- popular in the Eastern European market.
(A) complied (B) applied
(C) become (D) determined

SPARTA · Grammar Point 2

타동사 - 3/4형식

전체 동사의 90% 이상을 차지하는 타동사는 뒤에 목적어가 온다. 목적어 자리에는 명사, 대명사, to부정사, 동명사, 명사절 등이 올 수 있다. 동작의 의미적 특징에 따라 3형식, 4형식, 5형식 구조로 세분화시켜서 학습해야 한다.

A. 3형식 타동사

3형식 동사는 동작을 직접 하는 주어와 동작을 당하는 목적어가 앞뒤로 온다.

자동사로 착각하기 쉬운 타동사

access 접근하다	greet 환영하다	discuss 토론하다
approach 접근하다	marry 결혼하다	approve 승인하다
accompany 동반하다	mention 언급하다	await 기다리다
address 처리하다	reach 도달하다	enter 들어가다
attend 참석하다	resemble 닮다	exceed 초과하다
disclose 폭로하다	contact 연락하다	explain 설명하다
describe 묘사하다	compose 구성하다	

The manager should **address** the issues of increasing customer complaints.
매니저는 증가하는 고객 불만 건에 대한 이슈를 처리해야 한다.

B. 4형식 타동사

"주다"라는 의미의 4형식 동사는 간접목적어인 사람 목적어(~에게), 직접 목적어인 사물 목적어(~을) 2개의 목적어를 취한다.

TOEIC 빈출 4형식 동사

give 주다	grant 수여하다	award (상을) 주다
forward 전달해주다	assign 할당하다	offer 제공하다

이 외에도, "말해주다" 라는 의미로 tell 과 유사하게 사용되는 빈출 동사를 기억하도록 하자.

advise, inform, assure, notify, convince, remind	+	사람 목적어 (회사/기관 포함) ~에게	+	사물 목적어 (내용) ~을/를

I am e-mailing to **notify** you of a problem with the items we delivered.
저희가 배송한 상품에 문제가 있음을 알려드리고자 이메일을 보냅니다.

SPARTA Check-UP 2

The company ------- all the employees that they should check their completion of this quarter's training session.

(A) announced (B) informed
(C) explained (D) accounted

SPARTA — Grammar Point 3

타동사 - 5형식

5형식은 목적어와 목적보어를 취하고, 동사의 의미에 따라 목적보어로 to부정사, 형용사, 분사, 명사, 그리고 동사원형이 올 수 있다.

A. "시키다" 류 동사

직접적으로 시키는 동작은 아니지만, **권유/허가/요청/명령/희망/예상** 등의 동작을 바탕으로 주로 **사람 목적어**에게 **앞으로 할 일**을 지시하는 의미를 지니고, 사람 목적어 뒤에 to부정사를 보어로 취한다.

권유, 요청, 허용	encourage 독려하다	ask 요구하다	require 요구하다	enable 가능토록 하다
	allow 허락하다	permit 허락하다	request 요구하다	invite 권유하다
강요, 명령	get ~하게 하다	forbid 금지하다	force 강요하다	command 지시하다
희망, 기대	want 희망하다	expect 예상하다	would like 희망하다	

Most of the analysts **expect** the domestic economy **to** increasingly **deteriorate**.
대부분의 분석가들은 내수 경기가 점점 악화될 것으로 예상한다.

B. 사역 동사

앞서 살펴본 '시키다' 류 동사와 다르게 직접적으로 시키는 의미를 지니고, 사람 목적어 뒤에 동사원형을 보어로 취한다.

사역 동사	make	have	let	help	: ~에게 ~하도록 시키다

➡ help의 경우, 목적보어 자리에 to부정사가 올 수도 있다.

The teacher always **makes** students repeatedly **read** the sentences and vocabulary words.
그 교사는 늘 학생들에게 문장과 어휘를 반복적으로 읽도록 시켰다.

C. 상태/판단 동사

목적어의 **상태**나, **판단** 결과를 나타내기 위해 목적 보어 자리에 **형용사/분사/명사** 등이 등장한다.

상태 동사	make	leave	keep	: ~한 상태로 두다
판단 동사	consider	find		: ~라고 판단하다

The board of directors **found** the marketing strategy too **impractical**.
이사회는 그 마케팅 전략이 너무 실현 불가능하다는 것을 알았다.

D. 지각 동사

사람의 감각기관을 활용한 동작으로, **보고, 듣고, 느끼는** 것들을 의미한다. 목적보어 자리에 **동사원형과 분사**가 온다.

지각/감각 동사	feel 느끼다	see 보다	watch 보다	hear 듣다

We **saw** a lot of students bravely **marching** through the street.
우리는 용감하게 거리를 행진하는 많은 학생들을 보았다.

SPARTA Check-UP 3

정답 및 해설 p. 411

The state government decided to ------- the citizen to water their plants and lawns too frequently.

(A) forbid
(B) make
(C) consider
(D) fell

SPARTA Grammar Point 4

기타 필수 동사

시험에 자주 출제되는 동사로 자동사/타동사가 모두 가능한 것 중, 뜻이 같은 것과 달라지는 것을 비교하며 학습하도록 한다.

A. 자동사 & 타동사 모두 가능한 빈출 동사

의미가 같은 경우

search (for) 찾다	seek (for) 찾다	expand (into) 확장하다
increase 증가하다/증가시키다	decrease 감소하다/감소시키다	
prepare (for) 준비하다	reach (for) 도달하다	pay (for) 지불하다

의미가 다른 경우

자	attend to (대상을) 돌보다		자	allow for 감안/고려하다
타	attend 참석하다		타	allow 허락하다
자	account for 설명하다		자	return to (장소로) 돌아오다
타	account 간주하다		타	return 돌려주다, 반납하다
자	ask for 물어보다		자	lead to (장소/결과에) 이르다
타	ask 요구하다		타	lead 안내하다, 이어지다
자	leave for 떠나다		자	decline in 쇠하다
타	leave 남기다		타	decline 거절하다
자	serve as ~로 일하다		자	get to ~에 도달하다
타	serve 제공하다		타	get 얻다
자	succeed in 성공하다		자	benefit from 이익을 얻다
타	succeed ~을 잇다		타	benefit 유익하다

B. 3형식 타동사 + 목적어 Collocation

타동사		목적어
handle, treat, manipulate [다루다] solve, resolve, settle [해결하다]	문제점	problem, issue, conflict ...
follow, observe, obey, keep [준수하다, 지키다]	법/규정	regulation, rule, policy ...
assume, take over, hand over delegate ... [업무/권한 주고받는 동작]	업무/권한	수식어(to 대상) 수식어(from 주체)
provide, distribute, attribute submit, deliver ... [전달 관련동작]	물건/문서	수식어(to 사람) 수식어(for 사람)
obtain, acquire, get [획득] remove, extract [제거] prevent, prohibit, hinder [금지]	물건/회사 등	수식어(from ~)

SPARTA Check-UP

정답 및 해설 p. 411

The manager ------ materials for the workshop to those who attended Ms. Dana's presentation.

(A) acquired (B) distributed
(C) prohibited (D) contacted

SPARTA Practice Test

101. All of our customers ------- positively to the new model of the MVX-100 mobile phone developed by Charms Co.
    (A) responding
    (B) responses
    (C) responsibly
    (D) responded

102. The numerous products on the shelves ------- it difficult for customers to choose the one they want.
    (A) order
    (B) make
    (C) allow
    (D) watch

103. Mr. Samuel, who is in charge of the planning department, wants to give up his managerial position in order to ------- on his research about the market trends.
    (A) insist
    (B) focus
    (C) agree
    (D) deal

104. When forwarding company documents to others by e-mail, please keep them ------- by setting up the passwords for protecting them.
    (A) securing
    (B) to secure
    (C) secure
    (D) security

105. Charles's Dealership always ------- customers with reliable information and used cars at a reasonable price.
    (A) gives
    (B) provides
    (C) speaks
    (D) informs

106. The authorities announced that the banks needed to ------- borrowers who have a lot of outstanding debts from taking out additional loans.
    (A) enhance
    (B) refrain
    (C) prevent
    (D) determine

107. The initial comments on the Power Clean X10 vacuum cleaners indicate that reviewers found it ------- to use the device in any place.
    (A) convenience
    (B) convenient
    (C) conveniently
    (D) conveniences

108. Please ------- Mr. Swale that my visit to the Seoul branch has been rescheduled for March 20 because of other urgent tasks.
    (A) announce
    (B) leave
    (C) notify
    (D) confirm

109. Unless otherwise directed by your manager, all members should ------- with the current policies and regulations about the company's dress code.
    (A) respond
    (B) adhere
    (C) comply
    (D) follow

110. Kane Ltd.'s new mobile phones ------- enormous data storage capacity and impressive designs.
    (A) to feature
    (B) featuring
    (C) feature
    (D) features

111. The poor weather conditions can ------- the construction workers from making any progress.
    (A) prevent
    (B) invite
    (C) suggest
    (D) exist

112. Despite objection from the majority, Mr. Miller, the head of the marketing department, strongly ------- with the project.
    (A) to agree
    (B) agreeing
    (C) agreed
    (D) agreement

113. This is a chance for our graduate students to travel to Europe and ------- in the world-famous academic conference.
    (A) take place
    (B) attend
    (C) participate
    (D) convince

114. Pennecom has ------- that the company has a new plan to offer better and wider quality services to customers.
    (A) announce
    (B) announces
    (C) announced
    (D) announcement

115. Haneda Co. has asked headhunters to ------- for qualified and promising candidates for a managerial position in the public relations department.
    (A) apply
    (B) finish
    (C) search
    (D) replace

116. Because of his health problems, Mr. Earnest has ------- behind considerably on his ongoing project.
    (A) fallen
    (B) risen
    (C) enabled
    (D) helped

117. The Columbus city council strongly ------- its citizens to attend the Homecoming Festival at Ohio University.
    (A) responds
    (B) excels
    (C) maintains
    (D) encourages

118. Even though they have made every effort to develop a new item, the team still finds this project too ------- to complete before the deadline.
    (A) difficulty
    (B) difficulties
    (C) difficultly
    (D) difficult

119. The CEO ------- that the labor union never accepted the policy, which gives a 10% pay cut and slashes up to 200 jobs.
    (A) announced
    (B) told
    (C) convinced
    (D) reminded

120. The supervisor ------- the warehouse staff that fragile items must be carefully packed with polystyrene.
    (A) mentioned
    (B) noticed
    (C) reminded
    (D) explained

Questions 121-124 refer to the following e-mail.

To: Customer Service <customerservice@hwdpublishing.com>
From: Ken Hyland <k.hyland@firenetscape.com>
Subject: New Edition of the Book
Date: May 20

Dear Customer Service,

I just finished browsing your Web site for about 30 minutes, searching ------- a copy of the 7th
121.
edition of the *Language Adventure* series. Disappointingly, though, I could only see the 6th edition. Could you tell me if the 7th edition is currently available? If it is not for sale yet, could you tell me when it will be -------?
122.
I want to use it for a college prerequisite course on the introduction of linguistics I am starting this fall. -------. Could you send me an update on the
123.
issue date as soon as possible? I will ------- for
124.
your response before going to your Web site again.
Thank you so much in advance for your help.

Best Regards,

Ken Hyland

121. (A) among
(B) of
(C) for
(D) to

122. (A) informed
(B) released
(C) paid
(D) contacted

123. (A) Your collections of books are very impressive.
(B) The listed books on your Web site are easy to find.
(C) The revised edition is a required text for my students.
(D) I want to know the amount and price of the books available.

124. (A) wait
(B) charge
(C) postpone
(D) decide

SPARTA Grammar Review

(1) "증가/감소", "오고/가는" 의미의 동사들은 1형식 자동사이다.

(2) 주어의 상태나 변화를 나타내는 be, become, stay, remain 등은 2형식 자동사이다.

(3) 4형식 동사는 사람 목적어와 사물 목적어가 동시에 등장하는 "주다"라는 의미의 동사이다.

(4) **consider**와 **find**는 5형식에서 "~를 ...한 상태로 판단하다"라는 의미로 쓰인다.

(5) 권유/희망/요청/예상 등의 의미를 지닌 동사는 to부정사를 목적어로 하는 "시키다" 류 동사이다.

(6) **make, have, let, help** 등의 사역동사는 동사원형을 목적보어로 취한다.

DAY 6 수 일치와 태

SPARTA 유형 파악

매달 1문제 이상 출제되는 수 일치 문제는 주어와 동사의 수를 일치시키는 것으로, 단순히 수를 똑같은 형태로 맞춰 주는 것이 아니라, 주어인 복수 명사에 '-s'가 붙는다면, 동사는 '-s'를 붙이지 않는 것이 수 일치이다.

수동태는 동사 문제의 가장 대표적인 유형으로 매달 1~2문제 이상 출제된다. '수동'이란 동작을 당하는 대상(목적어)이 주어 자리로 오면서 강조되고, 그에 따라 동사의 형태가 <be+Ved>로 변형되는 것이다.

SPARTA 출제 포인트

☑ 수 일치의 기본 법칙

기본적으로 주어에 '-s'가 붙으면(복수 주어) 동사에 '-s'를 붙이지 않고, 주어에 '-s'가 붙어 있지 않으면(단수 주어) 동사에 '-s'를 붙인다.

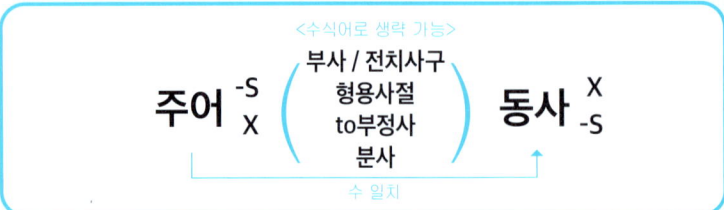

➡ 일반 동사의 경우 현재시제에서만 수 일치를 시킨다.
➡ 조동사(will, can, may, must, should) 뒤나, 주어가 없는 명령문은 동사원형이 온다.

	복수	단수
have	have	has
do	do	does
be(현재)	are	am/is
be(과거)	were	was

Most **consumers** always **consider** whether they purchase it or not.
대부분의 소비자들은 그들이 그것을 구매할지 말지 고민한다.

☑ 수동태의 기본 법칙

일반적으로 태를 확인하는 방법은 빈칸 뒤에 목적어(명사)가 있으면 능동태, 없으면 수동태임을 알 수 있다.

목적어 be 타Ved __(부사/전치사구/접속사절 등)__ ←수식어

➡ 강조하기 위해 목적어를 주어 자리로 이동시킨다.
➡ 동사를 <be 타Ved> 조합으로 변형시킨다.
➡ 행위자(주체)인 주어는 <by N> 형태로 문장 끝에 온다. (주로 생략)

Mr. Smith | ordered | some office supplies | last week. Smith 씨는 지난주에 사무용품을 주문했다.

↳ Some office supplies | were ordered | by Mr. Smith last week.

SPARTA 문제 풀이 비법

Items you already used will not -------- for a full refund.

(A) accept
(B) be accepted
(C) be accepting
(D) have accepted

당신이 이미 사용한 물품은 전액 환불을 받을 수 없습니다.

✅ 빈칸 뒤가 <전치사+명사>의 수식어구이므로 수동태인 (B)가 정답이다.
수동태가 되려면 동사구에 반드시 be와 Ved가 동시에 있어야 한다. <be+타Ving>인 진행, <have 타Ved>인 완료시제도, 이 조건을 충족시키지 못하므로 능동으로 목적어가 필요한 구조다.

SPARTA Grammar Point 1

주어와 동사의 수 일치

수식어를 제거한 후 주어의 형태를 확인하여 수 일치를 시킨다. 단순히 복수 어미 '-s'를 보고 일치시키는 것 이외에 응용 형태의 주어도 있으니 주의해야 한다.

A. 단수 주어와 단수 동사

주어에 '-s'가 붙지 않은 단수 주어에는 동사에 '-s'가 붙은 단수 동사가 따라온다.

> 단수 명사
> 고유 명사
> to부정사/동명사   + 단수 동사
> 명사절

Korean Airlines, founded in 1983, **is** one of the world-famous flight companies.
1983년에 설립된 Korean Airlines는 세계적으로 유명한 항공사 중 하나이다.

That employment rates are decreasing **has** been predicted before by professionals.
취업률이 떨어지고 있다는 것은 이전부터 전문가들에 의해서 예견되었다.

B. 복수 주어와 복수 동사

주어가 '-s'가 붙은 복수 명사인 경우 동사는 '-s'가 붙지 않은 복수 동사가 쓰인다. 주로 돈이나 규칙 관련 명사가 복수 명사 형태로 쓰인다.

> **funds** 자금, **earnings** 수입, **goods** 물품, **savings** 저금
> **belongings** 소지품, **resources** 자원, **standards** 기준
> **regulations** 규정, **customs** 세관, **procedures** 절차   + 복수 동사
> **requirements** 규정, **qualifications** 자격요건

➡ 주의) -s가 붙었어도, 과목이나 학문명은 단수 취급한다.
　　ex) news 소식, economics 경제학, politics 정치학, statistics 통계학 (단수 취급, 과목명 앞에 the 쓰지 ×)

The statistics released by the company **are** very reliable.
그 회사에 의해 발표된 통계수치들은 매우 신뢰할 만하다.

➡ statistics 앞에 the가 붙었다는 것은 "통계학"이라는 학문명으로 쓰인 것이 아님을 의미한다.
➡ 여기서는 "통계수치/통계자료"라는 의미로, 복수로 쓰였다.

SPARTA Check-UP

정답 및 해설 p. 414

The products our R&D team recently developed -------- very popular with customers in quality and price.

(A) have   (B) has
(C) are   (D) is

SPARTA Grammar Point 2

수량 표현과 수 일치

일반적인 수량 표현은 형용사로서 명사 앞에서 직접 수식하는 역할을 하고, 뒤에 나오는 명사의 속성과 형태를 결정하므로 직접적인 수 일치에 관여하지는 않는다. 하지만 뒤따르는 명사의 범위가 한정되면 대명사(부정대명사)로 쓰여 of와 함께 연결되는데, 이 경우의 수 일치에 대해 알아보도록 한다.

A. 수량과 수 일치의 원칙

수량 표현과 관련된 대명사들이 of와 연결되는 경우, of 뒤의 명사와 수 일치하는 것을 원칙으로 한다. 이들은 주로 부분과 관련된 수량 표현인 경우가 대부분이다.

➡ 수량 표현이 of와 함께 연결되면 뒤따르는 명사 앞에는 정관사(the)나 소유격이 와서 한정해야 한다.

All of the **parking lots** on campus were already filled with vehicles at 10 A.M.
교내의 모든 주차장이 오전 10시에 이미 차량들로 꽉 찼다.

B. 주어를 단수로 만드는 수량 표현

수량을 나타내는 대명사 중에서 of 뒤의 명사가 복수여도 주어 전체를 단수로 만드는 것들이 있다.

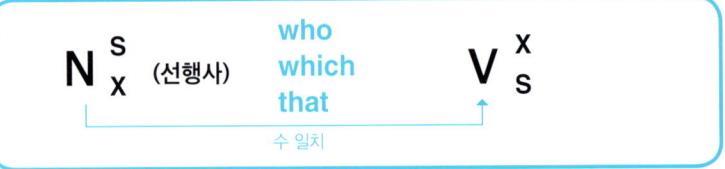

Each of the flight attendants needs to be educated thoroughly regarding the safety rules.
각각의 승무원들은 안전규정에 관하여 철저하게 교육 받을 필요가 있다.

C. 관계대명사(형용사절)의 선행사와 수 일치

주격 관계대명사(who/which/that) 뒤에는 주어가 없으므로, 수식을 받는 앞 명사(선행사)와 수 일치를 시킨다.

$$N \begin{smallmatrix}S\\X\end{smallmatrix} \text{ (선행사)} \quad \begin{matrix}\text{who}\\\text{which}\\\text{that}\end{matrix} \quad V \begin{smallmatrix}X\\S\end{smallmatrix}$$

Anyone who is planning to attend the seminar should submit the application form by this Friday.
누구든 세미나에 참석할 예정이라면 지원 양식을 이번 주 금요일까지 제출해야 합니다.

SPARTA Check-UP 2

정답 및 해설 p.414

------- of the changes in the terms and agreements have to be reported to all the customers in advance of its revision.

(A) One   (B) Each
(C) Either   (D) Most

SPARTA Grammar Point 3

수동태 응용 - 1

A. 4형식 수동태
4형식 동사는 목적어가 2개로 사람, 사물이 모두 있어야 능동태로 가능하다.

```
        S    4형식V(주다)    사람O    사물O        [능동]
  ➡ 사물O    be 4형식Ved    to 사람O   by S                  수동태
  ➡ 사람O    be 4형식Ved     사물O     by S
```

➡ 4형식의 수동태는 사물 목적어가 <be 타Ved> 뒤에 올 수 있다.
➡ 즉, 4형식의 경우 목적어가 하나라도 없으면 수동태가 된다.
➡ 빈출 4형식 동사를 기억하자. (give, forward, grant, award, advise, notify, inform, convince, assure, remind, tell 등)

As a plan to boost work productivity, devoted employees can **be given** a special incentive for their achievement.
노동 생산성 고양을 위한 계획으로서, 성실한 직원들은 그들의 성과에 대한 특별 보상을 받을 수 있다.

B. 5형식 타동사 : "시키다" 류 동사의 수동태
시키는 동작을 당하는 대상인 사람 목적어가 주어 자리로 오고, '앞으로 할 것'을 의미하는 to부정사 보어가 수동태 구조 뒤에 그대로 온다. 목적보어는 수동태에 관여하지 않으므로 그대로 둔다.

```
        S    5형식V(시키다 류)    사람O    to V      수동태에
  ➡ 사람O   be 5형식Ved(시키다 류)        to V       관여 안 함
```

➡ 권유/희망/예상/설득/명령 등의 의미를 지닌 "시키다" 류 동사를 기억하자.

| be allowed to V ~하도록 허락 받다 | be required to V ~하도록 요구 받다 | be asked to V ~하도록 요구 받다 |
| be encouraged to V ~하도록 격려 받다 | be expected to V ~할 예정이다 | be enabled to V ~가능하도록 되다 |

You **are invited** to attend the TESOL Conference in the Pittsburgh University.
피츠버그 대학에서의 TESOL 컨퍼런스에 귀하를 초대합니다.

SPARTA Check-UP 3

Successful candidates will ------- a job offer from the human resources department by phone call within seven business days.
(A) give   (B) be given
(C) to give   (D) giving

SPARTA Grammar Point 4

수동태 응용 - 2

5형식 동사 중에서, 허가/요청/권유 등의 "시키다" 류 동사 이외에 사람/사물 목적어의 상태 설명이나, 판단의 결과를 나타내는 동사 구조의 수동태를 이해한다. 그리고, 목적어가 없어서 수동태가 불가능한 자동사가 전치사와 함께 목적어를 취하는 경우에 대해 학습해 보자.

A. 5형식 타동사 : <상태/판단> 동사의 수동태

목적보어 자리에 형용사, 분사, 명사를 취하는 상태/판단 동사는 수동태 뒤에 해당 보어가 그대로 온다. 이때, 명사 보어는 목적어와 동격이므로, 수동태로 전환 시 주어와 동격 관계가 성립되는지를 확인한다.

$$S \quad 5형식V(상태/판단) \quad O \quad 형/분/명$$
$$\Rightarrow O \text{ be } 5형식Ved(상태/판단) \quad 형/분/명$$

(수동태에 관여 안 함)

➡ 수동태에서 명사 보어는 주어와 반드시 동격 관계가 성립되어야 한다.
　상태 동사: make, leave, keep, have, let (~를 ~한 상태로 두다)
　판단 동사: consider, find (~를 ~라고 판단하다)
　그 외 동사: elect(선출하다), appoint(임명하다)

Her advice **was considered** very |helpful| when he passed the exam.
그가 시험에 합격했을 때, 그녀의 충고가 매우 도움이 되었다고 여겨졌다.

B. 자동사의 수동태

기본적으로 수동태가 불가능한 자동사가 수동태로 쓰이는 경우가 있는데, 다음의 두 가지 조건을 충족해야 한다. (1) 자동사와 함께하는 전치사가 필요 (2) 전치사 뒤의 명사(전치사의 목적어)가 동작을 당하는 대상이어야 한다.

$$S \quad 1형식V \quad 전치사 \quad 명사$$
$$\Rightarrow 명사 \text{ be } 1형식Ved \quad 전치사$$

(전치사의 목적어가 주어로 이동)

The customer service center **dealt with** the issues that clients complained about.
➡ The issues that clients complained about **were dealt with** (by the customer service center).
고객 서비스 센터는 손님들이 불만을 제기한 이슈들을 처리했습니다.

➡ 모든 자동사가 위와 같은 수동태 구조를 만들 수 있는 것은 아니다.

deal with 다루다 / 처리하다	refer to 참고하다 / 참조하다
pay for 지불하다	dispose of 처분하다

➡ 위의 자동사는 수동태가 가능한 <자동사+전치사+목적어> 구조를 만들 수 있다.

SPARTA Check-UP 4

정답 및 해설 p.414

The movie *The Time Machine 2*, is considered very --------- because of its magnificent sounds and images.

(A) interest　　　　　　　　(B) interests
(C) to interest　　　　　　　(D) interesting

SPARTA Practice Test

101. When out-of-state students apply for a student loan, two forms of identification ------- presented to the financial aid staff.

(A) are
(B) is
(C) have
(D) do

102. Due to the problem with the company's online servers, the deadline to complete the project -------.

(A) to extend
(B) have extended
(C) to be extending
(D) has been extended

103. ------- of the graduate students attend the annual scholarship symposium hosted by the College of the Humanities on March 17.

(A) Each
(B) All
(C) Either
(D) The number

104. Procedures for applying for a driver's license ------- since a lot of citizens complained about their complexity.

(A) streamlining
(B) streamlines
(C) is streamlined
(D) have been streamlined

105. ------- interested in working overseas have to submit their applications by the end of the week.

(A) Employee
(B) Employees
(C) Employed
(D) Employing

106. Due to the company's restructuring, former members of the management ------- very few.

(A) remaining
(B) remain
(C) to remain
(D) are remained

107. Pollutants contaminating neighboring rivers and water sources should be effectively controlled and -------.

(A) removed
(B) are removing
(C) removes
(D) would be removing

108. ------- of our designers at Sharon Apparel is going to get a chance to participate in the 2024 Milano Fashion Week.

(A) One
(B) All
(C) Some
(D) Both

109. To celebrate its 20th anniversary, Power Digital Plaza is offering additional 20% discounts to anyone who ------- from October 1 to 20.

(A) visit
(B) visits
(C) to visit
(D) visiting

110. The authorities related to the Employment and Labor Administration are ------- regional infrastructure to make more jobs for local youths.

(A) renovate
(B) renovating
(C) renovated
(D) renovation

111. ------- posted on the company's Web site should be followed by and communicated to all the employees.
    (A) Regulator
    (B) Regulation
    (C) Regulations
    (D) Regulate

112. The filters of the air purifier must ------- at least once a month in order to keep the appliance working properly.
    (A) be cleaned
    (B) cleaning
    (C) have cleaned
    (D) clean

113. The public could be ------- that the government has a plan to expand existing medical activities more diversely and specifically.
    (A) assuredly
    (B) assurance
    (C) assured
    (D) assuring

114. To collect public opinions and reach an agreement ------- to be preceded by implementing the trade sanctions against the country.
    (A) need
    (B) needs
    (C) to need
    (D) needing

115. Dr. Smith's speech ------- very excellent among this year's forums we have hosted for the scholars.
    (A) considered
    (B) considers
    (C) is considered
    (D) will consider

116. Most American veterans ------- a large sum of money to the national charity foundation to develop talented soldiers.
    (A) has been donated
    (B) has donated
    (C) have been donated
    (D) have donated

117. Strict parking rules ------- in the downtown business district because of its traffic issues.
    (A) to enforce
    (B) are enforced
    (C) will enforce
    (D) are enforcing

118. The supervisors in the plant are ------- to treat workers with fairness in order to keep their workforce more productive.
    (A) required
    (B) requires
    (C) to require
    (D) requiring

119. David Mozes, the hard-line right conservative, was recently ------- governor of the state of Colorado.
    (A) elected
    (B) election
    (C) electing
    (D) elective

120. Junee's article about the current issue on the language education ------ to as the standard format to publish articles to the TESOL journal.
    (A) refers
    (B) is referred
    (C) has referred
    (D) referring

Questions 121-124 refer to the following notice.

**Chapel Hill Community Center
Rules and Regulations**

Chapel Hill Community Center Swimming Pool is open to citizens seven days a week from 6:00 A.M. to 9:00 P.M. Visitors are required to fully ------- with the following rules :
121.

- No diving from the high diving board between 1:30 P.M. and 3:30 P.M., Monday to Friday.
- No splashing or rough play in the pool at any time.
- No outdoor shoes should be worn in the pool area.
- A swimming cap should be worn.

The deep side of the pool is open to all swimmers from teenagers to adults. -------, parents or
122.
guardians should closely watch their children swimming there because there is no lifeguard on duty.

The rules ------- for the safety of all users.
123.

Those who break the above rules are forbidden to enter the pool. -------.
124.

121. (A) comply
(B) compliant
(C) complied
(D) compliance

122. (A) Similarly
(B) As an example
(C) Nevertheless
(D) Exceptionally

123. (A) enforce
(B) was enforcing
(C) are enforced
(D) to be enforced

124. (A) To register for regular courses, please call the customer service line at (711) 652-1241.
(B) In some cases, we may need to prohibit them from entering the center.
(C) Thank you for your understanding of this inconvenience during the construction.
(D) Our facility accepts members who have appropriate forms of identification.

SPARTA Grammar Review

(1) 수 일치의 기본은 주어에 '-s'가 붙으면 동사에 '-s'가 붙지 않는 것이다.
(2) 고유명사는 '-s'로 끝나도 단수 취급한다.
(3) <수량 표현+of the+명사> 구조에서는 가까이에 위치한 명사에 수 일치를 시킨다.
(4) 수량 표현 중에서, one, each, either, neither는 주어를 단수로 만드므로 동사에 '-s'가 붙는다.
(5) 빈칸 뒤에 목적어(명사)가 보이지 않으면 수동태이다.
(6) 빈칸 뒤에 to부정사가 있다면 주어와의 해석 관계를 통해 능동/수동을 구분한다.
(7) 4형식은 목적어가 하나라도 없으면 수동태이다.
(8) 5형식의 목적보어는 수동태에 관여하지 않는다. 단, 지각/사역 동사는 동사원형이 to부정사로 바뀐다.
(9) 판단/상태 동사의 목적보어인 형용사, 분사, 명사가 수동태 뒤에 남을 수 있다.
(10) 자동사는 일반적으로 수동태가 불가능하다.

DAY 7 동사의 시제와 가정법

SPARTA 유형 파악

시제란, 시간 수식어에 따라 동사의 시제가 결정되는 것이다. 앞선 챕터의 내용과 혼합하여 등장하고, <진-수-태-시> 구조에서 수동태/능동태를 파악한 후 시간 수식어 힌트를 빠르게 찾아 알맞은 동사의 형태로 결정하면 된다. 일반적으로 12시제라고 하지만, 실질적으로 시간을 나타내는 시제는 <현재-과거-미래> 3가지로 기본 시제를 판단한다.

SPARTA 출제 포인트

☑ 12시제의 변화

	현재	과거	미래
단순 시제	현재시제 I study TOEIC.	과거시제 I studied TOEIC.	미래시제 I will study TOEIC.
진행형	현재진행형 I am studying TOEIC.	과거진행형 I was studying TOEIC.	미래진행형 I will be studying TOEIC.
완료형	현재완료형 I have studied TOEIC.	과거완료형 I had studied TOEIC.	미래완료형 I will have studied TOEIC.
완료 진행형	현재완료 진행형 I have been studying TOEIC.	과거완료 진행형 I had been studying TOEIC.	미래완료 진행형 I will have been studying TOEIC.

➡ 실제로, 시제(tense)는 <현재-과거-미래>의 3가지 시간 기준을 기본으로 한다.
(진행형이나 완료형으로 바뀌어도, -ing라는 진행형이나, -ed라는 분사형은 변하지 않는다.)

☑ 과거에 대한 후회: 가정

기본적으로 접속사 if가 사용되는 문장은 조건문과 가정법 두 가지로 구분된다. 조건문은 사실을 전제로 하고, 가정법은 현재 사실에 반대되는 내용을 나타낸다. 해석으로 풀어 나가는 방법도 있으나 문장의 구조도 다르므로, 문장이 주는 힌트를 보고 조건문인지 가정법인지 확인하고 문제의 답을 찾자.

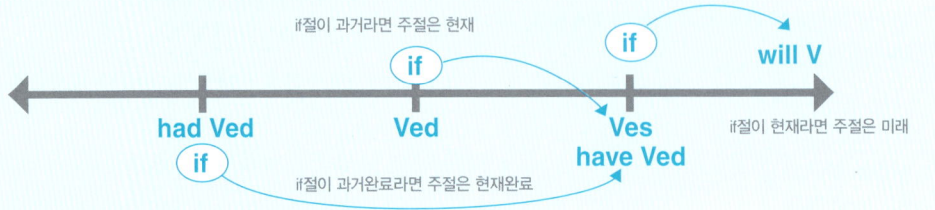

가정법은 조건문과 달리 주절과 if 절의 시제가 하나씩 차이가 난다. (+1의 법칙)

SPARTA 문제 풀이 비법

Mr. Kinder -------- to general manager of our Singapore branch last month.

(A) promotes
(B) promoted
(C) will be promoted
(D) was promoted

Kinder 씨는 지난달에 우리 싱가포르 지점의 총괄 매니저로 승진했습니다.

✅ last month(지난달)라는 시간 수식어를 통해 과거시제인 (D)가 답이 됨을 알 수 있다.
우선, 수 일치는 모두 이루어져 있다. 빈칸 뒤는 전치사 to로 시작하는 수식어구이므로 목적어가 없는 수동태 (C)와 (D) 중, 시간 수식어 last (지난)로 보아, 과거시제인 (D)가 가장 적절하다.

SPARTA Grammar Point 1

단순 시제

A. 현재 시제

시간 수식어가 없는 경우 기준 시제인 현재 시제가 정답이 된다. 그 밖에 "현재"를 알려주는 시점 부사와, "규칙", "반복"을 의미하는 빈도부사가 등장할 경우 현재 시제를 사용한다.

현재시점부사

| now 지금 | presently 현재 | currently 현재 | at present 현재 |

빈도 부사

always 항상	often 자주	usually 보통	sometimes 때때로
frequently 자주	generally 일반적으로	habitually 습관적으로	typically 전형적으로
regularly 정기적으로	periodically 주기적으로	every/each + 시점 매 ~마다	

The conference **is** usually held on the first Monday of each month.
그 컨퍼런스는 보통 매달 첫째 주 월요일에 열린다.

B. 과거 시제 : 과거를 나타내는 시간 수식어와 함께 사용된다.

과거 시점 표현

last/past + 명사 지난 ~	ago ~전에	recently 최근에	lately 최근에
at that time 그 당시	once 한 때	just now 방금 막	already 이미, 벌써
previously 이전에	formerly 예전에		

Mr. Jackson, who **joined** our marketing team **2 weeks ago**, shows outstanding performance.
2주전에 우리 마케팅 팀에 합류한 Jackson 씨는 뛰어난 실적을 보여주고 있다.

C. 미래 시제 : 미래를 나타내는 시간 수식어와 함께 사용된다.

미래 시점 표현

| next/following 다음의 | as of ~부터 | starting ~부터 | beginning ~부터 |
| effective (from) ~부터 | soon 곧 | shortly 곧 | sometime 언젠가 |

As of the next month, the new regulations **will be** in effect at all the branches.
다음달부터 새로운 규정들이 모든 지점에 효력을 발휘하게 될 것이다.

SPARTA Check-UP

정답 및 해설 p. 417

The board of directors -------- recently for the general meeting of stockholders because of the appointment of the new CEO.

(A) is gathered
(B) was gathered
(C) will be gathered
(D) has gathered

SPARTA | Grammar Point 2

완료 시제

완료 시제란, 과거에서 시작하여 현재, 과거, 미래까지 지속/완료되는 시간차의 시제 상태이다. 이렇게 시간차를 나타내는 수식어를 통해 완료 시제를 활용할 수 있다.

A. 현재 완료

<have + Ved> 구조의 현재 완료는 과거부터 현재까지 지속적인 동작, 또는 완료되는 동작을 나타낸다.

시간차 표현

since + 과거 시점 : ~이래로 [접속사/전치사/부사]		for / over / in + 과거 기간 : ~동안
already 이미, 벌써	finally 마침내	always 항상
lately 최근에	recently 최근에	continuously 지속적으로
consistently 꾸준히	continually 계속해서	repeatedly 반복적으로

For the last 10 years, Mr. Choi **has been dedicated** to improving our information infrastructure.
지난 10년동안, Choi 씨는 정보 기반을 개선하기 위해 헌신했다.

B. 과거 완료

<had + Ved> 구조의 과거 완료는 과거 시점 간의 시간차를 나타낸다. 더 먼저 일어난 일을 문법 용어로는 '대과거'라고 한다.

Before Ms. Karen **was** employed as our personnel director, she **had served** in a world-famous headhunting company.
Karren 씨가 우리 인사부장으로 채용되기 전, 그녀는 세계적으로 유명한 인재 스카우트 회사에서 일했었다.

C. 미래 완료

<will have + Ved> 구조의 미래 완료는 과거에 시작한 일이 앞으로 지속될 것을 나타낸다. 시간 수식어로는, 미래 시점 부사와 완료의 시간차를 보여주는 수식어가 동시에 나오는 경우가 많다.

Next year, Ms. Katrina **will have worked** here **for six years**. 내년에, Katrina 씨는 여기서 일한 지 6년이 될 것이다.
[미래 시점] [기간-완료 시간차]

그 외에, by the time(~할 때쯤)이라는 시간차 시간 부사절 접속사가 쓰일 경우 완료 시제가 등장한다.

> By the time S Ved(과거), S had Ved(과거완료)
> By the time S Ves(현재), S will have Ved(미래완료)

By the time the staff in the IT support center **repairs** the set-up box, our server **will have been activated** again.
IT 지원처의 직원이 그 셋업 박스를 수리할 때쯤, 우리 서버는 다시 활성화되어 있을 것 같습니다.

SPARTA Check-UP 2

정답 및 해설 p.417

Since she ------- the state governor, Ms. Cohen has instituted well-organized welfare policies.

(A) has been elected (B) was elected
(C) to elect (D) is elected

SPARTA — Grammar Point 3

예외적인 시제 구조

기본적인 시제 구조에서 진행형이 불가능한 형태와 시제 일치 예외적인 형태들이 등장한다.

A. 진행 불가 동사

대부분의 진행 시제는 단순 기본 시제와 마찬가지로 시간 수식어가 쓰인다. 단, '소유'나 '감정'의 동사들은 "~하는 중"이라는 의미의 <be + Ving> 진행 구조가 불가능하다.

| have 가지다 | feel 느끼다 | include 포함하다 | like 좋아하다 |

➡ 감정을 나타내는 형용사는 진행형과 쓰지 않는다.
➡ 순서를 나타내는 부사절 접속사 after / once / as soon as 뒤에 진행형을 쓰지 않는다.
➡ < be+having>이 "먹다"의 뜻일 경우 진행형이 가능하다.

This travel package ~~is including~~ a facility tour of King Chocolate World.
　　　　　　　　　➡ **includes**
이 관광 패키지는 King Chocolate World 시설 견학이 포함되어 있습니다.

B. 시간/조건 부사절 접속사

시간/조건의 부사절 접속사들은 이미 미래 시점이 내포되어 있기 때문에, 미래 시제 대신 현재 시제를 사용한다.

시간/조건 부사절 접속사 S Ved (과거), S Ved (과거)	[시제 일치]
시간/조건 부사절 접속사 S Ves (현재), S Ves (현재)	[시제 일치]
시간/조건 부사절 접속사 S Ves (현재), S will V (미래)	[시제 불일치]

➡ 시간/조건 부사절 접속사가 포함된 종속절의 시제가 현재일 때, 주절은 미래 시제가 나올 수 있다. 즉, 시간/조건 부사절 접속사 절에는 미래 (will V)시제를 쓸 수 없다.

시간/조건 접속사

| 시간 | when, as, while, as soon as, by the time, once(~하자마자) … |
| 조건 | if, once(일단 ~하면), unless, in case, in the event, as long as … |

If you **register** for our event before noon tomorrow, you **will get** a free gift card.
내일 정오 전까지 저희 행사에 등록하시면, 무료 상품권을 드립니다.

SPARTA Check-UP

정답 및 해설 p.417

As soon as the building ------ inspected for safety, you will do your original tasks again without any other directions.

(A) is
(B) has
(C) will be
(D) was

SPARTA Grammar Point 4

A. 가정법 기본 형태

| 가정법 과거 | If+주어+과거동사 ~, 주어+would / should / could / might+V (동사원형) |
| 가정법 과거완료 | If+주어+had+과거분사 ~, 주어+would / should / could / might+have Ved(p.p) |

If+주어+should+동사원형 ~, 주어+will/can/may/must/should+동사원형 (또는 명령문)

If+주어+현재동사 ~, 주어+will+동사원형

<u>If</u> you **acquired** the company, you <u>might</u> **regret** it because of its financial burden.
그 회사를 인수한다면, 회사의 재정적 부담으로 후회하게 될 텐데요.

➡ 주의) 가정법 과거에서 if절에 쓰이는 be동사는 인칭이나 수에 관계없이 were가 쓰이는 것이 원칙이다.
그러나 구어체에서는 인칭이나 수에 따라 was가 쓰이는 경우도 있다.

<u>If</u> the team **had finished** the project in time, we <u>would</u> **have released** new item at this fair.
그 팀이 프로젝트를 제 시간에 마쳤다면, 우리는 이번 박람회에서 신제품을 출시했을 텐데.

B. 가정법 도치

도치란, 문장 성분의 이동을 의미한다. 문장 성분을 이동시키는 이유는 강조하기 위함인데, 가정법(if절)의 강조어는 이미 주어보다 앞서 있는 if이다. 더 이상 앞으로 이동시킬 수 없으므로 if를 생략하고 문장 구조를 이동시킨다.
가정법(if절) 도치는 if절에서만 이루어진다. (주절은 아무 변화 없음)

가정법(if절) 도치 ➡ (if 생략) 조동사 + 주어 + 동사, 주어 + 동사

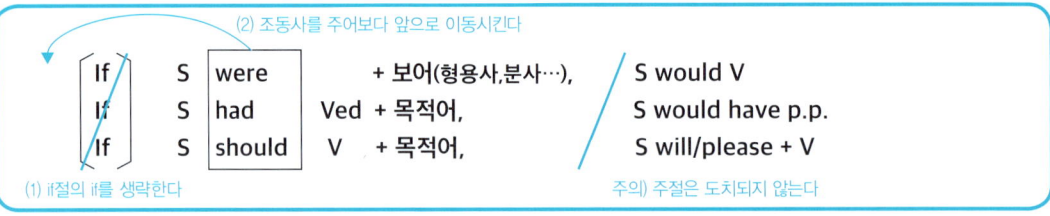

ex) If the art exhibitions **were** held throughout the country, more people could enjoy the famous paintings.
➡ **Were** the art exhibitions held throughout the county, more people could enjoy the famous paintings.
예술 전시회들이 전국에 걸쳐 열렸다면, 더 많은 사람들이 유명한 그림들을 즐길 수 있었을 텐데.

C. if 대용어구

if 접속사를 대신하여 쓰이는 대체 접속사와 전치사가 있다.

| 접속사 (만일 ~라면) | provided (that), providing (that), assuming (that), supposing (that) |
| 전치사 (~하지 않는다면) | without, but for, barring, if not for |

SPARTA Check-UP 4

정답 및 해설 p. 417

Our CEO could change his mind if marketing team ------ innovative strategies to attract more customers.
(A) propose (B) proposed
(C) will propose (D) would propose

SPARTA Practice Test

101. Mr. Schneider will explain the specific contents of the conference he -------- in Manchester last week.
(A) attends
(B) attended
(C) attending
(D) attend

102. Ms. Reina planned the construction of the company's new headquarters, and she -------- the maintenance team when it is complete next year.
(A) managed
(B) managing
(C) will manage
(D) had managed

103. The retirement of Ms. Serena --------- in the Grand Ballroom, on the second floor of the building at 8:00 P.M. next Friday.
(A) have been celebrated
(B) is celebrated
(C) will be celebrated
(D) will have celebrated

104. Over the last few years, Maxon Corporation -------- M&A experts in order to expand its business into the IT industry.
(A) is hiring
(B) were hiring
(C) has hired
(D) was hired

105. You should keep in mind that no application package received after the deadline --------.
(A) is considering
(B) considered
(C) will consider
(D) will be considered

106. Of the four candidates we considered for the position, Mr. Dan ------- to know the most about marketing strategies.
(A) will have appeared
(B) will appear
(C) appearing
(D) appears

107. T-Bone & Gourmet Food Corp.'s net profits for the last year -------- the management's prediction.
(A) surpassed
(B) surpassing
(C) to surpass
(D) having surpassed

108. Ms. Julian is substituted for the position of Mr. Nakata, who -------- from the Chief Financial Officer next week.
(A) has retired
(B) retired
(C) will retire
(D) retires

109. When Ms. Liao finishes her master's degree in English literature, she -------- for the doctorate program at Chicago University.
(A) apply
(B) applied
(C) is applied
(D) will apply

110. Ace Food Service -------- the best quality catering service to various events since it started its business in 2010.
(A) providing
(B) has provided
(C) will provide
(D) will be providing

111. When you ------- a question, our staff at the customer service center will respond to it quickly anytime.
(A) have
(B) has
(C) had
(D) will have

112. In 2015, Mr. Buncheon, the world-famous singer, -------- that he retired from the musical world and was planning to teach students in the college.
(A) announced
(B) was announced
(C) announcing
(D) will announce

113. By the time he gets promoted to executive, Mr. Gomez --------- at the company for thirty years.
(A) has worked
(B) had worked
(C) worked
(D) will have worked

114. Once the document is reviewed carefully, the Federal Award Committee ------- a winner of the State of the Year Award.
(A) choosing
(B) choose
(C) chose
(D) will choose

115. Ms. Lillian -------- innovative marketing ideas in the last two years since joining our team.
(A) developed
(B) has developed
(C) will develop
(D) develop

116. By next month, our media division ------- to a new office building with ample space in the Sangam Media area.
(A) relocate
(B) relocates
(C) will relocate
(D) to relocate

117. Because of the success of this promotion, our sales figures considerably increased more than we --------.
(A) are anticipating
(B) anticipate
(C) were anticipated
(D) had anticipated

118. If our staff had known the fact that some had a dietary restriction, we ------ the dish without any meat.
(A) serve
(B) would serve
(C) have served
(D) would have served

119. ------ you need further information about the conference schedule, please send me a request e-mail.
(A) Should
(B) Could
(C) Had
(D) Were

120. Provided that this quarter's sales profits ------, we might have secured funds to develop more innovative items.
(A) increased
(B) had increased
(C) will increase
(D) increase

Questions 121-124 refer to the following e-mail.

To : info@cismobileelec.net
From : grizman@commonmail.com
Date : October 10
Subject : Order : GX-Pro Tablet PC

To whom it may concern,

I am e-mailing you about an item I purchased. I am sorry to say that there ------- a significant amount of damage when I received it. For example, there were scratches on the surface, and the display was cracked. In its condition, it is ------- unusable. This product -------, of course. However, I don't know the best way to return it. Please e-mail me back to let me know whether I should send it back or bring it into one of your stores. -------.
121.
122. **123.**
124.

121. (A) is
(B) was
(C) are
(D) were

122. (A) currently
(B) previously
(C) shortly
(D) immediately

123. (A) was to have been returned
(B) has been returned
(C) was being returned
(D) must be returned

124. (A) I need to get some information about the next step I should take.
(B) I'm very disappointed that you refused my request on the matter.
(C) Thank you for giving me good service and the product I want.
(D) Please let me know who the best technician is in your company.

SPARTA Grammar Review

(1) 현재 시제에서, 빈도부사는 현재 시점 부사와 함께 쓰인다.

(2) ago나 last 등의 표현은 과거 시제의 시간 수식어이다.

(3) soon, shortly, next ~ 등의 표현은 미래 시제를 나타낸다.

(4) 완료 시제는 "시간차"를 나타낸다. 특히, since, for, over, in 등과 함께 쓰인다.

(5) 소유나 감정을 나타내는 동사는 진행형으로 잘 쓰이지 않는다.

(6) 시간/조건 부사절 접속사는 미래 시점을 포함한다.

(7) 가정법은 접속사 if와 주절에 조동사 would/could/might가 주로 함께 쓰인다.

(8) 과거에 대한 후회를 나타내는 가정법은, 주절과 if절의 시제가 하나씩 차이 난다.

(9) 조건문은 주절과 if절의 시제가 일치하거나, 현재 시제와 미래 시제의 일치 형태를 나타낸다.

(10) 가정법 도치는 if절의 if가 생략되고 문장의 어순이 <조동사+주어+동사>로 바뀐다.

(11) if 대신 접속사 provided/providing 또는 전치사 without이나 but for 등이 쓰일 수 있다.

DAY 8 to부정사와 동명사

SPARTA 유형 파악

to부정사와 동명사는 동사의 특징은 가지고 있으나, **동사 자리에 올 수 없는 준동사**이다. 문장 전체에서 to부정사 또는 동명사가 들어갈 알맞은 위치를 묻는 문제가 등장한다.

SPARTA 출제 포인트

☑ 준동사의 자리

동사 자리에 올 수 없는 다음의 준동사들이 문장에서 어느 자리, 어느 품사를 대체하는지 살펴본다.

문장에서의 위치			
to부정사 (to V) :	명사	형용사	부사
동명사 (-ing) :	명사		
분사 (-ing/p.p.) :		형용사	부사

☑ 동사 기능의 유지

동사 자리를 제외한 나머지 위치에 올 수 있는 준동사는 여전히 동사의 기능을 유지한다.

```
              (2) 동사처럼 부사가 수식한다
        ✗
       the      +  부사  +  to 타V    +  목적어
                           타Ving
(3) 동작이므로 셀 수 없고, 한정할 수 없다    (1) 동사처럼 목적어가 필요하다
```

Our board of directors asked managers **to** thoroughly **review** team members' job performance.
　　　　　　　　　　　　　　　　　　　　　(2) 부사 수식　　　　(1) 목적어

이사회는 매니저들에게 팀원들의 직무 수행을 철저하게 검토해 보라고 요구했다.

SPARTA 문제 풀이 비법

The newly appointed director tends to forcefully order his members ------ overtime.

(A) work
(B) works
(C) worked
(D) to work

새로 임명된 부장은 강압적으로 그의 직원들에게 추가 근무를 하도록 명령하는 경향이 있다.

✅ 이미 본동사인 tends가 있으므로 준동사인 to부정사 (D)가 정답이다.
tends(동사)+to order(목적어)+his member(to부정사의 목적어)로 문장이 제시되어 있고, order는 5형식의 "시키다" 류 동사이므로, 보어 자리에 to부정사가 와야 한다.

SPARTA　Grammar Point 1

to부정사 활용

to부정사는 문장에서 명사, 형용사, 부사의 품사를 대체해서 사용될 수 있다.

A. 명사 자리

(1) 주어 역할
To attract new customers is not easy in the recent condition of the economic recession.
신규 고객들을 모은다는 것은, 최근 경기 침체의 상황에서 쉽지 않다.
➡ 주어 자리에 to부정사가 나오면 단수 취급한다.

(2) 보어 역할
Our quarterly goal is **to exceed the sales figures of the preceding years**.
우리의 분기 목표는 이전의 판매 수치들을 초과하는 것이다.
➡ 보어 자리의 to부정사는 2형식의 경우 주어, 5형식의 경우 목적어의 "미래상태"(~할 것)를 나타낸다.

(3) 목적어 역할
The board of directors decided not **to hire additional employees this year**.
이사회는 올해 추가로 직원을 채용하지 않기로 결정했다.
➡ 목적어 자리의 to부정사는 미래 시점을 나타내는 동작 동사와 함께 쓴다.
➡ 전치사의 목적어(전치사 뒤)로 to부정사는 올 수 없다.

B. 형용사 자리

to부정사가 형용사를 대신할 때, 명사 뒤에 온다. 이때 to부정사의 수식을 받는 명사는 미래 시점이 내포되어 있다.

> **opportunity** (기회), **chance** (기회), **right** (권리)
> **authority** (권한), **ability** (능력), **effort** (노력)　＋　to부정사
> **plan** (계획), **attempt** (시도)

We should have a plan **to attract more tourists to the Indiana area**.
우리는 인디애나 지역으로 더 많은 관광객을 유치할 계획을 세워야 한다.

C. 부사 자리

to부정사가 부사를 대신할 때, 주로 목적(~하기 위해)의 의미로 쓰인다. 감정의 형용사나 감정 동사의 분사 뒤에서는 감정의 원인(~하게 되어)을 나타내기도 한다.

To reduce unnecessary expenses, we need to make every effort to improve our work procedures.
불필요한 비용을 줄이기 위해, 우리는 작업 절차를 개선하기 위한 모든 노력을 기울여야 합니다.
➡ 목적을 나타내는 to부정사의 "to"는 in order to V, 또는 so as to V와 바꾸어 쓸 수 있다.

We are pleased **to inform you that you pass the application process**.
저희는 당신이 이번 지원 과정에 통과하셨다는 것을 알려 드리게 되어 기쁩니다.

SPARTA　Check-UP

정답 및 해설 p. 420

Despite efforts ------- our customer service, most of our customers have increasingly left us because of our outdated online order system.

(A) improve　　　　　　　　(B) improvement
(C) to improve　　　　　　　(D) improving

SPARTA Grammar Point 2

동명사 활용

동명사는 명사 자리를 대신하는데, 명사가 올 수 있는 주어, 목적어 자리에 주로 쓰인다.

A. 명사 자리

(1) 주어 역할
Creating a new way to promote sales is our team's main responsibility.
판매를 촉진시킬 새로운 방법을 만드는 것이 우리 팀의 주된 업무이다.

➡ 동명사가 주어 자리에 올 때, "동작"을 나타내므로 단수 취급한다.

(2) 목적어 역할
Due to a lack of funds, we decided to postpone **sponsoring this charity event**.
자본의 부족으로, 우리는 이번 자선 행사의 후원을 미루기로 결정했다.

➡ 타동사의 목적어 자리에 올 수 있다.

B. 전치사의 목적어

to부정사와 달리 동명사는 전치사 뒤에 올 수 있는 준동사로, 전치사와 동명사가 연결되는 문제가 자주 출제된다. 특히, 전치사 to는 원칙상 동작을 나타내는 동명사(Ving)와 거의 사용되지 않는데, <to+V-ing> 구조가 가능한 일부 표현을 학습해 두자.

〈to + Ving〉

look forward to V-ing ~를 기대하다	be used to V-ing ~하는 데 익숙하다
object to V-ing ~에 반대하다	be subject to V-ing ~에 영향받기 쉽다
be accustomed to V-ing ~에 익숙하다	be opposed to V-ing ~에 반대하다
contribute to V-ing ~에 헌신하다	be committed to V-ing ~에 헌신하다
be dedicated to V-ing ~에 헌신하다	be devoted to V-ing ~에 헌신하다

그 밖에, 전치사와 동명사(Ving)가 함께 쓰여, 의미가 바뀌는 몇 가지 형태가 있다.

〈전치사 + Ving〉

by V-ing (수단) ~함으로써	on/upon V-ing (시점) ~하자마자
in V-ing (원인) ~하는 데 있어 (시점) ~할 때	for V-ing (원인) ~했기 때문에

The newly elected mayor has **contributed to making** our community better.
새로 당선된 시장은 우리 동네를 더 좋게 만드는 데 헌신하고 있다.

SPARTA Check-UP 2

------ familiar with a new language needs repeated exercise by speaking in the target language.

(A) Become
(B) Have become
(C) Becoming
(D) Became

SPARTA Grammar Point 3

to부정사 & 동명사 응용

to부정사와 동명사가 둘 다 가능한 위치에서의 문제 접근법, 그리고 동명사를 활용한 관용어구들을 살펴보도록 한다.

A. to부정사 vs. 동명사

to부정사와 동명사는 주어와 목적어 자리 등에서 to부정사는 "~할 것"이라는 뜻으로 미래 시점을 나타낼 때 쓰이고, 동명사는 "~하는, 하던 것"의 현재-과거 의미를 나타낼 때 쓴다. 이 둘을 구분하는 것은 주로 타동사의 목적어 자리인데, 본동사를 확인하고 알맞은 준동사의 형태를 고르도록 한다.

(1) to부정사를 목적어로 취하는 동사

> hope (희망하다), want (원하다), wish (기원하다),
> promise (약속하다), choose (고르다), plan (계획하다), + to부정사
> decide (결정하다), offer (제안하다), refuse (거절하다)

Howard Consulting Co. **decided** to change its operating system in order to attract more customers.
Howard Consulting 사는 고객을 더 모집하기 위해 운영 시스템을 바꾸기로 결정했다.

(2) 동명사를 목적어로 취하는 동사

> mind (꺼리다), enjoy (즐기다), give up (포기하다),
> avoid (피하다), postpone (연기하다), advise (충고하다),
> suggest (제안하다), stop (멈추다), include (포함하다), + 동명사
> deny (부정하다), recommend (추천하다), consider (고려하다),
> finish (마치다), complete (완료하다)

Mr. Jason **finished** correcting some errors in the article scheduled to be published on Friday.
Jason 씨는 금요일에 발간될 예정인 기사의 오류를 수정하는 것을 마쳤다.

B. 동명사 빈출 Collocation

go -ing -하러 가다	remember -ing -을 기억하다	It's no use -ing -해도 소용없다
feel like -ing -을 하고 싶다	spend 시간/돈 -ing -하느라 돈/시간을 쓰다	be worth -ing -할 가치가 있다
be busy -ing -하느라 바쁘다	keep -ing 계속해서 -하다	on/upon -ing -을 하자마자
have difficulty (problem / trouble) -ing -하느라 어려움/문제를 겪다		
prevent/stop/hinder/keep A from -ing (B) A가 B하는 것을 막다/방해하다		

Mr. Dave's family **spent** most of their time **visiting** Western American cities during the vacation.
Dave의 가족은 휴가 동안 대부분의 시간을 미국의 서부 도시들을 방문하는 데 썼다.

SPARTA Check-UP 3

정답 및 해설 p. 420

The management strongly suggested ------- new employees before becoming too busy in preparation for this Christmas holiday.

(A) hire (B) to hire
(C) hiring (D) hired

SPARTA　Grammar Point 4

A. 의미상 주어 (to부정사 vs 동명사)

to부정사나 동명사는 동사(동작) 의미를 지니고 있기 때문에, '누가' 해당 동작을 수행하는지에 대한 '주어'를 필요로 한다. 하지만 문장 전체의 본동사는 아니기 때문에 모양을 변형시키는데, to부정사는 주로 <for + 명사> 형태로, 동명사는 <소유격> 형태로 의미상 주어를 나타낸다.

- 가주어 it (2형식)과 의미상 주어
  It is 보어(형용사/분사) for 명사 to V
- 가목적어 it (5형식)과 의미상 주어
  S V it 보어(형용사/분사) for 명사 to V
- 동명사와 의미상 주어
  소유격 + 타Ving + 목적어

It is very important for me to study English for getting a job.
취업을 위해 영어를 공부하는 것은 매우 중요하다.

This book makes it easy for me to study English.
이 책은 내가 영어 공부하는 것을 쉽게 해준다.

The board of directors hates our investing in a risky business.
이사회는 우리가 위험한 사업에 투자하는 것을 싫어한다.

B. -ing 형태 구분하기 (동명사 vs 능동형 현재 분사)

형태상 동사에 -ing가 붙어서 똑같이 보일 수 있지만, 동명사와 능동형 분사는 전혀 다른 기능을 담당한다.

- 꼭 필요한 필수 자리: 동명사 ➡ 생략 불가능한 주어/목적어 역할
- 생략 가능 수식어 자리: 분사 ➡ 생략 가능한 형용사/부사 역할

When a lot of new vehicles are currently being released, selling the used cars is too difficult for its dealers.
　　　　　　　　　　　　　　　　　주어 역할을 하는 동명사 ⬅　　➡ 명사 앞 형용사(수식어) 역할을 하는 분사
새로운 차량들이 현재 엄청 출시되는 때에, 중고차를 판매하는 것은 딜러들에게 꽤나 어려운 일이다.

SPARTA Check-UP 4

With your generous donation and supports, we could succeed in ------ this charitable event.

(A) organize
(B) organized
(C) organizing
(D) organization

SPARTA Practice Test

101. ------ a memorable commercial film to the public through a television is one of our marketing strategies.

(A) Show
(B) Showing
(C) Shown
(D) Shows

102. Although costs of raw materials were considerably lowered last quarter, Fannenca Expressway Inc. failed ------ a net profit.

(A) make
(B) making
(C) made
(D) to make

103. Their ------ an outdated version of the security software can cause severe errors in the company's computers by spreading electronic viruses.

(A) use
(B) to use
(C) using
(D) used

104. The National Teachers' Forum next month will focus on effective ways ------ the issue of bullying among students in the school.

(A) handle
(B) had handled
(C) have handled
(D) to handle

105. Lafayette University of North Carolina has a longstanding commitment to ------ existing treatments for diabetic patients.

(A) improved
(B) improving
(C) improve
(D) be improved

106. Most of our employees insist that the conference be postponed until next month because the entire staff is really busy ------ for the quarterly audit.

(A) prepare
(B) preparation
(C) preparing
(D) to prepare

107. Thanks to ------ responding to the emergency situation, many people avoided severe damage at the moment of the car accident in the tunnel.

(A) prompt
(B) promptly
(C) prompting
(C) to prompt

108. Those who are planning to participate in this annual forum are required ------ to the provided brochures about the schedules and contents of this event.

(A) referring
(B) to refer
(C) referred
(D) reference

109. By -------- in the online survey, anyone can get a free coupon for one regular-sized beverage in all our stores through the mobile application.

(A) participate
(B) participant
(C) participating
(D) participated

110. If you expand your branches into other continents by constraint, you may go bankrupt and have no way of ------ the funds recovered.

(A) get
(B) to get
(C) getting
(D) gotten

111. The new security team has been posted at the entrance ------ check company ID cards of people entering the building.

    (A) considerably
    (B) in order to
    (C) nevertheless
    (D) as a result of

112. Before ------ the event hall for the retirement ceremony for Mr. Tao, we need to ask him about a possible date and time.

    (A) reserve
    (B) reserved
    (C) reserving
    (D) reservation

113. The accounting director reminded all employees that plans for the new payroll system were still subject to -------.

    (A) change
    (B) changed
    (C) changing
    (D) changeable

114. If anyone would like ------ an order outside Europe, please visit our Web site and click the International Shipping section.

    (A) to place
    (B) placement
    (C) placing
    (D) placed

115. Using symbols makes it possible ------- a large amount of information on a single map without any detailed descriptions.

    (A) put
    (B) putting
    (C) to put
    (D) to putting

116. Even if there are no immediate plans to ------ a new headquarters building, management will soon consider whether to do it.

    (A) construct
    (B) constructed
    (C) will construct
    (D) constructing

117. As we mentioned at the last meeting, the building renovations are scheduled ------ on May 1 and end by May 30.

    (A) to begin
    (B) begin
    (C) begins
    (D) will begin

118. ------- the editor to make an essential revision, all articles should be submitted a week before the publication date.

    (A) So that
    (B) That
    (C) In order for
    (D) By

119. Because of ------- our labor costs, the board of directors decided to construct our plants for the assembly line in the State of Arizona.

    (A) to reduce
    (B) reduced
    (C) reducing
    (D) reduction

120. Smartphone users tend to consider ------- their mobile phones once a year because most products become outdated quickly.

    (A) replace
    (B) replaces
    (C) replacing
    (D) to replace

Questions 121-124 refer to the following e-mail.

To: Chris Brown <c.brown@t-mail.com>
From: Joshua Debora, Advance Realty <j.debora@advancerealty.net>
Date: March 20
Subject: Commonwealth Boulevard property

Dear Mr. Brown,

I am writing about your inquiries yesterday about the vacant space on Commonwealth Boulevard. I was really pleased to meet you, and I was so glad to hear that the vacant store meets your requirements perfectly.

To respond to your question about the possibility of a rent negotiation, in my experience, the landlord is more likely ------- a reduced rent if
                                    121.
the tenant is willing to pay one year's rent in advance. So before I contact the owner, kindly let me know if this would be possible. In this challenging situation retailers encounter, I'm confident that an agreement can be reached to benefit your new business.

I look forward to ------- from you soon. -------.
                    122.   **123.**
If you are interested, Advance Realty also has a select list of excellent building developers ------- can help with the renovation of the
124.
commercial space.

Sincerely,

Joshua Debora
Manager, Advance Realty

121. (A) accepts
  (B) accepting
  (C) accepted
  (D) to accept

122. (A) hear
  (B) hearing
  (C) heard
  (D) hears

123. (A) You should note that the date of entry will be April 10.
  (B) Please notify the landlord of the date before May 1.
  (C) In addition, legal services regarding the contract will be provided.
  (D) After this, we can contract the building with others.

124. (A) who
  (B) these
  (C) they
  (D) whichever

SPARTA Grammar Review

(1) to부정사는 동사 자리와 전치사 뒤를 제외하고는 문장 어디에나 올 수 있다.

(2) 동명사는 주어, 목적어 자리에 쓰이는데, 전치사 뒤에도 올 수 있다.

(3) to부정사, 동명사 둘 다 동사의 기능을 유지하기 때문에, 타동사일 경우 목적어가 필요하고, 부사의 수식을 받는다.

(4) to부정사는 앞으로 "할 것", 동명사는 "하는 것/하던 것"을 나타낸다.

(5) 5형식 "시키다 류" 동사의 경우, 목적보어 자리에는 to부정사만 가능하다.

(6) 전치사 to와 어울리는 V-ing 표현을 익히자.

DAY 9 분사

SPARTA 유형 파악

분사는 수식어를 대체하는 준동사의 하나로, 형용사 또는 부사를 대신하는 특징이 있다. 현재분사(능동형)과 과거분사(수동형) 두 가지로 나뉘어지는데, 각 위치 별로 어떠한 특징이 있는지 알아 보도록 한다.

SPARTA 출제 포인트

☑ 분사의 자리

생략 가능한 부사 자리, 명사 앞뒤에서 수식하는 형용사 자리, 2형식 또는 5형식 보어 자리에 온다. 현재분사(능동형)는 "~하는, ~주는", 과거분사(수동형)는 "~되는, ~완료된"의 의미로 쓰인다.

문장에서의 위치

타Ving + O 타Ved (수식어)	타Ving 타Ved	N	타Ving + O 타Ved (수식어)	2V	타Ving + O 타Ved (수식어)
부사 자리	명사 앞 형용사		명사 뒤 형용사		보어 자리 형용사

➡ 대부분의 분사는 능동형 -ing 뒤에는 목적어가, 수동형 -ed 뒤에는 수식어가 덩어리로 등장해 수식 또는 보충해 주는 역할을 한다. 단, 명사 앞은 -ing 또는 -ed형 분사가 직접 수식하므로 해석으로 접근한다.

➡ 수동형이 불가능한 자동사의 경우, -ing가 붙은 능동형 분사만 가능하다.

The **finalized** marketing plan is likely to attract more new customers.
최종 마무리된 마케팅 기획이 더 새로운 고객들을 끌어모을 것 같다.

➡ 명사 앞자리에서 형용사를 대신하여 분사가 직접 수식

The idea **proposed by Ms. Sonya** was very innovative and creative.
Sonya 씨에 의해 제안된 그 아이디어는 매우 혁신적이고 창의적이었다.

➡ 명사 뒤에서 앞의 명사를 수식하는데, "구"의 형태인 2단어 이상으로 수식한다.

SPARTA 문제 풀이 비법

Our library's Web site has provided us with a great amount of ------ information on the academic materials.

(A) detail
(B) details
(C) detailing
(D) detailed

우리 도서관 웹사이트는 우리에게 학술 자료에 대한 엄청난 양의 세부 정보를 제공하고 있다.

✅ 명사(information) 앞에서 형용사를 대신하는 수식어인 분사 (D) detailed가 가장 적절하다.
명사 앞 자리에 알맞은 분사로 (C) detailing과 (D) detailed가 가능, 뒤따르는 명사 "정보"는 "설명되는" 동작의 대상이므로, 수동형 분사인 (D)가 답이 된다.

SPARTA Grammar Point 1

형용사 자리
명사 앞뒤 그리고 2형식과 5형식 보어 자리에 등장할 수 있다.

A. 명사 앞
명사 앞 분사에 포함되어 있는 동사의 의미와, 뒤따르는 명사와의 동작 관계를 의미적으로 접근해서 풀어야 한다.

[동작 타V -ing/-ed] N
- 명사가 동작을 하는
- 명사가 동작을 당하는

You can take advantage of our free trial service for a (limiting/**limited**) time only.
➡ 뒤에 나온 "시간"이라는 명사는 "제한하다"라는 동작을 당하는 대상
여러분은 무료 시험 서비스를 제한된 시간 동안에만 이용할 수 있습니다.

B. 명사 뒤
명사 뒤의 경우, 수식 받는 명사보다 수식어가 길어서 뒤로 가는 경우이므로 구의 형태로 등장한다.

N [타V -ing + 목적어 / -ed (수식어)]

Customers (**using**/used) our online banking system complained about its inconvenience.
➡ 명사 뒤에서 수식할 때는 -ing 능동형의 경우 목적어(명사)와 함께 구를 형성한다.
우리 온라인뱅킹 시스템을 이용하는 고객들은 이것의 불편함에 불만을 토로했다.

C. 보어 자리
2형식이나 5형식의 보어 자리에서 각각 주어 또는 목적어의 상태를 설명하기 위해 형용사를 대체하여 분사가 등장한다.

| 2형식: be, become, stay, remain + 보어(형용사/분사) |
| 5형식: leave, keep, consider, find + 목적어 + 보어(형용사/분사) |

The Study Abroad Foundation has been **operated** for college students since 2010. <2형식>
Study Abroad Foundation은 대학생들을 위해 2010년 이래로 계속 운영되고 있다.

The board of directors considered him **interested** in the marketing fields. <5형식>
이사회는 그가 마케팅 분야에 관심을 가지고 있다고 판단했다.

SPARTA Check-UP

정답 및 해설 p. 423

We are seeking for qualified employees who will be hired for the newly ------ managerial positions in the East Asia branches.

(A) create
(B) creating
(C) created
(D) creator

SPARTA | Grammar Point 2

부사 자리

완전한 문장을 제외한 나머지 부분에 분사로 문장 전체를 수식하는 형태이다. 이를 분사구문이라고 부른다.

A. 분사구문

분사구문은 분사로 구를 형성해 부사절 문장을 대체하여 문장 전체를 수식한다. 분사구문을 만드는 순서를 확인하고 이해한다.

> **분사구문 만들기**
>
> Step 1. 부사절 접속사의 생략
> Step 2. 부사절 접속사의 주어 생략 (주절의 주어와 같은 경우)
> Step 3. 시제가 같다면 부사절의 동사에 Ving, 시제가 다르다면 부사절 동사를
>   Having Ved 형태로 만든다.
>   (Being Ved 형태에서 being은 생략 가능하다.)

While he edited the articles in the magazine, Mr. John found some errors in most sections.
➡ **Editing the articles in the magazine**, Mr. John found some errors in most sections.
   그가 잡지 기사문을 편집하는 동안, John 씨는 대부분의 섹션에서 오류를 발견했다.

➡ (1) 접속사 while 생략, (2) 동일 주어인 he 생략, (3) 시제가 같으므로 동사를 Editing으로 변경.
➡ 부사 자리의 분사는 위와 같이 구의 형태이므로 Ving 능동형 뒤에는 목적어가, Ved 수동형 뒤에는 생략 가능한 수식어가 온다. 단, 자동사는 능동형 분사만 가능하다.

B. 시간/조건 부사절 접속사와 분사구문

시간/조건 부사절 접속사의 경우, 분사구문을 만들 때, 해당 접속사를 생략하지 않고 남겨 둘 수 있다.

> 시간/조건 부사절 접속사 + { 타Ving + O / 타Ved (수식어) / 형용사 / 전치사 + 명사 } , 주어 + 동사 ~

➡ 중복되는 주어와 의미가 없는 be동사(being)가 생략되는 경우, 분사 이외에 보어 역할을 하던 형용사나 전치사구가 나올 수 있다.
➡ 명사는 주격 보어로 주어와 같기 때문에 분사구문이 만들어지면서 주절의 주어와 같기 때문에 생략되므로 시간/조건 부사절 접속사에 연결되지 못한다. (명사는 전치사로 연결)

When applying for the position, please submit the application package with three recommendation letters.
그 직책에 지원하실 때, 3부의 추천서와 함께 지원 패키지를 제출하세요.

SPARTA Check-UP

정답 및 해설 p. 423

------ by the board of directors, the restructuring plan can help make company's work procedures more efficient than before.

(A) Propose (B) To propose
(C) Proposing (D) Proposed

SPARTA Grammar Point 3

분사 응용 표현

분사를 활용한 응용 패턴으로 감정 동사의 분사형과 형용사로 굳어진 표현들이 있다.

A. 감정 동사의 분사

동사의 의미가 동작이 아닌 "감정"을 의미하는 경우, 능동형(-ing)은 사물 명사와, 수동형(-ed)은 사람 명사와 함께 쓰인다.

```
감정    타 V  -ing  N   명사가 감정의 원인인 "사물"
              -ed       명사가 감정을 느끼는 "사람"
```

➡ 동작 동사의 분사와 달리, 감정 동사의 분사는 문장의 어느 위치에 오든지, 구의 형태가 아닌 한 단어로 수식 또는 보충하면서, 명사와의 관계로만 결정된다.

GNQ Asset Co. is **pleased** to announce the promotion of three employees to managerial positions in each department.
GNG Asset 사는 세 명의 직원을 각 부서의 관리직으로의 승진을 발표하게 되어 기쁩니다.

감정 동사			
excite 흥분시키다	bore 지루하게 하다	interest 흥미를 주다	confuse 혼란시키다
satisfy 만족시키다	embarrass 당황하게 하다	surprise 놀라게 하다	disappoint 실망시키다
astonish 놀라게 하다	bewilder 혼란스럽게 하다	overwhelm 압도하다	distract 산만하게 하다
startle 놀라게 하다	exhaust 기진 맥진하게 만들다	alarm 놀라게 하다	tire 피곤하게 하다

B. 분사형 형용사

-ing나 -ed인 분사형이 형용사로 굳어져 사용되는 표현을 학습하자.

-ing 형용사		
demanding 까다로운	challenging 힘든	encouraging 고무적인
rewarding 가치 있는	promising 전도유망한	missing 잃어버린
surrounding 둘러싼	following 다음의	entertaining 즐겁게 하는

➡ 그 밖의 V-ing형 형용사로 쓰이는 것들은 "증가", "감소" 또는 "2형식" 자동사로 만들어진 분사이다.

-ed 형용사		
renowned 이름난	experienced 능숙한	motivated 동기 부여된
talented 재능 있는	dedicated 헌신하는	skilled 숙련된
distinguished 유명한	recognized 인식되는	qualified 자격을 갖춘

➡ 위의 분사형들은 동사의 수동형(타Ved)이지만, 주로 "사람" 명사를 수식/보충한다.

SPARTA Check-UP

정답 및 해설 p. 423

As the thanksgiving holiday is approaching, the sales of gift items in all our branches have become -------.
(A) overwhelm (B) overwhelmed
(C) overwhelming (D) overwhelmingly

SPARTA — Grammar Point 4

어휘형 분사의 쓰임

동작을 당하는 수동형 분사인 경우 주로 사물과 함께 쓰이지만, 사람 명사가 등장하는 경우가 있다. 그리고 분사 자체가 형용사로 쓰여서 사람/사물 구분을 따로 하지 않는 경우가 있다.

A. -ing 분사 = 형용사

ing형 분사가 형용사 역할로 쓰이는 경우를 확인하도록 한다.

alarming 경각심을 일깨워주는	beginning 초보의	challenging 어려운
demanding 까다로운	encouraging 고무적인	existing 존재하는
growing 커져가는	incoming 들어오는	lasting 지속되는
limiting 제한하는	leading 선두의	operating 운영의
promising 유망한	remaining 남아 있는	rewarding 보람 있는
rising 증가하는	surrounding 둘러싼	worrying 걱정스러운

➡ 증가/감소, 오고/가는(이동)과 관련된 "자동사"들은 원래 능동형(Ving)분사만 가능하다.

The courses of civil engineering are some of the most **demanding** and **time-consuming** programs at our college. 토목 공학 강좌는 우리 대학에서 가장 힘들고 시간 소비적인 프로그램 중 일부이다.

B. -ed 분사 = 형용사

-ed형 분사가 형용사 역할로 쓰이는 경우를 확인하도록 한다.

complicated 복잡한	crowded 붐비는	detailed 자세한
distinguished 유명한	enclosed 첨부된	experienced 능숙한
expired 기간이 만료된	involved 포함된	motivated 동기부여 받은
renowned 유명한	tired 피곤한	skilled 능숙한
specialized 전문적인	talented 재능 있는	valued 소중한
dedicated 헌신하는	devoted 헌신하는	committed 헌신하는

➡ 이중에서, '유명한, 능숙한, 재능 있는, 헌신하는'의 의미는 주로 사람 명사를 수식/보충하는 역할을 한다.

Ms. Sue, one of our teachers, is a very **dedicated** and **talented** member of our language education team.
우리 교사 중 한 명인 Sue 씨는 우리 언어교육 팀의 매우 헌신적이고 재능 있는 일원이다.

SPARTA Check-UP

정답 및 해설 p. 423

Because our copy machine was out of order, we asked the general affairs department to call an ------- technician as soon as possible.

(A) experience
(B) experiences
(C) experiencing
(D) experienced

SPARTA Practice Test

101. The primary purpose of the ------ research is to acquire detailed information about newly implemented policies.
(A) propose
(B) proposed
(C) proposing
(D) proposal

102. Due to ------- time to finalize the proposal, all of the employees should work overtime and cooperatively communicate with each department.
(A) limit
(B) limited
(C) limits
(D) limitation

103. Once your application is submitted, you will receive an automatic e-mail, ------ your application status for the position.
(A) confirm
(B) confirmed
(C) confirming
(D) confirms

104. Those who are ------- in the seminar on how to start doing E-trading should register for it electronically in advance.
(A) interest
(B) interests
(C) interested
(D) interesting

105. ------- on practical methods for teaching children, our college's curriculum is highly recognized in the U.S.
(A) Focused
(B) To focus
(C) Is focused
(D) Focus

106. Because of low profitability, the board of directors decided to disclose the ------ plants in South Carolina.
(A) exist
(B) existing
(C) existed
(D) exists

107. Please make sure that you mark the sentences and words with a red pen when ------ the article that was received from the writer.
(A) revising
(B) revises
(C) revised
(D) revise

108. ------- to last quarter's profit statistics, this quarter's sales figures are much better than we expected early this month.
(A) Comparing
(B) Comparison
(C) Compared
(D) Compare

109. The new accountant ------ our team next week has extensive knowledge and experience in the field of auditing corporate finances.
(A) joining
(B) joined
(C) join
(D) will join

110. Most customers were very ------ because the store had never apologized for the inconvenience caused by the delay in shipment.
(A) disappointing
(B) disappointed
(C) disappoint
(D) disappointment

111. The parking zone ------- with yellow lines is designated for handicapped people visiting our store.
    (A) marked
    (B) marking
    (C) that mark
    (D) are marked

112. As the Vietnam is emerging, the ------- for learning Vietnamese language is gradually increasing all over the world.
    (A) demanding
    (B) demand
    (C) demander
    (D) demanded

113. As of tomorrow, all the applicants will be ------ into twelve groups for various types of successive interviews for a week.
    (A) divided
    (B) dividing
    (C) divide
    (D) to divide

114. INNOBIZ Ltd. posted a job opening seeking ------ applicants for a legal assistant position.
    (A) qualify
    (B) qualification
    (C) qualifies
    (D) qualified

115. Event notices will be e-mailed to all employees for the banquet ------ Ms. Krisha, who will be retiring on August 20.
    (A) honored
    (B) honoring
    (C) honorable
    (D) honor

116. Lingua Language Lab would be ------- to recruit Mr. Kramsch, who is widely renowned for establishing innovative and creative language theories.
    (A) delight
    (B) delightful
    (C) delighted
    (D) delighting

117. In response to the newly constructed department store's ------ popularity, the executives decided to expand its stores into the wings.
    (A) grown
    (B) grows
    (C) growing
    (D) grew

118. Analysts were ------- by the number of consumers who selected to purchase luxury sedan rather than a cheap one.
    (A) startle
    (B) startled
    (C) startling
    (D) to startle

119. The company plans to recruit a finance expert that will be ------- to systemizing our financial structures.
    (A) dedication
    (B) dedicated
    (C) dedicating
    (D) dedicates

120. ------- that the amount of certain items is limited, we can expect that a lot of people will wait in a long line to buy them on Black Friday.
    (A) To consider
    (B) Consideration
    (C) Consider
    (D) Considering

Questions 121-124 refer to the following e-mail.

To: Ms. Emma Watson <e.watson0605@nixonenergy.net>
From: Business Month Magazine <customerservice@businessmonth.org.us>
Date: July 30
Subject: Business Month

Dear Ms. Watson,

We are writing about the earlier ------- notice regarding your annual subscription to *Business Month* magazine.
121.

Because you registered to extend your subscription for another 12 months under the delayed payment program, your first installment payment will not be due until September 1. -------, you can pay at any time before the date of
122.
the installment.

We are glad to inform you that you can get free access to the online edition of our magazine, ordinarily a $100 value. Subscribers ------- this site will be charged no additional fee. -------.
123. **124.**

Thank you again for reading *Business Month*.

Sincerely,

Anne Isaiah
Subscription Director

121. (A) refund
(B) exchange
(C) percentage
(D) renewal

122. (A) Nevertheless
(B) For example
(C) Of course
(D) Meanwhile

123. (A) used
(B) using
(C) have used
(D) will use

124. (A) In fact, payments can now be made online at your convenience.
(B) You may send feedback through the online survey form.
(C) The next issue will be delivered on September 20.
(D) You can access it right now at www.buisnessmonth.org.us.

SPARTA Grammar Review

(1) -ing 분사는 동작을 "직접 하는" 능동형, -ed 분사는 동작을 "당하는" 수동형 분사로 이해한다.

(2) 명사 앞에서는 한 단어로 직접 수식하는 분사로 뒤따르는 명사와의 의미 관계를 통해 선택한다.

(3) 그외 자리는 구 형태로 수식하므로 능동형(타Ving)은 목적어와, 수동형(타Ved)은 수식어와 함께 한다.

(4) 자동사는 수동형이 불가능, 능동형 분사(자Ving)만 가능하다.

(5) 감정 동사로 분사를 쓸 때는, 사물 명사와는 능동형(감정Ving), 사람 명사와는 수동형(감정Ved)을 선택한다.

(6) V-ing 또는 V-ed 형으로 굳어진 형용사 표현들을 암기해 두도록 한다.

DAY 10 명사절과 형용사절

SPARTA 유형 파악

명사절은 <주어+동사>가 포함된 절의 형태가 주어, 목적어, 보어 자리인 명사 자리를 대신한다. 형용사절은 <주어+동사>가 포함된 절의 형태가 명사 뒤에서 수식하는 기능을 한다. 명사절/형용사절 모두 종속절의 한 종류로, 문장의 큰 틀에 속하는 문장 덩어리인데, 종속절의 종류에는 무엇이 있는지 확인해 보자.

SPARTA 출제 포인트

☑ 종속절의 종류

문장이라는 큰 틀에서 명사, 형용사, 부사를 대신하여 쓰이는 절을 종속절이라 하고, 이를 연결해 주는 접속사가 종속접속사이다. 문장 안에서의 위치에 따라 그 쓰임이 달라진다.

문장에서의 위치

구조		역할	종류
주어 + 타동사 + ___접속사+주어+동사___.		[목적어 자리] :	명사절
주어 + 타동사 + 목적어 (명사) ___접속사+주어+동사___.		[명사 수식] :	형용사절
___접속사+주어+동사___, 주어 + 타동사 + 목적어.		[부사 자리] :	부사절

☑ 명사절의 종류

명사절은 사실 여부와 관련된 것을 다룬다. 100% 사실을 나타내는 접속사 that, 아직 결정되지 않는 사실을 나타내는 whether나 if, 전체 정보 중 특정 정보를 묻는 wh- 의문사로 나눌 수 있다. 알맞은 것을 선택하기 위해 동사의 의미를 파악해서 가장 어울리는 접속사를 찾도록 한다.

☑ 형용사절 생성 원리

형용사절 접속사란, 앞에 나온 명사(선행사)를 수식하는 절을 연결하는 관계사를 가리킨다. 앞서, 명사절에서 보았던 의문사 대부분이 형용사절(관계사절)에도 사용된다. 관계대명사는 <접속사+대명사> 역할을 하면서 선행사를 수식하고, 관계부사는 <접속사+부사> 역할을 하면서 선행사를 수식한다.

I have learned English, [and] [it] is very interesting to me.
　　　　　　　　　　(선행사) 접속사 대명사

➡ I have learned English, [which] is very interesting to me.
　　　　　　　　　　　　　　<접속사+대명사(주어)>

저는 매우 흥미로운 영어를 배웠습니다.

SPARTA 문제 풀이 비법

Most of our citizens obviously know ------ our city's healthcare system is the best in the country.

(A) in that
(B) that
(C) in order that
(D) now that

대부분의 우리 시민들은 우리 시의 의료보호 제도가 전국에서 최고라는 것을 명백히 알고 있다.

✅ know라는 타동사 뒤 목적어(명사) 자리에 <주어+동사>인 절이 나왔으므로 명사절, 이를 연결하는 (B) that이 정답이다. (A) in that ~라는 점에서(원인), (C) in order that ~하기 위해(목적), (D) now that ~이기 때문에(원인)의 접속사들은 모두 부사절 접속사이다. 보기 중 명사절 접속사는 (B) that이 유일하다.

SPARTA Grammar Point 1

명사절 접속사 that

A. that의 위치

100% 사실을 이야기하는 명사절 접속사 that은 주어, 목적어, 보어 자리의 절(주어+동사)를 연결해 준다.

$$\underline{\text{That S V O}} \quad \text{타} \: V \quad \underline{\text{that S V O}}$$

➡ 주의) 명사절 접속사 that은 전치사의 목적어(전치사 뒤)에는 올 수 없다. 수식어 자리인 콤마(,) 뒤에도 올 수 없다.
➡ 명사절이 주어 자리에 오면 단수 취급한다.

That the company attracted a lot of new customers **is** deeply related to their marketing strategies.
그 회사가 많은 신규 고객을 모았다는 것은 그들의 마케팅 전략과 깊은 관련이 있다.

B. 사실 의미의 형용사와 that

"사실" 여부와 관련된 형용사가 나오면 that 명사절이 올 수 있다.

> sure (확신하는) certain (확신하는) confident (확신하는)
> aware (알고있는) afraid (염려하는) concerned (걱정하는) **that S V O**

The analysts are |confident **that**| we can recover from this economic recession.
분석가들은 우리가 이번 경기침체로부터 회복될 수 있다고 확신했다..

whether/if: 명사절 접속사 vs. 부사절 접속사

아직 결정되지 않은 사실을 이야기할 때 "~인지 아닌지"의 의미로 사용된다.

	명사절 접속사	부사절 접속사
if	~인지 아닌지	만일 ~라면
whether		~인지 아닌지

A. whether와 if의 위치

whether는 명사 자리(주어, 목적어, 보어) 어디든 올 수 있다.

Mr. Kim e-mailed me to ask **whether there is a train station near our office**.
Kim 씨는 우리 사무실 근처에 기차역이 있는지 물어보려고 이메일을 보냈다.

Whether employees want to proceed with the project |**or**| **not**, we should do it.
직원들이 그 프로젝트를 진행하기를 원하든 원하지 않든, 우리는 그것을 해야 한다.

➡ 부사절(부사 자리)의 whether는 or가 반드시 필요하다.
➡ if가 명사절 접속사로 쓰일 때, 타동사의 목적어(동사 뒤) 자리에만 올 수 있다.
➡ 부사절 접속사로 쓰일 때는 "~라면"이라는 뜻의 조건/가정의 접속사로 쓰인다.

SPARTA Check-UP

정답 및 해설 p. 426

The consultant recommended ------ our company make a detailed handbook for new recruits in order for them to adapt to the work effectively.

(A) what (B) that
(C) when (D) whether

SPARTA Grammar Point 2

명사절 접속사 wh- 의문사

특정 사항에 대한 의문이 있을 때 쓰는 접속사로, 사람/사물/상황에 대해 묻는 의문대명사와, 시간/장소/이유/방법에 대해 묻는 의문부사로 나뉜다.

A. 의문대명사

<접속사+대명사> 기능을 하면서 주어나 목적어 자리 등에 오는 사람/사물/상황에 대한 의문사이다. 의문대명사 뒤에 연결되는 문장은 주어나 목적어가 없는 불완전한 구조가 된다.

who / which / what + **(S) 타V O**
(사람) (사물) (사물/상황) **S 타V (O)**

➡ 자동사나 수동태의 경우, 주어 또는 전치사의 목적어가 없는 구조가 등장한다.

After finishing the recruitment process, we will consider **who is best suitable for the position**.
채용 절차가 마무리된 후, 우리는 누가 그 직책에 가장 적합할지 고민할 것이다.

➡ 사람이 "주어"역할을 하므로 주어가 없는 불완전 구조

B. 의문부사

<접속사+부사> 기능을 하면서 문장에서 부사(수식어) 역할을 하는 요소에 대한 의문을 제기할 때 쓰인다. 시간/장소/원인/방법에 대한 요소가 문장에서 수식어 역할을 하므로 연결되는 문장은 완전한 구조가 된다.

when / where / why / how + **S 타V O**
(시간) (장소) (이유) (방법)

➡ 수동태나 자동사는 원래 목적어가 필요 없으므로 완전한 구조이다.
➡ how가 "얼마나"(정도)를 의미하는 경우, <how + 형용사/부사 + 주어 + 동사> 구조로 나올 수 있다.

We should learn **how Quix Electornics has accomplished its considerable success in the field**.
우리는 Quix Electronics 사가 어떻게 그 분야에서 엄청난 성공을 달성했는지 배워야 한다.

➡ "방법"은 부사적 의미이기 때문에 뒤에 완전한 구조가 연결된다.

C. wh- 의문사와 to부정사

wh-로 시작하는 의문사는 to부정사와 연결되어 명사구 역할을 할 수 있다. while(~동안/반면에), whereas(반면에)는 wh-로 시작하지만 의문사가 아닌 부사절 접속사 중 하나이다.

We need to know **whether to plan to hire additional workers in the Atlanta plant**.
우리는 애틀란타 공장에 추가 노동자들을 고용할 계획인지 알 필요가 있다.

SPARTA Check-UP 2

정답 및 해설 p. 426

Members of each city council in Pennsylvania are under negotiation to determine ------ will host the National Sports Tournament.

(A) when
(B) which
(C) where
(D) whereas

SPARTA Grammar Point 3

관계대명사

A. 관계대명사의 격

일반 대명사에도 자리에 따른 격(형태 변화)이 있듯이, 관계대명사도 선행사의 종류와 뒤따르는 문장에서의 위치에 따라서 관계대명사의 격(형태)이 달라진다.

선행사	주격	소유격	목적격
사람	who	whose	who(m)
사물	which	whose of which	which
사람·사물	that	/	that

➡ 전치사의 목적어(전치사 뒤) 자리에서는 사람 선행사의 경우 whom만 가능하다.
➡ 선행사가 사람이든 사물이든 소유격은 whose로 쓸 수 있다.
➡ 사람/사물 선행사가 상관없는 that은 소유격이 없다.

The manager **who(m) we always report** will be out of the office for a while because of his illness.
우리가 항상 보고하는 그 매니저는 아파서 한동안 사무실을 비울 것이다.

The bridge **which has been under construction** will be open to the public soon.
공사중인 그 다리는 곧 대중에게 개방될 것이다.

B. 소유격 관계대명사 whose의 쓰임

소유격 관계대명사 whose는 선행사로 사람/사물 모두 가능하고, 뒤따르는 명사를 반드시 한정해야 한다. 이때, 뒤따르는 명사는 대명사나 동명사가 아닌 관사 없는 일반 명사가 와야 한다.

명사 + [**whose 명사** + (주어) + 동사 + (목적어)]

➡ <whose+명사>의 구조가 주어 역할을 할 때, 완전한 문장처럼 보일 수 있다.

The professor **whose class I have been taking this semester** has gradually become popular among students.
이번 학기에 내가 수강하는 수업의 교수가 학생들 사이에서 점점 인기를 얻고 있다.

SPARTA Check-UP

정답 및 해설 p. 426

The new employees ------ complete this on-the-job training session are given their tasks as a member of each team.

(A) who (B) which
(C) whose (D) what

SPARTA Grammar Point 4

관계부사

<접속사+부사> 기능으로 뒤에 완전한 문장을 연결한다.

A. 관계부사와 선행사

선행사	관계부사	전치사 + 관계대명사
the time(시간)	when	in/on/at which
the place(장소)	where	in/on/at which
the reason(이유)	why	for which
the way(방법)	how	by which

➡ 선행사의 속성만 파악하면 바로 답을 고를 수 있는 유형으로 출제된다.
➡ how는 선행사가 포함되었으므로, the way 또는 how 둘 중 하나만 사용한다.

장소 This building is [the place] **where** crucial decisions are made. 이 건물은 중요한 결정이 이루어지는 장소이다.
시간 We don't know [the time] **when** the funds are transferred into our account.
     우리는 자금이 우리 계좌로 이체되는 시간을 알 수 없다.
이유 Find out [the reason] **why** sales of our new products are decreasing. 우리 신제품들의 판매가 감소하는 이유를 찾으세요.
방법 This is **how** we learn the TOEIC test. (= This is [the way] **by which** we learn the TOEIC test.)
     이것은 우리가 토익 시험을 공부하는 방법이다.

B. 전치사와 관계대명사

<전치사 + 관계대명사 (whom/which)>는 관계부사와 같은 기능을 한다.

명사 [전치사 + whom / 전치사 + which] S 타V O 완전한 문장

This is the place **in which** you will be trained for the following two weeks.
= This is the place **where** you will be trained for the following two weeks.
여기는 여러분이 앞으로 2주동안 훈련을 받게 될 곳입니다.

C. 복합 관계사

wh-로 시작하는 의문사와 부사인 ever가 합쳐진 합성어로, 명사절, 부사절 등으로 사용된다. 즉, 선행사가 포함된 형태로, 선행사인 명사 뒤에서 수식할 수 없다.

	명사절	부사절
whoever	= anyone who	no matter who
whichever	= anything that	no matter which
whatever	= anything that	no matter what
whenever	=	no matter when
wherever	=	no matter where
however + 형용사/부사	=	no matter how + 형용사/부사

➡ -ever가 붙으면서 선행사가 포함된다. 뒤따르는 문장의 완성도는 변함없이 불완전한 문장이다.
➡ however가 접속사(얼마든지)로 쓰일 경우, 반드시 형용사 또는 부사가 뒤따라야 한다. (그렇지 않을 경우, 부사 '하지만'으로 쓰인 것임)

SPARTA Check-UP

정답 및 해설 p. 426

Articles published and reviewed by prestigious scholars explain the most common reasons ------ big companies hesitate to invest in the stock.

(A) when   (B) where   (C) which   (D) why

194 |

SPARTA Practice Test

101. Of our home appliances you asked about, we cannot be sure about ------ product is the best for your home if you do not give us detailed information.
(A) when
(B) why
(C) which
(D) where

102. When we heard breaking news about a sudden change in oil prices, we were afraid ------ the prices of raw materials will rise considerably.
(A) that
(B) whether
(C) which
(D) whoever

103. Our manager notified us ------ we should work overtime during the peak season to support the store's clerks.
(A) that
(B) what
(C) which
(D) where

104. ------ Broad & Speed Network Co. will accept our business proposal or not remains to be seen for a while.
(A) That
(B) Whether
(C) Which
(D) What

105. Two weeks before and after Christmas is ------- our sales figures are rapidly increasing because of the purchase of gifts.
(A) how
(B) for
(C) when
(D) what

106. At this meeting, the planning division should discuss ------ to make a strategy for our future business.
(A) whereas
(B) while
(C) how
(D) which

107. We would like to know ------ the delegation of Taiwan can attend this summit talk in Korea on July 20.
(A) even as
(B) if
(C) even if
(D) as if

108. ------- Cowa Industry Co. invested in the stock is very surprising in that it always purchase stable stocks.
(A) That
(B) Which
(C) What
(D) When

109. It is essential ------ the company gives their employees the same opportunities to show their job performance.
(A) during
(B) how
(C) about
(D) this

110. Our team members will decide ------ will be prepared for our quarterly outing and check the number of attendees.
(A) if
(B) that
(C) what
(D) whether

111. Users ------- want to renew the product's warranty should notify each service center at least 40 days before its expiration date.
    (A) which
    (B) whose
    (C) whom
    (D) who

112. The executives are planning to attend the annual conference ------- will be held in Austin, Texas, in the U.S next week.
    (A) what
    (B) which
    (C) who
    (D) when

113. Any old company computers ------- need to be replaced should be checked and reported to the general affairs division.
    (A) this
    (B) that
    (C) these
    (D) those

114. The hotel management discussed plans for the construction of the new event hall, ------- is expected to open in the new year.
    (A) which
    (B) whose
    (C) when
    (D) where

115. Graduate students, most of ------- graduated from prestigious universities, have shown great performance in various academic fields.
    (A) it
    (B) whom
    (C) which
    (D) those

116. Current investors in Anan Cove Co. ------ shares are over 10 millions may lose their money due to its tax investigation.
    (A) whose
    (B) which
    (C) what
    (D) who

117. Well-Done Stationery is located slightly past the Penn Intersection, ------ the Innobiz Center is located on the right side of the street.
    (A) near
    (B) beside
    (C) where
    (D) which

118. Papago Electronics will unveil its newly developed refrigerator for restaurant owners, ------ is the most efficient in energy saving.
    (A) both
    (B) which
    (C) besides
    (D) since

119. ------- willing to donate their used items needs to notify the city community center about the list of them by Friday.
    (A) Anyone
    (B) Whatever
    (C) Who
    (D) Whoever

120. The ------ which are presented by each manager should be reliable in their statistics based on their market research.
    (A) reported
    (B) reporting
    (C) report
    (D) reports

Questions 121-124 refer to the following review.

Little Pythagoras

By Joe Clein

The latest fall blockbuster is *Little Pythagoras*. ------- **121.**. It is about a young boy named Amatheus, ------- **122.** shows signs of genius in math and does not hesitate to answer all the mathematical questions.

He is brave, decisive, smart, and surely is a positive role model for teenagers. All parents with underaged kids will consider his adventures ------- **123.**.

This movie's only fault is that the complicated plot makes it confusing, ------- **124.** is especially problematic for children under 10 years old. Also, I think that its running time of nearly two hours is somewhat long for them.

The overall story, however, is highly fantastic and exciting, so I would like to strongly recommend it to everyone.

---

121. (A) It was first found in a novel about Mesopotamia.
(B) It was written and directed by Michael Straus.
(C) This formula is very useful for our daily life.
(D) Maybe you will have difficulty getting a ticket.

122. (A) for
(B) as
(C) who
(D) neither

123. (A) to interest
(B) interesting
(C) have interested
(D) will interest

124. (A) who
(B) which
(C) that
(D) why

SPARTA Grammar Review

<명사절>

(1) 명사절 접속사 that은 사실에 근거해 기술하면서, 완전한 문장을 연결한다.

(2) 명사 뒤 접속사 that(형용사절 접속사)은 불완전한 문장을 연결한다.

(3) whether는 명사절에서 or not이 생략 가능하지만 부사절에서는 or를 반드시 함께 써야 한다.

(4) 명사절 접속사 if(인지 아닌지)는 타동사 뒤 목적어 자리에만 가능하다.

(5) 의문대명사(who/which/what)는 뒤에 불완전한 문장이 온다.

(6) 의문사들은 to부정사와 연결되어 명사구 역할을 한다.

<형용사절>

(1) 선행사(명사)가 빈칸 앞에 나오면 오답이 되는 what, how, wh-ever에 주의한다.

(2) 선행사가 사람인지 사물인지 구분한다.

(3) 뒤따르는 문장의 완성도를 확인한다. who/which/what은 뒤에 불완전한 문장이 이어진다.

(4) when/where/why/how는 완전한 문장을 이끈다.

(5) 동사 뒤 that(명사절)은 완전한 문장, 명사 뒤 that(형용사절)은 불완전한 문장을 이끈다.

(6) whose는 앞뒤로 명사가 오는데, 뒤에는 일반 명사가 온다.

(7) 선행사 뒤의 <전치사+관계대명사>는 완전한 구조를 이끈다.

books.english.co.kr

PART 7
독해

DAY 11 | 주제/목적 찾기 유형
DAY 12 | 세부사항 및 추론 유형
DAY 13 | 문장 넣기 유형
DAY 14 | 의도 파악 및 유의어 유형
DAY 15 | 다중 지문 유형

PART 7 접근법

PART 7은 어휘에 대한 기본 지식과 문장을 구성하는 문법적 지식이 통합되는 파트로, 이에 따른 문장 분석 및 문제 풀이 순서를 명확하게 인지하고 문제를 풀어야 한다.

🛡 문제 풀이 전략

① 글의 종류 확인 → ② 주제/목적 찾기(글의 초반부) → ③ 문제 분석의 순서로 글을 읽는 연습을 한다. 각 지문의 종류 별로 요구하는 키워드(Key Word)가 있으니 확인하고, 첫 문단 또는 2-3문장을 먼저 읽어 글의 목적과 전개 방식을 예측한다. 그리고 나서 보기를 확인하면서 문제의 내용과 매칭시켜 나간다.

Question 1 refers to the following notice.

> **Millnersville University**
> **Orientation Day**
>
> 11:00 A.M.–4:00 P.M.
> August 25
>
> Millnersville University is delighted to announce its annual Orientation Day to welcome students joining us for the new semester, which will start on September 1. This is the perfect opportunity for new students to find out more about available lectures, course hours, tuitions, and the practical certifications we offer.
>
> It will also provide a chance to join seminars including "Webinars"(our online class system). In addition, this will be the first time we hold special information sessions for working students who may need assistance in adapting to school life. You will also have an opportunity to meet department coordinators, professors and administrative personnel.
>
> Complimentary refreshments will be served in our snack bars throughout the day. Hope to see you there!
>
> Participation in the Orientation Day is limited to students. We ask that parents and friends of students come to our Open House Day, held each summer semester.

(1) 글의 종류 확인
 : 공지문
 → 무엇을 공지하는가?

(2) 지문 초반 읽기
 : 주제 / 목적 찾기
 → 신입생을 위한 Orientation Day에 대해 알려 주고자 하는 글

Q1. What is the main purpose of the notice? 주제/목적 찾기
 (A) To inform prospective students their admission
 (B) To discuss the availability for specific classes
 (C) To advertise their event for new students
 (D) To notify faculty members of new information

(3) 문제 분석
 : 보기까지 해석
 → 글의 내용 매칭

해석 이 공지문의 주된 목적은 무엇인가?
 (A) 예비 학생들에게 그들의 입학 허가를 알려주기 위해
 (B) 특정 수업의 이용 가능성을 논의하기 위해
 (C) 신입생들을 위한 행사를 알리기 위해
 (D) 교직원들에게 새로운 정보를 알려주기 위해

해설 글의 첫 번째 문단, 첫 문장 "to announce its annual Orientation Day to welcome students joining us for the new semester,"를 통해 신입생 오리엔테이션을 알리기 위한 것임을 알 수 있으므로 (C)가 정답이다.

Question 2 refers to the following letter.

Supreme-Mart

July 30

Mr. Cavin Feige
92 Fleming Avenue
Indiana, PA 15701

Dear Mr. Feige,

Congratulations!
Your essay has been awarded the first prize in the regular category of the Supreme Mart and I Contest sponsored by Supreme Mart. We wish to celebrate your accomplishment at an award ceremony on Friday, August 5, at the Eagles Ballroom. –[1]–. Upon entering our store, turn left and walk past the information desk to get to the conference floor, where the ceremony will be held. –[2]–.

The winning essays will be published in the Supreme Mart Newsletter, which is sent to our members, and posted on our Web site. In addition, they will be printed out and displayed in all Supreme Mart stores. –[3]–. As a first-place winner, you will receive a 300-dollar gift voucher redeemable at any Supreme Mart stores before December 31. –[4]–.
Again, congratulations on your outstanding essay!

Sincerely,
Brad Triana
Brad Triana, Manager
Supreme Mart Co.

Q2. In which of the positions marked [1], [2], [3] and [4] does the following sentence best belong?

> "You can pick it up at the award ceremony, or sent it to you with an address which you wrote on the submission."

(A) [1]
(B) [2]
(C) [3]
(D) [4]

해석

Supreme-Mart

7월 30일

Cavin Feige 씨
92 Fleming Avenue
Indiana, PA 15701

Feige 씨에게,

축하합니다!
귀하의 수필이 Supreme Mart가 후원하는 "Supreme Mart와 나"라는 주제의 일반 범주에서 1등을 수상하였습니다. 저희는 8월 5일 금요일 Eagles Ballroom에서 열리는 시상식에서 귀하의 수상을 축하했으면 합니다. 저희 매장으로 들어오시자마자, 왼쪽으로 안내데스크를 지나서 시상식이 열리는 컨퍼런스 층쪽으로 오세요.
수상작들은 Supreme Mart의 뉴스레터에 실릴 것이고, 이는 저희 회원들에게 보내지고 웹사이트에 게시될 것입니다. 게다가, 그것들은 출력되어 모든 Supreme Mart 매장에 전시될 것입니다. 1등 수상자로서, 귀하는 12월 31일 전까지 모든 Supreme Mart에서 사용할 수 있는 300달러 상당의 상품 교환권을 받게 됩니다. 그것을 시상식에서 수령하시거나, 제출물에 적힌 주소로 보내드릴 수 있습니다.
다시 한번, 당신의 훌륭한 수필에 대해 축하 드립니다!

진심으로,
Brad Triana
Brad Triana, 매니저
Supreme Mart 사

Q2. [1], [2], [3] 그리고 [4]로 표시된 곳 중 다음 문장의 위치로 가장 적절한 곳은 어디인가?

"그것을 시상식에서 수령하시거나, 제출물에 적힌 주소로 보내드릴 수 있습니다."

(A) [1]
(B) [2]
(C) [3]
(D) [4]

해설 "~ pick it up ~"에서 it은 '수령하는 물건'으로, [4] 앞 문장에서 "300달러 상당의 상품 교환권(a 300-dollar gift voucher)을 받게 된다"고 했으므로 [4]가 가장 적절하다.

Tip
PART 7의 문장 위치 찾기 유형의 접근법은 "지시어"와 "연결어"를 중심으로 한다는 점에서 PART 6와 유사하다. PART 6의 경우, 정해져 있는 위치에 문맥상 알맞은 "문장"을 넣는 데 반해, PART 7은 제시된 문장을 문맥상 알맞은 "위치"에 대입시키는 것이다.
PART 7의 문장 위치 찾기 유형의 경우, 글의 유형을 파악한 뒤 제시 문장을 먼저 읽고, 지문을 읽어 나가면서 알맞은 위치를 찾아야 한다.

DAY 11 주제/목적 찾기 유형

SPARTA 유형 파악

PART 7에서 비중이 높은 주제/목적 찾기 유형이다. 글의 초반부를 통해 해당 지문의 글이 의도하는 바와, 글을 쓴 주제/목적을 찾으면서 글의 전체적인 전개 내용을 예측하며 읽어야 한다.
주제/목적을 묻는 질문은 Why 또는 What으로 묻는다. 이때, 질문에는 purpose, subject, topic, total, goal, intention, about 등이 주로 쓰인다.

Why was the e-mail written? 이메일을 쓴 이유는 무엇인가?
Why has this letter been sent? 편지를 보낸 이유는 무엇인가?
Why was the notice posted? 공지를 게시한 이유는 무엇인가?
What is the purpose of the notice? 공지의 목적은 무엇인가?
What is this information about? 정보는 무엇에 관한 것인가?

SPARTA 문제 풀이 비법

첫 번째 문제가 주제 또는 목적을 묻는다면, [제목 + 첫 2~3 문장]을 읽으면서 키워드를 찾는다. 거의 대부분의 주제/목적 문제가 지문 초반부를 통해 해결되지만, 일부 지문은 전체 맥락을 통해 유추될 수도 있고 글의 마지막에 단서가 등장하는 경우도 간혹 있으니 주의한다.

e.g) 후반부 주제/목적 등장의 맥락
➡ 권유, 요청, 허가 등의 의미를 지닌 맥락의 문장 또는, 서비스 관련한 불만 사항 제기 사항

1. 편지/이메일
편지/이메일을 주고받는 수신자-발신자 확인하기
주로 초반부에서 [~ to부정사 또는 about ~, that ~] 구조를 통해 제시된다.

2. 기사문
기사의 소재가 되는 항목을 찾고, 그에 대한 중심 키워드를 체크한다.
예측, 예상, 의심 등의 보기는 오답일 확률이 높다.

3. 메모-회람
발신자와 수신자가 거의 대부분 [회사 <-> 직원, 지점]의 관계이다.
회사 입장에서 전달하려는 특이 사항 또는 변경 사항이 무엇인지 찾는다.

4. 정보
해당 정보의 대상이 누군지를 파악하면 그 목적을 알 수 있다.

5. 공지문
무엇(what)을 왜(why) 공지하는지 파악하는 것이 첫 번째 순서이다.
공지의 주체와 대상이 누구인지를 동시에 밝혀내야 한다.

SPARTA 주제/목적 찾기 유형 TIP

글의 초반부를 집중적으로 공략함으로써 전체 내용을 예측하며 읽는 훈련을 한다. 제시된 문제를 사실 근거를 바탕으로 분석하며 정보를 매칭해 나가는 것이 필요하다.

Reading Point

Question 1 refers to the following postcard.

Bloomington Department Store
Get up to 60% off

Invitation Code: TL401034

Our fantastic Black Friday sale starts on November 15, and you need to hurry because it will be very popular. We have got a wide range of bargains and clearance items.
There will be big savings on everything from goose down jackets to fabric coats, and from adult apparel to children's clothing. Our friendly staff will be happy to help you!

Bring this postcard with you to get an additional 10% off anything in all our stores.

Don't have time to come into our store? No problem. Go to our online store at www.bloomingtondept.net to find the same great bargains. Enter the invitation code at the left top of this card when you place an order to get the same discounted prices available in our offline store.

In addition, when you shop online, this number automatically registers you for a special event we prepared such as a drawing for a $500 voucher, Random Lucky Box, and so on.

Q1. What is the purpose of the postcard?

(A) To advertise a promotion
(B) To explain membership procedures
(C) To announce a store's holiday
(D) To demonstrate new items

**블루밍턴 백화점
최대 60% 할인을 잡아라!**

초대코드. TL401034

저희의 환상적인 블랙 프라이데이 세일이 11월 15일에 시작하고, 이것은 매우 인기 있기 때문에 서두르셔야 합니다. 저희는 다양한 싼 물건과 재고정리 품목을 판매합니다.
거위털 재킷부터 직물 코트, 성인 의류부터 아이들 의류까지 모든 물건에서 크게 절약하실 수 있습니다. 저희 친절한 직원들이 기쁘게 여러분을 도와드릴 것입니다!

이 엽서를 가지고 오시면 모든 매장에서 10%의 추가 할인을 해 드립니다.

매장으로 직접 오실 시간이 없으세요? 문제없습니다. 저희 온라인 스토어 www.bloomingtondept.net으로 오셔서 이 좋은 세일과 똑같은 것을 찾으실 수 있습니다. 엽서 왼쪽 상단에 있는 초대코드를 주문 시 입력해 주세요, 여러분은 오프라인 매장에서 이용 가능한 할인된 가격으로 똑같이 주문하실 수 있어요.

추가로, 온라인에서 쇼핑하실 때, 이 번호는 저희가 마련해 둔 500달러 상당의 상품권, 랜덤 럭키박스 등의 특별 이벤트에 자동으로 등록됩니다.

Q1. 엽서의 목적은 무엇인가?

(A) 홍보 활동을 알리기 위해
(B) 회원 절차를 설명하기 위해
(C) 매장의 휴일을 알리기 위해
(D) 신제품들을 시연하기 위해

▶ 첫 번째 문장 (Our fantastic Black Friday sale starts on November 15, and you need to hurry because it will be very popular.)에서 할인 판매 시작에 대해 알려주고 있다. 그리고 제목에서 백화점 할인율이 명시되어 있으므로, 판매 촉진을 위한 홍보 활동임을 알 수 있다. 따라서 정답은 (A)이다.

어휘 invitation ⓝ 초대 bargain ⓝ 거래, 염가품 goose ⓝ 거위 fabric ⓝ 직물 apparel ⓝ 의류 discounted ⓐ 할인된 register for ⓥ 등록하다 random ⓐ 무작위의

> **Tip**
> 〈주제-목적〉은 대부분 지문 초반부에 단서가 등장한다. 따라서 첫 1~2문장을 통해 주제를 파악하는 것을 목표로 한다. 기사/광고/메모/공지는 도입부, 편지/이메일은 첫 1~2문장이 핵심이다. 제목이 있는 지문은 제목에서 주제/목적을 유추할 수 있다.

SPARTA Check-UP

Question 1 refers to the following e-mail.

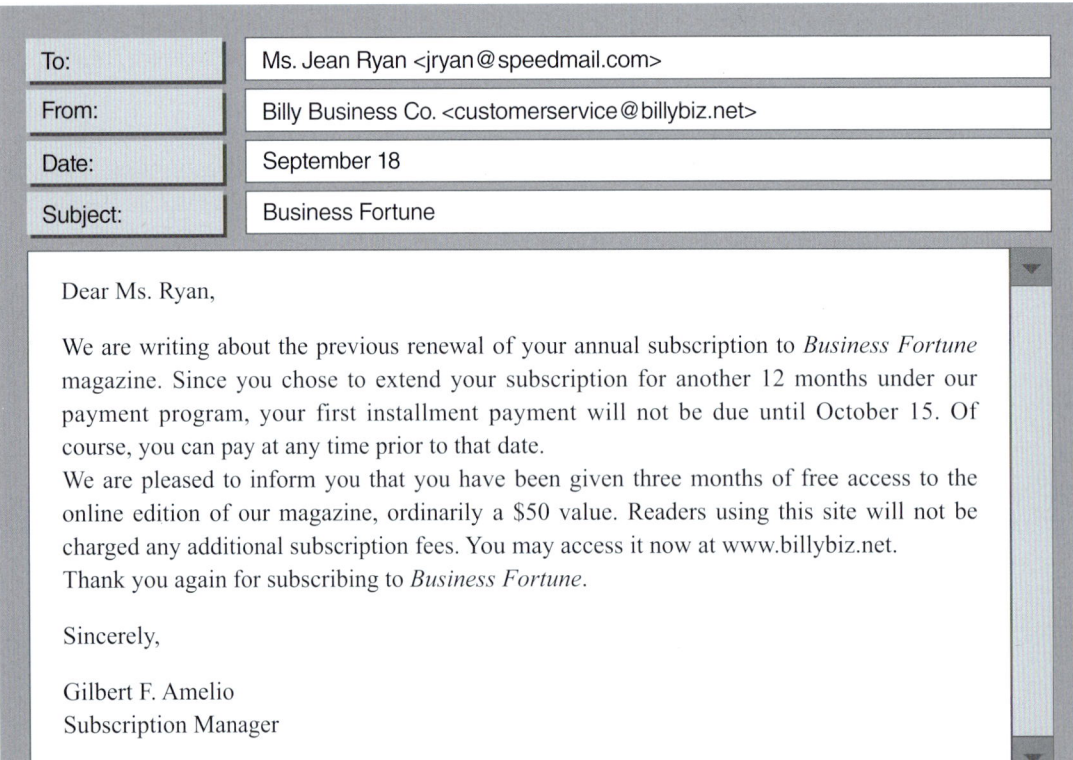

Q1 What is the purpose of the e-mail?

(A) To celebrate a customer's new registration
(B) To notify a customer of updated information
(C) To complain about the current services
(D) To give a customer new financial tips

Question 2 refers to the following notice.

Millnersville University
Orientation Day

11:00 A.M.–4:00 P.M.
August 25

Millnersville University is delighted to announce its annual Orientation Day to welcome students joining us for the new semester, which will start on September 1. This is the perfect opportunity for new students to find out more about available lectures, course hours, tuitions, and the practical certifications we offer.

It will also provide a chance to join seminars including "Webinars"(our online class system). In addition, this will be the first time we hold special information sessions for working students who may need assistance in adapting to school life. You will also have an opportunity to meet department coordinators, professors and administrative personnel.

Complimentary refreshments will be served in our snack bars throughout the day.
Hope to see you there!

Participation in the Orientation Day is limited to students. We ask that parents and friends of students come to our Open House Day, held each summer semester.

Q2. What is the main purpose of the notice?

(A) To inform prospective students their admission
(B) To discuss the availability for specific classes
(C) To advertise their event for new students
(D) To notify faculty members of new information

SPARTA Practice Test

Questions 1-3 refer to the following e-mail.

To: Daniel Joseph <daniel.joseph@bettyzoo.net>
From: Esther Jasmin, Judith Travel <e.jasmin@judithtravel.com>
Date: May 10
Subject: Business Trip

Dear Mr. Joseph,

You are now scheduled to depart for Beijing two days earlier than planned. This will give you the time you need to attend the board of directors meeting the day after you return. I am pleased to confirm that a rental car, a luxury Cancoon model, will be waiting for you at Northern China Airport. You may also be interested to know that you are entitled to a 5% discount on all Holliday Lodge rooms since you are a Travel VIP cardholder. Moreover, you will not have to make reservations 24 hours in advance to receive that discount.

If you need to make a change to your itinerary, the best way to do this is to go to www.judithtravel.com/customers/itinerary and enter your reservation number. Otherwise, you could call me on my desk line directly at 804-211-0445 or fax 804-211-0553. Talking to someone at the airline in person is also possible, but I am concerned that could be a slow process.

I wish you good luck on your trip!

Best regards,

Esther Jasmin
International Manager, Judith Travel

---

1. Why was the e-mail written?

    (A) To advertise a company's new card
    (B) To ask a customer to join a Web site
    (C) To confirm a traveler's reservation
    (D) To notify employees of trip schedules

2. According to the e-mail, how can Mr. Joseph receive a discount?

    (A) By giving the numbers of his rental car
    (B) By having a certain card
    (C) By using a certain hotel chain
    (D) By reserving 24 hours in advance

3. What is the best way to change his itinerary for Mr. Joseph?

    (A) By using the Internet
    (B) By calling Ms. Jasmin
    (C) By contacting the airlines
    (D) By visiting the agency

Questions 4-7 refer to the following e-mail.

To: Colin Hunter, Membership Division
From: Dixie Amanda, General Manager, X-Fit Gym Center
Date: Monday, April 1
Subject: Identity Checks

Dear Mr. Hunter,

I am pleased to see that the number of new memberships is continuously rising. This can definitely help increase our overall revenue. Meanwhile, I noticed that some important tasks are sometimes overlooked. Specifically, the policy of our company is that people applying for memberships should present at least two forms of certified identification such as a driver's license, passport, or a similar government-issued document with a photo.

Copies of them must be saved in the format of a document file, and they must be delivered to each branch manager and the main center manager. In addition, these are entered into our customer database server and storage. However, some of our employees are not doing this.

Staff should not deal with a new membership without this proof; they also should not create a membership and then wait for new members to come back later with the proper identification. This process should be finished at the time of application when they bring the appropriate IDs.

Some people may think that it is just a minor or impractical issue. Yet, it is more important than they may think, in that it increases the systemized work efficiency. Staff should also assure new prospective members that all personal information is kept completely confidential. Detailed information on this issue is on our company Web site and in our brochures. The front desk staff will also hand out their business cards to all visitors in case visitors have questions they want to ask later.

Again, I ask each manager to hold a special workshop for employees focusing on this regulation. This is to ensure that this part of the application process is not ignored. The workshop should be done by this Friday. Please e-mail me with the report after the session has been finished.

Thank you,

Dixie Amanda

4. What is the purpose of the e-mail?

   (A) To remind Mr. Hunter of appropriate procedures
   (B) To request membership information
   (C) To get some customer feedback
   (D) To advertise policy changes

5. What problem has happened?

   (A) Security officials are supposed to inspect the facility.
   (B) Some enrollment steps are not being followed by the staff.
   (C) Customers have complained about the service.
   (D) The personal database has been leaked online.

6. According to the e-mail, where can people find membership details?

   (A) On the membership cards
   (B) In the attachment of the e-mail
   (C) Through the online page
   (D) On the posters displayed in branches

7. By when should the session be held?

   (A) April 5
   (B) April 6
   (C) April 7
   (D) April 8

Questions 8-12 refer to the following e-mails and notice.

To: Alan Schwartz <aschwartz@qualcomcore.net>
From: Punit Renjen <prenjen@qualcomcore.net>
Date: November 20
Subject: Issues for the Meeting
Attachment: REVISION.docx

Alan,

I was really pleased to meet you at the meeting of department heads on Thursday. Since you moved to the Buffalo office, we have hardly had a chance to speak with each other. At the meeting, we discussed some issues with the blueprint of the new headquarters building. As the head of sales, I have some suggestions, which are not just related to our department.

The north-facing side of the roof is unsuitable for solar panels. There is no cover or awning on the balcony, so it may be very inconvenient in the rain. The floor of the display and showroom is invisible from the main street. We need to set up smaller windows at the front to put some advertising signs there. I have changed the design to reflect these issues. The attachment with this e-mail contains my revisions to the design. I'm not a professional architect, so please understand that it is very unprofessional, just using handwritten notes.

I am going to be on vacation as of tomorrow, but please feel free to contact me at your convenience.

Renjen

To: Punit Renjen <prenjen@qualcomcore.net>
From: Alan Schwartz <aschwartz@qualcomcore.net>
Date: November 21
Subject: Re: Issues for the Meeting

Punit,

I really appreciate your interest in the plans. I strongly believe that the company's success could depend largely on this construction of the new headquarters, and I am pleased that you have given me these design considerations for our company.

In my team's view, we agree with all of your suggestions except the one about the section of advertising signs. We have another solution for that issue. Unfortunately, I cannot open the document you attached, so I cannot comment on that. Would you mind resending it by e-mail or fax it as a paper copy?

If we are to meet the April 30 deadline for the completion of construction, we need to review these issues with the executives and submit them to the architect as soon as possible.

Best regards,

Alan Schwartz

Notice

Date May 10

Attention All Staff:

Construction of the new headquarters will be completed on May 30. Unfortunately, we will be too busy at that time to move our offices into the new ones. On June 2, a moving company will come and transfer all of our office furniture and equipment to the new headquarters. Please ensure that your section is completely ready for this move by packaging and wrapping smaller items and first-priority documents by the evening of May 30. Boxes can be picked up from the storage rooms on each floor.

8. What is the purpose of Ms. Renjen's e-mail?
   (A) To provide minutes on a meeting to others
   (B) To recommend changes to a building's plan
   (C) To suggest a suitable location for a headquarters
   (D) To propose the customer response to the plan

9. What is NOT indicated about Ms. Renjen?
   (A) She will take a vacation soon.
   (B) She is the head of a department.
   (C) She works in a different location from Mr. Schwartz.
   (D) She is expected to retire from the company.

10. What problem does Mr. Schwartz have?
    (A) He thinks that there is a lack of budget.
    (B) He does not have time to consider the issues.
    (C) He cannot open the file Ms. Renjen sent.
    (D) He is not pleased with Ms. Renjen's suggestions.

11. Which of Ms. Renjen's suggestions does Mr. Schwartz disagree with?
    (A) Reducing the size of the windows
    (B) Repositioning a showroom
    (C) Providing a sheltered balcony
    (D) Redesigning the roof

12. What is implied about the construction project?
    (A) It did not reflect any of Ms. Renjen's recommendations.
    (B) It used less budget on the plan than expected.
    (C) It failed to hire the best-qualified architect.
    (D) It did not satisfy its original deadline.

DAY 12 세부사항 및 추론 유형

SPARTA 유형 파악

글의 세부 정보(specific information)를 묻는 유형으로, 일반적인 세부 사항을 묻는 유형, 진위 확인 유형(True/Not true), 추론 유형 등이 이에 속한다. 특히, 정답 선택지가 지문 내용을 패러프레이징(paraphrasing)하여 제시되므로, 정확한 의미 파악 능력이 요구된다.

SPARTA 문제 풀이 비법

[일반적 세부사항 유형]
육하원칙(누가, 무엇을, 언제, 어디서, 어떻게, 왜)에 해당하는 의문사(Who / What&Which / When / Where / How / Why)를 체크하고, 동사 시제(해당 행위를 한 시점)에 유의하여 보기 내용과 일치하는 정보를 찾는다.

[진위 확인 유형]
소거법으로 풀어야 하는 유형으로, NOT이 문제에 제시될 경우, 지문 내용과 일치하는 내용의 보기를 하나씩 지워가며 확인한다. NOT이 있다고 해서 지문에 전혀 없는 내용이 아니라, 지문에 제시되었으나 문제에서 요구하는 것이 아닐 수 있으니 주의해야 한다.
채용 관련 지문에서 자격 요건을 묻는 문제의 경우, 선호/우대 사항은 필수 조건이 아니므로 구별할 줄 알아야 한다.

[추론 유형]
문제에서 inferred / implied / indicated / suggested / probably / most likely 등이 제시되는 경우를 추론 유형이라 하는데, 추론이란, "추측/상상"하는 것이 아니라, 지문에 드러난 사실 정보를 패러프레이징(paraphrasing)한 보기 문장을 선택하는 것이므로, 상상력을 동원해서 풀지 않도록 주의한다.
특히, 지문에서 언급하는 '기대하다/예상하다/추측하다/조사 중이다/의심된다' 등의 내용은 사실 정보가 아니므로 주의해야 한다.

SPARTA 세부사항 및 추론 유형 TIP

1. **대상 추론**: For who is the information likely intended?

2. **출처 추론**: Where would the information most likely be found?

3. **사람 추론**:
   Who로 시작하는 문제는 해당 인물의 단순 직업을 묻는 경우가 대부분이다.
   What으로 시작하는 사람 문제는 해당 인물이 한 행위를 묻는다. 이 경우, 보기를 미리 읽고 각 보기에서 키워드(동사와 목적어 중심)를 체크하고 지문과 대조한다.
   직업이나 과거 이력(업종/경력/학력), 향후 계획 등을 묻는다.

4. **회사 이름**: 회사 이름이 질문의 키워드인 경우 전체 지문을 거의 다 봐야 세부 사항에 대한 항목 정보를 찾을 수 있다.
   ➡ 업종 / 본사 (지역) / 지사 / 설립 연도 / 직원 / 향후 계획 (지점 확장 오픈/신규직원 채용)

SPARTA Reading Point

Question 1 refers to the following article.

Power Prime to Open New Warehouse

Power Prime Co., the world's second-largest online retailer, has announced the opening of a new warehouse in Busan, South Korea, in July. Power Prime Co. currently has 50 warehouses strategically placed around the world to fulfill orders from its customers. Last year, it sold around 20 million items a day during the holiday season and this winter it expects to record the highest sales figure of 30 million per day.

The new warehouse will be built on the site of a new pier and will be its biggest shipping center in Asia. Matthew Nicks, who works at its headquarters in San Diego, U.S., says that many people are surprised at the fact that there are no automated systems within Power Prime's immense warehouses. Instead, hundreds of workers use bar codes to find and ship the ordered items. According to Nicks, this is much more economical than implementing and using a warehouse robot. Reportedly, Power Prime will need an additional 150 workers for its latest warehouse.

Q1. What is indicated about Power Prime Co.?

(A) It made 20 million dollars last year.
(B) It runs an Internet shopping business.
(C) It has fifty storage facilities in the U.S.
(D) Its head office is located in Busan.

*Power Prime*이 새로운 창고를 오픈했습니다!

세계에서 두 번째로 큰 온라인 소매업체 Power Prime 사는 7월에 한국의 부산에 새로운 물류 창고를 오픈한다고 발표했습니다. Power Prime 사는 고객들의 주문을 충족시키기 위해 전세계의 전략적인 위치에 현재 50개의 물류 창고를 보유하고 있습니다. 작년에 그들은 휴가 시즌 동안 하루에 2,000만 개의 물품을 팔았고, 이번 겨울에는 하루에 3,000만 개의 최고 판매 수치를 기록할 것으로 예상하고 있습니다.

새로운 물류 창고는 신 항만 지역에 건설될 예정이고, 이는 아시아 최대 규모의 물류 센터가 될 것입니다. 미국 샌디에이고 본사에 근무하는 Matthew Nicks는 많은 사람들이 Power Prime 사의 거대한 물류 창고 안에 자동화 시스템이 없다는 사실에 놀라워 한다고 했습니다. 대신, 수백 명의 노동자들이 바코드를 이용하여 주문품을 찾고 배송합니다. Nicks에 따르면, 이것은 창고 로봇을 실행하고 이용하는 것보다 훨씬 경제적이라고 합니다. 전하는 바에 따르면, Power Prime 사는 최신 물류 창고에 추가로 150명 정도가 더 필요할 거라고 합니다.

Q1. Power Prime 사에 대해 알 수 있는 것은 무엇인가?
(A) 작년에 2000만 달러를 벌어들였다.
(B) 인터넷 쇼핑 사업을 운영한다.
(C) 미국에 50개의 저장 시설을 가지고 있다.
(D) 부산에 본사가 위치해 있다.

▶ 첫 문장에서, "Power Prime Co., the world's second largest online retailer, has announced the opening of a new warehouse in Busan, South Korea, in July."라고 했으므로 인터넷을 기반으로 한 사업과 관련된 언급을 한 (B)가 정답이다.

어휘 warehouse [n] 물류 창고 retailer [n] 소매업자 strategically [adv] 전략적으로 fulfill [v] 충족시키다 pier [n] 항만
immense [a] 거대한 automated [a] 자동화된 according to [prep] ~에 따르면 economical [a] 경제적인, 효율적인
reportedly [adv] 전하는 바에 따르면

Tip indicated/inferred/implied/suggested가 등장하는 세부 사항을 묻는 유형으로, 추측이나 상식을 바탕으로 문제에 접근하는 것이 아니라 지문에 등장하는 명확한 근거를 통해 답을 찾아야 한다.

Question 1 refers to the following article.

Monthly Book Choice

by Jason Kang

For the general public, one of the most drastically changed industries is surely the stock market. Now, we introduce to you how to buy and sell stocks as a private investor online with little help from professionals. However, please be aware that there is too much information available on the web, so most first-time investors are puzzled and even at a loss as to where to start. For these investors, we recommend the most helpful book, named *Easy Steps for Access and Success in Online Trading* by Charles Hunter, one of the renowned analysts of the U.S the stock market. This book provides basic instructions, such as how to choose online banking services and where to obtain trustworthy information. The introduction chapter is a must-read for all first-time investors. In this chapter, Mr. Hunter warns people to be attentive to investment risks and to get useless data from the Internet. In addition, he encourages novice investors to practice first by playing online simulated stock investment.

Q1 What is suggested about investing online?

(A) It requires the help of analysts.
(B) It should be done by experts.
(C) It is difficult to obtain related information.
(D) It can be confusing for beginners.

Question 2 refers to the following invoice.

Fast Laundry Corporation
1930 Kovalchick Center

September 9
Invoice to: Tommy Stark
890 Fleming Avenue

Dear Mr. Stark,

Please find your invoice for our services below. Payment is due as of the date above and can be made by:
- Using cash or a money order (in our store)
- Completing a business check* issued by Fast Laundry Corporation
- Sending credit or debit card information by fax to 719-281-2921

Please note our automated response system for the payment is currently being upgraded and will be temporarily unavailable until September 20. Our web page is under construction at the moment.

Description	Details	Price
Dry cleaning and Home delivery service	Shirts/Blouses x 8 Pants/Jeans x 4 Jackets x 6	$220.45
Subtotal		$220.45
10% Regular Customer Discount		$22.05
$10 Discount Coupon		$10.00
Total		$188.4

Sorry, no personal checks are accepted. The total should be paid in US dollars ($).

Q2 What can be inferred from the invoice?

(A) The items were picked up at the store.
(B) Some pants were not cleaned.
(C) Mr. Stark got a reduction on the price.
(D) Canadian dollars are accepted as well.

Questions 1-2 refer to the following advertisement.

Special Offer at Green Wood Suite and Villa Resort

Situated in the exclusive Northern National Park area, Green Wood Suite and Villa Resort invites you to experience its incredible services and hospitality. You can find fantastic scenery and majestic mountains within walking distance. So, we guarantee that our guests will have the best and most relaxing vacation possible. Currently, we offer discounted rates for our suites. Book now to take advantage of the limited time offer.

Superior Suite

Extensive 2,000-square-foot suite
Overlooking a tropical garden
Overlooking a 15-mile green wood forest
An open-air whirlpool bathtub in each unit
Special rate of only $350 per night

Standard Suite

Spacious 1,500-square-foot suite
Overlooking a tropical garden
A private hot tub in each unit
Special rate of only $200 per night

All suites and villas include a complimentary breakfast, fully equipped gym, wireless Internet connection, and scheduled shuttle service to a range of attractions for tourists in the national park and downtown.

1. What is suggested about Green Wood Suite and Villa Resort?

   (A) All guest rooms have mountain views.
   (B) Different types of rooms are available.
   (C) Suites are offered at the best rate in the area.
   (D) Guests can use its private terrace.

2. What is offered only to Superior Suite guests?

   (A) A tropical garden view
   (B) Ample room
   (C) A free breakfast
   (D) An outdoor bathtub

Questions 3-7 refer to the following advertisement and résumé.

WANTED

Geoplex Logistics is a fast-growing new company based in Toronto, Canada. If you have passion and diligence, we offer a variety of global opportunities. We are seeking a specialist to manage our distribution warehouses in Eastern Europe.

The position will be based in Poland but will require extensive travel throughout Eastern Europe, especially to Croatia, Slovenia, Bulgaria, Hungary, and so on. The primary responsibility of the job is the general management of the distribution and checking the inventory status in the company's Eastern European markets. Fluency in English or other European languages is required. The successful candidate must have communication and leadership skills, a bachelor's degree in a business-related field, and at least three years of sales experience at a managerial level. Competence in computer skills is preferred.

For more information, please call Ms. Elaine Helena, the human resources officer, and send your résumé with your career history to Mr. Peter Dixon by July 20 at dixon@geoplex.net.

Jonathan Erving
390 Fleming Avenue
Indiana, PA 16701
714-9201-1029
erving@calmonlogi.com

Objective:
To become a dedicated manager with an emerging company

Experience:
Distribution Manager 2016–2017
Gourmet Dish Catering Distribution Center, Altoona, PA
Responsibilities: Controlling inventory for catering foods at a large warehouse

Sales Manager 2014–2015
Target Incorporation, Fairfax, VA
Responsibilities: Hiring, training, and managing store sales representatives

Education:
MA, Business Administration (2012), West Virginia University, WV, the United States

3. Where is Geoplex Logistics' headquarters located?

   (A) Poland
   (B) Croatia
   (C) Toronto
   (D) Hungary

4. What position is available?

   (A) Sales representative
   (B) Personnel manager
   (C) Warehouse manager
   (D) Computer programmer

5. What is NOT required for the position?

   (A) Speaking in English or European languages
   (B) Having a bachelor's degree in business
   (C) Dealing with computer software
   (D) Having leadership skills

6. In the résumé, the word "inventory" in line 11, is closest in meaning to

   (A) account
   (B) garage
   (C) invention
   (D) stock

7. Why might Mr. Erving's application be rejected?

   (A) He doesn't meet the years of experience.
   (B) He doesn't have a bachelor's degree.
   (C) His residential area is too far.
   (D) He wants high wages.

Questions 8-12 refer to the following e-mail and advertisement.

To:	Tim Haywood <t.haywood@solarrealty.com>
From:	Jerry Fisherman <fisherman@vegaslawfirm.net>
Re:	Rent_Office Space

Dear Mr. Haywood,

While browsing your Web site www.solarrealty.com, I saw a lot of properties you have for rent in Pittsburgh. I am planning to relocate my office to the downtown area of the city as of March 5th, so I need to rent some space.

I would like the location of my next office to be in proximity to public transportation such as the Amtrack Pittsburgh Station or the Grey Hound Bus Terminal. In addition, there should be some parking spaces for my clients using their cars. I strongly believe that your company meets my needs with various properties.

I'm scheduled to travel to Philadelphia soon and want to make arrangements with your agent in order to look around available properties. If possible, could you e-mail me the space information on file with their floor plans?

Best Wishes,

Jerry Fisherman
Vegas Law Firm

Pittsburgh Office Space For Lease

How large a space does you need?
How far from the business district do you prefer?
Solar Realty sincerely welcomes anyone who is looking for properties in the downtown Pittsburgh area in order for their business to flourish.

Shadyside Property

Location: 5743 Walnut Street Pittsburgh, PA 15232
(2 Blocks East of Walnut Street Business District)
Rent: $2,100 Plus Utilities
Parking: Using the public parking lot (free for just half an hour)

Oakland Property

Location: 3360 5th Avenue, Pittsburgh, PA 15213
(within 5 minutes' walking distance from the station)
Rent: $2,250 Plus Utilities
Parking for 4~5 Vehicles

Lucernmines Property

Location: 51 11th Street, Pittsburgh, PA 15221
(left side of the road by Grey Hound Terminal)
Rent: $1,725 (Utilities included)
Free Wi-fi

Filbert Street Property

Location: 732 Filbert Street, Pittsburgh, PA 15232
(Great Location! Right in the middle of the business district)
Rent: $2,300 (Utilities included)
Parking for only one vehicle

8. What is Mr. Fisherman concerned about?

   (A) The size of the office space
   (B) The available parking spaces
   (C) The amount of utility fees
   (D) The rent for the office space

9. Who is Mr. Fisherman?

   (A) A real estate agent
   (B) An employee at a law office
   (C) A secretary of a lawyer
   (D) Mr. Haywood's colleague

10. Which space is likely to be suitable for the Vegas Law Firm?

    (A) Shadyside Property
    (B) Lucenrmines Property
    (C) Oakland Property
    (D) Filbert Street Property

11. What is indicated about the Shadyside Property?

    (A) It is near a bus terminal in the downtown area.
    (B) It doesn't have its own parking spaces.
    (C) It is in proximity to a residential area.
    (D) It is the most expensive property.

12. How would Solar Realty send the information to Mr. Fisherman?

    (A) By e-mail
    (B) In person
    (C) By fax
    (D) By mail

DAY 13 문장 넣기 유형

SPARTA 유형 파악

문장 넣기 유형은 앞뒤 문장과의 맥락을 파악하는 유형으로, PART 6에서는 문장의 위치가 정해져 있으나, PART 7은 제시된 문장을 보고 지문 안에서 알맞은 위치를 골라야 한다. PART 6의 문장 넣기 유형과 마찬가지로, 연결어인 접속부사와의 문맥 연결 상태, 지시어(대명사, 정관사)의 매칭 관계를 통해 문맥상 가장 적절한 곳을 고르면 된다. 제시 문장을 먼저 파악하고 지문을 읽도록 한다.

SPARTA 문제 풀이 비법

[질문 + 제시 문장]으로 제시된다.

In which of the positions marked [1], [2], [3] and [4] does the following sentence best belong?
"Previous customer service experience is preferred, but not required."

(A) [1]　　　(B) [2]　　　(C) [3]　　　(D) [4]

지문에 표시된 [1], [2], [3] 그리고 [4] 중에서 다음 문장이 들어가기에 가장 좋은 위치는?
"이전의 고객 서비스 경력이 선호되기는 하지만, 필수는 아니다."
(A) [1]　　　(B) [2]　　　(C) [3]　　　(D) [4]

[문제 풀이 순서]
1. 글의 종류를 파악한 후, 제시 문장을 먼저 해석하고, 지문을 읽는다.
2. 지문의 숫자 앞뒤에 단서가 될 만한 지시어나 연결어에 표시하며 읽는다.
3. 제시 문장과 매칭되는 단서에 표시해 둔다.
4. 선택한 숫자 위치에 제시 문장을 넣은 후, 앞뒤 문장과의 문맥이 자연스럽게 연결되는지를 확인한다.

SPARTA 문장 넣기 유형 TIP

(1) 지시어 확인
- 대명사:
  - this/these　앞 문장에 나온 명사 또는 문장 전체의 내용을 대신 받는다.
  - that/those　앞에 등장한 사물의 단수/복수 명사를 대신 받는다.
  - one　앞에 언급된 같은 종류의 명사를 대신 받는다.
- 정관사: the　앞에 이미 언급된 명사가 반복될 때 붙는다.

(2) 연결어 확인
- 접속 부사:
  - 결과　therefore, hence, consequently, in sum
  - 반전　nevertheless, nonetheless, however
  - 추가　in addition, additionally, also, moreover, furthermore
  - 예시　for example, for instance, to illustrate it
  - 전환　otherwise, meanwhile, in the meantime

(3) 동사의 시제
- 대부분 이어지는 앞뒤 문장의 동사 시제는 서로 일치되거나, 시간 순서대로 나열된다.

SPARTA Reading Point

Question 1 refers to the following memo.

To: All employees
From: Human Resources Department, General Accounting Co.
Date: May 20
Subject: Mr. Jacob

Dear All,

As you already know, Mr. Jacob will be retiring at the end of July. He was hired at General Accounting Co. as a sales representative 30 years ago. —[1]—. His leadership was widely known as the best, and over the years he has been in charge of company's various tasks in each department. —[2]—. These include the sales, planning, marketing, and financial departments. His performance in finance was outstanding, and he has devoted himself to the huge growth in our profits. —[3]—. To celebrate his accomplishments, we are planning to hold a retirement ceremony for him. It will take place at the Pacific Blue Ballroom at the Grand Comfort Hotel on July 30. —[4]—. Please let me know whether you will be able to attend by June 30.

Q1. In which of the positions marked [1], [2], [3], and [4] does the following sentence best belong?

"This is the reason he has worked as chief financial officer and one of the reasons why he will be so sorely missed."

(A) [1]
(B) [2]
(C) [3]
(D) [4]

수신: 전 직원
발신: 인사과, General Accounting 사
날짜: 5월 20일
제목: Jacob 씨

모두에게,

이미 아시다시피, Jacob 씨가 7월 말에 퇴임할 것입니다. 그는 General Accounting 사에 30년 전 판매사원으로 고용되었습니다. 그의 리더십은 최고라고 널리 알려져 있고, 지난 수년간 회사의 각 부서에서 다양한 직무를 담당했습니다. 이것은 판매, 기획, 마케팅 그리고 재정부서까지 포함합니다. 재정에 있어서 그의 업무 수행은 두드러졌고, 그는 우리의 수익이 엄청난 성장을 하는 데 자신을 헌신했습니다. 이것이 그가 자금 관리 이사로 일해 온 이유이고, 앞으로 그가 몹시 그리워질 이유 중 하나입니다. 그의 업적을 축하하기 위해, 우리는 그의 퇴임식을 진행할 예정입니다. 퇴임식은 7월 30일 Grand Comfort 호텔의 Pacific Blue Ballroom에서 열릴 것입니다. 참석 가능 여부를 6월 30일까지 알려 주시기 바랍니다.

Q1. [1], [2], [3] 그리고 [4]로 표시된 자리 중에서 뒤에 문장이 어디에 가장 적합하게 속하는가?
"이것이 그가 자금 관리 이사로 일해 온 이유이고, 앞으로 그가 몹시 그리워질 이유 중 하나입니다."

(A) [1]　　　　　　(B) [2]　　　　　　**(C) [3]**　　　　　　(D) [4]

▶ 제시 문장에서 This가 앞 문장의 내용에 연결해서 부연하고 있다. 이것이 그가 CFO로 일하는 이유라고 했으므로, 그가 회사에서 이뤄낸 업적을 설명하는(~ devoted himself to the huge growth in our profits) [3]이 가장 적절하다.

어휘 retire ⓥ 퇴임하다　sales representative ⓝ 판매사원　be in charge of ⓥ ~을 담당하다　performance ⓝ 직무 수행　outstanding ⓐ 두드러진　devote oneself to ⓥ ~에 헌신하다　huge ⓐ 거대한　accomplishment ⓝ 업적, 실천　take place ⓥ 발생하다

Tip 퇴임식과 같은 행사(event) 진행 공지가 자주 나오는데, 이때 TPO 즉, 시간(Time), 장소(Place), 목적(Objective)를 중심으로 정보를 확인한다.

Question 1 refers to the following letter.

Supreme Mart

July 30
Mr. Cavin Feige
92 Fleming Avenue
Indiana, PA 15701

Dear Mr. Feige,

Congratulations!
Your essay has been awarded the first prize in the regular category of the Supreme Mart and I Contest sponsored by Supreme Mart. We wish to celebrate your accomplishment at an award ceremony on Friday, August 5, at the Eagles Ballroom. —[1]—. Upon entering our store, turn left and walk past the information desk to get to the conference floor, where the ceremony will be held. —[2]—.
The winning essays will be published in the Supreme Mart Newsletter, which is sent to our members, and posted on our Web site. In addition, they will be printed out and displayed in all Supreme Mart stores. —[3]—. As a first-place winner, you will receive a 300-dollar gift voucher redeemable at any Supreme Mart stores before December 31. —[4]—.
Again, congratulations on your outstanding essay!

Sincerely,

Brad Triana

Brad Triana, Manager
Supreme Mart Co.

Q1 In which of the positions marked [1], [2], [3] and [4] does the following sentence best belong?

"You can pick it up at the award ceremony, or sent it to you with an address which you wrote on the submission."

(A) [1]
(B) [2]
(C) [3]
(D) [4]

Question 2 refers to the following review.

A Review of *Rose for Katrina* in Dublin

By Nancy Gibbs

Fans have been waiting a long time for this new mysterious and grotesque story by Carla Dorothy. I am confident that they'll be pleased with the release of the novel. Dorothy has gradually grown as a writer, and I think this book is probably the very best she has ever written. There are a wide variety of characters, and the plot is well-organized, with factors making readers excited. —[1]—. The complicated relationships among the main characters can make them attractive and hold the reader's attention. In the plot, Mr. Harry, the third person introduced in the story, finds the solution to a mysterious issue. One thing that could be improved is the ending. —[2]—. However, I believe that the book's other strengths can fully make up for this weakness. —[3]—. It goes without saying that she will continue to have dedicated fans waiting for her next novel. —[4]—.

Q2 In which of the positions marked [1], [2], [3], and [4] does the following sentence best belong?

"It is very typical of her writing, and many fans will no doubt predict the outcome from early on."

(A) [1]
(B) [2]
(C) [3]
(D) [4]

SPARTA Practice Test

Questions 1-4 refer to the following information.

Extra Parking Slots Available to Building Tenants

With the completion of the new parking lot, TF Square Premise is pleased to announce that new parking slots are available to tenants in our building. Unfortunately, tenants who have at least three years of lease agreement will be given priority on them because the spaces are limited. —[1]—.

To apply for the additional parking space, please fill in and submit an application form to the building administration office by May 10. —[2]—. All applicants must meet the following requirements. The registration fees must be paid by the date stated above. —[3]—. A copy of an official vehicle registration card needs to be accompanied as a proof of its car ownership. Tenants applying for this should currently have no parking slots. If tenants have already one or more parking spaces, they are no longer eligible.

Applications will be reviewed until the end of May, and parking slots will be designated by the first day of June. —[4]—. If you have any questions or concerns, please feel free to contact us at 959-0505.

TF Square Premise
707 Middle Boulevard
Tel. 959-0505
www.tfsquarepremise.com

---

1. What is suggested about new parking slots at TF Square Premise?

(A) They can be shared with other tenants.
(B) They should be paid for once a month.
(C) They are more expensive than before.
(D) They are mainly available to long-term contractors.

2. What is NOT a stated requirement for applying for a parking slot?

(A) Related documents should be submitted by the deadline.
(B) Fees for new parking slots should be paid before moving in.
(C) Each tenant should prove their car ownership.
(D) Applicants should have no parking slot at present.

3. What should applicants submit when applying for a parking slot?

(A) A proof of car payment
(B) Driver's license
(C) Car registration documents
(D) Monthly statement

4. In which of the positions marked [1], [2], [3], and [4], does the following sentence belong?

"Tenants for less than three years will be given second priority."

(A) [1]
(B) [2]
(C) [3]
(D) [4]

Questions 5-8 refer to the following letter.

June 5
Mr. Daniel McKenzie
Beoulegit Corporation
450 Oakvalley Street, Podalski
Prague, 230573

Dear Sir,

I would like to express my opposition to the proposed Vltava River Revitalization. —[1]—. As a property owner and long-time resident of Vltava River, I am concerned about the numerous negative impacts your project may have on our community. —[2]—. Although the construction of a large-scale shopping complex may seem attractive because it could bring more visitors and revenue to the community, it may also cause road congestion and impose a serious burden on the town's potential problems with public security such as robbery, noise, and so on.

—[3]—. Moreover, the nearby Vltava city park which is currently a conservation area for a variety of birds, insects, and other small animals may be adversely affected by the development. I feel we should be working to preserve nature instead of damaging it. I plan to formally voice my concerns at the resident meeting held by Beoulegit Corporation on July 10. —[4]—.

Regards,

Erica Yeshiva
Erica Yeshiva

5. What can be inferred about Ms. Yeshiva?

   (A) She manages a souvenir store near the Vltava River.
   (B) She has enjoyed having a party on the river.
   (C) She recently transferred to the Vltava area.
   (D) She has lived in the Vltava River area for years.

6. What does Beoulegit Corporation plan to do?

   (A) Open a luxurious hotel
   (B) Build a shopping center
   (C) Develop a wildlife reserve
   (D) Set up a government facility

7. What is NOT mentioned as a concern of Ms. Yeshiva?

   (A) The project may ruin the tourist industry.
   (B) The project may cause serious traffic jams.
   (C) The project may harm to the citizens.
   (D) The project may have adverse effects on animals.

8. In which of the positions marked [1], [2], [3] and [4] does the following sentence best belong?

   "I hope that Beoulegit Corporation will carefully consider the way to deal with these issues at that time."

   (A) [1]
   (B) [2]
   (C) [3]
   (D) [4]

Questions 9-12 refer to the following e-mail.

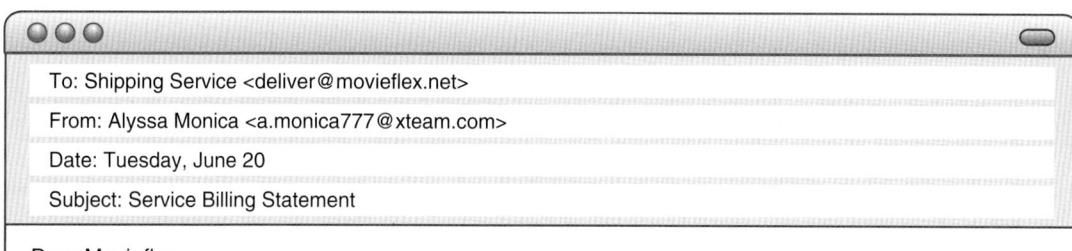

To: Shipping Service <deliver@movieflex.net>
From: Alyssa Monica <a.monica777@xteam.com>
Date: Tuesday, June 20
Subject: Service Billing Statement

Dear Movieflex,

I have been ordering a lot of movies from your Internet protocol television(IPTV) service for over three years. Most items I have watched are independent films that are usually hard to find. I have been mostly satisfied with the service, but your company has recently made a mistake regarding the service I have subscribed to on the billing statement for May. –[1]–.

Now I am using the Deluxe service for $75, including $5 for the value-added tax(VAT). On the May statement, $100 was charged, and I think that it is your Premium service fee. In addition, I got a new set-up box suddenly for the UHD IPTV service. I have never upgraded my service at all, as I have been really satisfied with my current service. When I checked my service status through your Web site, it still remains the same as before. –[2]–.

When I called your customer service line, I was informed that there was a mistake in the electronic data processing. By discussing the issue with your employee, I decided to deduct the price difference on the following month's bill without any additional complaints. –[3]–.

By the way, I have one more question about the set-up box. I don't know how I should send back the box I received. When I called the customer service center and talked to an employee there — Lilian Trisha — about this, she told me that the issues with returns and shipping are dealt with by your department. Furthermore, she informed me of your e-mail address. Could you let me know how to return this item? I look forward to hearing from you as soon as possible. –[4]–.

Thank you,

Alyssa Monica

---

9. What is indicated about Movieflex?

   (A) All of its customers got a chance to upgrade the service.
   (B) Customers feel that its movie genres are not various.
   (C) It deals with all customer complaints only via e-mail.
   (D) Its tasks are divided among departments.

10. What is suggested about Ms. Monica?

    (A) She recently got equipment for upgrading.
    (B) She is a first-time customer.
    (C) She is dissatisfied with the current service.
    (D) She needs to pay an extra charge.

11. What did Ms. Trisha do?

    (A) Talked to her supervisor
    (B) Explained a mistake
    (C) Sent an e-mail to Ms. Monica
    (D) Processed an express order

12. In which of the positions marked [1], [2], [3], and [4] does the following sentence best belong?

    "I was happy with the assurance that the matter was resolved."

    (A) [1]
    (B) [2]
    (C) [3]
    (D) [4]

DAY 14 의도 파악 및 유의어 유형

SPARTA 유형 파악

의도 파악 유형은 온라인 대화문 형태로 제시되어, 2~3인이 나누는 대화 속 특정 표현의 의도를 가장 잘 나타낸 문장을 고르는 것이다.
유의어 유형은 제시된 단어의 뉘앙스를 파악한 후 문맥상 가장 적절한 대체 단어를 찾는 것이다.

SPARTA 문제 풀이 비법

[의도 파악 유형]

[중략]

Rene [3:48 P.M.]
I'll confirm that with Connie when he comes, but for now Junee and I will go ahead and finish the slideshow without that data. It'll actually make our job easier.

Junee [3:50 P.M.]
I'm all for it.

Q. At 3:50 P.M., what does Ms. Junee most likely mean when she writes, "I'm all for it"?
 (A) She is happy that the job can be finished soon.
 (B) She agrees with including data in a presentation.
 (C) She is concerned that the meeting will take too long.
 (D) She prefers to attend the meeting in three weeks.

➡ 제시 문장이 바로 앞 사람이 한 말(Rene 3:48)에 대해 긍정하는 내용인지, 부정하는 내용인지를 파악한다.
➡ "I'm all for it"은 앞에 나온 "우선 지금은 데이터 없이 Junee와 본인이 작업을 진행해서 슬라이드쇼를 마치겠다"는 말에 긍정적인 반응을 한 것으로, 그녀는 그 일이 곧 마무리될 수 있음에 좋아한다는 (A)가 정답이다.

참고 의도 파악 유형이 포함된 온라인 대화문 종류
- 회사 내 동료들 간의 업무 관련 대화
- 동료, 친구 간의 일상적인 대화
- 고객과 고객센터 직원 간의 대화

[대화문의 구성] 문제점 확인 ➡ 문제에 대한 세부사항 확인 ➡ 해결 방안 (추후 행동)

온라인 대화문 CHECK POINT
- 전체적인 맥락 흐름보다는 앞뒤 대화 상황을 중점으로 파악한다.
- 대화 참여자의 이름, 직책, 또는 성별을 혼동하지 않도록 한다.
- 3인 이상의 다자간 대화에서 참여자들을 혼동하지 않도록 표시하며 읽는다.

[유의어 유형]

[중략]

Also, I spent a semester abroad in Hong-Kong doing my research. As mentioned in my résumé,, I am a suitable person who you are looking for and hope to be considered.

I look forward to hearing back from you soon regarding my application package.

Sincerely,
Mr. Graham

Q. In the e-mail, the word "regarding" in paragraph 3, line 1, is closest in meaning to
(A) Respecting
(B) Viewing
(C) Explaining
(D) Concerning

➡ 제시어만 보면 regard는 명사로 "존경"이라는 의미가 있으므로 respecting과, 동사로 "간주하다"의 의미로 보면 viewing과, regarding이 전치사로 "~에 관하여"라는 뜻이므로 concerning과도 유사하다고 볼 수 있다. 따라서 문맥을 명확히 파악해 답을 골라야 한다.

➡ 마지막 문장을 보면 "저는 제 지원 패키지에 관하여 당신에게 곧 답변을 듣고 싶습니다"라고 했으므로 전치사로 "~에 관하여"라는 concerning이 가장 가까운 의미로 쓰였음을 알 수 있다.

참고 헷갈리는 기출 유의어 표현

기출 어휘	의미	유의어	기출 어휘	의미	유의어
property	부동산	location, real estate	cover	다루다	deal with, handle
	특성	characteristic, feature		보도하다	report
	소유물	possession, belongings	outstanding	뛰어난, 두드러진	exceptional, impressive
critical	비판적인	negative		미납의	unpaid, payable
	중대한	essential, important	issue	발행하다	publish
meet	충족시키다	fulfill, satisfy		문제(점)	problem, matter, question
	만나다	get together, encounter		권, 호	edition, volume
significant	중대한	important	follow	(법/규정 등을) 따르다	obey, observe, adhere to
	거대한	enormous, huge		뒤를 잇다	succeed, take over from, come after
draw	끌어당기다, 유치하다	attract		동반하다, 함께 가다	accompany
	그리다	paint, design			
	추첨	lottery			

* Part 7 유의어 유형은 다의어를 활용한 문제가 출제되므로, 단어의 뜻 하나만으로 유의어를 찾으려 하지 말고, 제시어가 포함된 문장과 함께 앞뒤 문맥을 따져 가장 적절한 단어를 골라야 한다.

SPARTA 의도 파악 및 유의어 유형 TIP

의도 파악 유형은 대화에 등장하는 인물들의 관계와 대화 전후 상황을 고려하여 제시된 표현의 의미를 파악해야 한다. 즉, 단순한 의미적 접근이 아닌, 종합적 이해를 바탕으로 접근해야 한다.

유의어 유형은 의미상 제시어를 대체할 수 있는 단어를 찾는 문제로, 해당 제시어가 포함된 문장뿐만 아니라 앞뒤 문맥과 연계해 함께 파악해야 한다.

Reading Point

Question 1 refers to the following online chat discussion.

Lillian, Jessie	[5:30 P.M.]	I'm considering preparing for a yacht reservation for our year-end party. I'd like to get some information from the agency first. What do you think?
Richard, Simon	[5:31 P.M.]	Do we have to prepare for the meal or provide it on board?
Lillian, Jessie	[5:33 P.M.]	The yacht I'm looking at has meals included but we can have other options to stop at near restaurants.
Angela, Beth	[5:35 P.M.]	I think it's a great idea. I'm concerned about the cost of dinner, Is there enough budgets?
Lillian, Jessie	[5:37 P.M.]	More than enough. In fact, it's cheaper than the place we usually use at Grand Hotel.
McClaster, Bon	[5:39 P.M.]	Let's not forget that Grand Hotel is one of our biggest clients. We've supplied all of their uniforms for 10 years.
Angela, Beth	[5:45 P.M.]	Bon, that's an excellent point. It could be risky if we do not use them.
Richard, Simon	[5:47 P.M.]	Grand Hotel is right next to the river. We could enjoy the party on the yacht and then stop off at their banquet hall.
Lillian, Jessie	[5:50 P.M.]	We could eat at their restaurant instead of the banquet hall. I'm confident that it'll be much cheaper.
McClaster, Bon	[5:52 P.M.]	Jessie, is there a cruise that will let us get off at the Grand Hotel and wait for us to finish?
Lillian, Jessie	[5:54 P.M.]	I'll look into it.

Q1. At 5:37 P.M., what does Ms. Lillian mean when she writes, "More than enough"?

(A) She thinks there is sufficient time to eat.
(B) She wants the room to be larger.
(C) She believes that budget is suitable for meals.
(D) She hopes to avoid the hotel restaurant.

Lillian, Jessie	[5:30 P.M.]	우리 연말 파티를 위해 요트 예약을 준비할까 해. 우선 여행사 같은 곳에서 먼저 정보를 얻으려고 하는데, 어떻게 생각해?
Richard, Simon	[5:31 P.M.]	식사를 우리가 준비해야 돼? 아니면 선상에서 제공해 줘?
Lillian, Jessie	[5:33 P.M.]	내가 고려하고 있는 요트는 식사가 포함되지만 근처 식당에 들르는 다른 옵션도 있어.
Angela, Beth	[5:35 P.M.]	그거 좋은 생각인 것 같아. 근데 저녁식사 비용이 좀 걱정이네. 예산이 충분해?
Lillian, Jessie	[5:37 P.M.]	충분하고도 남아. 사실, 우리가 보통 이용하는 Grand Hotel보다 더 저렴할 거야.
McClaster, Bon	[5:39 P.M.]	Grand Hotel은 우리의 큰 고객 중 하나라는 것을 잊으면 안돼. 우리는 10년 동안 그들에게 유니폼을 공급하고 있어.
Angela, Beth	[5:45 P.M.]	Bon, 중요한 지적이야. 우리가 그들을 이용하지 않으면 위험할 수도 있어.
Richard, Simon	[5:47 P.M.]	Grand Hotel은 바로 강 옆에 있어. 우리는 요트 위에서 파티를 즐기고, 그들의 연회장에 들를 수 있어.
Lillian, Jessie	[5:50 P.M.]	연회장에서 먹는 대신 거기 식당에서 먹을 수도 있어. 확신하건대 훨씬 저렴할 거야.
McClaster, Bon	[5:52 P.M.]	Jessie, 우리를 Grand Hotel에 내려 주고 식사 끝날 때까지 기다려 줄 배가 있어?
Lillian, Jessie	[5:54 P.M.]	알아볼게.

Q1. 오후 5:37에, Lillian 씨가 쓴 " More than enough"는 무엇을 의미하는가?

(A) 그녀는 먹을 시간이 충분하다고 생각한다.
(B) 그녀는 더 큰 공간을 원한다.
(C) 그녀는 식사를 위한 예산이 적절하다고 믿는다.
(D) 그녀는 호텔 식당은 피하고 싶어 한다.

▶ 앞 문장에서 Beth가 "is there enough budget?"(예산이 충분해?)라고 물었고, 이에 대해 "More than enough"라는 답은 식사를 위한 예산이 충분하다는 의미이다.

 yacht ⓝ 요트   year-end party ⓝ 연말파티   on board ⓐ 선상의, 승선한   included ⓐ 포함된   concerned ⓐ 걱정하는   risky ⓐ 위험한   banquet ⓝ 연회   instead of prep 대신에   get off ⓥ 내리다   wait for ⓥ 기다리다

Tip 온라인 대화문은 대화의 이슈가 등장하고 해당 이슈를 서로 논의하는 내용으로 전개된다. 구어체(회화체)로 쓰인 표현의 의도를 묻는 문제는 앞 사람이 서술한 내용에 대한 동의 또는 거절의 표현이 답이 된다.

Question 2 refers to the following e-mail.

To: Giant Eagle Retail Human Resources <recruit@gianteagleretail.net>

From: Juliano Nikita <j.nikita@cupgraduate.com>

Date: April 10

Subject: Application Process

To whom it may concern,

I'm sorry that I'm writing only by e-mail because I'm currently working in Vietnam.

In my attached résumé, you can see that I graduated from Clarion University of Portland four years ago. Since then, I have experienced a variety of jobs related to dealing with customers in many different commercial environments such as clothing shops, gasoline stations, and restaurants. Therefore, I am confident I could take care of visitors well in your stores.

My father is Spanish and my mother is American, so I speak both languages very fluently. In addition, I am proficient in French, which I minored.
I look forward to hearing from you soon.

Sincerely,
Juliano Nikita

Attached File ▶ *Nikita_Resume.docx*

Q2. The word "environments" in paragraph 2, line 3, is closest in meaning to

(A) natures
(B) situations
(C) payments
(D) motions

수신: Giant Eagle Retail Human Resources <recruit@gianteagleretail.net>
발신: Juliano Nikita <j.nikita@cupgraduate.com>
날짜: 4월 10일
제목: 지원 절차

관계자 분께,

제가 현재 베트남에서 일하고 있어서 이메일로만 쓰는 것을 유감으로 생각합니다.

제가 첨부한 이력서에서, 제가 Clarion University of Portland를 4년 전에 졸업한 것을 보실 수 있을 것입니다. 그때부터 저는 의류 매장, 주유소, 식당 등 다양한 상업 환경에서 고객을 다루는 것과 관련된 여러 직무를 경험하고 있습니다. 따라서 저는 귀하의 매장에서 방문객들을 매우 잘 다룰 수 있을 거라고 확신합니다.

제 아버지는 스페인 사람이고 어머니는 미국인이기 때문에, 저는 이 두 언어를 매우 유창하게 구사합니다. 게다가, 저는 부전공 했던 불어도 능숙합니다.
귀하로부터의 답장을 기다리겠습니다.

Juliano Nikita 드림

첨부파일 ▶ Nikita_Resume.docx

Q2. 두 번째 단락, 세 번째 줄의 "environments"와 의미상 가장 가까운 단어는?

(A) 자연
(B) 상황
(C) 지불
(D) 움직임

▶ I have experienced a variety of jobs related to dealing with customers in many different commercial environments ~ (저는 다양한 상업 환경에서 고객을 다루는 것과 관련된 여러 직무를 경험하고 있습니다)에서, '환경'은 일하는 '상황'을 나타내므로 보기 중 가장 적절한 것은 (B)이다.

어휘 attached ⓐ 첨부된 graduate from ⓥ 졸업하다 experience ⓥ 경험하다 related ⓐ 관련된 deal with ⓥ 다루다 commercial ⓐ 상업의 environment ⓝ 환경 clothing ⓝ 의류 gasoline station ⓝ 주유소 take care of ⓥ 돌보다 fluently adv 유창하게 proficient ⓐ 능숙한 look forward to ⓥ 바라다

Tip 유의어 유형은 우선 제시어의 위치를 빠르게 찾아서 표시한 후, 보기에서 대체 가능한 것을 찾는다.

SPARTA Check-UP

Question 1 refers to the following text-message chain.

Gilbert Amelio [2:20 P.M.]
I'm in front of Terra Tech Co. now, but no one is here I guess.
I've pushed the bell five times with no answer.

Dixie Lynn [2:22 P.M.]
Now? That's highly unusual.
Let me call the sales manager immediately,
and then I will tell you the situation. Don't go anywhere.

Gilbert Amelio [2:23 P.M.]
I won't. I don't want to come here again by bus!

Dixie Lynn [2:30 P.M.]
OK, Amelio. Now they are all attending the seminar in Wisconsin.
They apologized for forgetting to notify us.
Apparently, a superintendent is in the office next to the entrance.
You can leave the relevant documents with him.

Gilbert Amelio [2:33 P.M.]
Great. I won't message you again if there is no problem.
See you later.

Q1 At 2:23 P.M., what does Mr. Amelio mean when he writes, "I won't"?

   (A) He will not come to the office.
   (B) He will wait for Ms. Lynn's response.
   (C) He will not accept Ms. Lynn's offer.
   (D) He will ring the buzzer again.

Question 2 refers to the following article.

Serengeti Wildlife Park

By Mugabe Mbape

Since 1971, Serengeti Wildlife Park in Mid Africa has been providing shelter to orphaned and injured animals from all the continents, including pumas, lions, elephants, and various species of birds. The 3,000-acre park is privately owned and relies heavily on donations from individuals, companies, and organizations.

Jonathan Spilbergh, widely known as the director of the popular sci-fi movie *The Kingdom of Universe*, donated $10 million to the Serengeti Wildlife Park after spending a one-month family holiday at a log cabin located within the park. "I was really impressed by the efforts of the volunteers and employees at the park and wanted to support them," Spilbergh said.

Q2 The word "shelter" in paragraph 1, line 1, is closest in meaning to

(A) sanctuary
(B) product
(C) donation
(D) treatment

SPARTA Practice Test

Questions 1-3 refer to the following online chat discussion.

New Chat

Matthew Johns [10:10 A.M.]
Hi everyone. I'd like to check that you know the arrangements for this weekend's fair.

Reuben Sylvia [10:12 A.M.]
I know where it is and what time the building opens, but I'm not clear on when I go there.

Matthew Johns [10:15 A.M.]
Ms. Sylvia, because you're responsible for arranging the items on display, you need to get there around 8:30 A.M. I'll be there soon after, so I can give you a hand if possible. Just remember to arrange the products at a low-level for children.

Fang Liao [10:16 A.M.]
Mr. Min and I have arranged to drive there in his car. We should arrive there at 10, right?

Matthew Johns [10:17 A.M.]
That's right. Be sure you go through the sales descriptions thoroughly. I'd like you to really focus on the educational aspects of our products when talking to the parents.

Fang Liao [10:18 A.M.]
I'm already on it. Mr. Min e-mailed me the contents last night.

DK Min [10:20 A.M.]
Don't we have a confirmed time for the item demonstration on the main stage yet?

Matthew Johns [10:22 A.M.]
Not yet, but it's likely to be after lunch. You can decide who will show the trial on the day. I'm sure any of you would do an excellent job. Ms. Sylvia, I sent you the list of items you need to take, didn't I?

Reuben Sylvia [10:23 A.M.]
You did. I'll go down to the storage floor soon to confirm everything is there, and then move the items into my car tomorrow.

Matthew Johns [10:25 A.M.]
Great. I'll go there with you. Thanks, everyone.

Send

1. What kind of company does Mr. Johns most likely work for?

    (A) A conference center
    (B) A tutoring institute
    (C) A toy manufacturer
    (D) A children's apparel company

2. Who will arrive at the event first?

    (A) Mr. Johns
    (B) Ms. Sylvia
    (C) Ms. Liao
    (D) Mr. Min

3. At 10:18 A.M., what does Ms. Liao mean when she writes, "I'm already on it"?

    (A) She has been reviewing the contents.
    (B) She is willing to make a demonstration.
    (C) She is one of the parents participating in the fair.
    (D) She is invited to make a speech in the forum.

Questions 4-8 refer to the following Web page and e-mail.

http://www.nottinghillbook.com

Nottinghill Bookstore
The source of England's most unique books!

A short walk from Grand Forest Square, you can come across some unique editions of England's greatest literature. In our collections, we have books written by masters from England, Wales, Ireland, and Scotland. All publications are original texts and written in their original languages.

We also provide advice on book storage and preservation as well as an effective restoration service. Visit us for a free consultation with our conversant staff in these old books.

Please click to see our online catalog, where you can order books and even get them delivered to your home at very reasonable rates.

ONLINE CATALOG

To:	Customer Service <nottinghill.cs@notinghillbook.com>
From:	Alex Williams <a.williams@newmexico.edu>
Date:	March 10
Subject:	Great Expectations by Charles Dickens

To Whom It May Concern:

Yesterday I was in Portsmouth and had an opportunity to visit your brilliant store. I happened to notice that you had a copy of Charles Dickens' *Great Expectations*. Unfortunately, I had realized that I had left my wallet at my hotel at that time. I had to attend the annual scholarship symposium on classical literary works and did not have time to bring my wallet back and buy the book. When I came back to your store again after the event, your store had already closed. I saw this e-mail address when I looked at the show window of your bookstore.

I would like to ask whether it would be possible to have the book shipped to my home in the U.S. This forum will be held in another country next year, so I will be unlikely to visit London again in the near future. I'm looking forward to hearing from you soon.

Sincerely,

Alex Williams

4. What is NOT suggested about Nottinghill Bookstore?

   (A) It retains various books in diverse languages.
   (B) It is located in Portsmouth, England.
   (C) It only sells newly released books.
   (D) It can ship a book to a customer's address.

5. On the Web page, the phrase "come across" in paragraph 1, line 1, is closest in meaning to

   (A) discover
   (B) pass over
   (C) benefit from
   (D) conform to

6. In what field does Mr. Williams most likely work?

   (A) Construction
   (B) Book restoration
   (C) Accounting
   (D) Education

7. What is the purpose of the e-mail?

   (A) To inquire about the availability of a book
   (B) To ask about the store's shipping policy
   (C) To mention an error in the online catalog
   (D) To request a discount on some unique books

8. What is indicated about Mr. Williams?

   (A) He lives in the United States of America.
   (B) He went to London for sightseeing with his family.
   (C) He visited Nottinghill Bookstore three times.
   (D) He has a plan to visit the store soon.

Questions 9-13 refer to the article, schedule, and e-mail.

BOSTON — When David Conte, who is a native of Boston, was just 4 years old, his parents were cognizant of his gift for music, especially playing the piano. When he reached age 6, his parents enrolled him in a school program for gifted children, affiliated with Berklee College of Music in Boston. Two years later, after completing his basic musical programs, he had a chance to be on stage at the Massachusetts Music Festival. By age 12, Conte had composed more than 100 pieces in various genres.

David Conte, now just 15 years old, has already swept a lot of awards locally and internationally in different musical award ceremonies. Nowadays, Conte is living in New York City and working in various fields of musical activities such as directing music for movies, composing for TV commercials, and collaborating with musical performances.

Conte would like to perform a regular recital in his hometown once a year, so we will notify you of performance information as soon as getting his plan.

XD GARDEN THEATER NOVEMBER EVENTS

Benjamin's Standing Show Tour – November 5, 6 P.M.
Lauded by peers and critics alike, Benjamin is one of our generation's strongest comedic voices. As a nationally renowned comedian, he has provided a healthy laugh to the public.
Caution) No cell phones, cameras, or recording devices will be allowed during this show.

David Conte – November 12, 6 P.M.
The greatest musical genius ever produced on Boston soil, David Conte will perform a variety of pieces. These include a collection he composed during his time at the music academy in Berklee College of Music. This teenager prodigy will not return to the XD Garden Theater until next year, so don't miss the chance to listen to his brilliant piano melodies!

ELF the Musical – November 19, 7 P.M.
Everyone's favorite ELF will make his return to Boston this holiday season with *ELF the Musical* at the XD Garden Theater!
ELF the Musical is the hilarious tale of Buddy, a young orphan child who mistakenly crawls into Santa's bag of gifts and is transported back to the North Pole.

Rolling Hollywood's Concert – November 26, 5 P.M.
The top-ranked and best-selling artists Rolling Hollywood will bring *A Fantastic Christmas Concert* to the XD Garden Theater for their special performance. This California-based rock band has toured throughout the U.S., and finally arrived here!
They notified us that this concert would be very meaningful in that they released a new song "Rolling Christmas!"

```
To:        Information <info@xdgardentheater.org>
From:      Joshua Melisa <j.melisa@bkportal.net>
Subject:   Seats Availability for disabled person
Date:      November 19
```

Dear XD Garden Theater,

Now I am in a wheelchair, and I had never been to your theater because I thought that I would not be able to see the performances well due to my difficulties. However, I recently had a great experience in your theater, and I appreciate the consideration you take for disabled people like me. I was so surprised by how much I was able to enjoy Benjamin's stand-up show. I could see and hear very well from my seat in the front row, and I didn't need to compete with the crowded situation in the central aisle with others.

I am concerned that I cannot secure a seat for your final event. I will try to get a ticket as soon as possible, but I would like to ask whether seats for the disabled are still available or not.

I'm looking forward to hearing about it from you soon.

Best wishes,

Joshua Melisa

9. What is indicated about Mr. Conte?

   (A) He graduated from the College of Music.
   (B) He studied music formally since age 4.
   (C) He is now appearing in commercials.
   (D) He no longer lives in Boston.

10. How old was Mr. Conte when he played at a local festival for the first time?

    (A) 4
    (B) 6
    (C) 8
    (D) 12

11. In the e-mail, the word "compete" in paragraph 1, line 5, is closest in meaning to

    (A) contest
    (B) play
    (C) struggle
    (D) offend

12. What does Mr. Melisa NOT mention about his seat at the theater?

    (A) It was conveniently located near the stage.
    (B) There were no obstacles visually.
    (C) It had plenty of legroom.
    (D) It did not require passing through the center.

13. Which performance does Mr. Melisa want to attend next?

    (A) Benjamin's Standing Show Tour
    (B) David Conte
    (C) ELF the Musical
    (D) Rolling Hollywood's Concert

DAY 15 다중 지문 유형

SPARTA 유형 파악

이중 지문(double passages)과 삼중 지문(triple passages)은 한 세트당 5문제로 구성, 총 5세트가 출제된다. 2~3개의 지문 중, 각 문제가 몇 번째 지문에 해당하는지 반드시 체크하면서 읽도록 한다. 문제를 보고 글을 읽을 때, 몇 번째 지문인지 표시를 해둬야, 필요한 부분으로 넘어가서 답의 근거가 되는 지문을 바로 확인할 수 있다. 다중 지문은 각 지문간의 연계 문제가 등장하므로, 정보를 꼼꼼하게 살펴보고 매칭시키는 맥락 완성 이해력이 요구된다. 단일 지문(single passage)과 마찬가지로, 각 지문의 도입부를 빠르게 읽으며 문제를 분석한다.

SPARTA 문제 풀이 비법

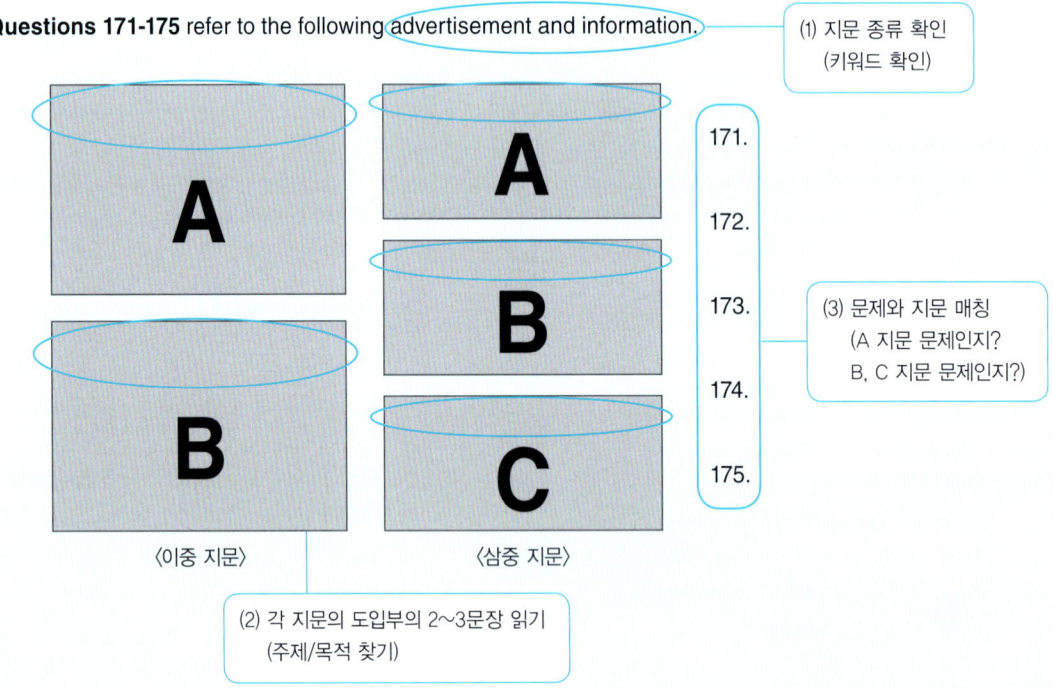

1. 빈출 지문 유형 파악하기
    예) 편지/이메일: 기본 정보 탐독 → 제목, 수신인, 발신인, 날짜, 이메일 주소
        기타 양식: 날짜, 돈, 수량과 같은 숫자에 유의하여 체크해 두기

2. 연계 문제 개수 파악하기
    이중 지문은 최소 1문항, 삼중 지문은 최소 2문항의 연계 문제 출제
    보통 육하원칙이나 추론 질문 유형(세부 사항)으로 출제되는 경향이 있음.

3. 지문 간의 관계 파악하기
    각 지문은 반드시 하나의 상황에 연관된 사람, 사건, 행사 등을 두고 이야기가 전개되기 때문에 그 연관성을 예측하며 읽기를 통해 문제를 분석해야 한다.

상황 예시) 첫 번째 환급 양식의 제출자 이름이 두 번째 이메일에서 발신자 이름과 같다.
→ 회사에 환급금 요청을 위한 양식을 제출하고, 이에 대한 추가적인 문의나 혹은 변경 사항 등을 해당 부서에 알리고자 쓰는 글일 수 있다는 상황의 연관성 예측

세 번째 지문에서 회계부서가 양식 제출자에게 다시 이메일을 보낸 경우
→ 두 번째 이메일에서 발신자(즉, 환급 신청서 양식 제출자)가 요청 또는 문의한 사항에 대한 대응(요구사항 승인, 반영, 거절 등)

[유형 엿보기] 이중 지문

이메일(일정 변경 요청) & 이메일(일정 변경 제안)
이메일(일자리 제안) & 편지(일자리 수락)
광고(상품/제품 광고) & 기사/정보(보증서/설명서)
광고(구인 광고) & 이메일(이력서, 문의)
공고(매장 오픈/행사, 제품 출시) & 이메일(가격표, 기능 문의)
기사(행사/인물 평가) & 이메일(행사 안내문/인물 소개)
양식(설문지, 스케줄, 송장 등) & 이메일(문의, 요청 목적)

[유형 엿보기] 삼중 지문

공지 & 양식(요청서/신청서) & 이메일(승인 여부)
구인/구직 광고 & 이메일(인사 담당자/구직자 작성) & 지원서
제품/서비스 광고 & 송장(주문 내역) & 편지/이메일(처리 결과)
이메일(일정 확인) & 여정/일정표 & 이메일(일정 확정 또는 변경)
행사 관련 기사 & 행사 초대장 & 진행 상황 보고

SPARTA 다중 지문 유형 TIP

이중 지문, 삼중 지문 모두 각 글의 주제/목적을 찾고, 문제를 분석해 가면서 몇 번째 글에 해당하는 문제인지 표시해 둔다. 이중 지문의 경우, 연계 문제가 5문제 중에서 주로 세 번째 또는 다섯 번째 순서로 등장한다. 삼중 지문도 비슷하지만 <첫 번째+두 번째>, <두 번째+세 번째>, <첫 번째+세 번째> 형태 중에서 어떤 지문끼리의 연계 정보를 물어보는지 파악해야 한다. 대부분의 경우, 문제의 순서와 정답 단서가 나오는 순서가 유사하므로 순서대로 문제를 풀도록 한다.

연계 문제 단서	첫 번째 문제	두 번째 문제	세 번째 문제	네 번째 문제	다섯 번째 문제
예시 1	A지문	A지문	B지문	C지문	C+B지문
예시 2	A지문	B지문	A+B지문	C지문	C지문
예시 3	A지문	B지문	B지문	A+C지문	C지문

위 예시처럼 연계 문제는 중간 이후에 주로 등장하는데, 글의 전개 순서와 문제 순서가 유사하므로 각 문제가 어떤 지문에 해당하는지 표시해 두도록 한다.

1. 지시문을 보고 지문의 종류 확인
2. 각 지문의 연관 관계 파악하고 글의 흐름 예측하기
3. 질문을 읽고 몇 번째 지문의 글과 관련되어 있는지 표시
4. 해당 지문의 핵심어구 (고유명사, 장소-시간 정보) 찾기
5. 연계 문제의 관련 단서를 글의 전개 순서에 따라 판단하기

SPARTA — Reading Point

Question 1 refers to the following e-mail and document.

To : info@prudentinsure.com
From : diana.avril@fundametalcorp.net
Date : June 30
Subject : Coverage

To whom it may concern:

I am currently a Silver Plan member, but would like to upgrade to your most comprehensive plan as soon as possible. I have received a promotion that takes effect next month, and that new income will enable me to bring my husband and two daughters under my coverage.
In addition, there is a new local doctor in our area, Vaan Hunterar, and he has already gotten many good reviews from patients. However, I did not see him on the list of your Complete Care. Can I use him with this plan? Please e-mail me back to let me know about my requests.

Thanks,
Diana Avril

Prudent Insurance Company
Plans to Cover Your Needs

Health Insurance Plans

Plan Name	Type	Monthly Fee	Total Medical Expense Coverage *
Bronze	Individual	$150	$300,000
Silver	Individual	$250	$600,000
Gold	Spouse	$400	$900,000
Platinum	Family	$500	$1,800,000

Enrollment is August 1 to August 30 for coverage that begins the next year. Our auto-renew function ensures that your plan is extended every year on September 1.

*Medical expense coverage is only for clinics, hospitals, and other facilities within the list of the Complete Care healthcare provider network.

Q1. What plan does Ms. Avril want?

(A) Bronze
(B) Silver
(C) Gold
(D) Platinum

수신: info@prudentinsure.com
발신: diana.avril@fundametalcorp.net
날짜: 6월 30일
제목: 보험 적용 범위

관계자분께,

저는 현재 Silver Plan 회원인데, 가능한 한 빨리 귀사의 가장 종합적인 상품으로 업그레이드를 하고자 합니다. 저는 다음달 효력이 생기는 홍보물을 받았고, 새로운 수입이 제 남편과 두 딸을 제 보험 보장 범위 아래에 둘 수 있을 것 같습니다.

이에 더하여, 우리 지역에 Vaan Hunterar라는 의사 선생님이 계신데, 그는 환자들로부터 좋은 평가를 많이 받고 있습니다. 하지만 저는 귀사의 Complete Care 목록에서 이 분을 찾을 수 없습니다. 이 상품으로 그 분을 이용할 수 있을까요? 그와 관련한 제 요청에 대해 이메일로 알려주시기 바랍니다.

감사합니다.

Diana Avril

Prudent 보험 회사
당신의 요구를 보장할 계획

의료 보험 상품

상품명	유형	월 보험료	총 의료 지출 보장 범위
Bronze	개인	$150	300달러
Silver	개인	$250	600달러
Gold	배우자	$400	900달러
Platinum	가족	$500	1800달러

내년에 시작하는 보장 상품의 등록은 8월 1일부터 8월 30일까지입니다. 저희 자동 갱신 기능은 귀하의 보험 상품이 매년 9월 1일에 연장됨을 보장합니다.

* 의료 지출 보장은 오직 *Complete Care* 의료 제공자 네트워크 목록에 있는 의료원, 병원이나 기타 시설들에서만 가능합니다.

Q1. Avril 씨가 원하는 보험 상품은?

(A) Bronze
(B) Silver
(C) Gold
(D) Platinum

▶ 첫 번째 이메일에서 현재 Silver 회원인데, "most comprehensive(가장 종합적인)" 것으로 업그레이드하기를 원하면서, my husband and two daughters까지 넣고 싶다고 했으므로, 아래의 차트에서 family type 최상위 유형인 (D)가 정답이다.

어휘 comprehensive ⓐ 종합적인   plan ⓝ 계획, 보험상품   promotion ⓝ 홍보(물)   coverage ⓝ 보장범위   rate ⓝ 등급, 평가   insurance ⓝ 보험   enrollment ⓝ 등록, 등록 인원   function ⓝ 기능   clinic ⓝ 의료원   expense ⓝ 지출   spouse ⓝ 배우자

Tip 첫 번째 이메일과 두 번째 문서(양식)의 연계 문제 유형이다.
첫 번째 이메일에서 현재 Silver 회원인데, "most comprehensive(가장 종합적인)" 것으로 업그레이드를 원하면서, my husband and two daughters까지 넣고 싶다고 했으므로, 아래의 차트에서 family type의 최상위 보험 상품을 찾아 확인하면 된다.

SPARTA Check-UP

Question 1 refers to the following booklet, e-mail, and notice.

Premium Resort
The biggest resort near the downtown area, attracting thousands of people each year.

Countless trees, various wildlife, and clean and pure water in the valley greet everyone who wants to take a break by getting away from the hubbub of urban life and enjoy fresh nature.

Activities & Areas:

Green Valleyside	**Skihut Wood**	**Zulu Fields**
Bicycle rentals	Hiking trails	Basketball courts
Skate rentals	Bicycle paths	Soccer Field
Canoe rentals	Jogging paths	Badminton courts
		Volleyball courts

Mountain Adventure
Reserved picnic spots
Scenic views of the surrounding city
Birds, flowers and wildlife viewing (please do no feed the animals)

> There is something for everyone here. Please enjoy responsibly and follow all resort regulations while visiting our areas.

Nick Hamilton
General Director of the Resort

To: Gary D. Cohn
From: Melissa Beth
Date: May 2
Subject: Outing

Dear Mr. Cohn,

Thanks for leaving the Premium Resort brochure on my desk. I've been there only once or twice, at the reserved picnic areas.

I think your idea about going there is good for our annual outing in June. In my opinion, a lot of our employees enjoy volleyball and basketball, so I know that they would like participating in those activities. In addition, I believe we can build up strong teamwork. Matching groups with one another is also favorable.

Iris Stella's group – Min-sung, Whitney and Brian – are all fanatical hikers. They could have a nice time trekking the trails in the wood.

I would like to finalize and announce this plan. Please ask Ms. Alyssa to handle the estimates and other paperwork within our department budget.

After all of those things are complete, we will announce this outing plan at the next department meeting on May 12.

Thanks,

Melissa Beth
Department Head

Notice

Issued on May 3

Premium Resort

We welcome everyone to our wonderful place.
Please note the changes implemented recently.

Online payment:
Individuals or organizations that want to pay for resort services or activities are encouraged to do so through our Web site or mobile application. Visitors using the app get a 3% discount.

Sports area:
All spaces in Zulu Fields are temporarily closed for renovation over the next 5 months. We sincerely apologize for any inconvenience about this sudden construction plan.

Pathway along the valley:
Please keep in mind that paths along the valley are too narrow. Bikes must refrain from using these trails. Be sure to wear protective gear --- such as helmets, kneepads, and other similar items --- throughout all the areas.

Q1 Where has Ms. Beth already visited at the resort?

(A) Green Valleyside
(B) Skihut Wood
(C) Zulu Fields
(D) Mountain Adventure

SPARTA Practice Test

Questions 1-5 refer to the following advertisement and article.

Greenwich Stock Trade Corporation

Fairfax, Virginia

The Glare Metal Fund

Now you can enjoy excellent financial benefits from our most competitive stock funds available: the Glare Metal Fund. The fund specializes in stocks from some of the largest, oldest, and safest companies operating their headquarters in South Africa, Kenya, Ethiopia, and other countries in Africa.

The fund has averaged an impressive 20% growth rate in the past three years, easily beating other funds in its category. The growth was outstanding, so it was even mentioned in *The Magazine of Top Stock Trade*.

It is easy for anyone to invest in this stock fund. All you have to do is sign up either at one of our local branches or online. Afterwards, the amount you designate will be automatically transferred from your bank deposit account to the Glare Metal Fund every month.

Furthermore, you can change that amount easily with our online stock exchange. You can also temporarily stop your automatic transfers at any time.

Find out more information and details at www.greenwichstock.com/glaremetalfund.

* A minimum of $1,000 or the equivalent amount in U.S. dollars as a starting deposit is required to open an account.

---

http://www.topstocktrade.com

Making Your Money Work for You

By Lynn M. Martin, a Writer in the Finance
Posted: October 1, 10:20 A.M.

Investing in particular stock funds used to be time-consuming and complex. However, this procedure is quickly changing today. Investment companies wanting to attract new customers are becoming much more flexible in their trading methods, with an online trading system that can make it easier to transfer money from consumers' accounts to stock funds. The Glare Metal Fund is an exceptional example of this innovative method.

The only problem is that the account opening requirements, like those of Greenwich, are commonly asking customers to agree with it in person. Greenwich says that this procedure is not unreasonable. Yet, on the contrary, I strongly think that it is a little inconvenient in terms of visiting each branch, and it cannot be entirely Web-based as an online trading system.

In my October 10 article, online visitors will have a chance to watch my real-time webcast interview with Dorothy Rebecca, the fund's senior manager, on this matter and the general prospects of the fund.

1. According to the advertisement, what does the Glare Metal Fund focus on?

   (A) Small companies
   (B) New companies
   (C) International companies
   (D) American companies

2. Why was *The Magazine of Top Stock Trade* mentioned?

   (A) To announce new stock funds
   (B) To explain why growth rates deteriorated
   (C) To support a service's advantages
   (D) To suggest new investment rules

3. What is NOT a stated advantage of the Glare Metal Fund?

   (A) Accessing advice from experts
   (B) Using an online system
   (C) Choosing any monthly amount
   (D) Depositing either dollars or other currencies

4. What feature of the Glare Metal Fund does Mr. Martin disagree with?

   (A) Difficulties in making transfers
   (B) The need to verify the process offline
   (C) Lack of data for the growth rates
   (D) The delays in trading starting procedures

5. What will happen on October 10?

   (A) A chart for a fund's growth rates will be uploaded.
   (B) Webservers will be updated in the security section.
   (C) A writer will talk with the person in charge of the fund.
   (D) All the passwords for the trading will be changed.

Questions 6-10 refer to the following memorandum and e-mail.

To: All Staff Members
From: Director, Human Resources Department
Re: Application Procedures

If anyone wants to apply for a promotion in their department, please submit the following documents by next week, May 1st;

- An official application form with a copy of the photo identification
- Three letters of recommendation and reference contact information from your previous or current supervisors

The admission committee will thoroughly review your application packages, and only three candidates in each department can get a chance to perform five-minute presentations on their work capacity and prospective planning ability on May 20. That will be followed by a couple of interviews before the board decides which candidate is suitable for being promoted. After the final decision, the successful candidates will be notified via e-mail by the beginning of June. If you have any inquiries, send me an e-mail at timberton@dreamculture.org, and I will send an e-mail back to you as soon as possible. Thank you for your attention.

Best Regards,

Ganette Timberton
Personnel Division

To: Ganette Timberton <timberton@dreamculture.org>
From: Jacy Swift <j.swift@dreamculture.org>
Subject: Application for Promotion

I'm writing to ask you a few questions about the recommendation letters I should submit along with my application package. I have been working here at Dream Culture Co. for only a year and unfortunately, one of my three bosses, Mr. Daven, resigned from his position six months ago, so just two bosses remain. Now, not only do I have no way to contact him, but also he does not know about my job performance well because of just working with him for a few months. My other current bosses, Ms. Rebecca and Mr. Steven, have agreed to write a letter of recommendation.
Do I still have to submit one more letter to apply for the promotion? Or should I still ask Mr. Daven to write a letter of recommendation for me in spite of his resignation? Please let me know as soon as possible, because contact with him will likely take more time than I expected.

Sincerely,

Jacy Swift
Marketing Division (Extension: 7810)

6. Which of the following is NOT scheduled before the end of May?

   (A) Interviews
   (B) Presentations
   (C) Form submission
   (D) Promotion notification

7. What is Jacy Swift worried about?

   (A) Her photo ID
   (B) Her previous careers
   (C) Her communication skills
   (D) Her references

8. What can be inferred about Jacy Swift?

   (A) She has shown excellent job performance.
   (B) She may try to contact a boss.
   (C) She is working in another branch at present.
   (D) Her supervisor declined her request.

9. Who is Ms. Rebecca?

   (A) The personnel manager
   (B) An employee in the marketing department
   (C) A director of the sales division
   (D) One of the admission committee members

10. When was the e-mail most likely written?

    (A) In April
    (B) In May
    (C) In June
    (D) In July

Questions 11-15 refer to the following menu, order form, and e-mail.

Gourmet Catering Co. Menu
76 Lunger Drive #80, Bloomsburg, PA 17815, USA

Lunch - $25 per person
11:00 A.M. – 2:00 P.M.
Two pasta dishes (See pasta menu)

Light Dinner - $25 per person
5:00 P.M. – 6:00 P.M.
Two pasta dishes (See pasta menu)

Superior Dinner - $50 per person
5:00 P.M. – 9:00 P.M.
Includes two main dishes and two plates from the deluxe menu as well as drinks and desserts

Burger Bites - $15 per person
10:00 A.M. – 1:30 P.M.
A selection of burgers served by our chef
Available through August 30

Deluxe Dinner - $30 per person
6:00 P.M. – 8:00 P.M.
Two pasta dishes (See pasta menu) with salad

Oriental Cuisine - $32 per person
5:00 P.M. – 8:00 P.M.
Includes a variety of popular Southeast Asian dishes
Available on Friday and Saturday evenings only

Please note :
All orders must be made at least two days beforethe the delivery time.
Free delivery within Bloomsburg, Pennsylvania, for orders for over 30 people. For orders for under 50 people, there is a 5% surcharge to deliver to the places more than 20 miles outside Bloomsburg.

Gourmet Catering Co. (GCC) Online Order Confirmation

Please check the following information of your order carefully before clicking the "Complete" button. Be sure to print this page as your proof of purchase.

Order No. : AU2019921
Deliver to : Randall Seedorff (Angel Power Energy)
Delivery date and time : Friday, August 20
11:30 A.M. (Lunch), 6:30 P.M.(Dinner)
Address : 32 Ideal Park Road, Catawissa, PA 17820
Telephone : 570-799-5006
E-mail : r.seedorff@angelpowerenergy.net

Order Date/Time : August 17, 2:35 P.M.
Bill to : Angel Power Energy
Address : 145 Brooklyn Avenue, Brooklyn, NY, 111213
Telephone : 718-735-4400

Item	Quantity	Price per person	Total
Lunch	48 people	$25.00	$1,200.00
Superior Dinner	45 people	$50.00	$2,250.00
		Delivery 5%	$172.50
		Sales Tax 7%	$241.50
		Grand Total	$3,864.00

Notes : Please send me a text message at 710-2083-1923 when you arrive as I may not be at the delivery place at that time.

| Order processed by : | Scott Fitzgerald | |

To: GCC Orders <orders@gourmentcatering.com>
From: Randall Seedorff <r.seedorff@angelpowerengery.net>
Subject: Order Number AU2019921
Date: August 19

Dear Sir/Madam,

I would like to change my order submitted on August 17. We will have some additional visitors to our firm set for the lunch service, so I would like to change the order from 48 people to 55 people. Additionally, I would like to add the Burger Bites set for 15 people to be served at 12:30. I would appreciate it if you could recalculate the invoice and send it back to me as soon as possible.

Regards,

Randall Seedorff
Manager, Human Resources Department
Angel Power Energy

---

11. Which is NOT a menu item to be delivered on August 20?

(A) Pasta
(B) Salad
(C) Asian dish
(D) Beverage

12. What is indicated about Mr. Seedorff's order?

(A) It is for a group of more than 100 people.
(B) It qualifies for free desserts and delivery.
(C) It requires a delivery of over 20 miles from Bloomsburg.
(D) It was placed over the phone two days before the delivery.

13. What is the purpose of the e-mail?

(A) To celebrate a company
(B) To update an order
(C) To ask for the best menu for an event
(D) To request a discount

14. Who most likely is Scott Fitzgerald?

(A) A guest of Mr. Seedorff
(B) An HR manager in Angel Power Energy
(C) A person who is in charge of delivery
(D) A staff member of the catering company

15. Why might Mr. Seedorff's request for additional menu items be rejected?

(A) Gourmet Catering requires two days' notice.
(B) It is temporarily out of stock.
(C) It is only available during a limited period.
(D) The address is beyond the limit of their delivery.

스파르타 토익
750⁺
LC & RC

실전 모의고사

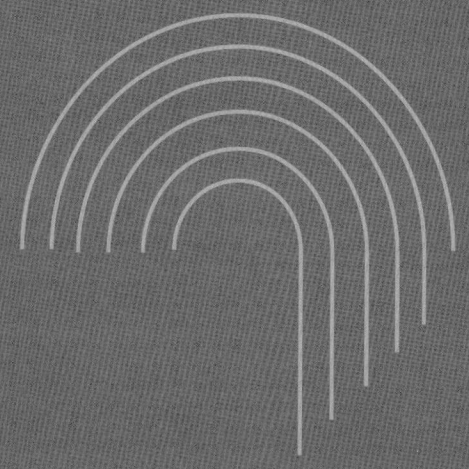

정답 p. 448
(OMR 및 해설은 http://books.english.co.kr에서 다운로드 가능)

LISTENING TEST

In the Listening test, you will be asked to demonstrate how well you understand spoken English. The entire Listening test will last approximately 45 minutes. There are four parts, and directions are given for each part. You must mark your answers on the separate answer sheet.
Do not write your answers in your test book.

PART 1

Directions: For each question in this part, you will hear four statements about a picture in your test book. When you hear the statements, you must select the one statement that best describes what you see in the picture. Then find the number of the question on your answer sheet and mark your answer.
The statements will not be printed in your test book and will be spoken only one time.

Sample Answer
Ⓐ ● Ⓒ Ⓓ

Statement (B), "They're shaking hands," is the best description of the picture, so you should select answer (B) and mark it on your answer sheet.

1.

2.

3.

4.

5.

6.

PART 2

Directions: You will hear a question or statement and three responses spoken in English. They will not be printed in your test book and will be spoken only one time. Select the best response to the question or statement and mark the letter (A), (B), or (C) on your answer sheet.

7. Mark your answer on your answer sheet.
8. Mark your answer on your answer sheet.
9. Mark your answer on your answer sheet.
10. Mark your answer on your answer sheet.
11. Mark your answer on your answer sheet.
12. Mark your answer on your answer sheet.
13. Mark your answer on your answer sheet.
14. Mark your answer on your answer sheet.
15. Mark your answer on your answer sheet.
16. Mark your answer on your answer sheet.
17. Mark your answer on your answer sheet.
18. Mark your answer on your answer sheet.
19. Mark your answer on your answer sheet.
20. Mark your answer on your answer sheet.
21. Mark your answer on your answer sheet.
22. Mark your answer on your answer sheet.
23. Mark your answer on your answer sheet.
24. Mark your answer on your answer sheet.
25. Mark your answer on your answer sheet.
26. Mark your answer on your answer sheet.
27. Mark your answer on your answer sheet.
28. Mark your answer on your answer sheet.
29. Mark your answer on your answer sheet.
30. Mark your answer on your answer sheet.
31. Mark your answer on your answer sheet.

PART 3

Directions: You will hear some conversations between two or more people. You will be asked to answer three questions about what the speakers say in each conversation. Select the best response to each question and mark the letter (A), (B), (C), or (D) on your answer sheet. The conversations will not be printed in your test book and will be spoken only one time.

32. Where most likely are the speakers?
    (A) In a presentation hall
    (B) In a hallway
    (C) In a security office
    (D) In a supply room

33. What are the speakers concerned about?
    (A) Preparing for a presentation
    (B) Forgetting a password
    (C) Changing the security code
    (D) Being late for work

34. What does the woman suggest they do?
    (A) Post a notice
    (B) Contact their supervisor
    (C) Ask someone for help
    (D) Lock all the doors

35. What are the speakers talking about?
    (A) A new system
    (B) Taking inventory
    (C) Tracking an order
    (D) A store's rules

36. What problem does the woman mention?
    (A) There has been a shortage of parts.
    (B) Some software is not operating properly.
    (C) System testing has been delayed.
    (D) Costs have been higher than she expected.

37. What does the man ask the woman to do?
    (A) Submit a report
    (B) Launch a marketing campaign
    (C) Compile some design specifications
    (D) Assemble a device

38. Where does the man most likely work?
    (A) At an optician's
    (B) At a medical clinic
    (C) At an auto mechanic
    (D) At a bookstore

39. Why is the woman visiting the shop?
    (A) She wants to have a vision test.
    (B) She wants to buy a frame.
    (C) Her item does not fit right.
    (D) Her item is damaged.

40. What does the man offer to do?
    (A) Change to a new product
    (B) Test the woman's eyes
    (C) Extend warranty
    (D) Order some parts

41. What is the conversation mainly about?
    (A) A reservation for a hotel room
    (B) Alternative transportation to a meeting place
    (C) Different types of negotiations
    (D) Some information on a flyer

42. Who most likely is Mr. Renquist?
    (A) A mechanic
    (B) A train conductor
    (C) A job candidate
    (D) A client

43. What will the man do next?
    (A) Talk to a presenter
    (B) Cancel the meeting
    (C) Call for a taxi
    (D) Review the document

Go on to the next page

44. Where most likely are the speakers?

(A) At a restaurant
(B) On the road
(C) In an office kitchen
(D) In a coffee shop

45. What does the woman imply when she says, "Have you finished your newspaper"?

(A) She would like to leave.
(B) She would like to borrow the man's newspaper.
(C) She is interested in the man's opinion.
(D) She wants to drink another coffee.

46. What will the man do next?

(A) Buy some food
(B) Wait for the woman
(C) Go to his workplace
(D) Make a phone call

47. What does the woman ask the man to do?

(A) Go to the printers together
(B) Authorize her work
(C) Print some documents
(D) Give her some advice

48. Why does the man ask to meet again tomorrow?

(A) He has no time right now.
(B) He needs the woman to meet a deadline.
(C) He wants to learn how to use new equipment.
(D) He is waiting for a document to arrive.

49. What does the man say about the company?

(A) It made a deal.
(B) It reduced working time.
(C) It hired more staff.
(D) It helped with a summer promotion.

50. What problem does the man mention?

(A) He broke tiles at a store.
(B) He is unable to locate a product.
(C) He forgot the product number.
(D) He lost an invoice.

51. What does the woman mean when she says, "Please do"?

(A) She will cancel a purchase.
(B) She plans to double an order.
(C) She wants to get a piece of information.
(D) She thinks the man will participate in an event.

52. What will the man probably do next?

(A) Place a special order
(B) Visit another store
(C) Pay for an order
(D) Exchange his cash

53. Where most likely are the speakers?

(A) At a convention
(B) At a plant
(C) At a laboratory
(D) At a fashion show

54. What do the women imply about their company?

(A) It only focuses on large firms.
(B) It specializes in international law.
(C) It helps reduce IT budgets.
(D) It works with state-of-the-art technologies.

55. What will the man probably do next?

(A) Order some business cards
(B) Set up an appointment
(C) Find out more information at another place
(D) Sign a contract with women's company

56. Why did the man travel to Venice?
    (A) To make some deliveries
    (B) To visit relatives
    (C) To make a deal
    (D) To open a café

57. What is the man's problem?
    (A) He sent the wrong address.
    (B) He had trouble remembering some information.
    (C) He could not meet the clients.
    (D) He could not purchase the items he wanted.

58. According to the woman, what will be included in a handbook?
    (A) Easy recipes
    (B) Travel information
    (C) Sales strategies
    (D) Product descriptions

59. What are the speakers working on?
    (A) An interior design project
    (B) A menu upgrade
    (C) An interview
    (D) A lecture series

60. Why are the speakers concerned?
    (A) They need to expand a team.
    (B) A client doesn't want to change the deadline.
    (C) Some information is incomplete.
    (D) They didn't attend the meeting.

61. What does the woman say she will do next?
    (A) Contact a client
    (B) Call off the project
    (C) Cancel her meetings
    (D) Review some documents

Current Price List

Number	Price
500	$110
1000	$140
2000	$180
3000	$210

62. What does the woman notice?
    (A) A modification to a company's product prices
    (B) A greater need for advertisement distribution
    (C) A mistake on some newly printed brochures
    (D) A change in a printing company's ownership

63. Look at the graphic. How much did the company pay for brochures the last time?
    (A) $55
    (B) $70
    (C) $90
    (D) $105

64. What does the man want the woman to do in the future?
    (A) Restock certain items earlier
    (B) Make their brochure more effective
    (C) Try to negotiate a discounted price
    (D) Find a more suitable printing company

Go on to the next page

Bestsellers Section

	Title	Author
1	Matilda	John Hopkins
2	Two Lovers	Luise Secker
3	The Giver	Royald Dal
4	Wonder	Jess Kini

European Jazz Festival

7–11 March

Millennium Park

Tickets £20

65. Where do the speakers most likely work?

   (A) At a publishing company
   (B) At a library
   (C) At a shoe store
   (D) At a bookstore

66. Look at the graphic. Who does the man want to invite to an event?

   (A) John Hopkins
   (B) Luise Secker
   (C) Royald Dal
   (D) Jess Kini

67. What does the woman ask the man to do?

   (A) Contact the writer
   (B) Delay a book signing event
   (C) Get in touch with the publisher
   (D) Consult with an expert

68. What project will the speakers be working on?

   (A) Restoring some artworks
   (B) Creating a park
   (C) Designing a building
   (D) Writing some lyrics

69. Look at the graphic. Which date will the woman attend the festival?

   (A) On March 7
   (B) On March 8
   (C) On March 9
   (D) On March 11

70. Who is Switzerland Basel?

   (A) A conductor
   (B) An event organizer
   (C) A singer
   (D) A music critic

PART 4

Directions: You will hear some talks given by a single speaker. You will be asked to answer three questions about what the speaker says in each talk. Select the best response to each question and mark the letter (A), (B), (C), or (D) on your answer sheet. The talks will not be printed in your test book and will be spoken only one time.

71. Where is the announcement taking place?
    (A) In a bus
    (B) At an airport
    (C) In a train
    (D) At an electricity firm

72. What caused the problem?
    (A) A train failure
    (B) A blackout
    (C) Traffic congestion
    (D) A car accident

73. What is the company going to provide for some inconvenienced passengers?
    (A) Taxi coupons
    (B) Free snacks at Town Hall Station
    (C) Discount tickets
    (D) Another form of transportation

74. What is the purpose of the announcement?
    (A) To announce a job opening
    (B) To report a personnel change
    (C) To welcome a new director
    (D) To report sales results

75. How long has Megan Drummond worked as a sales director?
    (A) For three years
    (B) For five years
    (C) For seven years
    (D) For ten years

76. Why would some employees contact the speaker?
    (A) To apply for a position
    (B) To participate in a party
    (C) To give him some money
    (D) To receive a gift

77. Who is the speaker?
    (A) An accountant
    (B) A human resources director
    (C) The factory supervisor
    (D) An assembly line employee

78. According to the speaker, what should the listeners do with the security cards?
    (A) Carry them the whole time
    (B) Return them to the receptionist
    (C) Insert them into the card reader
    (D) Enter the card number

79. What will the listeners hear about later?
    (A) Production quotas
    (B) Sales figures
    (C) Strategic plans
    (D) Computer programs

80. Why has the meeting been held at the last minute?
    (A) To introduce the new dishware
    (B) To announce a new policy
    (C) To provide the contents of a contract
    (D) To inform employees of an error

81. Why does the speaker say, "It's been a week"?
    (A) To express a concern about a delay
    (B) To praise a team's performance
    (C) To ship the boxes themselves
    (D) To change the business strategies

82. What is Min asked to do?
    (A) Call a shipping company
    (B) Verify some addresses
    (C) Inform some staff about the change
    (D) Give a speech

Go on to the next page

83. Which department does the listener most likely work in?
    (A) Research & development
    (B) Sales
    (C) Public relations
    (D) Human resources

84. What does the speaker mean when she says, "we've already received 100 candidates"?
    (A) An application period should be extended.
    (B) Some application materials should be shortened.
    (C) Some candidates have already been selected.
    (D) A job advertisement has been successful.

85. What does the speaker ask Miyaki to do?
    (A) Submit an application
    (B) Arrange workspaces
    (C) Look over a document
    (D) Fill out a questionnaire

86. What does Briton Company plan to do in March?
    (A) Hold a press conference
    (B) Expand overseas branches
    (C) Construct a facility
    (D) Donate books to the library

87. Who is Rachel Kim?
    (A) A city official
    (B) A professional entertainer
    (C) A building manager
    (D) A company worker

88. What are the listeners asked to do next?
    (A) Look at the materials
    (B) Hand out some brochures
    (C) Set up the equipment
    (D) Attend the welcoming party

89. Who is the talk for?
    (A) Conference participants
    (B) Authors
    (C) New employees
    (D) Event volunteers

90. What will the listeners probably do first?
    (A) Go to the security office
    (B) Take a tour
    (C) Set up their laptops
    (D) Proofread a report

91. What does the speaker say has recently changed?
    (A) A work shift
    (B) An employment directory
    (C) A meeting schedule
    (D) An office layout

92. What is Ted's known for?
    (A) Used-car sales
    (B) Automotive items
    (C) Office supplies
    (D) Vehicle rentals

93. What service has Ted's recently added?
    (A) On-site maintenance
    (B) Reasonable vehicle inspection
    (C) Online appointments
    (D) Free tow assistance

94. According to the advertisement, what can the listeners do on the Web site?
    (A) Make an appointment in advance
    (B) Get discount information
    (C) Check an available product
    (D) See the store location

Summer Jazz Sessions

Theodore Grant	July 3rd
Sam James	July 10th
Melinda Thames	July 20th
Maria Garcia	August 4th

95. What problem does the speaker mention?
    (A) Some maintenance work will occur.
    (B) Inclement weather is predicted.
    (C) Some instruments have been lost.
    (D) A stage has been damaged.

96. Look at the graphic. Which musician's performance will be rescheduled?
    (A) Theodore Grant
    (B) Sam James
    (C) Melinda Thames
    (D) Maria Garcia

97. What is available on the Web site?
    (A) A performance schedule
    (B) Weather information
    (C) Park directions
    (D) Concert locations

Queens department store Directory

1st Floor: Footwear & Jewelry
2nd Floor: Women's Clothing
3rd Floor: Men's Clothing
4th Floor: Electronic Appliances
5th Floor: Cafe & Dining Bar

98. Why is the announcement being held?
    (A) To inform shoppers of special event
    (B) To clear out old merchandise
    (C) To announce a 10th anniversary party
    (D) To welcome a celebrity

99. Look at the graphic. Which floor is the sale on this week?
    (A) The second floor
    (B) The third floor
    (C) The fourth floor
    (D) The fifth floor

100. According to the speaker, what is available near the elevators?
    (A) A free sample
    (B) A flyer
    (C) A discount coupon
    (D) A membership card

Go on to the next page

READING TEST

In the Reading test, you will read a variety of texts and answer several different types of reading comprehension questions. The entire Reading test will last 75 minutes. There are three parts, and directions are given for each part. You are encouraged to answer as many questions as possible within the time allowed.

You must mark your answers on the separate answer sheet. Do not write your answers in the test book.

PART 5

Directions: A word or phrase is missing in each of the sentences below. Four answer choices are given below each sentence. Select the best answer to complete the sentence. Then mark the letter (A), (B), (C), or (D) on your answer sheet.

101. Of the four applicants, two have a variety of experience, but ------- do not have any in the related field.

(A) others
(B) the others
(C) other
(D) another

102. Employees should have ------- from the management for taking additional vacations.

(A) approval
(B) approve
(C) approved
(D) approving

103. Each of the applicants for the position ------- very competitive in all sections this year.

(A) is
(B) are
(C) been
(D) being

104. Start-up businesses are becoming increasingly ------- on online marketing channels such as social networking services.

(A) dependable
(B) dependent
(C) depend
(D) depended

105. The board of directors ------- employees of the new payroll system they decided to change.

(A) talked
(B) announced
(C) mentioned
(D) notified

106. ------- still remains our assembly-line branch in Seoul despite our efforts to expand our factories to the local areas.

(A) There
(B) It
(C) He
(D) They

107. If a new item ------- by rival manufacturers next year, our company will start producing a better one quickly.

(A) released
(B) will release
(C) will be released
(D) is released

108. Before ------- the report to their immediate supervisor, all employees should carefully look through their papers.

(A) submit
(B) submitted
(C) submitting
(D) to submit

109. Customers who want to know more information can find the answer ------- their devices on our Web site.
    (A) about
    (B) according to
    (C) beside
    (D) in addition to

110. All flights to New York City will be delayed or canceled ------- there will be inclement weather in NYC for three days in a row.
    (A) because
    (B) as long as
    (C) even as
    (D) even if

111. Anyone ------- is planning to attend the seminar should fill in the form by picking it up from the human resources department.
    (A) who
    (B) whom
    (C) which
    (D) what

112. ------- the volunteers have done in the on-campus bazaar was very helpful to homeless people around Allegheny County.
    (A) What
    (B) That
    (C) Whether
    (D) Because

113. ------- the firefighters arrive at the scene of the fire, the building will have been terribly damaged.
    (A) In order that
    (B) By the time
    (C) Owing to
    (D) Furthermore

114. Mr. Kevin should be in charge of handling payroll procedures because he is the most -------.
    (A) approved
    (B) knowledgeable
    (C) complex
    (D) confirmed

115. The Creative Architecture Award is annually given to an architect who has ------- recognition in the field of industrial design.
    (A) achieved
    (B) afforded
    (C) endured
    (D) arrested

116. All employees can pick up the ------- version of the company's employee manual in front of the main entrance.
    (A) numerous
    (B) updated
    (C) certain
    (D) aware

117. All construction workers should follow the ------- specified in the employee safety handbook.
    (A) advantages
    (B) permissions
    (C) regulations
    (D) progressions

118. This year's movie magazine will feature stories about the lives of the top-five animation directors ------- the direction of the Animation Movie Association.
    (A) under
    (B) either
    (C) among
    (D) beyond

119. When installing a household generator, homeowners must follow the set-up instructions ------- to prevent any malfunction.
    (A) directly
    (B) precisely
    (C) rightfully
    (D) indefinitely

120. This notice reminds tenants that the apartment management office will inspect the apartment building next week ------- check for any damage.
    (A) even if
    (B) in order to
    (C) after all
    (D) given that

Go on to the next page

121. Pitt's main subway station is ------- located near commuter parking areas that lead to the region's largest shopping mall.
   (A) conveniently
   (B) consistently
   (C) continually
   (D) commonly

122. Ms. Heather began working at the Brown Municipal Library five years ago and has ------- served as the manager.
   (A) ever
   (B) yet
   (C) so
   (D) since

123. Over the last decade, *Seoul Business News* has built a ------- as one of the most reliable and informative programs on global business.
   (A) privilege
   (B) character
   (C) reputation
   (D) consequence

124. Before Mr. Brown starts working with several different agencies, he needs to obtain the permits ------- for collaboration.
   (A) required
   (B) requiring
   (C) requires
   (D) will require

125. With ticket sales increasing, the first film that Mike Moore directed turned out to be ------- a success.
   (A) clear
   (B) clearly
   (C) clearer
   (D) clearing

126. All employees at Johns Construction Inc. must ------- a request form for paid sick leave to their immediate supervisor for approval.
   (A) apply
   (B) submit
   (C) vacate
   (D) oppose

127. A sales representative is trained to ------- the proper method of replacing an old toner cartridge with a new one.
   (A) demonstrate
   (B) respond
   (C) inquire
   (D) visit

128. To gather nominations for the Employee of the Year Award, the executives ------- asked each manager to choose outstanding employees from their departments.
   (A) nervously
   (B) utterly
   (C) specifically
   (D) densely

129. The release of online advertisements helped create a ------- demand for our new products.
   (A) redundant
   (B) plentiful
   (C) sizable
   (D) durable

130. ------- the spread of remote-control applications, more and more people can control their home appliances in their absence.
   (A) Because of
   (B) Instead of
   (C) In spite of
   (D) As much as

PART 6

Directions: Read the texts that follow. A word, phrase, or sentence is missing in parts of each text. Four answer choices for each question are given below the text. Select the best answer to complete the text. Then mark the letter (A), (B), (C), or (D) on your answer sheet.

Questions 131-134 refer to the following notice.

At Ventelo Books Online, we do our best to ship orders as promptly as possible. If you are concerned because your order has not yet ------- **131.**, please note the following information. ------- **132.**. An estimated delivery date is provided at the time of your purchase. Although we aim to make the most accurate estimate possible, some shipments may take ------- **133.** to be delivered. If your order is significantly delayed, please contact us. We'll investigate and ------- **134.** you of your shipment status.

131. (A) arrive
(B) been arrived
(C) arrived
(D) arriving

132. (A) As your warranty will expire soon, you need to update your contract.
(B) We should improve our customer service because our customer is dissatisfied with the refund procedure.
(C) Delivery times range from 2 to 3 weeks, depending on the shipping method selected during the order.
(D) All of our staff can always respond to an issue regarding any types of complaints caused by a contractor.

133. (A) longest
(B) longer
(C) length
(D) lengthy

134. (A) stay
(B) explain
(C) notify
(D) address

Questions 135-138 refer to the following e-mail.

To : All Staff
From : Jonathan Rose
Date : May 14
Subject : Upgrade of Computer

All computers of our offices will be notified of messages this afternoon to update an essential security software.

-------. You can continue to use your personal computers while installing the set-up files, although
135.
you may ------- that your computer speed is a bit slower than usual. After these security updates,
136.
you need to restart your computers. -------, if you have urgent tasks, you can defer the installation
137.
until you are in your spare time for the update. We sincerely apologize for any ------- and
138.
inconvenience because of it and thank you for understanding again.

135. (A) Those updates are connected with other mobile devices.
(B) Do not hesitate to contact us about the questions.
(C) These updates will be implemented automatically at 5 P.M.
(D) The latest model of computers is very popular with the public.

136. (A) notice
(B) convince
(C) enhance
(D) commence

137. (A) Similarly
(B) Rather
(C) However
(D) Therefore

138. (A) disrupt
(B) disruptive
(C) disruption
(D) disruptively

Questions 139-142 refer to the following article.

Chuck Taylor has spent 25 years selling and repairing pianos in Madison City. Starting April, he will ------- stop his work and begin his new career at the Wisconsin College of Music and Art in Milwaukee. -------. "I've loved my work, but now it's time for me to learn more specialized skills and share my field experiences." he said. Before he closes the store, Mr.Taylor wants to dispose his stocks to the public. On this occasion, people can get excellent ------- at highly discounted prices. Additional accessories for a piano will ------- be for sale. Anyone who is interested in this event just visits his store and buys something with competitive prices.

139. (A) regret
 (B) regrets
 (C) regretful
 (D) regretfully

140. (A) The prices of pianos are more competitive than other retailers who are selling grand pianos.
 (B) Mr.Taylor will take advanced courses about tuning a piano, working as a teaching assistant.
 (C) His skills of tuning pianos have already been recognized in the U.S. widely.
 (D) Mr.Taylor had spent his youth learning and experiencing audio equipment in the field of music.

141. (A) paintings
 (B) sculptures
 (C) instruments
 (D) electronics

142. (A) reciprocally
 (B) generally
 (C) instead
 (D) also

Go on to the next page

Questions 143-146 refer to the following memo.

To : All Prudent Insurance Staff
From : Kathy Stella, CEO, Prudent Insurance
Re : M&A Issue
Date : August 20

I am happy to notify all the staff that the merger between Prudent Insurance and Standard Bank will be accomplished on August 30. From that date ------- **143.**, the company's name will be changed into Prudent Bancassurance Group. This merger enables us to grow one of the largest ------- **144.** of commercial bank and insurance companies in the Europe.

Don't worry about your current status! Based on your current employment contract, your position, benefits package and salaries will remain the same without any changes. ------- **145.**.

As a result, the merger will cause changes of company policies in some parts. ------- **146.** will be shared during the formal company-wide conference on September 2 at 2:00 P.M. in the grand auditorium. If you have a question about the merger, please feel free to bring your inquiries there.

143. (A) forward
 (B) still
 (C) besides
 (D) last

144. (A) provide
 (B) provider
 (C) provided
 (D) providing

145. (A) The modified rules were under negotiation between Prudent and Standard.
 (B) Actually, our company needs additional experienced staff in many departments.
 (C) Please complete the formal document with three recommendation letters.
 (D) In case some revisions are needed, look through your document thoroughly.

146. (A) Both
 (B) Neither
 (C) These
 (D) Other

PART 7

Directions: In this part you will read a selection of texts, such as magazine and newspaper articles, e-mails, and instant messages. Each text or set of texts is followed by several questions. Select the best answer for each question and mark the letter (A), (B), (C), or (D) on your answer sheet.

Questions 147-148 refer to the following advertisement.

Posting Item: X2 Power Generator
Price: $300
Location: Indiana, PA

Posting Description
Bought at a store a year ago. Paid $650 for it. Had a 1-year warranty.
Fuel pump is not working and must be replaced by the buyer.
Otherwise in good condition. (Sorry, no pictures available).

$300 firm, as is.

First come first served, or call to reserve

Reply to: Call or text me for address (721) 214-9247

147. What is NOT indicated about the item?
 (A) It needs a repair.
 (B) Its price is fixed.
 (C) It had a certified document.
 (D) A manual is enclosed.

148. What is the seller willing to do?
 (A) Send photos upon request
 (B) Extend the current warranty
 (C) Hold the item for a prospective buyer
 (D) Deliver the item to a buyer's home

Go on to the next page

Questions 149-151 refer to the following information.

RADE DRINKS INTERNATIONAL

Rosa Stephens
Director, Personnel Division

A respected and innovative leader, Ms. Stephens oversees our global distribution chains for RADE Drinks International. She was employed 15 years ago and has been in charge of several essential tasks in various departments since that time.

In her previous role as a senior personnel manager, Ms. Stephens supervised RADE's on-the-job training for all employees, substantially increasing work productivity. She also planned, systemized and established company's human resources structure.

In addition, Ms. Stephens has been recognized as an eloquent speaker and presenter in the company. With these abilities, she also teaches at Great Pacific University, where as a student she received the Cobuild Award for her research on market trends in 4th generation industry. Fluent in both English and French, Ms. Stephens worked in the field of hospitality in France for five years before joining RADE.

149. What is the purpose of the information?

(A) To explain conditions for promotion
(B) To summarize an employee's current research
(C) To introduce a company staff
(D) To announce the winner of an award

150. What is NOT indicated as one of Ms. Stephens's strengths?

(A) She speaks more than one language.
(B) She recruits highly-qualified employees.
(C) She has done various tasks in the company.
(D) She is an experienced public speaker.

151. What is suggested about Ms. Stephens?

(A) She began her career at RADE before receiving her university degree.
(B) She has been a senior human resources manager for eight years.
(C) She does not work in a field related to her university studies.
(D) She did not always work in the beverage industry.

Questions 152-153 refer to the following online chat.

	Kate Morris 11:05 A.M.	I'm still writing some lists of accommodations for your Santa Fe business trip – where you're preparing for meeting clients.
	Tony Mcfaden 11:06 A.M.	Okay, how many options can I choose?
	Kate Morris 11:08 A.M.	There are some choices, but I recommend Premium Santa Fe Inn, which is close to the airport. And, it's famous for good amenities.
	Tony Mcfaden 11:10 A.M.	I'd prefer something near the client offices. We'll have to prepare materials related to the building design for our clients at the hotel before meeting them.
	Kate Morris 11:13 A.M.	Oh, I fully understand what you mean. Well… There's Mevius Hotel – It's just within walking distance from the client's office – although it's more expensive than one I mentioned above.
	Tony Mcfaden 11:18 A.M.	That sounds much better I guess. Then, could you make a reservation there?

152. For what kind of business does Mr. Mcfaden most likely work?

(A) A cosmetic company
(B) A clothing corporation
(C) An education institute
(D) An architectural agency

153. At 11:13 A.M., what does Ms. Morris most likely mean when she writes, "Oh, I fully understand what you mean"?

(A) She wants to know his intention.
(B) She can notify him of a suitable place.
(C) She reschedules his meeting time.
(D) She checks their meeting agenda.

Questions 154-155 refer to the following notice.

Edgewood Dentistry
5732 Ellsworth Avenue
Pittsburgh, PA 15232

10 May

James McNab
FN 1155
Spring Meadow Apartment
Oakwood Street
Pittsburgh, PA 15232

At Edgewood Dentistry, ensuring that you have the current information of your account with us is a priority. As of next month, all invoices not paid at the time of service must be paid within 30 days. Please find enclosed a detailed explanation of the revised billing schedule.

This essential revision allows us to continue to provide dental care to you and your family without increasing the cost of services this year. Should you need to seek alternative payment methods, please contact our office manager, Bruce Parker, at 412-441-7874.

Sincerely,

Donald Edgewood
Enclosure

154. Why was the letter sent to Mr. McNab?
(A) To correct a billing mistake
(B) To publicize a newly opened clinic
(C) To announce a policy change
(D) To reschedule an appointment

155. What is indicated about Edgewood Dentistry?
(A) It has hired a new office manager.
(B) It hopes to avoid an increase in fees.
(C) It teaches dental students.
(D) It has updated its operation hours.

Questions 156-158 refer to the following memo.

From: Jamie Karen
To: All Employees
Date: April 20
Subject: Renovation Issues – Parking Lot

Dear coworkers,

Please be aware that the Culpepper parking lot will be unavailable from May 15 through May 20 as it undergoes improvements. —[1]—. The scheduled date for reopening the lot is Monday, May 21. —[2]—. Employees are encouraged to use public transportation and may talk with their managers about the possibility of working at home. Please note that any expenses incurred while using alternative parking lots (e.g., Oak Groove Parking Lot) will be fully reimbursed later. —[3]—.

Also note that once the renovation has been completed, two additional spaces will be added to the parking lot. —[4]—. These areas will be allocated via a drawing to interested full-time employees. If you would like to enter the drawing, please contact me at extension 8103. Thank you.

Jamie Karen

156. According to the memo, what can employees discuss with their managers?

(A) The best alternative parking areas
(B) The possibility of working remotely
(C) Taking part in a drawing for a parking spot
(D) Transitioning to full-time employment

157. What is suggested about the Oak Groove Parking Lot?

(A) It requires a fee to use.
(B) It was recently expanded.
(C) It will be closed on May 21.
(D) It is far from the Culpepper office.

158. In which of the positions marked [1], [2], [3], and [4] does the following sentence best belong?

"The surface will be waterproofed and a fence will be put up."

(A) [1]
(B) [2]
(C) [3]
(D) [4]

Questions 159-161 refer to the following announcement.

August 10

Flavors for Fall

Attention all employees!

As this summer season is becoming over, we need to discuss our new strategies for the next season. In general, a fall season tends to drop the sales drastically. As one of these strategies, we are expected to hold a contest called "Choose Your Flavor." Employees will have the chance to come up with unique ideas to be featured at Meadow Ice Cream from September through November. The winner will receive a $200 gift card, which can be used in any section of Nelly Department Store, our corporate partner.

Application forms for the contest can be picked up in the employee lounge of each floor. The deadline for submission is August 20. Your submissions will be judged depending on being favored by a wide range of customers, convenience of procuring ingredients and low production cost.

Good luck!

159. What is the purpose of the announcement?

    (A) To provide sales figures to the staff
    (B) To invite staff to an ice cream event
    (C) To notify staff company's competition
    (D) To inform the staff of a new hiring process

160. What is indicated about Nelly Department Store?

    (A) It is affiliated with Meadow Ice Cream.
    (B) It features a seasonal menu.
    (C) It is closed during the summer.
    (D) It launched new sections.

161. What is NOT mentioned as an aspect of a good product?

    (A) Being inexpensive to make
    (B) Being liked by a wide range of people
    (C) Having components that are easy to obtain
    (D) Having an attractive appearance

Questions 162-163 refer to the following advertisement.

LIFE INSURANCE FOR CHILDREN?

Of course you have life insurance for yourself, maybe even for your husband.

But life insurance for your children? What should I say? Simply this: your kids won't be kids forever, and when they grow to adulthood they are going to need all the financial power they can get to help themselves. A life insurance plan started in childhood can help to secure student loans, personal loans, mortgages, even business loans, as well as provide basic financial coverage in the event of death. And the premiums never go up. At Alert Financial Insurance, we've been insuring youth and assuring the future since 1970. Call and consult with us today for more detailed information.

162. According to the advertisement, what is the main advantage of the insurance?

(A) It can give some discounts to parents.
(B) The cost increases gradually in the future.
(C) It provides money in case of illness.
(D) It can help the children get financial aid later.

163. What assumption is made in the advertisement?

(A) Children are always weak.
(B) The reader of the advertisement is a man.
(C) The reader has life insurance.
(D) The reader's husband has life insurance.

Questions 164-167 refer to the following text-message chain.

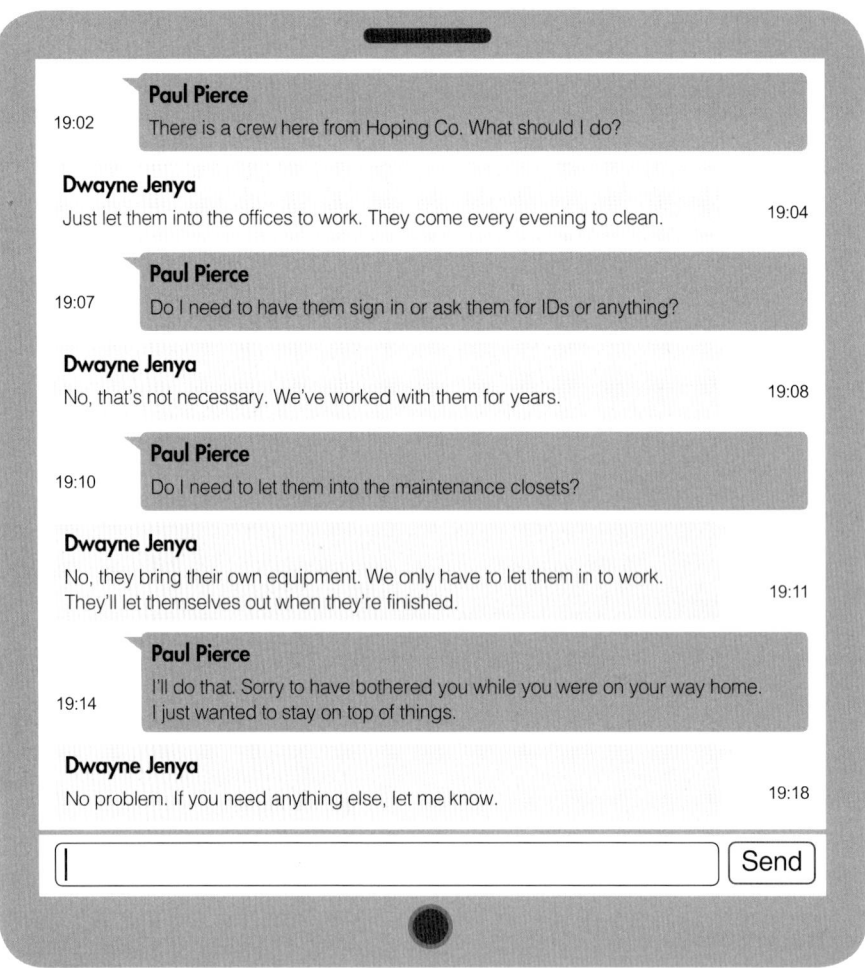

164. Why did Mr. Pierce write to Mr. Jenya?
    (A) To inquire about how to attend to an outsider
    (B) To check the expenses for a cleaning service
    (C) To announce a way to outsource a service
    (D) To help someone to check into their accommodation

165. What is indicated about Hoping Co.?
    (A) It caters special events.
    (B) It repairs machines.
    (C) It performs cleaning.
    (D) It consults businesses.

166. At 19:14, what does Mr. Pierce mean when he writes, "I just wanted to stay on top of things."?
    (A) He wants a good position.
    (B) He wants to stay informed.
    (C) He wants to win a competition.
    (D) He wants to learn from the best people.

167. What will Mr. Pierce do next?
    (A) Provide someone with additional tools
    (B) Open the office to cleaning service members
    (C) Confirm service hours during business days
    (D) Send an e-mail to his immediate supervisor

Questions 168-171 refer to the following notice.

Public Museum of Atlanta City

Modern Art Classes

- June 1
- June 10
- June 20
- June 30

Seminar room 101F, 4:30 P.M.
Register online: atlantacitymuseum.org
[No registration through the reception desk]

We are pleased to announce the opening of modern art classes next month as part of our ongoing public art projects for our citizens. —[1]—. Led by prominent professors from our local universities, these will be an excellent opportunity for anyone who wants to get a basic knowledge of modern art. —[2]—.

Topics included in the classes:

- The beginning of modern art
- Contemporary and renowned artists of modern art
- Modern art factors throughout our lives
- Trends and predictions for the future of modern art

—[3]—. These classes are all free and open to citizens, but there is limited space for only 50 people, so applications are accepted on a first come, first served basis. Participants who register for the classes successfully should print out their confirmation document and bring it on the first day of class. —[4]—.

---

168. According to the notice, what is true about the museum?

(A) It is planning to renovate the building of the museum.
(B) It is operating various programs to attract the public.
(C) It is expected to exhibit different paintings from recognized artists.
(D) It is scheduled to open seminars in a local university.

169. What is NOT mentioned as a topic to be covered in the classes?

(A) The historical background of an art style
(B) The amount of artwork in our society
(C) Relationships between our lives and the art
(D) Future prospects for art

170. What should attendees bring to the June 1 class?

(A) An application form
(B) A certificate in the related field
(C) Proof of registration
(D) A form of photo identification

171. In which of the following positions marked [1], [2], [3], and [4] does the following sentence best belong?

"It will be especially helpful to citizens and those who simply want to know more about artistic techniques."

(A) [1]
(B) [2]
(C) [3]
(D) [4]

Questions 172-175 refer to the following article.

(April 10) Appalachian Municipal Resort has been a space for rest and relaxation for decades. Thousands of people visit here every year from all over the country. Some areas of the resort, such as Tahoma Valley and Fiorenti Garden, have become one of the special attractions for family groups in the U.S.

However, the municipal-resort official said that they have been operating their areas with far smaller funds recently. It is impossible for them to hire additional staff who respond to too many inquiries and deal with issues within the resort.

Kevin Feige, the resort manager, has appealed for the local residents to be interested in the local resort. "We really need a continuous interest and support in order to maintain our resort and boost regional economy together," he said in the interview. "For this reason, we have a plan to carry on a campaign to attract prospective donors and volunteers, and raise funds for the resort. If we cannot do that, the current popularity of the resort will wane rapidly and economic vitalization of region could step backward." he added.

172. What is indicated about the resort?
(A) Its employees need to be trained.
(B) Its budget is insufficient for its needs.
(C) Its main office is located in Tahoma.
(D) Its operation has been just for a year.

173. The word "prospective" in paragraph 3, line 5, is closest in meaning to
(A) fundamental
(B) potential
(C) contrary
(D) eligible

174. What is the purpose of the current campaign?
(A) To ask for assistance from the citizens
(B) To evaluate its work efficiency
(C) To promote its special event
(D) To systemize its staffing process

175. Why is Mr. Feige concerned about the resort?
(A) Lack of care in the community
(B) Decreased visitors to the resort
(C) Outdated strategies for the promotion
(D) Difficulties to recruit a talented person

Go on to the next page

Questions 176-180 refer to the following the article and e-mail.

Los Angeles — CAL Air's popular calendar came about due to a digital photography contest for its members five years ago. As part of a learning incentive program, CAL Air let its crew members show their best photographs taken at its destination cities, with a $100 gift voucher given for the best one. The top 12 pictures were included in the charity calendar.

The calendars were printed and sold on board CAL Air flights. To the surprise and delight of the airline staff, the first 600 copies sold out in just 4 days. CAL Air Managing Director Steven Nash, donated the $6,840 proceeds to Saving Children, a global charity specializing in children's education, a few months later at a ceremony in L.A.

Since then, the airline company has made the charitable calendar every year. This year's calendar features an extra 3 pages containing maps of Seoul, Dubai, and Berlin, the three most frequent destinations of CAL Air.

Copies are available onboard CAL Air flights, at calair.com, and at Saving Children charity shops in the U.S., Asia, and Europe.

To: Timothy Paulson <tpaulson@calair.com>

From: Katie Yoon <kyoon@savingchildren.org>

Date: September 9, 10:30 A.M.

Subject: Thank you for your contribution

Dear Mr. Paulson,

Thank you for your continued support of Saving Children. Thanks to your company's generous donation, this year our organization was able to offer scholarships to 5 students who are under financial difficulties, and help establish two new children's learning centers in Ethiopia. Please know that your company's efforts have made a big difference in the lives of these children.

In addition, I purchased several copies of your calendar for myself as well as for my friends, and I was very impressed. The maps are beautiful, and I have hung them in my house. I have never traveled much myself, but the pictures truly stimulate my imagination. My friends have also found the bonus pages extremely helpful. I hope your calendar will be widely recognized throughout the world.

Sincerely,

Katie Yoon
Saving Children

176. What does the article imply about the calendar?

(A) It costs $100 for each item.
(B) It is made from pictures from the contest.
(C) It contains pictures of flight attendants.
(D) It had been planned for many years.

177. Where are people NOT able to purchase the calendar?

(A) On CAL Air flights
(B) At international airports
(C) From a company's Web site
(D) At an organization's store

178. What is indicated about Saving Children?

(A) It focuses on medical treatments.
(B) It has been operated domestically.
(C) It has been in business for 5 years.
(D) It provides students with education.

179. What feature of the calendar did Ms. Yoon's friends find helpful?

(A) The city maps
(B) The item catalog
(C) The flight brochure
(D) The donation information

180. What can be inferred about Ms. Yoon?

(A) She works at CAL Air.
(B) She does not fly frequently.
(C) She received a financial reimbursement.
(D) She is interested in the culture of the cities.

Go on to the next page

Questions 181-185 refer to the following brochure and e-mail.

Prime Worldwide Co.
Your Food Service Industry Container Solution

Prime Worldwide Co., a subsidiary of Prime Material International Corporation, offers a full range of food-grade packaging solutions to clients across Europe. No matter what your business is, Prime Co. definitely has the solutions you are seeking. We offer both reusable and disposable products providing excellent hygienic packaging and hot/cold insulation at a reasonable price. We are strongly confident that our wrapping technology is recognized in quality due to using advanced materials. For detailed information, please visit us www.primefw.eu.

Dear Prime Worldwide Co.,

I am the manager of a local convenience store chain in the Benelux area (Belgium, the Netherlands, and Luxembourg). We operate twenty stores and have recently moved toward the food service industry because our sandwiches and salads are becoming increasingly popular. Our current supplier is unable to provide a full range of disposable containers customized with our needs, such as the company name, logo, and color. We are therefore in need of a customized line of food containers that can help us keep costs down while raising our brand awareness as a food service company. I have a question regarding whether you serve large-scale buyers like us. Clearly, we are an international business, but operate regional chains in Western Europe, and we would typically purchase disposable cups and take-out containers in lots of 40,000 or more. Please contact me at your earliest convenience to discuss orders and options. I look forward to hearing from you.

Sincerely,

Reuben Anderson
Local Manager
Harvest Market O Food

181. What product would Prime Worldwide Co. most likely offer?

(A) Dishwashing detergent
(B) Garbage disposal
(C) Plastic plates
(D) Tinted glasses

182. What information about Prime Worldwide does the brochure provide?

(A) Features of its products and services
(B) Historical information about the company
(C) Locations of its local branches
(D) Strategies to improve its perception

183. What does Reuben Anderson say about his business?

(A) It includes branches in several continents.
(B) Its service has been changed into another industry.
(C) It was recently established.
(D) Its productivity is growing rapidly.

184. Why does Mr. Anderson ask whether Prime Worldwide can serve his company?

(A) Customizing containers from the business is satisfying.
(B) Redesigning his company logo may be necessary.
(C) The scale of orders is not mentioned in the brochure.
(D) Prime Worldwide prefers to serve distribution businesses.

185. What is Harvest Market O Food probably hoping to purchase from Prime Worldwide?

(A) Educational materials
(B) Throwaway bowls
(C) Cartons for shipping
(D) Shipping containers

Go on to the next page

Questions 186-190 refer to the following advertisement, form, and e-mail.

Urgently Wanted
Movie & TV Extras

Green Beam Media is looking for extras (background actors) to fill a number of vacancies on TV and movie sets in the Arlington area. Previous experience is not essential; however, priority will be given to applicants who have previously worked on-screen, and to those with special talents (especially martial arts skills, musical competence, and an ability to speak in various accents). Due to the variety of views in our city, more and more production companies are shooting here. If you want to earn extra income, have fun, and possibly meet your favorite stars, visit www.greenbeam.net to complete our online form. After taking one of our daily training sessions, you can receive opportunities right after the training day!

Daily Pay Rates

Outdoor filming: Speaking: $100; Non-speaking: $60
Indoor filming: Speaking: $80; Non-speaking: $40

* In case of action scenes, additional fees will be negotiated.

Green Beam Application Form for Extras

Name	: Stephen Kameron
Address	: 701 W Road, Arlington, TX 76012
E-mail address	: s.kameron@utarlington.edu
Age	: 22
Relevant experience	: Appeared on *"Texas Has Talent 2016"* audition program in the actor category. Played a minor role as neighbor no. 2 in the TV series *Good Village* (now running).
Headshot attached?	: [✔] YES [ ] No
Things we should know	: I am a college student in the Department of Theater and Film. In the near future, I want to be a famous actor. In particular, I am interested in acting outside rather than doing so in the studio. Through this opportunity, I would like to speak and get some lines on the screen.
Availability	: From May 20. All days except Sunday. I can shoot scenes both early mornings and late nights.
Preferred date for training	: May 17
Skills	: I am proficient in a British English accent, as it was essential in my department because most classical literature is composed of this language and played on the stage.

From : Kevin Trisha <k.trisha@greenbeam.net>
To : Stephen Kameron <s.kameron@utarlington.edu>
Date : May 5
Subject : Your application

Dear Mr. Kameron,

Thank you for your interest in joining Green Beam Media as an extra in the Arlington area. Your profile is very impressive, and we are therefore sure that we can give you various roles in TV & movie series. Your ability to do a British English accent is probably suitable for our upcoming historical soap opera called *Discovering the New Continent*.

As for the training session, the date you gave on your application form is a Friday, and unfortunately, our office is closed on Fridays. We have reserved a place for you on the following day, Saturday. We hope you can make it.

Best regards,

Kevin Trisha
Casting Manager
Green Beam Media

186. According to the advertisement, what is causing increased job opportunities in Arlington?
(A) The good economic conditions
(B) The scenery of the area
(C) The attractive accent of citizens
(D) The high quality of local products

187. What pay rate would Mr. Kameron receive according to his preferences?
(A) $40 per day
(B) $60 per day
(C) $80 per day
(D) $100 per day

188. What is suggested about Mr. Kameron?
(A) He was born in England.
(B) He works as a theater manager on Sundays.
(C) He lives outside the company's designated area.
(D) He sent the company his photo.

189. In the e-mail, the word "suitable" in paragraph 1, line 3, is closest in meaning to
(A) fit
(B) stable
(C) convenient
(D) demanding

190. When will Mr. Kameron most likely receive training?
(A) On May 5
(B) On May 17
(C) On May 18
(D) On May 20

Questions 191-195 refer to the following advertisement and e-mails.

Oriental Culture Fair

March 10–24

Place: The Kovalchick Convention Center
Time: 10:00 A.M.–7:00 P.M. Monday–Friday, 11:00 A.M.–8:00 P.M. Saturday & Sunday
Event Details: The event is designed to provide the local community with an opportunity to experience wonderful Asian cultures.
Entertainment: Traditional dances will be performed by four different countries for visitors three times a day—11:00 A.M., 1:00 P.M., and 5:00 P.M. If a large group requests an additional performance, it will be added only one more time. So, a group that wants to make this request should make a reservation at least two days before the visit. In addition, there are various workshops on oriental music and its history on the 2nd floor throughout the day.
Movie: This year's film is *Bi-Cheon*, which is a story about a heavenly maid. It will be screened at 1:30 P.M. and at 5:30 P.M. To cover costs, an additional $5 will be charged on top of the admission fee. There is a discount of 10 percent for groups of seven or more.
Food: Enjoy traditional Asian food served at lunchtime and dinnertime from our buffet cafeteria on the 3rd floor.
Admission: Adults - $15, Children under 12 - $10, Senior citizens - $12.
Admission includes access to rides and dance performances.
Contact information: Visit the Web site at www.kovalchick.com/2018events/orient
E-mail us at service@kovalchick.com

To:	Service Center <service@kovalchick.com>
From:	Ulla Connor <u.connor@oxbridge.net>
Subject:	Questions about the Movie
Date:	March 2

Every year, I enjoy the cultural fairs hosted by Kovalchick Convention Center. I saw the advertisement for this year's fair in the "Now On" section of the *Indiana Gazette* newspaper. On Thursday, I plan to attend it with some colleagues, all of whom have business connections in East Asia. We would like to see *Bi-Cheon* as a group. There are nine of us in total. I wonder if it would be possible to arrange an afternoon viewing, as many of us are not available in the late afternoon. Also, is it possible to buy tickets in advance, or should we pay at the box office there?

Sincerely,

Ulla Connor

To:	Ulla Connor <u.connor@oxbridge.net>
From:	Service Center <service@kovalchick.com>
Subject:	Re: Questions about the Movie
Date:	March 3

Thank you for your inquiry about *Bi-Cheon*. We have had quite a few people requesting viewings during the daytime, so we are providing additional screenings. On weekdays, there will be one at 11:00 A.M and another at 3:00 P.M. On the weekend, there will be one more screening at 6:00 A.M. We are offering a 10 percent discount for groups of seven or more for *Bi-Cheon*. It is possible to purchase tickets at the venue, but they may sell out, so we advise buying them in advance. Please understand that admission to the fair is separately charged in addition to the cost of movie tickets.

Sincerely,

Nancy Helena
Oriental Culture Fair Organizing Committee

191. What is NOT part of the Oriental Culture Fair?

(A) Dance performances
(B) Cooking classes
(C) Traditional food
(D) Musical workshops

192. What is mentioned about the advertisement?

(A) It included various discount coupons.
(B) It contains some errors in its information.
(C) It was designed by the Kovalchick Center.
(D) It was posted in a newspaper.

193. What is indicated about Ms. Connor?

(A) She will gather a group of students.
(B) She will provide entertainment.
(C) She will get discounted movie tickets.
(D) She will write an article on the upcoming event.

194. When will Ms. Connor most likely view *Bi-Cheon*?

(A) At 11:00 A.M.
(B) At 1:30 P.M.
(C) At 5:30 P.M.
(D) At 6:00 P.M.

195. In the second e-mail, the word "admission" in line 6, is closest in meaning to

(A) connection
(B) approval
(C) decision
(D) entrance

Questions 196-200 refer to the following advertisement, e-mail, and online review.

Pine Hill Interiors

190 Ottley Dr NE, Atlanta, GA 30324
Phone: 404-897-5551
Monday to Friday, 9 A.M. to 5 P.M.

DON'T MISS OUR THANKSGIVING CLEARANCE SALE!

Wednesday, November 1 to Sunday, November 18
Floor Area Rugs 10% off
Window Shades 15% off
Bedroom and living room furniture 25% off
Kitchen and dining room furniture 25% off
Home decoration items 30% off

Please note that the store will close at 2:00 P.M. on Tuesday, October 31 in order to prepare for the clearance sale. Sales prices are available on both in-store and online purchases. Sign up for Pine Hill Interiors' Platinum membership to get free delivery. Our experienced sales representatives are always available to answer your questions.

To : All employees

From : Alan Smith <alansmith@Ph.interior.com>

Subject : Schedule

Date : October 25

To all employees,

We are working overtime on October 31 and will need employees to record inventory, attach new prices, and move items and merchandise. I have prepared a special breakfast for all volunteers at Ruby Thursdays in addition to incentive pay during the shift. Please notify me by October 28 if you are able to work then.

Sincerely,

Alan Smith
Store Director

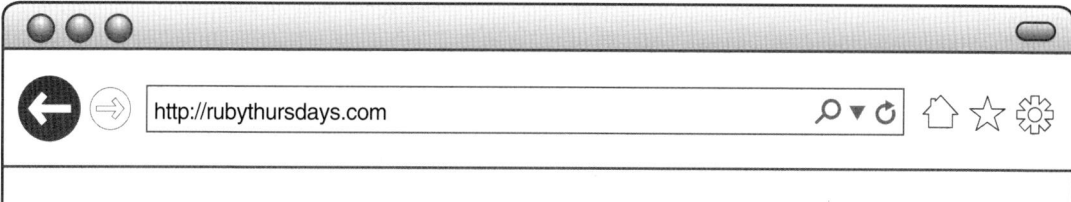

196. According to the advertisement, what will happen on October 31?

(A) A membership program will begin.
(B) A furniture sale will take place.
(C) Some new merchandise will arrive.
(D) A store will close early.

197. What does Mr. Smith ask employees to do?

(A) Attend some training sessions
(B) Demonstrate an assembly process
(C) Prepare for an upcoming event
(D) Pay attention to details

198. In the e-mail, the word "prepared" in line 2, is closest in meaning to

(A) arranged
(B) recognized
(C) displayed
(D) positioned

199. How many employees responded to Mr. Smith's request?

(A) 10
(B) 25
(C) 30
(D) 50

200. What is NOT mentioned in the online review?

(A) The level of customer service
(B) The competitiveness of the price
(C) The quality of the food
(D) The proximity to the workplace

books.english.co.kr

스파르타 토익

750⁺
LC & RC

정답 및 해설

LC PART 1 | 사진 묘사

DAY 1 인물 등장 사진

SPARTA Check-UP
p.22

1. (B)   2. (C)   3. (A)   4. (A)

1.

(A) He's folding the net with other people.
(B) He's holding a fishing pole.
(C) He's ready for diving.
(D) He's boarding a boat.

(A) 그는 다른 사람들과 함께 그물을 접고 있다.
(B) 그는 낚싯대를 들고 있다.
(C) 그는 다이빙을 할 준비를 하고 있다.
(D) 그는 배에 탑승하고 있다.

해설 한 남자가 낚시를 하고 있는 모습이다. (A) 그물이 없고 사람한 명만 보이므로 틀렸다. (C) 다이빙을 준비하는 동작이 아니기 때문에 오답, (D) 배도 보이지 않고 타려는 행동도 보이지 않으므로 오답이다.

어휘 fold 접다   net 그물   fishing pole 낚싯대   be ready for ~를 준비하다   board 탑승하다

2.

(A) They're getting out of the aircraft.
(B) They're facing each other.
(C) They're climbing up the stairs.
(D) They're loading their luggage into the truck.

(A) 그들은 비행기에서 내리고 있다.
(B) 그들은 서로 마주 보고 있다.
(C) 그들은 계단을 오르고 있다.
(D) 그들은 트럭에 짐을 싣고 있다.

해설 승객 두 명이 비행기에 탑승하고 있는 사진이다. 사진에서 마지막으로 계단을 오르는 남자가 가방을 메고 있다. (A)는 내리는 동작이 아니라서 오답. (B)는 마주 보고 있지 않으므로 동작 묘사 오류, (D)는 짐이나 트럭은 보이지 않는다.

어휘 get out of 내리다   aircraft 항공기   face 마주하다
climb 오르다   load 짐을 싣다   luggage 짐, 수하물

3.

(A) Shelves are stocked with items.
(B) A man is lying on a bed.
(C) Customers are purchasing some goods at the cash register.
(D) An armchair is being positioned by a drawer.

(A) 선반이 제품들로 채워져 있다.
(B) 한 남자가 침대에 누워 있다.
(C) 고객들이 계산대에서 물건들을 구입하고 있다.
(D) 안락의자가 서랍장 옆에 놓여지고 있다.

해설 매장에 물건이 진열되어 있고 사람들이 매장을 둘러보고 있는 사진으로, 선반에 제품들이 채워져 있다고 묘사한 (A)가 정답이다. (B) 남자는 누워 있지 않고 침대 쪽으로 몸을 구부리고 (bend over) 있다. (C) 계산대에서 구매 중인 고객은 보이지 않아 오답, purchase/buy/pay for라는 표현이 들린다면 물건을 구매하고 있는 사진이어야 답이 될 수 있다. (D) 의자를 놓고 있는 사람은 안 보이므로 행동을 나타내는 〈be being p.p.〉 형태는 답이 될 수 없다.

어휘 stock 채우다   lie 눕다   cash register 계산대
armchair 안락의자   drawer 서랍

4.

(A) There are many people at an outdoor market.
(B) A woman is writing something on the board.
(C) A vendor is putting on an apron.
(D) A cooking demonstration is taking place.

(A) 야외 시장에 많은 사람들이 있다.
(B) 여자가 게시판에 무언가를 적고 있다.

(C) 상인이 앞치마를 입고 있다.
(D) 요리 시연회가 열리고 있다.

해설 야외 시장에 있는 많은 사람들의 모습으로, 이를 묘사한 (A)가 정답이다. 주변에 사람들이 많이 있고 한 여자가 무언가 잡으려고 손을 뻗고 있다. (B) 여자의 행동이 무언가를 적고 있는 모습이 아니므로 동작 불일치 오답. (C) 상인은 앞치마를 이미 착용하고(wearing) 있으므로 오답. (D) 요리 시연회를 하는 상황은 아니다.

어휘 outdoor 야외의   board 게시판   apron 앞치마
demonstration 시범, 시연   take place 발생하다

(A) 옷이 선반에 정리되어 있다.
(B) 물건들이 바닥에 펼쳐져 있다.
(C) 점원이 진열대에서 코트를 접고 있다.
(D) 여자 중 한 명이 거울을 보고 있다.

해설 의류 매장으로 보이는 장소에서 여자가 선반에 있는 옷을 살펴보고 있다. 사진 속 인물의 동작이 아닌, 옷이 선반에 정리되어 있는 상태를 묘사한 (A)가 정답이다. (B) 바닥에 어떤 물건이 있는지는 보이지 않는다. (C) 동작 불일치 오답, (D) 거울은 보이지 않으며 동작 묘사도 틀렸다.

어휘 rack 선반, 걸이   spread (out) (물건 등을) 늘어놓다   clerk 점원   fold 접다   display stand 진열대   mirror 거울

SPARTA Practice Test
p.23

| 1. (B) | 2. (A) | 3. (D) | 4. (C) | 5. (A) |
| 6. (C) | 7. (D) | 8. (A) | 9. (A) | 10. (A) |

1.

(A) She's jogging on the street.
(B) She's carrying a bag on her shoulder.
(C) She's opening the store's door to enter.
(D) She's trying on a jacket.

(A) 그녀는 거리에서 조깅을 하고 있다.
(B) 그녀는 어깨에 가방을 메고 있다.
(C) 그녀는 들어가려고 가게 문을 열고 있다.
(D) 그녀는 재킷을 입어 보고 있다.

해설 여자가 어깨에 가방을 멘 채 제품을 들여다보고 있다. (A) 조깅 중이 아니므로 동작 묘사 오류. (C) 이미 가게 안에 있으므로 오답, (D) 재킷을 입어 보고 있는 동작이 아니므로 오답이다.

어휘 enter 들어가다   try on ~을 입어 보다

2.

(A) Clothing is arranged on racks.
(B) Items are spread out on the floor.
(C) A clerk is folding a coat on a display stand.
(D) One of the women is looking at the mirror.

3.

(A) The men are mowing the grass.
(B) One man is handing a phone to the other.
(C) The men are sitting on the lawn.
(D) The men have parked their bicycles.

(A) 남자들이 잔디를 깎고 있다.
(B) 한 남자가 다른 남자에게 전화기를 건네주고 있다.
(C) 남자들이 잔디에 앉아 있다.
(D) 남자들이 그들의 자전거를 주차했다.

해설 남자들이 앉아서 쉬고 있고 그 앞에는 자전거가 주차되어 있는 사진으로, 이를 묘사한 (D)가 정답이다. (A) 잔디를 깎고 있지 않으므로 동작 불일치 오답. (B) 한 남자가 전화기를 보고 있지만 건네고 있지는 않다. (C) 남자들이 앉아 있는 곳은 잔디 위가 아니다.

어휘 mow the grass[lawn] 잔디를 깎다   hand 건네다
park 주차하다

4.

(A) Performers are leaving the stage.
(B) The audience is clapping to a presenter.
(C) The audience is seated in rows.
(D) People have gathered on the stage.

(A) 연주자들이 무대를 떠나고 있다.
(B) 관중들이 발표자에게 박수를 보내고 있다.

(C) 청중들이 여러 줄로 앉아 있다.
(D) 사람들이 무대 위에 모여 있다.

해설 여러 줄로 앉아 있는 사람들을 묘사한 (C)가 정답이다. (A) 공연이나 연기를 하는 사람은 보이지 않고, 무대를 떠나고 있다는 설명도 동작 묘사 오류, (B) 박수를 치고 있는 사람들은 보이지 않는다. (D) 무대 위에 모인 사람도 보이지 않으므로 틀렸다.

어휘 performer 연주자, 연기자   leave 떠나다   stage 무대
audience 청중, 관중   clap 박수 치다   presenter 발표자
in rows 여러 줄로   gather 모이다

(C) 식탁보가 테이블 위에 드리워져 있다.
(D) 램프를 벽에 붙이고 있다.

해설 레스토랑 내부의 모습을 담은 사진으로, 테이블이 세팅되어 있고 유니폼을 입은 종업원들이 보인다. 식탁보가 테이블 위에 펼쳐져 있다고 한 (C)가 정답이다. (A) 음식을 서빙하고 있는 웨이터는 보이지 않고, (B) 유니폼을 이미 입고 있으므로 오답, (D) 램프를 벽에 고정시키려는 사람은 보이지 않으므로 오답이다.

어휘 serve 제공하다   customer 고객   tablecloth 식탁보
drape 씌우다, 걸치다   attach 붙이다, 부착하다

5.

(A) All the people are having a conversation.
(B) Some people are seated behind the counter.
(C) A suitcase is being pulled through the hallway.
(D) One man is handing a drink to another.

(A) 모든 사람들이 대화를 하고 있다.
(B) 몇몇 사람들이 카운터 뒤에 앉아 있다.
(C) 여행가방을 복도에서 끌고 가고 있다.
(D) 한 남자가 다른 사람에게 음료를 건네고 있다.

해설 창구에서 상담 중인 두 사람과 뒤에서 기다리는 두 사람이 서로 대화 중이다. 이를 묘사한 (A)가 정답이다. (B) 앉아 있는 사람은 보이지 않는다. (C) 여행가방을 끌고 가는 사람도 보이지 않는다. (D) 음료를 건네고 있는 남자는 없으므로 동작 묘사 오류.

어휘 have a conversation 대화를 나누다   pull 끌다
hallway 복도

6.

(A) Waiters are serving food to customers.
(B) Some people are trying on their uniforms.
(C) Tablecloths are draped on the tables.
(D) The lamps are being attached to the wall.

(A) 종업원들이 손님들에게 음식을 제공하고 있다.
(B) 몇몇 사람들이 유니폼을 입어 보고 있다.

7.

(A) A customer is paying for the bread.
(B) Some people are baking some bread in the oven.
(C) People are waiting in the lobby.
(D) The lights are hanging from the ceiling.

(A) 고객이 빵값을 지불하고 있다.
(B) 몇몇 사람들이 오븐에 빵을 굽고 있다.
(C) 사람들이 로비에서 기다리고 있다.
(D) 전등이 천장에 매달려 있다.

해설 식당 안에서 사람들이 주문을 하기 위해 기다리고 있는 사진이다. 배경에 표지판이 세워져 있고 천장에는 전등이 매달려 있다. 천장에 매달린 전등을 묘사한 (D)가 정답이다. (A) 돈을 지불하고 있는 사람은 보이지 않는다. (B) 빵을 굽고 있는 사람들은 보이지 않아 오답. (C) 장소 불일치 오답이다.

어휘 pay for 대금을 지불하다   bake 굽다   oven 오븐
hang 걸다, 매달리다   ceiling 천장

8.

(A) They're waiting for their baggage.
(B) One of the women is picking up her bag.
(C) Luggage is being unloaded from the carousel.
(D) One of the men is pulling his suitcase.

(A) 그들은 짐을 기다리고 있다.
(B) 여자 중 한 명이 가방을 들어올리고 있다.

(C) 짐이 수화물 찾는 곳에서 내려지고 있다.
(D) 남자 중 한 명이 여행가방을 끌고 있다.

해설 수화물 찾는 곳에서 사람들이 짐을 기다리고 있고 컨베이어 벨트에 짐들이 놓여 있는 사진으로, 이와 일치하는 (A)가 정답이다. (B) 가방을 집어 올리는 여자는 보이지 않아 오답, (C) 짐이 컨베이어 벨트 위에 놓여 있으므로 오답, (D) 여행가방을 끌고 있는 남자는 보이지 않는다.

어휘 unload (짐을) 내리다   carousel 수화물 찾는 곳

(A) 그들은 안전 장비를 착용하고 있다.
(B) 중장비가 공사장에서 작동되고 있다.
(C) 인부들이 삽으로 땅을 파고 있다.
(D) 도로가 재포장되고 있다.

해설 안전 장비를 착용한 인부들이 도로에서 작업하고 있는 사진으로, 이를 묘사한 (A)가 정답이다. (B) 사진 속에 중장비는 보이지 않는다. (C) 삽으로 땅을 파고 있는 인부는 보이지 않아 오답, (D) 도로를 포장하고 있는 상황이 아니다.

어휘 safety gear 안전 장비   heavy machinery 중장비
construction site 공사장   dig 파다   shovel 삽
repave 재포장하다

9.

(A) The woman is using a device.
(B) The woman is getting off the subway.
(C) The woman is holding a phone to her ear.
(D) The woman is looking at the route on the wall.

(A) 여자가 장치를 사용하고 있다.
(B) 여자가 지하철에서 내리고 있다.
(C) 여자가 휴대폰을 귀에 대고 있다.
(D) 여자가 벽에 있는 노선을 보고 있다.

해설 여자가 버스에 앉아서 휴대폰을 보고 있는 사진으로 이를 묘사한 (A)가 정답이다. phone이 device로 패러프레이징 되었다. (B) 내리는 동작이 아니라 틀렸고, (C) 휴대폰을 귀에 대고 있지 않으므로 오답, (D) 벽에 걸린 노선표를 보고 있지 않으므로 동작 불일치 오답이다.

어휘 device 장치   get off 내리다   route 노선

10.

(A) They're wearing safety gear.
(B) Heavy machinery is being operated at a construction site.
(C) Workers are digging the soil with a shovel.
(D) The road is being repaved.

DAY 2 사물/풍경 사진

SPARTA Check-UP
p.26

1. (D) 2. (A) 3. (B) 4. (D)

1.

(A) Glasses are being filled with water.
(B) A napkin is unfolded beside the cutlery.
(C) Diners are having a meal in the restaurant.
(D) The table has been set neatly.

(A) 유리잔에 물이 채워지고 있다.
(B) 냅킨이 식탁용 날붙이류 옆에 펼쳐져 있다.
(C) 손님들이 식당에서 식사하고 있다.
(D) 식탁이 깔끔하게 차려져 있다.

해설 레스토랑의 식탁이 깔끔하게 세팅되어 있는 사진이다. 포크와 나이프 사이에 냅킨이 놓여 있고 바구니에는 빵이 보인다. (A)는 사람이 없으므로 채우고 있는 동작을 확인하기 어렵고 이미 잔에는 음료가 채워져 있다. (B)는 냅킨이 접혀 있으므로 오답, (C) 식사하는 사람들이 보이지 않으므로 오답이다.

어휘 glass 유리잔 fill 채우다 unfold 펼치다 cutlery (수저나 포크 같은) 날붙이류 diner 식사하는 사람 neatly 단정하게

2.

(A) The bookshelf is filled with reading materials.
(B) Potted plants are arranged on the windowsill.
(C) Books are being placed on the shelves.
(D) Some shelves are being assembled.

(A) 책꽂이가 읽을 거리로 가득 차 있다.
(B) 화분들이 창턱에 배열되어 있다.
(C) 책이 선반에 놓여지고 있다.
(D) 선반들이 조립되고 있다.

해설 책꽂이에 책들이 가득 차 있는 사진으로, 이를 묘사한 (A)가 정답이다. (B) 창턱에는 아무것도 없고 화분도 보이지 않으므로 오답, (C) 선반에 책을 놓는 사람은 보이지 않으므로 오답, (D) 선반이 조립되고 있는 상황도 아니다.

어휘 bookshelf 책꽂이 be filled with ~로 가득 차다 reading materials 읽을 거리 potted 화분에 심은 arrange 마련하다 windowsill 창턱 assemble 조립하다

3.

(A) A van is being parked behind the boxes.
(B) Containers have been stacked beside the road.
(C) Some cartons are being loaded onto a truck.
(D) A worker is pushing a wheelbarrow.

(A) 승합차가 박스들 뒤에 주차되고 있다.
(B) 용기들이 길 옆에 쌓여 있다.
(C) 종이 박스들이 트럭에 실리고 있다.
(D) 인부가 손수레를 밀고 있다.

해설 길가에 박스들이 쌓여 있고 그 뒤에는 승합차가 주차되어 있다. 도로 옆에 용기들이 쌓여 있다고 한 (B)가 정답이다. 여기서 box를 container(용기)로 표현했다. (A) 승합차는 이미 주차되어 있고, (C) 박스를 트럭에 싣는 사람은 보이지 않는다. (D) 수레를 밀고 있는 인부도 보이지 않는다.

어휘 stack 쌓다 carton 종이 상자 wheelbarrow 손수레

4.

(A) Many boats are tied up at the harbor.
(B) Some people are swimming in the water.
(C) The bridge is being built over the river.
(D) There are some tall buildings in the distance.

(A) 많은 배들이 항구에 묶여 있다.
(B) 몇몇 사람들이 물에서 수영하고 있다.
(C) 다리가 강 위에 세워지고 있다.
(D) 저 멀리 고층 빌딩들이 있다.

해설 다리 아래로 배가 지나가고 있고 저 멀리 빌딩들이 보인다. 이를 묘사한 (D)가 정답이다. (A) 항구는 사진에서 보이지 않으므로 오답, (B) 수영 중인 사람들도 보이지 않는다. (C) 다리는 이미 세워져 있으므로 틀렸다.

어휘 harbor 항구 bridge 다리 in the distance 저 멀리

SPARTA Practice Test
p.27

| 1. (A) | 2. (B) | 3. (B) | 4. (B) | 5. (C) |
| 6. (A) | 7. (A) | 8. (C) | 9. (C) | 10. (D) |

1.

(A) The lamps have been turned on in the bedroom.
(B) There are two paintings above the beds.
(C) The curtains have been pulled shut.
(D) The beds are being made in the room.

(A) 램프가 침실에 켜져 있다.
(B) 침대 위에 그림이 두 개 있다.
(C) 커튼이 닫혀 있다.
(D) 침구가 방에서 정리되고 있다.

해설 침대 두 개가 나란히 있고 그 사이에 램프가 켜져 있다. 이를 묘사한 (A)가 정답. (B) 그림은 보이지 않고, (C) 커튼은 열려 있으며, (D) 침구를 정리 중인 사람은 보이지 않아 오답이다.

어휘 turn on 켜다 pull shut 당겨서 닫다

2.

(A) Umbrellas are unfolded on the patio.
(B) All the chairs are unoccupied outdoors.
(C) The railing is being installed around the restaurant.
(D) Tables are being moved into the shop.

(A) 우산이 파티오에 펼쳐져 있다.
(B) 야외에 모든 의자들이 비어 있다.
(C) 난간이 레스토랑 주위에 설치되고 있다.
(D) 테이블이 가게 안으로 옮겨지고 있다.

해설 식당의 야외 테이블이 보이고 사람은 보이지 않으며 파라솔은 접혀 있다. 의자들이 모두 비어 있다고 한 (B)가 정답이다. (A) 우산이 접혀 있으므로 오답, (C) 설치 중인 난간은 보이지 않고, (D) 가게 안으로 테이블을 옮기고 있는 사람도 보이지 않아 오답이다.

어휘 unfold 펴다 patio 파티오, 테라스 unoccupied 빈 railing 난간 install 설치하다

3.

(A) Documents are being handed out.
(B) Some chairs are arranged around the table.
(C) The monitor is mounted on the wall.
(D) Chairs are stacked on top of each other.

(A) 서류를 나눠 주고 있다.
(B) 몇 개 의자들이 테이블 주위에 배열되어 있다.
(C) 모니터가 벽에 고정되어 있다.
(D) 의자들이 차곡차곡 쌓여 있다.

해설 회의실의 테이블 주위에 놓여 있는 의자들을 묘사한 (B)가 정답. (A) 서류를 나눠 주고 있는 사람은 보이지 않고, (C) 벽에 고정된 모니터는 보이지 않는다. (D) 의자가 쌓여 있는 상태는 아니므로 오답.

어휘 hand out 나눠 주다 mount 고정시키다 stack 쌓다

4.

(A) Cars are being parked in the parking lot.
(B) Vehicles are on multiple stories.
(C) There is heavy traffic at the intersection.
(D) Cars are entering a garage.

(A) 차들이 주차장에 주차되고 있다.
(B) 차량들이 여러 층에 있다.
(C) 교차로에 교통이 혼잡하다.
(D) 차들이 차고로 들어가고 있다.

해설 여러 층으로 구성된 주차장에 차들이 주차되어 있는 사진으로, 이를 묘사한 (B)가 정답이다. (A) be being p.p. 오답 함정으로, 차를 주차하고 있는 사람은 보이지 않고, (C) 교차로나 교통 혼잡 상황 역시 보이지 않는다. (D) 차고로 들어가고 있는 차는 사진에 보이지 않는다.

어휘 multiple 많은 stories (건물의) 층 heavy traffic 교통 혼잡 intersection 교차로 garage 차고

해설 팩스기가 나란히 놓여 있는 사진으로, 이를 묘사한 (A)가 정답이다. (B) 서랍은 닫혀 있고, (C) 벽에 걸린 시계는 보이지 않는다. (D) 수리 중인 복사기는 보이지 않으므로 틀렸다.

어휘 side by side 나란히 drawer 서랍 hang 걸다 repair 수리하다

5.

(A) Lines are being painted on the road.
(B) Vehicles are stopped at the traffic signal.
(C) Bicycles are parked in a line.
(D) Tires have been removed from the bikes.

(A) 도로에 선들이 그려지고 있다.
(B) 차량들이 신호등에 멈춰 있다.
(C) 자전거들이 일렬로 주차되어 있다.
(D) 자전거의 타이어가 빠져 있다.

해설 길에 일렬로 주차되어 있는 자전거들을 묘사한 (C)가 정답이다. (A) 도로에 선을 그리고 있는 사람은 보이지 않고, (B) 신호등에 멈춰 서 있는 차들도 보이지 않는다. (D) 타이어가 자전거에서 빠져 있지 않으므로 오답이다.

어휘 traffic signal 신호등 in a line 일렬로 remove 제거하다

7.

(A) A carving is positioned behind the fence.
(B) The grass is being cut.
(C) Trees are being planted in the park.
(D) There are some lamp posts along the road.

(A) 조각품이 울타리 뒤에 놓여 있다.
(B) 잔디가 깎이고 있다.
(C) 공원에서 나무를 심고 있다.
(D) 길을 따라 가로등이 서 있다.

해설 공원으로 보이는 사진으로, 울타리 뒤에 조각상이 하나 있고 주변에 나무와 가로등이 보인다. 이와 묘사가 일치하는 것은 (A)이다. (B)와 (C)는 be being p.p. 오답 함정으로, 잔디를 깎거나 나무를 심는 사람은 보이지 않는다. (D) 길을 따라 놓인 가로등은 보이지 않는다.

어휘 carving 조각품 position 두다, 위치하다 fence 울타리 lamp post 가로등

6.

(A) Fax machines are placed side by side.
(B) A cabinet drawer has been left open in the office.
(C) A clock is hanging on the wall.
(D) Copy machines are being repaired.

(A) 팩스기가 나란히 놓여 있다.
(B) 사무실에 서랍이 열려 있다.
(C) 시계가 벽에 걸려 있다.
(D) 복사기가 수리 중이다.

8.

(A) All of the seats are occupied.
(B) A clock is being removed form a wall.
(C) Some chairs have been set around a table.
(D) Some lights are being installed.

(A) 좌석이 모두 차 있다.
(B) 시계가 벽에서 떨어지고 있다.
(C) 의자 몇 개가 테이블 주위에 놓여 있다.
(D) 조명이 설치되고 있다.

해설 테이블 주위에 의자 몇 개가 놓여 있는 사진으로, 이를 묘사한 (C)가 정답이다. (A) 좌석은 모두 비어 있고, (B) 벽에 시계가 걸려 있는 상태이고, (D) 조명기구가 보이지만 설치되고 있는 상황은 아니다.

어휘 occupy 차지하다, 사용하다   install 설치하다

해설 한 건축물의 그림자가 땅에 드리워져 있는 사진으로, 이를 묘사한 (D)가 정답이다. (A) 지어지고 있는 건물은 보이지 않고, (B) 야외 광장에는 사람들이 전혀 보이지 않으며, (C) 가로등이 보이지만 줄지어 있는 상태는 아니다.

어휘 construct 건설하다   outdoor 야외의   area 구역
walkway 통로, 보도   shadow 그림자
cast (그림자를) 드리우다

9.

(A) A passenger is waiting at the bus stop.
(B) A bus has been stopped at a gas station.
(C) There are some pictures attached to the side of a vehicle.
(D) Some people are getting off the bus.

(A) 승객이 버스 정류장에서 기다리고 있다.
(B) 버스가 주유소에 멈춰 있다.
(C) 차량 옆면에 사진들이 붙어 있다.
(D) 몇몇 사람들이 버스에서 내리고 있다.

해설 버스 정류장에 버스 한 대가 서 있고 버스 옆면에 광고용 사진이 붙어 있다. 이를 묘사한 (C)가 정답. 사진에 사람이 보이지 않으므로 (A)와 (D)는 오답, (B)는 장소 불일치 오답이다.

어휘 passenger 승객   gas station 주유소   attach 붙이다

10.

(A) A building is being constructed.
(B) An outdoor area is crowded with people.
(C) Lamp posts are lining a walkway.
(D) Shadows are being cast on the ground.

(A) 건물이 시공 중이다.
(B) 야외 공간이 사람들로 붐빈다.
(C) 가로등이 보행로에 줄지어 서 있다.
(D) 그림자가 땅에 드리워져 있다.

LC PART 2 | 질의 응답

DAY 3 Who/When/Where 의문문

SPARTA Check-UP
p.38

1. (B)   2. (B)   3. (A)   4. (A)   5. (C)

1. Who's going to help us with the annual fundraiser?
(A) It's on Friday.
(B) Louise volunteered to do it.
(C) Lucy is the best driver.

누가 연례 모금 행사에 우리를 도와줄 건가요?
(A) 금요일이에요.
(B) Louise가 자원했어요.
(C) Lucy는 모범 운전사예요.

해설 도와줄 수 있는 사람을 묻는 질문이다. (A) who로 물었는데 시간을 언급한 오답. (C)는 Lucy라는 이름이 들리지만 모범 운전사라는 엉뚱한 내용이 언급되었다. (B) Louise가 돕는 것을 자원했다는 내용으로 질문에 적절한 응답이다.

어휘 annual 연례의 fundraiser 모금 행사 volunteer 자원하다

2. When was the last time you played tennis?
(A) For a long time.
(B) A week ago.
(C) I played the piano last week.

테니스를 마지막으로 친 게 언제였나요?
(A) 오랫동안이요.
(B) 일주일 전이요.
(C) 지난주에 피아노를 쳤어요.

해설 테니스를 마지막으로 친 시점을 묻는 질문이다. (A)는 when 질문에서 자주 나오는 오답으로, 시점을 물었는데 기간을 언급하고 있다. (C)는 last week만 듣고 혼동할 수 있는 오답 함정이다. (B) 일주일 전에 테니스를 쳤다는 말로, 질문에 적절한 응답이다.

3. Where is the paper for the copier?
(A) We've run out.
(B) Every Tuesday.
(C) It's not mine.

복사용지는 어디에 있나요?
(A) 다 썼어요.
(B) 화요일마다요.
(C) 제 것이 아니에요.

해설 용지의 위치를 묻는 질문으로, (B)는 When 의문문의 답변이고, (C)는 질문과 어울리지 않는 응답이다. 다 써서 종이가 없다는 내용의 (A)가 정답이다.

어휘 run out 다 쓰다   mine 내 것

4. When is the sales report due?
(A) By the end of today.
(B) It was a nice proposal.
(C) To the marketing department.

판매 보고서 마감이 언제인가요?
(A) 오늘까지예요.
(B) 멋진 제안이었어요.
(C) 마케팅 부서로요.

해설 보고서 마감 예정일을 묻는 질문으로, 오늘까지라고 한 (A)가 정답이다. (B) 질문과 전혀 다른 대답이고 (C)는 Where 의문문에 어울리는 응답이다.

어휘 sales report 판매 보고서   due ~하기로 되어 있는
proposal 제안

5. Where did Ms. Suzuki work when she first started here?
(A) For almost seven years.
(B) Is it near the lobby?
(C) In the public relations office.

Suzuki 씨는 여기에서 처음 일을 시작했을 때 어디에서 일했나요?
(A) 거의 7년 동안이요.
(B) 로비 근처에 있나요?
(C) 홍보 부서에서요.

해설 과거에 일한 곳을 묻는 질문으로, (A)는 기간을 묻는 질문에 대한 답이고, (B)는 장소를 언급했지만 내용상 어색하다. 전형적인 Where 의문문의 대답으로, 근무했던 부서를 언급하는 (C)가 답이다.

어휘 almost 거의   public relations 홍보부

SPARTA Practice Test
p.39

1. (C)   2. (A)   3. (C)   4. (A)   5. (B)
6. (B)   7. (A)   8. (A)   9. (A)   10. (A)
11. (A) 12. (A) 13. (B) 14. (B) 15. (B)
16. (C) 17. (C) 18. (B) 19. (A) 20. (A)
21. (B) 22. (A) 23. (A) 24. (C) 25. (A)

1. When do you leave the office today?
(A) Does Yukiko also work there?
(B) I put it on the shelf.

(C) I still have a lot of assignments to do.

오늘 언제 퇴근할 건가요?
(A) Yukiko도 역시 거기에서 일하나요?
(B) 그것을 선반에 뒀어요.
(C) 저는 여전히 해야 할 업무가 많아요.

해설 퇴근하는 시점을 묻는 질문으로, (A) 질문과 맞지 않는 내용의 응답, (B) 연상 어휘 leave-put를 이용한 오답 함정이다. 해야 할 일이 많아서 언제 퇴근할지 모른다는 뜻의 (C)가 정답이다.

어휘 leave the office 퇴근하다   assignment 업무

2. Where's the user manual for our new software?
   (A) It's only available online.
   (B) His laptop computer is on the desk.
   (C) A week from today.

새 소프트웨어 사용 설명서는 어디에 있나요?
(A) 그것은 온라인에서만 이용 가능해요.
(B) 그의 노트북은 책상 위에 있어요.
(C) 오늘부터 일주일 뒤요.

해설 설명서의 위치를 묻는 질문에, 온라인상에 설명서가 있다는 (A)가 정답이다. (B) 컴퓨터 위치를 언급한 오답, (C) When 의문문으로 잘못 들을 경우 고를 수 있는 오답 함정이다.

어휘 user manual 사용 설명서

3. Who's leading the design workshop?
   (A) I can lead you there.
   (B) Susan likes to read.
   (C) We're still deciding.

누가 디자인 워크숍을 이끌 건가요?
(A) 제가 당신을 거기로 데리고 갈게요.
(B) Susan은 독서를 좋아해요.
(C) 아직 논의 중이에요.

해설 워크숍을 누가 이끄는지를 묻는 질문으로, (A)는 질문에 나온 lead를 이용한 함정. (B) 역시 leading-read를 이용한 함정으로, 사람 이름이 들린다고 바로 고르지 말고 문맥을 파악해서 풀어야 한다. (C)는 '몰라요' 유형의 답변으로, 아직 결정되지 않았다는 내용의 적절한 응답이다.

어휘 lead 이끌다   decide 결정하다

4. Who's in charge of booking Mr. Kim's hotel?
   (A) Sarah will make the arrangements.
   (B) Yes, it's on the calendar.
   (C) I booked the room for my vacation.

누가 Kim 씨의 호텔 예약을 담당하고 있나요?
(A) Sarah가 준비할 겁니다.
(B) 네, 달력에 있어요.
(C) 저는 휴가를 위해 방을 예약했어요.

해설 호텔 예약 담당자를 묻는 질문으로, Sarah가 준비할 거라는 내용의 (A)가 정답이다. Who's in charge of ~?는 Who 의문문에서 꾸준히 나오는 유형이다. (B) 의문사 의문문에 Yes는 올 수 없으므로 오답, (C)는 book을 반복한 오답 함정이다.

어휘 in charge of ~을 담당하는   book 예약하다
arrangement 준비, 마련   calendar 달력   vacation 휴가

5. Where are the new fax machines being made?
   (A) Mr. Cruz fixed them already.
   (B) In Sydney.
   (C) Tomorrow will be fine.

어디에서 새 팩스기기를 만드나요?
(A) Cruz 씨가 이미 그것들을 고쳤어요.
(B) 시드니에서요.
(C) 내일이 좋을 것 같네요.

해설 팩스기를 만드는 장소를 묻는 질문으로, 장소를 언급한 (B)가 정답이다. (A) fix-fax 유사 발음의 함정으로, 고치는 사람을 묻는 질문의 응답으로 적절하다. (C)는 의문사를 When으로 잘못 들었을 경우 고를 수 있는 오답 함정이다.

어휘 fax machine 팩스기   fix 고치다   already 이미

6. Who's going to be the new manager for the planning department?
   (A) It's on the 10th floor.
   (B) They're still interviewing candidates.
   (C) Sam likes living in the new apartment.

누가 기획부 신임 부장이 될 건가요?
(A) 10층에 있어요.
(B) 아직 후보자들을 인터뷰 중이에요.
(C) Sam은 새 아파트에서 사는 것을 좋아해요.

해설 신임 부장이 누가 될 건지를 묻는 질문으로, 아직 지원자들을 인터뷰 중이라 결정되지 않았다는 내용의 (B)가 정답이다. (A)는 위치를 언급한 오답, (C) department-apartment의 유사 발음 함정.

어휘 planning department 기획부   candidate 후보자

7. When can we meet again?
   (A) How about the day after tomorrow?
   (B) Nice to meet you, too.
   (C) Why not?

우리 언제 다시 만날 수 있죠?
(A) 모레는 어때요?
(B) 저 역시 만나서 반가워요.
(C) 좋아요.

해설 언제 다시 볼 수 있는지를 묻는 질문에, (A) 모레가 어떠냐며 제안하는 (A)가 정답이다. (B) meet을 반복한 함정이고, (C) 수락의 답변으로 내용상 어색하다.

어휘 the day after tomorrow 모레

8. Whose turn is it to take inventory?

   (A) I did it last time.
   (B) Turn right on Main Street.
   (C) Let's take a rest.

   재고 조사는 누구 차례인가요?
   (A) 지난번에 제가 했어요.
   (B) Main Street에서 우회전하세요.
   (C) 쉽시다.

   해설 누구의 순서인지를 묻는 질문으로, 자기는 지난번에 했다 즉, 이번에는 자기 순서가 아니라는 의미의 (A)가 정답이다. (B) 방향을 언급하고 있어 내용상 어색하고, (C) 질문의 take를 반복한 오답 함정이다.

   어휘 take inventory 재고 조사하다   take a rest 쉬다

9. When is the engineering conference scheduled for?

   (A) Check your calendar.
   (B) To start a conference call.
   (C) In the banquet hall.

   공학 학회는 언제로 일정이 잡혀 있나요?
   (A) 달력을 확인해 보세요.
   (B) 전화 회담을 시작하기 위해서요.
   (C) 연회장에서요.

   해설 학회 일정을 묻는 질문으로, 달력을 확인해 보라는 우회적 답변의 (A)가 정답이다. (B) 이유를 묻는 질문에 대한 답변, (C)는 Where 의문문으로 착각할 경우 고를 수 있는 오답이다.

   어휘 conference 회의   conference call 전화 회담   banquet 연회

10. When are you going to New York?

    (A) At the end of the year.
    (B) For a couple of months.
    (C) To get a new job.

    언제 뉴욕으로 갈 건가요?
    (A) 올해 말에요.
    (B) 2달 동안이요.
    (C) 새 직장을 얻기 위해서요.

    해설 뉴욕으로 언제 가는지를 묻는 질문에, 올해 말이라는 시점을 언급하고 있는 (A)가 정답이다. for를 이용해 기간을 언급한 (B)는 오답 함정, (C) Why 의문문에 어울리는 응답이다.

    어휘 a couple of 몇 개의, 둘의

11. Where will the overseas clients be staying?

    (A) We won't know until September.
    (B) She oversees the Tokyo branch.
    (C) For three days.

    해외 고객들은 어디에 머물 거예요?
    (A) 9월이 되어야 알아요.
    (B) 그녀는 도쿄 지점을 감독해요.
    (C) 3일 동안이요.

    해설 고객이 머무는 장소를 묻는 질문으로, 9월이 되어야 안다 즉, '현재는 모른다'는 의미의 (A)가 정답이다. (B) 장소가 언급되었지만 누군지 알 수 없는 She가 등장한 오답이다. (C) 기간을 묻는 질문에 어울리는 응답이다.

    어휘 overseas 해외의   client 고객   oversee 감독하다   branch 지점

12. Who's the head manager here?

    (A) It's me.
    (B) We don't charge.
    (C) The department store is across the street.

    누가 여기 지점장이에요?
    (A) 전데요.
    (B) 저희는 요금을 청구하지 않아요.
    (C) 백화점은 길 건너에 있어요.

    해설 누가 지점장인지를 묻는 질문으로, 본인이라고 답하는 (A)가 정답이다. (B)는 질문과 전혀 관계없는 내용의 오답. (C) 위치를 묻는 질문에 대한 응답이다.

    어휘 charge (요금을) 청구하다   department store 백화점   across 건너편에

13. When did Joanne ask for new software?

    (A) In an hour.
    (B) Sometime last week.
    (C) I knew that.

    언제 Joanne이 새 소프트웨어를 요청했나요?
    (A) 한 시간 뒤요.
    (B) 지난주 언젠가요.
    (C) 그것을 알고 있었어요.

    해설 요청한 시점을 묻는 질문으로, 지난주라고 특정 과거 시점을 언급한 (B)가 정답이다. (A) 미래 시점을 언급해 시제상 어색하고, (C)는 new-knew 유사 발음을 이용한 오답 함정이다.

    어휘 ask for 요청하다

14. Where should I put these documents?

    (A) I haven't seen them.
    (B) Just leave them on my desk.
    (C) Because your boss wants to see them.

    이 서류들을 어디에 둬야 하나요?
    (A) 그것들을 보지 못했어요.
    (B) 그냥 제 책상 위에 두세요.
    (C) 왜냐하면 사장님이 그들을 보고 싶어서요.

해설 서류를 둘 위치를 묻는 질문에, 책상에 두라고 하는 (B)가 적절한 응답이다. (A) 그것을 보지 못했다고 하는 응답은 내용상 어색, (C) Why 의문문에 대한 응답이다.

어휘 document 서류   leave 두다   boss 상사

15. When are those books due back?
(A) Yes, they must be returned.
(B) Today! Thanks for reminding me.
(C) I think they've already come back.

저 책들을 언제까지 돌려줘야 하나요?
(A) 네, 그것들은 반납해야 합니다.
(B) 오늘이요! 상기시켜 줘서 고마워요.
(C) 그들이 이미 돌아온 것 같아요.

해설 책 반납일을 묻는 질문으로, 오늘이라며 상기시켜 줘서 고맙다고 덧붙이는 (B)가 어울린다. (A) 의문사 의문문에 Yes로 답해 오답이고, (C) 질문에 나온 back을 반복한 오답 함정이다.

어휘 be due ~할 예정이다   return 반납하다, 돌아오다
remind 상기시키다

16. Where's the Sunset Conference Room?
(A) I need more room in my office.
(B) Steve's presentation is before mine.
(C) There's a map near the front desk.

선셋 컨퍼런스 룸은 어디에 있나요?
(A) 제 사무실에 더 많은 공간이 필요해요.
(B) Steve 발표는 제 발표 전이에요.
(C) 안내데스크 근처에 지도가 있어요.

해설 컨퍼런스 룸의 위치를 묻는 질문에, 지도의 위치를 대신 알려주는 (C)가 정답이다. (A) 질문에 나온 room을 반복한 오답 함정, (B) conference-presentation의 연상 어휘 함정이다.

어휘 presentation 발표   map 지도   front desk 안내데스크

17. When can we deliver this order?
(A) Delivery is free.
(B) In alphabetical order.
(C) The customer just canceled it.

언제 이 주문을 배달할 수 있나요?
(A) 배송은 무료예요.
(A) 알파벳 순서로요.
(C) 고객이 방금 취소했어요.

해설 배달 가능 시기를 묻는 질문으로, 고객이 방금 취소해서 배송할 필요가 없다는 의미의 (C)가 정답이다. (A) 배송비를 묻는 질문에 어울리는 응답으로, deliver-delivery 유사 발음 함정이다. (B) 방법을 묻는 질문에 대한 응답으로 어울린다.

어휘 deliver 배달하다   alphabetical 알파벳순의

18. Where can I store this manual until the orientation?
(A) No, I don't think so.
(B) In the cabinet over there.
(C) To hire new employees.

오리엔테이션 때까지 이 설명서를 어디에 저장할까요?
(A) 아니요, 저는 그렇게 생각하지 않아요.
(B) 저기 있는 서랍장예요.
(C) 새로운 직원들을 고용하기 위해서요.

해설 설명서를 저장할 장소를 묻는 질문에, 구체적인 위치를 언급하는 (B)가 정답으로, 사무실에서 물건을 두는 장소로 drawer(서랍), cabinet(캐비닛), supply closet(비품 창고) 등이 자주 등장한다. (A) 의문사 의문문에 No로 답한 오답, (C) 이유를 묻는 질문에 어울리는 응답이다.

어휘 store 저장하다   manual 설명서   over there 저쪽에
hire 고용하다

19. Who will take over for Francesco?
(A) It depends on our supervisor.
(B) No, it didn't go as planned.
(C) Fran also felt the same.

누가 Francesco 일을 인계 받을 건가요?
(A) 상사한테 달려 있어요.
(B) 아니요, 계획대로 진행되지 않았어요.
(C) Fran 역시 같은 것을 느꼈어요.

해설 일을 인계 받을 사람이 누군지 묻는 질문으로, 구체적인 인물을 언급하는 대신 상사에 의해 결정된다고 우회적으로 답변하는 (A)가 정답이다. (B) 의문사 의문문에 No로 답한 오답, (C) 질문의 Francesco과 유사 발음인 Fran으로 혼동을 노린 오답 함정이다.

어휘 take over 인계 받다   depend on ~에 달려 있다
supervisor 상사

20. Where did Jamal begin working here?
(A) In customer service.
(B) She usually takes the bus.
(C) A couple of years ago.

Jamal은 여기 어디에서 일을 시작했나요?
(A) 고객 서비스부에서요.
(B) 그녀는 보통 버스를 타요.
(C) 2년 전이요.

해설 일을 시작했던 곳, 부서를 묻는 질문으로, 고객 서비스부에서 일을 시작했다는 (A)가 정답이다. (B)는 방법을 묻는 How 의문문에 어울리는 응답, (C) 시기를 묻는 When 의문문에 대한 응답이다.

어휘 customer service 고객 서비스

21. Who processed this purchase order?

(A) The training is required.

(B) I guess Camilla did.

(C) Are you ready to order?

누가 이 구매 주문 건을 처리했나요?
(A) 교육이 필요합니다.
(B) Camilla가 한 것 같아요.
(C) 주문하시겠어요?

해설 주문 건을 진행한 사람이 누구인지를 묻는 Who 의문문으로, Camilla가 한 것 같다고 한 (B)가 정답이다. (A) 질문과 관련 없는 내용, (C) 질문에 나온 order를 반복한 오답 함정이다.

어휘 process 처리하다 purchase 구매 order 주문
required 필수의, 필요한

22. When will this recreational area be open to the public?

(A) The first week of August.

(B) At the public park.

(C) A playground and a bike path.

이 휴양 단지는 언제 대중에게 공개되나요?
(A) 8월 첫째 주요.
(B) 공원에서요.
(C) 운동장과 자전거 도로요.

해설 휴양지가 대중에게 공개되는 시기를 묻는 When 의문문으로, 구체적인 때를 언급한 (A)가 정답이다. (B) Where 의문문으로 잘못 들었을 경우 고를 수 있는 오답 함정, (C) recreational area를 듣고 연상 가능한 오답 함정이다.

어휘 recreational area 휴양 단지 public 일반 사람들, 대중
playground 운동장

23. Where can I see today's schedule of events?

(A) It's posted on the door.

(B) Probably around 2 P.M.

(C) I don't have time to attend.

오늘 행사 일정은 어디에서 볼 수 있나요?
(A) 문에 게시되어 있어요.
(B) 아마도 오후 2시 정도요.
(C) 참석할 시간이 없어요.

해설 행사 일정을 어디에서 볼 수 있냐는 Where 의문문으로, 문에 붙어 있다며 구체적인 장소를 언급한 (A)가 정답이다. (B) When 의문문에 어울리는 응답, (C) events-attend의 연상 어휘 함정이다.

어휘 post 게시하다 probably 아마 attend 참석하다

24. Where should I move these boxes of paper?

(A) It is too heavy to carry.

(B) On Friday morning.

(C) Andrew will organize all the supplies.

이 종이 상자들을 어디로 옮겨야 되나요?
(A) 그것은 들기에 너무 무거워요.
(B) 금요일 아침에요.
(C) Andrew가 모든 물품을 정리할 거예요.

해설 박스들을 어디로 옮길지를 묻는 Where 의문문으로, Andrew가 정리할 거라서 옮길 필요가 없다는 의미의 (C)가 정답이다. (A) 대명사가 일치하지 않고, (B) When 의문문에 어울리는 응답이다.

어휘 organize 정리하다 supplies 물품

25. Who's responsible for updating the employee handbook?

(A) What needs to be changed?

(B) It's handy to use.

(C) I don't know who's coming.

누가 직원 안내서 업데이트를 담당하나요?
(A) 무엇을 바꿔야 되나요?
(B) 그것은 사용하기에 편해요.
(C) 누가 오는지 몰라요.

해설 안내서 업데이트 담당자를 묻는 Who 의문문으로, 특정 인물을 지칭하는 대신 수정되어야 할 게 있는지를 되묻는 (A)가 응답으로 자연스럽다. (B)는 handbook-handy 유사 발음 함정, (C)는 질문의 who's를 반복해 혼동을 노린 오답 함정이다.

어휘 responsible for ~에 책임이 있는 employee
handbook 직원 안내서 handy 유용한, 편리한

DAY 4 — What&Which/How/Why 의문문

SPARTA Check-UP
p.43

1. (C) 2. (C) 3. (C) 4. (A) 5. (C)

---

1. What photo should I use for my article?
   (A) He's a photographer.
   (B) Use the camera on the phone.
   (C) Whichever you want.

제 기사에 어떤 사진을 사용해야 하나요?
(A) 그는 사진사예요.
(B) 휴대폰에 있는 카메라를 사용하세요.
(C) 당신이 원하는 걸로요.

[해설] 기사에 사용할 사진을 묻는 질문으로, 원하는 걸로 선택하라는 (C)가 정답이다. (A) 주어 he가 가리킬 만한 대상이 없고 photo–photographer를 이용한 유사 어휘 함정, (B) photo–camera 연상 어휘를 이용한 오답 함정이다.

[어휘] article 기사 whichever 어느 쪽이든

2. Which movie star will be interviewed on the news today?
   (A) I enjoy seeing the film.
   (B) After the business news.
   (C) The one who won the Best Actor award.

오늘 뉴스에서 어떤 영화 배우를 인터뷰하게 되나요?
(A) 영화 보는 것을 좋아해요.
(B) 비즈니스 뉴스 이후에요.
(C) 최고의 배우상을 받은 사람요.

[해설] 인터뷰 대상을 묻는 질문으로, Which 의문문은 the one으로 시작하는 답변이 정답일 확률이 높다. 따라서 (C)가 정답이다. (A) 질문의 movie를 듣고 연상 가능한 film을 이용해 혼동을 노린 함정, (B) news를 반복한 오답 함정으로, When 의문문에 어울리는 응답이다.

[어휘] enjoy 즐기다 actor 배우 award 상

3. How is the repair service at Canton Electronics Store?
   (A) Please fix my laptop computer.
   (B) Do you think so?
   (C) I'm satisfied with it.

Canton 전자제품 매장의 수리 서비스는 어때요?
(A) 노트북을 고쳐 주세요.
(B) 그렇게 생각해요?
(C) 만족해요.

[해설] 전자제품 매장의 수리 서비스가 어떤지 의견을 묻는 질문으로, 만족한다는 내용의 (C)가 정답이다. (A) repair service–fix를 이용한 오답 함정, (B) 질문과 내용상 관련 없다.

[어휘] repair 수리(하다) electronics store 전자제품 매장 fix 고치다 be satisfied with ~에 만족하다

4. Excuse me. How soon can you fix my watch?
   (A) Can I have a look at it?
   (B) Seven miles an hour.
   (C) I can repair it.

실례합니다. 시계를 얼마나 빨리 고칠 수 있나요?
(A) 한번 볼까요?
(B) 한 시간에 7마일이에요.
(C) 제가 고칠 수 있어요.

[해설] 얼마나 빨리 고칠 수 있는지를 묻는 질문으로, 시점을 말하는 대신, 한번 보자는 뜻의 (A)가 응답으로 어울린다. (B) 거리를 묻는 질문(How far ~?)에 어울리는 응답, (C) 연상 어휘 fix–repair을 이용한 오답 함정이다.

[어휘] how soon ~ 얼마나 빨리 ~

5. Why is the self-assessment still not finished?
   (A) Help yourself.
   (B) Because she completed the annual report.
   (C) Didn't you get the notice?

왜 자기 평가서를 아직 안 끝냈어요?
(A) 마음껏 드세요.
(B) 왜냐하면 그녀가 연례 보고서를 끝냈기 때문이에요.
(C) 공지 못 받았어요?

[해설] 자기 평가서를 아직 끝내지 않은 이유를 묻는 질문으로, 관련 공지를 못 받았는지를 되묻는 (C)가 응답으로 어울린다. (A) self–yourself를 이용한 유사 발음 함정, (B) because로 시작해 답으로 착각할 수 있지만 she가 누구인지 알 수 없다.

[어휘] self-assessment 자기 평가 complete 완성하다, 마치다 annual 연례의 notice 공지

SPARTA Practice Test
p.44

1. (C) 2. (A) 3. (A) 4. (C) 5. (C)
6. (B) 7. (A) 8. (A) 9. (B) 10. (C)
11. (C) 12. (A) 13. (A) 14. (C) 15. (B)
16. (A) 17. (C) 18. (B) 19. (C) 20. (B)
21. (A) 22. (B) 23. (A) 24. (C) 25. (A)

1. What do you think of the revised travel policy?
   (A) I will update it.
   (B) I had a good time.
   (C) I like the flexible schedule.

변경된 여행 방침에 대해 어떻게 생각하세요?
(A) 제가 업데이트할게요.
(B) 좋은 시간을 가졌어요.
(C) 융통성 있는 일정이 맘에 들어요.

해설 의견을 묻는 질문에, 맘에 든다며 자신의 생각을 말하는 (C)가 정답이다. (A) 질문의 revised의 연상 어휘인 update로 혼동을 노린 오답 함정. (B) travel-good time을 이용한 연상 함정이다.

어휘 revise 수정하다   policy 방침   update 업데이트하다
flexible 융통성 있는

2. Why didn't you make it to the party?
   (A) I couldn't finish work in time.
   (B) I took a taxi.
   (C) I came with my friends.

왜 파티에 안 왔어요?
(A) 일을 제때 끝낼 수 없었어요.
(B) 택시를 탔어요.
(C) 제 친구랑 왔어요.

해설 파티에 오지 않은 이유를 묻는 질문에, 일을 끝내지 못해서 못 갔다고 하는 (A)가 정답이다. (B) 교통수단을 묻는 How 의문문에 어울리는 응답, (C) 질문과 관련 없는 내용이다.

어휘 make it 참석하다   in time 제시간에

3. Which restaurant should we take our clients to this evening?
   (A) I thought we were having dinner catered.
   (B) They're waiting in the lobby.
   (C) The food is really good.

오늘 저녁에 우리 고객들을 어느 레스토랑으로 데리고 가야 하나요?
(A) 출장요리업체를 부르는 걸로 생각했는데요.
(B) 그들은 로비에서 기다리고 있어요.
(C) 음식이 정말 맛있어요.

해설 고객을 어느 레스토랑으로 데리고 갈지를 묻는 질문에, 출장 요리업체를 부르는 걸로 알고 있다는 (A)가 적절한 응답이다. (B)는 where 의문문에 어울리는 응답, (C) restaurant-food 연상 어휘를 이용한 오답 함정이다.

어휘 cater (음식을) 공급하다

4. How many positions will we have this year?
   (A) In the advertising field.
   (B) She said she really likes the job.
   (C) It depends on the budget.

올해 일자리가 얼마나 날까요?
(A) 광고 분야에서요.
(B) 그녀는 그 일을 정말 좋아한다고 말했어요.
(C) 예산에 따라 달라요.

해설 일자리가 얼마나 생길지를 묻는 질문에, 예산에 따라 달라진다는 '몰라요' 유형의 답변 (C)가 정답이다. (A) positions-advertising 연상 어휘 함정, (B) she를 가리킬 만한 대상이 언급되지 않았다.

어휘 position 일자리   advertising 광고   field 분야
depend on ~에 달려 있다   budget 예산

5. Which carton should we use to ship these parts?
   (A) About four days.
   (B) You'd be better off.
   (C) The smallest one.

이 부품들을 배송하기 위해 어느 상자를 사용해야 하나요?
(A) 약 4일이요.
(B) 더 나아질 거예요.
(C) 가장 작은 거요.

해설 배송을 위해 사용해야 할 상자가 어느 것인지 묻는 질문으로, 가장 작은 박스를 사용하라는 (C)가 정답이다. Which 의문문의 정답으로 the one을 이용한 보기가 자주 등장한다. (A) 기간을 묻는 질문의 응답, (B) 질문과 관련 없는 내용이다.

어휘 carton 상자   part 부품   be better off 더 나아지다

6. How can I get some more paper for the copier?
   (A) There's storage space available.
   (B) Mr. Wang takes care of that.
   (C) Can I have a cup of coffee?

복사기 용지를 어떻게 더 얻을 수 있어요?
(A) 이용 가능한 저장 공간이 있어요.
(B) Wang 씨가 그걸 관리해요.
(C) 커피 한잔 마셔도 되나요?

해설 용지를 더 얻는 방법을 묻는 질문에, 본인은 모르고 Wang 씨가 그 일을 맡고 있으니 그에게 물어보라는 "몰라요" 유형의 (B)가 정답이다. (A) 질문과 관련 없는 응답, (C) copier-coffee 유사 발음을 이용한 오답 함정이다.

어휘 copier 복사기   storage space 저장 공간
take care of ~ 돌보다, 처리하다

7. How are we going to accommodate ten extra people?
   (A) By adding more chairs in the back.
   (B) The address is written on the invitation.
   (C) Patti has the guest list.

어떻게 10명의 추가 인원을 수용할 건가요?
(A) 뒤에 의자들을 더 추가해서요.
(B) 주소는 초대장에 쓰여 있어요.
(C) Patti가 고객 명단을 가지고 있어요.

해설 추가 인원을 어떻게 수용할지를 묻는 질문에, 의자를 더 추가하자며 방법을 제시하는 (A)가 정답이다. (B) 질문과 관련 없는 내용, (C) people-guest list 연상 어휘를 이용한 오답 함정이다.

어휘 accommodate 수용하다　extra 추가의　add 추가하다
invitation 초대장　guest list 고객 명단

8. Why have they blocked off Highway 15?
(A) For the repaving work.
(B) I'm caught in traffic.
(C) Yes, I believe it's true.

그들은 왜 15번 고속도로를 막았나요?
(A) 재포장 공사를 위해서요.
(B) 차가 막혔어요.
(C) 네, 그게 사실이라고 믿어요.

해설 도로를 막은 이유를 묻는 질문에, 도로 포장 작업 때문이라고 이유를 언급하는 (A)가 정답이다. (B) Highway-traffic 연상 어휘 함정, (C) 의문사 의문문에 Yes로 답할 수 없다.

어휘 block off 막다　highway 고속도로　repave 재포장하다

9. What time is the new employee orientation?
(A) Room 303.
(B) It hasn't been decided yet.
(C) It finishes at 6 P.M.

신입 사원 오리엔테이션은 몇 시에 있나요?
(A) 303호실이요.
(B) 아직 결정되지 않았어요.
(C) 저녁 6시에 끝나요.

해설 행사 시작 시간을 묻는 질문에, 아직 결정되지 않았다는 "몰라요" 유형의 (B)가 정답이다. (A) 방 번호를 답하는 어색한 내용의 오답, (C) time-6 P.M.의 연상 어휘 함정이다.

어휘 new employee 신입 사원　orientation 오리엔테이션
decide 결정하다

10. Why did Rick Studio cancel our appointment?
(A) Yes, that's a good point.
(B) Just tomorrow morning.
(C) Due to a scheduling conflict.

왜 Rick 스튜디오가 우리 예약을 취소했나요?
(A) 네, 좋은 지적이에요.
(B) 내일 아침만요.
(C) 일정이 겹쳐서요.

해설 예약이 취소된 이유를 묻는 질문에, 일정이 겹쳐서라며 이유를 말하는 (C)가 정답이다. (A) 의문사 의문문에 Yes로 답할 수 없고, (B) When 의문문에 어울리는 응답이다.

어휘 appointment 약속　point 요점　due to ~때문에
scheduling conflict 일정 겹침

11. How much does the tennis club membership cost?
(A) Fill out an online registration form.
(B) Once a month.
(C) Wait a minute. Let me get my manager.

테니스 클럽 회원비는 얼마인가요?
(A) 온라인 신청서를 작성하세요.
(B) 한 달에 한 번이요.
(C) 잠시만요. 매니저를 모셔 올게요.

해설 회원비를 묻는 질문에, 본인은 모르고 매니저를 데리고 오겠다는 "몰라요" 유형의 (C)가 정답이다. (A) 등록 방법을 묻는 질문에 어울리는 답변, (B) 횟수를 묻는 질문(how often ~?)에 어울리는 응답이다.

어휘 membership 회원　registration form 신청서

12. Which applicant did you hire?
(A) It's still under consideration.
(B) Ten people applied for the position.
(C) It is higher than expected.

어떤 지원자를 고용했나요?
(A) 여전히 고려 중이에요.
(B) 10명이 그 일자리에 지원했어요.
(C) 예상보다 더 높아요.

해설 지원자들 중 누구를 고용했는지를 묻는 질문에, 아직 결정하지 못했다는 (A)가 정답이다. (B) 지원자 수를 묻는 질문에 어울리는 응답, (C) hire-higher 유사 발음 함정이다.

어휘 applicant 지원자　hire 고용하다　under consideration 고려 중인　apply for 지원하다　expect 예상하다

13. What do you want me to do with these old files?
(A) Just recycle them.
(B) No, that's not what I wanted.
(C) As soon as the new office opens.

이전 파일들로 제가 무엇을 하기를 원하시나요?
(A) 그냥 재활용하세요.
(B) 아니요, 제가 원했던 게 아니에요.
(C) 새 사무실이 열자마자요.

해설 이전 파일을 어떻게 했으면 좋겠냐는 질문에, 재활용하라고 방법을 제시하는 (A)가 정답이다. (B) 의문사 의문문에 No로 답할 수 없고, (C) When 의문문에 어울리는 응답이다.

어휘 recycle 재활용하다　as soon as ~하자마자

14. Why was our research proposal rejected?
(A) A large research laboratory.
(B) Tim will propose a possible solution.
(C) Because of the shortage of funding.

왜 우리 연구 제안서가 거절되었나요?
(A) 큰 연구소요.
(B) Tim이 가능한 해결책을 제안할 거예요.
(C) 자금 부족 때문이죠.

해설 제안서가 거절된 이유를 묻는 질문에, 자금 부족 때문에 거절됐다고 하는 (C)가 정답이다. (A) 질문의 research를 반복해 혼동을 노린 오답 함정, (B) proposal-propose 유사 발음 함정이다.

어휘 research 연구   reject 거절하다   research laboratory 연구소   propose 제안하다   possible 가능한   solution 해법   shortage 부족   funding 자금

15. How long do we have to wait for the lights to be fixed?
(A) Some damaged parts.
(B) It'll all be finished by noon.
(C) Yeah, we should contact him right away.

전등을 고치는 데 얼마나 기다려야 할까요?
(A) 몇 개 손상된 부품들이요.
(B) 정오까지는 모두 끝날 거예요.
(C) 네, 우리는 그에게 바로 연락해야 해요.

해설 수리하는 데 걸리는 시간을 묻는 질문에, 정오까지는 마무리된다는 (B)가 정답이다. (A) fixed-damaged 연상 어휘 함정, (C) 의문사 의문문에 Yes로 답할 수 없으며, him을 가리킬 만한 대상도 언급되지 않았다.

어휘 light 전등   fix 수리하다   damaged 손상된   part 부품   contact 연락하다

16. How did you read this book so quickly?
(A) It was just very interesting.
(B) Look at the user's manual.
(C) An author will sign this book.

어떻게 이 책을 그렇게 빨리 읽었어요?
(A) 그냥 너무 재미있었거든요.
(B) 사용 설명서를 보세요.
(C) 작가가 이 책에 사인할 거예요.

해설 책을 빨리 읽은 이유를 묻는 질문에, 재미있어서 빨리 읽었다고 이유를 말하는 (A)가 정답이다. (B) 사용법을 묻는 질문에 어울리는 응답, (C) book-author의 연상 어휘 함정이다.

어휘 user's manual 사용자 매뉴얼, 사용 설명서   author 작가   sign 서명하다

17. Why did Sylvia come to work late?
(A) I'm not sure how it works.
(B) I'm not late.
(C) She missed the bus.

Sylvia는 왜 지각했나요?
(A) 어떻게 그것이 작동하는지 몰라요.
(B) 저는 지각하지 않았어요.
(C) 그녀는 버스를 놓쳤어요.

해설 Sylvia가 늦은 이유를 묻는 질문에, 버스를 놓쳐서 늦었다고 이유를 말하는 (C)가 정답이다. (A) 질문의 work를 반복한 오답 함정, (B) 주어도 일치하지 않고 late를 반복해 혼동을 주고 있다.

어휘 miss 놓치다

18. Why was the television show discontinued?
(A) Earlier this year.
(B) It received negative comments.
(C) Yes, I'll watch it with you.

왜 텔레비전 쇼가 중단되었나요?
(A) 올해 초예요.
(B) 부정적인 반응을 받았어요.
(C) 네, 당신과 함께 그걸 볼 거예요.

해설 쇼가 중단된 이유를 묻는 질문에, 부정적인 반응 때문에 중단됐다는 (B)가 정답이다. (A) When 의문문에 어울리는 응답, (C) 의문사 의문문에 yes로 답할 수 없다.

어휘 discontinue 중단하다   receive 받다   negative 부정적인   comment 논평, 비판

19. How was the lecture about eating habits yesterday?
(A) Actually, I couldn't attend it.
(B) It depends on the weather.
(C) More than two years of managerial experience.

어제 식습관에 대한 강연은 어땠어요?
(A) 사실 참석할 수 없었어요.
(B) 날씨에 따라 달라요.
(C) 2년 이상의 경영 경험이요.

해설 강연이 어땠는지 의견을 묻는 질문에, 참석하지 못해 알 수 없다는 "몰라요" 유형의 (A)가 정답이다. (B), (C) 모두 질문과 어울리지 않는 내용의 답변이다.

어휘 lecture 강의   eating habits 식습관   attend 참석하다   depend on ~에 달려 있다   weather 날씨   managerial 경영의   experience 경험

20. What's the price of these comfortable shoes?
(A) Great products.
(B) There may be a discount.
(C) They look nice.

이 편안한 신발은 얼마죠?
(A) 멋진 제품들이에요.

(B) 할인할지도 모르겠네요.
(C) 그것들은 좋아 보여요.

해설 신발의 가격을 묻는 질문에, 할인 수도 있다는 (B)가 정답이다. (A)와 (C)는 질문과 어울리지 않는 내용의 답변이다.

어휘 comfortable 편안한   discount 할인

21. How do I enter the convention center?
(A) I'll show you. Follow me.
(B) It lasted for two hours.
(C) It can accommodate about 100 participants.

컨벤션 센터에 어떻게 들어가나요?
(A) 보여 줄게요. 저 따라오세요.
(B) 2시간 동안 지속됐어요.
(C) 100명의 참석자들을 수용할 수 있어요.

해설 컨벤션 센터에 들어가는 방법을 묻는 How 의문문으로, 길을 직접 안내해 주겠다는 (A)가 정답이다. (B) 걸리는 기간을 묻는 How long 의문문에 어울리는 응답, (C) 참석자 수를 묻는 How many 의문문에 적합한 응답이다.

어휘 enter 들어가다   last 지속되다   accommodate 수용하다   participant 참석자

22. In which room is Angela staying at the hotel?
(A) I'll stay for another hour.
(B) Let's call her.
(C) At the front desk.

Angela는 호텔의 어느 룸에 머물고 있어요?
(A) 한 시간 더 머물 거예요.
(B) 그녀에게 전화합시다.
(C) 프런트에서요.

해설 Angela가 어느 방에서 묵는지 묻는 Which 의문문으로, 전화해서 물어보자는 "몰라요" 유형의 (B)가 정답이다. (A)는 기간을 묻는 How long 의문문에 어울리는 응답, (C) 질문의 hotel을 듣고 연상 가능한 front desk로 혼동을 주고 있다.

어휘 stay 머물다

23. Why can't I print this document?
(A) You can just e-mail it to me.
(B) A documentary film.
(C) It is difficult to read.

왜 이 서류는 인쇄되지 않는 걸까요?
(A) 그냥 메일로 보내 주세요.
(B) 다큐멘터리 영화요.
(C) 그건 읽기 어려워요.

해설 서류 인쇄가 왜 안 되는지를 묻는 Why 의문문으로, 그냥 메일로 보내 달라는 (A)가 정답이다. (B) document–documentary 유사 발음 함정, (C) document–read의 연상 어휘 함정이다.

어휘 print 인쇄하다   document 문서   difficult 어려운   documentary film 기록 영화

24. How much will it cost to send these parcels?
(A) Approximately three days.
(B) The packaging is weak.
(C) When do you want them to arrive?

이 소포들을 보내는 데 비용이 얼마나 들까요?
(A) 대략 3일이요.
(B) 포장재가 약해요.
(C) 그것들이 언제 도착하길 원하시나요?

해설 배송 비용을 묻는 How much 의문문으로, 언제 도착하기를 원하는지 되묻는 (C)가 정답이다. (A)는 걸리는 기간을 답한 How long 의문문에 어울리는 응답, (B) parcel–packaging의 연상 어휘 함정이다.

어휘 parcel 소포   approximately 대략   packaging 포장(재)

25. What is your opinion about that presenter?
(A) I wish she could train my team.
(B) I think it's a good present.
(C) About twice a week.

발표자에 대해 어떻게 생각하세요?
(A) 그녀가 제 팀의 교육을 담당했으면 좋겠어요.
(B) 좋은 선물이라고 생각해요.
(C) 대략 일주일에 두 번이요.

해설 발표자에 대한 의견을 묻는 What 의문문으로, 발표자가 자기 팀을 교육해 줬으면 좋겠다 즉, 맘에 든다는 의미의 (A)가 정답이다. (B)는 presenter–present의 유사 발음 함정, (C) 횟수를 묻는 How often ~?에 어울리는 응답이다.

어휘 opinion 의견   presenter 발표자   present 선물

DAY 5 일반/부정/부가의문문

SPARTA Check-UP
p.48

1. (A) 2. (B) 3. (C) 4. (A) 5. (B)

1. Has Ms. Han left for the dentist?
(A) No, her appointment isn't until 2 P.M.
(B) Thanks, I'm feeling much better.
(C) Please wait in the lobby.

Han 씨는 치과에 갔어요?
(A) 아니요, 그녀의 예약은 오후 2시예요.
(B) 고마워요, 훨씬 좋아졌어요.
(C) 로비에서 기다리세요.

해설 Han 씨가 치과에 갔는지를 묻는 질문으로, not until을 이용해 2시에 예약되어 있다는 (A)가 정답이다. (B), (C)는 내용상 어색한 응답이다.

어휘 dentist 치과, 치과의사   not until ~이 되어서야

2. Do you know where the food court is in this building?
(A) The courthouse is around the corner.
(B) It's in the basement.
(C) Let's meet at noon.

이 빌딩에 푸드코트가 어디에 있는지 알아요?
(A) 법원은 모퉁이를 돌면 있어요.
(B) 지하에 있어요.
(C) 정오에 만납시다.

해설 푸드코트가 어디에 있는지 묻는 간접 의문문으로, Yes가 생략된 채 위치를 언급한 (B)가 정답이다. 질문에서 Do you know 뒤에 나오는 부분을 잘 들어야 한다. (A) court–courthouse 유사 발음 함정, (C)는 When 의문문에 어울리는 응답이다.

어휘 courthouse 법원   corner 모퉁이   basement 지하(층)

3. Hasn't the ship been loaded yet?
(A) Delivery is free of charge.
(B) Sure, they'll download that program.
(C) Some maintenance work is causing a delay.

배에 아직 짐이 안 실렸나요?
(A) 배달비가 무료예요.
(B) 그럼요, 그들이 프로그램을 다운로드할 거예요.
(C) 몇 가지 정비 작업이 지연되고 있어요.

해설 배에 짐을 실었는지 묻는 질문에, No 생략 후 부연 설명이 이어진 (C)가 정답이다. (A) ship–delivery 연상 어휘 함정, (B) load–download 유사 발음 함정이다.

어휘 load (짐을) 싣다   free of charge 무료로   maintenance work 정비, 보수 작업   cause 야기하다   delay 지연

4. The warehouse is locked, isn't it?
(A) Yes, but Tom will give you the key.
(B) I restocked all the items in there.
(C) Please close it.

창고가 잠겼죠, 그렇죠?
(A) 네, 근데 Tom이 당신에게 열쇠를 줄 거예요.
(B) 거기 안에 모든 물건들을 다 채웠어요.
(C) 그걸 닫아 주세요.

해설 창고가 잠겼는지 확인하는 질문에, 잠기긴 했지만 Tom이 열쇠를 줄 거라는 (A)가 정답이다. (B) warehouse–restocked 연상 어휘 함정, (C) locked–close 연상 어휘 함정이다.

어휘 lock 잠그다   restock 다시 채우다

5. Melissa has the copies of the sales report, doesn't she?
(A) A yearly salary increase.
(B) Let's check on her desk.
(C) It was a great success.

Melissa가 판매 보고서 사본을 가지고 있죠, 그렇죠?
(A) 연간 임금 인상이요.
(B) 그녀의 책상을 확인해 봅시다.
(C) 대성공이었어요.

해설 Melissa가 보고서 사본을 가지고 있는지 확인하는 질문으로, 그녀의 책상을 확인해 보자는 (B)가 응답으로 어울린다. (A) sales report–increase 연상 어휘 함정, (C) 질문과 관련 없는 내용이다.

어휘 sales report 판매 보고서   yearly 연간의   salary 급여

SPARTA Practice Test
p.49

1. (A) 2. (A) 3. (B) 4. (C) 5. (C)
6. (C) 7. (B) 8. (A) 9. (A) 10. (B)
11. (B) 12. (B) 13. (B) 14. (C) 15. (A)
16. (A) 17. (B) 18. (B) 19. (A) 20. (C)
21. (B) 22. (B) 23. (B) 24. (B) 25. (B)

1. Can you tell me where Yukiko went?
(A) Maybe to the archives.
(B) No, I don't know the way.
(C) It was at eleven thirty.

Yukiko가 어디에 갔는지 말해 주시겠어요?
(A) 아마 기록 보관실에 갔을 거예요.
(B) 아니요, 저는 그 길을 몰라요.
(C) 11시 30분이었어요.

해설 Yukiko가 어디로 갔는지 묻는 간접 의문문으로, 기록 보관실이라고 구체적 장소를 언급한 (A)가 정답이다. (B) where-the way 연상 어휘로 혼동을 주는 오답 함정, (C) When 의문문에 어울리는 응답이다.

어휘 archives 기록 보관실

2. You bought the musical tickets, didn't you?

(A) I didn't think I could go.

(B) I'll play the piano.

(C) An action film.

뮤지컬 티켓을 구입했죠, 그렇죠?
(A) 못 가는 줄 알았어요.
(B) 피아노를 연주할 거예요.
(C) 액션 영화요.

해설 티켓을 구입했는지 묻는 부가 의문문으로, No가 생략된 채, 못 가는 줄 알고 안 샀다는 의미의 (A)가 정답이다. (B)와 (C)는 각각 musical tickets의 연상 어휘(piano-film)를 이용한 오답 함정이다.

어휘 play 연주하다 film 영화

3. Don't you think Rita Parks is the most experienced candidate?

(A) A few more résumés.

(B) No, she just graduated from university.

(C) An opportunity in the marketing division.

Rita Parks가 가장 경험이 많은 지원자라고 생각하지 않아요?
(A) 이력서 몇 부 더요.
(B) 아니요, 그녀는 대학을 막 졸업했어요.
(C) 마케팅 부서에서 기회예요.

해설 Rita Parks가 후보자로 괜찮지 않은지를 묻는 부정 의문문으로, 대학을 막 졸업해서 질문에 동의하지 않는다는 의미의 (B)가 정답이다. (A) candidate의 연상 어휘 résumés로 혼동을 노린 오답 함정, (C) 역시 candidate의 연상 어휘 marketing division를 이용한 오답이다.

어휘 experienced 경험 많은 candidate 지원자, 후보 résumé 이력서 graduate 졸업하다 opportunity 기회 division 부서

4. We're not receiving our bonuses this month, right?

(A) I can't remember when it was.

(B) My salary increased by ten percent.

(C) I haven't heard that.

이번 달에는 보너스 안 받는 거죠, 그렇죠?
(A) 언제였는지 기억 안 나요.
(B) 제 월급은 10퍼센트 인상됐어요.
(C) 들은 게 없어요.

해설 이번 달에 보너스를 받는지 묻는 부가 의문문으로, 들은 게 없다 즉, '모른다'는 뉘앙스의 (C)가 응답으로 어울린다. (A) 질문의 시제와 맞지 않는 오답, (B) bonuses-salary 연상 어휘 함정이다.

어휘 remember 기억하다 salary 월급 increase 증가하다

5. Are you planning to attend a conference in Melbourne?

(A) Go to Conference Room A or B.

(B) At least a few hundred people from Sydney.

(C) I'm still waiting to find out who the speakers will be.

멜버른에 있는 학회에 참석할 계획인가요?
(A) A 회의실 아니면 B 회의실로 가세요.
(B) 적어도 시드니에서 온 몇 백 명의 사람들이요.
(C) 누가 연설자인지 알려고 기다리고 있어요.

해설 학회에 참석할지를 묻는 일반 의문문으로, 연설자가 누구인지 확인하기 위해 기다리고 있다 즉, 아직 참석 여부를 정하지 않았다는 (C)가 정답이다. (A) conference 어휘 반복 함정, (B) Melbourne-Sydney의 연상 어휘 함정이다.

어휘 conference room 회의실 at least 적어도 find out 알아내다

6. Isn't your store closed for the holiday?

(A) It can be stored here.

(B) I'm going to Hawaii.

(C) No, it's our busiest season.

가게가 휴일에 문을 닫지 않나요?
(A) 그것은 여기에 저장될 수 있어요.
(B) 저는 하와이로 갈 거예요.
(C) 아니요, 가장 바쁜 시즌이에요.

해설 휴일에 가게 문을 닫냐고 묻는 부정 의문문으로, 가장 바쁜 시즌이라서 문을 닫지 않는다는 (C)가 정답이다. (A) store-stored 유사 발음 함정, (B) holiday를 듣고 연상 가능한 이용한 Hawaii로 혼동을 노린 오답이다.

어휘 store 가게; 저장하다 busiest 가장 바쁜 season 계절, 시즌

7. Have you read the e-mail about the budget cut?

(A) I bought it at an affordable price.

(B) I haven't checked.

(C) I'll send the money soon.

예산 삭감에 대한 메일을 읽었나요?
(A) 저렴한 가격으로 샀어요.
(B) 확인 안 했어요.
(C) 곧 돈을 보내 줄게요.

해설 메일을 읽었는지 묻는 일반 의문문으로, No 생략 후 아직 확인하지 못했다고 하는 (B)가 정답이다. (A)와 (C)는 질문의 budget의 연상 어휘 함정(price-money)이다.

어휘 budget cut 예산 삭감 affordable (가격이) 알맞은

8. You're not going to wear that suit to the company luncheon, are you?

  (A) You don't like it?
  (B) Yes, it suits you.
  (C) No, I don't know where she is.

회사 오찬 갈 때 저 정장 입는 거 아니죠, 그렇죠?
(A) 마음에 안 들어요?
(B) 네, 당신한테 잘 어울려요.
(C) 아니요, 그녀가 어디에 있는지 몰라요.

해설 행사 갈 때 정장을 입을 건지 묻는 부가 의문문으로, 마음에 안 든다고 반문하는 (A)가 정답이다. (B) 주어 불일치 오답, (C) wear-where 유사 발음 함정이다.

어휘 luncheon 오찬 suit 정장; 어울리다

9. Are we supposed to submit this report by tomorrow?

  (A) Yes, to our immediate supervisor.
  (B) I suppose the report is fine.
  (C) Yes, keep it until next month.

내일까지 이 보고서를 제출하기로 했나요?
(A) 네, 저희 직속 상사에게요.
(B) 보고서가 괜찮다고 생각해요.
(C) 네, 다음 달까지 그것을 보관하세요.

해설 내일까지 보고서를 제출해야 하는지 묻는 일반 의문문으로, 직속 상사에게 제출하라는 (A)가 정답이다. (B) 질문에 나온 suppose-report를 반복한 오답 함정, (C) tomorrow-next month 연상 어휘 함정이다.

어휘 be supposed to ~하기로 되어 있다 submit 제출하다 immediate supervisor 직속 상사 suppose 생각하다, 가정하다 keep 보관하다

10. You looked over the new candidate's résumés, didn't you?

  (A) Professional work experience.
  (B) Not yet, but I'll do it soon.
  (C) The working hours are flexible.

후보자들의 이력서를 검토했죠, 그렇죠?
(A) 전문적인 경력이요.
(B) 아직이요, 하지만 곧 할 거예요.
(C) 근무 시간이 자유로워요.

해설 이력서를 검토했는지 묻는 부가 의문문으로, 아직 안 했지만 곧 할 거라는 (B)가 어울린다. (A)와 (C)는 candidate's résumés의 연상 어휘(work experience-working hours) 함정이다.

어휘 look over 검토하다 résumé 이력서 professional 전문적인 work experience 경력 flexible 유연한

11. Isn't Nakamura coming to the opera with us?

  (A) Sit in the front row.
  (B) No, he doesn't have time.
  (C) I'm looking forward to this performance.

Nakamura는 우리와 같이 오페라에 안 가나요?
(A) 앞줄에 앉으세요.
(B) 아니요, 그는 시간이 없어요.
(C) 이 공연을 기대하고 있어요.

해설 Nakamura가 오페라에 함께 가는지를 묻는 부정 의문문으로, 바빠서 못 간다고 하는 (B)가 정답이다. (A), (C)는 질문의 opera의 연상 어휘(front row-performance) 함정이다.

어휘 front 앞쪽 row 줄 look forward to ~을 기대하다

12. Do you know who isn't coming to the banquet tonight?

  (A) He was invited to the celebration.
  (B) No, let me go check.
  (C) I'll be waiting, so please get ready.

오늘밤 연회에 누가 안 오는지 알아요?
(A) 그는 축하 행사에 초대 받았어요.
(B) 아니요, 제가 확인할게요.
(C) 기다릴 테니, 준비하세요.

해설 연회에 누가 오는지를 묻는 일반 의문문으로, 모르지만 확인해 보겠다는 "몰라요" 유형의 (B)가 정답이다. (A) banquet의 연상 어휘(celebration) 함정, (C)는 질문 내용과 연관 없는 응답이다.

어휘 banquet 연회 invite 초대하다 celebration 축하 행사

13. Didn't Ms. Miyaki leave me a message?

  (A) The leaves are falling to the ground.
  (B) No, she just said she would call you again.
  (C) You should leave it on my desk.

Miyaki 씨께서 저한테 메시지 안 남겼나요?
(A) 낙엽이 바닥으로 떨어지고 있어요.
(B) 아니요, 그냥 다시 전화한다고 했어요.
(C) 제 책상 위에 두세요.

해설 Miyaki 씨가 메시지를 남겼는지 묻는 부정 의문문으로, No로 부정한 후 다시 전화하겠다고 했다며 부연 설명하는 (B)가 정답이다. (A) leave-leaves의 유사 발음 함정, (C) leave를 그대로 반복한 오답 함정이다.

어휘 leave 남기다, 떠나다   leaves 낙엽   ground 땅바닥

14. Ms. Debby has been working here quite a long time, hasn't she?

(A) No, a managing director.
(B) How much longer does she need?
(C) Yes, for almost 15 years.

Debby 씨는 여기에서 꽤 오랫동안 일하고 있죠, 그렇죠?
(A) 아니요, 경영 이사예요.
(B) 그녀는 얼마나 더 필요한가요?
(C) 네, 거의 15년 동안이요.

해설 Debby 씨가 여기에서 일한 지 오래됐는지를 묻는 부가 의문문으로, Yes로 긍정한 후 15년 동안 일하고 있다는 (C)가 정답이다. (A) working의 연상 어휘 managing director로 혼동을 주고 있고, (B) long-longer를 이용한 유사 발음 함정이다.

어휘 quite 꽤   almost 거의

15. Is the room big enough for the product seminar?

(A) Only five people have signed up for it.
(B) Susan is one of the best presenters.
(C) It'll be very informative.

제품 세미나를 위한 룸이 충분히 크나요?
(A) 5명만 등록했어요.
(B) Susan은 최고의 발표자 중 한 명이에요.
(C) 매우 유익할 거예요.

해설 세미나 룸이 충분히 큰지 묻는 일반 의문문으로, 5명밖에 등록하지 않아서 충분하다는 (A)가 정답이다. (B)와 (C)는 seminar의 연상 어휘(presenters-informative) 함정이다.

어휘 sign up 신청하다, 등록하다   informative 유익한

16. Haven't we received the order yet?

(A) Yes, yesterday evening.
(B) We're not ready to order yet.
(C) No, the receptionist is on the phone.

주문품 아직 안 받았나요?
(A) 네, 어제 저녁에요.
(B) 아직 주문할 준비가 안 됐어요.
(C) 아니요, 접수 담당자가 통화 중이에요.

해설 주문품을 받았는지 묻는 부정 의문문으로, 받았다고 한 후 받은 시점을 부연 설명한 (A)가 정답이다. (B) 질문에 나온 단어 order yet를 반복한 오답 함정, (C) received-receptionist을 이용한 유사 발음 함정이다.

어휘 receptionist 접수 담당자

17. The escalator on this floor hasn't been fixed yet, has it?

(A) To the next floor.
(B) Mr. Taya took care of that.
(C) By taking the escalator.

이 층의 에스컬레이터가 아직 수리 안 됐죠, 그렇죠?
(A) 다음 층으로요.
(B) Taya 씨가 그걸 처리했어요.
(C) 에스컬레이터를 타고요.

해설 에스컬레이터가 고쳐졌는지 묻는 부가 의문문으로, 제3자가 처리했다고 하는 (B)가 정답이다. (A) escalator의 연상 어휘(next floor) 함정, (C) 질문에 나온 escalator를 그대로 반복한 오답 함정이다.

어휘 fix 고치다   floor 층   take care of ~를 돌보다

18. Don't you know how to use the new fax machine?

(A) Really? I didn't know that.
(B) Yes, I'll show you.
(C) No, he fixed the machine.

새 팩스기 사용하는 법 몰라요?
(A) 정말요? 몰랐어요.
(B) 네, 보여 드릴게요.
(C) 아니요, 그가 기계를 고쳤어요.

해설 기계 사용법을 아는지 묻는 부정 의문문으로, 안다면서 직접 보여주겠다는 (B)가 질문에 어울리는 응답이다. (A) 질문의 know 반복 및 시제 불일치 오답, (C) fax-fix의 유사 발음 함정이다.

어휘 machine 기계

19. The shredding machine was repaired yesterday, wasn't it?

(A) No, a technician will come tomorrow.
(B) Several large devices.
(C) Yes, I have one.

파쇄기가 어제 수리됐죠, 그렇죠?
(A) 아니요, 기술자가 내일 올 거예요.
(B) 몇 개의 큰 기기들이요.
(C) 네, 하나 가지고 있어요.

해설 기계가 고쳐졌는지 묻는 부가 의문문으로, No로 부정한 후 내일 기술자가 고치러 온다는 (A)가 정답이다. (B) machine-devices를 이용한 연상 어휘 함정, (C) 부연 설명의 내용이 어색하다.

어휘 shredding machine 파쇄기   several 몇몇의

20. Have you met Ms. Lee, the new executive director?
    (A) A board meeting next Tuesday.
    (B) The accounting department.
    (C) Oh, we were coworkers.

    신임 이사 Lee 씨를 만나 봤어요?
    (A) 다음주 화요일 이사회의요.
    (B) 회계부서요.
    (C) 아, 저희는 동료였어요.

    해설 새로 온 이사를 만나 봤는지 묻는 일반 의문문으로, 예전에 함께 일했던 동료라고 하는 (C)가 정답이다. (A) director-board meeting 연상 어휘 함정, (B) director-accounting department 연상 어휘 함정이다.

    어휘 executive director 이사 coworker 동료

21. Didn't you hear anything from Jackson?
    (A) Yes, you can use mine.
    (B) No, he didn't tell me.
    (C) Yes, he will be.

    Jackson한테서 무슨 소식 안 들었어요?
    (A) 네, 제 것을 쓰세요.
    (B) 아니요, 그는 말하지 않았는데요.
    (C) 네, 그가 있을 거예요.

    해설 Jackson에게서 들은 소식이 없는지를 묻는 부정 의문문으로, 그가 말하지 않아서 모른다는 (B)가 정답이다. (A) 질문과 관련 없는 내용, (C) 시제 및 내용상 어색하다.

22. Are you serious about quitting your job?
    (A) The monthly lecture series.
    (B) Yeah, I want to try something new.
    (C) Look for marketing consultants.

    정말 일 그만두는 거예요?
    (A) 매달 시리즈 강의예요.
    (B) 네, 새로운 무언가를 해보고 싶어요.
    (C) 마케팅 컨설턴트를 찾으세요.

    해설 일을 정말 그만두는지를 묻는 일반 의문문으로, 그렇다면서 그만두는 이유에 대해 부연 설명하는 (B)가 정답이다. (A) serious-series을 이용한 유사 발음 함정, (C) job-consultants의 연상 어휘 함정이다.

    어휘 serious 심각한 quit one's job 일을 그만두다 lecture series 연속 강의

23. Simon hasn't filled out his time sheet, has he?
    (A) I didn't have any time.
    (B) He's back from vacation next week.
    (C) John can work that day.

    Simon은 근무 시간 기록표를 작성하지 않았죠, 그렇죠?
    (A) 시간이 없었어요.
    (B) 그는 다음 주에 휴가에서 돌아와요.
    (C) John이 그날 일할 수 있어요.

    해설 Simon이 근무 시간을 작성했는지를 묻는 부가 의문문으로, 휴가 중이라 다음 주에 돌아온다는 (B)가 정답이다. (A) 질문의 time을 반복한 오답 함정, (C)는 질문의 time sheet를 듣고 연상 가능한 내용으로 혼동을 주고 있다.

    어휘 fill out 작성하다 time sheet 근무 시간 기록표

24. Is Ms. Parker's flight due to arrive on schedule this afternoon?
    (A) She prefers a non-stop flight.
    (B) It left on time from Mumbai.
    (C) At the airport.

    Parker 씨의 비행기는 오늘 오후에 도착할 예정인가요?
    (A) 그녀는 직항을 선호해요.
    (B) 뭄바이에서 정각에 떠났어요.
    (C) 공항에서요.

    해설 Parker 씨가 탄 비행기가 오늘 오후에 도착하는지 묻는 일반 의문문으로, 정각에 출발했다 즉, 예정대로 도착할 거라는 뉘앙스의 (B)가 정답이다. (A) 질문의 flight를 반복한 오답 함정, (C) flight-airport을 이용한 연상 어휘 함정이다.

    어휘 be due to ~할 예정이다 on time 정각에, 시간을 어기지 않고

25. Hasn't the managers meeting been delayed this week?
    (A) I had a problem with it.
    (B) Yes, it will be on Wednesday.
    (C) Overqualified managers.

    이번 주 간부 회의가 연기되지 않았나요?
    (A) 문제가 있었어요.
    (B) 네, 수요일에 할 거예요.
    (C) 필요 이상으로 자격을 갖춘 부장들이요.

    해설 회의가 연기되지 않았냐고 묻는 부정 의문문으로, 연기되어서 수요일에 할 거라는 (B)가 정답이다. (A) 대명사가 어색하고, (C) 질문의 managers를 반복한 오답 함정이다.

    어휘 delay 미루다 overqualified 필요 이상으로 자격을 갖춘

DAY 6 제안/요청문

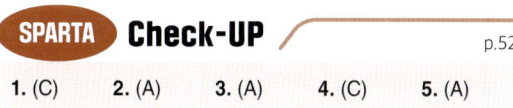 p.52

1. (C)   2. (A)   3. (A)   4. (C)   5. (A)

1. Why don't we stop discussing it and just go out for lunch?
   (A) Because we've talked enough.
   (B) I agree. Let's discuss it more.
   (C) Good idea!

   토론 그만하고 그냥 점심 먹으러 나가는 게 어때요?
   (A) 우리는 충분한 이야기를 했기 때문이죠.
   (B) 동의해요. 그것을 더 토론합시다.
   (C) 좋은 생각이에요!

   해설 토론을 그만하고 점심 먹으러 나가자는 제안문으로, 좋은 생각이라며 동의하는 (C)가 정답이다. (A)는 이유를 묻는 Why 의문문으로 착각할 경우 고를 수 있는 오답 함정, (B)는 앞부분이 I don't agree로 시작한다면 답이 될 수도 있다.

   어휘 discuss 논의하다   enough 충분한   agree 동의하다

2. Could you take a look at this revised document?
   (A) I'm afraid I am busy right now.
   (B) On my desk.
   (C) I think it has a beautiful view.

   수정된 보고서 좀 봐주시겠어요?
   (A) 죄송하지만 지금은 너무 바빠요.
   (B) 제 책상 위에요.
   (C) 전망이 아름다운 것 같아요.

   해설 서류를 봐달라는 요청문으로, 지금은 바쁘다고 거절하는 (A)가 정답이다. (B)는 Where 의문에 어울리는 응답, (C) look-view를 이용한 연상 어휘 함정이다.

   어휘 revise 수정하다   right now 지금 당장   view 전망

3. Should we eat out for lunch in the new Italian restaurant?
   (A) Sorry, I brought something from home today.
   (B) You're right. It was delicious.
   (C) Our new product is launching soon.

   새로 생긴 이탈리아 식당에서 점심 먹을까요?
   (A) 미안하지만, 오늘 집에서 음식을 싸 왔어요.
   (B) 당신 말이 맞네요. 그건 맛있었어요.
   (C) 우리의 신제품이 곧 출시됩니다.

   해설 새로 생긴 식당에서 점심을 먹자는 제안에, 집에서 점심을 싸 왔다며 거절하는 (A)가 정답이다. (B) lunch-delicious 연상 어휘 함정, (C)는 lunch-launching 유사 발음 함정이다.

   어휘 eat out 외식하다   launch 출시하다

4. Would you mind coming to our office?
   (A) Office supplies will be delivered soon.
   (B) The banquet room is available on that day.
   (C) No, that would be convenient for me, too.

   우리 사무실로 오지 않을래요?
   (A) 사무용품이 곧 배달될 거예요.
   (B) 연회장은 그날 이용 가능합니다.
   (C) 네, 저도 그게 편하겠네요.

   해설 사무실로 와 달라는 요청으로, Would you mind ~? 유형은 직역해서 답을 찾아야 한다. No(꺼리지 않는다)라고 한 후, 그게 자기도 편할 것 같다고 덧붙이는 (C)가 정답이다. (A)는 질문의 office를 그대로 반복한 오답 함정, (B) 질문과 관련 없는 내용이다.

   어휘 office supplies 사무용품   available 이용할 수 있는   convenient 편리한

5. Why don't we hand in the request form by the end of the day?
   (A) I already submitted it.
   (B) It was handy to use.
   (C) Sure, we did.

   오늘까지 신청서를 제출하는 게 어때요?
   (A) 제가 이미 제출했어요.
   (B) 그것은 사용하기 편리해요.
   (C) 그럼요, 우리가 했죠.

   해설 오늘까지 신청서를 제출하자는 제안에, 이미 자기가 제출했다는 (A)가 정답이다. (B) hand in-handy 유사 발음 함정, (C) Sure 뒤에 이어지는 내용의 시제가 어색하다.

   어휘 hand in 제출하다(= submit)   request form 신청서   handy 편리한

 p.53

1. (A)	2. (A)	3. (A)	4. (A)	5. (A)
6. (C)	7. (C)	8. (A)	9. (A)	10. (A)
11. (C)	12. (A)	13. (C)	14. (A)	15. (B)
16. (B)	17. (A)	18. (B)	19. (A)	20. (C)
21. (A)	22. (A)	23. (B)	24. (A)	25. (C)

1. Can we recruit more employees?
   (A) No, it's not in the budget this quarter.
   (B) I think it still has a vacancy.
   (C) Several new résumés.

더 많은 직원을 고용할 수 있을까요?
(A) 아니요, 이번 분기는 예산이 안 돼요.
(B) 여전히 비어 있다고 생각해요.
(C) 새 이력서 몇 부요.

해설 직원을 더 고용해도 되는지 묻는 요청문으로, 예산이 부족해서 안 된다는 (A)가 정답이다. (B), (C)는 질문의 recruit를 듣고 연상 가능한 어휘(vacancy–résumés)를 이용한 오답 함정이다.

어휘 recruit 채용하다   budget 예산   vacancy 공석
résumé 이력서

2. Could you work my day shift on Thursday?
   (A) Did you ask the supervisor first?
   (B) It shipped already.
   (C) I am busy on Friday.

   목요일에 저 대신 주간 근무를 해 줄 수 있어요?
   (A) 관리자한테 먼저 물어 봤어요?
   (B) 이미 배송됐어요.
   (C) 금요일에는 바빠요.

   해설 대신 일해 줄 수 있는지 묻는 요청문으로, 먼저 상사에게 물어봤냐고 되묻는 (A)가 정답이다. (B) shift–shipped의 유사 발음 함정, (C) Thursday–Friday 연상 어휘 함정이다.

   어휘 shift 교대 근무   supervisor 상사, 감독자

3. Would you like me to draft the contract now?
   (A) That's so kind of you.
   (B) She will write it up for you.
   (C) An e-mail address.

   제가 계약서 초안을 지금 작성할까요?
   (A) 정말 친절하시네요.
   (B) 그녀가 당신을 위해 적어 둘 거예요.
   (C) 메일 주소요.

   해설 계약서 초안을 작성해 주겠다는 제안에, 감사의 표현을 하는 (A)가 어울리는 응답이다. (B) She를 지칭할 만한 대상이 언급되지 않았고, (C) 질문과 관련 없는 내용이다.

   어휘 draft (초안을) 작성하다   contract 계약서
   write up 작성하다

4. Why don't you join the financial workshop with us?
   (A) Sorry, I don't have time to go.
   (B) For personal reasons.
   (C) In the conference hall.

   금융 워크숍에 함께 가는 게 어때요?
   (A) 미안해요, 갈 시간이 없네요.
   (B) 개인적인 문제로요.
   (C) 회의장에서요.

   해설 함께 워크숍에 가자는 권유에, 그럴 시간이 없다고 거절하는 (A)가 정답이다. (B)는 이유를 묻는 Why 의문문으로 착각할 경우 고를 수 있는 오답 함정, (C)는 workshop–conference hall 연상 어휘 함정이다.

   어휘 financial 금융의   personal 개인적인
   conference hall 회의장

5. Should I make some tea?
   (A) That would be nice.
   (B) It's really hot.
   (C) The dessert looks delicious.

   차 좀 드릴까요?
   (A) 좋아요.
   (B) 그것은 너무 뜨거워요.
   (C) 그 디저트는 맛있어 보여요.

   해설 차를 마시겠냐고 묻는 제안문으로, 승낙하는 표현의 (A)가 정답이다. (B)와 (C)는 tea의 연상 어휘(hot–dessert)를 이용한 오답 함정이다.

   어휘 dessert 후식   delicious 맛있는

6. Would you be interested in giving a speech at the company's 10th anniversary ceremony?
   (A) I enjoyed your lecture very much.
   (B) I'd love to speak with the customers.
   (C) When is it being held?

   회사 10주년 창립 기념식에서 연설할 생각 있어요?
   (A) 당신의 강의가 진짜 좋았어요.
   (B) 고객들과 말하고 싶어요.
   (C) 언제 열리는데요?

   해설 연설할 의향이 있는지 묻는 제안문으로, 언제 열리는지 반문하는 (C)가 정답이다. (A)는 speech–lecture 연상 어휘 함정, (B)는 speech–speak의 유사 발음 함정이다.

   어휘 be interested in ~에 관심이 있다   give a speech 연설하다   anniversary ceremony 창립 기념식   lecture 강의

7. Can you pass the scissors?
   (A) Why don't you cut it in half?
   (B) Some office supplies.
   (C) Sure, here you are.

   가위 좀 건네주시겠어요?
   (A) 반으로 자르는 게 어때요?
   (B) 사무용품이요.
   (C) 그럼요, 여기 있어요.

   해설 물건을 건네달라는 요청에, 여기 있다며 전해 주는 (C)가 응답으로 어울린다. (A)와 (B)는 질문의 scissors를 듣고 연상 가능한 어휘(cut–office supplies)를 이용한 함정이다.

   어휘 pass 건네주다   scissors 가위   in half 절반으로
   office supplies 사무용품

8. Would you like to see the play with us tonight?

   (A) No, thanks. Today is my mother's birthday.
   (B) He will be late today.
   (C) Yes, it was already sold out.

   오늘밤에 저희랑 연극 볼래요?
   (A) 아뇨, 괜찮아요. 오늘은 어머니 생신이에요.
   (B) 그는 오늘 늦을 거예요.
   (C) 네, 이미 다 매진됐어요.

   해설 연극을 같이 보러 가자는 제안에, 다른 일정이 있다고 거절하는 (A)가 응답으로 자연스럽다. (B) He를 가리킬 만한 대상이 언급되지 않았고, (C) Yes와 부연 설명이 내용상 어색하다.

   어휘 play 연극   sold out 매진된

9. Could you please send those e-mails to human resources?

   (A) Sure, when I return to my office.
   (B) I haven't received anything.
   (C) To train new staff members.

   인사과로 메일 좀 보내 주시겠어요?
   (A) 당연하죠, 사무실로 돌아가면요.
   (B) 아무것도 받지 못했어요.
   (C) 신입사원을 교육하기 위해서요.

   해설 메일을 보내 주라는 요청에, 사무실에 가면 그러겠다는 (A)가 정답이다. (B)는 send-receive를 이용한 연상 어휘 함정, (C) human resources-staff members 연상 어휘 함정이다.

   어휘 human resources 인사과   train 교육시키다

10. Would you mind if I opened the window?

   (A) Not at all. Go ahead.
   (B) Keep that in mind.
   (C) You can close the backdoor.

   창문을 여는 걸 꺼리세요?
   (A) 전혀요. 그렇게 하세요.
   (B) 명심하세요.
   (C) 뒷문을 닫으세요.

   해설 정중한 요청 표현인 Would you mind ~?로 창문을 열어도 되는지를 묻고 있다. 전혀 꺼리지 않는다 즉, 열어도 된다고 하는 (A)가 정답이다. (B)는 질문에 나온 mind를 그대로 반복한 오답 함정, (C) open-close의 연상 어휘 함정이다.

   어휘 keep in mind 명심하다   backdoor 뒷문

11. Can I talk to you for a minute?

   (A) Here's your report.
   (B) Ms. Kim will be in charge of that.
   (C) My next meeting is about to start.

   잠깐 이야기할 수 있을까요?
   (A) 여기 당신의 보고서가 있어요.
   (B) Kim 씨가 그것을 담당할 거예요.
   (C) 다음 회의가 곧 시작해요.

   해설 잠깐 대화를 나누자는 요청문으로, 곧 회의가 있다며 거절하는 (C)가 정답이다. (A)와 (B)는 질문과 관계 없는 답변이다.

   어휘 in charge of ~을 담당하는   be about to 막 ~하려는 참이다

12. Why don't we stop working for a moment?

   (A) This report is due tomorrow.
   (B) Yes, he's on the phone.
   (C) Because you're behind schedule.

   잠시 일을 멈추는 게 어때요?
   (A) 이 보고서가 내일까지예요.
   (B) 네, 그는 통화 중이에요.
   (C) 당신이 예정보다 늦어서요.

   해설 잠깐 일을 쉬자는 제안에, 보고서 기한이 내일이다 즉, 쉴 시간이 없다는 뜻의 (A)가 정답이다. (B)는 He를 지칭할 만한 대상이 나오지 않았고, (C)는 이유를 묻는 Why 의문문으로 착각할 경우 고를 수 있는 오답이다.

   어휘 for a moment 잠시 동안   behind schedule 예정보다 늦게

13. Could you help me install the chairs for our meeting?

   (A) How many handouts do you need?
   (B) Yes, I met him earlier in the morning.
   (C) Sorry, I'm not feeling good today.

   회의용 의자 설치하는 것 좀 도와주시겠어요?
   (A) 몇 장의 인쇄물이 필요하세요?
   (B) 네, 아침 일찍 그를 만났어요.
   (C) 죄송하지만 오늘 몸이 안 좋아서요.

   해설 의자 설치하는 걸 도와달라는 요청에, 몸이 안 좋다고 거절하는 (C)가 정답이다. (A) meeting-handouts 연상 어휘 함정이고, (B) him을 지칭할 만한 대상이 나오지 않았다.

   어휘 install 설치하다   handout 인쇄물

14. Can I make an announcement before the performance begins?

   (A) Okay, but please keep it short.
   (B) She'll start the work at four o'clock.
   (C) The opening act was impressive.

   공연을 시작하기 전에 제가 발표해도 될까요?
   (A) 좋아요, 근데 짧게 해 주세요.
   (B) 그녀는 4시에 일을 시작할 거예요.
   (C) 개막 공연이 인상적이었어요.

해설 공연 전에 발표를 해도 되는지 허락을 구하는 질문에, 대신 짧게 하라는 (A)가 정답이다. (B) She를 지칭할 만한 대상이 언급되지 않았고, (C) performance의 연상 어휘(opening act) 함정이다.

어휘 make an announcement 발표하다 impressive 인상적인

15. Could you please refrain from using any electronic devices before we take off?

(A) I thought I did.

(B) Oh, sorry. I didn't realize it was on.

(C) I'm on a business trip.

이륙하기 전에 전자기기 사용을 삼가 주시겠어요?
(A) 제가 했다고 생각했어요.
(B) 아, 미안해요. 켜져 있는지 몰랐어요.
(C) 저는 출장 중이에요.

해설 전자기기를 꺼 달라는 요청에, 켜져 있는지 몰랐다고 하는 (B)가 정답이다. (A), (C) 모두 질문과 맞지 않는 내용이다.

어휘 refrain 삼가다 electronic device 전자기기 take off 이륙하다 business trip 출장

16. Should I call a repairperson?

(A) I'm returning your call.

(B) Let's take a look at the manual first.

(C) I want to buy a pair of shoes.

제가 수리공에게 전화할까요?
(A) 저한테 전화하셨다면서요.
(B) 설명서를 먼저 봅시다.
(C) 신발 한 켤레를 사고 싶은데요.

해설 수리공에게 연락할지를 묻는 제안문으로, 전화하기 전에 설명서를 먼저 보자는 (B)가 정답이다. (A) call을 그대로 반복한 함정, (C) repair–pair의 유사 발음 함정이다.

어휘 repairperson 수리공 manual 설명서

17. Let's use meeting room A rather than room B.

(A) But five people will attend.

(B) Somewhere around the Chicago Hotel.

(C) An annual charity banquet.

B 회의실 대신 A 회의실을 사용합시다.
(A) 하지만 5명이 참석할 거예요.
(B) 시카고 호텔 어딘가요.
(C) 연례 자선행사요.

해설 B 회의실 대신 A 회의실을 쓰자는 제안에, But으로 시작해 이의를 제기하고 있는 (A)가 정답이다. (B) room–hotel의 연상 어휘 함정, (C) meeting room을 듣고 연상 가능한 banquet으로 혼동을 주고 있다.

어휘 attend 참석하다 annual 연례의 charity 자선 banquet 연회

18. Could you make some copies?

(A) I have two copies of today's paper.

(B) How many do you need?

(C) Sure, I'm busy now.

복사 좀 해주시겠어요?
(A) 오늘 신문을 2부 가지고 있어요.
(B) 몇 부 필요하세요?
(C) 그럼요, 저는 지금 바빠요.

해설 복사해 달라는 요청에, 몇 부가 필요한지 되묻는 (B)가 응답으로 자연스럽다. (A) copies를 그대로 반복한 오답 함정, (C) Sure로 승낙한 다음 이어지는 부연 설명이 어색하다.

어휘 paper 신문

19. Should we take our clients to the restaurant in the Burwood Mall?

(A) It's always crowded in there.

(B) For an important business meeting.

(C) I'll have today's special.

Burwood Mall에 있는 레스토랑에 고객들을 데리고 갈까요?
(A) 거기는 항상 붐벼요.
(B) 중요한 비즈니스 회의를 위해서요.
(C) 오늘의 추천 요리로 주세요.

해설 고객들을 특정 레스토랑에 데리고 가자는 제안에, 거기는 사람이 많으니 다른 곳으로 가자는 뉘앙스의 (A)가 정답이다. (B) clients–business meeting의 연상 어휘 함정, (C)는 restaurant을 듣고 연상 가능한 today's special로 혼동을 주고 있다.

어휘 crowded 붐비는 today's special 오늘의 추천 요리

20. Let's move the paper closer to the copy machine.

(A) I haven't used it for a long time.

(B) The fax machine is out of order.

(C) I'll take care of that.

용지를 복사기와 더 가까운 곳으로 옮깁시다.
(A) 오랫동안 그것을 사용하지 않았어요.
(B) 팩스기가 고장이에요.
(C) 제가 할게요.

해설 용지를 복사기 근처로 옮기자는 제안에, 자신이 하겠다는 (C)가 응답으로 자연스럽다. (A)는 질문과 관련 없는 내용의 오답, (B)는 machine을 반복한 오답 함정이다.

어휘 copy machine 복사기 out of order 고장 난 take care of 돌보다, 처리하다

21. Could you fix my laptop?

  (A) I'd be delighted to.

  (B) I can't remember the name.

  (C) Fax me by this Friday.

제 노트북 좀 고쳐 주시겠어요?
(A) 기꺼이 해드리죠.
(B) 이름이 기억나지 않아요.
(C) 이번 주 금요일까지 팩스로 보내 주세요.

해설 컴퓨터를 고쳐 줄 수 있냐는 요청문으로, 승낙의 표현으로 답한 (A)가 정답이다. (B) 질문과 관련 없는 내용, (C) fix–fax의 유사 발음 함정이다.

어휘 fix 고치다 | delighted 매우 기뻐하는

22. How about stopping by my office before you leave the office?

  (A) Sure, I'd be happy to.

  (B) My office is on the second floor.

  (C) Look at the map.

퇴근 전에 제 사무실에 잠깐 들를래요?
(A) 그럼요, 그렇게 할게요.
(B) 제 사무실은 2층에 있어요.
(C) 지도를 보세요.

해설 How about ~?는 상대방의 의향을 묻는 표현으로, 사무실에 들를 수 있냐는 말에 그러겠다고 수락하는 (A)가 정답이다. (B) office를 반복한 오답 함정, (C) 길을 물었을 때 가능한 응답이다.

어휘 stop by 잠시 들르다 | leave the office 퇴근하다

23. Would you like me to review the annual report before you send it?

  (A) Of course, I have an interview in 2 weeks.

  (B) Mandy already looked over it.

  (C) She's a good reporter.

연례 보고서를 보내시기 전에 제가 검토할까요?
(A) 물론이죠, 2주뒤에 면접이 있어요.
(B) Mandy가 이미 검토했어요.
(C) 그녀는 좋은 기자예요.

해설 Would you like me to ~? 제안할 때 쓸 수 있는 표현으로, Mandy가 이미 했다며 제안을 거절하는 (B)가 정답이다. (A) review–interview 유사 발음을 이용한 오답 함정, (C) She가 지칭할 만한 대상이 언급되지 않았다.

어휘 review = look over 검토하다 | annual 연례의 | reporter 기자

24. Could you send the next year's sales projections?

  (A) Yoko emailed it to you this morning.

  (B) Yes, it's on sale.

  (C) I bought the projector.

내년 예상 매출을 보내주실 수 있어요?
(A) Yoko가 오늘 아침에 당신한테 이메일로 보냈어요.
(B) 네, 그것은 할인 중입니다.
(C) 영사기를 샀어요.

해설 Could you ~?를 이용한 요청문으로, Yoko가 이미 보냈다고 한 (A)가 정답이다. (B) sale을 반복한 오답 함정, (C) projection–projector의 유사 발음 함정이다.

어휘 projections 예상, 예측 | on sale 할인 중인 | projector 영사기

25. Would you mind fixing the copier this afternoon?

  (A) Why not? I can make the coffee.

  (B) He repaired the fax machine.

  (C) No, I don't mind.

오늘 오후에 복사기 좀 고쳐 주실래요?
(A) 물론이죠, 제가 커피를 만들 수 있어요.
(B) 그가 팩스기를 고쳤어요.
(C) 그럼요.

해설 Would you mind ~?를 이용한 요청문으로, 그렇게 하겠다고 수락하는 (C)가 정답이다. (A) copier–coffee 유사 발음 함정, (B) He를 지칭할 만한 대상이 언급된 바 없다.

어휘 fix 고치다 | copier 복사기 | repair 수리하다

DAY 7 선택 의문문/평서문

SPARTA Check-UP
p.56

1. (A) 2. (A) 3. (C) 4. (B) 5. (C)

1. Should we invite everyone to the presentation or just the clients?
   (A) The room is big enough.
   (B) They are waiting in the lobby.
   (C) The revised agenda topics.

   모든 사람들을 프레젠테이션에 초대해야 하나요, 아니면 고객들만 초대하나요?
   (A) 그 방은 충분히 커요.
   (B) 그들이 로비에서 기다리고 있어요.
   (C) 수정된 안건 의제요.

   해설 모든 사람을 초대할지 아니면 고객만 초대할지 묻는 선택 의문문으로, 방이 충분히 크다 즉, 모든 사람을 초대해도 된다는 뜻의 (A)가 정답이다. (B) 질문과 관련 없는 내용의 오답, (C) presentation의 연상 어휘 agenda topics로 혼동을 주고 있다.

   어휘 invite 초대하다   revised 수정된   agenda 안건

2. Have we been selling more raspberry pie or apple pie?
   (A) About the same of both.
   (B) I'll have some dessert.
   (C) With milk.

   라즈베리 파이가 더 팔리나요, 아니면 애플 파이가 더 팔리나요?
   (A) 둘 다 거의 비슷해요.
   (B) 디저트를 좀 먹을게요.
   (C) 우유랑요.

   해설 어떤 파이를 더 많이 팔리는지 묻는 선택 의문문에, 둘 다 잘 팔린다는 뜻의 (A)가 정답이다. (B), (C)는 질문의 pie를 듣고 연상 가능한 어휘(dessert-milk)를 이용해 혼동을 주고 있다.

   어휘 dessert 후식

3. The office feels cold today.
   (A) I have a bad cold.
   (B) Turn on the air conditioner.
   (C) I have a jacket you could borrow.

   사무실이 오늘 추운 것 같아요.
   (A) 저는 독감에 걸렸어요.
   (B) 에어컨을 켜요.
   (C) 재킷을 빌려줄게요.

   해설 사무실이 춥다는 의견을 전하는 평서문으로, 재킷을 빌려주겠다는 (C)가 응답으로 어울린다. (A) 질문의 cold를 반복한 오답 함정, (B) 춥다는 말에 에어컨을 켜라는 응답은 어색하다.

   어휘 cold 추운; 감기   turn on 켜다   borrow 빌리다

4. Would you like to sit indoors or outdoors?
   (A) It's a very comfortable chair.
   (B) Isn't it too windy outside?
   (C) Table for three, please.

   실내에 앉을래요, 아니면 밖에 앉을래요?
   (A) 의자가 정말 편하네요.
   (B) 밖에 바람이 너무 불지 않나요?
   (C) 3명 테이블로 주세요.

   해설 실내와 실외 중 어디 앉을 건지를 묻는 선택 의문문으로, 밖에 바람이 많이 불지 않냐며 안에 앉자는 뉘앙스로 답한 (B)가 정답이다. (A)는 sit-chair의 연상 어휘 함정, (C) 질문과 관련 없는 응답이다.

   어휘 indoors 실내에서   outdoors 실외에서   comfortable 편안한   windy 바람이 부는

5. I was very impressed with Mr. Martin's address yesterday.
   (A) Please give the address to him.
   (B) Here's his business card.
   (C) I think he was really well prepared.

   어제 Martin 씨의 연설은 매우 인상적이었어요.
   (A) 그에게 선물을 주세요.
   (B) 여기 그의 명함입니다.
   (C) 그가 정말 준비를 잘한 것 같아요.

   해설 연설이 매우 인상적이었다는 의견을 전하는 평서문으로, 잘 준비한 것 같다며 상대방의 말에 동의하는 (C)가 정답이다. (A)는 질문의 address를 반복한 오답 함정으로 전혀 다른 의미로 쓰였으며, (B)는 관련 없는 내용이다.

   어휘 impressed 감명 받은   address 연설, 주소   business card 명함   well prepared 잘 준비된

SPARTA Practice Test
p.57

1. (C) 2. (A) 3. (C) 4. (C) 5. (B)
6. (B) 7. (B) 8. (A) 9. (B) 10. (C)
11. (B) 12. (C) 13. (B) 14. (C) 15. (C)
16. (B) 17. (A) 18. (B) 19. (B) 20. (C)
21. (B) 22. (B) 23. (B) 24. (A) 25. (B)

1. I really need the revised annual sales report.
   (A) 20 percent off every department.
   (B) It wasn't reasonable.
   (C) I'll forward it soon.

수정된 연례 매출 보고서가 꼭 필요해요.
(A) 모든 코너에서 20퍼센트 할인이요.
(B) 합리적이지 않아요.
(C) 곧 보내 줄게요.

해설 보고서가 필요하다는 평서문으로, 곧 보내주겠다는 (C)가 응답으로 자연스럽다. (A)와 (B)는 sales report의 연상 어휘(20 percent–reasonable) 함정이다.

어휘 annual 연례의　department 부서, 코너　reasonable 합리적인　forward 보내다

2. Would you like the chicken or the beef?
   (A) What would you recommend?
   (B) It's delicious.
   (C) Yes, grilled, please.

   닭고기를 드릴까요, 아니면 소고기를 드릴까요?
   (A) 뭘 추천하시겠어요?
   (B) 그것은 맛있어요.
   (C) 네, 구워서 주세요.

   해설 메뉴를 고르라는 선택 의문문으로, A나 B 중 고르는 전형적인 답변이 아니라 어떤 걸 추천하겠냐고 되묻는 (A)가 정답이다. (B)는 It이 무엇을 지칭하는지 알 수 없고, 연상 어휘(delicious)로 혼동을 주고 있다. (C)는 선택 의문문에 Yes로 답해 어색하다.

   어휘 recommend 추천하다　delicious 맛있는　grilled 구운

3. Would you like the two o'clock or the three o'clock appointment with Dr. Wong?
   (A) The nearby medical clinic.
   (B) Twice a week.
   (C) I'll check my schedule.

   Wong 박사와의 예약을 2시로 하실래요, 아니면 3시로 하실래요?
   (A) 가까운 병원이요.
   (B) 일주일에 두 번이요.
   (C) 제 일정을 확인할게요.

   해설 약속 시간을 고르라는 선택 의문문으로, 일정을 먼저 확인하겠다는 (C)가 정답이다. (A) 연상 어휘(medical clinic) 오답 함정, (B) 질문의 시간 표현을 듣고 혼동하도록 만든 오답 함정이다.

   어휘 appointment 예약　nearby 인근의　medical clinic 병원

4. The luncheon with the clients is Thursday.
   (A) Four steaks, please.
   (B) I'm not sure that he did.
   (C) That's not what I heard.

   고객과의 오찬은 목요일입니다.
   (A) 스테이크 네 접시 주세요.
   (B) 그가 했는지 확실하지 않아요.
   (C) 제가 들은 거랑 다른데요.

   해설 오찬이 목요일이라는 정보를 제공하는 평서문으로, 본인이 아는 바와 다르다는 뜻의 (C)가 정답이다. (A) luncheon–steaks로 혼동을 주고 있고, (B) he를 지칭할 만한 대상이 나오지 않았다.

   어휘 luncheon 오찬　client 고객

5. Shall we take a lunch break or keep working?
   (A) Let's move the desk later.
   (B) I'm not hungry yet.
   (C) It's a ten-minute walk from our office.

   점심 먹고 할까요, 아니면 계속 일할까요?
   (A) 책상을 나중에 옮깁시다.
   (B) 아직 안 배고파요.
   (C) 사무실에서 걸어서 10분 거리예요.

   해설 점심을 먹고 일할 건지 계속 일할 건지를 묻는 선택 의문문으로, 지금은 배가 안 고프니 계속 일하자는 의미로 말한 (B)가 정답이다. (A) 질문과 관련 없는 내용, (C) work–walk 유사 발음 함정이다.

   어휘 keep 계속하다

6. I'm going to take off my sweater.
   (A) The evening weather report.
   (B) I could turn down the heater.
   (C) They haven't decided yet.

   스웨터를 벗을래요.
   (A) 저녁 일기예보요.
   (B) 히터를 줄일게요.
   (C) 그들은 아직 결정하지 않았어요.

   해설 스웨터를 벗겠다는 말에, 히터를 줄여 온도를 낮추겠다는 (B)가 응답으로 어울린다. (A) 질문과 관련 없는 내용, (C) 결정하지 않아 모른다는 내용은 질문과 논리적으로 맞지 않는다.

   어휘 take off 벗다　weather report 일기예보　turn down (온도 등을) 낮추다　decide 결정하다

7. This e-mail from Mohammad is rather complex.
   (A) Yesterday afternoon.
   (B) I didn't understand it either.
   (C) Please send it by mail.

   모하메드로부터 온 메일이 꽤 복잡해요.
   (A) 어제 오후요.
   (B) 저도 이해 못했어요.
   (C) 그것을 우편으로 보내 주세요.

   해설 특정 메일이 복잡하다는 평서문으로, 본인도 이해하지 못했다며 동의하는 (B)가 정답이다. (A)는 질문과 관련 없는 내용, (C) email–mail 유사 발음 함정이다.

   어휘 rather 꽤, 다소　complex 복잡한　by mail 우편으로

8. Do you want to tell Marco about the funding cut, or should I?

   (A) Well, it certainly wasn't my idea.

   (B) Yes, he told everyone.

   (C) I want to cut my hair.

   자금 삭감에 대해 당신이 Marco에게 말할래요, 아니면 제가 할까요?
   (A) 음, 확실히 제 생각은 아니었어요.
   (B) 네, 그는 모든 사람에게 말했어요.
   (C) 머리를 자르고 싶어요.

   해설 자금 삭감에 대해 누가 말할 건지 묻는 선택 의문문으로, 본인의 생각이 아니었다 즉, 상대방에게 말하라는 뉘앙스의 (A)가 정답이다. (B) Yes 뒤에 이어지는 부연 설명이 내용상 어색하고, (C) 질문에 나온 cut을 반복한 오답 함정이다.

   어휘 funding cut 자금 삭감 certainly 분명히

9. I just received the monthly sales figures.

   (A) I prefer the department store on Peterson Street.

   (B) The numbers were quite surprising.

   (C) The manager is away on business.

   월별 판매 수치를 방금 받았어요.
   (A) Peterson 가에 있는 백화점이 더 좋아요.
   (B) 수치가 꽤 놀라웠어요.
   (C) 부장님은 업무차 자리를 비웠어요.

   해설 월별 판매 수치를 방금 받았다는 평서문으로, 수치를 보고 놀랐다는 (B)가 응답으로 자연스럽다. (A) 질문과 관련 없는 내용, (C) 역시 전혀 관련 없는 내용이다.

   어휘 sales figures 매출액 prefer 선호하다 surprising 놀라운 on business 업무로

10. I don't think we should walk to the subway station.

    (A) I like that radio station, too.

    (B) It arrives every hour.

    (C) But it is within walking distance.

    지하철역까지 걸어가지 않는 게 좋겠어요.
    (A) 저도 그 라디오 방송국을 좋아해요.
    (B) 그것은 매시간마다 도착해요.
    (C) 하지만 걸어갈 수 있는 거리예요.

    해설 지하철역까지 걸어가지 않는 게 좋겠다는 의견에, 걸어갈 만한 거리라고 한 (C)가 응답으로 어울린다. (A) 질문에 나온 station을 반복한 오답 함정, (B) subway만 듣고 고를 수 있는 연상 함정이다.

    어휘 walking distance 도보 거리

11. Can I bring you the dessert menu or a bill?

    (A) 30 euros each.

    (B) Give me the receipt, please.

    (C) The cookies were great.

    디저트 메뉴를 가져올까요, 아니면 계산서를 드릴까요?
    (A) 각 30유로예요.
    (B) 영수증을 주세요.
    (C) 쿠키가 정말 맛있었어요.

    해설 디저트를 먹을 건지, 바로 계산할 건지를 묻는 선택 의문문으로, 영수증을 달라 즉, 바로 계산하겠다는 의미의 (B)가 정답이다. (A) bill을 듣고 연상 가능한 오답 함정, (C)는 dessert-cookies 연상 어휘 함정이다.

    어휘 bill 계산서 receipt 영수증

12. Ms. Rartez wants everyone to be at the meeting at ten.

    (A) She hasn't decided.

    (B) Nine participants.

    (C) I have an interview with a candidate then.

    Rartez 씨는 모든 사람들이 10시 회의에 참석하길 원해요.
    (A) 그녀는 결정하지 못했어요.
    (B) 9명의 참석자들이요.
    (C) 저는 그때 지원자와 면접이 있어요.

    해설 Rartez 씨가 10시 회의에 모두 참석하길 원한다는 뜻의 평서문으로, 그 시간에 다른 일정이 있어서 참석이 어렵다는 의미의 (C)가 응답으로 자연스럽다. (A) 질문과 관련 없는 내용, (B) meeting-participants 연상 어휘 함정이다.

    어휘 participant 참석자 candidate 지원자

13. Could you please schedule our team meeting for Thursday or Friday morning?

    (A) No, I don't have any plans.

    (B) When is everyone available?

    (C) It usually lasts about an hour.

    팀 회의를 목요일로 잡아주시겠어요, 아니면 금요일 아침으로 잡아주시겠어요?
    (A) 아니요. 저는 계획이 없어요.
    (B) 다들 언제 가능한가요?
    (C) 보통 약 한 시간 정도 지속돼요.

    해설 회의를 언제로 잡는 게 좋을지 묻는 선택 의문문으로, 모든 사람들이 가능한 시간대가 언제인지 되묻는 (B)가 정답이다. (A) 선택 의문문에 No로 답해 어색하고, (C) meeting을 이용한 연상 함정이다.

    어휘 schedule 일정을 잡다 usually 보통 last 지속되다

14. We should plan the event for the 20th anniversary celebration.
(A) More than 50 people.
(B) Congratulations.
(C) Let's choose the venue first.

20주년 창립 기념일을 위한 행사를 계획해야 해요.
(A) 50명 이상이요.
(B) 축하해요.
(C) 장소부터 먼저 고릅시다.

해설 회사 기념일 행사를 계획해야 한다는 평서문으로, 우선 장소부터 고르자는 (C)가 정답이다. (A)와 (B)는 질문의 event/celebration를 듣고 고르도록 한 연상 함정이다.

어휘 anniversary 기념일 celebration 기념 행사 venue 장소

15. Would you like to come this afternoon or in the evening?
(A) It's necessary.
(B) For a week.
(C) Sorry, I can't make it today.

오늘 오후에 오실 건가요, 아니면 저녁에 오실 건가요?
(A) 그것이 필요해요.
(B) 일주일 동안이요.
(C) 미안해요, 오늘은 못 가요.

해설 오늘 오후나 저녁 중 언제 올 수 있는지 묻는 선택 의문문에, 오늘은 못 간다는 (C)가 응답으로 어울린다. (A), (B)는 질문과 관련 없는 내용이다.

어휘 necessary 필요한 make it (모임 등에) 가다, 참석하다

16. Can you give me a hand counting the items, or are you too busy?
(A) I used to work as an accountant.
(B) I need some assistance.
(C) Sorry, I'm tied up now.

물품 세는 거 도와줄 수 있어요, 아니면 많이 바빠요?
(A) 회계사로 일했어요.
(B) 도움이 필요해요.
(C) 미안하지만, 지금 매우 바빠요.

해설 도와줄 수 있는지를 묻는 선택 의문문으로, 바쁘다 즉, 지금은 도와줄 수 없다는 (C)가 정답이다. (A)는 counting-accountant의 유사 발음 함정, (B) 도움이 필요한 주체가 뒤바뀐 오답 함정이다.

어휘 count 세다 accountant 회계사 assistance 도움 tied up 바쁜

17. I'd like to see Mr. Burner for my loan consultation.
(A) He is no longer at this bank.
(B) No, two o'clock is better.
(C) She can lend some money.

대출 상담을 위해 Burner 씨를 만나고 싶은데요.
(A) 그는 더 이상 이 은행에 있지 않아요.
(B) 아니요, 2시가 더 좋아요.
(C) 그녀는 약간의 돈을 빌려줄 수 있어요.

해설 대출 상담을 위해 Burner 씨를 만나고 싶다는 평서문으로, 그는 현재 이 은행에서 일하지 않는다는 (A)가 정답이다. (B) 질문과 관련 없는 내용, (C) loan-lend money를 이용한 연상 함정이다.

어휘 loan 대출 consultation 상담 lend 빌려주다

18. Should I bring my driver's license or my passport?
(A) No, we don't accept copies.
(B) Either one would be fine.
(C) It expired last month.

운전 면허증을 가져와야 하나요, 아니면 여권을 가져와야 하나요?
(A) 아니요, 저희는 복사본을 받지 않아요.
(B) 아무거나 괜찮습니다.
(C) 그것은 지난달에 만료됐어요.

해설 운전 면허증과 여권 중 무엇을 가져와야 하는지를 묻는 선택 의문문으로, 둘 다 괜찮다는 (B)가 정답이다. (A) 선택 의문문에 No로 답해 어색하고, (C)는 질문의 driver's license or my passport를 듣고 연상 가능한 오답 함정이다.

어휘 driver's license 운전 면허증 passport 여권 accept 받아들이다 expire 만료되다

19. Should we meet inside the gallery or in front of it?
(A) Yes, we've been busy.
(B) I like this exhibit.
(C) How about by the information desk?

갤러리 안에서 만날까요, 아니면 그 앞에서 만날까요?
(A) 네, 우리는 바빴어요.
(B) 저는 이 전시회가 맘에 들어요.
(C) 안내 데스크 옆은 어때요?

해설 갤러리 안과 그 앞 어디서 만날지를 묻는 선택 의문문으로, A나 B가 아닌 제3의 장소를 제안하는 (C)가 정답이다. (A)는 선택 의문문에 Yes로 답해 어색하고, (B)는 gallery-exhibit의 연상 어휘 함정이다.

어휘 exhibit 전시회 information desk 안내소

20. I saw the accident on my way to work.

　　(A) I'm sorry. Did you get hurt?

　　(B) I'm not late.

　　(C) Oh, how bad was it?

출근길에 사고를 봤어요.
(A) 유감이에요. 다쳤어요?
(B) 늦지 않았어요.
(C) 아, 얼마나 심각했어요?

해설 사고를 목격했다는 평서문으로, 사고가 얼마나 심각했는지를 반문하는 (C)가 응답으로 자연스럽다. (A), (B)는 질문의 accident를 듣고 연상 가능한 함정이다.

어휘 accident 사고　get hurt 다치다

21. There isn't enough capacity in Room B.

　　(A) He's capable of leading his team.

　　(B) We'll have to book another room then.

　　(C) I want a room with an ocean view.

B호는 인원을 수용하기에 충분하지 않아요.
(A) 그는 팀을 이끌 수 있어요.
(B) 그러면 다른 방을 예약해야겠네요.
(C) 바다 전망이 보이는 방으로 주세요.

해설 현재 B호는 정원을 수용할 수 없다는 문제점을 언급하는 평서문으로, 그럼 다른 방을 예약해야겠다며 해결책을 제시하는 (B)가 정답이다. (A) He를 지칭할 만한 대상은 나오지 않았고, (C) 질문의 room을 반복한 오답 함정이다.

어휘 capacity 수용력　capable 할 수 있는　lead 이끌다　ocean view 바다가 보이는 전망

22. Do we have enough tables for the party, or should we add some more?

　　(A) No, it's more than twenty people.

　　(B) I guess we don't need any more.

　　(C) I met only a few people.

파티용 테이블이 충분히 있나요, 아니면 추가해야 하나요?
(A) 아니오, 20명 이상이에요.
(B) 더 이상 필요하지 않을 것 같아요.
(C) 몇 명의 사람들만 만났어요.

해설 파티용 테이블이 충분한지, 추가로 더 필요한지를 묻는 선택의문문으로, 더 필요하지 않을 것 같다는 (B)가 정답이다. (A)는 선택 의문문에 No로 답해 어색하고, (C)는 party-people를 이용한 연상 함정이다.

어휘 enough 충분한　add 추가하다

23. The shoes I ordered online have finally arrived.

　　(A) Yes, it's in alphabetical order.

　　(B) What caused the delay?

　　(C) Right in front of your desk.

온라인으로 주문한 신발이 마침내 도착했어요.
(A) 네, 알파벳 순이에요.
(B) 배송이 지연된 원인이 뭐예요?
(C) 당신의 책상 바로 앞이요.

해설 주문한 상품이 마침내 도착했다고 말에, 배송이 지연된 이유를 묻는 (B)가 정답이다. (A)는 질문에 나온 order을 이용한 함정이고, (C)는 내용상 어색하다.

24. Is the annual report due on Tuesday or Wednesday?

　　(A) Actually, the deadline has been postponed until Friday.

　　(B) You should report it to your immediate supervisor.

　　(C) It's due to arrive at 10 A.M.

연례 보고서 마감이 화요일까지인가요, 아니면 수요일까지인가요?
(A) 사실, 마감일이 금요일까지로 연기됐어요.
(B) 직속 상사에게 그것을 보고해야 해요.
(C) 오전 10시에 도착할 예정이에요.

해설 보고서 마감이 화요일인지 수요일인지 묻는 선택 의문문으로, A도 B도 아닌 C 즉, 금요일까지 연기됐다는 뜻의 (A)가 정답이다. (B) 질문의 report를 반복한 오답 함정, (C) 시간 표현으로 혼동을 주고 있다.

어휘 postpone 연기하다　immediate 직속의　supervisor 상사

25. Diego has been promoted to director of the product development team.

　　(A) It was working properly.

　　(B) That's good to hear. He is very competent.

　　(C) Are we planning to launch a new product?

Diego가 제품 개발팀 팀장으로 승진했어요.
(A) 그건 잘 작동했어요.
(B) 좋은 소식이네요. 그는 정말 유능하죠.
(C) 새로운 상품을 출시할 계획인가요?

해설 동료의 승진 소식을 전하는 평서문으로, 좋은 소식이라며 동료를 칭찬하는 (B)가 정답이다. (A) product-working properly의 연상 어휘 함정, (C) 질문의 product를 그대로 반복해 혼동을 노린 오답이다.

어휘 promote 승진시키다　development 개발　properly 제대로　competent 실력 있는, 유능한　launch 출시하다

LC PART 3 | 대화문

DAY 8 주제/목적, 장소/직업

SPARTA Check-UP
p.63

1. (C) 2. (D) 3. (B) 4. (D) 5. (C)
6. (B)

[1-3]

> M: Ms. Larson, are you satisfied with the instrument arrangement on the stage? Is everything in the right place?
> W: Yes, it looks good. However, can you make sure there will be enough background lights? I want all the members of my band to be visible.
> M: No problem. Let me know when the rehearsal starts with your band so I can adjust the lighting to be certain.
> W: All right. We'll get together for lunch and then we're coming back to the stage to rehearse.
>
> M: Larson 씨, 무대 악기 배치에 만족하세요? 모든 것이 알맞은 장소에 있나요?
> W: 네, 좋아요. 하지만 배경에 빛이 충분한지 확인해 주실래요? 밴드의 모든 멤버들이 잘 보였으면 해서요.
> M: 그러죠. 밴드가 언제 리허설을 시작하는지 알려 주시면 확실히 전등을 조절할 수 있어요.
> W: 알았어요. 점심 먹고 나서 리허설을 위해 무대로 다시 돌아올게요.

어휘 be satisfied with ~에 만족하다 instrument 악기 arrangement 배열, 배치 background 배경 light 빛 visible 눈에 보이는 rehearsal 리허설 adjust 조절하다 lighting 조명 certain 확실한 get together 만나다

1. Who most likely is the man?
   (A) A dancer
   (B) A musician
   (C) A stage director
   (D) An audience member

   남자는 누구인 것 같은가?
   (A) 댄서
   (B) 음악가
   (C) 무대 감독
   (D) 관중

해설 직업은 주로 대화 초반에 단서가 나온다. 남자가 "are you satisfied with the instrument arrangement on the stage?"라며 무대 악기 배치가 마음에 드는지 여자에게 묻고 있으므로 남자는 (C) 무대 감독으로 볼 수 있다.

2. What does the woman ask about?
   (A) An instrument arrangement
   (B) A guest list
   (C) Some seating assignments
   (D) Some lights

   여자는 무엇에 관해 묻는가?
   (A) 악기 배치
   (B) 손님 명단
   (C) 좌석 배치
   (D) 전등

해설 여자가 묻고 있는 것을 물었으므로 여자의 대사를 집중해야 한다. 여자가 대화 중반에 "can you make sure there will be enough background lights?"라며 불빛이 충분한지 묻고 있으므로 정답은 (D)이다.

3. What will the woman do next?
   (A) Conclude a task
   (B) Have lunch
   (C) Adjust the lighting
   (D) Start the rehearsal

   여자는 다음에 무엇을 할 것인가?
   (A) 일을 끝낸다
   (B) 점심을 먹는다
   (C) 조명을 조절한다
   (D) 리허설을 시작한다

해설 다음으로 할 일은 대화 후반부에 단서가 나온다. 마지막에 여자가 "We'll get together for lunch and then we're coming back to the stage to rehearse."라면서 점심 먹고 리허설하러 오겠다고 했으므로 (B)가 정답이다.

[4~6]

> W: Hi, Mr. Collins. This is Lucy calling from Watson's Photography Studio. Unfortunately, we have to cancel your appointment with us this afternoon to have your picture taken. Our ceiling is leaking after heavy rain this morning. So, we're not open today, as we're working on fixing it. I'm really sorry.

M: Actually, I can't reschedule the appointment anytime soon because I'm really busy nowadays. It was hard to make this appointment. So, could you recommend other places that could take me today?

W: Give me a second. Yes, I know a studio that doesn't require you to make an appointment at all: MD Studio nearby. If you go there now, you might have to wait a bit, but it shouldn't take too long.

W: 안녕하세요, Collins 씨. Watson 사진관의 Lucy입니다. 불행히도 오늘 오후에 사진을 찍기로 한 예약을 취소해야 해서요. 오늘 아침에 폭우로 저희 천장에 누수가 있네요. 그래서 오늘 수리해야 해서 문을 열지 않아요. 정말 죄송합니다.

M: 사실 제가 요즘 너무 바빠서 일정을 바로 조정할 수가 없어요. 이 예약도 잡기 힘들었거든요. 오늘 사진 찍을 수 있는 다른 곳을 추천해 주시겠어요?

W: 잠깐만요. 네, 근처에 MD 스튜디오라고 있는데, 예약을 안 하셔도 됩니다. 지금 가시면 조금 기다리실 순 있지만 오래 걸리지 않을 거예요.

어휘 unfortunately 불행히도   appointment 약속
reschedule 일정을 다시 잡다   nowadays 요즘
recommend 추천하다   nearby 인근에

4. Why is the woman calling the man?
(A) To remind him about an appointment
(B) To tell him about an exclusive deal
(C) To inform him that some photographs are ready
(D) To notify him about a cancellation

여자는 남자에게 왜 전화하는가?
(A) 약속에 대해 상기시키기 위해
(B) 독점 계약에 대해 말하기 위해
(C) 사진이 준비된 것을 알리기 위해
(D) 취소에 대해 알리기 위해

해설 여자가 전화한 목적을 묻는 문제로, 여자의 첫 대사를 집중해서 들어야 한다. 여자가 "Unfortunately, we have to cancel your appointment ~."라면서 예약을 취소해야 한다고 했으므로 정답은 (D)이다. (A)는 함정으로, 키워드인 appointment가 들린다고 선택하면 안 된다.

5. What problem does the man mention?
(A) His photos are not ready.
(B) He plans to return later.
(C) He has difficulty arranging a schedule.
(D) He will be a little late.

남자는 무슨 문제를 언급하는가?
(A) 사진들이 준비되지 않았다.
(B) 나중에 돌아올 예정이다.
(C) 일정을 잡는 것이 어렵다.
(D) 조금 늦을 것이다.

해설 남자가 언급한 문제점을 묻는 문제로, 남자 대사에 집중하자. "I can't reschedule the appointment anytime soon because I'm really busy nowadays."라면서 바빠서 다시 예약 잡는 것이 어렵다고 했으므로 정답은 (C)이다.

6. What does the woman say about MD Studio?
(A) It is far from the man's workplace.
(B) It does not require any reservations.
(C) It has a good location.
(D) It has longer hours.

MD 스튜디오에 대해 여자는 뭐라고 말하는가?
(A) 남자의 직장에서 멀다.
(B) 어떤 예약도 필요하지 않다.
(C) 좋은 위치에 있다.
(D) 더 오랫동안 영업한다.

해설 여자가 MD 스튜디오에 대해 언급한 것을 묻고 있으므로 여자 대사에 집중하자. 후반부에 여자가 "I know a studio that doesn't require you to make an appointment at all: MD Studio nearby." MD 스튜디오는 예약할 필요가 없다고 했으므로 (B)가 정답이다.

SPARTA Practice Test   p.64

1. (B)	2. (D)	3. (C)	4. (B)	5. (A)
6. (A)	7. (D)	8. (B)	9. (A)	10. (C)
11. (B)	12. (A)	13. (A)	14. (A)	15. (B)
16. (A)	17. (C)	18. (A)	19. (B)	20. (D)
21. (C)	22. (A)	23. (B)	24. (D)	

Questions 1-3 refer to the following conversation.

W: Hi, George. It's Mariko from Sanwa Industries. I'm calling to let you know that I got a good impression of you at the interview last week. So, I'd like to offer you the position of field service engineer.

M: Thanks for calling. I'm very happy with the offer. However, to be honest, I'm considering all the travelling I'd have to do. I didn't realize I'd have to go on an overseas business trip at least once a month.

W: Yes, working in another country is mandatory in your field. If it helps, I'd be willing to discuss a different pay scale than what was initially offered. Perhaps that would make the job more attractive?

W: 안녕하세요, George 씨. 산와 산업의 Mariko입니다. 지난주 면접에서 당신에게 좋은 인상을 받았음을 알리고자 연락 드립니다. 그래서 현장 서비스 엔지니어 자리를 제안 드리고 싶은데요.
M: 전화 주셔서 감사합니다. 제안해 주셔서 매우 기쁩니다. 하지만 솔직히, 출장을 가야 하는 것에 대해 고려 중이에요. 적어도 한 달에 한 번 해외 출장을 가야 하는지 몰랐거든요.
W: 네, 당신의 분야는 다른 나라에서 일하는 것이 의무입니다. 선택에 도움이 된다면 제가 처음 제시한 급여와는 다른 급여 체계에 대해 논의할 의향이 있습니다. 그러면 더 끌리시겠죠?

어휘 impression 인상   overseas 해외의   mandatory 의무적인   pay scale 급여 체계   initially 처음에   attractive 마음을 끄는

1. Why is the woman calling?
   (A) To request a service
   (B) To offer a job
   (C) To reschedule an interview
   (D) To change a position

   여자는 왜 전화하는가?
   (A) 서비스를 요청하기 위해
   (B) 일자리를 제안하기 위해
   (C) 면접 일정을 다시 잡기 위해
   (D) 위치를 바꾸기 위해

   해설 여자가 전화한 이유는 여자의 대사에서 단서가 나온다. 여자의 첫 대사에서 "I'd like to offer you the position ~." 일자리 제안이 목적임을 알 수 있으므로 정답은 (B)이다.

2. What is the man concerned about?
   (A) He is interested in a job at another company.
   (B) He would have to relocate to an overseas country.
   (C) He is concerned that he is not qualified.
   (D) He would have to take many trips.

   남자는 무엇에 대해 염려하는가?
   (A) 그는 다른 회사의 일자리에 관심이 있다.
   (B) 그는 해외로 이전해야 할 것이다.
   (C) 그는 스스로 자격을 갖추지 못했다고 걱정한다.
   (D) 그는 출장을 많이 가야 할 것이다.

   해설 남자의 대사에서 "I'm considering all the travelling I'd have to do."에서 출장에 대해 고려 중이라고 했으므로 정답은 이와 의미가 통하는 (D)이다.

3. What part of the job is the woman willing to negotiate?
   (A) The amount of paid time off
   (B) The location
   (C) The salary
   (D) The job title

   여자는 직업의 어떤 부분에 대해 협상할 의지가 있는가?
   (A) 유급 휴가 수
   (B) 장소
   (C) 급여
   (D) 직책

   해설 남자가 그 일자리에 대해 고려 중이라고 하자, 여자가 후반에 "I'd be willing to discuss a different pay scale"라며 다른 급여 체계에 대해 논의하자고 했으므로 정답은 (C)이다.

Questions 4-6 refer to the following conversation.

M: Hello, Ms. Min. Thank you for reviewing the sales report I worked on. This is my first time preparing it. So, I wanted to make sure that it is correct.
W: No problem. It was organized clearly overall. The only issue is that you need to add more details about why the sales decreased last month, so we can come up with ways to increase sales at the next meeting.
M: Okay. I'll do that this afternoon. It would be helpful to analyze the sales figures from last month. Do you have any feedback other than this?
W: No. If you need more information, you should talk to Noriko. She's worked on the sales report before.

M: 안녕하세요, Min 씨. 제가 작성한 판매 보고서를 검토해 주셔서 감사해요. 이번이 제가 처음으로 준비한 거예요. 그래서 그것이 정확한지 확실히 하고 싶었어요.
W: 괜찮아요. 전반적으로 잘 정리되어 있었어요. 단지 문제는 저희가 다음 회의에서 매출을 올릴 방법을 생각해낼 수 있도록 왜 지난달에 매출이 감소했는지 더 세부 사항들을 추가해야 한다는 거예요.
M: 좋아요. 오늘 오후에 할게요. 지난달 판매 수치를 분석하는 것이 도움이 될 것 같네요. 이것을 제외하고 다른 피드백 있어요?
W: 아니요, 더 많은 정보가 필요하면 Noriko와 얘기하세요. 그녀가 전에 판매 보고서 관련 작업을 했어요.

어휘 correct 정확한   organize 준비하다   clearly 분명히   overall 전반적으로   come up with 생각해내다   analyze 분석하다   sales figures 판매 수치

4. What is the main topic of the conversation?

   (A) A new manager

   (B) A sales document

   (C) An office atmosphere

   (D) A project deadline

   대화의 주제는 무엇인가?
   (A) 새로운 매니저
   (B) 판매 관련 서류
   (C) 사무실 분위기
   (D) 프로젝트 마감일

   해설 대화 초반의 남자 대사에서 "Thank you for reviewing the sales report I worked on."을 보면 판매 보고서에 대해 언급하고 있고 이어지는 내용 또한 동일한 맥락이므로 정답은 (B)이다.

5. What does the man request?

   (A) Some opinions

   (B) Sales tax

   (C) Customers' feedback

   (D) A sample document

   남자가 요청하는 것이 무엇인가?
   (A) 의견
   (B) 판매세
   (C) 고객들의 후기
   (D) 견본 서류

   해설 초반부의 남자 대사 "I wanted to make sure that it is correct."에서 보고서가 정확한지 알고 싶다고 했고, 중반에 "Do you have any feedback other than this?" 또 다른 의견이 있는지 묻고 있으므로 정답은 (A)이다. 고객들의 피드백을 원하는 것은 아니므로 (C)는 오답이다.

6. What does the woman suggest the man do?

   (A) Speak with a coworker

   (B) Organize some files

   (C) Record the information

   (D) Send a memo

   여자는 남자에게 무엇을 하라고 제안하는가?
   (A) 동료와 얘기하기
   (B) 파일 정리하기
   (C) 정보 기록하기
   (D) 메모 보내기

   해설 대화 후반에 여자가, 더 많은 정보를 원하면 "you should talk to Noriko. She's worked on the sales report before."라며 다른 동료와 얘기해 보라고 했으므로 정답은 (A)이다.

Questions 7-9 refer to the following conversation.

> W: Hi, I'm Janice Kang. I'm calling about my mobile phone bill. It was much higher than usual.
> M: Okay, what is your account number?
> W: My number is 346700.
> M: Let me see… You used a lot of international data in Japan. Did you travel there?
> W: Yes, last month. But I only used my phone to take photos.
> M: Unfortunately, you're automatically charged when you use any data overseas. Before you went abroad, you should have read the policy carefully. That's why we sent you a notification instructing you to turn off the data-receiving feature on your phone when traveling.
> W: Oh, I didn't see that. Is there something you can do to reduce these fees? I've been a loyal customer for many years.
>
> W: 안녕하세요, 저는 Janice Kang입니다. 휴대폰 요금 청구서에 관해 연락했는데요. 요금이 평소보다 더 많이 나왔어요.
> M: 네, 계정 번호가 어떻게 되죠?
> W: 제 번호는 346700입니다.
> M: 한번 볼게요… 일본에서 국제 데이터를 많이 이용하셨네요. 거기에 가신 적 있으세요?
> W: 네, 지난달에요. 하지만 폰으로 사진만 찍었어요.
> M: 유감스럽게도 해외에서 데이터를 사용하셨을 때 자동으로 요금이 부과됩니다. 해외에 가기 전에 규정을 잘 읽어 보셔야 합니다. 그래서 여행 시 핸드폰 데이터 수신 기능을 끄도록 알림을 보내드립니다.
> W: 아, 제가 그것을 안 봤네요. 요금을 줄일 수 있는 방법이 있나요? 오랫동안 이용했어요.

어휘 than usual 평소보다   account 계정   international 국제적인, 국제의   automatically 자동적으로   overseas/abroad 해외에   notification 통보   instruct 알리다   feature 기능   reduce 줄이다   loyal customer 단골 고객

7. Why is the woman calling?

   (A) To order a mobile phone

   (B) To confirm a registration

   (C) To close an account

   (D) To complain about a bill

   여자는 왜 전화하고 있는가?
   (A) 휴대폰을 주문하기 위해
   (B) 등록을 확인하기 위해
   (C) 거래를 끊기 위해
   (D) 청구서에 대해 항의하기 위해

해설 전화한 목적은 지문 초반에 언급된다. 여자의 첫 대사 중 "I'm calling about my mobile phone bill. It was much higher than usual."에서 휴대폰 요금이 전보다 많이 나왔다고 했으므로 정답은 (D)이다.

8. What did the woman do last month?
   (A) She went on a business trip.
   (B) She traveled abroad.
   (C) She entered a photo contest.
   (D) She purchased a device.

   여자는 지난달에 무엇을 했는가?
   (A) 그녀는 출장을 갔다.
   (B) 그녀는 해외로 여행을 갔다.
   (C) 그녀는 사진 콘테스트에 참가했다.
   (D) 그녀는 기기를 샀다.

해설 대화 중반에 남자가 여자에게 "You used a lot of international data in Japan. Did you travel there?"라며 일본에 갔는지 물었고 이에 여자가 지난달에 갔다고 했으므로 정답은 (B)이다.

9. According to the man, what was the woman asked to do?
   (A) Switch off a device feature
   (B) Take many pictures
   (C) Rewrite a policy
   (D) Sign some documents

   남자에 따르면, 여자는 무엇을 하도록 요청 받았는가?
   (A) 기기 기능 끄기
   (B) 사진 많이 찍기
   (C) 규정 다시 쓰기
   (D) 서류에 사인하기

해설 남자가 여자에게 "That's why we sent you a notification instructing you to turn off the data-receiving feature on your phone when traveling."라며 여행할 때 휴대폰 데이터 수신 기능을 꺼야 함을 알리는 통보를 했다고 했으므로 정답은 (A)이다.

Questions 10-12 refer to the following conversation.

M: Mr. Lee just called. He wants to increase the number of T-shirts in the order for his employees.
W: That's good to hear. When do we have to complete the order? Has the deadline changed also?
M: No. Actually, there's no way we can make them on time that quickly.
W: So, why don't we add temporary employees to help with this extra work?
M: That's a good idea. Can you put up the job opening on the recruiting Web site?

M: Lee 씨가 방금 그의 직원들을 위한 티셔츠 주문량을 늘리고 싶다고 연락했어요.
W: 좋네요. 언제 주문 건을 끝내야 하나요? 마감일도 바뀌었죠?
M: 아니요. 사실 그렇게 빨리 제시간에 만들 수 있는 방법이 없어요.
W: 그럼, 이 추가 작업을 도와줄 임시직원을 충원하는 게 어때요?
M: 좋은 생각이네요. 채용 사이트에 구인 공고를 올려 주시겠어요?

어휘 increase 증가하다 complete the order 주문을 완성하다 deadline 마감일 temporary 임시의 job opening 일자리

10. Where do the speakers most likely work?
    (A) At a local hotel
    (B) At a recruiting agency
    (C) At a clothing manufacturer
    (D) At a laundry service

    화자들은 어디에서 일할 것 같은가?
    (A) 지역 호텔에서
    (B) 직업 소개소에서
    (C) 의류 제조업체에서
    (D) 세탁소에서

해설 화자들이 일하는 장소는 대화 초반에 주로 언급된다. 남자의 첫 대사 중 "Mr. Lee just called. He wants to increase the number of T-shirts in the order for his employees."에서 고객이 티셔츠 주문량을 늘리고 싶어 한다는 내용이 나온다. 이어지는 내용도 티셔츠 주문 처리에 대한 것이므로 화자들이 일하는 곳은 의류 제조업체임을 알 수 있다.

11. What problem does the man mention?
    (A) A machine is malfunctioning.
    (B) A completion date is not realistic.
    (C) An item is poorly made.
    (D) A supplier went out of business.

    남자는 무슨 문제점을 언급하는가?
    (A) 기계가 작동되지 않는다.
    (B) 완료 일정이 현실적이지 않다.
    (C) 제품이 형편없이 만들어졌다.
    (D) 공급업체가 폐업했다.

해설 남자가 언급한 문제가 무엇인지 묻고 있으므로 남자의 대사에 집중하자. 대화 중반에서 남자가 "there's no way we can make them on time that quickly."라며 제시간에 주문을 완성할 방법이 없다고 말하고 있다. 즉, (B) 마감일을 현실적으로 맞추기 힘들다는 (B)가 정답이다.

12. How will the speakers address the problem?

(A) By hiring more staff
(B) By working extra hours
(C) By updating the Web site
(D) By negotiating with a business

화자들은 어떻게 문제를 처리할 것인가?
(A) 직원들을 더 고용함으로써
(B) 초과 근무를 함으로써
(C) 웹사이트를 업데이트함으로써
(D) 업체와 협상함으로써

해설 대화 마지막에 여자가 "why don't we add temporary employees to help with this extra work?"라며 임시직원들을 고용하자고 했고 남자가 이어서 "Can you put up the job opening on the recruiting Web site?"라며 채용 사이트에 공고를 올려 달라고 했으므로 직원을 더 채용할 것임을 알 수 있다. 따라서 (A)가 정답이다.

Questions 13-15 refer to the following conversation.

> **M:** Hello, this is Robert from Glenside paint shop and I'm calling to confirm the visit date to deliver your items. Will you be at your home this Friday morning? Is that a good time for you?
> **W:** Sorry, no. I have a dental appointment that morning. Could I reschedule for Saturday instead?
> **M:** Let me see… Okay, I can do that day at 9:30 in the morning. Does that work for you?
> **W:** Yes, thanks. And I suggest that you park on Cremond Avenue, which is right behind my house. You cannot park in front of my house because the street is too narrow for a delivery truck.
>
> M: 안녕하세요. Glenside 페인트 가게의 Robert입니다. 귀하의 집에 물건을 배달하기 위한 방문 일정을 확인하려고 연락 드립니다. 이번 주 금요일 오전에 집에 계시나요? 시간 괜찮으실까요?
> W: 죄송하지만, 안 돼요. 그날 오전에 치과 예약이 있어서요. 토요일로 대신 일정을 잡아도 될까요?
> M: 한번 볼게요… 좋아요. 저는 그날 아침 9시 30분에 가능해요. 그 시간에 괜찮으신가요?
> W: 네, 감사합니다. 그리고 저희 집 바로 뒤에 있는 Cremond 가에 차를 주차해 주세요. 배달 트럭이 주차하기에는 길이 너무 좁아서 저희 집 앞에는 차를 댈 수 없어요.

어휘 confirm 확인하다   dental appointment 치과 검진
instead 대신에   narrow 좁은

13. Where does the man most likely work?

(A) At a paint store
(B) At a moving company
(C) At a dental clinic
(D) At a construction company

남자는 어디에서 일하는 것 같은가?
(A) 페인트 가게에서
(B) 이삿짐 센터에서
(C) 치과에서
(D) 건설 회사에서

해설 직업/신분은 대화 초반에 단서가 제시된다. 남자가 첫 대사에서 "this is Robert from Glenside paint shop ~"라며 페인트 가게라고 소개하고 있으므로 정답은 (A)이다.

14. Why is the woman unavailable on Friday?

(A) She will go to a medical office.
(B) She will paint her house.
(C) She will have a lot of work.
(D) She will have an appointment with her friend.

왜 여자는 금요일에 시간이 안 되는가?
(A) 그녀는 병원에 갈 것이다.
(B) 그녀는 집을 페인트칠할 것이다.
(C) 그녀는 일을 많이 할 것이다.
(D) 그녀는 친구와 약속이 있을 것이다.

해설 남자가 금요일에 방문해도 되는지 묻자 여자가 "I have a dental appointment that morning."이라며 오전에 치과에 가야 한다고 했으므로 정답은 (A)이다.

15. What does the woman recommend for the man?

(A) What to bring
(B) Where to park
(C) When to deliver
(D) Where to paint

여자는 남자에게 무엇을 제안하는가?
(A) 무엇을 가져올지
(B) 어디에 주차할지
(C) 언제 배달할지
(D) 어디를 페인트칠할지

해설 대화 후반에 여자가 "I suggest that you park on Cremond Avenue, which is right behind my house."라며 자기 집 뒤에 주차하라고 알려 주고 있으므로 정답은 (B)이다.

Questions 16-18 refer to the following conversation.

W: Mr. Kim, I know you wanted my company to design a new advertising campaign for your hair salon. How do the customers like it so far?
M: Well… they like it but we're concerned about the location. Since we relocated to the downtown area, we've started to feel the effects of competition. Business hasn't been as good since then. I'd like to have something special in the commercial.
W: I understand. It would help if I got a better sense of what customers like about your company. That's something we can emphasize throughout the campaign.
M: Okay. Patrons say they can change their trendy hair styles at a reasonable price and get a consultation with experienced designers to meet their expectations in our shop. I'm sure no other salons in the area can offer that service.

W: Kim 씨, 저희 회사가 당신 미용실의 새로운 광고를 기획하길 원하셨다고 아는데요. 고객들은 지금까지 광고에 대해 어떻게 생각하나요?
M: 음, 좋아하지만 단지 위치가 걱정이에요. 저희가 시내로 이전한 후 경쟁의 영향을 느끼고 있어요. 그때 이후로 사업이 그만큼 잘 안 돼요. 광고에서 특별한 무언가를 하면 좋겠어요.
W: 이해해요. 당신 회사에 대해 고객들이 무엇을 좋아하는지 제가 이해한다면 도움이 될 거예요. 그게 광고를 통해 우리가 강조할 수 있는 거죠.
M: 좋아요. 고객들은 우리 숍에서 저렴한 가격에 최신 유행의 헤어스타일로 바꿀 수 있고 기대를 충족시켜 주는 경력 있는 디자이너들과 상담할 수 있어서 좋다고 해요. 이 지역에서 이런 서비스를 제공하는 다른 미용실은 없다고 확신해요.

어휘 advertising campaign 광고 캠페인　so far 지금까지　relocate 이전하다　downtown area 도심 지역　effect 영향　competition 경쟁(자)　commercial 광고　emphasize 강조하다　reasonable 합리적인　consultation 상담　experienced 경력 있는　expectation 기대

16. What type of business does the man work for?
(A) A beauty parlor
(B) A real estate agency
(C) An advertising agency
(D) An equipment rental service

남자는 어떤 종류의 업체를 위해 일하는가?
(A) 미용실
(B) 부동산
(C) 광고 회사
(D) 장비 임대 서비스

해설 여자의 첫 대사 "I know you wanted my company to design a new advertising campaign for your hair salon."에서 여자는 광고 회사, 남자는 미용실에서 일하고 있음을 알 수 있다. 따라서 정답은 (A)이다.

17. What is the man worried about?
(A) Customers' complaints
(B) An expensive location
(C) An increase in competition
(D) A shortage of funds

남자는 무엇에 대해 걱정하는가?
(A) 고객의 불만
(B) 비싼 위치 선정
(C) 경쟁의 확대
(D) 자금 부족

해설 남자의 첫 대사 "Since we relocated to the downtown area, we've started to feel the effects of the competition."에서 시내로 이전하고 나서 경쟁의 영향을 느낀다고 말하고 있으므로 경쟁이 심화되는 것에 대해 걱정하고 있음을 알 수 있다. 따라서 정답은 (C)이다.

18. What does the man emphasize about the company?
(A) The affordable prices
(B) The number of branch offices
(C) The user-friendly Web site
(D) The trendy fashion styles

남자는 회사에 대해 무엇을 강조하는가?
(A) 합리적인 가격
(B) 지점의 개수
(C) 이용하기 편한 웹사이트
(D) 최신 유행의 패션 스타일

해설 대화 후반부에 남자가 "Patrons say they can change their trendy hair styles at a reasonable price ~."라며 고객들이 합리적인 가격으로 최신 유행 헤어스타일로 바꿀 수 있어서 좋아한다고 말하고 있으므로 정답은 (A)이다. (D)는 일부 단어가 언급된 오답 함정이다.

Questions 19-21 refer to the following conversation.

> W: Excuse me. I just heard an announcement saying that flight 102 to New York has been delayed for two hours. But, I didn't get any message from you in advance. I think you should have told me the status of the flight ahead of time.
> M: I'm so sorry, ma'am. Unfortunately, our company has been experiencing some technical problems with mobile updates for our passengers. So, we couldn't send you a text. Would you like me to see if there's an earlier flight?
> W: Yes, I have a very important meeting with our investors in New York at four, so I have to go in a hurry.

> W: 실례합니다. 뉴욕행 비행기 102편이 2시간 지연됐다는 안내 방송을 들었어요. 그런데 저는 사전에 어떠한 메시지도 받지 못했어요. 사전에 항공편의 상태를 저에게 말씀해 주셨어야 하는 것 같은데요.
> M: 정말 죄송합니다. 유감스럽게도 저희는 승객들의 휴대폰 업데이트를 하는 데 기술적 문제를 겪고 있어요. 그래서 귀하께 문자를 보낼 수 없었습니다. 더 일찍 출발하는 항공편이 있는지 알아볼까요?
> W: 네, 제가 4시에 뉴욕에서 투자자들과 매우 중요한 회의가 있어서 서둘러서 가야 합니다.

어휘 delay 지연시키다　status 상태　in advance/ahead of time 사전에　technical problem 기술적 문제　passenger 승객　investor 투자자　in a hurry 서둘러

19. Where are the speakers?
(A) On a flight
(B) In an airport
(C) In an office
(D) At a train station

화자들은 어디에 있는가?
(A) 기내에
(B) 공항에
(C) 사무실에
(D) 기차역에

해설 첫 대사에서 여자가 "I just heard an announcement saying that flight 102 to New York has been delayed for two hours."라며 비행편 지연 방송을 들었다고 하고 있으므로 화자가 있는 장소는 (B) 공항임을 알 수 있다.

20. What does the man offer to do?
(A) Cancel her flight
(B) Give her money back
(C) Upgrade her plane seat
(D) Check the possible flights

남자는 무엇을 해주겠다고 하는가?
(A) 비행편을 취소한다
(B) 돈을 돌려준다
(C) 비행기 좌석을 업그레이드한다
(D) 이용 가능한 비행기를 확인한다

해설 여자가 비행기 지연에 대한 불만을 말하자 남자가 "Would you like me to see if there's an earlier flight?"라며 더 이른 비행편이 있는지 확인해 주겠다고 했으므로 정답은 (D)이다.

21. Why should the woman go to New York in a hurry?
(A) To see her cousin
(B) To tour the city
(C) To meet some clients
(D) To attend an important workshop

왜 여자는 뉴욕으로 서둘러 가야 하는가?
(A) 사촌을 보기 위해
(B) 도시를 관광하기 위해
(C) 고객들을 만나기 위해
(D) 중요한 워크숍에 참석하기 위해

해설 대화 후반에 여자가 "I have a very important meeting with our investors in New York ~."라며 투자자들을 만나러 가야 한다고 하고 있으므로 정답은 (C)이다.

Questions 22-24 refer to the following conversation.

> W: Thank you for agreeing to meet me for this interview. The readers of Food World Magazine are eager to hear about your company's plans.
> M: We'll be opening some branches in Singapore soon. We already have a hundred chains nationwide. So we expect to expand our business abroad.
> W: All right. So do you have any plans to open a restaurant in the European market?
> M: Sure, we're planning on that for next year.

> W: 인터뷰를 위해 저를 만나는 데 동의해 주셔서 감사합니다. Food World Magazine 독자들은 귀사의 계획을 듣고 싶어 해요.
> M: 네, 저희는 싱가포르에 몇 개의 지점을 곧 열 겁니다. 이미 전국적으로 100개의 체인점을 가지고 있고요. 그래서 해외로 사업을 확장하는 것을 기대하고 있죠.
> W: 좋아요. 그러면 유럽 시장에 레스토랑을 열 계획이 있으신가요?
> M: 그럼요, 내년으로 계획하고 있습니다.

어휘 be eager to ~을 하고 싶어 하다   nationwide 전국적으로
expand 확장하다   abroad 해외로

22. Who most likely is the woman?

(A) A journalist
(B) A restaurant manager
(C) A potential applicant
(D) A chef

여자는 누구일 것 같은가?
(A) 기자
(B) 레스토랑 매니저
(C) 가능성 있는 지원자
(D) 요리사

해설 여자가 초반에 "Thank you for agreeing to meet me for this interview."라며 인터뷰에 응해 줘서 고맙다고 했으므로 여자의 직업은 (A) 기자임을 유추할 수 있다.

23. What is the main topic of the conversation?

(A) New restaurant menus
(B) The expansion of a business
(C) An increase in sales
(D) An article about food

대화의 주제는 무엇인가?
(A) 새로운 레스토랑 메뉴
(B) 사업 확장
(C) 매출 증가
(D) 음식에 관한 기사

해설 대화 초반에 남자가 "We'll be opening some branches in Singapore soon."라며 해외에서도 지점을 열 거라는 내용이 언급되었으므로 (B)가 정답이다.

24. According to the man, what will happen next year?

(A) New menus will be available.
(B) An advertising campaign will start.
(C) Many branches will be opened nationwide.
(D) Business will start in the European market.

남자에 따르면, 내년에 무슨 일이 일어날 것인가?
(A) 새로운 메뉴를 이용할 수 있을 것이다.
(B) 광고가 시작될 것이다.
(C) 전국적으로 많은 지점이 생길 것이다.
(D) 유럽 시장에서 사업이 시작될 것이다.

해설 여자의 마지막 대사에서 "So do you have any plans to open a restaurant in the European market?"라며 유럽 시장에 지점을 열 것인지를 묻고 있고 남자의 마지막 대사 Sure, we're planning on that for next year.를 통해 남자가 내년으로 계획하고 있다고 했으므로 정답은 (D)이다.

DAY 9 이유&세부 사항/문제점

SPARTA Check-UP   p.68

1. (C)   2. (B)   3. (C)   4. (D)   5. (C)
6. (D)

[1~3]

W: Diego, were you at the sales meeting yesterday? I couldn't make it because I was on the phone with an important client. Can you fill me in?
M: Okay, you got a copy of the meeting materials, right?
W: Yeah, but the part about how to get money back for travel expenses was really complicated. Do you know if there's more documents on that?
M: Oh, you can look at them electronically. You'll see… there's a link to our internal Web site where you can find more details on reimbursement procedures.

W: Diego, 어제 영업 회의에 있었어요? 저는 중요한 고객과 통화 중이라서 참석할 수 없었어요. 자세히 좀 알려주시겠어요?
M: 네, 회의 자료 사본을 가지고 있죠, 그렇죠?
W: 네, 하지만 출장 경비를 상환 받는 법이 너무 복잡했어요. 혹시 거기에 관한 자료가 더 있나요?
M: 아, 컴퓨터로 볼 수 있어요. 우리 상환 절차에 대한 더 많은 정보가 있는 내부 웹사이트가 링크되어 있어요.

어휘 fill in 자세히 알려주다   materials 자료   travel expenses 여행 경비   complicated 복잡한   electronically 컴퓨터로   internal 내부의   reimbursement 상환   procedure 절차

1. Why did the woman miss a meeting?

(A) She was not feeling well.
(B) She forgot the meeting time.
(C) She was talking to a client.
(D) She did not receive the invitation.

왜 여자는 회의를 놓쳤는가?
(A) 몸이 좋지 않았다.
(B) 회의 시간을 잊었다.
(C) 고객과 대화 중이었다.
(D) 초대장을 받지 못했다.

해설 여자가 회의에 못 간 이유를 묻는 질문에, 여자의 첫 대사 중 "I was on the phone with an important client."에서 고객과 통화 중이라서 회의에 못 갔다고 했으므로 정답은 (C)이다.

2. What is the woman confused about?
(A) The details of an assignment
(B) A reimbursement process
(C) The terms of a contract
(D) A travel itinerary

여자는 무엇에 관해 혼란스러워 하는가?
(A) 업무의 세부 사항
(B) 상환 과정
(C) 계약 조건
(D) 여행 일정

해설 대화 중반에 여자가 "the part about how to get money back for travel expenses was really complicated."라며 비용을 상환 받는 법에 대해 혼란스러워하는 것을 알 수 있다. 따라서 정답은 (B)이다.

3. According to the man, what should the woman do?
(A) Restart a computer
(B) Talk to the manager about the meeting
(C) Refer to the electronic version of the data
(D) Upgrade the Web site

남자에 따르면, 여자는 무엇을 하겠는가?
(A) 컴퓨터를 다시 시작한다
(B) 회의에 대해 매니저에게 말한다
(C) 자료의 전자 버전을 참고한다
(D) 웹사이트를 업그레이드한다

해설 대화 후반에 남자가 여자에게 "there's a link to our internal Web site where you can find more details ~."라며 회사 웹사이트에 필요한 정보가 있다고 말하고 있다. 따라서 (C)가 정답이다. Web site가 electronic version으로 패러프레이징되었다.

[4~6]

W: Thanks for visiting, Mr. Flynn. Your work crew did a good job painting the hallway of our building. It goes well with our other rooms. So could I ask you a favor? As you can see, the restroom on the 10th floor also needs to be painted because of leaking from the ceiling. I know you are so busy.
M: Hmm… Actually, my team is fully scheduled this week. Is it urgent? By when should I complete the work?
W: To be honest, I hope you'll be able to take care of this soon.
M: All right. I'll check our work schedule again and let you know by the end of the day.

W: 방문해 주셔서 감사합니다, Flynn 씨. 당신의 작업조가 우리 빌딩 복도 페인트칠을 잘했어요. 다른 방이랑도 잘 어울리고요. 그래서 말인데 한 가지 부탁해도 될까요? 아시다시피 천장 누수 때문에 10층 화장실을 페인트칠 해야 합니다. 당신이 매우 바쁜 건 알고 있어요.
M: 흠… 사실 저희 팀이 이번 주에는 일정이 다 찼어요. 급하신가요? 언제까지 작업을 끝내야 하나요?
W: 솔직히 말하면 당신이 이 일을 빨리 맡을 수 있으면 좋겠어요.
M: 좋아요. 제가 다시 작업 일정을 확인해 보고 오늘까지 알려 드릴게요.

어휘 work crew 작업반 | go well with ~와 잘 어울리다 | ask a favor 부탁하다 | leaking 누수 | ceiling 천장 | take care of ~을 신경 쓰다

4. What problem does the woman mention?
(A) A painting is blurry.
(B) A restroom is dirty.
(C) A job is incomplete.
(D) A ceiling is damaged.

여자는 무슨 문제를 언급하는가?
(A) 그림이 흐리다.
(B) 화장실이 더럽다.
(C) 일이 완성되지 않았다.
(D) 천장에 하자가 생겼다.

해설 문제점은 주로 대화 초반에 언급된다. 여자의 첫 대사 중 "the restroom on the 10th floor also needs to be painted because of leaking from the ceiling."에서 천장 누수 문제를 언급했으므로 정답은 (D)이다.

5. What does the man ask the woman about?
(A) A crew member's name
(B) A start time
(C) A completion date
(D) Inexperienced workers

남자는 여자에게 무엇에 관해 묻는가?
(A) 작업반의 이름
(B) 시작 시간
(C) 완성 날짜
(D) 경험이 부족한 노동자들

해설 대화 중반에 남자가 "By when should I complete the work?"라며 언제까지 작업을 끝내야 하는지 묻고 있으므로 (C)가 정답이다.

342

6. What does the man say he will do right away?
   (A) Reduce the working hours
   (B) Contact the supplier
   (C) Finish some works
   (D) Adjust a schedule

   남자는 지금 당장 무엇을 하겠다고 말하는가?
   (A) 작업 시간 줄이기
   (B) 공급 업체에 연락하기
   (C) 작업 마무리하기
   (D) 일정 조정하기

   해설 대화 후반에 남자가 "I'll check our work schedule again ~."라며 일정을 확인해 보겠다 즉, 일정을 조정해 보겠다는 의미이므로 정답은 (D)이다.

SPARTA Practice Test   p.69

1. (B)	2. (C)	3. (D)	4. (B)	5. (C)
6. (D)	7. (D)	8. (B)	9. (A)	10. (A)
11. (C)	12. (A)	13. (B)	14. (C)	15. (B)
16. (A)	17. (B)	18. (C)	19. (B)	20. (A)
21. (D)	22. (B)	23. (C)	24. (D)	

Questions 1-3 refer to the following conversation.

M: Hi. I'm looking for a hammer but I can't find one. Aren't they in the gardening section?
W: No, they're over there in aisle five. If you follow me, I'll show you exactly where they are. Are you doing a little work?
M: Well, last weekend I picked up a beautiful antique mirror at a garage sale and now I need to hang it up. It's big and heavy so it's quite challenging. I had a hard time carrying it to my house in a wheelbarrow, even though it was only two blocks away.
W: You're kidding! Do you mean the garage sale on Oak Street? We live right next to that house!

M: 안녕하세요. 망치를 찾고 있는데 안 보이네요. 정원용품 섹션에 있지 않나요?
W: 아니요. 그것들은 저기 5번 통로에 있어요. 따라오시면 정확히 어디에 있는지 보여 드릴게요. 간단한 작업을 하시려는 건가요?
M: 음, 지난 주말에 중고 물품 세일에서 멋진 골동품 거울을 샀는데 그것 좀 걸려고요. 크고 무거워서 꽤 어렵네요. 수레로 저희 집으로 가져오는 데 애먹었어요. 겨우 두 블록 떨어져 있는데 말이죠.
W: 설마요! Oak 가에서 하는 중고 물품 세일을 말씀하시는 건가요? 저희는 거기 바로 옆에 살아요!

어휘 hammer 망치   gardening 정원 가꾸기   aisle 통로
antique 골동품   garage sale 중고 물품 세일
challenging 어려운, 도전적인   wheelbarrow 손수레

1. What is the man unable to find?
   (A) Some furniture
   (B) A hand tool
   (C) A protective device
   (D) Some cleaning supplies

   남자는 무엇을 찾을 수 없는가?
   (A) 가구
   (B) 수공구
   (C) 보호 장치
   (D) 청소용품

   해설 첫 대사에서 남자가 "I'm looking for a hammer."라며 망치를 찾고 있다고 했으므로 정답은 (B)이다.

2. What did the man do last weekend?
   (A) He purchased a small vehicle.
   (B) He visited an art gallery.
   (C) He obtained an old object.
   (D) He worked in the garden.

   남자는 지난 주말에 무엇을 했는가?
   (A) 소형차를 샀다.
   (B) 미술관을 방문했다.
   (C) 오래된 물건을 구했다.
   (D) 정원에서 일했다.

   해설 대화 중반에 남자가 "last weekend I picked up a beautiful antique mirror at a garage sale ~."라며 지난 주말에 골동품 거울을 샀다고 했으므로 이를 패러프레이징 한 (C)가 정답이다.

3. Why most likely is the woman surprised?
   (A) She has met the man before.
   (B) She thinks the work is too hard.
   (C) She was not aware of the sale.
   (D) She knows the place the man said.

   왜 여자는 놀라는 것 같은가?
   (A) 남자를 전에 만난 적이 있다.
   (B) 작업이 너무 어렵다고 생각한다.
   (C) 세일에 대해 알지 못했다.
   (D) 그녀는 남자가 말한 장소를 안다.

   해설 대화 후반에 여자가 "Do you mean the garage sale on Oak Street? We live right next to that house!"라면서 바로 옆에 산다고 말하고 있으므로 정답은 (D)이다.

Questions 4-6 refer to the following conversation.

M: Didn't we go over this an hour ago? It seems like I'm rereading the same pages. We should really get some rest.
W: I think so, too. I'm getting sleepy anyway. Why don't we get together first thing tomorrow morning?
M: That'll be good. Shall we have breakfast at Spicoli's? They're open at 7:00 A.M. And then let's start the work.
W: That is a good time, but I want to go to the Breakfast Nook just around the corner. I prefer their home-style pancakes.
M: Okay, let's meet there at seven.

M: 한 시간 전에 이걸 검토하지 않았나요? 같은 페이지를 읽는 것 같아요. 우리는 정말 쉬어야겠어요.
W: 그래요. 슬슬 잠이 오네요. 내일 아침 일찍 만나는 게 어때요?
M: 좋아요. Spicoli's에서 아침 먹을까요? 오전 7시에 문을 열어요. 그러고 나서 일을 시작합시다.
W: 시간은 괜찮은데, 저는 모퉁이를 돌면 있는 Breakfast Nook에 가고 싶어요. 그들의 가정식 팬케이크를 좋아하거든요.
M: 알았어요. 거기에서 7시에 봐요.

어휘 get some rest 쉬다   get together 만나다

4. What do the two speakers have in common?
   (A) Both are hungry.
   (B) Both are tired.
   (C) Both want to go to Spicoli's.
   (D) Both prefer home-style pancakes.

두 화자의 공통점은 무엇인가?
(A) 둘 다 배고프다.
(B) 둘 다 피곤하다.
(C) 둘 다 Spicoli's에 가고 싶다.
(D) 둘 다 가정식 팬케이크를 선호한다.

해설 대화 초반에 남자가 "We should really get some rest."라며 쉬어야겠다고 했고, 여자가 뒤이어 "I think so, too. I'm getting sleepy anyway."라며 남자의 말에 동조하면서 졸리다고 했으므로 (B)가 정답이다.

5. Why does the woman want to go to the Breakfast Nook?
   (A) It opens at 7 A.M.
   (B) She knows the owner.
   (C) She likes the food there.
   (D) It is cheaper than Spicoli's.

왜 여자는 Breakfast Nook에 가고 싶어 하는가?
(A) 그곳은 오전 7시에 문을 연다.
(B) 그녀는 가게 주인을 안다.
(C) 그녀는 그곳 음식을 좋아한다.
(D) Spicoli's보다 싸다.

해설 여자가 "I prefer their home-style pancakes."라면서 그 가게의 가정식 팬케이크를 좋아한다고 했으므로 정답은 (C)이다.

6. What are the speakers going to do next?
   (A) Continue reading the pages
   (B) Get a bite to eat
   (C) Continue their discussion
   (D) Get some rest

화자들은 다음에 무엇을 할 것인가?
(A) 페이지를 계속 읽는다
(B) 간단히 먹는다
(C) 토론을 계속한다
(D) 휴식을 취한다

해설 다음에 할 일은 주로 대화 후반에 단서가 등장하지만 이 문제처럼 전체 흐름을 파악해야 풀 수 있는 경우도 있다. 두 사람은 오늘은 이만 쉬고 내일 일찍 다시 만나기로 약속하고 있으므로 정답은 (D)이다.

Questions 7-9 refer to the following conversation.

M: Hello, Ms. Matsuda? I'm calling from TOP electronics store. I'm so sorry, but the refrigerator you ordered was accidentally left off this morning's delivery schedule. We discovered the oversight after the delivery truck left.
W: Oh, no. Three days from now, an inspection will be carried out in our restaurant. So we need the refrigerator to be installed by tomorrow. Our refrigerator is too outdated.
M: Hmm… That doesn't leave us with much time. Please give me a second. I'm going to contact my manager. I think she'll be able to deal with this problem.

M: 안녕하세요, Matsuda 씨? TOP 전자제품 매장에서 연락 드립니다. 주문하신 냉장고가 오늘 아침 배송 일정에서 어쩌다가 빠져 버렸습니다. 배송 트럭이 떠난 후에 알았어요.
W: 아, 안 돼요. 3일 후에 저희 레스토랑에서 점검이 있을 거예요. 그래서 내일까지 설치해야 해요. 저희 냉장고가 너무 오래됐거든요.
M: 음… 시간이 많지 않네요. 잠시만요. 매니저한테 연락해 볼게요. 그녀가 이 문제를 처리할 수 있을 거예요.

어휘 **accidentally** 뜻하지 않게, 어쩌다가   **leave off** ~을 빼다
oversight 실수   **inspection** 점검   **outdated** 구식인
deal with 다루다

7. What problem does the man mention?
(A) Some defective items
(B) The shortage of a product
(C) A broken truck
(D) A delivery error

남자는 무슨 문제를 언급하는가?
(A) 결함 있는 물건
(B) 물품 부족
(C) 고장 난 트럭
(D) 배송 실수

해설 남자의 첫 대사에서 "I'm so sorry, but the refrigerator you ordered was accidentally left off this morning's delivery schedule."라며 배송 실수로 주문한 냉장고가 누락 됐다고 했으므로 정답은 (D)이다.

8. What does the woman say is planned in three days?
(A) A product launch
(B) An inspection
(C) A cooking class
(D) A product demonstration

여자는 3일 뒤에 무엇이 계획되어 있다고 말하는가?
(A) 제품 출시
(B) 점검
(C) 요리 수업
(D) 제품 시연회

해설 대화 초반에 여자가 "Three days from now, an inspection will be carried out in our restaurant."라며 3일 뒤에 점검이 있다고 했으므로 정답은 (B)이다.

9. What does the man say he will do?
(A) Call a supervisor
(B) Install a device
(C) Extend a warranty
(D) Contact the woman's manager

남자는 무엇을 하겠다고 말하는가?
(A) 상사에게 전화하기
(B) 기기 설치하기
(C) 보증 기간 연장하기
(D) 여자의 매니저에게 연락하기

해설 남자가 하겠다고 하는 것을 묻고 있으므로 남자의 대사에 집중한다. 대화 후반에 남자가 "I'm going to contact my manager."라며 본인의 매니저에게 연락해서 문제를 해결하겠

다고 했으므로 정답은 (A)이다.

Questions 10-12 refer to the following conversation.

W: Hi, David. I saw your e-mail about the safety training at 11 A.M. this Thursday. But I have to meet with clients at that time.
M: Oh, I didn't know you had a meeting. How long will it take?
W: Around an hour. I have to negotiate the terms of the contract. Is there any way that you could start the training later in the day?
M: I don't think so. The rest of our team isn't available this afternoon. But if it's okay with you, I can just email you the training materials to review on your own. If you have any questions, contact me anytime.

W: 안녕하세요, David. 이번 주 목요일 오전 11시에 있는 안전 교육에 관한 메일을 봤어요. 하지만 그 시간에 저는 고객을 만나야 해요.
M: 아, 회의가 있는 줄은 몰랐네요. 얼마나 걸릴까요?
W: 한 시간 정도요. 계약 조건을 협상해야 하거든요. 교육을 오후에 시작할 수 있는 방법이 없을까요?
M: 아니요. 나머지 팀원들이 오후에 시간이 안 돼요. 당신만 괜찮다면 혼자서 검토할 수 있도록 교육 자료를 메일로 보내 줄게요. 질문이 있으면 언제든지 연락 주세요.

어휘 **safety** 안전   **negotiate** 협상하다   **terms** 조건
material 자료   **on one's own** 혼자서   **contact** 연락하다

10. What is the woman's problem?
(A) There is a scheduling conflict.
(B) There are no projectors available.
(C) A contract is incorrect.
(D) A deadline has been moved up to Friday.

여자의 문제는 무엇인가?
(A) 일정이 겹친다.
(B) 이용할 수 있는 프로젝터가 없다.
(C) 계약서가 잘못되었다.
(D) 마감일이 금요일로 앞당겨졌다.

해설 여자가 교육 시간을 언급하면서 "But I have to meet with clients at that time."라면서 그 시간에 고객과 약속이 있다고 말하고 있으므로 일정이 겹친다는 (A)가 정답이다.

11. What does the woman inquire about?
(A) Negotiating the prices
(B) Winning the contract
(C) Putting off a training session
(D) Arranging a teleconference

여자는 무엇에 대해 문의하는가?
(A) 가격을 협상하는 것
(B) 계약을 따는 것
(C) 교육을 미루는 것
(D) 전화 회의를 준비하는 것

해설 여자가 문의하는 것을 묻고 있으므로 여자의 대사에 집중한다. 여자가 일정이 겹친다면서 "Is there any way that you could start the training later in the day?"라며 교육을 늦게 시작할 수 없는지 묻고 있다. 따라서 정답은 (C)이다.

12. What does the man say he will do?
(A) Forward some documents
(B) Review the materials
(C) Speak with a supervisor
(D) Contact a client

남자는 무엇을 하겠다고 말하는가?
(A) 서류 보내기
(B) 자료 검토하기
(C) 상사와 말하기
(D) 고객에게 연락하기

해설 남자가 하겠다고 한 것을 물었으므로 남자의 대사에 집중한다. 남자가 "I can just email you the training materials to review on your own."라면서 검토용 교육 자료를 보내주겠다고 했으므로 정답은 (A)이다. (B)는 여자가 하게 될 행동이다.

Questions 13-15 refer to the following conversation.

W: Hi, a patron returned an expensive designer suit this morning. Do you know the reason he brought it back?
M: Actually, I do. The suit's label said the wrong size, and he bought it without trying it on. I checked the other suits on that same rack just now, and I found out there are some more suits with the wrong label. So, we need to check all the labels of the items at our store.
W: Okay. I'll check the racks of the other types of suits. Can you check the shirts and coats?

W: 안녕하세요. 고객이 오늘 아침에 비싼 디자이너 정장을 반납했어요. 다시 가져온 이유 알아요?
M: 사실 알아요. 정장의 라벨이 잘못된 사이즈로 표기되어 있었고 그는 입어 보지도 않고 구매했죠. 방금 전에 같은 옷걸이에 걸려 있는 다른 정장들을 확인했고 잘못된 라벨이 있는 정장들이 더 있는 걸 발견했어요. 그래서 우리 매장 모든 상품의 라벨을 확인해야 해요.
W: 좋아요. 제가 다른 종류의 정장이 있는 옷걸이를 확인할게요. 당신이 셔츠와 코트를 확인해 주시겠어요?

어휘 patron 고객   return 반납하다   suit 정장   label 라벨   rack 걸이

13. Where do the speakers most likely work?
(A) At a furniture warehouse
(B) At a retail store
(C) At a laundry
(D) At a law firm

화자들은 어디에서 일할 것 같은가?
(A) 가구 창고에서
(B) 소매점에서
(C) 세탁소에서
(D) 법률 회사에서

해설 여자의 첫 대사에서 "a patron returned an expensive designer suit this morning."라면서 고객이 옷을 반납했다고 했다. 이를 통해 화자들이 의류 매장에서 일한다는 것을 알 수 있으므로 (B)가 정답이다.

14. What is the problem?
(A) Some merchandise is broken.
(B) A receipt is missing.
(C) The information on some labels is incorrect.
(D) An order has not arrived.

문제가 무엇인가?
(A) 일부 상품이 망가졌다.
(B) 영수증이 없어졌다.
(C) 라벨 정보가 잘못됐다.
(D) 주문품이 도착하지 않았다.

해설 문제점은 대화 초반에 주로 등장한다. 남자가 "I found out there are some more suits with the wrong label."라며 라벨이 잘못되어 있다고 했으므로 정답은 (C)이다.

15. What will the speakers probably do next?
(A) Mail a discount voucher
(B) Inspect some products
(C) Talk to a store owner
(D) Check the inventory

화자들은 다음에 무엇을 할 것 같은가?
(A) 메일로 할인권 보내기
(B) 제품 검사하기
(C) 가게 주인과 말하기
(D) 재고 확인하기

해설 대화 후반에 여자가 "I'll check the racks of the other types of suits. Can you check the shirts and coats?"라며 본인은 정장을 확인할 테니 남자에게 셔츠와 코트를 확인하라고 했으므로 정답은 (B)이다.

Questions 16-18 refer to the following conversation.

> M: Hi, Melanie. Thanks for coming here so quickly. One of the servers for this company event is out sick today. Also, we haven't finished preparing the catering service yet.
> W: You're welcome. But, I was in such a rush that I forgot my apron.
> M: Oh, you don't have to worry about that. I always carry some extras in the car.
> W: Great. So, what kind of the event is this?
> M: It's a luncheon for the workers at the university administration facility. We've never catered here before, and if it goes well, I think we'll get more work from them in the future.
>
> M: 안녕하세요, Melanie. 이렇게 빨리 와주셔서 고마워요. 이 회사 행사의 웨이터 중 한 명이 아파서 못 나왔어요. 아직 출장연회 서비스 준비도 끝내지 못했는데 말이에요.
> W: 천만에요. 그런데 급하게 오는 바람에 앞치마를 깜빡했어요.
> M: 아, 걱정할 필요 없어요. 저는 항상 차에 여분을 가지고 다니거든요.
> W: 좋아요. 그래서 이번에는 무슨 행사인가요?
> M: 대학교 행정 시설에서 일하는 사람들을 위한 오찬이에요. 전에 한번도 여기에 음식을 제공한 적이 없어요. 만약에 잘 되면 앞으로 그들과 더 많은 일을 할 것 같아요.

어휘 catering service 출장연회 서비스   in a rush 급하게   apron 앞치마   extra 여분   luncheon 오찬   administration facility 행정 시설

16. What kind of business do the speakers work for?

(A) A catering company
(B) A café
(C) A university
(D) A clothing manufacturer

화자들은 어떤 종류의 회사에서 일하는가?
(A) 출장연회 서비스 업체
(B) 카페
(C) 대학교
(D) 의류 제조업체

해설 첫 대사에서 남자가 여자를 환영하면서 "~ we haven't finished preparing the catering service yet."라며 출장연회 서비스 준비를 아직 못 끝냈다고 했다. 따라서 정답은 (A)이다.

17. What did the woman forget to bring?

(A) A mobile phone
(B) An apron
(C) Some medicine
(D) A wallet

여자는 무엇을 가져오는 것을 잊어버렸는가?
(A) 핸드폰
(B) 앞치마
(C) 약
(D) 지갑

해설 여자가 "I was in such a rush that I forgot my apron."라면서 급하게 오느라 앞치마 가져오는 걸 깜빡했다고 했으므로 정답은 (B)이다.

18. What does the man mention about the event?

(A) It is a charity fundraiser.
(B) It has been catered several times before.
(C) It will be able to lead to more business.
(D) Its attendees are well known.

남자는 행사에 대해 뭐라고 언급하는가?
(A) 자선 모금 행사이다.
(B) 전에 출장 음식을 몇 번 제공했었다.
(C) 더 많은 거래로 이어질 수 있다.
(D) 참석자들이 유명하다.

해설 대화 후반에 남자가 행사를 언급하면서 "~ if it goes well, I think we'll get more work from them in the future."라며 잘 진행되면 향후에 더 많은 일이 들어올 거라고 했으므로 정답은 (C)이다.

Questions 19-21 refer to the following conversation.

> M: Excuse me, I'm looking for a DSL camera. I've never used one before, but I'm planning to go backpacking next month. So I want to take a lot of nice pictures. Could you make some suggestions?
> W: Sure. It'll help to know what your specific needs are and how much you'd like to spend.
> M: Well, I plan to use it mostly during holidays. I have a couple of trips by myself coming up, and I'd like to record my experiences to hold onto my memories. So I want a camera with a good selfies feature and that is easy to operate for basic users.
> W: In that case, I'd recommend the Dixcon 90. It is the best product for the basics. If you buy it today, I can give you 20 percent off of the regular price. Don't miss this opportunity.
> M: Wow! Okay, I'll take it.

M: 실례합니다. DSL 카메라를 찾고 있는데요. 전에 한번도 써 본 적은 없지만 다음 달에 배낭여행을 갈 거라서요. 그래서 멋진 사진을 많이 찍고 싶어요. 추천 좀 해주시겠어요?
W: 그럼요. 특별히 원하시는 사항과 얼마를 지불하실지를 알면 도움이 될 것 같아요.
M: 음, 거의 휴가 동안 사용할 거예요. 두 번 정도 혼자 여행 갈 거고 추억을 간직하기 위해 경험을 기록하고 싶어요. 그래서 셀프 촬영 기능이 좋고 초급자들이 사용하기 쉬운 카메라를 원해요.
W: 그런 경우라면 Dixcon 90을 추천합니다. 기본을 위한 가장 좋은 상품이죠. 오늘 사시면 정가에서 20퍼센트 할인해 드릴 수 있어요. 이런 기회를 놓치지 마세요.
M: 와! 좋아요. 그걸로 할게요.

어휘 go backpacking 배낭여행을 가다 specific 특정한, 구체적인
record 기록하다 experience 경험 memory 기억
selfies feature 셀프 촬영 기능 operate 작동시키다
basics 기본 regular price 정가 opportunity 기회

19. What does the man want the woman to do?
(A) Change a camera
(B) Recommend a product
(C) Explain a feature
(D) Plan a backpacking trip

남자는 여자가 무엇을 하기를 원하는가?
(A) 카메라 바꾸기
(B) 상품 추천하기
(C) 특징 설명하기
(D) 배낭여행 계획하기

해설 첫 대사에서 남자가 배낭여행을 위한 카메라를 찾고 있다면서 "Could you make some suggestions?"라며 추천해 달라고 했으므로 정답은 (B)이다.

20. What does the man say he will do with the camera?
(A) Document his trips
(B) Teach a class
(C) Record music
(D) Make a commercial

남자는 카메라로 무엇을 할 거라고 말하는가?
(A) 여행 기록하기
(B) 수업 가르치기
(C) 음악 녹음하기
(D) 광고 만들기

해설 남자가 여행하는 동안 카메라를 쓸 계획이라면서 "I'd like to record my experiences to hold onto my memories."라며 추억을 간직하기 위해 경험을 기록하고 싶다고 했으므로 정답은 (A)이다.

21. What is the feature of the Dixcon 90?
(A) It has a long battery life.
(B) It is for experts.
(C) It is a new model.
(D) It is easy to operate.

Dixcon 90의 특징은 무엇인가?
(A) 배터리 수명이 길다.
(B) 전문가를 위한 것이다.
(C) 새로운 모델이다.
(D) 사용하기 쉽다.

해설 남자가 사용하기 쉬운 것을 원한다고(So I want a camera with a good selfies feature and that is easy to operate for basic users.) 했고 여자가 "It is the best product for the basics."라며 기본을 위한 가장 좋은 제품이라고 했다. 따라서 정답은 (D)이다.

Questions 22-24 refer to the following conversation.

W: Excuse me, there is a mistake on my receipt. I was charged for two drinks, but I only ordered one.
M: Oh, I'm really sorry about that. I'll revise this right away and bring you a new bill.
W: Thank you. I have a question. Does your restaurant offer a catering service? I'm having a company retreat next month.
M: Sure, could you wait a few minutes? I'll bring over the catering manager for you. She's talking to another customer.

W: 실례합니다. 제 영수증에 착오가 있네요. 전 음료를 한 잔 주문했는데 두 잔으로 요금이 부과됐어요.
M: 아, 정말 죄송합니다. 지금 바로 수정해서 새로운 영수증을 가져다드릴게요.
W: 고마워요. 질문이 있는데요. 이 레스토랑은 출장연회 서비스도 제공하나요? 다음 달에 회사 단합 대회가 있거든요.
M: 물론이죠. 잠시만 기다려 주시겠어요? 출장연회 담당 매니저를 불러 오겠습니다. 그녀가 다른 고객과 이야기 중이거든요.

어휘 mistake 실수 receipt 영수증 charge 청구하다
revise 수정하다 company retreat 회사 단합 대회

22. What problem does the woman mention?
(A) A meal is cold.
(B) A bill is incorrect.
(C) An order is not processed.
(D) A receipt is missing.

여자는 어떤 문제를 언급하는가?
(A) 음식이 차갑다.
(B) 청구서가 잘못되었다.
(C) 주문이 진행되지 않았다.
(D) 영수증을 분실했다.

해설 여자가 언급한 문제를 묻는 질문으로, 여자의 첫 대사에서 "there is a mistake on my receipt."라며 영수증에 착오가 있다고 언급했다. 이를 나타낸 (B)가 정답이다. mistake가 incorrect로 패러프레이징 되었다.

23. What does the woman say she wants to do?
(A) Speak to the chef
(B) Fill out a comment card
(C) Get some details about a service
(D) Upgrade the catering order

여자는 무엇을 하고 싶다고 말하는가?
(A) 요리사와 이야기한다
(B) 의견 카드를 작성한다
(C) 서비스에 관한 세부 설명을 듣는다
(D) 음식 공급을 개선한다

해설 여자가 원하는 것을 물었으므로 여자의 대사에 집중해야 한다. "Does your restaurant offer a catering service?"라며 출장연회 서비스가 가능한지를 묻고 있다. 즉 서비스에 대한 정보를 원한다는 것을 알 수 있으므로 (C)가 정답이다.

24. Why is the woman asked to wait?
(A) A special dish takes time to cook.
(B) Some food is being packaged.
(C) There are so many customers.
(D) A staff member is busy.

왜 여자는 기다려 달라고 요청 받는가?
(A) 특별 음식을 요리하는 데 시간이 걸린다.
(B) 음식이 포장되고 있다.
(C) 고객들이 너무 많다.
(D) 직원이 바쁘다.

해설 남자가 후반에 "I'll bring over the catering manager for you. She's talking to another customer."라며 담당 매니저를 불러 오겠다고 한 후 지금 다른 고객과 대화하고 있다고 했으므로 정답은 (D)이다.

DAY 10 요청&제안/다음에 할 일

SPARTA Check-UP
p.73

1. (C) 2. (B) 3. (B) 4. (A) 5. (C)
6. (D)

[1-3]

M: Hi, Ms. Rartez. I'm calling about your laptop computer case design you sent over last week. I wanted to let you know that we should be able to manufacture them here at our plastics factory next week.
W: Okay, I'm glad to hear that. To begin, we'd like to start with 1,000 cases and then hand them out to some field testers to get their feedback. Can you tell me how much it would cost for that?
M: If you make them all the same pattern, it'll be cheaper for you. Also we'll be able to complete them faster.

M: 안녕하세요, Rartez 씨. 지난주에 보내신 노트북 컴퓨터 케이스 디자인 때문에 연락 드립니다. 다음 주에 여기 플라스틱 공장에서 그것들을 제조할 수 있게 되어 말씀 드리려고요.
W: 네, 기쁘네요. 먼저 1000개 케이스를 시작했으면 하고, 그러고 나서 피드백을 받기 위해 현장의 검사자들한테 나눠주면 좋겠네요. 그렇게 하면 비용이 얼마나 드는지 알려 주시겠어요?
M: 만약 모두 같은 패턴으로 만든다면 더 저렴할 겁니다. 그리고 더 빨리 완성할 수도 있고요.

어휘 manufacture 제조하다 factory 공장 hand out 나눠 주다 field 현장 pattern 모양 complete 완성하다

1. Where does the man most likely work?
(A) At an electronics store
(B) At a clothing distributor
(C) At a manufacturing plant
(D) At a computer manufacturer

남자는 어디에서 일할 것 같은가?
(A) 전자제품 매장에서
(B) 의류 유통 회사에서
(C) 제조 공장에서
(D) 컴퓨터 제조업체에서

해설 남자의 첫 대사 "I wanted to let you know that we should be able to manufacture them here ~."에서 여자가 보낸 컴퓨터 케이스를 자신의 공장에서 만들 수 있게 됐다고 했으므로 정답은 (C)이다. (D)는 어휘 반복 함정이다.

2. What does the woman ask about?

(A) The size of an order

(B) The price quote

(C) Customer survey results

(D) Testers' feedback

여자는 무엇에 대해 물어보는가?
(A) 주문품의 사이즈
(B) 가격 견적
(C) 고객 설문조사 결과
(D) 검사자들의 피드백

해설 대화 중반에 여자가 "Can you tell me how much it would cost for that?"라며 비용이 얼마나 드는지를 묻고 있다. 즉, 제품의 견적을 묻고 있으므로 (B)가 정답이다.

3. What does the man recommend regarding the order?

(A) Changing the pattern

(B) Limiting pattern options

(C) Calling a different supplier

(D) Completing the form first

남자가 주문에 대해 추천하는 것은 무엇인가?
(A) 패턴을 바꾸는 것
(B) 패턴 옵션을 제한하는 것
(C) 다른 공급 업체에 연락하는 것
(D) 먼저 양식을 작성하는 것

해설 대화 후반부에 남자가 "If you make them all the same pattern, it'll be cheaper for you."라며 같은 모양으로 만든다면 더 싸고 빠르게 할 수 있다고 했다. 즉 패턴의 선택을 제한하라는 의미이므로 (B)가 정답이다.

[4-6]

M: Jenny, some of our hotel's guests asked me if we could get tickets for the opera performance tomorrow night. So, I've contacted the ticket office several times, but nobody answered the phone. I just got a recording.

W: Well, I've got a pamphlet about another musical performance happening tomorrow night at a different venue. You could ask them if they'd be interested in seeing that show instead. It also received good reviews.

M: Great! I'll ask them. If they want to go there, I'll stop by your office after lunch to get more information.

M: Jenny, 저희 호텔 고객 몇 분이 내일 밤에 있는 오페라 공연 티켓을 구할 수 있는지 물었어요. 그래서 몇 번이나 매표소에 전화했는데 아무도 안 받네요. 녹음 메시지만 들려요.

W: 내일 밤에 다른 장소에서 열리는 음악 공연 팜플렛을 가지고 있어요. 그들에게 그 공연 대신 보는 것에 관심이 있는지 물어보세요. 그 공연도 평이 좋았어요.

M: 좋아요! 물어볼게요. 만약에 그들이 가기를 원하면 점심 시간 후에 정보를 얻으러 당신 사무실에 들를게요.

어휘 performance 공연 several 몇몇의 venue 장소 review 논평 stop by 들르다

4. Where do the speakers work?

(A) At a hotel

(B) At a concert hall

(C) At a phone company

(D) At a playhouse

화자들은 어디서 일하는가?
(A) 호텔에서
(B) 콘서트 홀에서
(C) 전화 회사에서
(D) 극장에서

해설 일하는 장소는 주로 대화 앞부분에서 단서가 나온다. 남자의 첫 대사 중 "some of our hotel's guests asked me ~."에서 화자들은 호텔에서 일하는 것을 알 수 있으므로 정답은 (A)이다.

5. What is the man concerned about?

(A) No rooms are available at the hotel.

(B) Tickets are sold out.

(C) Ticket agents didn't answer the phone.

(D) Guests canceled their reservations.

남자는 무엇에 대해 염려하는가?
(A) 호텔에 방이 없다.
(B) 티켓이 매진되었다.
(C) 매표소 직원이 전화를 받지 않았다.
(D) 고객들이 예약을 취소했다.

해설 남자의 걱정거리는 남자의 대사에 집중해서 들어야 한다. "I've contacted the ticket office several times, but nobody answered the phone."라며 매표소로 연락이 안 된다고 했으므로 정답은 (C)이다.

6. What will the man do after lunch?

(A) Stop by the ticket office

(B) Send the pamphlet

(C) Buy some tickets

(D) Visit the woman's office

남자는 점심 시간 후에 무엇을 할 것인가?
(A) 매표소에 들른다
(B) 팜플렛을 보낸다
(C) 티켓을 산다
(D) 여자의 사무실을 방문한다

해설 대화 후반에 남자가 "I'll stop by your office after lunch to get more information."라며 정보를 얻으러 여자의 사무실에 가겠다고 했으므로 정답은 (D)이다. 여기서 stop by만 듣고 (A)를 선택하면 안 된다.

SPARTA Practice Test

p.74

1. (A)	2. (D)	3. (A)	4. (A)	5. (D)
6. (C)	7. (A)	8. (B)	9. (D)	10. (D)
11. (A)	12. (B)	13. (B)	14. (A)	15. (B)
16. (D)	17. (B)	18. (B)	19. (B)	20. (D)
21. (B)	22. (A)	23. (B)	24. (A)	

Questions 1-3 refer to the following conversation.

W: In short, Frank, you've been working hard here over the past year. So you're a valuable member of the department, which is why you continuously receive outstanding performance evaluations from the company.
M: I'm really satisfied with the opportunity to work here.
W: That's good to hear. We want you to have more responsibilities. We're expanding the branch in Tokyo next year and we'd like you to oversee that branch.
M: Really? That's wonderful. But I have to talk to my family first. By when should I make a decision?
W: How about meeting next week to discuss this?

W: 요컨대, Frank, 당신은 지난 몇 년간 여기에서 열심히 일했어요. 그래서 당신은 우리 부서의 인재이고, 그게 당신이 우리 회사에서 뛰어난 업무 능력 평가를 지속적으로 받는 이유이기도 하죠.
M: 저는 여기에서 일할 수 있어서 정말 만족해요.
W: 반가운 말이네요. 그래서 우리는 당신이 더 많은 업무를 맡았으면 해요. 우리는 내년에 도쿄에서 지점을 확장할 것이고 그 지점을 당신이 감독했으면 합니다.
M: 정말요? 멋지군요. 하지만 가족이랑 먼저 이야기해야 해요. 언제까지 결정해야 하나요?
W: 이 건을 논의하기 위해 다음 주에 만나는 게 어떠세요?

어휘 valuable 소중한   continuously 연달아   outstanding 뛰어난   performance 업무   evaluation 평가   be satisfied with ~에 만족하다   opportunity 기회   responsibility 책임   expand 확장하다   oversee 감독하다   make a decision 결정하다

1. What does the woman say about the man's job performance?
(A) He is a competent employee.
(B) He always meets his deadlines.
(C) He has creative ideas for new projects.
(D) He has increased company profits.

여자는 남자의 업무 능력에 대해 뭐라고 말하는가?
(A) 그는 능력 있는 직원이다.
(B) 그는 항상 마감일을 잘 맞춘다.
(C) 그는 새로운 프로젝트에 창의적인 아이디어를 낸다.
(D) 그는 회사 수익을 증가시켰다.

해설 여자가 초반에 남자에게 "~ you continuously receive outstanding performance evaluations from the company."라며 그의 업무 능력을 높게 평가한다고 말하고 있다. 이를 의미하는 (A)가 정답이다.

2. What does the woman ask the man to do?
(A) Attend a trade show
(B) Join a leadership council
(C) Meet the client in Tokyo
(D) Accept a new position

여자는 남자에게 무엇을 하도록 요청하는가?
(A) 무역 박람회에 참석한다
(B) 지도부 위원회에 가입한다
(C) 도쿄에서 고객을 만난다
(D) 새 직책을 맡는다

해설 여자가 "We're expanding the branch in Tokyo next year and we'd like you to oversee that branch."라며 내년에 사업을 확장할 것이고 남자에게 새 지점을 맡아 달라고 말하고 있다. 따라서 정답은 (D)이다.

3. What is the company planning to do next year?
(A) Open a new overseas office
(B) Extend the business hours
(C) Meet the staff's family
(D) Get feedback from employees

회사는 내년에 무엇을 할 계획인가?
(A) 신규 해외 지사를 연다
(B) 영업 시간을 연장한다
(C) 직원들의 가족을 만난다
(D) 직원들로부터 피드백을 얻는다

해설 대화 중반에 여자가 "We're expanding the branch in Tokyo next year ~."라며 내년에 도쿄에서 지점을 확장한다고 했으므로 해외 지점을 연다는 (A)가 정답이다.

Questions 4-6 refer to the following conversation.

M: Hi, Sunisa. We should begin an advertising campaign for our Food Community Fair on television and radio to attract more people. Unfortunately, many people in the area still aren't familiar with the event.
W: Actually, we probably cannot afford to do that. But why don't you forward me a budget proposal? I'll take a look at it and see if I can convince the board of directors.
M: Thank you. I'll put together the proposal right away. Just so you know, from next Monday the local broadcasting network is offering a big discount for first-time TV advertisers. It might be a great opportunity for us.

M: 안녕하세요, Sunisa. 우리는 음식 지역사회 박람회에 더 많은 사람들을 끌어 모으기 위해 텔레비전과 라디오 광고를 시작해야 해요. 안타깝게도 지역의 많은 사람들이 이 행사를 잘 몰라요.
W: 사실 저희는 그럴 여유가 없어요. 그래도 저한테 예산 기획안을 보내 보시겠어요? 제가 이사진을 설득할 수 있을지 한번 볼게요.
M: 고마워요. 지금 바로 기획안을 준비할게요. 참고로 말하자면, 다음주 월요일부터 지역 방송국이 첫 텔레비전 광고주들에게 대폭 할인을 제공해요. 저희에게 굉장한 기회가 될 거예요.

어휘 attract 끌다   be familiar with ~에 친숙하다
forward 보내다   budget 예산   convince 설득하다
board of directors 이사회   put together 준비하다
broadcasting 방송(업)   advertiser 광고주

4. What does the man recommend?
   (A) Advertising on television
   (B) Switching the day of an event
   (C) Conducting a survey
   (D) Entertaining people in the area

   남자는 무엇을 추천하는가?
   (A) 텔레비전에 광고하는 것
   (B) 행사 날짜를 바꾸는 것
   (C) 설문조사를 하는 것
   (D) 지역 사람들을 즐겁게 하는 것

   해설 남자의 첫 대사에서 "We should begin an advertising campaign for our Food Community Fair on television ~."라며 행사에 대한 텔레비전 광고를 시작해야 한다고 말하고 있다. 따라서 정답은 (A)이다.

5. What does the woman ask the man to do?
   (A) Communicate with employees
   (B) Reduce expenses
   (C) Attend a board meeting
   (D) Send a plan

   여자는 남자에게 무엇을 하라고 요구하는가?
   (A) 직원들과 소통한다
   (B) 지출을 줄인다
   (C) 이사회에 참석한다
   (D) 계획안을 보낸다

   해설 TV 광고를 해야 한다는 남자의 말에 여자가 그럴 여유가 없다면서 "why don't you forward me a budget proposal?" 예산 기획안을 보내보라고 했다. 따라서 (D)가 정답이다.

6. What does the man say will start on Monday?
   (A) A clearance sale
   (B) An important project
   (C) A special offer
   (D) A television show

   남자는 월요일에 무엇이 시작할 거라고 말하는가?
   (A) 재고 정리 세일
   (B) 중요한 프로젝트
   (C) 특별 할인
   (D) 텔레비전 쇼

   해설 대화 후반에 남자가 "from next Monday the local broadcasting network is offering a big discount ~."라며 월요일부터 지역 방송국이 대폭 할인을 제공할 거라고 말했으므로 정답은 (C)이다.

Questions 7-9 refer to the following conversation.

W: Hello, this is Kale Industries. You have reached the front desk. How may I help you today?
M: Hi, my name is Martin Miller. I bought the NCN Shredder last week, but it broke yesterday. I want to know if I can replace it with a new one.
W: I'm sorry to hear that. You'll be happy to know that all purchases at our store have a one-year warranty. So please drop by, and we will be happy to offer you a new shredder.
M: What a relief! I was worried that I had lost my money. Is there anything else I need to bring with me?
W: Yes. Please bring your original receipt.
M: Sure! I'll be there shortly.

W: 안녕하세요, Kale Industries입니다. 안내 데스크에 연결되셨습니다. 무엇을 도와드릴까요?
M: 안녕하세요. 제 이름은 Martin Miller입니다. 지난주에 NCN 파쇄기를 샀는데 어제 고장 났어요. 새것으로 교체할 수 있는지 해서요.
W: 유감이네요. 저희 매장의 모든 제품은 1년의 보증 기간이 있어요. 그러니 방문하시면 저희가 새 파쇄기로 드리겠습니다.
M: 다행이네요! 돈을 날렸을까 봐 걱정했어요. 그밖에 제가 가져가야 할 게 있나요?
W: 네, 영수증 원본을 가져오세요.
M: 네! 곧 갈게요.

어휘 shredder 파쇄기 replace 교체하다 warranty 품질보증서 drop by 들르다 relief 안도 receipt 영수증 shortly 곧

7. Why is the man calling?
(A) To inquire about a product
(B) To cancel an appointment
(C) To confirm a client's schedule
(D) To book a repair service

남자는 왜 전화하는가?
(A) 제품에 대해 문의하기 위해
(B) 약속을 취소하기 위해
(C) 고객의 일정을 확인하기 위해
(D) 수리 서비스를 예약하기 위해

해설 남자의 첫 대사에서 "I bought the NCN Shredder last week but it broke yesterday. I want to know if I can replace it with a new one."라며 지난주에 파쇄기를 샀는데 부서져서 새것으로 교체가 가능한지를 문의하고 있음을 알 수 있다. 따라서 정답은 (A)이다.

8. What does the woman offer to do?
(A) Schedule a repair
(B) Provide a replacement
(C) Waive a service fee
(D) Place an advertisement online

여자는 무엇을 해주겠다고 하는가?
(A) 수리 일정 정하기
(B) 교체품 제공하기
(C) 서비스 요금 면제하기
(D) 온라인에 광고하기

해설 여자가 해주겠다고 하는 것을 묻고 있으므로 여자의 대사에 집중하자. "~ we will be happy to offer you a new shredder."라며 새 기계로 바꿔주겠다고 했으므로 정답은 (B)이다.

9. What will the man most likely do next?
(A) Print a receipt
(B) Purchase a magazine
(C) Make a telephone call
(D) Visit a store

남자는 다음에 무엇을 할 것 같은가?
(A) 영수증 인쇄하기
(B) 잡지 구입하기
(C) 전화하기
(D) 가게 방문하기

해설 대화 후반에서 여자가 영수증 원본을 가지고 오면 물건을 바꿔주겠다고 하니 남자가 "I'll be there shortly."라며 곧 가겠다고 했다. 따라서 정답은 (D)이다.

Questions 10-12 refer to the following conversation.

W: You've reached Dook's Grill. What can I do for you?
M: Hello. I'd like to make a dinner reservation for 10 to 12 people.
W: Sure. We can accommodate the number of people you want. But, we have an extra service charge for groups of 10 or more. Is that okay?
M: No problem. Our company will pay for it. Please book the table this Friday at six.
W: Great. And you're in luck! This Friday we'll have a live jazz band playing, starting at seven. Many people really like it.

W: Dook's Grill입니다. 무엇을 도와드릴까요?
M: 안녕하세요. 10~12명 정도로 저녁 식사를 예약하고 싶은데요.
W: 네, 원하시는 인원을 수용할 수 있습니다. 하지만 10명 이상 단체일 때 추가 서비스 요금이 붙는데 괜찮으신가요?
M: 괜찮아요. 저희 회사가 지불할 거예요. 금요일 6시로 예약해주세요.
W: 좋습니다. 그리고 운이 좋으시네요! 이번 주 금요일 7시에 시작하는 재즈 라이브 공연이 있어요. 많은 사람들이 정말 좋아하는 공연이죠.

어휘 reach 연락하다 make a reservation 예약하다 accommodate 수용하다 charge 요금

10. What are the speakers mainly discussing?
(A) An itinerary
(B) A room schedule
(C) A dinner recipe
(D) A dining reservation

화자들은 주로 무엇에 대해 논의하는가?
(A) 여행 일정
(B) 방 사용 일정
(C) 저녁 조리법
(D) 식사 예약

해설 대화 초반에 남자가 "I'd like to make a dinner reservation ~."라며 저녁 예약을 원한다고 했으므로 정답은 (D)이다.

11. What does the woman notify the man about?

(A) An extra fee
(B) A long wait
(C) A lack of space
(D) A limited menu

여자는 남자에게 무엇에 대해 알려주는가?
(A) 추가 요금
(B) 오랜 대기
(C) 공간 부족
(D) 제한된 메뉴

해설 여자가 "~ we have an extra service charge for groups of 10 or more ~"라며 10명 이상일 경우 추가 요금을 내야 한다고 말하고 있다. 따라서 정답은 (A)이다.

12. According to the woman, what is scheduled for Friday evening?

(A) A play
(B) A musical performance
(C) A movie screening
(D) A cooking demonstration

여자에 따르면, 금요일 저녁에 무슨 일정이 있는가?
(A) 연극
(B) 음악 공연
(C) 영화 상영
(D) 요리 시연회

해설 대화 후반에 여자가 "This Friday we'll have a live jazz band playing, starting at seven."라며 금요일 저녁에 재즈 공연이 있다고 했으므로 정답은 (B)이다.

Questions 13-15 refer to the following conversation.

W: Excuse me, sir, but I think you're in my seat, 10A.
M: I'll check my ticket. Hmm… No, it says that the seat number is right. 10A as well.
W: Well, this is the first floor. Are you sure you're on the right floor?
M: Let me see. Oh, sorry, I'm 10A on the second floor. I've put my bags under the chair. So just give me a moment to get my belongings together.
W: No problem. Take your time.

W: 실례합니다만, 제 자리인 10A에 앉아 계신 것 같은데요.
M: 제 티켓을 확인해 볼게요. 흠… 아니요, 제 좌석 번호는 10A가 역시 맞아요.
W: 음, 이곳은 1층이에요. 맞는 층에 계신 게 확실한가요?
M: 확인해 볼게요. 아, 죄송합니다. 저는 2층 10A이네요. 좌석 아래에 제 가방이 있어요. 잠시 제 소지품 좀 챙길게요.
W: 그럼요. 천천히 하세요.

어휘 seat 좌석 floor 층 belongings 소지품 take time 천천히 하다

13. What are the speakers talking about?

(A) A performance time
(B) A seat assignment
(C) A ticket price
(D) A theater location

화자들은 무엇에 대해 말하고 있는가?
(A) 공연 시간
(B) 좌석 배치
(C) 티켓 가격
(D) 극장 위치

해설 첫 대화에서 여자가 "~ but I think you're in my seat, 10A."라며 남자에게 자기 자리에 앉아 있지 않냐면서 서로 좌석을 확인하는 내용이 이어지고 있다. 따라서 정답은 (B)이다.

14. What is the man's problem?

(A) He was confused about the seat area.
(B) He had the wrong ticket.
(C) He doesn't know the woman well.
(D) He lost his bags.

남자의 문제는 무엇인가?
(A) 그는 좌석 구역을 헷갈렸다.
(B) 그는 잘못된 티켓을 가지고 있었다.
(C) 그는 여자를 잘 모른다.
(D) 그는 가방을 잃어버렸다.

해설 여자가 "Are you sure you're on the right floor?"라며 남자의 좌석 층수를 확인해 보라고 하자 남자가 "sorry, I'm 10A on the second floor."라며 자기 좌석은 2층이라고 정정하고 있다. 즉, 좌석을 헷갈렸다는 (A)가 정답이다.

15. What does the man say he will do?

(A) Arrange the chairs

(B) Collect his possessions

(C) Refund the ticket

(D) Speak with an organizer

남자는 무엇을 할 거라고 말하는가?
(A) 의자 배열하기
(B) 소지품 챙기기
(C) 티켓 환불하기
(D) 주최자와 말하기

해설 대화 후반에 남자가 좌석을 옮기면서 "~ just give me a moment to get my belongings together."라며 짐을 챙기겠다고 했으므로 정답은 (B)이다.

Questions 16-18 refer to the following conversation.

W: Hello, I'm calling about my mobile phone bill. I haven't received last month's bill. I'm wondering what the problem is, since I already gave my new address when I moved two months ago. My name is Angela Nelson.

M: All right. I'll check it. Oh, I think we didn't update your account. Did you change your new address online by any chance?

W: Yes, I did it on your Web site.

M: Actually, our Web site had some errors last month, so your account has been affected. I'll revise your contact information right now. Sorry for the inconvenience.

W: 안녕하세요, 제 휴대폰 청구서 때문에 연락 드립니다. 지난달에 청구서를 못 받았어요. 뭐가 문제인지 궁금해서요. 제가 두 달 전에 이사했을 때 새 주소를 이미 줬거든요. 제 이름은 Angela Nelson입니다.

M: 알겠습니다, 확인할게요. 아, 당신의 계정을 업데이트하지 않은 것 같은데요. 혹시 새 주소를 온라인에서 바꾸셨나요?

W: 네, 웹사이트에서 했어요.

M: 사실, 지난달에 저희 웹사이트에 오류가 좀 있어서 귀하의 계정이 영향을 받은 것 같아요. 지금 바로 연락처를 수정하겠습니다. 불편을 드려 죄송합니다.

어휘 bill 청구서 account 계정, 계좌 by any chance 혹시라도 error 오류 affect 영향을 미치다 revise 변경하다 contact information 연락처 inconvenience 불편

16. What type of business is the woman calling?

(A) An Internet provider

(B) A computer store

(C) An accounting firm

(D) A phone company

여자는 어떤 업체에 연락하고 있는가?
(A) 인터넷 공급업체
(B) 컴퓨터 매장
(C) 회계사무소
(D) 전화 회사

해설 여자의 첫 대사에서 "I'm calling about my mobile phone bill."이라며 휴대폰 청구서 때문에 연락했다고 했으므로 정답은 (D)이다.

17. What does the man mention about the company?

(A) They replaced their ID cards.

(B) They had some system problems.

(C) They moved last month.

(D) They updated their Web site.

남자는 회사에 대해 무엇을 언급하는가?
(A) 신분증을 교체했다.
(B) 시스템 문제가 있었다.
(C) 지난 달에 이사했다.
(D) 웹사이트를 업데이트했다.

해설 여자가 웹 사이트에서 새 주소를 변경했다고 하자 남자가 "our Web Site had some errors last month ~."라며 지난 달에 회사 웹사이트에 오류가 있었다고 했다. 따라서 정답은 (B)이다.

18. What will the man probably do next?

(A) Change the phone number

(B) Update the account

(C) Give contact information

(D) Go to the convenience store

남자는 다음에 무엇을 할 것 같은가?
(A) 전화번호를 바꾼다
(B) 계정을 업데이트한다
(C) 연락처를 준다
(D) 편의점에 간다

해설 대화 후반부에 남자가 "I'll revise your contact information right now."라며 연락처를 수정하겠다고 했으므로 정답은 (B)이다.

Questions 19-21 refer to the following conversation.

M: Hi, Melanie. Since it's your first day here at the warehouse and we're about to receive a shipment, do you have any questions?
W: I learned a lot at the training this morning. It was very helpful, but I'm not exactly sure about the inventory system. How do we keep track of the shipments we've unloaded?
M: You just use the scanner here to scan each package as you unload it from the truck. Then place the package in the offloading zone.
W: Okay. I used a similar process at my previous job.
M: Good. If you have any more questions after today, there's information on page 15 of your training instructions.

M: 안녕하세요, Melanie. 당신은 여기 창고에서 일하는 첫날이고 우리는 곧 선적을 받을 예정인데, 질문 있나요?
W: 오늘 오전에 교육을 많이 받았어요. 정말 도움이 됐어요. 하지만 재고 관리 시스템에 대해 정확히 모르겠어요. 우리가 내리는 선적들을 어떻게 기록하나요?
M: 트럭에서 짐을 내릴 때 여기 스캐너로 스캔하면 돼요. 그러고 나서 하역 구역에 짐을 두면 됩니다.
W: 알겠어요. 전 직장에서 비슷한 과정을 했어요.
M: 좋네요. 오늘 이후에 질문이 있으면 교육 설명서 15페이지에 정보가 있어요.

어휘 warehouse 창고 shipment 선적 inventory 재고 keep track of ~을 기록하다 unload (짐을) 내리다 previous 이전의 instructions 설명(서)

19. Who is the woman?
(A) A delivery person
(B) A new employee
(C) A warehouse supervisor
(D) A truck driver

여자는 누구인가?
(A) 배달원
(B) 신입사원
(C) 창고 감독관
(D) 트럭 운전사

해설 첫 대사에서 남자가 여자에게 "it's your first day here at the warehouse ~."라며 근무 첫날이라고 했으므로 여자는 신입사원임을 알 수 있다. 따라서 정답은 (B)이다.

20. What does the woman ask about?
(A) Some delivery processes
(B) A training schedule
(C) Some manufacturing equipment
(D) An inventory process

여자는 무엇에 대해 묻는가?
(A) 배달 과정
(B) 교육 일정
(C) 제조 장비
(D) 재고 관리 절차

해설 여자의 대사 중 "I'm not exactly sure about ~ keep track of the shipments we've unloaded?"라며 재고 관리 시스템에 대해 잘 모르겠다면서 어떻게 하는지 물었으므로 답은 (D)이다.

21. According to the man, how can the woman find additional information?
(A) By contacting a supervisor
(B) By checking a training manual
(C) By visiting a Web site
(D) By posting questions on a bulletin board

남자에 따르면, 여자는 어떻게 추가 정보를 찾을 수 있는가?
(A) 감독관에게 연락함으로써
(B) 교육 설명서를 확인함으로써
(C) 웹사이트를 방문함으로써
(D) 게시판에 질문을 게시함으로써

해설 질문이 According to the man ~으로 시작하므로 남자의 대사에 집중하자. 대화 후반에 남자가 "~ there's information on page 15 of your training instructions."라면서 교육 설명서에 정보가 있다고 했으므로 정답은 (B)이다.

Questions 22-24 refer to the following conversation.

M: Thanks for coming. My name is William. I'm the head of this department. We're very excited to work with you. I was especially impressed with your skills in Web site design.
W: It's nice to meet you, William. You said I should start by looking over the company's various Web pages to find things to upgrade.
M: Yes, and we'd like you to present your creative ideas at our group meeting this Wednesday.
W: Sure, I can do that on Wednesday.

M: 와 주셔서 고마워요. 제 이름은 William입니다. 여기 부서장입니다. 당신과 같이 일하게 되어 정말 기뻐요. 특히 당신의 웹사이트 디자인 기술이 인상 깊었어요.
W: 만나서 반갑습니다, William. 업그레이드할 것을 찾기 위해 회사의 다양한 웹 페이지를 훑어보는 것부터 하라고 하셨죠.
M: 네, 그리고 당신이 이번 주 수요일에 있을 단체 회의에서 창의적인 아이디어를 제시해 주면 좋겠어요.
W: 당연하죠, 수요일에 그렇게 할 수 있어요.

어휘 department 부서   be impressed with ~에 감명 받다
look over 검토하다   various 다양한   creative 창의적인

22. Who is the woman?

(A) A Web designer
(B) A salesperson
(C) A personnel manager
(D) The head of the sales department

여자는 누구인가?
(A) 웹 디자이너
(B) 판매 사원
(C) 인사 부장
(D) 영업 부장

해설 화자의 신분/직업은 대화 초반에 주로 제시된다. 남자가 "I was especially impressed with your skills in Web site design."라며 여자의 웹사이트 디자인 기술에 감명 받았다고 했으므로 정답은 (A)이다.

23. What has the woman been assigned to do?

(A) Develop more efficient processes
(B) Review online materials
(C) Upgrade the computers
(D) Reach financial goals

여자는 무슨 일을 할당 받았는가?
(A) 더 효율적인 과정 개발하기
(B) 온라인 자료 검토하기
(C) 컴퓨터 업그레이드하기
(D) 재정 목표에 도달하기

해설 여자가 남자에게 "I should start by looking over ~ find things to upgrade."라며 다양한 웹페이지 검토를 지시 받았음을 언급했으므로 답은 (B)이다.

24. What does the man want the woman to do?

(A) Share her comments
(B) Select a group
(C) Change the meeting time
(D) Get familiar with other people

남자는 여자가 무엇을 하기를 바라는가?
(A) 의견 나누기
(B) 그룹 선택하기
(C) 회의 시간 바꾸기
(D) 다른 사람들과 친해지기

해설 대화 후반에 "we'd like you to present your creative ideas at our group meeting this Wednesday."라며 수요일 회의에서 창의적 아이디어를 발표해 달라고 했으므로 정답은 (A)이다.

DAY 11 의도 파악/시각 자료

SPARTA Check-UP
p.78

1. (A) 2. (D) 3. (B) 4. (B) 5. (C)
6. (D)

[1-3]

M: Alice, I just heard that <u>you will lead the orientation</u> for new employees in the legal department. It's a good opportunity for you.
W: It is. I'm doing it Tuesday after lunchtime. Can I ask a favor? I was wondering <u>if you might sit in on</u> this first class and give me some feedback afterward, because you are the most experienced lawyer in our firm.
M: Oh, I'm really sorry. I'm going to <u>go on an important business trip on Monday</u>. I won't be back until Wednesday. But maybe I can participate in your next class. When's the second class?
W: Thank you. Next Tuesday.

M: Alice, 법무부의 신입 사원들을 위한 오리엔테이션을 당신이 이끈다고 방금 들었어요. 당신한테 좋은 기회네요.
W: 네, 화요일 점심 이후에 해요. 부탁 하나 해도 될까요? 첫 수업에 앉아 있다가 나중에 피드백을 주실 수 있을까 해서요. 당신이 우리 회사에서 가장 경력 있는 변호사잖아요.
M: 아, 정말 죄송해요. 월요일에 중요한 출장을 갈 예정이에요. 수요일이나 되어야 돌아올 거예요. 하지만 아마 다음 수업에는 참석할 수 있을 것 같아요. 두 번째 수업이 언제죠?
W: 고마워요. 다음주 화요일이에요.

어휘 legal department 법무부   opportunity 기회   afterward 후에   experienced 경험 있는, 유능한   lawyer 변호사   business trip 출장   participate in ~에 참석하다

1. What is the woman doing on Tuesday?
   (A) Training new hires
   (B) Distributing legal documents
   (C) Moving to a new department
   (D) Going on vacation

   화요일에 여자는 무엇을 할 것인가?
   (A) 신입 사원들을 교육하는 것
   (B) 법률 자료들을 나눠주는 것
   (C) 새로운 부서로 이동하는 것
   (D) 휴가 가는 것

해설 남자의 첫 대사에서 "I just heard that you will lead the orientation for new employees."라며 신입사원 오리엔테이션을 한다고 들었다고 했고 여자가 이어서 화요일이라고 언급했다. 따라서 답은 (A)이다. new employees가 new hires로 패러프레이징 되었다.

2. Why does the woman say, "you are the most experienced lawyer in our firm"?
   (A) To get the man promoted
   (B) To revise a mistake
   (C) To remind a colleague of a new procedure
   (D) To explain a request

   여자는 왜 "당신이 우리 회사에서 가장 경력 있는 변호사잖아요"라고 말하는가?
   (A) 남자를 승진시키기 위해
   (B) 실수를 수정하기 위해
   (C) 동료에게 새로운 절차를 알려 주기 위해
   (D) 요청 사항을 설명하기 위해

해설 여자가 남자에게 자신의 수업에 참석 후 피드백을 달라면서 "You are the most experienced lawyer in our firm."라고 덧붙이고 있으므로 본인의 요청 사항을 설명하기 위해 한 말임을 알 수 있다. 따라서 정답은 (D)이다.

3. What will the man do on Monday?
   (A) Send some forms
   (B) Travel on company business
   (C) Participate in some negotiations
   (D) Attend the next class

   남자는 월요일에 무엇을 할 건인가?
   (A) 양식을 보낸다
   (B) 출장을 간다
   (C) 협상에 참여한다
   (D) 다음 수업에 참석한다

해설 대화 후반에 남자가 "I'm going to go on an important business trip on Monday."라며 월요일에 중요한 출장을 간다고 했으므로 정답은 (B)이다.

[4-6]

M: Hi, Tina. It's lunchtime. Why are you still working?
W: I'm not working. I'm looking for a used car on this Web site. Train ticket fares have gone up again, and a car actually works out <u>cheaper in the long run</u>.
M: I see. Well, how about this one? It's only three years old.

W: It's almost six thousand dollars! This one here looks good enough, and it's the cheapest I've found so far.
M: So, are you going to call the dealer? Someone else might get it before you.
W: I'll need to go home and ask my husband, Mike, first. He knows exactly how much we can afford to spend.

M: 안녕하세요, Tina. 지금 점심시간이에요. 왜 아직도 일하고 있어요?
W: 일하는 거 아니에요. 웹사이트에서 중고차를 보고 있어요. 기차표 요금이 계속 오르고 있어서 장기적으로는 자동차가 더 저렴하다는 계산이 나오거든요.
M: 그렇군요. 음, 이건 어때요? 3년밖에 안 됐어요.
W: 거의 6000달러네요! 이거면 충분히 좋을 것 같고 지금까지 본 것 중 제일 싸요.
M: 그럼 딜러에게 전화할 거죠? 당신이 사기 전에 다른 누군가 살 수도 있어요.
W: 먼저 집에 가서 남편 Mike한테 물어봐야 해요. 얼마나 지출할 수 있는지 그가 정확히 알거든요.

어휘 used car 중고차 fare 요금 in the long run 장기적으로 so far 지금까지 dealer 중개인 afford 여유가 되다

모델	가격
Candon	7,500달러
Zester	6,500달러
Promo	5,900달러
Santa	9,900달러

4. Why does the woman want to buy a car?
   (A) To drive to the train station
   (B) To save money
   (C) To enjoy her weekends
   (D) To get a driver's license

   왜 여자는 차를 사고 싶어 하는가?
   (A) 기차역으로 운전하기 위해
   (B) 돈을 절약하기 위해
   (C) 주말을 즐기기 위해
   (D) 운전 면허증을 따기 위해

   해설 여자의 첫 대사 중 "Train ticket fares have gone up again, and a car actually works out cheaper in the long run."에서 기차표 가격이 계속 올라서 차를 사는 것이 장기적으로 볼 때 더 싸다고 했으므로 이와 의미가 통하는 (B)가 정답이다.

5. Look at the graphic. What vehicle is the woman most interested in?
   (A) Candon
   (B) Zester
   (C) Promo
   (D) Santa

   도표를 보시오. 여자는 어떤 차량에 관심 있는가?
   (A) Candon
   (B) Zester
   (C) Promo
   (D) Santa

   해설 보기가 모델명으로 표기되어 있으므로 가격과 관련하여 단서가 제시될 것이다. 대화 중반부에 여자가 "It's almost six thousand dollars! This one here looks good enough, and it's the cheapest I've found so far."라며 거의 6,000달러이고 가장 저렴하다고 말하고 있다. 따라서 이 기준을 충족시키는 (C)가 정답이다.

6. What will the woman do later?
   (A) Look on another Web site
   (B) Borrow some money
   (C) Contact the car dealer
   (D) Consult her spouse

   여자는 나중에 무엇을 할 것인가?
   (A) 다른 웹사이트 보기
   (B) 돈 빌리기
   (C) 자동차 판매원에게 연락하기
   (D) 배우자와 상의하기

   해설 대화 후반에 남자가 빨리 사지 않으면 다른 사람이 살 수도 있다고 하자, 여자가 "I'll need to go home and ask my husband, Mike, first."라며 집에 가서 남편에게 먼저 물어봐야 한다고 했으므로 정답은 (D)이다.

SPARTA Practice Test
p.79

1. (C)	2. (A)	3. (B)	4. (B)	5. (B)
6. (A)	7. (B)	8. (D)	9. (C)	10. (C)
11. (B)	12. (A)	13. (B)	14. (A)	15. (D)
16. (A)	17. (B)	18. (B)	19. (D)	20. (C)
21. (D)	22. (D)	23. (A)	24. (A)	25. (A)
26. (B)	27. (D)			

Questions 1-3 refer to the following conversation and schedule.

W: Hi, Tom. I hope you're ready for your presentation today. I can't find the draft for my speech, and the science conference starts at eight this morning.

M: Sorry to hear that. Yes, I did have a chance to review some material last night. Do you need some help finding your draft? We can search your office together.

W: No, that's all right. I already looked everywhere. I'm going to call the organizer and ask him to delay my presentation for an hour. Maybe I can switch with Mr. West. That will give me time to reprint the details and look them over.

M: That's a good idea. I'll see you there later.

W: 안녕하세요, Tom. 오늘 발표가 준비되었기를 바랍니다. 제 연설 원고를 못 찾겠어요. 그리고 과학 학회는 오늘 아침 8시에 시작하고요.

M: 안됐네요. 네, 저는 지난밤에 자료를 검토했어요. 원고를 찾는 거 도와드릴까요? 당신 사무실에서 함께 찾아요.

W: 아니요, 괜찮아요. 이미 모든 곳을 찾아 봤어요. 주최자한테 전화해서 제 발표를 한 시간 미뤄 달라고 요청하려고요. 아마 West 씨와 바꿀 수 있을 것 같아요. 그러면 세부 사항들을 다시 인쇄해서 훑어볼 수 있을 거예요.

M: 좋은 생각이네요. 나중에 거기에서 봐요.

어휘 draft 원고 organizer 주최자 delay 미루다 switch 바꾸다 look over 훑어보다

제45회 과학 학회
Golan 타워 1층

시간	발표자
오전 8시 ~ 8시 50분	Lucy Hynam
오전 9시 ~ 9시 50분	Derrick West
오전 10시 ~ 10시 50분	Paula Collins
오전 11시 ~ 11시 50분	Samantha Smith

1. Why is the woman concerned?
   (A) She thinks a printer is broken.
   (B) She didn't send her résumé.
   (C) She lost the draft for a speech.
   (D) She forgot about an appointment.

   왜 여자는 걱정하는가?
   (A) 그녀는 프린터가 고장 났다고 생각한다.
   (B) 그녀는 이력서를 보내지 않았다.
   (C) 그녀는 연설 원고를 잃어버렸다.
   (D) 그녀는 약속에 대해 잊어버렸다.

   해설 대화 초반에 여자가 "I can't find the draft for my speech."라며 연설 원고를 찾을 수 없다고 했으므로 정답은 (C)이다.

2. What did the man do last night?
   (A) Prepare for his speech
   (B) Checked his flight schedule
   (C) Went to the woman's office
   (D) Wrote an e-mail

   남자는 지난밤에 무엇을 했는가?
   (A) 연설을 준비했다
   (B) 비행 일정을 확인했다
   (C) 여자의 사무실에 갔다
   (D) 메일을 썼다

   해설 남자의 첫 대사에서 "I did have a chance to review some material last night."라며 지난밤에 자료를 검토했다고 했으므로 연설 준비를 했다는 (A)가 정답이다.

3. Look at the graphic. What time will the woman probably give her presentation?
   (A) 8:00 A.M.
   (B) 9:00 A.M.
   (C) 10:00 A.M.
   (D) 11:00 A.M.

   도표를 보시오. 여자는 발표를 몇 시에 할 것 같은가?
   (A) 오전 8시
   (B) 오전 9시
   (C) 오전 10시
   (D) 오전 11시

   해설 여자가 주최자에게 연설을 한 시간 연기해 달라고 요청할 거라고 한 후 "Maybe I can switch with Mr. West."라며 West 씨와 바꿀 수 있을 거라고 했다. 표를 보면 West 씨는 9시에 연설하므로 정답은 (B)이다.

Questions 4-6 refer to the following conversation.

W: Hey, Albert. I haven't seen you around much lately. Are you working on a new assignment or something?

M: They've got me traveling weekly now that I'm in the sales department. There's still a lot to learn, but so far the relationships I'm forming with our customers are very rewarding.

W: Oh, that's right! It's quite a change for you.

M: Yes, but a good one. I'm much happier now coming to work each day. The hotels and time away from family is already tiring me out, but now, I like that my work is different every day.

360

W: 안녕하세요, Albert. 최근에 못 본 것 같은데요. 새로운 일이나 다른 일을 하고 있어요?
M: 일주일 출장 다녀 왔어요. 제가 지금 판매부에 있거든요. 여전히 배울 게 많지만 지금까지 제가 고객들과 맺는 관계들이 매우 보람 있어요.
W: 아, 맞네요! 당신한테 꽤 변화가 되겠어요.
M: 네, 하지만 좋은 것은요. 저는 매일 일하러 오는 지금이 정말 행복해요. 가족들과 떨어져 있는 시간과 호텔 생활에 벌써 지쳤지만 지금 제 업무가 매일 달라서 좋아요.

어휘 lately 최근에 assignment 임무, 배치 relationship 관계 form 구성하다 rewarding 보람 있는 quite 꽤 tire out 녹초가 되게 만들다

4. Why hasn't the woman seen the man lately?
(A) He is busy with projects.
(B) He started a new position.
(C) He is training a coworker.
(D) He traveled to many countries.

왜 여자는 최근에 남자를 못 봤는가?
(A) 그는 프로젝트로 바쁘다.
(B) 그는 새로운 일을 시작했다.
(C) 그는 동료를 교육하고 있다.
(D) 그는 많은 나라들을 여행 다녔다.

해설 여자가 남자에게 최근에 자주 못 봤다고 하자, 남자가 "They've got me traveling weekly now that I'm in the sales department."라며 현재 판매부에서 일하고 있다 즉, 새로운 일을 시작한 것임을 알 수 있다. 따라서 정답은 (B)이다.

5. What does the woman mean when she says, "Oh, that's right"?
(A) She is looking forward to working with the man.
(B) She agrees with the man's situation.
(C) She remembers her time working in sales.
(D) She failed to finish her assignment on time.

여자가 "아, 맞아요"라고 말할 때 의도하는 것은 무엇인가?
(A) 그녀는 남자와 일하는 것을 기대하고 있다.
(B) 그녀는 남자의 상황에 동의한다.
(C) 그녀는 판매부에서 일한 시간을 기억한다.
(D) 그녀는 시간에 맞춰 일을 끝내는 데 실패했다.

해설 남자가 판매부에서 새로운 일을 시작했다고 하자 여자가 "Oh, that's right!"이라고 한 후 "It's quite a change for you."라며 꽤 변화가 생겼겠다고 했다. 남자의 말에 동의를 표하며 한 말이므로 정답은 (B)이다.

6. What doesn't the man like about his job?
(A) Staying in hotels
(B) Working with his coworkers
(C) Getting to know clients
(D) Learning new things

남자는 그의 업무에 대해 무엇을 좋아하지 않는가?
(A) 호텔에 머무는 것
(B) 그의 동료들과 일하는 것
(C) 고객들을 알아 가는 것
(D) 새로운 것들을 배우는 것

해설 후반부의 남자의 대사에서 "The hotels and time away from family is already tiring me out, ~"라며 호텔 생활에 지쳐간다고 했으므로 정답은 (A)이다.

Questions 7-9 refer to the following conversation.

W: Mr. Collins, I heard you just opened your own bakery. How's the business doing?
M: Great so far! More and more people are coming to buy our baked goods. And next week there's going to be a feature about us in Health Food magazine. I'm really looking forward to that.
W: Congratulations! That should help you attract a lot of customers.
M: I think so. The reporter is going to mention our facilities and atmosphere. Also, the article will focus more on our special popular goods, like the tart we offer.
W: That's nice. I haven't tried your tart.
M: From 11 everyday, you can try it at our store.
W: Okay, maybe I'll come by tomorrow.

W: Collins 씨, 얼마 전에 빵집을 열었다는 소식을 들었어요. 사업은 잘 되나요?
M: 지금까지는 좋아요! 점점 더 많은 사람들이 빵을 사러 오고 있어요. 그리고 다음 주에 Health Food 잡지에 특집 기사로 실릴 거예요. 정말 기대돼요.
W: 축하해요! 많은 고객들을 끌어모으는 데 도움이 되겠네요.
M: 저도 그렇게 생각해요. 기자가 저희 시설과 분위기를 언급할 거예요. 그리고 우리가 제공하는 타르트처럼 특히 인기 있는 빵에 기사가 초점을 맞출 거예요.
W: 멋져요. 타르트는 안 먹어 봤어요.
M: 매일 11시부터 저희 가게에서 맛볼 수 있어요.
W: 좋아요, 그러면 내일 들를게요.

어휘 bakery 빵집 more and more 점점 더 많은 feature 특집 기사 attract 끌다 mention 언급하다 facilities 시설 atmosphere 분위기 come by 들르다

7. What did the man recently do?

   (A) He wrote an article.

   (B) He started a business.

   (C) He won an award.

   (D) He published a book.

   남자는 최근에 무엇을 했는가?
   (A) 그는 기사를 썼다.
   (B) 그는 사업을 시작했다.
   (C) 그는 상을 받았다.
   (D) 그는 책을 출판했다.

   해설 대화의 첫 부분에서 여자가 "I heard you just opened your own bakery."라며 남자에게 새로 문을 연 빵집에 대해 언급하고 있다. 따라서 남자가 새로 사업을 시작했다는 것을 알 수 있으므로 정답은 (B)이다.

8. What is the man looking forward to?

   (A) Some baked goods

   (B) A cash prize

   (C) A radio interview

   (D) A magazine article

   남자는 무엇을 기대하고 있는가?
   (A) 빵
   (B) 상금
   (C) 라디오 인터뷰
   (D) 잡지 기사

   해설 남자가 "next week there's going to be a feature about us in Health Food magazine. I'm really looking forward to that."이라며 다음 주에 특집 기사가 잡지에 실릴 것이 기대된다고 했으므로 정답은 (D)이다.

9. Why does the man say, "you can try it at our store"?

   (A) To give an assignment

   (B) To suggest a different time

   (C) To extend an invitation

   (D) To express dissatisfaction

   남자는 왜 "저희 가게에서 맛볼 수 있어요"라고 말하는가?
   (A) 업무를 주기 위해
   (B) 다른 시간을 제안하기 위해
   (C) 초대하기 위해
   (D) 불만을 표현하기 위해

   해설 여자가 타르트를 안 먹어 봤다고 하자, "From 11 everyday, you can try it at our store."라며 매일 11시 이후에 먹어볼 수 있다고 했다. 즉 초대하려는 의도로 볼 수 있으므로 정답은 (C)이다.

Questions 10-12 refer to the following conversation and map.

M: Good morning. I passed by here on my way to work yesterday and saw you have some plots available in Highgate. I wonder if you could show me a brochure or something.

W: No problem, sir. Here is a layout of the site. There are currently four plots available, all at the same price.

M: Hmm… I didn't realize it was so close to the main road. It wouldn't be good for my young children.

W: What about one of the plots set back from the road?

M: Those trees may block the sun there, but the other plot looks perfect. Could we take a look now? If it's as good as it looks, I could have the money ready tomorrow.

W: Really? Wow! I'll show you right now.

M: 안녕하세요. 어제 출근 길에 여기를 지나가다가 Highgate에 이용할 수 있는 부지가 좀 있는 걸 봤어요. 책자나 자료를 보여 주실 수 있을까 해서요.
W: 그럼요. 이게 부지의 배치도예요. 현재는 4개의 부지가 이용 가능하고 가격은 모두 동일합니다.
M: 흠… 대로와 이렇게 가까운 곳인지는 몰랐네요. 저희 아이들한테는 안 좋을 것 같아요.
W: 도로에서 멀찍이 떨어져 있는 것 중 하나는 어때요?
M: 나무들이 거기에서 햇빛을 차단할지도 모르지만 다른 쪽 부지는 완벽하네요. 지금 봐도 될까요? 만약 실제로도 좋아 보이면 내일 돈을 준비할 수 있어요.
W: 정말요? 와! 지금 당장 보여 드리죠.

어휘 pass by ~의 옆을 지나가다 plot 부지, 작은 땅
brochure 책자 layout 배치도 currently 현재
block 막다

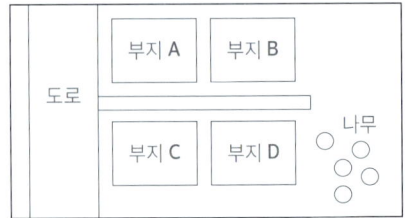

10. Where did the man learn about the land for sale?

    (A) On the Internet

    (B) On the radio

    (C) In the shop window

    (D) From a colleague

남자는 부지를 판다는 것을 어디서 알았는가?
(A) 인터넷에서
(B) 라디오에서
(C) 상점 진열장에서
(D) 동료로부터

해설 남자가 초반에 "I passed by here on my way to work yesterday and saw you have some plots available in Highgate."라며 어제 출근하는 길에 봤다고 했으므로 정답은 (C)이다.

11. Look at the graphic. Which plot is the man interested in?

    (A) Plot A
    (B) Plot B
    (C) Plot C
    (D) Plot D

    도표를 보시오. 남자는 어떤 부지에 관심 있는가?
    (A) 부지 A
    (B) 부지 B
    (C) 부지 C
    (D) 부지 D

해설 남자가 대로 근처는 아이들에게 좋지 않을 거라고 했고(It wouldn't be good for my young children), 이어서 한 말 "Those trees may block the sun there, but the other plot looks perfect."에서 어떤 부지는 햇빛이 차단될 수 있지만 다른 부지는 완벽해 보인다고 했다. 따라서 남자가 관심 있는 땅은 부지 B이다.

12. What is the woman surprised by?

    (A) The quick decision
    (B) The man's occupation
    (C) The opinion of the man's children
    (D) The location of a parking lot

    여자는 무엇에 놀라는가?
    (A) 빠른 결정
    (B) 남자의 직업
    (C) 남자의 아이들의 의견
    (D) 주차장의 위치

해설 대화 후반에서 남자가 "If it's as good as it looks, I could have the money ready tomorrow."라며 부지를 보고 마음에 들면 내일 돈을 준비할 수 있다고 하자, 여자가 놀라는 상황이다. 이는 남자의 빠른 결정에 놀라는 것으로 볼 수 있으므로 정답은 (A)이다.

Questions 13-15 refer to the following conversation.

W: We're about to leave to provide food for the event at the Medison Architecture firm, but we don't have enough dishes. Where can I find some?
M: Oh, no. I ordered some from our supplier three days ago, but they haven't arrived yet. This is the third time this has happened.
W: I think we should cancel that order. I'll stop by the store on the way to buy more. We don't have time because we're supposed to start setting up our tables at Medison Architecture by ten.
M: Okay. I'll call the vendor to cancel it and next time we'll just find another supplier.
W: I think you're right.

W: Medison 건축 회사 행사를 위한 음식을 제공하러 가려고 하는데요. 접시가 충분하지 않아요. 어디에 있나요?
M: 아, 안 돼요. 3일 전에 공급업체에 주문했는데 아직 도착하지 않았네요. 이런 일이 일어난 게 이번이 세 번째예요.
W: 주문을 취소해야 할 것 같아요. 제가 물건 사러 가는 길에 가게에 들를게요. 왜냐하면 10시까지 Medison 건축 회사에 테이블 설치를 시작하려면 시간이 없거든요.
M: 알았어요. 업체에 전화해서 취소하고 다음에는 다른 업체를 찾아야겠어요.
W: 당신 말이 맞는 것 같네요.

어휘 provide 제공하다 architecture firm 건축 회사
supplier 공급업체 on the way 도중에 set up 설치하다
vendor 판매사

13. Where do the speakers most likely work?

    (A) At an architecture firm
    (B) At a catering company
    (C) At a supermarket
    (D) At a medical clinic

    화자들은 어디에서 일하는 것 같은가?
    (A) 건축 회사에서
    (B) 출장 요리 업체에서
    (C) 슈퍼마켓에서
    (D) 병원에서

해설 대화 초반에 여자가 "We're about to leave to provide food for the event at the Medison Architecture firm, ~."라며 회사 행사를 위해 음식을 제공하러 간다고 했으므로 화자들이 일하는 곳은 출장 요리 업체임을 알 수 있다. 따라서 정답은 (B)이다.

14. Why does the man say, "This is the third time this has happened"?

(A) He is very disappointed with a vendor.
(B) He does not agree with an idea.
(C) He knows when the items are delivered.
(D) He is satisfied with a supplier.

남자는 왜 "이런 일이 일어난 게 이번이 세 번째예요"라고 말하는가?
(A) 그는 판매사에 매우 실망했다.
(B) 그는 그 생각에 동의하지 않는다.
(C) 그는 물품이 언제 배달되는지 안다.
(D) 그는 공급업체에 만족한다.

해설 남자가 "I ordered some from our supplier three days ago, but they haven't arrived yet."라며 3일 전에 주문했는데 아직 안 왔다고 한 후 한 말이므로, 공급업체에 실망감을 표현하고 있다는 것을 알 수 있다. 따라서 정답은 (A)이다.

15. What will the man most likely do next?

(A) Call the architecture firm
(B) Speak with a manager
(C) Stop by the store
(D) Call off the order

남자는 다음에 무엇을 할 것 같은가?
(A) 건축 회사에 전화하기
(B) 부장과 말하기
(C) 가게에 들르기
(D) 주문 취소하기

해설 대화 후반에 남자가 "I'll call the vendor to cancel it ~."라며 회사에 전화해서 취소하겠다고 했으므로 정답은 (D)이다.

Questions 16-18 refer to the following conversation.

M: Hi, Sarah. Our supervisor said you are in charge of training our new employees.
W: Yeah. Actually, the training begins next Monday. But I still have a lot of work to prepare the training documents. I haven't had any time to do other tasks.
M: Well, I've already completed my work. Can I give you a hand?
W: Thanks a lot! Could you bring the employee name tags from the security office for the new hires? I already requested them last week, but I haven't been informed about them yet.
M: Of course. I'll go there right away.

M: 안녕하세요, Sarah. 팀장님이 당신이 신입사원 교육을 담당한다고 하던데요.
W: 네, 사실, 교육은 다음주 월요일에 시작해요. 하지만 교육용 자료를 준비할 게 여전히 너무 많네요. 다른 업무 할 시간이 없었어요.
M: 음, 저는 이미 제 일을 끝냈어요. 도와드릴까요?
W: 정말 고마워요! 경비실에 가서 신입사원들을 위한 직원용 명찰을 가져다주시겠어요? 제가 이미 지난주에 신청했는데 아직 아무 소식이 없네요.
M: 물론이죠. 지금 바로 갈게요.

어휘 in charge of ~을 담당해서   document 문서   task 업무   give a hand 도와주다   name tag 명찰   new hire 신입사원

16. What are the speakers talking about?

(A) Training materials
(B) A job interview
(C) New employees
(D) Sales figures

화자들을 무엇에 대해 말하고 있는가?
(A) 교육 자료
(B) 일자리 면접
(C) 신입직원들
(D) 매출액

해설 대화의 주제는 주로 앞부분에 언급된다. 대화 초반에 여자가 "I still have a lot of work to prepare the training documents."라며 준비해야 할 교육용 문서가 많다고 했고 남자가 도와주겠다는 내용이 이어지고 있다. 따라서 정답은 (A)이다.

17. What does the man imply when he says, "I've already completed my work"?

(A) He wants comments on an assignment.
(B) He wants to offer assistance.
(C) He would like to leave for the day.
(D) He wants to train new hires.

남자가 "저는 이미 제 일을 끝냈어요"라고 말할 때 의도하는 것은 무엇인가?
(A) 그는 과제에 대한 의견을 원한다.
(B) 그는 도움을 주고 싶어 한다.
(C) 그는 퇴근하고 싶어 한다.
(D) 그는 신입사원들을 교육하고 싶어 한다.

해설 여자가 교육 자료 준비할 게 많다고 하자, 남자가 자신은 일을 끝냈다면서 "Can I give you a hand?"라며 도움이 필요한지를 묻고 있다. 따라서 정답은 (B)이다.

18. What will the man most likely do next?
   (A) Call the security office
   (B) Take care of the request
   (C) Contact the new hires
   (D) Make name tags

   남자는 다음에 무엇을 할 것 같은가?
   (A) 경비실에 전화하기
   (B) 요청 사항 처리하기
   (C) 신입사원들에게 연락하기
   (D) 명찰 만들기

   해설 대화 후반에 여자가 "Could you bring the employee name tags from the security office for the new hires?"라며 신입사원들을 위한 명찰을 가져와 달라고 요청하자, 남자가 "I'll go there right away."라며 지금 바로 가겠다고 했다. 따라서 정답은 (B)이다.

Questions 19-21 refer to the following conversation and map.

> M: Melissa, I've been asked to reposition the desks on our floor because the B Team keeps complaining about the windows being behind them. They say it's hard to see their computer screens with the reflections from outside.
> W: Why don't you put them by the door so the windows aren't a problem?
> M: They don't like the distraction of people coming and going.
> W: Okay, I've got it. They're the ones who print the most documents, so put them next to the photocopier. That would be convenient and take care of all their complaints.
>
> M: Melissa, B팀 사람들이 뒤에 있는 창문에 대해 계속 불평해서 이 층 책상 위치를 바꾸라는 요청을 받았어요. 그들은 밖에서 들어오는 빛이 반사되어서 컴퓨터 화면을 보기 힘들다고 하네요.
> W: 창문이 문제되지 않도록 사람들을 문 옆으로 배치하는 건 어때요?
> M: 그들은 오고 가는 사람들로 일을 방해 받는 걸 좋아하지 않아요.
> W: 좋아요, 이해했어요. 그들이 대부분의 서류를 인쇄하니까 복사기 옆에 앉게 해요. 그러면 편리하기도 하고 그들의 불평사항도 처리할 수 있겠네요.

어휘 reposition 위치를 바꾸다   reflection (빛) 반사
distraction 주의 산만   photocopier 복사기
convenient 편리한   complaint 불평 사항

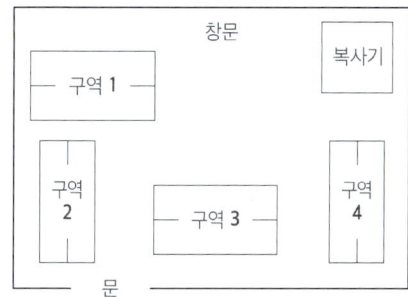

19. What has the man been asked to do?
   (A) Assign new projects
   (B) Schedule a window cleaning
   (C) Research new computers
   (D) Rearrange the office layout

   남자는 무엇을 하도록 요청 받았는가?
   (A) 새로운 프로젝트를 배정하는 것
   (B) 창문 청소 일정을 잡는 것
   (C) 새 컴퓨터를 조사하는 것
   (D) 사무실 레이아웃을 재배치하는 것

   해설 대화 초반에 남자가 "I've been asked to reposition the desks on our floor ~."라며 이 층의 책상 위치를 바꾸라는 요청을 받았다고 했으므로 정답은 (D)이다.

20. What is the B Team's problem with their current desk location?
   (A) They dislike the breeze.
   (B) They are bored with it.
   (C) The sunlight bothers them.
   (D) The view outside is distracting.

   현재의 책상 위치로 인한 B팀의 문제는 무엇인가?
   (A) 그들은 미풍을 좋아하지 않는다.
   (B) 그들은 책상 위치가 지겹다.
   (C) 햇빛이 그들을 방해한다.
   (D) 바깥 전망이 집중을 방해한다.

   해설 남자의 대사 중 "They say it's hard to see their computer screens with the reflections from outside."에서 B팀이 밖에서 들어오는 빛 반사로 컴퓨터 화면을 보기 힘들어 한다는 것을 알 수 있으므로 정답은 (C)이다.

21. Look at the graphic. Where does the woman finally think the B Team should be put?
   (A) In Block 1
   (B) In Block 2
   (C) In Block 3
   (D) In Block 4

도표를 보시오. 여자는 최종적으로 B팀을 어디에 둬야 한다고 생각하는가?
(A) 구역 1에
(B) 구역 2에
(C) 구역 3에
(D) 구역 4에

해설 대화 후반에 여자가 "They're the ones who print the most documents, so put them next to the photocopier."라며 그들이 인쇄 작업을 많이 하니 복사기 옆에 두자고 말하고 있다. 도표에서 복사기 옆은 Block 4이므로 정답은 (D)이다.

Questions 22-24 refer to the following conversation.

M: Olivia, have you reviewed the questionnaire we did last week?
W: Not yet. What were the results? Were there any problems about our medical clinic here?
M: Well, almost all patients pointed out that they wanted more time to talk to the doctors during their visits. They usually spend about 10 minutes with their doctor. So I think our clinic needs to extend the counseling time for them.
W: That would require important changes to our scheduling process. But we're not able to revise it ourselves. It'll be up to the members of the board to decide.

M: Olivia, 지난주에 실시한 설문지 검토했어요?
W: 아직이요. 결과가 어때요? 우리 병원에 대한 문제가 있나요?
M: 글쎄요. 대부분의 환자들이 방문 시 의사와 이야기하는 시간을 더 갖고 싶다는 의견을 냈어요. 그들은 보통 의사와 10분 정도 시간을 보내요. 그래서 그들을 위해 상담 시간을 연장할 필요가 있는 것 같아요.
W: 그것은 우리 일정 조율 절차에 중요한 변화를 요구하는데요. 하지만 우리가 수정할 수는 없어요. 이사진들이 결정하기에 달렸어요.

어휘 questionnaire 설문지 patient 환자 point out 지적하다
extend 연장하다 counseling 상담 revise 수정하다
be up to ~에 달려 있다

22. What are the speakers mainly discussing?
   (A) A job opening
   (B) A new product
   (C) A medical clinic location
   (D) Some survey results

화자들은 주로 무엇에 대해 이야기하는가?
(A) 일자리
(B) 신상품
(C) 병원 위치
(D) 설문조사 결과

해설 대화의 주제는 주로 도입부에 제시된다. 첫 대사에서 남자가 "~ have you reviewed the questionnaire we did last week?"라며 설문조사 결과를 봤는지에 대해 물은 후 세부적으로 대화가 이어지고 있으므로 정답은 (D)이다.

23. According to the man, what is the problem?
   (A) Patients are not satisfied with the meeting times with doctors.
   (B) Doctors need to have more experience.
   (C) Patients wait for a long time to see the doctors.
   (D) It is hard to make an appointment.

남자에 따르면, 문제가 무엇인가?
(A) 환자들은 의사와의 대면 시간에 만족하지 못한다.
(B) 의사들은 더 많은 경험이 필요하다.
(C) 환자들은 의사를 보기 위해 오래 기다린다.
(D) 예약하는 데 힘들다.

해설 대화 중반에 남자가 "~ almost all patients pointed out that they wanted more time to talk to the doctors during their visits."라며 환자들이 의사들과 더 많은 시간을 보내고 싶어 한다고 했으므로 정답은 (A)이다.

24. What does the woman imply when she says, "That would require important changes to our scheduling process"?
   (A) She doubts a change will be implemented.
   (B) She thinks more employees should be hired.
   (C) She needs more time to decide.
   (D) She believes some data is incorrect.

여자가 "그것은 우리 일정 조율 절차에 중요한 변화를 요구하는데요"라고 말할 때, 의도한 것은 무엇인가?
(A) 그녀는 이 변화가 실행될지 의문이다.
(B) 그녀는 새로운 직원들이 고용되어야 한다고 생각한다.
(C) 그녀는 결정하는 데 더 많은 시간을 필요로 한다.
(D) 그녀는 일부 데이터가 잘못됐다고 생각한다.

해설 남자가 의사와 대면하는 시간을 늘렸으면 한다고 하자, 여자가 일정 조율 절차에 변화가 필요한데 "But we're not able to revise it ourselves."라며 우리가 수정할 수는 없다고 덧붙이고 있다. 즉, 그 변화가 실행될지 확신하지 못하고 있는 뉘앙스이므로 정답은 (A)이다.

Question 25-27 refer to the following conversation and graph.

W: I've been looking at our bill from the paper supplier. We're spending too much on paper. I think it's wasteful. Take a look at this graph; it shows how much each department is using.
M: I see, but the training department can't reduce it because they have to print out a lot of materials and things.
W: You're right, but look at this one. I think if we gave them all tablet computers, we could cut down this 500-dollar amount.
M: It'll cost more in the short run, though.
W: I know, but it's not just about money. Can you get in touch with James? I'd like to hear his opinion.
M: Sure. I'll contact him right away.

W: 종이 공급업체에서 온 청구서를 보고 있는데요. 저희가 너무 많은 종이를 쓰고 있어요. 너무 낭비인 것 같아요. 이 그래프 좀 봐요. 각 부서가 얼마나 많은 종이를 쓰는지요.
M: 알겠어요. 하지만 교육부는 용지 사용을 줄일 수 없어요. 왜냐하면 그들은 많은 자료들을 인쇄해야 하거든요.
W: 맞아요. 그런데 이것 좀 봐요. 우리가 그들 모두에게 태블릿 PC를 준다면 500달러를 줄일 수 있어요.
M: 하지만 단기적으로는 비용이 많이 들겠네요.
W: 알아요. 하지만 돈에 관한 것만은 아니에요. James한테 연락해 줄래요? 그의 의견을 듣고 싶어요.
M: 물론이죠. 제가 지금 바로 연락할게요.

어휘 supplier 공급업자 wasteful 낭비하는 reduce 줄이다 cut down 줄이다 in the short run 단기적으로 get in touch with 연락하다 opinion 의견 contact 연락하다

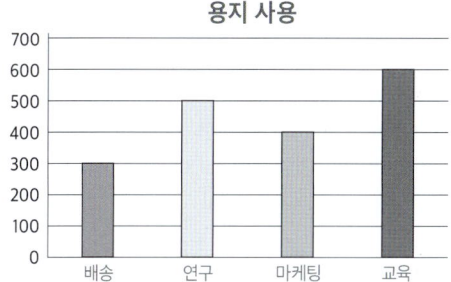

25. What are the speakers talking about?
    (A) A waste of stationery items
    (B) A billing problem
    (C) Moving to another department
    (D) A staff training event

화자들은 무엇에 대해 말하고 있는가?
(A) 문구류의 낭비
(B) 청구서 문제
(C) 다른 부서로의 이동
(D) 직원 교육 행사

해설 대화의 주제는 주로 도입부에 언급된다. 대화 초반에 여자가 "We're spending too much on paper. I think it's wasteful."라며 종이를 많이 쓰고 있다면서 문제점을 지적하고 있다. 따라서 정답은 (A)이다.

26. Look at the graphic. Which department does the woman suggest giving the tablet computers to?
    (A) Shipping
    (B) Research
    (C) Marketing
    (D) Training

도표를 보시오. 여자는 어떤 부서에 태블릿 PC를 제공해야 한다고 제안하는가?
(A) 배송
(B) 연구
(C) 마케팅
(D) 교육

해설 여자의 대사에 집중하면 "I think if we gave them all tablet computers, we could cut down this 500-dollar amount."라며 500달러치의 종이를 쓴 부서에 컴퓨터를 주자고 한 것이므로 정답은 (B)이다.

27. What is the man asked to do?
    (A) Check a price
    (B) Explain a process
    (C) Purchase the tablets computers
    (D) Contact a colleague

남자는 무엇을 하도록 요청 받는가?
(A) 가격 확인하기
(B) 과정 설명하기
(C) 태블릿 PC 구매하기
(D) 동료에게 연락하기

해설 대화 후반에 여자가 남자에게 "Can you get in touch with James?"라며 James에게 연락해 달라고 부탁했으므로 (D)가 정답이다.

LC PART 4 | 담화문

DAY 12 광고/방송

SPARTA Check-UP p.90

1. (A)   2. (C)   3. (B)   4. (D)   5. (C)
6. (C)

Question 1-3 refer to the following advertisement.

> Are you having trouble sleeping? Then come to the renowned Cypress Sleeping Center for help from our professional experts. You'll spend the night at our clinic, and our medical staff will monitor your sleep patterns with the latest equipment in the sleep laboratory. The data we collect from these sessions can help improve your sleep. However, if you don't want to stay overnight in a sleep lab, don't worry. We have a day program in our clinic that can perform the studies during the day. All you need is an appointment for four hours. For more information, look at our Web site, www.cypresssleepcenter.or.kr. Don't lose another night's sleep again. To make an appointment, please call our center at 777-9191 or visit our Web site. Thank you.

수면 장애를 겪고 계시나요? 그러면 전문가들이 도움을 주는 유명한 Cypress 수면센터로 오세요. 저희 병원에서 밤을 보내면 저희 의료 직원들이 수면 실험실에서 최신 장비로 당신의 수면 패턴을 추적 관찰할 것입니다. 이 시간에 모은 데이터는 당신의 수면이 향상되도록 도울 수 있습니다. 하지만 만약에 수면 실험실에서 일박하는 것을 원하지 않으신다면, 걱정 마세요. 저희는 낮 동안 연구할 수 있는 프로그램이 있습니다. 당신이 할 일은 4시간 동안의 예약을 하는 것입니다. 더 많은 정보를 원하신다면 저희 웹 사이트 www.cypresssleepcenter.or.kr을 보세요. 다시는 잠을 설치지 마세요. 예약을 원하시면 저희 센터 777-9191로 전화하시거나 웹사이트를 방문하시면 됩니다. 감사합니다.

어휘 renowned 유명한   professional 전문적인   expert 전문가   latest 최신의   equipment 장비   sleep laboratory 수면 실험실   collect 모으다   session 기간   stay overnight 하룻밤 머무르다   perform 행하다   during the day 낮 동안

---

1. What is being advertised?
(A) A medical clinic
(B) A bookstore
(C) A bed
(D) A sports center

무엇이 광고되고 있는가?
(A) 병원
(B) 서점
(C) 침대
(D) 스포츠센터

해설 담화 초반부에 수면 문제에 대해 언급하면서 "Then come to the renowned Cypress Sleeping Center for help from our professional experts."라며 전문가가 있는 수면센터로 오라고 말하고 있다. 따라서 수면 전문 병원의 광고임을 알 수 있으므로 정답은 (A)이다.

2. According to the speaker, what special option is available?
(A) An online cancelation system
(B) Complimentary training
(C) Daytime appointments
(D) Reduced fees

화자에 따르면, 어떤 특별 옵션이 가능한가?
(A) 온라인 취소 시스템
(B) 무료 교육
(C) 낮 시간 예약
(D) 할인된 요금

해설 지문에서 만약에 하룻밤을 병원에서 묵지 못한다면 "We have a day program in our clinic that can perform the studies during the day."라며 특별히 낮 프로그램도 있다고 소개하고 있다. 따라서 정답은 (C)이다.

3. How can the listeners get more information?
(A) By attending the training
(B) By visiting the homepage
(C) By contacting the service center
(D) By looking at the manual

청자들은 어떻게 더 많은 정보를 얻을 수 있는가?
(A) 교육에 참석함으로써
(B) 홈페이지를 방문함으로써
(C) 서비스 센터에 연락함으로써
(D) 설명서를 봄으로써

해설 광고에서 추가 정보를 얻는 방법은 주로 후반에 단서가 나온다. 후반부 "For more information, look at our Web site ~."에서 추가 정보를 원하면 웹사이트를 보라고 했으므로 정답은 (B)이다.

Questions 4-6 refer to the following news report.

This is Naomi Leslie, your reporter for KMD News, reporting live this week from the Global Motor Show. Throughout the week, I'll be showing you some of the latest vehicles on display here. Right now, I'm standing in front of the latest car from Ambiquest, the Speedo 30. What's really special about this vehicle is its revolutionary design. Ambiquest has developed an environmentally friendly material for the inside and outside of the car. If you're coming to the motor show this week, be sure to check out this car at the Ambiquest booth in aisle one.

이번 주 KMD 뉴스의 기자 Naomi Leslie가 글로벌 모터쇼에서 생방송으로 알려드립니다. 일주일 내내 저는 여기에 있는 최신 차량의 일부를 보여드릴 것입니다. 저는 지금, Ambiquest의 최신 자동차인 Speedo 30 앞에 서 있습니다. 혁신적인 디자인으로 정말 특별하죠. Ambiquest는 자동차 내부와 외부를 위해 친환경 소재를 개발했습니다. 이번 주에 모터쇼에 오신다면 1번 통로의 Ambiquest 부스에서 이 차종을 확인하시기 바랍니다.

어휘 throughout 내내, ~동안　revolutionary 혁신적인　develop 개발하다　environmentally friendly 친환경의　material 소재, 재료　aisle 통로

4. What product is the reporter discussing?
   (A) A laptop computer
   (B) A mobile phone
   (C) A DVD player
   (D) An automobile

   기자는 어떤 제품을 말하고 있는가?
   (A) 노트북
   (B) 휴대 전화
   (C) DVD 플레이어
   (D) 자동차

   해설 담화 초반 "~ reporting live this week from the Global Motor Show."에서 기자가 모터쇼에 있다는 것을 알 수 있으므로 정답은 (D)이다.

5. What is unique about the product?
   (A) Its logo design
   (B) Its reasonable price
   (C) Its material
   (D) Its size

   제품의 무엇이 독특한가?
   (A) 로고 디자인
   (B) 합리적인 가격
   (C) 소재
   (D) 크기

   해설 중반에 "Ambiquest has developed an environmentally friendly material for the inside and outside of the car."라며 친환경 소재를 개발했다고 했으므로 정답은 (C)이다.

6. What does the speaker suggest some listeners do?
   (A) Call a customer service number
   (B) Replace older parts
   (C) Stop by the booth
   (D) Visit a Web site

   화자는 일부 청자에게 무엇을 하도록 제안하는가?
   (A) 고객 서비스 번호로 전화하기
   (B) 오래된 부품 교체하기
   (C) 부스에 들르기
   (D) 웹사이트 방문하기

   해설 담화 후반에 "~ be sure to check out this car at the Ambiquest booth in aisle one."라며 자동차를 보러 부스에 오라고 언급하고 있으므로 정답은 (C)이다.

SPARTA Practice Test p.91

1. (D)	2. (A)	3. (C)	4. (B)	5. (B)
6. (C)	7. (B)	8. (D)	9. (B)	10. (B)
11. (D)	12. (A)	13. (B)	14. (A)	15. (C)
16. (B)	17. (D)	18. (A)	19. (B)	20. (D)
21. (B)	22. (D)	23. (A)	24. (B)	

Questions 1-3 refer to the following broadcast.

Good morning, you're listening to local news from WZA Radio. City officials have reported that last weekend's fundraising charity concert at Riverside Park was a huge success. More than $30,000 was raised for the creation of a new city public library downtown. Even though the original event was rescheduled due to heavy rain, attendance was higher than expected. However, the city still needs to raise another $20,000 before construction can begin on the new facility. For more information, or to make a donation, please visit the city's library donation Web site.

좋은 아침입니다. WZA 라디오 지역 뉴스를 듣고 계십니다. 지난 주말에 Riverside 공원에서 한 자선 모금 콘서트가 큰 성과를 이루었다고 공무원들이 보고했습니다. 시내에 새로운 공공 도서관을 설립하기 위한 자금으로 3만 달러 이상이 모금되었습니다. 폭우로 인해 기존 행사 일정이 조정되었음에도 불구하고 참석자가 예상보다 더 많았습니다. 하지만 시는 새 시설 공사를 시작하기 전에 아직 2만 달러를 더 모아야 됩니다. 더 많은 정보를 원하거나 기부를 하고 싶다면 시 도서관 기부 웹사이트를 방문하세요.

어휘 city official 시 공무원 fundraising 자선 모금 charity 자선 단체 raise 자금을 모으다 creation 창조 original 원래의 attendance 참석자 수 construction 건설 donation 기부

1. What event took place last weekend?
   (A) An art exhibit
   (B) An opening ceremony
   (C) An outdoor flea market
   (D) A live performance

   지난 주말에 어떤 행사가 있었는가?
   (A) 미술 전시회
   (B) 개업식
   (C) 야외 벼룩 시장
   (D) 라이브 공연

   해설 담화 초반에 "~ last weekend's fundraising charity concert ~."라고 했으므로 콘서트를 패러프레이징 한 (D)가 정답이다.

2. Why is the city raising money?
   (A) To construct a library
   (B) To build a new city hall
   (C) To reopen a museum
   (D) To create a monument

   왜 시는 돈을 모으는가?
   (A) 도서관을 짓기 위해
   (B) 새 시청을 짓기 위해
   (C) 박물관을 다시 열기 위해
   (D) 기념비를 만들기 위해

   해설 지문 중반에 "More than $30,000 was raised for the creation of a new city public library downtown."이라며 도서관을 짓기 위해 3만 달러 이상을 모았다고 했으므로 정답은 (A)이다.

3. Why was the event rescheduled?
   (A) Expensive tickets
   (B) An inconvenient location
   (C) Inclement weather
   (D) Low attendance

   왜 행사 일정을 다시 잡았는가?
   (A) 비싼 티켓
   (B) 불편한 위치
   (C) 악천후
   (D) 낮은 참석률

   해설 담화 중반에 "~ the original event was rescheduled due to heavy rain ~"라며 폭우 때문에 일정이 변경됐다고 했으므로 (C)가 정답이다. 지문에 thunderstorm, foggy, snowstorm 등과 같은 날씨 표현이 나오면 정답은 inclement[=bad/poor/severe] weather 등으로 나온다.

Questions 4-6 refer to the following broadcast.

And now we have an FM Radio 10 public service announcement. Next Monday afternoon, the Carson Community Center is holding a free workshop for people who want to practice public speaking skills. The workshop will give you speaking tips for presentations, lectures, interviews, and more. Attendees are also invited to stay afterwards for a networking event with workshop lecturers to ask questions they might have. But there is limited space, so please be sure to enroll beforehand. You can sign up by calling the center at 333-7080 or visiting their Web site at carsoncommunity.org.

이제 FM 라디오 10의 공익 광고 시간입니다. 다음 주 월요일 오후 Carson 커뮤니티센터는 연설 기술을 연습하고자 하는 사람들을 위한 무료 워크숍을 개최할 것입니다. 워크숍은 여러분에게 프레젠테이션, 강의, 인터뷰 등에 필요한 말하기 팁을 제공할 것입니다. 참석자들은 또한 이후에 워크숍 강사와 진행하는 교류 행사에 참여해서 궁금한 점을 질문할 수 있습니다. 하지만 공간이 한정되어 있으므로 반드시 미리 등록하시기 바랍니다. 333-7080으로 전화하시거나 carsoncommunity.org 웹사이트를 방문하시면 등록하실 수 있습니다.

어휘 public service announcement 공익 광고 practice 연습하다 attendee 참석자 tip 조언 afterwards 이후에 lecturer 강연자 beforehand 사전에 sign up 등록하다

4. What is the topic of the workshop?
   (A) Interview strategies
   (B) Speaking techniques
   (C) Leadership skills
   (D) Writing practice

워크숍의 주제는 무엇인가?
(A) 인터뷰 전략
(B) 말하기 기술
(C) 리더십 기술
(D) 작문 연습

해설 주제는 담화 초반에 주로 언급된다. 화자가 "~ the Carson Community Center is holding a free workshop for people who want to practice public speaking skills."이라며 무료 워크숍에 대해 안내하면서 연설 기술을 연습하고 싶은 사람들을 위한 내용이라고 언급하고 있다. 따라서 정답은 (B)이다.

5. What can participants do after the workshop?
(A) Receive a free meal coupon
(B) Speak with lecturers
(C) Register for another workshop
(D) Attend an awards banquet

워크숍 후에 참가자들은 무엇을 할 수 있는가?
(A) 무료 식사 쿠폰을 받는다
(B) 강사와 이야기한다
(C) 다른 워크숍에 등록한다
(D) 시상식 연회에 참석한다

해설 담화 중반부에 "Attendees are also invited to stay afterwards for a networking event with workshop lecturers ~."라며 강사와 만나서 교류할 수 있다고 언급했으므로 정답은 (B)이다.

6. What does the speaker encourage the listeners to do?
(A) Refer a friend
(B) Call the radio station
(C) Register ahead of time
(D) Process a payment

화자는 청자들에게 무엇을 하도록 권하는가?
(A) 친구를 추천한다
(B) 라디오 방송국에 전화한다
(C) 사전 등록한다
(D) 지불을 처리한다

해설 담화 후반에 "But there is limited space, so please be sure to enroll beforehand."라며 공간이 제한되어 있으므로 미리 등록하도록 권하고 있으므로 정답은 (C)이다.

Questions 7-9 refer to the following radio broadcast.

Hello, listeners. I'm Judy McAuley with *Book Time*. Today you'll be hearing from writers appearing at this weekend's Hawksbury Literature Festival. Later in the show, my guests will include mystery author Susan Snell and German novelist Klaus Bender. To get us started, I'm delighted to welcome the festival's guest of honor, Vince Rathbone, two-time winner of the National Poetry Award. Vince has published a dozen acclaimed volumes of verse, and this year released his first novel, *Childhood in South Africa*. He'll read a couple of new poems for us. But first, the traffic news with Barbara Kim after the commercial break.

안녕하세요, 청취자 여러분. 저는 〈Book Time〉의 Judy McAuley입니다. 오늘 여러분은 이번 주말에 Hawksbury 문학 축제에 출연하는 작가들의 이야기를 듣게 되실 겁니다. 행사의 후반부에는 미스터리 작가 Susan Snell과 독일 소설가 Klaus Bender가 게스트로 참여할 예정입니다. 시작하면서 저는 이번 축제의 귀빈이자 National Poetry Award를 2회 수상한 Vince Rathbone 씨를 환영하게 되어 기쁩니다. Vince는 십여 편의 호평을 받은 시집을 출간했으며, 올해는 남아공에서 첫 번째 소설인 〈Childhood in South Africa〉를 냈습니다. 그는 우리를 위해 새로운 시 몇 편을 낭독할 겁니다. 하지만 먼저, 광고 후에 Barbara Kim의 교통 방송이 진행됩니다.

어휘 appear 나타나다 author 작가 novelist 소설가 guest of honor 귀빈 dozen 다수 publish 출판하다 acclaimed 칭찬을 받고 있는 verse 시 release 발표하다 commercial break 광고 시간

7. What will the speaker do?
(A) Introduce a weekend event
(B) Interview writers
(C) Review best-selling books
(D) Provide book rankings

화자는 무엇을 할 것인가?
(A) 주말 행사를 소개한다
(B) 작가들을 인터뷰한다
(C) 베스트셀러 도서를 검토한다
(D) 도서 순위를 제공한다

해설 라디오 프로그램 진행자가 "~ you'll be hearing from writers appearing at this weekend's Hawksbury Literature Festival."라며 이번 주말 문학 축제에 출연하는 작가들의 이야기를 듣겠다는 것은 화자가 그들을 인터뷰하겠다는 걸로 볼 수 있으므로 정답은 (B)이다.

정답 및 해설 | 371

8. What did Vince Rathbone do this year?
  (A) Won an award
  (B) Founded an organization
  (C) Organized a festival
  (D) Published a book

  Vince Rathbone는 올해 무엇을 했는가?
  (A) 상을 받았다
  (B) 기관을 설립했다
  (C) 축제를 준비했다
  (D) 책을 출간했다

  [해설] 담화 후반에 "~ this year released his first novel, Childhood in South Africa."라며 첫 소설을 출간했다고 했으므로 정답은 (D)이다.

9. What will listeners hear next?
  (A) A traffic update
  (B) An advertisement
  (C) An author interview
  (D) A poetry reading

  청자는 다음에 무엇을 들을 것인가?
  (A) 교통 소식
  (B) 광고
  (C) 저자 인터뷰
  (D) 시 낭송

  [해설] 담화 후반에 "But first, the traffic news with Barbara Kim after the commercial break."라며 광고 후 교통 방송이 있다고 했으므로 광고를 먼저 들은 후 교통 방송을 듣게 될 것이다. 따라서 정답은 (B)이다.

Questions 10-12 refer to the following news report.

> Good morning, I'm Benjamin Smith for Radio 105.5. In today's business news, we'll announce an innovation in the automobile industry. The Auto Kindy Company, a local manufacturer of automotive parts, has just invented a new type of brakes for vehicles. These brakes are made from a special lightweight material that cools down more quickly after use, which means these brakes will last much longer than ordinary brakes in the market. Auto Kindy, which was founded just ten years ago, will demonstrate their new brakes at the annual international trade expo in September before bringing them to the market the following month. Stay tuned for further news after the commercial breaks.

> 좋은 아침입니다. 라디오 105.5의 Benjamin Smith입니다. 오늘의 비즈니스 뉴스에서는 자동차 산업의 혁신에 대해 알려 드릴 것입니다. 자동차 부품을 생산하는 현지 제조업체인 Auto Kindy 사는 새로운 차량용 브레이크를 발명했습니다. 이 브레이크는 특수 경량 소재로 만들어져 브레이크 사용 후 더 빨리 냉각되는데, 이것은 시중의 일반 브레이크보다 훨씬 오래간다는 것을 의미합니다. 10년 전에 설립된 Auto Kindy는 다음 달에 시중에 출시하기 전인 9월에 개최되는 연례 국제 무역 엑스포에서 새로운 브레이크를 선보일 예정입니다. 광고 후에 더 많은 뉴스가 나오니 채널 고정하세요.

[어휘] innovation 혁신 automobile 자동차 industry 산업 manufacturer 제조사 invent 발명하다 lightweight 가벼운 ordinary 보통의, 평범한 demonstrate 시연하다 stay tuned 채널 고정하다

10. What type of business is being discussed?
  (A) A repair shop
  (B) An auto parts manufacturer
  (C) A car manufacturer
  (D) An advertising agency

  어떤 업체가 논의되고 있는가?
  (A) 정비소
  (B) 자동차 부품 제조업체
  (C) 자동차 제조업체
  (D) 광고 대행사

  [해설] 담화 초반에 회사를 소개하면서 "The Auto Kindy Company, a local manufacturer of automotive parts, ~."라며 자동차 부품 제조업체라고 언급했으므로 정답은 (B)이다.

11. According to the speaker, what is special about a new product?
  (A) It is made of recycled materials.
  (B) It has various models.
  (C) It was introduced a decade ago.
  (D) It is made to last longer.

  화자에 따르면, 신제품의 특별한 점은 무엇인가?
  (A) 재활용 재료로 만들어졌다.
  (B) 다양한 모델을 가지고 있다.
  (C) 10년 전에 소개되었다.
  (D) 더 오래 지속되도록 만들어졌다.

  [해설] 담화 중반에 "~, which means these brakes will last much longer than ordinary brakes in the market."라며 시중에 나온 제품보다 더 오래 지속된다고 제품의 특징을 언급하고 있다. 따라서 정답은 (D)이다.

12. According to the speaker, what will take place in September?

(A) A trade show
(B) An advertising campaign
(C) An opening ceremony
(D) An anniversary party

화자에 따르면, 9월에 무슨 일이 일어날 것인가?
(A) 무역 박람회
(B) 광고 캠페인
(C) 개회식
(D) 창립 기념 행사

해설 담화 후반에 "~ will demonstrate their new brakes at the annual international trade expo in September ~."라며 9월에 연례 국제 무역 박람회에서 제품 시연을 한다고 했으므로 정답은 (A)이다.

Questions 13-15 refer to the following advertisement.

Does your fitness tracker take too much effort to use? Well, not anymore with the Health Monitor, which is worn around your wrist like a watch. With most wearable devices, you have to push a button in the middle of your exercise routine to access your heart rate tracker or to see how many calories you've burned. Who wants to do that? The Health Monitor will automatically display these features on its screen so you can see this information easily without interrupting your workout. Plus, the price of a Health Monitor has been reduced by 10 percent for the next month in honor of its debut on the market. So order one now.

건강 추적기를 사용하는 게 너무 수고스럽나요? 자, 손목에 시계처럼 차는 Health Monitor와 함께라면 더 이상 힘들지 않습니다. 대부분의 착용이 가능한 기기들은 심박수 추적기를 사용하거나 얼마나 많은 칼로리를 소모하였는지 보기 위해 운동 중 버튼을 눌러야 합니다. 누가 그렇게 하고 싶겠어요? Health Monitor는 이러한 기능이 자동으로 화면에 표시되므로 운동을 방해하지 않고도 정보를 쉽게 볼 수 있어요. 게다가, 다음 달 동안 Health Monitor의 출시를 기념하여 가격을 10%까지 인하했습니다. 그러니 지금 주문하세요.

어휘 fitness 건강 effort 수고, 노력 wrist 손목 wearable 착용이 가능한 heart rate 심박동수 burn 태우다 automatically 자동으로 feature 특징 interrupt 방해하다, 중단하다 debut 출시

13. What is the Health Monitor?

(A) A television program
(B) A wearable device
(C) A medical Web site
(D) A fitness center

Health Monitor는 무엇인가?
(A) TV 프로그램
(B) 착용 가능한 장치
(C) 의료 웹사이트
(D) 헬스클럽

해설 담화 초반에 "Well, not anymore with the Health Monitor, which is worn around your wrist like a watch."라며 손목에 차는 시계처럼 착용 가능한 장치라고 했다. 따라서 정답은 (B)이다.

14. What does the speaker mean when she says, "Who wants to do that"?

(A) A task is inconvenient.
(B) A project requires more volunteers.
(C) An event is no longer popular.
(D) An application period has begun.

화자가 "누가 그것을 하고 싶겠어요"라고 말할 때, 의도한 것은 무엇인가?
(A) 작업이 불편하다.
(B) 프로젝트는 더 많은 자원 봉사자를 필요로 한다.
(C) 행사는 더 이상 인기가 없다.
(D) 원서 접수 기간이 시작되었다.

해설 해당 표현 앞에서 다른 제품들은 칼로리 소모를 확인하기 위해 버튼을 눌러야 한다며 누구도 하고 싶지 않은 불편한 일이라는 것을 강조하려는 의도로 볼 수 있다. 따라서 정답은 (A)이다.

15. Why are listeners encouraged to order now?

(A) Some stores are closing.
(B) Tickets are almost sold out.
(C) A product is temporarily discounted.
(D) A deadline has been changed.

청자들은 왜 지금 주문하도록 권유 받는가?
(A) 일부 매장이 문을 닫는다.
(B) 표가 거의 매진되었다.
(C) 상품이 일시적으로 할인된다.
(D) 기한이 변경되었다.

해설 담화 후반에 "~ the price of a Health Monitor has been reduced by 10 percent for the next month ~."라며 출시 기념으로 10퍼센트 할인됨을 알리면서 지금 주문하라고 했으므로 정답은 (C)이다.

Questions 16-18 refer to the following advertisement.

I needed to get back in shape, but after three knee surgeries, I couldn't work out the way I used to. That's why I use the Flex Trainer 100. It's a low-impact workout that's easy on my knees, legs, and back, yet it still gives me a full workout. Here's how it works: The treadmill moves both forward and up and down. This provides enough resistance to benefit all your muscle groups. All it takes is one 30-minute workout three to four times a week, and you'll see the results in three months or less. I just lost eight pounds and five percent of my body fat in only one month with the Flex Trainer 100. You can too. Just call 777-8282 to order the Flex Trainer 100 today.

다시 건강해지려고 했는데 무릎 수술을 세 번 하고 나니 예전처럼 운동할 수 없었죠. 그래서 Flex Trainer 100을 사용합니다. 무릎, 다리, 등에 적은 충격을 주는 쉬운 운동이지만 그래도 충분히 운동이 됩니다. 여기에 작동법이 있어요: 러닝머신이 앞으로 나아가면서 위아래로 움직입니다. 이것은 여러분의 모든 근육에 이로운 충분한 저항력을 제공합니다. 일주일에 서너 번씩 30분 정도만 운동하면 3개월 이내에 결과를 보게 될 겁니다. 저는 Flex Trainer 100으로 불과 한 달 만에 8파운드와 체지방 5%를 감량했어요. 당신도 할 수 있습니다. 오늘 777-8282로 전화하셔서 Flex Trainer 100을 주문하세요.

어휘 get back in shape 다시 건강해지다 surgery 수술
low-impact 충격이 적은 workout 운동 treadmill 러닝머신 forward 앞으로 resistance 저항력
benefit 유익하다 muscle 근육

16. Who is the advertisement aimed at?
 (A) People who dislike treadmill exercises
 (B) People who cannot train too hard
 (C) Professional body builders
 (D) Judges of sports game

광고는 누구를 겨냥한 것인가?
(A) 러닝머신 운동을 싫어하는 사람
(B) 과도하게 운동할 수 없는 사람
(C) 전문적인 보디 빌더
(D) 스포츠 경기 심판

해설 도입부에서 "I needed to get back in shape, but after three knee surgeries, I couldn't work out the way I used to."라면서 수술 후 예전처럼 운동할 수 없었다고 말하면서 광고를 시작하고 있다. 따라서 정답은 (B)이다.

17. What does the woman mean when she says, "Here's how it works"?
 (A) She will explain her job.
 (B) She has found what she was looking for.
 (C) She has bad knees.
 (D) She will demonstrate a product.

여자가 "여기에 작동하는 방법이 있어요"라고 말할 때 의도하는 것은 무엇인가?
(A) 그녀는 자신의 일을 설명할 것이다.
(B) 그녀는 찾고 있던 것을 찾았다.
(C) 그녀는 무릎이 안 좋다.
(D) 그녀는 제품을 설명할 것이다.

해설 화자가 해당 표현 뒤에 "The treadmill moves both forward and up and down."라며 제품 사용법에 대해 설명하고 있으므로 정답은 (D)이다.

18. What does the woman emphasize about this product?
 (A) It can help with weight loss.
 (B) It can be used anywhere.
 (C) It can gain the user body fat.
 (D) It can be made from a variety of materials.

여자는 제품에 대해 무엇을 강조하는가?
(A) 체중 감량에 도움이 된다.
(B) 어디서든 사용할 수 있다.
(C) 체지방이 늘 수 있다.
(D) 다양한 소재로 만들 수 있다.

해설 담화 후반에 "I just lost eight pounds and five percent of my body fat in only one month with the Flex Trainer 100."라면서 몸무게와 체지방을 감량했다고 했으므로 정답은 (A)이다.

Questions 19-21 refer to the following report.

A spokesperson for Nickson Automotive Company made an announcement at a press conference this morning. The company is reducing production at its engine plant in Potland City. The factory provides more than 300 jobs to local residents. However, declines in market demand have led to a partial closure of the plant. Since the plant's foundation a decade ago, it has had a maximum capacity of 40 units per day. Unfortunately, it has never operated at full capacity, and production was continuously decreased to 20 and now only 15 per day. A spokesperson said production will be reduced to ten each day from next month.

Nickson 자동차 회사 대변인이 오늘 아침에 기자 회견에서 발표했습니다. 회사는 Potland 시의 엔진 공장에서 생산량을 줄이고 있습니다. 그 공장은 지역 주민들에게 300개 이상의 일자리를 제공합니다. 그러나 시장 수요의 감소가 공장의 부분적인 폐쇄를 이끌었습니다. 10년 전에 공장을 설립한 이후로, 하루에 40개의 최대 용량을 만들었습니다. 불행히도 전 용량으로 가동되지 못해서 생산량이 지속적으로 20개까지로 감소했고 지금은 하루에 15개만 생산하고 있습니다. 대변인은 다음 달부터 하루에 10개로 줄 거라고 말했습니다.

어휘 spokesperson 대변인 press conference 기자 회견 reduce 줄이다 production 생산량 local resident 지역 주민 decline 감소 market demand 시장 수요 foundation 설립 maximum capacity 최대 용량 continuously 지속적으로 per day 하루에

19. What is the main topic of the report?
(A) The opening of a new assembly plant
(B) Production cuts at a local factory
(C) An increase in the number of jobs
(D) A merger of two corporations

보도의 주제는 무엇인가?
(A) 새로운 조립 공장의 개관식
(B) 지역 공장의 생산 단축
(C) 일자리 수의 증가
(D) 두 회사의 합병

해설 담화 초반에 "The company is reducing production at its engine plant in Potland City."라며 Potland 시의 생산 감소를 발표했다고 했으므로 정답은 (B)이다.

20. When was the plant built?
(A) Three years ago
(B) Five years ago
(C) Seven years ago
(D) Ten years ago

공장은 언제 세워졌는가?
(A) 3년 전에
(B) 5년 전에
(C) 7년 전에
(D) 10년 전에

해설 담화 중반에 "Since the plant's foundation a decade ago, ~."라며 10년 전 설립한 이후라고 했으므로 정답은 (D)이다. decade가 10 years로 패러프레이징 되었다.

21. How many units are now produced each day at the factory?
(A) 10
(B) 15
(C) 20
(D) 40

현재 하루에 몇 개의 엔진이 공장에서 생산되는가?
(A) 10개
(B) 15개
(C) 20개
(D) 40개

해설 숫자를 묻는 경우, 여러 개의 숫자가 등장하기 때문에 헷갈릴 수 있으므로 질문을 먼저 정확히 파악해야 한다. "~ now only 15 per day."를 통해 (B)가 정답임을 알 수 있다.

Questions 22-24 refer to the following broadcast.

Good evening, and welcome to *Better Life in Health*, a weekly program devoted to keeping listeners up to date on the latest health trends. Today's guest speaker is Dr. Rhonda Collins, a renowned health trainer nationwide. I'm eager for you to hear about her recent research study on the beneficial effects of exercise like walking and cycling. Did you know that walking and cycling have certain impacts that help you to lose weight? Dr. Collins will be explaining this benefit and a lot more in detail. But first, we'll hear a short commercial.

안녕하세요, 최신 건강 경향을 청취자들에게 꾸준히 전달하는 주간 프로그램 "건강을 위한 더 나은 인생"에 오신 것을 환영합니다. 오늘의 초청 게스트는 전국적으로 유명한 헬스 트레이너 Rhonda Collins 박사입니다. 걷기와 자전거 타기 같은 운동의 유익한 효과에 관한 그녀의 최신 연구에 대해 알려 드리고 싶습니다. 걷기와 자전거 타기가 체중을 감량하는 데 확실한 영향을 준다는 걸 알고 계시나요? Collins 박사님이 좀 더 세부적으로 이점들을 설명할 거예요. 그보다 먼저, 짧은 광고부터 듣겠습니다.

어휘 devoted to ~에 전념하는 guest speaker 초청 연사 renowned 유명한 nationwide 전국적인 eager 열렬한 beneficial 유익한 effect 효과 impact 영향 explain 설명하다 commercial 광고

22. Who most likely is the speaker?
(A) A health trainer
(B) A research assistant
(C) A renowned nutritionist
(D) A radio show host

화자는 누구일 것 같은가?
(A) 헬스 트레이너
(B) 연구 조교
(C) 유명 영양사
(D) 라디오 쇼 진행자

해설 화자의 신분/직업은 담화 앞부분에 언급된다. 여기에서는 본인을 직접 소개하지는 않지만 "~ welcome to *Better Life in Health*, a weekly program devoted to keeping listeners up to date on the latest health trends."에서 라디오 프로그램을 소개하고 있으므로 화자는 라디오 프로그램 진행자임을 알 수 있다. 따라서 정답은 (D)이다.

23. What is Dr. Collins's specialty?
(A) Workouts
(B) Sports broadcasting
(C) Health food
(D) Food distribution

Collins 박사의 전문 분야는 무엇인가?
(A) 운동
(B) 스포츠 중계
(C) 건강식품
(D) 식품 유통

해설 진행자가 Collins 박사를 소개하면서 "Today's guest speaker is Dr. Rhonda Collins, a renowned health trainer ~."라며 유명 헬스 트레이너라고 했으므로 전문 분야는 운동과 관련 있음을 알 수 있다. 따라서 정답은 (A)이다.

24. What is the advantage of the exercise mentioned?
(A) It is easy to follow.
(B) It can help your diet.
(C) It can make you sleep well.
(D) It can build muscle.

언급된 운동의 장점은 무엇인가?
(A) 따라 하기 쉽다.
(B) 다이어트에 도움을 준다.
(C) 잠을 잘 잘 수 있도록 도와준다.
(D) 근육을 키울 수 있다.

해설 담화 후반 "Did you know that walking and cycling have certain impacts that help you to lose weight?"에서 걷기와 자전거 타기가 체중을 감량하는 데 효과가 있다고 언급했으므로 정답은 (B)이다.

DAY 13 전화 메시지

SPARTA Check-UP
p.94

1. (C) **2.** (A) **3.** (B) **4.** (B) **5.** (B)
6. (C)

Questions 1-3 refer to the following telephone message.

Hi, Sofia, this is Daniel from reception downstairs. Could you come down here as soon as possible, please? I have a package addressed to you. The sender's name is Stephen Wong from Sun Talk Corporation, and the package is marked as urgent. The delivery person, James, has it at the desk, but unfortunately, only you can sign for it; otherwise, it can't be received. It's 10:35 now. If you can't come within the next 15 minutes, James will have to take it with him and come back later. I hope to hear from you soon. Thanks.

안녕하세요, Sofia 씨, 아래층에 있는 접수처의 Daniel입니다. 가능한 한 빨리 여기로 오실 수 있나요? 당신 앞으로 온 소포가 있습니다. 보낸 사람 이름은 Sun Talk 사의 Stephen Wong이고, 소포에 '긴급'으로 표시되어 있습니다. 배달원 James 씨가 소포를 가지고 데스크에 있어요. 하지만 안타깝게도 당신만 이 소포에 서명할 수 있어요. 그렇지 않으면 소포를 받을 수 없습니다. 지금 10시 35분이니까 15분 안에 오실 수 없으면 James 씨는 소포를 가지고 가서 나중에 다시 와야 합니다. 연락 기다리겠습니다. 감사합니다.

어휘 downstairs 아래층에서   package 상자, 포장물
address to ~의 앞으로 보내다   mark 표시하다
urgent 긴급한

1. What is the main purpose of the message?
(A) To get a schedule
(B) To receive an update
(C) To request a visit
(D) To ask about a product

메시지의 주된 목적이 무엇인가?
(A) 일정을 얻기 위해
(B) 최신 정보를 받기 위해
(C) 방문을 요청하기 위해
(D) 제품에 대해 묻기 위해

해설 담화 초반에 화자가 청자에게 "Could you come down here as soon as possible, please?"라며 아래층으로 내려오라고 요청하고 있으므로 정답은 (C)이다.

2. What is Sofia asked to do?
   (A) Provide a signature
   (B) Call a delivery person
   (C) Meet Stephen Wong
   (D) E-mail Sun Talk Corporation

   Sofia 씨는 무엇을 하도록 요청 받는가?
   (A) 서명하기
   (B) 배달원에게 전화하기
   (C) Stephen Wong 만나기
   (D) Sun Talk 사로 이메일 보내기

   해설 청자가 요청 받는 것을 묻고 있다. 담화 중반에 화자가 "only you can sign for it."라며 서명이 필요하다고 했으므로 정답은 (A)이다.

3. According to the speaker, how long will James remain at the front desk?
   (A) For 10 minutes
   (B) For 15 minutes
   (C) For 30 minutes
   (D) For 35 minutes

   화자에 따르면, James는 안내 데스크에 얼마나 머물 것인가?
   (A) 10분 동안
   (B) 15분 동안
   (C) 30분 동안
   (D) 35분 동안

   해설 담화 후반에 "If you can't come within the next 15 minutes, James will have to take it with him ~."라며 15분 내로 안 오면 배달원인 James가 다시 소포를 가져갈 거라고 했으므로 정답은 (B)이다.

Questions 4-6 refer to the following recorded message.

You have reached RT Transportation Corporation. Please choose one of the following options. If you are calling to report damage to a rail line, please hang up and dial 983-555-5561. For train schedules and a list of stations, please press 1. For information on fares and monthly passes, please press 2. For ticket refunds, please press 3. For information about employment opportunities, please press 4. You can find more information about the services we offer at www.rtcorporationonline.co.ca. If you wish to speak to a customer service representative, please call back during regular office hours. Thank you.

RT 운수 회사에 연결되셨습니다. 다음 옵션 중 하나를 선택해 주십시오. 철도 훼손을 신고하시는 경우, 전화를 끊고 983-555-5561로 전화하십시오. 기차 운행 일정 및 역 목록은 1번을 누르십시오. 운임 및 월 통행권에 대한 정보는 2번을 누르십시오. 티켓 환불은 3번을 누르십시오. 고용 기회에 관한 정보는 4번을 누르십시오. 저희가 제공하는 서비스에 대한 더 많은 정보는 www.rtcorporationonline.co.ca에서 찾으실 수 있습니다. 고객 서비스 담당자와 통화하시려면 정규 업무 시간에 다시 전화해 주시기 바랍니다. 감사합니다.

어휘 damage 피해, 훼손 rail line 철도 hang up 전화를 끊다 fare 요금 monthly pass 한달 정기권 refund 환불 employment opportunity 고용 기회

4. What type of business has the listener called?
   (A) A news organization
   (B) A transportation company
   (C) A recruitment agency
   (D) A utilities center

   청자는 어떤 업체에 전화했는가?
   (A) 언론사
   (B) 운수업체
   (C) 채용 대행업체
   (D) 공익사업 센터

   해설 담화 도입부에 "You have reached RT Transportation Corporation."라며 운수 회사에 연락하셨다고 언급하고 있으므로 정답은 (B)이다.

5. How can the listener get information on prices?
   (A) By dialing another number
   (B) By pressing two
   (C) By pressing four
   (D) By visiting a Web site

   청자는 어떻게 가격 정보를 얻을 수 있는가?
   (A) 다른 번호로 전화를 걸어서
   (B) 2번을 눌러서
   (C) 4번을 눌러서
   (D) 웹사이트를 방문해서

   해설 중반에 "For information on fares and monthly passes, please press 2."라며 운임 및 월 통행권에 대한 정보는 2번을 누르라고 했으므로 정답은 (B)이다.

6. Why is the message being heard?
   (A) Customer service representatives are busy.
   (B) The Web site address has changed.
   (C) The office is currently closed.
   (D) Office hours have been extended.

왜 이 메시지가 나오는가?
(A) 고객 서비스 상담원이 바쁘다.
(B) 웹사이트 주소가 변경되었다.
(C) 사무실이 현재 닫혀 있다.
(D) 근무 시간이 연장되었다.

> **해설** 메시지가 남겨진 있는 이유를 묻고 있다. 메시지를 남기는 이유는 주로 도입부에 언급되나, 이 문제처럼 후반부에 등장하기도 한다. "If you wish to speak to a customer service representative, please call back during regular office hours."라며 고객 상담원과의 전화 연결을 원하면 정규 업무 시간에 다시 전화하라고 했으므로 현재는 업무 시간이 아님을 알 수 있다. 따라서 정답은 (C)이다.

SPARTA Practice Test p.95

1. (D)	2. (D)	3. (A)	4. (A)	5. (B)
6. (B)	7. (D)	8. (D)	9. (C)	10. (A)
11. (B)	12. (B)	13. (A)	14. (B)	15. (C)
16. (A)	17. (C)	18. (D)	19. (C)	20. (D)
21. (A)				

Questions 1-3 refer to the following telephone message.

> Hello, Ms. Matsuda, this is Luisa Monica from Burnado Publishing House. First of all, I'd like to congratulate you on how well your book is selling. In fact, it's been one of the best-selling books this year. Also, we'd like to have a second edition of your novel at the end of this year. And so we want to talk about it with you. If you are interested in this, we'll advertise the release as soon as possible. Please get back to me so we can discuss more details. Thank you.
>
> 안녕하세요, Matsuda 씨, Burnado 출판사의 Luisa Monica입니다. 우선 당신의 책이 잘 팔리고 있다는 걸 축하하고 싶네요. 사실은 올해 베스트셀러 중 하나예요. 또한, 저희는 올해 말에 당신 소설의 재판을 출간하고 싶습니다. 그리고 그것에 대해 당신과 이야기 나누고 싶어요. 의향이 있으시면 저희는 가능한 한 빨리 출간 광고를 할 거예요. 세부 사항에 대해 논의할 수 있도록 연락 주세요. 감사합니다.

어휘 congratulate 축하하다   novel 소설   release 출시, 발간   get back to 답례 전화를 하다   details 세부 사항

1. Why does the speaker congratulate Ms. Matsuda?
   (A) She started a publishing company.
   (B) She finished the research project.
   (C) She won the Best Author prize.
   (D) Her novel is very popular.

   화자는 왜 Matsuda 씨를 축하하는가?
   (A) 그녀는 출판사를 차렸다.
   (B) 그녀는 연구 프로젝트를 마쳤다.
   (C) 그녀는 최고의 작가상을 받았다.
   (D) 그녀의 소설이 매우 인기가 있다.

   > **해설** 초반에 화자가 "First of all, I'd like to congratulate you on how well your book is selling."이라며 그녀의 책이 잘 팔린다고 언급했으므로 정답은 (D)이다.

2. What does the speaker want to have happen at the end of this year?
   (A) A television show will begin.
   (B) A book signing will take place.
   (C) A new film will be introduced.
   (D) A new edition will be published.

   올해 말에 화자는 무슨 일이 생기길 바라는가?
   (A) 텔레비전 쇼가 시작될 것이다.
   (B) 책 사인회가 있을 것이다.
   (C) 새로운 영화가 소개될 것이다.
   (D) 새 증보판이 출판될 것이다.

   > **해설** 화자가 중반부에 "~ we'd like to have a second edition of your novel at the end of this year."라며 올해 말에 청자의 책을 증쇄하고 싶다고 언급했으므로 정답은 (D)이다.

3. Why is the listener asked to return the call?
   (A) To discuss more particulars
   (B) To talk about the grand opening
   (C) To schedule an interview
   (D) To confirm an itinerary

   왜 청자는 다시 연락하도록 요청 받는가?
   (A) 더 자세한 내용을 논의하기 위해
   (B) 개점에 대해 이야기하기 위해
   (C) 면접 일정을 잡기 위해
   (D) 여행 일정을 확인하기 위해

   > **해설** 담화 후반에 "Please get back to me so we could discuss more details."라며 세부 사항에 대해 논의하기 위해 연락 달라고 했으므로 정답은 (A)이다.

Questions 4-6 refer to the following telephone message.

> Hello, Ms. Denby. This is Milton Reynolds, director of human resources at Watson Printing Company. I'm calling to let you know that your résumé has been approved. We are particularly impressed by your extensive experience in print advertising production in the publishing industry. As you know, we're eager to fill the position with someone who's got fresh talent in newspaper advertising. Please get back to me about when you are available for an interview. I'll be conducting the interview together with one of our HR directors, Sandra Gilbert. Thanks.
>
> 안녕하세요, Denby 씨. Watson 인쇄소의 인사부장 Milton Reynolds입니다. 당신의 이력서가 승인되었음을 알려 드리고자 연락 드립니다. 저희는 특히 출판업계의 인쇄 광고 제작에 대한 당신의 폭넓은 경험에 깊은 인상을 받았습니다. 아시다시피 저희는 신문 광고에 새로운 재능을 가진 사람으로 충원하고 싶습니다. 언제 면접이 가능한지 연락 주세요. 인사부 책임자 중 한 명인 Sandra Gilbert 씨와 함께 면접을 진행할 예정입니다. 감사합니다.

어휘 approve 승인하다   particularly 특히   impress 깊은 인상을 주다   extensive 광범위한   industry 업계   be eager to ~을 하고 싶어 하다   fresh 새로운   talent 재능   conduct 하다

4. Why does the speaker call Ms. Denby?
   (A) She has applied for a job.
   (B) Her proposal has been approved.
   (C) Her interview was successful.
   (D) The position has already been filled.

   화자가 Denby 씨에게 전화하는 이유는 무엇인가?
   (A) 그녀가 일자리에 지원했다.
   (B) 그녀의 제안이 승인되었다.
   (C) 그녀의 인터뷰가 성공적이었다.
   (D) 일자리가 이미 충원되었다.

   해설 담화 초반에 "I'm calling to let you know that your résumé has been approved."라며 청자의 이력서가 통과되었다고 했다. 즉 그녀가 일자리에 지원했음을 알 수 있으므로 정답은 (A)이다.

5. Who is Milton Reynolds?
   (A) A newspaper writer
   (B) A personnel director
   (C) A candidate
   (D) A vice president

   Milton Reynolds는 누구인가?
   (A) 신문 기자
   (B) 인사부장
   (C) 지원자
   (D) 부사장

   해설 Milton Reynolds는 화자로, "This is Milton Reynolds, director of human resources ~."라며 자기 소개하는 부분에서 인사부장이라고 언급했으므로 정답은 (B)이다.

6. Why does the speaker ask Ms. Denby to return the call?
   (A) To correct some information
   (B) To schedule an interview
   (C) To conduct a survey
   (D) To give some directions

   화자는 왜 Denby 씨에게 다시 연락 달라고 요청하는가?
   (A) 정보를 수정하기 위해
   (B) 면접 일정을 잡기 위해
   (C) 설문 조사를 하기 위해
   (D) 몇 가지 지시를 하기 위해

   해설 메시지 후반에 "Please get back to me about when you are available for an interview."라며 인터뷰 가능한 시간을 알려 달라고 했으므로 정답은 (B)이다.

Questions 7-9 refer to the following telephone message.

> Hi, Ms. Larson. This is Sam from the Westwood Library. I'm calling to let you know that the book you wanted to check out, *Business Ethics*, has been returned and is now available. We'll put it aside for you for three days, but feel free to call if you need additional time. The number is 666-7789. And keep in mind that the library is now on summer hours, so we close at 6 P.M. instead of 7 P.M. Thanks, Ms. Larson, and have a nice day.
>
> 안녕하세요, Larson 씨. Westwood 도서관의 Sam입니다. 저는 당신이 대출하려는 책인 〈Business Ethics〉가 반납되어 현재 대출 가능하다는 것을 알려드리고자 전화 드립니다. 저희는 3일 동안 당신을 위해 책을 따로 보관하겠지만, 만약에 추가로 시간이 필요하시면 언제든지 전화 주십시오. 전화번호는 666-7789입니다. 그리고 도서관은 현재 여름 시간대로 오후 7시가 아닌 오후 6시에 문을 닫는다는 것을 명심하세요. Larson 씨, 감사합니다. 좋은 하루 보내세요.

어휘 check out 대출하다   put aside 따로 떼어 놓다   additional 추가적인   keep in mind 명심하다   instead of ~대신에

7. Why does the speaker call Ms. Larson?
   (A) To offer her a membership card
   (B) To ask her to return some reading materials
   (C) To invite her to a book club
   (D) To notify her that a book is available

   왜 화자는 Larson 씨에게 전화하는가?
   (A) 회원 카드를 제공하기 위해
   (B) 책들을 반납하라고 요청하기 위해
   (C) 북 클럽에 초대하기 위해
   (D) 책이 대출 가능함을 알리기 위해

   해설 화자가 전화한 이유는 초반에 언급된다. "I'm calling to let you know that the book you wanted to check out, Business Ethics, has been returned and is now available."이라며 원하는 책이 반납되어 대출 가능하다는 것을 알리기 위해 전화했다고 했으므로 정답은 (D)이다.

8. What can Ms. Larson request?
   (A) A free voucher
   (B) A receipt
   (C) A discounted price
   (D) An extra time

   Larson 씨는 무엇을 요청할 수 있는가?
   (A) 무료 상품권
   (B) 영수증
   (C) 가격 할인
   (D) 추가 시간

   해설 화자가 기본 3일 정도 책을 따로 보관할 예정이고 시간이 더 필요하면 언제든지 전화하라고 했으므로(feel free to call if you need additional time) 정답은 (D)이다.

9. What does the speaker remind the listener about?
   (A) An e-mail address
   (B) A late fee
   (C) Reduced operating hours
   (D) Parking permission

   화자는 청자에게 무엇에 대해 알려 주는가?
   (A) 메일 주소
   (B) 연체료
   (C) 단축된 운영 시간
   (D) 주차 허가

   해설 담화 후반에 "~ we close at 6 P.M. instead of 7 P.M."라며 7시가 아닌 6시에 닫는다고 언급했다. 즉 운영 시간이 단축되었음을 알리고 있으므로 정답은 (C)이다.

Questions 10-12 refer to the following recorded message.

Hello, you've reached the customer service center at JK Logistics. We specialize in international shipping services. We're happy to announce that starting September 1st we're finally offering shipping services to Mexico. Before that, note that if you are planning to ship to any location overseas, you must provide proof of ownership. Your call may be recorded, and the recording could be used for quality-control or training purposes. Thank you.

안녕하세요, JK Logistics의 고객 서비스 센터입니다. 저희는 국제 운송 서비스를 전문으로 하고 있습니다. 9월 1일부터 드디어 멕시코로 배송 서비스를 제공하게 됨을 알리게 되어 기쁩니다. 그 전에, 해외로 출하를 계획하신다면 소유권 증명서를 제공하셔야 합니다. 귀하의 전화가 녹음될 수 있으며 녹음은 품질 관리 또는 교육 목적으로 사용될 수 있습니다. 감사합니다.

어휘 reach 연락하다 specialize in ~을 전문으로 하다
international 국제의 shipping 배송 location 위치
overseas 해외에 proof 증거 ownership 소유
quality-control 품질 관리 purpose 목적

10. What type of facility is the message about?
    (A) A shipping company
    (B) A law firm
    (C) A university
    (D) A travel agency

    메시지는 어떤 기관에 대한 것인가?
    (A) 운송 회사
    (B) 법률 회사
    (C) 대학교
    (D) 여행사

    해설 도입부에서 화자가 "We specialize in international shipping services."라며 국제 배송을 전문으로 한다고 소개하고 있으므로 정답은 (A)이다.

11. What will the company do beginning on September 1st?
    (A) Win the contract
    (B) Provide service to a new country
    (C) Offer free shipping
    (D) Hire more employees

    9월 1일부터 회사는 무엇을 할 것인가?
    (A) 계약하기
    (B) 새로운 국가에 서비스 제공하기

(C) 무료 배송 제공하기
(D) 더 많은 직원 고용하기

해설 담화 중반에 "~ starting September 1st we're finally offering shipping services to Mexico."라며 멕시코에서도 배송 서비스가 가능하다고 했으므로 정답은 (B)이다.

12. What does the speaker indicate about the call?
    (A) It will be transferred to a different department.
    (B) It will be recorded for future use.
    (C) It will take several minutes until a representative answers.
    (D) It will be answered promptly.

    화자는 통화에 대해 무엇을 언급하는가?
    (A) 다른 부서로 돌려줄 것이다.
    (B) 나중에 이용하기 위해 녹음될 것이다.
    (C) 상담원이 대답할 때까지 몇 분 걸릴 것이다.
    (D) 즉시 답변될 것이다.

    해설 담화 후반부에 "Your call may be recorded, and the recording could be used for quality-control or training purposes."라며 더 나은 서비스를 위해 통화가 녹음된다고 했으므로 정답은 (B)이다.

Questions 13-15 refer to the following telephone message.

> Hi, this is a message for Cindy Guard. This is Sam, the owner of the apartment building on George Street. You were very interested in the two-bedroom unit I showed you yesterday and said you needed a day to think it over. Well, I'm calling because I just showed the same place to someone else today, and she'd like to rent this apartment right away. But I prefer you as a tenant because it sounds like you plan to rent the apartment for longer. If I don't hear from you by tomorrow before noon, I'm going to have to offer it to this other party. So if you're still interested, let me know what you'd like to do. My number is 556-9090.
>
> 안녕하세요, Cindy Guard에게 남기는 메시지입니다. 저는 George 가에 있는 아파트 주인 Sam입니다. 당신은 제가 어제 보여 드린 방 2개짜리 집에 매우 관심이 있으셨고, 하루 정도 생각할 시간이 필요하다고 말씀하셨습니다. 오늘 같은 장소를 다른 분께 보여 드렸는데 지금 당장이라도 이 아파트를 임대하고 싶다고 해서 연락을 드립니다. 하지만 저는 당신이 더 장기간 아파트를 임대할 계획인 것 같아서 당신을 세입자로 더 원합니다. 만약 내일 정오 전까지 당신에게서 연락을 받지 못한다면 다른 사람에게 이 집을 제공해야 할 것 같습니다. 따라서 여전히 관심이 있으시다면 원하는 바를 알려 주세요. 제 번호는 556-9090입니다.

어휘 owner 주인 think over ~를 심사숙고하다 tenant 세입자 party (소송계약 등의) 당사자

13. Who is the speaker?
    (A) A landlord
    (B) A tenant
    (C) A building manager
    (D) A hotel receptionist

    화자는 누구인가?
    (A) 집주인
    (B) 세입자
    (C) 건물 관리자
    (D) 호텔 접수 담당자

    해설 화자의 신분은 주로 도입부에 언급된다. "This is Sam, the owner of the apartment building ~."라며 아파트 주인이라고 본인을 소개하고 있으므로 정답은 (A)이다.

14. Why does the speaker prefer to work with Cindy Guard?
    (A) She is a celebrity.
    (B) She wants to have a longer contract.
    (C) She does not want to reduce the rent.
    (D) She is familiar with the area.

    화자가 Cindy Guard와 함께 하는 것을 선호하는 이유는 무엇인가?
    (A) 그녀는 유명인사이다.
    (B) 그녀는 더 장기 계약을 원한다.
    (C) 그녀는 집세를 낮추고 싶어 하지 않는다.
    (D) 그녀는 그 지역을 잘 알고 있다.

    해설 담화 중반에 "I prefer you as a tenant because it sounds like you plan to rent the apartment for longer."라며 그녀가 더 오랫동안 아파트를 임대하고 싶어 하기 때문에 선호한다고 언급했으므로 정답은 (B)이다.

15. When is the deadline for Cindy Guard to make a decision?
    (A) This morning
    (B) This evening
    (C) Tomorrow morning
    (D) Tomorrow evening

    Cindy Guard의 결정 기한은 언제인가?
    (A) 오늘 아침
    (B) 오늘 저녁
    (C) 내일 아침
    (D) 내일 저녁

    해설 담화 후반에 화자가 "If I don't hear from you by tomorrow before noon, ~"라며 내일 정오 전까지 답을 달라고 했으므로 정답은 (C)이다.

Questions 16-18 refer to the following telephone message.

Hello, this is Anand Patel from Ace Furniture Store. This message is for Ms. Jiang. I'm calling regarding the order we received from you at our online shop last Friday. We will be able to deliver the bed and frame you ordered this afternoon. Unfortunately, we currently do not have the matching bedside table in stock. If you would prefer that the bedside table be shipped with the other furniture together, you should wait for about a week. Please call me back directly at extension 550 to let me know what you want to do. Sorry for the inconvenience.

안녕하세요, 저는 Ace 가구점의 Anand Patel입니다. Jiang 씨에게 메시지를 남깁니다. 지난주 금요일에 온라인 매장에서 주문하신 것과 관련하여 연락 드립니다. 귀하께서 주문하신 침대와 프레임을 오늘 오후에 배송 가능합니다. 유감스럽게도, 어울리는 침대 옆 탁자가 현재 재고가 없습니다. 만약 다른 가구와 같이 침대 옆 탁자가 배송되길 원하시면 일주일 정도 기다리셔야 합니다. 내선번호 550으로 바로 연락 주셔서 원하시는 바를 알려 주세요. 불편을 드려 죄송합니다.

어휘 regarding ~에 관하여 currently 현재 matching 어울리는 extension 내선번호 inconvenience 불편

16. Where does the speaker probably work?
(A) At a retail store
(B) At a bed factory
(C) At an Internet provider
(D) At a shipping company

화자는 어디에서 일하는 것 같은가?
(A) 소매점에서
(B) 침대 공장에서
(C) 인터넷 서비스 제공업체에서
(D) 배송 업체에서

해설 초반에 "~ this is Anand Patel from Ace Furniture Store."라며 가구점에서 전화하는 누구라고 본인을 소개했으므로 (A)가 정답이다.

17. What problem is mentioned about the order?
(A) The Web site is currently unavailable.
(B) The payment has not been completed.
(C) An item is out of stock.
(D) A table was damaged in transit.

주문에 대해 무슨 문제가 언급되는가?
(A) 웹사이트를 현재 이용할 수 없다.
(B) 지불이 완료되지 않았다.
(C) 제품이 품절이다.
(D) 탁자가 운송 중에 파손되었다.

해설 담화 중반에 "~ we currently do not have the matching bedside table in stock."이라며 현재 침대 옆 탁자의 재고가 없다고 언급했기 때문에 (C)가 정답이다.

18. Why does the speaker ask the listener to call him later?
(A) To talk about the shipping method
(B) To renew the contract
(C) To cancel the order
(D) To inform him of her preference

화자는 왜 청자에게 나중에 전화 달라고 하는가?
(A) 배송 방법에 대해 논의하기 위해
(B) 계약을 갱신하기 위해
(C) 주문을 취소하기 위해
(D) 선호 사항을 알리기 위해

해설 담화 후반에 "Please call me back directly at extension 550 to let me know what you want to do."에서 전화해서 원하는 바를 알려 달라고 했으므로 (D)가 정답이다.

Questions 19-21 refer to the following telephone message and instructions.

Hello. This is Valeria Lopez calling from Dr. Hellman's office. It is concerning your consultation this morning at the clinic. I need to inform you of an important mistake on your prescription instructions. The dosage for Fantex should be half of what is stated. The dosage of Fantex and Tydol should always be the same. We are so sorry. If you have already taken Fantex, you don't have to take any more today. Please get back to me at reception within the next two hours to confirm this message. If you do not, Dr. Hellman will have to visit your home this evening.

안녕하세요. Hellman 병원의 Valeria Lopez입니다. 오늘 아침 병원에서 상담한 것에 관한 내용입니다. 처방전에 중대한 실수가 있었어요. Fantex의 복용량은 적힌 양의 절반이어야 합니다. Fantex와 Tydol의 양은 항상 같아야 합니다. 정말 죄송합니다. 이미 Fantex를 복용했다면 오늘 더 이상 복용할 필요 없습니다. 이 메시지를 확인하시고 2시간 이내에 접수처로 전화 주십시오. 그렇지 않으면 Hellman 박사님이 오늘 저녁에 댁에 방문해야 합니다.

어휘 consultation 상담   prescription 처방전   instructions 설명, 지시 사항   dosage 복용량   confirm 확인하다

약물	복용량
Aspirin	2
Tydol	3
Vitamin B12	4
Fantex	6

19. Who most likely is the caller?

(A) A doctor

(B) A patient

(C) A clinic receptionist

(D) A pharmaceutical sales representative

전화한 사람은 누구인 것 같은가?
(A) 의사
(B) 환자
(C) 병원 접수원
(D) 제약 회사 영업사원

해설 담화 초반에 "This is Valeria Lopez calling from Dr. Hellman's office."라며 Hellman 병원에서 전화했다고 소개하고 있으므로 화자는 (C) 병원 접수원으로 볼 수 있다.

20. Look at the graphic. Which quantity is no longer accurate?

(A) 2

(B) 3

(C) 4

(D) 6

도표를 보시오. 어느 양이 더 이상 정확하지 않은가?
(A) 2
(B) 3
(C) 4
(D) 6

해설 화자가 처방전이 잘못되었다면서 "The dosage for Fantex should be half of what is stated."라며 Fantex는 명시된 것의 반으로 줄여야 한다고 했으므로 정답은 (D)이다.

21. What is the listener asked to do?

(A) Contact the caller

(B) Wait at home

(C) Visit a clinic

(D) Send some medicine

청자는 무엇을 하도록 요청 받는가?
(A) 전화 건 사람에게 연락하기
(B) 집에서 기다리기
(C) 병원 방문하기
(D) 약 보내기

해설 요청 사항은 주로 담화 후반에 언급된다. "Please get back to me at reception within the next two hours ~."라며 2시간 내로 연락 달라고 했으므로 정답은 (A)이다.

DAY 14 안내/공지

SPARTA Check-UP
p.98

1. (C)   2. (A)   3. (B)   4. (C)   5. (A)
6. (B)

Questions 1-3 refer to the following talk.

> We're now in the town of Delft. Where we stand now is where the original town center was rebuilt after a gunpowder explosion in 1654. You may recognize this area from the Vermeer painting we saw yesterday. This is the exact same spot. First of all, we're going to visit the place where William of Orange is buried, which is in the New Church. After that, we'll head over to the Museum Lambert van Meerten to have a look at what Delft is famous for—its pottery. After lunch, feel free to go shopping on your own. I'm handing out a list of shops that we recommend for purchasing the best in Delft pottery. Just remember to be back here by 4:30 P.M.
>
> 우리는 지금 Delft 시에 있습니다. 우리가 지금 서 있는 곳은 1654년에 화약 폭발 후 본래 도심지가 재건된 곳입니다. 어제 보았던 Vermeer 그림에서 이 지역을 볼 수 있어요. 정확히 같은 지점이거든요. 우선, 우리는 New Church에서 William of Orange가 묻힌 곳을 방문할 것입니다. 그 후에 Delft 시의 유명한 도자기를 보기 위해 Lambert van Meerten 박물관으로 향할 겁니다. 점심 식사 후에 혼자 쇼핑하러 가셔도 좋습니다. Delft 최고의 도자기를 구입할 수 있는 추천 상점 목록을 나눠 드리겠습니다. 오후 4시 30분까지 여기로 돌아오는 것을 잊지 마세요.

어휘 original 원래의   town center 번화가   rebuild 재건하다   gunpowder explosion 화약 폭발   recognize 알아보다   exact 정확한   buried 묻힌   pottery 도자기   hand out 나눠 주다

1. Who is the speaker?
   (A) A Delft businessman
   (B) A potter
   (C) A tour guide
   (D) A tourist visiting Delft

   화자는 누구인가?
   (A) Delft 시의 사업가
   (B) 도예가
   (C) 여행 가이드
   (D) Delft를 방문한 관광객

해설 담화 초반의 "We're now in the town of Delft."에서 Delft 시에 있다면서 장소를 설명하고 있다. 이를 통해 화자가 가이드임을 알 수 있으므로 답은 (C)이다.

2. What did the visitors see yesterday?
   (A) A work of art
   (B) New church
   (C) A shopping center
   (D) A pottery shop

   방문객들은 어제 무엇을 보았는가?
   (A) 예술작품
   (B) 신축 교회
   (C) 쇼핑센터
   (D) 도자기 상점

해설 yesterday가 키워드로, 담화 앞부분 "You may recognize this area from the Vermeer painting we saw yesterday."에서 어제 본 그림에서 나왔던 장소라고 설명하고 있으므로 정답은 (A)이다.

3. At the end of the talk, what will the speaker distribute?
   (A) A map of Delft
   (B) Shopping information
   (C) A small piece of pottery
   (D) Discount coupons for pottery

   담화가 끝나면, 화자는 무엇을 배포하겠는가?
   (A) Delft 시의 지도
   (B) 쇼핑 정보
   (C) 작은 도자기 조각
   (D) 도자기 할인 쿠폰

해설 담화 후반에 "I'm handing out a list of shops that we recommend for purchasing the best in Delft pottery."라며 최고의 도자기를 살 수 있는 상점 목록을 나눠 준다고 했으므로 정답은 (B)이다.

Questions 4-6 refer to the following talk.

> Good morning, everyone. We hope you've been enjoying the conference on medical science this week. Tomorrow, in addition to our workshops and presentations, you can go to one of the sites we suggested after leaving the convention center. There is a list of the medical centers in the area. You can tour one of the local hospitals on the list. These tours are free, and we expect them to be very popular. But we have limited seats on the buses, so please be sure to register ahead of time at the front desk by the entrance.

좋은 아침입니다, 여러분. 여러분들이 이번 주 의학 학회를 즐기고 계시길 바랍니다. 내일은 워크숍 및 발표 이외에, 컨벤션 센터를 나온 후 저희가 제안한 장소 중 한 곳으로 갈 수 있습니다. 지역의 의료 센터 목록이 있습니다. 여러분들은 목록에 있는 지역 병원 중 한 곳을 투어할 수 있습니다. 이 투어는 무료이며 매우 인기 있을 것으로 예상됩니다. 하지만 버스 좌석 수가 제한되어 있으므로 입구 옆의 프런트 데스크에서 미리 등록해 주시기 바랍니다.

어휘 conference 학회 medical science 의학 in addition to ~에 더하여 limited 제한된 register 등록하다 ahead of time 미리 entrance 입구

4. At what event is the announcement being made?
(A) A book signing
(B) A product launch
(C) A professional conference
(D) A charity fundraiser

어떤 행사에서 안내되고 있는가?
(A) 책 사인회
(B) 제품 출시회
(C) 전문 학회
(D) 자선기금 모금 행사

해설 담화 초반 "We hope you've been enjoying the conference on medical science this week."에서 의학 학회인 것을 알 수 있으므로 정답은 (C)이다.

5. What does the speaker suggest that some listeners do tomorrow?
(A) Go on a tour
(B) Attend an opening ceremony
(C) Participate in a presentation
(D) Make a list

화자는 일부 청자에게 내일 무엇을 하도록 제안하는가?
(A) 견학 가기
(B) 개회식에 참석하기
(C) 프레젠테이션에 참여하기
(D) 목록 만들기

해설 담화 중반부에 "Tomorrow, ~ you can go to one of the sites we suggested after leaving the convention center."라며 내일 센터를 나온 후 제안된 장소 중 한 곳으로 갈 수 있다고 했으므로 정답은 (A)이다.

6. What are the listeners instructed to do?
(A) Use a different entrance
(B) Sign up early
(C) Complete a questionnaire
(D) Sit in a designated seat

청자는 무엇을 하도록 지시 받는가?
(A) 다른 입구 이용하기
(B) 조기 등록하기
(C) 설문지 작성하기
(D) 지정석에 앉기

해설 담화 후반에 "~ please be sure to register ahead of time at the front desk by the entrance."라며 좌석 제한으로 미리 등록하라고 요청하고 있으므로 정답은 (B)이다.

SPARTA Practice Test p.99

1. (B)	2. (C)	3. (B)	4. (D)	5. (C)
6. (D)	7. (D)	8. (C)	9. (A)	10. (D)
11. (C)	12. (D)	13. (D)	14. (C)	15. (B)
16. (B)	17. (A)	18. (D)	19. (D)	20. (C)
21. (B)				

Questions 1-3 refer to the following announcement.

Good morning, everyone, and welcome to Pearl Academy. Since I created the academy many years ago, it has been my privilege to sponsor the annual management seminar for business students. This year, we will feature twenty speakers from around the world, including Jason West. Mr. West will share his ideas on how to make your company a resounding success. All participants will receive a detailed schedule of the week's activities. If you wish to attend this special event, please fill in the application form in front of you and give it to me after this explanatory meeting. I am looking forward to seeing many of you at this event.

여러분, 안녕하세요. Pearl Academy에 오신 것을 환영합니다. 수년 전에 제가 학교를 설립한 이래로 경영학 전공 경영학 학생들을 위한 연례 경영 세미나를 후원할 수 있어서 영광이었습니다. 올해는 Jason West를 비롯하여 전세계 20명의 연사들로 특별 구성될 것입니다. West 씨는 회사를 어떻게 완전한 기업으로 만드는지에 대한 아이디어를 공유할 거예요. 모든 참가자는 주간 활동에 대한 세부 일정을 받게 될 것입니다. 특별 행사에 참석하고 싶으시면 여러분 앞에 있는 신청서를 작성해서 이 설명회가 끝나면 제출하세요. 이 행사에서 많은 분들을 만나기를 기대하겠습니다.

어휘 privilege 영광 sponsor 후원하다 management seminar 경영 세미나 feature 특징으로 하다 resounding 완전한, 굉장한 explanatory meeting 설명회

1. Who most likely is the speaker?
   (A) A city official
   (B) A school founder
   (C) A salesperson
   (D) A hotel staff member

   화자는 누구인 것 같은가?
   (A) 시 공무원
   (B) 학교 설립자
   (C) 영업사원
   (D) 호텔 직원

   해설 담화 초반에 화자가 "Since I created the academy many years ago ~."라며 수년 전에 학교를 설립했다고 언급했으므로 정답은 (B)이다.

2. What is mentioned about the management seminar?
   (A) It serves complimentary beverages.
   (B) It will last for one day.
   (C) It has some speakers invited from overseas.
   (D) It will start tomorrow afternoon.

   경영 세미나에 관해 언급된 내용은 무엇인가?
   (A) 무료 음료를 제공한다.
   (B) 하루 동안 진행된다.
   (C) 해외에서 초청된 연사들이 있다.
   (D) 내일 오후에 시작한다.

   해설 담화 초중반에 "This year, we will feature twenty speakers from around the world, ~."에서 올해에는 전세계 연사들로 구성된다고 했으므로 정답은 (C)이다.

3. What does the speaker suggest the listeners do?
   (A) Arrive at the academy early
   (B) Submit a form
   (C) Review a schedule for an event
   (D) Access a company's Web site

   화자는 청자들에게 무엇을 하도록 제안하는가?
   (A) 학교에 일찍 도착하기
   (B) 양식 제출하기
   (C) 행사 일정 검토하기
   (D) 회사 웹사이트 들어가기

   해설 담화 후반에 "~ please fill in the application form in front of you and give it to me after this explanatory meeting."라며 신청서를 작성해서 설명회가 끝난 후 제출하라고 했으므로 정답은 (B)이다.

Questions 4-6 refer to the following announcement.

Good afternoon, and thanks for waiting for me. I work on the 6th floor at the stadium; unfortunately, the elevator near my office isn't installed yet. Okay, let's begin the tour. Once the renovation is completely finished, this basketball arena will be the largest one in the country. The court and the locker rooms are completed, so we'll see those areas. Also, there is a gift shop on the second level, but we aren't displaying any merchandise in it right now, so there isn't much to see there. Now, I'd like to give a special greeting to the delegates from Sky Financial Institute who are here with us today. They made investments to bring a professional basketball team to Belmont.

안녕하세요, 기다려 주셔서 감사합니다. 저는 경기장 6층에서 일합니다. 불행히도, 제 사무실 근처 엘리베이터가 아직 설치되지 않았습니다. 그래도 투어를 시작합시다. 일단 보수 공사가 완전히 끝나면 이 농구 경기장은 국내에서 가장 큰 경기장이 될 것입니다. 코트와 탈의실은 완료되어, 그곳을 보게 될 것입니다. 또한 2층에 선물 가게가 있지만 지금은 상품들을 진열하고 있지 않습니다. 그래서 거기에는 볼 게 없어요. 자, 오늘 저희를 방문한 Sky 금융기관 대표자들을 특별히 환영해 주시길 바랍니다. 그들은 Belmont에 전문 농구팀을 데려오는 데 투자했습니다.

어휘 stadium(=arena) 경기장 install 설치하다
renovation 보수, 수리 merchandise 상품
greeting 인사 delegate 대표 investment 투자
professional 전문의

4. What problem does the speaker mention?
   (A) A renovation will be delayed.
   (B) The shipment has not arrived.
   (C) The elevator is broken again.
   (D) The elevator isn't set up.

   화자가 언급한 문제가 무엇인가?
   (A) 보수 공사가 지연될 것이다.
   (B) 선적이 도착하지 않았다.
   (C) 엘리베이터가 또 고장 났다.
   (D) 엘리베이터가 설치되지 않았다.

   해설 지문 초반에 "~ unfortunately, the elevator near my office isn't installed yet."라며 엘리베이터가 아직 설치되지 않았다고 언급하고 있다. 이처럼 unfortunately 뒤에 주로 문제점이 언급된다. 따라서 정답은 (D)이다. install의 동의어인 set up을 외워 두자.

5. What does the speaker say about the gift shop?
   (A) It is on the 6th floor.
   (B) It is completed.
   (C) It is not stocked with items.
   (D) It is having an opening event.

   화자는 선물 가게에 대해 뭐라고 하는가?
   (A) 6층에 있다.
   (B) 완성됐다.
   (C) 물건들이 채워지지 않았다.
   (D) 개업 행사를 하고 있다.

   해설 지문 중반 "~ we aren't displaying any merchandise in it right now, ~"에서 현재는 물건이 진열되어 있지 않다고 했으므로 답은 (C)이다. merchandise가 items, display가 stock으로 패러프레이징 되었다.

6. Who does the speaker welcome as special guests?
   (A) Athletes
   (B) Sports magazine reporters
   (C) Stadium architects
   (D) Financial experts

   화자는 특별 게스트로서 누구를 환영하는가?
   (A) 운동선수들
   (B) 스포츠 잡지사 기자들
   (C) 경기장 건축가들
   (D) 재정 전문가들

   해설 지문 후반 "I'd like to give a special greeting to the delegates from Sky Financial Institute who are here with us today."에서 금융 기관에서 온 대표자들을 환영하고 싶다고 했으므로 정답은 (D)이다.

Questions 7-9 refer to the following announcement.

Before we open our restaurant today, I want to talk about some seasonal menu changes. I just heard from the corporate headquarters that there will be new nuts and berry drinks on the dessert menu starting next week. One of the new drinks is called "Healthy Nuts Delight". I've got some samples of it here for everyone to try. Now, a number of different syrup flavors such as peanut or hazelnut can be added to this drink, so I'd like to ask you to be extra careful when taking customers' orders. We want to make sure they get exactly what they want.

오늘 우리 레스토랑을 열기 전에 계절 메뉴 변화에 대해 말하고자 합니다. 다음주부터 디저트 메뉴에 견과류와 베리 음료가 들어갈 거라는 소식을 방금 본사로부터 들었습니다. 새로운 음료 중 하나는 "Healthy Nuts Delight"라고 불립니다. 모든 사람들이 먹어볼 수 있도록 샘플이 몇 개 있어요. 이제 땅콩이나 헤이즐넛 같은 많은 다양한 시럽이 음료에 첨가될 것이므로, 고객 주문을 받을 때 각별히 주의하시기 바랍니다. 저희는 정확히 그들이 원하는 것을 얻도록 하고 싶습니다.

어휘 seasonal 계절적인   corporate 기업의   headquarters 본사   flavor 맛   exactly 정확히

7. Who most likely is the speaker?
   (A) A customer
   (B) A waiter
   (C) A food critic
   (D) A restaurant manager

   화자는 누구일 것 같은가?
   (A) 고객
   (B) 웨이터
   (C) 음식 비평가
   (D) 레스토랑 매니저

   해설 담화 도입부에서 "Before we open our restaurant today, I want to talk about some seasonal menu changes."라며 레스토랑을 열기 전에 메뉴 변화에 대해 말하고자 한다고 언급했기 때문에 (D) 레스토랑 매니저로 볼 수 있다.

8. According to the speaker, what will happen next week?
   (A) A new oven will be installed.
   (B) The headquarters will be relocated.
   (C) New menu items will be added.
   (D) Seasonal dishes will be removed.

   화자에 따르면, 다음 주에 무슨 일이 일어날 것인가?
   (A) 새 오븐이 설치될 것이다.
   (B) 본사가 이전할 것이다.
   (C) 새로운 메뉴가 추가될 것이다.
   (D) 계절 요리가 사라질 것이다.

   해설 다음 주(next week)라는 키워드를 기억하고 듣자. "~ there will be new nuts and berry drinks on the dessert menu starting next week."라며 디저트 메뉴에 새로운 음료가 생길 거라고 했으므로 메뉴가 새로 추가된다는 (C)가 정답이다.

9. What does the speaker instruct listeners about?
   (A) Taking orders carefully
   (B) Cleaning the dining hall
   (C) Setting the table neatly
   (D) Taking inventory daily

화자는 청자들에게 무엇에 대해 지시하는가?
(A) 주의해서 주문 받기
(B) 식당 청소하기
(C) 깔끔히 테이블 차리기
(D) 매일 재고 정리하기

해설 담화 후반에 "~ I'd like to ask you to be extra careful when taking customers' orders."에서 주문 받을 때 각별히 조심할 것을 요청하고 있으므로 (A)가 정답이다.

Questions 10-12 refer to the following tour information.

During this special tour of Sanwa laptop manufacturing plant, I'll show you exactly how our scientists and engineers develop our laptop computers, as well as how our production team manufactures the final products. Sanwa has become one of the leading companies in the electronics industry, and we always try our best to create innovative and state-of-the-art products. When we finish the tour, you'll have the opportunity to hear from Jamal Megumi, one of our best scientists here at Sanwa. Dr. Megumi will talk about some of our newest research and products. Please remember that photography is prohibited during the tour, as it bothers our workers. Now let's get started!

Sanwa 노트북 제조 공장의 특별 투어를 하는 동안 저는 저희 과학자들과 기술자들이 어떻게 노트북을 개발하고, 생산팀이 어떻게 최종 완성품을 만드는지 정확히 보여 드리겠습니다. Sanwa는 전자 산업 분야에서 일류 회사 중 하나이고, 저희는 혁신적인 최신 제품을 만들기 위해 항상 최선을 다합니다. 투어가 끝날 때 Sanwa에서 최고의 과학자 중 한 명인 Jamal Megumi의 연설을 들을 기회를 가지실 겁니다. Megumi 박사는 우리의 최신 연구와 제품에 대해 얘기할 것입니다. 투어를 하는 동안 직원들에게 방해가 되지 않도록 사진 촬영을 금지하고 있으니 기억하세요. 이제 시작해 봅시다!

어휘 manufacturing plant 제조 공장 develop 개발하다 leading 선두적인 electronics industry 전자 산업 innovative 혁신적인 state-of-the-art 최신식의 photography 사진 찍기 prohibit 금하다 bother 방해하다

10. What product will listeners learn about on the tour?
(A) Mobile phones
(B) Batteries
(C) Cameras
(D) Computers

청자들은 투어에서 무슨 제품에 대해 배울 것인가?
(A) 휴대폰
(B) 배터리
(C) 카메라
(D) 컴퓨터

해설 담화 도입부의 "During this special tour of Sanwa laptop manufacturing plant, ~."에서 노트북 제조 공장 투어라고 언급했으므로 정답은 (D)이다.

11. Who is Jamal Megumi?
(A) A tour guide
(B) A news reporter
(C) A scientist
(D) A plant supervisor

Jamal Megumi는 누구인가?
(A) 투어 가이드
(B) 뉴스 기자
(C) 과학자
(D) 공장 감독관

해설 담화 중반에 "~ you'll have the opportunity to hear from Jamal Megumi, one of our best scientists here at Sanwa."에서 과학자라고 소개하고 있으므로 정답은 (C)이다. 특정 인물의 직업을 묻는 질문은 문제를 통해 이름을 잘 기억하고 듣자.

12. What is mentioned about the tour?
(A) Oversized bags are prohibited.
(B) The group size is limited.
(C) Pre-registration is required.
(D) Taking pictures is not allowed.

투어에 대해 무엇이 언급되는가?
(A) 너무 큰 가방은 금지된다.
(B) 단체의 규모가 제한된다.
(C) 사전 등록이 요구된다.
(D) 사진 찍는 것이 허용되지 않는다.

해설 담화 후반에 "Please remember that photography is prohibited during the tour ~"에서 사진 촬영을 금지한다고 했으므로 정답은 (D)이다. "Please remember ~." 뒤에 정답 단서가 자주 등장한다.

Questions 13-15 refer to the following announcement.

Before we start today's presentation, I'd like to say a few words. There has been a slight change in the schedule, so you might want to make a note of it on the program with your invitation. Actually, the first speaker, Dr. Rhonda Collins, will be starting off the program as planned, but she will be immediately followed by Dr. Wong. But the rest of the schedule will be conducted as scheduled. After a 20-minute break, Dr. Collins will give a speech. We have some time now, so please help yourselves to some coffee, tea, and some snacks at the back of the hall.

오늘 발표를 시작하기 전에 할 얘기가 있어요. 일정이 약간 변경되었으므로 프로그램이 적힌 초대장에 함께 메모하셔도 좋습니다. 사실, 첫 번째 연설자인 Rhonda Collins 박사가 계획대로 프로그램을 시작할 예정이지만 Wong 박사가 바로 이어서 하게 되었어요. 나머지 일정들은 계획대로 진행될 것입니다. 20분간 휴식을 취한 후 Collins 박사께서 연설할 것입니다. 우리는 잠시 시간이 있습니다. 따라서 홀 뒤쪽에 있는 커피와 차, 간식을 맘껏 즐기시기 바랍니다.

어휘 slight 약간의   make a note of ~을 적다   invitation 초대장   be followed by ~이 계속되다   immediately 즉시, 바로   help oneself to (음식을) 마음대로 먹다

13. Why is the announcement being made?
(A) To distribute a program to the audience
(B) To award a prize to some speakers
(C) To close the presentation session
(D) To notify the audience of some schedule changes

왜 안내가 이뤄지고 있는가?
(A) 청중에게 프로그램을 나눠 주기 위해
(B) 몇 명의 연설자들에게 상을 수여하기 위해
(C) 발표 세션을 마무리하기 위해
(D) 청중에게 일정 변경을 알리기 위해

해설 안내의 목적은 주로 담화 초반에 언급된다. 초반에 "There has been a slight change in the schedule ~."라며 일정이 변경되었다고 했으므로 정답은 (D)이다.

14. What have the attendees received?
(A) Postcards
(B) Business cards
(C) Printed invitations
(D) Meal vouchers

참석자들은 무엇을 받았는가?
(A) 우편 엽서
(B) 명함
(C) 인쇄된 초대장
(D) 식권

해설 화자가 변경된 일정에 대해 언급하면서 "~ so you might want to make a note of it on the program with your invitation."에서 청자들이 받은 초대장에 메모하라고 했으므로 정답은 (C)이다.

15. What will the listeners probably do next?
(A) Ask questions about the presentation
(B) Get some refreshments
(C) Sign their names on a sheet
(D) Make some tea

청자들은 다음에 무엇을 할 것인가?
(A) 발표 내용에 대해 질문한다
(B) 다과를 먹는다
(C) 용지에 서명한다
(D) 차를 만든다

해설 안내를 마무리하면서 "please help yourselves to some coffee, tea, and some snacks ~."라며 커피와 간식을 맘껏 먹으라고 했으므로 정답은 (B)이다.

Questions 16-18 refer to the following excerpt from a speech.

I believe that this year's Sydney Fun Run was the most successful race yet. One reason for that was the extra funding we received from our sponsor at Max Athletics. And I would like to express my appreciation to event planners for making that deal. Next year, we'll hold our first Camper River boat race. I'm sure this team is very capable of handling this event. Nevertheless, we really need to plan this carefully. If the event doesn't go well in the first year, we won't have another opportunity next time.

저는 올해 Sydney Fun Run이 가장 성공적인 경기였다고 생각합니다. 그 이유 중 하나는 Max Athletics의 후원자에게서 받은 추가 자금 때문이었습니다. 그 거래를 성사시킨 행사 기획자들에게 감사를 표하고 싶습니다. 내년에는 Camper River 보트 경주를 처음으로 개최할 예정입니다. 저는 이 팀이 행사를 매우 잘 수행할 거라고 확신합니다. 그렇지만 우리는 정말 신중하게 계획해야 합니다. 첫해에 행사가 잘 진행되지 않는다면, 다음에 또 다른 기회는 없을 것입니다.

어휘 successful 성공적인　race 경기　funding 자금
sponsor 후원자　appreciation 감사　event planner
행사 기획자　deal 거래　capable 유능한　opportunity
기회

16. What does the speaker thank organizers for?

(A) Publicizing a product launch

(B) Obtaining corporate sponsorship

(C) Evaluating a performance

(D) Reviewing a proposal

화자는 주최자들에게 무엇을 감사하는가?
(A) 제품 출시를 홍보한 것
(B) 기업 후원을 받은 것
(C) 성과를 평가하는 것
(D) 제안서를 검토하는 것

해설 담화 초반에 "One reason for that was ~ I would like to express my appreciation to event planners for making that deal."라며 스폰서에게 후원을 받게 한 행사 기획자들에게 감사를 표하고 싶다고 했으므로 정답은 (B)이다.

17. What kind of event will be provided next year?

(A) A boat competition

(B) A theatrical production

(C) A clearance sale

(D) A marathon race

내년에 어떤 종류의 행사가 제공될 것인가?
(A) 보트 경기
(B) 연극 제작
(C) 창고 정리 세일
(D) 마라톤 경주

해설 담화 중반에 "Next year, we'll hold our first Camper River boat race."라며 내년에 보트 경기가 처음 열린다고 했으므로 정답은 (A)이다.

18. What does the speaker mean when she says, "we won't have another opportunity next time"?

(A) They should request a policy change.

(B) Another team will be in charge next year.

(C) The project's budget is limited.

(D) The event's success is very important.

화자가 "다음에 또 다른 기회는 없을 것입니다"라고 말할 때 의도한 것은 무엇인가?
(A) 그들은 정책 변경을 요청해야 한다.
(B) 내년에 다른 팀이 담당할 것이다.
(C) 프로젝트의 예산이 제한되어 있다.
(D) 행사의 성공 여부가 매우 중요하다.

해설 담화 후반에 행사 준비의 중요성을 언급하면서 "If the event doesn't go well in the first year, ~."에서 첫해에 행사가 잘 진행되어야 함을 강조하고 있으므로 정답은 (D)이다.

Questions 19-21 refer to the following announcement and schedule.

Good morning, everyone. I hope you'll enjoy these sessions today at this year's Convention on Mobile Game Development. Our company is proud to include many capable guest speakers today for amateur game developers like you. I have an announcement that there is one change to today's schedule. Unfortunately, Olly Whitfield can't join us today because she is sick. So Chris Watana will substitute for Olly Whitfield. He'll give a speech on designing platform software that can be used to create many different games. Also, remember to hand in your opinion forms by the end of the day. All those who submit these forms will automatically be entered into a contest for 1,000 dollars cash.

여러분, 좋은 아침입니다. 오늘, 올해의 모바일 게임 개발 컨벤션에서 이 세션들을 즐기시길 바랍니다. 저희 회사는 귀하와 같은 아마추어 게임 개발업체들을 위해 많은 유능한 초청 연사들을 초빙하게 되어 자랑스럽습니다. 오늘 일정에 변경 사항이 하나 있습니다. 안타깝게도, Olly Whitfield는 아파서 오늘 저희와 함께 할 수 없게 되었습니다. 그래서 Chris Watana가 Olly Whitfield를 대신하게 될 것입니다. 그는 다양한 많은 게임을 만드는 데 사용할 플랫폼 소프트웨어 디자인에 대해 연설할 것입니다. 또한 오늘까지 귀하의 의견 양식 제출하는 것을 잊지 마십시오. 이 양식을 제출하는 모든 사람들은 1,000달러를 받기 위한 콘테스트에 자동으로 참가하게 될 것입니다.

어휘 development 개발　capable 유능한　guest speaker
초청 연사　substitute for ~을 대신하게 되다
give a speech 연설하다　hand in 제출하다
automatically 자동으로

Session 1	Sam Black
Session 2	Greta Grimes
Session 3	Olly Whitfield
Session 4	Helen Chang

19. Who most likely is the audience of this event?

(A) Photojournalists

(B) Mobile phone sellers

(C) Graphic designers

(D) Mobile game developers

행사의 관객은 누구인 것 같은가?
(A) 사진 기자
(B) 휴대전화 판매인
(C) 그래픽 디자이너
(D) 모바일 게임 개발자

해설 화자가 행사의 세션을 소개하면서 "~ you'll enjoy these sessions today at this year's Convention on Mobile Game Development."라고 언급한 부분에서 행사 주제가 모바일 게임 개발임을 알 수 있으므로 정답은 (D)이다.

20. Look at the graphic. Which session has been changed?
    (A) Session 1
    (B) Session 2
    (C) Session 3
    (D) Session 4

도표를 보시오. 어떤 세션이 변경되었는가?
(A) 세션 1
(B) 세션 2
(C) 세션 3
(D) 세션 4

해설 담화 중반에 "Olly Whitfield can't join us today because she is sick. So Chris Watana will substitute for Olly Whitfield."에서 Whitfield 씨가 아파서 함께 할 수 없게 되어 Watana 씨가 대신하게 되었다고 했으므로 정답은 (C)이다.

21. How can listeners enter a contest?
    (A) By submitting a work sample
    (B) By giving some feedback
    (C) By making a deposit
    (D) By attending a Q&A session

청자는 어떻게 대회에 참가할 수 있는가?
(A) 작업 샘플 제출함으로써
(B) 피드백을 제공함으로써
(C) 입금함으로써
(D) 질의응답 시간에 참여함으로써

해설 담화 후반에 "~ remember to hand in your opinion forms by the end of the day."에서 오늘까지 의견을 제출하라고 했으므로 정답은 (B)이다.

DAY 15 회의/소개

SPARTA Check-UP
p.102

1. (B) 2. (C) 3. (C) 4. (B) 5. (B)
6. (C)

Questions 1-3 refer to the following introduction.

Thank you for attending the Local Business Seminar. I'm happy to introduce our first guest speaker, Sophie Moore. She's the founder of Moore Accounting Firm. Her company specializes in tax preparation and has many branches nationwide. Recently, she published the book *How to Manage Your Tax Wisely*, which is a best-seller. Today she'll share some tips on the strategies she used when she started her firm ten years ago working from her home. As you know, if you have questions for our speaker, you should raise your hands after the speech. She'll answer any questions you have. Without further delay, please help me welcome Sophie Moore.

지역 비즈니스 세미나에 참석해 주셔서 감사합니다. 저는 첫 초청 연사인 Sophie Moore 씨를 소개하려고 합니다. 그녀는 Moore 회계법인의 설립자입니다. 그녀의 회사는 세금 준비를 전문으로 하고 있으며 전국적으로 많은 지점을 가지고 있습니다. 최근에는 베스트셀러 〈현명하게 세금을 관리하는 방법〉이라는 책을 출간했습니다. 오늘 그녀는 10년 전에 재택 근무로 회사를 시작하면서 사용했던 전략에 관한 조언을 공유할 것입니다. 아시다시피, 연사에게 질문이 있으시면 연설 후에 손을 들어 주세요. 그녀는 어떤 질문에도 답해 드릴 것입니다. 더 지체하지 않고, Sophie Moore 씨를 환영해 주시기 바랍니다.

어휘 local 지역의 guest speaker 초청 연사 founder 설립자 accounting firm 회계법인 specializes in ~을 전문으로 하다 tax 세금 preparation 준비 nationwide 전국적인 strategy 전략 raise 올리다 delay 지체

1. What field does Sophie Moore work in?
   (A) Event planning
   (B) Accounting
   (C) Tourism
   (D) Financial loans

Sophie Moore는 어떤 분야에서 일하는가?
(A) 행사 계획
(B) 회계
(C) 관광
(D) 금융 대출

해설 담화 초반에 "I'm happy to introduce our first guest speaker, Sophie Moore. She's the founder of Moore Accounting Firm."라면서 회계법인 설립자라고 소개하고 있으므로 정답은 (B)이다.

2. What has Sophie Moore recently done?
   (A) Started her own business
   (B) Worked from home
   (C) Wrote a book
   (D) Published an article

Sophie Moore는 최근에 무엇을 했는가?
(A) 그녀의 사업을 시작했다
(B) 재택근무를 했다
(C) 책을 썼다
(D) 기사를 발표했다

해설 질문의 키워드는 recently로, 담화 중반에 "Recently, she published the book ~."라며 책을 출간했다고 했으므로 정답은 (C)이다. (A)는 10년 전에 사업을 시작했다고 했으므로 오답 함정이다.

3. What does the speaker request the listeners do?
   (A) Take a handout before they leave
   (B) Submit their questions in writing
   (C) Put their hands up for inquiries
   (D) Divide into small discussion groups

화자는 청자들에게 무엇을 하도록 요청하는가?
(A) 떠나기 전에 유인물 가져가기
(B) 서면으로 질문 제출하기
(C) 질문하고 싶으면 손 들기
(D) 소규모 토론 그룹으로 나누기

해설 담화 후반에 "~ you should raise your hands after the speech."라며 연설 후에 손을 들고 질문하라고 했으므로 정답은 (C)이다. (B)는 질문하는 것은 맞지만 서면 제출하라는 내용은 언급된 바 없다.

Questions 4-6 refer to the following talk.

Good morning to all board members, and thank you for coming to this meeting. As you know, our residential project has been delayed, but we need to complete it within two months. To speed up the process, we're thinking of recruiting a team of temporary workers. We will post an advertisement online and in the newspapers with a list of requirements. Construction experience, willingness to work in a team, and customer service skills are the qualifications we need. If you have ideas about other requirements that are essential for our job, please share them with the group.

이사님들, 좋은 아침입니다. 그리고 회의에 와 주셔서 감사합니다. 아시다시피 저희의 주거 건축 사업이 연기되었습니다만, 저희는 두 달 내로 그것을 완성해야 합니다. 진행 속도를 높이기 위해 임시 근로자 한 팀 정도를 고용해야 할 것 같습니다. 신문과 온라인에 자격 요건들과 함께 광고를 게재할 것입니다. 건설 경험과 팀에서 일하고자 하는 의지, 고객 서비스 기술들이 우리가 필요로 하는 자격 요건입니다. 만약 우리 일에 필수적인 다른 조건이 있다면 그룹과 같이 공유해 주세요.

어휘 residential project 주거 건축   delay 지연시키다   recruit 채용하다   temporary 임시의   requirement 필요 조건   willingness 기꺼이 하는 마음, 의지   qualification 자격   essential 필수적인   share 공유하다

4. Where is the talk most likely taking place?
   (A) In a school
   (B) In a conference room
   (C) In a newspaper
   (D) In a department store

담화는 어디서 일어나고 있는 것 같은가?
(A) 학교에서
(B) 회의실에서
(C) 신문사에서
(D) 백화점에서

해설 담화 도입부에서 "~ thank you for coming to this meeting."라며 회의에 와 주셔서 감사하다고 했으므로 장소가 (B) 회의실임을 짐작할 수 있다.

5. What does the speaker plan to do?
   (A) Organize an event
   (B) Hire employees
   (C) Make a manual
   (D) Conduct a survey

화자는 무엇을 하려고 계획하는가?
(A) 행사를 준비한다
(B) 직원들을 고용한다
(C) 설명서를 만든다
(D) 설문조사를 실시한다

해설 담화 앞부분 "~ we're thinking of recruiting a team of temporary workers."에서 임시 직원들을 고용할 것을 고려 중이라고 했으므로 정답은 (B)이다. recruit가 hire로, workers가 employees로 패러프레이징 되었다.

6. What does the speaker ask the listeners to do?
(A) Apply for a job
(B) Register for a seminar
(C) Share their suggestions
(D) Leave the office early

화자는 청자들에게 무엇을 하도록 요청하는가?
(A) 일자리에 지원한다
(B) 세미나에 등록한다
(C) 그들의 의견을 공유한다
(D) 일찍 퇴근한다

해설 담화 후반 "If you have ideas about other requirements that are essential for our job, please share them with the group."에서 청자들에게 아이디어가 있다면 그것들을 공유해 달라고 했으므로 (C)가 정답이다. ideas가 suggestions으로 패러프레이징 되었다.

SPARTA Practice Test   p.103

1. (B)	2. (A)	3. (D)	4. (A)	5. (C)
6. (A)	7. (C)	8. (D)	9. (D)	10. (C)
11. (A)	12. (B)	13. (C)	14. (A)	15. (D)
16. (A)	17. (D)	18. (A)	19. (C)	20. (B)
21. (D)				

Questions 1-3 refer to the following excerpt from a meeting.

Thank you for coming to the meeting. I'm very pleased to see all of you. I'd like to discuss Mojo, a woman's clothing brand we will start selling in our stores next month. As you know, our stores bring in younger shoppers nowadays. With recent fashion trends, the marketing department has discovered that customers aged 20 to 28 prefer styles that come in a lot of different colors. We chose Mojo as a new vendor for this very reason. Please look at the color selection in these samples and then tell me what you think. Next, You-Jin from the finance department will review the expected costs and profit estimates.

회의에 참석해 주셔서 감사합니다. 여러분 모두를 만나서 매우 기쁩니다. 다음 달에 저희 매장에서 판매할 여성 의류 브랜드 Mojo에 대해 이야기하려고 합니다. 아시다시피 저희 매장은 요즘 더 젊은 쇼핑객들을 끌어들입니다. 최신 패션 경향으로, 마케팅 부서에서 20~28세의 고객들이 다양한 색상으로 제공되는 스타일을 선호한다는 사실을 발견했습니다. 우리는 바로 이러한 이유로 Mojo를 새 업체로 선택했습니다. 이 샘플들의 색상 선택 항목을 보고 생각하시는 바를 알려 주세요. 그 다음에, 재무 부서의 유진이 예상 비용과 이익 추정치를 검토할 것입니다.

어휘 nowadays 요즘   discover 발견하다   vendor 판매회사, 상인   finance 재정의   profit 이익, 수익   estimate 추정치

1. What kind of product does Mojo produce?
(A) Jewelry
(B) Clothing
(C) Art supplies
(D) Shoes

Mojo는 무슨 종류의 상품을 생산하는가?
(A) 보석
(B) 옷
(C) 미술용품
(D) 신발

해설 담화 초반 "Mojo, a woman's clothing brand we will start selling in our stores next month."에서 Mojo를 여성의류 브랜드라고 소개하고 있으므로 정답은 (B)이다.

2. Why does the speaker say, "Please look at the color selection in these samples"?
(A) To support a decision
(B) To assign a task
(C) To describe a design
(D) To introduce a new skill

화자는 왜 "이 샘플들의 색상 선택 항목을 살펴보세요"라고 말하는가?
(A) 결정을 지지하기 위해
(B) 업무를 할당하기 위해
(C) 디자인을 묘사하기 위해
(D) 새로운 기술을 소개하기 위해

해설 해당 문장 앞에서 "We chose Mojo as a new vendor for this very reason."라며 새 공급업체를 선택한 이유로 샘플 색상을 언급했으므로 본인의 결정 사항을 뒷받침하기 위한 의도로 볼 수 있다. 따라서 정답은 (A)이다.

3. What will You-Jin do?
   (A) Present competitor data
   (B) Conduct a survey
   (C) Introduce an advertising technique
   (D) Check financial information

   유진은 무엇을 할 것인가?
   (A) 경쟁사의 자료 보여 주기
   (B) 설문조사 실시하기
   (C) 광고 기술 소개하기
   (D) 재정 정보 확인하기

   해설 담화 후반에 "You-Jin from the finance department will review the expected costs and profit estimates."라며 재무 부서에 있는 유진이 재정 관련 정보를 검토할 거라고 했으므로 (D)가 정답이다.

Questions 4-6 refer to the following excerpt from a meeting.

> I'm very pleased to tell everyone that the interior details of the office have been completed, so construction is scheduled to start next week. I've reviewed the new floor plan for a few days, but I've had a lot of assignments this week. So it's been delayed to announce officially. I know you're probably eager to see where you'll be sitting. I think those of you in the marketing department are going to be excited with the design you will have in your work areas. Now, if you have any questions about the renovation project, please ask me.
>
> 여러분께 사무실 인테리어의 세부 요소들이 마무리되었음을 알리게 되어 정말 기쁩니다. 그래서 다음 주에 공사가 시작될 예정입니다. 며칠 동안 새로운 평면도를 검토했는데, 저는 이번 주에 업무가 많았어요. 그래서 공식적으로 발표하는 것이 지연되었습니다. 여러분들이 어디에 앉게 될지 알고 싶다는 거 알아요. 마케팅 부서에 계신 여러분들은 작업 공간에 적용될 디자인에 기뻐할 것 같군요. 자, 만약 사무실 개조 계획에 대해 질문이 있으시면 저한테 물어보세요.

어휘 construction 공사 floor plan 평면도 assignment 임무, 과제 officially 공식적으로 be eager to ~을 하고 싶어 하다 renovation 개조, 보수

4. What is the speaker talking about?
   (A) Refurbishing an office
   (B) Designing a company logo
   (C) Delaying a construction schedule
   (D) Remodeling a cafeteria

화자가 무엇에 대해 얘기하는가?
(A) 사무실 개조하기
(B) 회사 로고 디자인하기
(C) 시공 일정 연기하기
(D) 구내식당 개조하기

해설 담화의 주제는 초반에 언급된다. 화자가 "~ the interior details of the office have been completed,"라며 사무실의 인테리어 세부 요소들이 완성됐음을 전하고 있다. 따라서 정답은 (A)이다.

5. Why does the speaker say, "but I've had a lot of assignments this week"?
   (A) To complain about his project
   (B) To ask for help
   (C) To make an excuse
   (D) To thank colleagues

   화자는 왜 "하지만 저는 이번 주에 업무가 많았어요"라고 말하는가?
   (A) 프로젝트에 대해 불평하기 위해
   (B) 도움을 청하기 위해
   (C) 변명하기 위해
   (D) 동료들에게 감사하기 위해

   해설 해당 문장 뒤에 "So it's been delayed to announce officially."라며 업무가 많아서 발표가 지연되었다고 덧붙이고 있으므로 변명하기 위한 의도로 볼 수 있다. 따라서 정답은 (C)이다.

6. What does the speaker think the marketing staff will like?
   (A) The design of a work area
   (B) The type of lighting
   (C) The variety of computer programs
   (D) The size of an office

   화자는 마케팅 직원들이 무엇을 좋아할 거라고 생각하는가?
   (A) 작업 공간의 디자인
   (B) 조명의 종류
   (C) 다양한 컴퓨터 프로그램
   (D) 사무실의 크기

   해설 담화 후반의 "~ those of you in the marketing department are going to be excited with the design you will have in your work areas."에서 마케팅 부서 직원들이 작업 공간의 디자인을 보면 기뻐할 거라고 언급했으므로 정답은 (A)이다.

Questions 7-9 refer to the following excerpt from a meeting.

> As you all know, I'm leaving my position at the restaurant this month, so I'm really pleased to announce today that we've found someone to take over my position. Let me introduce your new executive chef, Steve Suh. Steve has worked at Illua Hotel for the last ten years, where he received high praise for his creative cooking. Also, he won the Best Chef Award last year. He has tried using modern technology to transform traditional dishes, and many of his new methods have been featured in Best Cooking magazine. Steve will begin training with me from today. Please welcome him.
>
> 여러분 모두 알다시피, 저는 이번 달에 식당을 떠나게 되었고, 그래서 오늘 제 자리를 대신할 사람을 찾았다는 것을 알리게 되어 정말 기쁩니다. 새로운 총괄 주방장 Steve Suh를 소개할게요. Steve는 Illua 호텔에서 지난 10년간 근무하면서 창의적인 요리로 극찬을 받았어요. 또한 작년에 최우수 요리사 상도 받았죠. 그는 그의 요리에서 전통적인 요리법을 바꾸기 위해 현대적인 기술을 시도하였고, 그의 새로운 방식들이 Best Cooking 잡지에 실렸습니다. Steve는 오늘부터 저와 함께 교육을 시작할 겁니다. 그를 환영해 주세요.

어휘 leave the position 직책을 떠나다　take over 인계 받다　executive chef 총괄 주방장　praise 칭찬　creative 창의적인　transform 변형시키다　traditional 전통적인　method 방법　feature 특집 기사에 실리다

7. Where do the listeners most likely work?
   (A) At a magazine publisher
   (B) At a culinary school
   (C) At a restaurant
   (D) At a hotel

   청자들이 일하는 곳은 어디일 것 같은가?
   (A) 잡지사에서
   (B) 요리 학교에서
   (C) 식당에서
   (D) 호텔에서

   해설 담화 초반에 "I'm leaving my position at the restaurant this month."라며 이번 달에 레스토랑을 떠나게 됐음을 언급한 후 그를 대신할 요리사를 소개하고 있다. 따라서 정답은 (C)이다.

8. What does Steve Suh specialize in?
   (A) Hosting cooking demonstrations
   (B) Excellent customer service
   (C) Publishing many recipes
   (D) Innovative cooking skills

   Steve Suh는 무엇을 전문으로 하는가?
   (A) 요리 시연 실시
   (B) 우수한 고객 서비스
   (C) 많은 요리법 출판
   (D) 혁신적인 요리 기술

   해설 화자가 Steve Suh를 소개하면서 "~ where he received high praise for his creative cooking."라며 창의적인 요리로 극찬을 받았다고 했으므로 정답은 (D)이다.

9. What will Steve Suh do from today?
   (A) Open another restaurant
   (B) Finalize a certificate program
   (C) Write an article
   (D) Train for a position

   Steve Suh는 오늘부터 무엇을 할 예정인가?
   (A) 다른 식당 열기
   (B) 인증서 프로그램 마무리하기
   (C) 기사 쓰기
   (D) 해당 직무 교육하기

   해설 담화를 마무리하면서 "Steve will begin training with me from today."라며 오늘부터 교육을 시작할 거라고 했으므로 정답은 (D)이다.

Questions 10-12 refer to the following introduction.

> Good morning, everyone. As you know, today is the first day of our training program for new employees. This is a four-day program in which you'll learn the basics of what you need to know to achieve excellence as an employee of Naeil Travel. Today and tomorrow, we're going to focus on common subjects to every position in the company, including our regulations for how to deal with customers and the public. And then you'll be divided into groups for more specialized training. During these sessions, I'll be training those of you as tour agents in the travel agency and as employees in the accounting, and personnel divisions. Now, I'll pass out the material. So please take one and hand the rest on.
>
> 모두 좋은 아침이에요. 여러분들도 아시다시피 오늘은 신입사원들을 위한 교육 프로그램의 첫날입니다. Naeil Travel의 직원으로서 탁월함을 얻기 위해 알아야 할 기초를 배우는 4일짜리 프로그램입니다. 오늘과 내일은 고객과 대중을 다루는 방법에 대한 규정을 포함하여, 회사 내의 모든 직책에 공통된 주제를 중점으로 할 것입니다. 그런 다음, 더 전문적인 교육을 위해 그룹으로 나뉠 예정입니다. 이 교육에서는 회계 부서, 인사 부서에서 일하는 여행사 직원으로서 교육을 받게 될 겁니다. 이제 자료를 나눠드릴게요. 하나를 가지시고 나머지는 넘겨주시기 바랍니다.

어휘 achieve 달성하다, 성취하다   excellence 뛰어남, 탁월함
focus on ~에 초점을 맞추다   common 공통의
regulations 규칙   divide into ~으로 나누다
pass out 나눠주다   hand on 넘겨주다

10. How long will the training program last?
(A) One day
(B) Two days
(C) Four days
(D) Seven days

교육 프로그램은 얼마 동안 지속되는가?
(A) 1일
(B) 2일
(C) 4일
(D) 7일

해설 담화 초반에 "This is a four-day program ~."라며 4일짜리 프로그램이라고 언급했으므로 정답은 (C)이다.

11. Who will the speaker give training to?
(A) Travel agents
(B) Personnel executives
(C) Visitors
(D) Office clerks

화자는 누구에게 교육을 제공할 것인가?
(A) 여행사 직원들
(B) 인사 간부들
(C) 방문객들
(D) 사무원들

해설 담화 초반 "you'll learn the basics of what you need to know to achieve excellence as an employee of Naeil Travel."에서 여행사 직원들이 교육을 받게 될 것임을 알 수 있다. 따라서 정답은 (A)이다.

12. What will happen next?
(A) The listeners will tour the office.
(B) Handouts will be distributed.
(C) A slide show will be presented.
(D) The listeners will visit a Web site.

다음에 어떤 일이 일어날 것인가?
(A) 청자들이 사무실을 견학할 것이다.
(B) 유인물이 배포될 것이다.
(C) 슬라이드 쇼가 발표될 것이다.
(D) 청자들이 웹사이트를 방문할 것이다.

해설 담화 후반에 "Now, I'll pass out the material. So please take one and hand the rest on."이라며 자료들을 나눠주겠다고 했으므로 정답은 (B)이다.

Questions 13-15 refer to the following excerpt from a meeting.

Good morning. Congratulations on creating such a successful marketing campaign for our Nato Gelato ice cream. We've dramatically increased this product's sales since the launch of the television commercial. So I'd like you to expand this marketing campaign to our other products as well, like cookies. According to the market research, many customers really like the images of the families eating together that they saw in the commercials. So to keep the success going, I'd like to discuss this concept and share some ideas for our other products. We'll have a meeting at this time next week. Before then, please send me some opinions by the end of the week.

좋은 아침입니다. Nato Gelato 아이스크림 마케팅 캠페인의 성공을 이룬 것을 축하합니다. TV 광고 출시 이후 제품의 매출이 급격히 증가했습니다. 그래서 이 마케팅 캠페인을 쿠키 같은 다른 제품에도 확장하셨으면 합니다. 시장 조사에 따르면, 많은 고객들은 광고에 가족이 함께 식사하는 모습이 나오는 것을 정말 좋아한다고 합니다. 그래서 성공을 지속하기 위해 이 컨셉에 대해 논의하고 다른 제품에 대한 아이디어를 공유하고 싶습니다. 다음 주 이 시간에 회의를 가질 예정입니다. 그 전에, 이번 주까지 몇 가지 의견을 제게 보내 주세요.

어휘 dramatically 급격히   launch (상품을) 출시하다; 출시
commercial 광고   expand 확장하다   market research 시장 조사

13. Who is the speaker congratulating?
(A) Advertisers
(B) A new business partner
(C) Marketing personnel
(D) Food critics

화자는 누구를 축하하고 있는가?
(A) 광고주들
(B) 새로운 비즈니스 파트너
(C) 마케팅 직원들
(D) 음식 비평가들

해설 축하하고 있는 대상, 즉 청자가 누구인지를 묻고 있다. 담화 초반에 "Congratulations on creating such a successful marketing campaign ~."라며 성공적인 마케팅 캠페인을 축하한다고 했으므로 마케팅 직원들이 청자임을 알 수 있다. 따라서 정답은 (C)이다.

14. According to the speaker, what do customers like about the commercial?

(A) The scene with families
(B) The various flavors
(C) The celebrities
(D) The background music

화자에 따르면, 고객은 광고에 대해 무엇을 좋아하는가?
(A) 가족이 있는 장면
(B) 다양한 맛
(C) 유명 인사
(D) 배경 음악

해설 담화 중반 "~ many customers really like the images of the families eating together that they saw in the commercials."에서 많은 고객들이 가족들이 함께 식사하는 장면을 좋아한다고 했으므로 정답은 (A)이다.

15. What will listeners most likely do by Friday?

(A) Meet candidates
(B) Send the products
(C) Check some sales figures
(D) Forward some ideas

청자들은 금요일까지 무엇을 할 것 같은가?
(A) 후보자들 만나기
(B) 제품 보내기
(C) 매출액 확인하기
(D) 아이디어 보내기

해설 다음에 할 일은 주로 담화 후반에 언급된다. "please send me some opinions by the end of the week."라며 이번 주까지 의견들을 보내 달라고 했으므로 정답은 (D)이다.

Questions 16-18 refer to the following introduction.

> Thank you for coming to this retirement ceremony for our president, Jane Kennedy. I'd like to say a big thank you to Jane for her 30 years of dedication to this company. She has accomplished so much during her time here. Most of all, she played a key role in our company's international growth. When she started working here, we were a very small company that had only a few offices in Australia. Since then, she has extended the business to over ten overseas countries and managed them. Now, we'd like to invite Jane to the stage. We'll give her a plaque to express our appreciation.

> Jane Kennedy 사장님 퇴임식에 와 주셔서 감사합니다. 30년 동안 이 회사에 헌신하신 Jane에게 큰 감사의 말씀을 전하고 싶습니다. 그녀는 여기에서 매우 많은 성과를 냈습니다. 무엇보다도, 회사의 국제적인 성장에 중요한 역할을 했죠. 그녀가 여기에서 일을 시작할 때, 우리는 호주에 사무실 몇 개밖에 없는 작은 회사였어요. 그 이후로 그녀는 10개국 이상의 해외로 사업을 확장했고 관리했습니다. 지금 Jane을 무대로 모실게요. 감사함을 표현하기 위한 상패를 드리려고 합니다.

어휘 retirement 은퇴 dedication 헌신 accomplish 성취하다 most of all 무엇보다도 played a key role 중요한 역할을 하다 international 국제적인 growth 성장 extend 확장하다 plaque 감사패, 상패 express 표현하다 appreciation 감사

16. Why is the event being held?

(A) To show gratitude to an executive
(B) To introduce a new president
(C) To attract more customers
(D) To launch a new product

왜 행사가 열리고 있는가?
(A) 간부에게 감사를 표현하기 위해
(B) 새로운 사장을 소개하기 위해
(C) 더 많은 고객을 끌기 위해
(D) 신상품을 출시하기 위해

해설 담화 초반에 Jane이 회사 사장임을 언급했고 "I'd like to say a big thank you to Jane for her 30 years of dedication to this company."에서 그녀가 이 회사에 헌신해 준 것에 감사함을 표현하고 있다. 따라서 정답은 (A)이다.

17. What did Jane Kennedy achieve?

(A) She developed a product.
(B) She won a big contract.
(C) She created more efficient processes.
(D) She expanded a company internationally.

Jane Kennedy는 무엇을 이루었는가?
(A) 그녀는 상품을 개발했다.
(B) 그녀는 큰 계약을 체결했다.
(C) 그녀는 더 효율적인 과정을 만들었다.
(D) 그녀는 국제적으로 회사를 확장했다.

해설 담화 중반에 "~ she has extended the business to over ten overseas countries and managed them."라며 10개국 이상의 해외로 사업을 확장했다고 언급했으므로 정답은 (D)이다.

18. What will most likely happen next?

(A) A plaque will be presented.
(B) A short video will play.
(C) A speech will be given.
(D) Refreshments will be served.

다음에 무슨 일이 일어날 것 같은가?
(A) 감사패가 수여될 것이다.
(B) 짧은 비디오가 상영될 것이다.
(C) 연설을 할 것이다.
(D) 다과가 제공될 것이다.

해설 다음에 일어날 일은 주로 지문 후반에 나온다. 담화 끝부분 "We'll give her a plaque to express our appreciation."에서 감사패를 전달할 예정이라고 했으므로 정답은 (A)이다.

Questions 19-21 refer to the following excerpt from a meeting and chart.

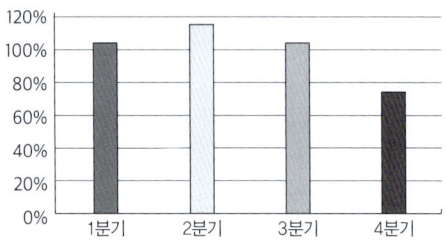

Thank you for staying late today. We're going to talk about the accounting reports. The graph shows our sales output as percentages of the quarterly goals that were set before the first quarter. As you can see, the first through the third quarters were above 100 percent, which is great. However, the fourth-quarter sales were below 80 percent. We need to find out the cause of this in order to recover sales in the next quarter. But before doing this, I want to discuss the quarter with the highest percentage. I think we should share ideas about what factors contributed to the sales output during that quarter. Let me say my opinions first, and after that I will welcome any questions you may have.

오늘 늦게까지 계셔 주셔서 감사합니다. 저는 회계 보고서에 대해 말하려고 합니다. 그래프는 1분기 전에 정한 분기별 목표의 퍼센트로 매출 생산량을 보여 줍니다. 보시다시피 1분기에서 3분기까지 100 퍼센트가 넘었습니다. 대단하죠. 하지만 4분기 매출이 80퍼센트 아래로 내려갔습니다. 저희는 다음 분기에 매출을 회복하기 위해 원인을 알아내야 합니다. 하지만 그 전에, 가장 높은 퍼센트 분기에 대해 논의하고자 합니다. 무슨 요소들이 이 분기 동안 매출 생산에 기여했는지 의견을 공유해야 할 것 같아요. 제 의견을 먼저 말할게요. 그러고 나서 여러분들의 질문을 받겠습니다.

어휘 accounting 회계 output 생산량 quarterly 분기별 goal 목표 cause 원인 recover 회복하다, 되찾다 factor 요소 be contributed to ~에 기여하다

19. What is the purpose of the meeting?
(A) To introduce a new accountant
(B) To arrange a meeting date
(C) To review financial data
(D) To prepare for a merger

회의의 목적은 무엇인가?
(A) 새 회계사를 소개하기 위해
(B) 회의 날짜를 정하기 위해
(C) 재무 자료를 검토하기 위해
(D) 합병을 준비하기 위해

해설 회의의 목적은 초반에 언급된다. "We're going to talk about the accounting reports."라며 회계 보고서에 대해 이야기하자고 했으므로 이와 의미가 통하는 (C)가 정답이다.

20. Look at the graphic. What quarter will the speaker talk about first?
(A) First quarter
(B) Second quarter
(C) Third quarter
(D) Fourth quarter

그래프를 보시오. 화자는 어떤 분기에 대해 먼저 말할 것인가?
(A) 1분기
(B) 2분기
(C) 3분기
(D) 4분기

해설 그래프가 나오면 가장 높은 것과 낮은 것을 눈여겨보자. 담화 중반에 "But before doing this, I want to discuss the quarter with the highest percentage."라며 가장 높은 퍼센트의 분기를 먼저 다루자고 했으므로 정답은 (B)이다.

21. What will the speaker most likely do next?
(A) Leave the office
(B) Share customers' opinions
(C) Ask questions
(D) Give his ideas

화자는 다음에 무엇을 할 것 같은가?
(A) 퇴근한다
(B) 고객의 의견을 공유한다
(C) 질문을 한다
(D) 그의 생각을 말한다

해설 담화 후반에 화자가 "Let me say my opinions first, ~."라며 본인의 의견을 먼저 말하고 청자들에게 질문을 받는다고 했으므로 정답은 (D)이다.

RC PART 5&6 | 단문/장문 채우기

DAY 1 명사와 대명사

SPARTA Check-UP p.119

1. (A) 2. (B) 3. (D) 4. (D)

1. CEO는 직원들에게 자기 계발을 위한 워크숍에 참석하도록 독려했다.

해설 encourage 목적어로 명사가 필요한 자리이다. (D)의 동명사는 목적어가 필요하므로 탈락이다. 의미상, (A) 직원들 (B) 고용주들 (C) 취업 중, CEO가 독려하는 대상으로는 (A)가 가장 적절하다.

어휘 encourage ⓥ 독려하다 self-improvement ⓝ 자기 계발

정답 (A)

2. Bradley & Joy Wood 사에서 만들어진 상품들은 유럽시장에서 매우 인기 있다.

해설 made부터 Wood까지 수식어로 묶으면 동사는 has이다. 그러므로 주어는 -s가 붙지 않는 단수여야 하므로 (A)는 오답이다. 이 중, (C) Desk와 (D) Employer는 셀 수 있는 가산 명사이므로 단독 사용이 불가능해 오답이다. (B) Merchandise는 셀 수 없는 불가산 명사이므로 단독 사용 가능하여 정답이다.

어휘 popular ⓐ 인기 있는 merchandise ⓝ 상품

정답 (B)

3. 디자인 팀은 CEO가 신제품 제안서를 직접 승인했다는 사실을 들었다.

해설 주어(CEO)와 동사(had approved) 사이 부사 자리인데, 재귀대명사(D)만이 위치할 수 있다.

어휘 inform ⓥ 알려주다 proposal ⓝ 제안(서)

정답 (D)

4. 그 직책의 5명의 후보자들 중, 두 명은 해당 분야의 공인된 자격증이 필요하지만, 나머지는 그 업무에 매우 적합하다.

해설 빈칸 뒤에 are가 있으므로 복수가 필요한데, of the five ~라는 숫자로 범위가 정해져 있으니 정관사 the가 쓰인 (D)가 정답이다.

어휘 candidate ⓝ 후보자 certified 공인된 highly ⓐdv 매우 qualified ⓐ 자격을 갖춘

정답 (D)

SPARTA Practice Test p.123

101. (B)	102. (C)	103. (B)	104. (B)	105. (C)
106. (C)	107. (D)	108. (B)	109. (C)	110. (D)
111. (B)	112. (C)	113. (D)	114. (D)	115. (C)
116. (A)	117. (A)	118. (C)	119. (A)	120. (B)
121. (B)	122. (B)	123. (A)	124. (A)	

| PART 5 |

101. 축제 참가 예정인 방문자 수를 아는 것은 기획 위원회한테 매우 중요하다.

해설 빈칸 앞 great이라는 형용사 뒤 명사가 필요하므로 (B)가 정답이다.

어휘 be planning to ⓥ ~할 예정이다 planning ⓝ 기획 committee ⓝ 위원회

정답 (B)

102. 여행자들은 항공권이 실제 그들의 것인지 확인하기 위해 그들의 여정 문서들을 확인하도록 지시 받았습니다.

해설 are (be) 동사 뒤는 보어 자리 소유대명사인 (C)가 정답이다.

어휘 itinerary ⓝ 여정 verify ⓥ 확인하다

정답 (C)

103. 추천서들을 기반으로 하여 새로운 직원을 채용하고자 하는 부서장들은 먼저 인사과에서 허가를 받아야 한다.

해설 get 뒤에 목적어 자리이므로 명사 (B)가 가장 적절하다.

어휘 based on prep ~에 근거하여 recommendation ⓝ 추천(서)

정답 (B)

104. Rachel 씨는 팀원들에게 그 직책에 대한 지원서를 정리하는 것을 도와 달라고 부탁했다.

해설 help의 목적어 자리로 "사람"을 도와주도록 해야 하므로 (B)가 정답이다.

어휘 arrange ⓥ 정리하다 application ⓝ 지원서

정답 (B)

105. JBM 소프트웨어 사는 ARB 사와의 합병에 관한 이슈를 협상 중이라고 발표했다.

해설 under라는 전치사 뒤 명사 자리로, (D)는 사람 명사로 셀 수 있으므로, 단독 사용이 불가능하다. 따라서 (C)가 정답이다. under negotiation(협상 중)을 알아두자.

어휘 merger ⓝ 합병

정답 (C)

106. 회사에 관리 직원이 없어서 Eric은 어제 복사기를 직접 고쳤다.
- 해설: Mr. Eric 이하가 완전한 문장이므로 빈칸은 부사 자리다. 부사 자리에 올 수 있는 재귀대명사 (C)가 정답이다.
- 어휘: absence n 부재 maintenance n 유지, 보수
- 정답: (C)

107. 비록 그의 모든 그림이 현실에 바탕을 두었지만, McGrady 씨는 그 작업을 완성하기 위해 상상에 의존하는 경우가 가끔 있다.
- 해설: his라는 소유격 한정사 뒤에는 명사인 (D)가 가능하다.
- 어휘: painting n 그림 reality n 현실성 depend on v 의존하다 imagine v 상상하다
- 정답: (D)

108. 캠퍼스 사교 모임은 신입생들을 환영하고 그들의 가입을 승인하는 바입니다.
- 해설: 인칭대명사의 격을 묻는 문제로, 빈칸은 명사 앞 소유격 자리다. 따라서 (B) Our가 정답이다.
- 어휘: social club n 사교 모임 enrollment n 가입
- 정답: (B)

109. 마케팅 부장은 대형 유통업체와의 계약 조건들을 면밀히 검토했다.
- 해설: huge라는 형용사 뒤, company라는 명사 앞 자리에 가장 적절한 것은 명사 (C)로, distribution company(유통업체)라는 복합명사가 만들어진다.
- 어휘: review v 검토하다 term n 조건 contract n 계약 huge a 큰 distribute v 배포하다
- 정답: (C)

110. Terry의 부서원 모두는 그들의 전자제품 라인 개선에 헌신을 다했다.
- 해설: wh-로 시작하는 것은 접속사이므로 동사가 추가되어야 하고, each other/one another(서로 서로)는 주어 자리에 불가능하므로 (D)가 정답이다.
- 어휘: division n 부서 dedicated to a ~에 헌신하는 electronic a 전자의 line of products n 제품 라인
- 정답: (D)

111. Warren Finance 사는 최근의 신입사원 그룹이 생산 절차를 배우도록 방콕 공장으로 보냈다.
- 해설: of라는 전치사 뒤 명사 자리로, (B) recruits(신입사원들)과 (D) recruitment(채용) 중에서, 보내는(sent) 동작을 당하는 목적어로 사람 목적어인 (B)가 적절하다.
- 어휘: procedure n 절차 recruit v 채용하다; n 신입사원
- 정답: (B)

112. 제 동료가 연간 학술 포럼에서 영문학과를 대표할 것입니다.
- 해설: 이중 소유격으로 〈a colleague/coworker/friend of + 소유대명사〉 구조는 〈소유격 + 명사〉와 같다. 따라서 소유대명사 (C)가 정답이다.
- 어휘: represent v 대표하다 scholarship n 학술
- 정답: (C)

113. 이사회는 전 직원을 위해 회사의 예외적인 규정들을 일반적인 상세 항목으로 전환시켰다.
- 해설: general이라는 형용사 뒤 명사 자리인데, specific은 형용사, 명사 둘 다 된다. 명사로 "상세 항목"이라는 뜻의 셀 수 있는 명사이므로, 단독 사용이 불가능하여 (D)가 정답이다.
- 어휘: convert v 전환시키다 unusual a 일반적이지 않은 specifically adv 구체적으로 specific a 구체적인; n 상세 항목
- 정답: (D)

114. 4개의 소프트웨어 중 하나는 승인을 받았지만, 나머지들은 논리적 오류 때문에 거부되었다.
- 해설: have가 동사이므로 복수 주어가 필요한데, 숫자 (four)로 범위가 정해져 있으므로 정관사 the가 포함된 (D)가 정답이다.
- 어휘: logical a 논리적인 error n 오류
- 정답: (D)

115. 다가오는 축제의 빠듯한 예산은 행사 주최가 직면하는 문제 중 하나일 뿐이다.
- 해설: of라는 전치사와 the라는 정관사 뒤 명사가 필요한데, 〈one of the + 복수명사〉 구조로 (C) problems가 정답이다.
- 어휘: tight a 빠듯한 upcoming a 다가오는 face v 직면하다
- 정답: (C)

116. 클럽 회원들 모두 CEO가 그 제안에 호의적일 거라고 기대합니다.
- 해설: (B) One, (C) Either, (D) Each 모두 주어를 단수로 만드는 수량대명사이므로 동사는 expects가 와야 한다. 따라서 (A)가 정답이다.
- 어휘: in favor of~ prep ~에 호의적인, 찬성하여
- 정답: (A)

117. 저희 웹사이트에서 환불 요청 제출의 확인을 위해 이 이메일을 제시해 주셔야 합니다.
- 해설: as라는 전치사 뒤에 명사가 필요하므로 (A)가 정답이다.
- 어휘: present v 제시하다
- 정답: (A)

118. 구매 영수증을 소지하고 계시면 각 기계 부품은 보증됩니다.

해설 of 앞 명사 자리에 (D) every는 올 수 없고, of 뒤에 복수 명사가 왔고, 동사가 is(단수)이므로 주어를 단수로 만드는 (C) each가 정답이다.

어휘 guarantee ⓥ 보증하다 receipt ⓝ 영수증

정답 (C)

119. 지침에 따르면, 당신의 세미나 참석이 승진을 위해 필수적이다.

해설 your라는 소유격 뒤 명사 자리로, (A)와 (B) 중 승진을 위해 요구되는 것은 '참석'이라는 의미의 (A)이다.

어휘 according to prep ~에 따라 guideline ⓝ 지침
promote ⓥ 승진시키다 participate ⓥ 참석하다

정답 (A)

120. Rhys 씨가 장학금을 수차례 받았기 때문에, 그녀의 학과는 많은 외부 연구 과제를 따올 수 있었다.

해설 department라는 명사 앞에는 소유격 (B)가 적절하다.

어휘 now that conj ~이기 때문에 award ⓥ 수여하다
scholarship ⓝ 장학(금) grant ⓥ 수여하다
external ⓐ 외부의

정답 (B)

| PART 6 |

(121–124) 다음 광고를 참조하세요.

> Alpha 사는 새로운 Bubble DX200을 소개하게 되어 자랑스럽습니다. DX200은 '섬세한 (세탁)'부터 '강력한 (세탁)'까지 4개의 다양한 세탁 모드를 갖고 있고, 특별한 기능들도 있습니다. 또한, 사용하기 쉽고 엄청 편리한 이 세탁기는 매우 에너지 효율적인데, 일반 모델들이 사용하는 전기량의 3분의 2를 소비합니다. 게다가, 아주 작은 사이즈로 디자인되었습니다. 이것은 당신의 집 가장 좁은 공간에도 적합할 것입니다. 우리는 당신이 이 가전제품을 좋아할 것이라 확신하고, 바이백 보증을 통해 지원합니다. DX200이 만족스럽지 못하다면, 당신은 전액 환불을 위해 구매일로부터 45일 이내에 언제든 그것을 돌려보내시면 됩니다. 추가 정보를 위해, 우리 웹사이트인 www.alphaco.com으로 방문해 보세요.

어휘 delicate ⓐ 섬세한 heavy-duty ⓐ 무거운, 튼튼한, 강력한
energy efficient ⓐ 에너지 효율적인 typical ⓐ 일반적인
furthermore adv 게다가 compact ⓐ 작고 경제적인
suitable ⓐ 적합한

121. 명사

해설 special이라는 형용사 뒤에는 수식을 받는 명사가 와야 한다. '기능'이라는 명사는 셀 수 있는 명사이므로 (B)가 정답이다.

정답 (B)

122. 문장 넣기

(A) 세탁 중 추가 세탁물을 쉽게 넣을 수 있습니다.
(B) 이것은 당신의 집 가장 좁은 공간에도 적합할 것입니다.
(C) 일부 대량 세탁을 처리할 용량을 가지고 있습니다.
(D) 많은 세탁물을 세탁하기 위한 시간을 절약할 수 있습니다.

해설 앞 문장에서 compact size로 '크기'에 대해 언급했으므로 공간의 크기에 대해 부연 설명하는 (B)가 정답이다.

정답 (B)

123. 명사-어휘

해설 (A) 가전제품, (B) 발명, (C) 의류, (D) 거주 중에서 문맥상 어울리는 것은 (A)이다.

정답 (A)

124. 대명사

해설 앞에 나온 DX200의 환불/교환 방식을 설명하므로 단수 사물인 (A) it가 정답이다.

정답 (A)

DAY 2 형용사와 부사

SPARTA Check-UP p.127

1. (C)   2. (B)   3. (A)   4. (D)

1. 수정된 주간 보고서를 제출하지 않은 사람들은 오늘까지 반드시 제출해야 합니다.

해설 소유격 뒤 명사를 수식하는 형용사 자리인데, 형용사가 없어서 분사로 대체하는 자리이다. 보고서(report)는 수정하다(revise)라는 동작을 당하는 대상이므로 (C)가 정답이다.

어휘 weekly ⓐ 주간의   revise ⓥ 수정하다

정답 (C)

2. 출장에 대한 회사 환급 정책의 잦은 변경으로 모든 직원들은 매우 당혹스러워했다.

해설 every는 셀 수 있는 단수 명사를 수식하므로 (B)가 정답이다.

어휘 embarrassed ⓐ 당혹스러운   frequent ⓐ 잦은   reimbursement ⓝ 환급(금)

정답 (B)

3. 우리는 버지니아 주 페어팩스 지역 새로운 주상복합 아파트 건설을 위한 공개 입찰에 최근 합류했다.

해설 현재완료(have Ved)시제와 함께 사용할 수 있는 것은 (A) recently이다. ago(전에)는 단순 과거 시제, shortly(곧)는 미래 시제, yet(아직)은 부정문이나 to부정사와 함께 사용한다.

어휘 bidding ⓝ 입찰   complex ⓝ 복합단지

정답 (A)

4. DG홀딩스는 직원들에게 사내 과외 활동을 제공함으로써 기술을 쌓을 수 있는 훨씬 더 많은 기회들을 제공하고 있다.

해설 비교급 more를 강조할 수 있는 부사는, far/a lot/still/even/much이기 때문에 (D)가 정답이다.

어휘 opportunity ⓝ 기회   extracurricular ⓐ 본 업무 외의

정답 (D)

SPARTA Practice Test p.131

101. (B)	102. (A)	103. (A)	104. (C)	105. (D)
106. (B)	107. (C)	108. (A)	109. (D)	110. (B)
111. (A)	112. (A)	113. (C)	114. (A)	115. (D)
116. (B)	117. (B)	118. (A)	119. (B)	120. (A)
121. (D)	122. (A)	123. (C)	124. (C)	

| PART 5 |

101. 이번 모터쇼에서 새롭게 선보인 차량들 중에서 Hoax-3 모델이 가장 효율적인 엔진을 탑재했다.

해설 명사(engine) 앞 형용사를 고르는 문제로 (B)가 정답이다.

어휘 launched ⓐ 출시된   vehicle ⓝ 차량   efficient ⓐ 효율적인

정답 (B)

102. 공지 없이 그 행사가 취소되는 경우, 여러분의 티켓 비용은 신용카드로 바로 환불될 것입니다.

해설 〈be + 타Ved〉 수동태 뒤의 수식어 자리이므로 "즉시/바로"의 의미의 (A) directly가 정답이다.

어휘 in case of prep ~의 경우   notice ⓝ 공지   refund ⓥ 환불하다   credit card ⓝ 신용카드

정답 (A)

103. 애슐리 여행사는 이번 겨울까지 막바지 호텔 예약 특가 상품을 제공하고 있습니다.

해설 deal(거래/상품)의 명사 앞 형용사 (A)가 정답이다.

어휘 special deal ⓝ 특가 상품   reservation ⓝ 예약

정답 (A)

104. Fiorentina 시는 '중세 문화 중심지'로 널리 알려져 있고, 전세계의 방문객들을 끌어들이고 있다.

해설 〈be ____ 타Ved〉 수동태 사이에 들어오는 수식어로 부사인 (C)가 정답이다.

어휘 Medieval ⓐ 중세의

정답 (C)

105. Office Depot 사의 모든 정규직원은 사내 웹 시스템을 위한 보안패스를 받게 될 것입니다.

해설 빈칸 뒤 employee는 사람 명사로 셀 수 있는 단수 명사이므로 (D) Every가 가장 적절하다. (C) Other는 셀 수 있는 명사의 경우 복수 명사가 나와야 한다.

어휘 full-time ⓐ 정규직의   security pass ⓝ 보안패스

정답 (D)

106. 다양한 이슈 때문에, 새로운 홍보 전략들이 우리 판매 목표를 어떻게 맞출지 아직 확정되지 않았다.

해설 (A) ever는 짝이 되는 단어 또는 과거 시점과, (C) soon은 미래 시제와, (D) almost (거의/대략)는 숫자를 수식하므로 "여전히"를 의미하는 (B) still이 정답이다.

어휘 various ⓐ 다양한 promotional ⓐ 홍보의

정답 (B)

107. Schmidt Trans의 기사들은 승객들의 요금을 인상하는 것과 관련한 규정에는 거의 영향을 미치지 못한다.

해설 빈칸 뒤 명사(influence)는 가산/불가산 둘 다 가능한데, few/many는 뒤에 반드시 복수 명사를, any는 부정문/조건문에 등장하므로 (C)가 가장 적절하다.

어휘 have influence on ⓥ ~에 영향을 미치다

정답 (C)

108. 시장조사에 따르면, TerraPower 사의 새로운 태양 판넬의 판매 수치는 향후 3년 동안 거의 30퍼센트 증가할 것이다.

해설 빈칸 뒤 숫자를 수식하는 부사로 '거의, 대략'이라는 뜻의 (A)가 정답이다.

어휘 solar ⓐ 태양의 panel ⓝ 판

정답 (A)

109. 모든 세계적 기업들은 해외 지사를 운영하는 데 점점 더 외국인 노동자에 의존하는 경향이 있다.

해설 be동사 뒤 보어 자리로 형용사가 와야 하는데, (A)의 rely는 자동사로 수동형 분사가 불가능하다. (C) '신뢰할 만한', (D) '의존하는' 중에서 문맥상 (D)가 적절하다.

어휘 tend to ⓥ ~하는 경향이 있다 run ⓥ 운영하다

정답 (D)

110. 여러모로 힘든 시기 동안, Jerry의 팀은 회사의 위기를 극복하기 위해 다른 사람들에게 그들의 노력과 열정을 꾸준히 증명해 보이고 있다.

해설 〈has Ved〉 현재완료 시제 사이 자리에 수식어인 부사 (B)가 정답이다.

어휘 tough ⓐ 힘든 in many ways adv 여러모로 passion ⓝ 열정 overcome ⓥ 극복하다

정답 (B)

111. 그 지역에 새로운 건물을 건설할 때에는 바닥 표면을 완전히 평평하게 해야 함을 명심하세요.

해설 be동사 is 뒤, 부사 completely의 수식을 받을 수 있는 형용사 (A)가 정답이다.

어휘 surface ⓝ 표면 completely adv 완전히 flat ⓐ 평평한

정답 (A)

112. John Anthony가 영업부서를 구조 조정한 이래로, 분기 판매 수익이 상당히 증가하고 있다.

해설 증가/감소의 자동사는 "상당히"라는 의미의 부사와 어울리므로 (A)가 정답이다.

어휘 restructure ⓥ 구조 조정하다 quarterly ⓐ 분기의

정답 (A)

113. 그 직책에 지원하기 전, 회사 웹사이트에 게시된 그 일에 대한 직무를 확인해 보세요.

해설 복수 명사 앞에 위치하는 수량 형용사로 (C)가 정답이다.

어휘 responsibility ⓝ 책임, 업무

정답 (C)

114. 많은 경제 전문가들은 베트남의 불안정한 정책이 인플레이션을 초래하는 것을 예방하기 위해 반드시 개선되어야 한다고 강하게 믿고 있다.

해설 미래 시제와 함께 "곧"이라는 의미의 부사 (A) soon이 가장 적절하다.

어휘 unstable ⓐ 불안정한 prevent ⓥ 예방하다

정답 (A)

115. 시애틀 대학의 대학원 프로그램은 지원자들에게 그들의 지도 교수로부터 3부의 인상적인 추천서를 받아 제출할 것을 요구했다.

해설 명사 앞 형용사 자리로, (C) impressed는 감정 동사에 -ed가 붙어서 만들어진 분사이므로 사람 명사와 함께 쓰여야 한다. '인상적인, 뛰어난'이라는 의미의 (D)가 정답이다.

어휘 graduate program ⓝ 대학원 프로그램 academic advisor ⓝ 지도 교수

정답 (D)

116. 박사 논문을 위한 Scott의 글은 경제학과의 논문 심사위원들에 의해 호의적인 평가를 받았다.

해설 〈been ___ Ved〉의 수동 구조 사이에 들어가는 "부사" 자리로 (B)가 정답이다.

어휘 dissertation ⓝ 박사 논문 paper examiner ⓝ 논문 심사위원

정답 (B)

117. RED-허가증을 소지하신 직원들은 추가 금액 없이 지정된 장소에 차량을 주차할 수 있습니다.

해설 명사 앞 형용사 자리로 (B)가 정답이다.

어휘 designated ⓐ 지정된 charge ⓝ 부과금

정답 (B)

118. 유의미한 데이터베이스를 수집하는 것은 시민들과 인터뷰를 하고 그것을 파일로 옮기는 작업을 함으로써 현재 거의 완료되었다.

해설 부사 중에서 (A) 거의, (B) 근처에, (C) 언제든지, (D) 아직 중에서 문맥상 '완료, 충족'의 의미를 내포하는 어휘와 어울리는 (A)가 정답이다.

어휘 meaningful ⓐ 유의미한 transcribe ⓥ 옮겨 적다

정답 (A)

119. 우리 시설물을 개선하고 업데이트하는 것은 이곳을 자주 방문하고 둘러보는 잠재 고객들에게 시설들을 더 매력적으로 보이게 할 수 있습니다.

해설 make라는 5형식 상태 동사의 보어 자리로 형용사인 (B)가 가장 적절하다.

어휘 potential ⓐ 잠재적인 frequently adv 자주 tour ⓥ 둘러보다

정답 (B)

120. Heinle 종합 운동장 수리가 아직 끝나지 않았지만, 그 곳의 일부 매장은 이미 문을 열고 손님들을 끌어들이고 있다.

해설 빈칸 앞에 부정어 not과 어울릴 수 있는 부사는 (A)가 가장 적절하다. (B), (C)는 빈도부사로 현재시제와 어울리고, (D)는 부정어이다.

어휘 renovation ⓝ 수리 attract ⓥ 끌어들이다

정답 (A)

| PART 6 |

(121-124) 다음 편지를 참조하세요.

Global Charity Fund
843 Lincoln Boulevard
Nashville, Tennessee

6월 20일
Nelson Kim
370 Central Street
Busan, Republic of Korea

Kim 씨께,

저는 Global Charity Fund에 후원하는 것을 당신에게 요청하기 위해 글을 쓰고 있습니다. 하루에 1달러도 없이 살아 가는 수백만의 사람들이 전세계에 있습니다. 게다가, 그들은 때때로 아주 기본적인 의료보장도 받지 못하고 있습니다. 그러므로, 정말 작은 도움도 다른 이들에게는 엄청난 차이를 만들 수 있습니다. 우리 모두는 특히, 전세계 어린이들의 기근의 영향에 대해 걱정하고 있습니다. 그것을 멈추게 하기 위해, 여러분이 기부하실 수 있는 얼마가 되든 상관없이 당신의 수표를 선불 봉투 안에 넣어 저희에게 보내주세요. 당신께서 해주시는 기여에 저희는 매우 기쁠 것입니다.

진심으로,

Ezekiel Nikomo
Global Hunger Fund

어휘 charity ⓝ 자선 assistance ⓝ 도움 considerable ⓐ 상당한 starvation ⓝ 기근 donate ⓥ 기부하다 contribution ⓝ 기부 urgently adv 긴급하게

121. 문장 넣기
(A) 반대로, 파트너쉽을 원하는 사람들은 당신의 도움이 급하게 필요합니다.
(B) 이러한 상황에도 불구하고, 생활 조건은 더 악화되고 있습니다.
(C) 예를 들어, 우리는 그들에게 훌륭한 초등 교육을 제공합니다.
(D) 게다가, 그들은 때때로 아주 기본적인 의료보장도 받지 못하고 있습니다.

해설 앞/뒤 문맥을 보면 도움이 필요한 사람들의 안 좋은 상황을 언급하고 있기 때문에 (D)가 가장 적절하다.

정답 (D)

122. 대명사
해설 전치사 뒤 명사 자리로, (A) every는 형용사로만 쓰이기 때문에 뒤에 명사가 필요하고, (B) much는 셀 수 없는 명사를 수식하고, (D) both는 양쪽을 의미하므로 일반적인 '다른 사람들'을 나타내는 (C)가 적절하다.

정답 (C)

123. 형용사(분사)
해설 be동사 뒤 분사 자리에 형용사를 대신하여 분사를 위치시키는데, worry(걱정시키다)는 감정동사이므로 주어가 사람이면 수동형 Ved인 (C) worried가 정답이 된다.

정답 (C)

124. 형용사(분사)
해설 명사 앞 형용사 자리로, 봉투(envelope)는 '선불하다(prepay)'라는 동작을 당하는 대상이므로 (C)가 정답이다.

정답 (C)

DAY 3 전치사

SPARTA Check-UP
p.135

1. (B)   2. (C)   3. (A)   4.(C)

1. 우리 시설에서 특정 직원과 이야기하고 싶으시면, 4번을 누르고 삐 소리 이후 그 사람의 내선번호를 누르세요.

해설 (A) 기간, (B) 시점, (C) 시점, (D) 기간의 전치사 중에서 문맥상 "~ 후에"라는 의미의 (B)가 가장 적절하다.

어휘 particular ⓐ 특정한   press ⓥ 누르다   beep ⓝ 삐 소리

정답 (B)

2. 사무실에 필요한 추가 자료들과 용품들은 9층 데이터 저장소 옆에 있는 912호에 보관되어 있다.

해설 (A) among은 "셋 이상 사이"의 의미이므로 복수 명사가 와야 하고, (B) on은 표면/선의 개념으로 층/거리 등이, (D) beneath는 표면 아래에 붙어 있는 장소를 의미하므로 "~옆에"라는 장소의 전치사 (C)가 가장 적절하다.

어휘 material ⓝ 자료   supplies ⓝ 용품

정답 (C)

3. 대학원생을 제외하고는 누구도 제2언어의 효과적인 작문에 대한 Jacob 박사의 발표를 이해하지 못했다.

해설 (A) ~을 제외하고 (B) 다음의 (C) ~을 통해 (D) ~의 결과로 전치사들 중에 문맥상 "제외"의 의미를 지닌 (A) except가 가장 적절하다.

어휘 graduate student ⓝ 대학원생   effective ⓐ 효과적인

정답 (A)

4. 연간 컨퍼런스에 참석하고자 하는 사람들은 사진이 있는 신분증 없이는 해당 행사장에 입장할 수 없다.

해설 빈칸 뒤 명사를 연결할 전치사가 필요하므로, (C) without이 정답이다.

어휘 admittance ⓝ 입장 허가   identification ⓝ 신분증

정답 (C)

SPARTA Practice Test
p.139

101. (B)	102. (D)	103. (A)	104. (B)	105. (A)
106. (C)	107. (A)	108. (C)	109. (A)	110. (B)
111. (B)	112. (D)	113. (D)	114. (B)	115. (A)
116. (C)	117. (A)	118. (C)	119. (D)	120. (D)
121. (A)	122. (A)	123. (B)	124. (D)	

PART 5

101. 증권거래소에 새롭게 목록으로 오른 종목은 2년 이내에 30퍼센트까지 증가할 것으로 예상된다.

해설 two years는 기간을 나타내므로 (B)가 정답이다. (A) about (~경에), (C) toward(~쯤), (D) following(~이후)는 의미상 어색하다.

어휘 stock exchange ⓝ 증권거래소

정답 (B)

102. Lohbson Apparel은 남는 재고를 올해 말까지 20퍼센트로 줄이려고 노력할 것이다.

해설 "연말(the end of the year)"은 "시점"을 나타내므로 (D)가 정답이다.

어휘 redundant ⓐ 잉여의, 남는

정답 (D)

103. Ian Schmitt은 뛰어난 업무 실적을 보여주었기 때문에, 올해의 직원 상 후보로 오르게 되었다.

해설 빈칸 뒤가 〈주어 + 동사〉 구조이므로 접속사 (A)가 정답이다.

어휘 outstanding ⓐ 뛰어난

정답 (A)

104. 우리는 Monica 씨가 회사에서 가장 영광스러운 '올해 최고의 직원상'에 마침내 지명되었다는 사실을 듣게 되어 기쁩니다.

해설 nominate(후보자로 추천/지명하다)와 어울리는 전치사로 (B)가 정답이다. be nominated for ~를 덩어리째 알아두자.

어휘 finally adv 마침내   honorable ⓐ 영광스러운

정답 (B)

105. 개인 거래의 증가와 관계없이, 전반적으로 유럽의 주식 시장이 4주 연속 고전하고 있습니다.

해설 of와 함께 "~와 관계없이"라는 표현을 이루는 (A) regardless가 정답이다.

어휘 regarding prep ~에 관하여   trading ⓝ (주식)거래   consecutive ⓐ 연속적인

정답 (A)

106. 지난 10년 동안 Lafayette 초등학교의 학생 수가 3천명 증가했습니다.

해설 빈칸 뒤에 "지난 10년"이라는 기간이 나오고 주절에 현재완료가 왔으므로, (C) over가 정답이다.

어휘 elementary school ⓝ 초등학교 the number of ~의 수

정답 (C)

107. 교육 훈련이 시작되자마자 신입사원들에게 직원 업무 편람이 제공될 것입니다.

해설 [upon/on + -ing] 구조로 "~하자마자"의 의미를 나타내는 (A)가 가장 적절하다.

어휘 employee manual ⓝ 업무 편람 recruit ⓝ 신입사원

정답 (A)

108. 이 웹페이지는 출발지와 목적지 사이가 얼마나 먼지 또는 적절한 경로들을 어떻게 운전하고 이용할지에 대한 질문에 대응해줍니다.

해설 [between A and B] 구조로 두 지점 사이를 의미하는 전치사 (C) between이 정답이다.

어휘 destination ⓝ 목적지 appropriate ⓐ 적절한

정답 (C)

109. 비록 그녀가 지난달에 회계 관리자로 승진되었지만, 대리로서의 그녀의 이전 업무들이 여전히 똑같이 남아 있다.

해설 빈칸 뒤 명사를 연결하고, 신분이나 직책의 명사와 함께 쓰이는 전치사로 "~로서" 의미의 (A)가 적절하다.

어휘 duty ⓝ 업무 deputy ⓝ 대리(인)

정답 (A)

110. 심한 가격 경쟁에도 불구하고, 그 회사의 분기 결과물은 세계 광고 시장에서 뛰어난 능력을 보여주었다.

해설 우선 전치사가 아닌 (D) in spite (부사)는 빈칸 뒤 명사를 연결하지 못하므로 제외되고, (A) 제외 (B) 반전 (C) 장소/순위의 전치사 중 문맥상 (B)가 가장 적절하다.

어휘 outstanding ⓐ 뛰어난 competition ⓝ 경쟁

정답 (B)

111. 캘리포니아 주 도처에 설치되어 있는 많은 판넬은 햇빛으로부터 더 많은 전기를 발생시킬 것이다.

해설 전기가 햇빛에서 오는 것이므로 시작/출발점을 나타내는 전치사 (B) from이 가장 적절하다.

어휘 an array of ⓐ 많은 generate ⓥ 발생시키다

정답 (B)

112. Hannah 씨는 그녀의 교육적, 학문적 배경들 때문에 곧 실험실 리더로 임명될 것입니다.

해설 (A) ~앞에(전치사), (B) 바로 맞은편에(전치사), (C) 결과적으로(부사), (D) ~ 때문에(전치사) 중에서, 문맥상 원인을 나타내는 (D)가 적절하다.

어휘 appoint ⓝ 임명하다 academic ⓐ 학문적인

정답 (D)

113. 모든 계정 번호는 일반적으로 IT 지원부서장에 의해 12시에 설정됩니다.

해설 〈be + 타Ved + by〉 수동태 구조로, 빈칸 뒤 행위 주체를 통해 '~에 의해'라는 의미의 (D)가 적절하다.

어휘 account number ⓝ 계좌 번호, 계정 번호

정답 (D)

114. 작년 여름 축제의 인기를 고려해볼 때, 그 기관은 올해 방문객 수가 급격히 증가할 것으로 예상합니다.

해설 빈칸 뒤 명사구와 함께 수식어가 될 수 있는 전치사는 (B) Given이다.

어휘 popularity ⓝ 인기 organization ⓝ 기관 sharply ⓐdv 급격히 provided (that) ⓒonj ~라면 namely ⓐdv 즉

정답 (B)

115. 추가로 주문하고 싶으시면, 다음의 저희 회사의 협력 공급업체 목록을 참고하셔야 합니다.

해설 빈칸 앞의 list(목록)가 빈칸 뒤의 suppliers(공급업체)에 관한 것이기 때문에 (A) of(앞의 명사와 같은 속성, 동격)가 정답이다.

어휘 supplier ⓝ 공급업체

정답 (A)

116. 완성도 높은 하드웨어와 개인 컴퓨터를 생산하는 Plus Technology는 소프트웨어 산업까지 확장하는 중입니다.

해설 expand into가 '~로 확장하다'라는 의미의 표현으로, (C) into가 정답이다.

어휘 well-made ⓐ 완성도 높은

정답 (C)

117. 태블릿 PC의 새로운 버전이 월요일부터 판매되면서, CREBIZ 사는 모바일 기기 시장에서 가장 심한 경쟁에 직면하게 될 것입니다.

해설 '판매되는, 판매 중'의 의미로 sale과 가장 적절하게 연결되는 전치사 (A) on이 정답이다.

어휘 as of [prep] (미래) ~부로 face [v] 직면하다
competition [n] 경쟁 device [n] 장치, 장비
정답 (A)

118. 모든 수업 활동 완료 후, Yenjing 씨는 홍콩 대학으로부터 박사 학위 프로그램을 수료할 기회를 잡았다.
해설 빈칸 뒤의 명사구를 연결할 전치사는 (C)밖에 없다.
어휘 coursework [n] 수업 활동 admission [n] 입학
Ph.D. [n] 박사 학위
정답 (C)

119. C&T Broadband 사는 이용자들에게 빠른 속도의 인터넷 연결과 무제한 다운로드 용량을 포함한 다양한 서비스를 제공하고 있습니다.
해설 빈칸 앞의 다양한 서비스(a variety of services)에 대한 세부 항목을 설명하는 명사들이 이어지므로 '~을 포함하여'라는 의미의 (D)가 알맞다.
어휘 subscriber [n] 구독자, 이용자 connection [n] 연결
capacity [n] 용량
정답 (D)

120. 100개 이상의 제품을 대량 구매하신다면, 우리 제품 모두 20 퍼센트 할인을 받을 수 있습니다.
해설 in bulk가 '대량으로'라는 의미의 표현으로 (D)가 적절하다.
어휘 discount [v] 할인하다 bulk [n] 거대함, 대량
정답 (D)

121. 전치사
해설 choose from이 '~에서 택하다'라는 의미로 (A)가 정답이다.
정답 (A)

122. 동사
해설 would라는 조동사 뒤에 동사원형이 필요하므로 (A)가 정답이다.
정답 (A)

123. 동사
해설 would라는 조동사 뒤에 동사원형으로 (B) suit가 적절하다.
정답 (B)

124. 문장 넣기
(A) 여러분은 또한 미리 예약해야 합니다.
(B) 이 가격은 12월 30일까지만 유효합니다.
(C) 이 아파트는 지역 상점들과 멀리 떨어져 있습니다.
(D) 저희 매장은 주6일 오전 10시부터 오후 10시까지 엽니다.
해설 질문에 대한 대답을 해준다는 내용이 앞에 등장한 후, 해당 매장의 영업 시간을 알려주며 글을 마무리하는 흐름의 (D)가 자연스럽다.
정답 (D)

| PART 6 |

(121-124) 다음 광고를 참조하세요.

Ever PET World
모든 동물 애호가들을 환영합니다!

반려동물을 찾고 계시다면, 저희에게 와주세요. 여기 Ever PET World에서 고르실 수 있는 수백마리의 동물들이 있습니다. 강아지, 고양이, 토끼, 햄스터와 같은 것들이 고객분들께 인기 있는 선택입니다. 우리 매장의 전문가들은 여러분의 애완동물이 일반적으로 필요로 하는 관리 수준을 상세히 설명해줄 수 있습니다. 그들은 또한 당신에게 어떤 애완동물이 당신의 집과 아파트에 가장 적합한지 추천해줄 것입니다. 그들은 당신께서 갖고 계신 어떠한 질문에도 답해주는 것을 행복해할 것입니다. 저희 매장은 주6일 오전 10시부터 오후 10시까지 엽니다. 가능한 한 빨리 보러 오세요!

어휘 animal lover [n] 동물 애호가 hundreds of [a] 수백의
expert [n] 전문가 explain [v] 설명하다 care [n] 관리
normally [adv] 일반적으로

DAY 4 부사절 접속사

SPARTA Check-UP
p.143

1. (C) 2. (C) 3. (B) 4. (C)

1. 휴가 동안의 과중한 업무 때문에, 영업부장과 그녀의 팀은 모두 지쳐 있다.

해설 상관접속사를 묻는 문제로, both와 함께 쓰일 수 있는 접속사는 (C) and이다.

어휘 heavy work ⓝ 과중한 업무 exhausted ⓐ 지친

정답 (C)

2. 2019년 새로운 개발 계획을 발표한 이래로, 시의회는 신규 복합단지 건설에 대한 공개 입찰을 시작했다.

해설 부사절 접속사 중, 접속사의 시제가 과거, 주절의 시제가 현재완료가 나오는 경우는 '~이래로'라는 의미의 (C) since이다. ⟨S have(has) Ved + since S Ved⟩ 구조이다.

어휘 city council ⓝ 시의회 launch ⓥ 개시하다 public bid ⓝ 공개 입찰 multiplex ⓝ 복합 단지

정답 (C)

3. Emily 씨는 영어와 불어 둘 다 유창하게 한다는 점에서 다른 후보자들보다 유리하다.

해설 부사절 접속사를 묻는 문제이다. (A) [목적] ~하기 위해, (B) [원인] ~라는 점에서, (C) [반전] 비록 ~일지라도, (D) [제외] ~을 제외하고 중에서, 주절 및 종속절의 의미 관계상 (B)가 적절하다.

어휘 advantage ⓝ 장점 fluently adv 유창하게

정답 (B)

4. 회사 메인 서버에 최신 보안 소프트웨어를 설치하는 동안, 우리 웹사이트가 오전 10시부터 11시까지 일시적으로 멈출 것입니다.

해설 빈칸 뒤의 -ing형 분사를 연결할 수 있는 것은 시간/조건 부사절 접속사로 동시 동작을 나타내는 (C) While이 정답이다.

어휘 install ⓥ 설치하다 shut down ⓥ 멈추다

정답 (C)

SPARTA Practice Test
p.147

101. (A)	102. (C)	103. (A)	104. (C)	105. (B)
106. (A)	107. (C)	108. (B)	109. (C)	110. (C)
111. (B)	112. (D)	113. (A)	114. (A)	115. (D)
116. (D)	117. (A)	118. (B)	119. (B)	120. (A)
121. (B)	122. (C)	123. (C)	124. (B)	

PART 5

101. 영수증 원본과 당신의 물건이 판매자에게 배송될 때까지 우리는 전액 환불을 해드릴 수 없습니다.

해설 빈칸 뒤 ⟨주어 + 동사⟩ 구조가 있으므로 접속사가 필요하다. 전치사인 (C) in case of와 (D) given은 오답이다. 그리고 부사절 접속사 자리에 (B) whether가 오려면 or를 동반해야 하므로 (A) until이 정답이다.

어휘 refund ⓥ 환불하다 deliver ⓥ 보내다

정답 (A)

102. BTA-300 모델의 판매율이 지난 시즌보다 낮음에도 불구하고, 총수익은 평균을 훨씬 넘었다.

해설 빈칸 뒤 ⟨주어 + 동사⟩를 연결할 접속사가 필요하다. (A) 전치사 (B) 접속부사 (C) 접속사 (D) 전치사 중에서 (C)가 정답이다.

어휘 lower ⓐ 더 낮은 revenue ⓝ 수익

정답 (C)

103. 새로운 전담반을 설립하는 것은 정부가 전략을 강화하는 데 도움될 뿐만 아니라 현재의 경기 침체를 벗어나도록 도와주기도 한다.

해설 'A뿐만 아니라 B도'라는 의미의 not only A but (also) B를 이루는 (A)가 정답이다.

어휘 task force ⓝ 전담반 enhance ⓥ 강화시키다 escape ⓥ 벗어나다 recession ⓝ (경기)침체

정답 (A)

104. 다양한 자격요건을 신중히 검토한 후, 위원회는 Graham 씨의 입학을 승인하기로 결정했다.

해설 빈칸 뒤 -ing는 동명사일 수도, 능동형 현재분사일 수도 있는데, 동명사라면 전치사가, 능동분사라면 시간/조건 부사절 접속사가 가능하다. 우선 (D)는 접속 부사이므로 오답이고, 나머지 (A) ~라면 (B) ~옆에 (C) ~이후 중에서 문맥상 (C)가 가장 적절하다.

어휘 various ⓐ 다양한 requirement ⓝ 자격요건 admission ⓝ 입학

정답 (C)

105. 출장비 환급을 받고 싶은 직원들은 직접 수표를 수령하거나, 자동이체를 선택할 수 있다.

해설 빈칸 뒤에 동사원형이 있으므로, 빈칸 앞의 pick up과 대등한 구조를 이끄는 등위접속사가 필요하다. 보기 중에서 부사절 접속사 if와 완전한 문장이 필요한 so를 제거하면, or와 but 중 (B)가 의미상 알맞다.

어휘 reimbursement ⓝ 환급 travel expense ⓝ 출장비 in person adv 직접 automatic transfer ⓝ 자동이체

정답 (B)

106. 당신이 Sydney 공항에 도착할 때쯤, Luis 씨가 공항 주차장 Section Yellow B-2에서 당신을 기다리고 있을 겁니다.

해설 빈칸 뒤 〈주어 + 동사〉를 연결할 부사절 접속사 자리로, (D)를 제외하고 가능하다. 빈칸 뒤 종속절의 동사의 시제가 현재인데, 주절에 미래완료가 나올 수 있는 부사절 접속사는 시간차를 나타내 주는 "~할 때쯤" 의미의 (A)가 정답이다.

어휘 wait for ⓥ 기다리다

정답 (A)

107. 새로 개발된 소프트웨어 Hack-Security 45는 이전 모델보다 비싸지만, 그럼에도 불구하고 안전성이나 품질 면에서 훨씬 더 뛰어나다.

해설 (A) 그러나(등위 접속사), (B) ~하지 않는다면, (C) 반면에, (D) 언제든지 중에서, 문맥상 반전의 의미를 나타내는 (C)가 적절하다.

어휘 expensive ⓐ 비싼

정답 (C)

108. 신입사원들이 채용되자마자, 현장 직무 교육을 위해 그들을 302호로 보내주세요.

해설 빈칸 뒤에 〈주어 + 동사〉 구조이므로 전치사인 Other than과 In addition to는 오답, So that은 문장 맨 앞에 올 수 없다. '~하자마자'라는 의미의 시간 부사절 접속사 (B)가 정답이다.

어휘 on-the-job training ⓝ 현장 직무 교육

정답 (B)

109. 주식 구매를 결정하기 전에, 모든 투자자들은 회사의 재무제표를 신중하게 확인해야 합니다.

해설 빈칸 뒤 -ing가 분사로 쓰이므로 시간/조건 부사절 접속사가 가능한데, (B) since는 시간의 의미일 때 '~이래로'라는 뜻으로 주절에 현재완료(have Ved)가 와야 한다. 현재완료 시제가 없으므로 '~전에'라는 의미의 시간 접속사 (C)가 정답이다.

어휘 financial statement ⓝ 재무제표

정답 (C)

110. 이사회는 현재 시장 상황이 얼마나 불안정하든지 간에 새로운 사업에의 투자를 주장하고 있다.

해설 [however[=no matter how] + 형용사/부사 + 주어 + 동사 ~] 구조로, [주어 + 동사] 앞에 형용사/부사를 위치시킬 수 있는 접속사로는 how가 포함된 (C)가 적절하다.

어휘 insist upon ⓥ 주장하다   unstable ⓐ 불안정한

정답 (C)

111. Culpepper가 소스코드 정리를 일단 끝내면, 그들의 새로운 웹 주문 시스템이 내일 아침부터 이용 가능할 것입니다.

해설 빈칸 뒤 〈주어 + 동사〉를 연결할 접속사가 필요하다. so too와 not only는 부사이므로 오답이다. how는 명사절 접속사로 쓰이는데, 해당 빈칸은 완전한 문장 다음에 나온 부사절을 이끄는 접속사가 필요하므로 (B) once가 적절하다.

어휘 as of ⓟ ~부터   arrangement ⓝ 정리

정답 (B)

112. 일자리가 제한적일지라도, 우리는 그들이 뛰어난 자격조건들을 갖추고 있다면 추가로 직원을 뽑을 준비가 되어 있다.

해설 and와 짝을 이루는 (A) Both는 오답이다. (B) So that은 문장 맨 앞에 오지 못하기 때문에 오답이다. (C) Whether가 부사절 접속사로 쓰이려면 or와 동반해야 한다. 그러므로 반전을 나타내는 (D) Even though가 정답이다.

어휘 job opening ⓝ 일자리   qualification ⓝ 자격요건

정답 (D)

113. 운전면허증을 신청할 때, 여권, 신분증, 사회보장 카드 등 적어도 2개의 신분 증명서 양식을 제출하셔야 합니다.

해설 빈칸 뒤 능동형 현재분사를 연결할 수 있는 부사절 접속사는 "시간/조건"의 부사절 접속사만 가능하므로 (A)가 정답이다.

어휘 social security ⓝ 사회 보장   and so on (기타) 등등

정답 (A)

114. 주문을 빨리 처리하기 위해 웹사이트에 접속하셔서 당신의 정보를 입력해 주세요.

해설 빈칸 뒤 〈주어 + 동사〉를 연결할 접속사는 보기 중에서 '~하기 위해'라는 의미의 (A)이다.

어휘 log on ⓥ 접속하다   process ⓥ 처리하다

정답 (A)

115. 저는 Belkin 항공사에 취업한 이래로 전세계에 있는 다양한 사람들을 만날 기회를 갖고 있습니다.

해설 빈칸 뒤의 〈주어 + 동사〉를 연결할 부사절 접속사가 필요한데, (A)는 부사이므로 정답에서 제외, (C)는 형용사/부사가 나와야 하므로 오답이다. (B) while은 동시 동작의 경우 시제를 일치시켜 '반전'의 의미로 쓰일 수 있고, (D) since는 과거시제와 주절에 현재완료가 올 때 '~이래로'라는 의미로 쓰인다. 따라서 (D)가 적절하다.

어휘 employ ⓥ 채용하다

정답 (D)

116. 이 보고서에 포함된 모든 것은 연방법과 주법 하에 기밀이기 때문에 특정 상황에서만 그 정보가 공개되어야 한다.

해설 빈칸 뒤의 절을 이끄는 접속사 자리로, (A) 전치사, (B) 부사, (C) 부사이므로 접속사인 (D)가 정답이다.

어휘 confidential ⓐ 기밀의   federal ⓐ 연방의

정답 (D)

117. 비록 베트남에 있는 그 회사는 인건비에 있어 유리하지만, 유럽의 자동차 산업은 기술과 품질 면에서 강점이 있다.

해설 (B) That은 명사절로 쓰이므로 오답, (D) Whether는 부사절에서 or와 동반해야 하므로 오답, (A) Although(비록 ~일지라도) 반전 접속사와 (C) Until(~까지) 시간 접속사 중 문맥상 (A)가 자연스럽다.

어휘 labor cost ⓝ 인건비 automobile ⓝ 자동차

정답 (A)

118. 서버 점검이 정기적으로 실시되는 한, 우리 온라인 서비스는 고객들에게 더 신뢰할 만하고 품질이 좋아질 것입니다.

해설 빈칸 뒤 [주어 + 동사]를 연결할 접속사 중에서 문맥상 "~하는 한"의 (B) As long as가 적절하다.

어휘 inspection ⓝ 조사, 검사 conduct ⓥ 실행하다

정답 (B)

119. 구매일로부터 10일 이내에 물품을 반납하기만 하면, 우리는 기꺼이 전액 환불해 드릴 것입니다.

해설 부사절 접속사 (A) ~하지 않는다면, (B) ~하는 한, (C) 마치 ~인 것처럼, (D) 비록 ~일지라도 중에서, 한정적 조건을 나타내는 (B)가 가장 적절하다.

어휘 be willing to ⓥ 기꺼이 ~하다 in full adv 전액으로

정답 (B)

120. 뉴타운 건설이 완료되면, 거의 2,000가구의 추가 주택들이 Shippensburgh County에 제공될 것입니다.

해설 빈칸 뒤 완전한 문장을 연결할 수 있는 부사절 접속사로 (A) when이 적절하다.

어휘 almost adv 거의 county ⓝ (군 단위) 도시

정답 (A)

| PART 6 |

(121-124) 다음의 편지를 참조하세요.

8월 10일
Q-Main Electronics
130 Jayhawk Boulevard
Lawrence, KS 66045

고객 서비스부서에,

심사숙고 끝에, 저는 지난주 귀사의 온라인 매장을 통해 Power Fly 전자레인지 RS-2 모델을 구매했습니다. 사용 설명서에 따르면, 제품이 일정 온도에 도달하면 자동으로 꺼져야 합니다. 그러나 제가 구매한 전자레인지는 수동으로 스위치를 꺼야 할 때까지 유지됩니다. 조리기구의 온도조절기가 명백히 뭔가 잘못된 것 같고, 전액 환불을 위해 반송하고 싶습니다. 어쨌든, 너무 위험해서 지속적으로 사용할 수 없습니다. 특히, 이번 건은 제가 귀사의 제품을 처음 주문하는 거라서 계속 사용하고 싶었습니다. 어떻게 이 전자레인지를 반품해야 하는지 저에게 말해주세요. 답을 기다리겠습니다.

그럼 이만,

Robert Joshua

어휘 consideration ⓝ 고려 microwave ⓝ 전자레인지 manual ⓝ 사용설명서 turn off ⓥ 끄다 manually adv 수동으로 obviously adv 명백하게 temperature ⓝ 온도 controller ⓝ 조절기, 제어기

121. 전치사

해설 빈칸 뒤에 your online store라는 장소 명사가 왔으므로 전치사 자리다. (A) although는 접속사, (B) through는 전치사, (C) even as는 접속사, (D) only if는 접속사이므로 (B)가 정답이다.

정답 (B)

122. 동사

해설 접속사 if 뒤에 it이 주어, 그 뒤에 동사가 와야 하므로 (B) 동명사, (D) to부정사는 오답이고, 수 일치에 의해 (A) reach도 오답이다. 과거시제 동사인 (C) reached가 정답이다.

정답 (C)

123. 접속사

해설 (A) 어디든지, (B) 마치~인 것처럼, (C) ~까지, (D) 둘 중 하나 중에서, 빈칸 뒤 절을 이끄는 접속사로, 문맥상 '~까지'라는 의미의 (C)가 가장 적절하다.

정답 (C)

124. 문장 넣기
  (A) 다른 브랜드에 비해, 귀사의 제품은 가격이 두 배나 비쌉니다.
  (B) 어쨌든, 너무 위험해서 지속적으로 사용할 수 없습니다.
  (C) 귀사의 신제품에 대해 모든 정보를 듣고 싶습니다.
  (D) 게다가, 작업장에서는 안전 절차를 반드시 따라야 합니다.

해설 전자레인지에 문제가 있어서 환불을 받고 싶다고 했으므로, 더 이상 사용하지 못하겠다는 문맥의 (B)가 가장 적절하다.

정답 (B)

DAY 5 동사의 5형식

SPARTA Check-UP p.151

1. (C) 2. (B) 3. (A) 4. (B)

1. 새로 개발된 진공 청소기 X-10은 동유럽 시장에서 점점 인기를 얻고 있다.
해설 빈칸 뒤 형용사(popular)가 보어 역할을 하므로 2형식 동사가 필요하다. (A) 준수하다(1형식 자동사), (B) 신청하다(1형식 자동사), (C) ~되다(2형식 자동사), (D) 결정하다(3형식 타동사) 중에서 (C)가 정답이다.
어휘 vacuum cleaner ⓝ 진공 청소기
정답 (C)

2. 그 회사는 전 직원들에게 이번 분기 교육 훈련 수료를 확인해야 한다고 알렸다.
해설 빈칸 뒤에 사람 목적어가 먼저 등장했다. [----- 사람 O + 사물 O(that 명사절)] 구조와 함께 쓰일 수 있는 것은 4형식 동사로, (B)가 정답이다.
어휘 completion ⓝ 완성 quarter ⓝ 분기
정답 (B)

3. 주 정부는 시민들이 식물과 잔디에 너무 자주 물을 주는 것을 금지하도록 결정했다.
해설 〈----- + 사람 O + to V〉 구조로, '~에게 ~하게 하다'라는 뜻의 "시키다" 류 5형식 타동사가 필요하다. (A) forbid가 '~가 …하지 못하도록 하다'라는 뜻으로 정답이다.
어휘 water ⓥ 물을 주다 lawn ⓝ 잔디
정답 (A)

4. 매니저는 Dana 씨의 발표에 참석한 사람들에게 워크숍 자료를 배포했다.
해설 (A) 획득하다, (B) 배포하다, (C) 금지하다, (D) 연락하다 모두 3형식 타동사로, 빈칸 뒤에 목적어가 사물이고 to those who ~라는 수식어가 있으므로 '~에게 사물을 전달/배포/분배하는'이라는 의미의 (B)가 적절하다.
어휘 material ⓝ 자료
정답 (B)

SPARTA Practice Test p.155

101. (D) 102. (B) 103. (C) 104. (C) 105. (B)
106. (C) 107. (B) 108. (C) 109. (C) 110. (C)
111. (A) 112. (C) 113. (C) 114. (C) 115. (C)
116. (A) 117. (D) 118. (D) 119. (A) 120. (C)
121. (C) 122. (B) 123. (C) 124. (A)

| PART 5 |

101. 모든 고객들이 Charms 사에 의해 개발된 MVX-100 휴대폰 신제품에 긍정적인 반응을 보였다.
해설 빈칸은 동사 자리이므로 respond to(~에 대응하다)의 (D)가 가장 적절하다.
어휘 positively ⓐdv 긍정적으로 developed ⓐ 개발된
정답 (D)

102. 선반 위에 있는 수많은 제품들은 고객들이 그들이 원하는 최상의 물건을 고르는 것을 어렵게 만든다.
해설 〈동사 + it(가목적어) + 목적보어 + to부정사(진목적어)〉 구조로, 보기 중 5형식 동사인 (B)가 정답이다.
어휘 shelves ⓝ 선반 difficult ⓐ 어려운
정답 (B)

103. 기획부서를 맡고 있는 Samuel 씨는 시장 경향에 대한 연구에 집중하기 위해 관리직 직책을 포기하기를 원한다.
해설 자동사 (A) 주장하다, (B) 집중하다, (C) 동의하다, (D) 다루다 중에서, focus on(~에 집중하다)이 문맥상 적절하므로 (B)가 정답이다.
어휘 be in charge of ⓥ ~을 맡다, 담당하다 give up ⓥ 포기하다
정답 (B)

104. 이메일로 회사 문서를 타인에게 전달할 때는, 그것들을 보호하기 위해 비밀번호를 설정해서 안전하게 하세요.
해설 [keep/leave + 목적어 + 목적보어(형용사/분사)]의 5형식 상태 동사 구조로 "~을 ~한 상태로 두다"의 의미를 지닌다. 빈칸은 목적보어 자리이므로 형용사인 (C)가 정답이다.
어휘 secure ⓐ 안전한 set up ⓥ 설정하다 protect ⓥ 보호하다
정답 (C)

105. Charles's Dealership은 항상 고객들에게 신뢰할 만한 정보와 중고차를 합리적인 가격으로 제공한다.
해설 〈provide + 사람 목적어 + with + 사물 목적어〉(~에게 ~을 제공하다) 구조로 (B)가 적절하다.

정답 및 해설 | 411

어휘 reliable ⓐ 믿을 만한 used ⓐ 중고의
정답 (B)

106. 관계당국은 미지급된 부채를 많이 안고 있는 대출자들의 추가 대출을 금지할 필요가 있다고 발표했다.
해설 (A) 강화하다 (B) 금지하다 (C) 금지하다 (D) 결정하다 중에서 [prevent + 목적어 + from -ing](~가 ~하는 것을 금지하다) 구조의 (C)가 가장 적절하다.
어휘 outstanding ⓐ 미지급의 debt ⓝ 빚, 부채 loan ⓝ 대출
정답 (C)

107. Power Clean X10 청소기에 대한 초기 후기가 의미하는 것은 평가자들이 이것을 어느 장소에서나 사용하기 편리하다고 판단했다는 것이다.
해설 [consider/find + it(가목적어) + 목적보어 + to부정사(진목적어)](~을 ~라고 판단하다)의 5형식 구조로, 빈칸은 목적어의 상태를 설명하는 형용사로 (B)가 적절하다.
어휘 comment ⓝ 후기 indicate ⓥ 의미하다
정답 (B)

108. 다른 긴급한 업무 때문에, 제 서울 지사 방문이 3월 20일로 재조정되었다고 Swale 씨에게 알려 주세요.
해설 빈칸 뒤에 사람 목적어가 나오고 그 뒤에 명사절(that~)이 위치하므로 4형식 타동사로 (C)가 가장 적절하다.
어휘 urgent ⓐ 긴급한, 중요한 task ⓝ 업무
정답 (C)

109. 당신의 관리자한테서 따로 지시받지 않았다면, 모든 멤버들은 회사 복장 규정에 관한 현재 정책과 규정을 준수해야 합니다.
해설 (A) 대응하다 (B) 고수하다 (C) 준수하다 (D) 준수하다 중에서 빈칸 뒤 with와 함께 쓰이는 자동사이면서 문맥상 적절한 comply with(~을 준수하다/따르다)의 (C)가 정답이다.
어휘 otherwise ⓐⓓⓥ 다르게 dress code ⓝ 복장 규정
정답 (C)

110. Kane 사의 새로운 휴대폰은 엄청난 데이터 용량과 훌륭한 디자인이 특징이다.
해설 본동사 자리로, 복수 주어 뒤에는 (C)가 가장 적절하다.
어휘 enormous ⓐ 엄청난 storage ⓝ 저장 capacity ⓝ 용량 impressive ⓐ 인상적인, 훌륭한
정답 (C)

111. 안 좋은 날씨 상황은 건설 노동자들이 어떤 일도 진행하지 못하게 할 수 있다.
해설 [---- + O + from -ing] 구조로 "금지하다"의 의미를 지닌 (A)가 가장 적절하다.

어휘 make progress ⓥ 진행하다, 발전하다
정답 (A)

112. 다수의 반대에도 불구하고, 마케팅 부장 Miller 씨는 프로젝트에 강력히 동의했다.
해설 빈칸은 동사 자리이므로 (A), (B)는 제외. 과거시제 동사인 (C)가 정답이다.
어휘 objection ⓝ 반대 majority ⓝ 다수 agree with ⓥ ~에 동의하다
정답 (C)

113. 이것은 우리 대학원생들이 유럽을 여행하고 세계적으로 유명한 학술제에 참석할 수 있는 기회입니다.
해설 빈칸 뒤에 전치사가 있으므로 자동사가 필요한데, 자동사로는 (A) 발생하다, (B) 돌보다, (C) 참석하다가 있다. 문맥상 컨퍼런스에 '참석하다'가 자연스러우므로 (C)가 정답이다.
어휘 take place ⓥ 발생하다 participate in ⓥ 참석하다
정답 (C)

114. Pennecom은 더 좋고 광범위한 양질의 서비스를 고객들에게 제공할 새로운 계획을 가지고 있다고 발표했다.
해설 has 뒤에는 명사 목적어, Ved 완료시제, 의무의 to V를 사용할 수 있는데 빈칸 뒤 명사절(that)이 있으므로 능동태 구조로 명사절을 목적어로 취할 수 있는 [have 타Ved] 구조로 (C)가 정답이다.
어휘 quality ⓐ 양질의
정답 (C)

115. Haneda 사는 홍보부 관리직에 자격을 갖춘 전도유망한 후보자를 찾도록 헤드헌터들에게 요구했다.
해설 빈칸 뒤의 전치사 for와 함께 쓰이는 자동사를 찾아야 하는데, (A) apply for(신청하다)와 (C) search for(찾다) 중에서 문맥상 (C)가 가장 적절하다.
어휘 qualified ⓐ 자격을 갖춘 promising ⓐ 전도유망한
정답 (C)

116. 그의 건강 문제 때문에 Earnest 씨는 현재 진행 중인 프로젝트가 상당히 뒤쳐져 있다.
해설 빈칸 뒤에 부사 behind가 있으므로 자동사인 fall과 rise가 가능. fall behind(뒤쳐지다, 뒤떨어지다)를 이루는 (A)가 정답이다.
어휘 considerably ⓐⓓⓥ 상당히 ongoing ⓐ 진행 중인
정답 (A)

117. Columbus 시의회는 오하이오 대학에서 열리는 이번 홈커밍 축제에 시민들이 참석하기를 강력하게 권고합니다.

해설 〈---- 사람 목적어 + to V〉의 5형식 구조로 (D)가 가장 적절하다.

어휘 city council ⓝ 시의회   encourage ⓥ 독려하다

정답 (D)

118. 비록 그들은 신제품 개발에 온 힘을 기울였지만, 그 팀은 여전히 그 프로젝트가 너무 어려워서 마감기한을 맞추기 어렵다고 생각한다.

해설 〈find + O + 형/분〉인 5형식 구조로, 목적보어로 알맞은 형용사 (D)가 정답이다.

어휘 deadline ⓝ 마감기한   make an effort ⓥ 노력하다

정답 (D)

119. CEO는 노조가 임금의 10퍼센트 삭감과 최대 200개의 일자리를 없애겠다는 그 규정을 절대 승인하지 않을 것이라고 발표했다.

해설 빈칸 뒤 that 명사절을 목적어로 취하는 3형식 타동사가 필요한데 told, convinced, reminded는 4형식 타동사이므로 (A)가 정답이다.

어휘 labor union ⓝ 노조   pay cut ⓝ 임금 삭감   slash ⓥ 대폭 줄이다

정답 (A)

120. 관리자는 물류 창고 직원에게 깨지기 쉬운 제품은 폴리스티렌으로 조심스럽게 포장되어야 함을 상기시켰다.

해설 〈---- 사람 O + 사물 O(that 명사절)〉 구조로, 4형식 동사 (C)가 정답이다.

어휘 warehouse ⓝ 물류 창고   fragile ⓐ 깨지기 쉬운   polystyrene ⓝ 폴리스티렌

정답 (C)

| PART 6 |

(121-124) 다음 이메일을 참조하세요.

> 수신: 고객 서비스 〈customerservice@hwdpublishing.com〉
> 발신: Ken Hyland 〈k.hyland@firenetscape.com〉
> 제목: 새로운 개정판 도서
> 날짜: 5월 20일
>
> 고객 서비스부에,
>
> 저는 "언어 모험" 시리즈의 제7판을 찾으면서 거의 30분 정도 귀사의 웹사이트를 둘러보기를 방금 마쳤습니다. 하지만 실망스럽게도 6판만 보였습니다. 7판을 현재 구할 수 있는지 말씀해주시겠어요? 만약 아직 판매되지 않는다면, 언제 그것이 출판될지 알려주시겠어요? 저는 이번 가을에 시작하게 될 언어학 개론 수업을 주제로 한 대학교 필수 수업을 위해 그것이 필요합니다. 그 개정판이 제 학생들을 위한 필수 교재입니다. 가능하면 빨리 발행일에 대한 업데이트 정보를 좀 보내주실 수 있나요? 사이트를 다시 가보기 전에 답을 기다리겠습니다. 당신의 도움에 미리 감사드립니다.
>
> 그럼 이만
> Ken Hyland

어휘 browse ⓥ 둘러보다   edition ⓝ (간행물의) 판   prerequisite course ⓝ 필수 과목   linguistics ⓝ 언어학   introduction ⓝ 입문, 개론

121. 전치사

해설 search(~을 찾다)가 자동사로 쓰이면 찾는 목적을 나타내는 for가 함께 쓰이므로 (C)가 정답이다.

정답 (C)

122. 동사 어휘

해설 수동형 동사 (A) 알림 받다, (B) 출판되다, (C) 지불되다, (D) 연락되다 중에서, 해당 책이 언제 '출판되는지'를 뜻하는 (B) released가 정답이다.

정답 (B)

123. 문장 넣기
(A) 당신이 수집한 책들은 매우 인상적입니다.
(B) 귀사의 웹사이트 목록에 있는 책들은 찾기 쉽습니다.
(C) 그 개정판이 제 학생들을 위한 필수 교재입니다.
(D) 저는 이용 가능한 책들의 수량과 가격을 알고 싶습니다.

해설 앞 문장에서 발신자가 찾고 있는 책의 7판이 필수 과목용 교재임을 알 수 있고, 결과적으로 해당 수업의 필독 도서라는 의미의 (C)가 적절하다.

정답 (C)

124. 동사 어휘

해설 (A) 기다리다, (B) 부과하다, (C) 연기하다, (D) 결정하다 중에서 빈칸 뒤 전치사 for와 함께 쓸 수 있는 자동사로 (A) wait가 정답이다.

정답 (A)

DAY 6 수 일치와 태

SPARTA Check-UP p.159

1. (C) 2. (D) 3. (B) 4. (D)

1. 우리 R&D팀이 최근에 개발한 그 제품은 품질과 가격 면에서 소비자들에게 매우 인기가 있다.

   해설 주어는 The products로 복수이므로 have와 are가 가능한데, 빈칸 뒤에 형용사 보어가 있으므로 (C)가 정답이다.

   어휘 recently [adv] 최근에 quality [n] 품질

   정답 (C)

2. 이용약관 대부분의 변경사항들은 개정 전에 모든 고객들에게 전달되어야 합니다.

   해설 수량(부정)대명사 보기 중에 One, Each, Either는 주어를 단수로 만들기 때문에 has로 수 일치가 되어야 한다. 동사가 have이므로 (D) Most가 정답이다.

   어휘 terms and agreements [n] 이용약관 revision [n] 개정

   정답 (D)

3. 합격자들은 영업일 7일 이내에 전화를 통해 인사과로부터 일자리 제안을 받게 될 것이다.

   해설 조동사 can 뒤가 빈칸이므로 동사원형이 필요하다. 보기의 give(주다)는 대표적인 4형식 동사로, 사람 목적어가 맨 앞에 있고 사물 목적어인 a job offer가 빈칸 뒤에 왔으므로 수동태인 (B)가 정답이다.

   어휘 candidate [n] 후보자 business day [n] 영업일, 평일

   정답 (B)

4. 영화 〈타임머신-2〉는 웅장한 사운드와 이미지 때문에 매우 흥미롭다고 여겨졌다.

   해설 consider는 '~을 ~라고 간주하다'라는 뜻의 5형식 동사로, 목적보어 자리에 형용사 또는 분사가 온다. 수동태(is considered)로 되어 있으므로 목적어가 주어로 이동한 것으로, 분사 (D)가 정답이다.

   어휘 magnificent [a] 웅장한

   정답 (D)

SPARTA Practice Test p.163

101. (A) 102. (D) 103. (B) 104. (D) 105. (B)
106. (B) 107. (A) 108. (A) 109. (B) 110. (B)
111. (C) 112. (A) 113. (C) 114. (B) 115. (C)
116. (D) 117. (B) 118. (A) 119. (A) 120. (B)
121. (A) 122. (C) 123. (C) 124. (B)

| PART 5 |

101. 다른 주에서 온 학생들이 학자금대출을 신청할 때, 신분 증명에 대한 두 가지 양식이 학자금 지원처 직원에게 제시됩니다.

   해설 주어는 forms로 복수이고, '양식'은 '제출되는' 것이므로 (A) are가 적절하다.

   어휘 out-of-state [a] 다른 주의 financial aid [n] 학자금 지원

   정답 (A)

102. 회사의 온라인 서버 문제 때문에, 프로젝트 완료 마감 기한이 연장되었다.

   해설 주어는 deadline으로 단수, 빈칸 뒤에 목적어가 없으므로 수동태인 (D)가 정답이다.

   어휘 deadline [n] 마감 기한 extend [v] 연장하다

   정답 (D)

103. 대학원생들은 전부 3월 17일에 인문대가 개최하는 연간 학술 심포지움에 참석합니다.

   해설 동사가 attend로 복수이므로 단수 취급하는 (A), (C), (D)는 오답이다. 따라서 (B)가 정답이다.

   어휘 annual [a] 연간의 scholarship [n] 학문

   정답 (B)

104. 많은 시민들이 운전 면허증 신청을 위한 절차의 복잡함에 불만을 토론한 이래로 그것은 간소화되었다.

   해설 빈칸은 동사 자리로 뒤에 수식어(부사절)가 있으므로 수동태인 (C), (D) 중 가능한데, 주어가 복수(Procedures)이므로 (D)가 정답이다.

   어휘 streamline [v] 간소화하다 complexity [n] 복잡함

   정답 (D)

105. 해외에서 근무하는 것에 관심 있는 직원들은 이번 주말까지 지원서를 제출해야 합니다.

   해설 동사가 have로 복수이므로 복수 주어인 (B) Employees가 정답이다.

   어휘 overseas [adv] 해외에서

   정답 (B)

414

106. 회사의 구조조정 때문에 이전 운영진 멤버들은 거의 없다.

해설 보기의 remain은 2형식 자동사이므로 수동태가 불가능하다. 그러므로 (B)가 적절하다.

어휘 restructuring ⓝ 구조조정 former ⓐ 이전의

정답 (B)

107. 주변의 강들과 수자원을 오염시키는 오염 물질은 효과적으로 제어되고 제거되어야 합니다.

해설 등위 접속사 and 앞이 'be controlled' 수동 구조이므로, 동일하게 be removed가 와야 하는데 be동사 중복 제거로 (A)가 정답이다.

어휘 pollutant ⓝ 오염 물질 contaminate ⓥ 오염시키다 water source ⓝ 수자원

정답 (A)

108. Sharon Apparel의 우리 디자이너 중 한 명은 2024 밀라노 패션위크에 참석할 기회를 얻을 것입니다.

해설 of 뒤의 명사가 복수, 동사가 is인 단수로 나왔으므로 주어 전체를 단수로 만드는 (A) One이 정답이다.

어휘 chance ⓝ 기회 participate in ⓥ 참석하다

정답 (A)

109. 20주년을 축하하기 위해서 Power Digital Plaza는 10월 1일부터 20일까지 방문하시는 모든 분들에게 20% 추가 할인을 제공하고 있습니다.

해설 주격 관계대명사 who 앞의 선행사가 anyone이므로 단수동사인 (B)가 정답이다.

어휘 anniversary ⓝ 기념일 additional ⓐ 추가의

정답 (B)

110. 고용 노동청은 지역 청년들을 위한 더 많은 일자리를 창출하기 위해 지역 기반 시설을 개선하고 있다.

해설 빈칸 앞에 be동사가 있고 뒤에 목적어인 명사가 있으므로 능동태로 (B)가 정답이다.

어휘 authorities ⓝ 당국 regional ⓐ 지역의 infrastructure ⓝ 기반 시설

정답 (B)

111. 회사 웹사이트에 게시된 규정들은 준수되어야 하고 전직원에게 알려져야 합니다.

해설 빈칸은 주어 자리로 명사를 써야 하는데 사람 명사 (A) Regulator와 "규정"을 의미하는 (B) Regulation 모두 셀 수 있는 명사이므로 단독 사용이 불가능하다. 따라서 복수형 명사인 (C)가 정답이다.

어휘 post ⓥ 게시하다 follow ⓥ 따르다, 준수하다

정답 (C)

112. 그 공기청정기 필터는 해당 제품이 제대로 작동하는 것을 유지하기 위해 적어도 한 달에 한 번 세척되어야 한다.

해설 must라는 조동사 뒤에는 동사원형이 와야 하는데, 빈칸 뒤에 목적어가 없고 수식어만 있으므로 수동태인 (A)가 정답이다.

어휘 filter ⓝ 필터 air purifier ⓝ 공기청정기 appliance ⓝ 가전제품

정답 (A)

113. 대중은 정부가 현존하는 의료활동을 더 다양하고 구체적으로 확장할 계획을 가지고 있다는 사실을 확신 받을 수 있을 것이다.

해설 assure(확신시키다)는 4형식 동사로, 빈칸 뒤에 명사절(that)만 있으므로 빈칸 앞의 be동사와 수동형을 이루는 (C)가 정답이다.

어휘 existing ⓐ 현존하는 diversely ⓐⓓⓥ 다양하게

정답 (C)

114. 대중의 의견을 수집하고 합의에 도달하는 것은 그 나라에 대한 무역 제재 실행이 선행되어야 한다.

해설 빈칸 이하는 동사로, 주어가 to부정사이므로 단수 취급하여 (B) needs가 답이 된다.

어휘 precede ⓥ 선행하다 implement ⓥ 실행하다 sanction ⓝ 제재

정답 (B)

115. Smith 박사의 연설은 학자들을 위해 우리가 주최한 올해 포럼 중에서 매우 훌륭하다고 간주되었다.

해설 빈칸 뒤 형용사(excellent)는 목적어가 될 수 없으므로 타동사 consider의 수동형인 (C)가 정답이다.

어휘 excellent ⓐ 훌륭한 host ⓥ 주최하다

정답 (C)

116. 미국의 참전 용사 대부분이 재능 있는 군인들을 성장시키기 위해 국가 자선 재단에 많은 돈을 기부하고 있다.

해설 복수 주어에 빈칸 뒤 목적어인 명사가 있으므로 능동형인 (D) have donated가 정답이다.

어휘 veteran ⓝ 참전 용사 charity ⓝ 자선 단체 talented ⓐ 재능 있는

정답 (D)

117. 교통 이슈들로 인해, 도심의 상업 지구에는 엄격한 주차 규정이 실시된다.

해설 빈칸 뒤에 수식어만 있으므로 수동태인 (B)가 정답이다.

어휘 strict ⓐ 엄격한, 엄중한   enforce ⓥ 시행(실시)하다

정답 (B)

118. 공장의 감독관들은 노동자들의 노동력을 더 생산적으로 유지하기 위해 그들을 공정하게 대해야 한다.

해설 require(요구하다)는 대표적인 5형식 동사로 [V+O+to V] 구조가 능동형이 된다. 빈칸 뒤에 to부정사가 있고 목적어가 없는 수동형이므로, 빈칸 앞의 be동사와 함께 수동태를 이루는 (A)가 정답이다.

어휘 supervisor ⓝ 감독관   with fairness ⓐⓓⓥ 공정하게

정답 (A)

119. 강경 노선의 우파 보수주의자인 David Mozes 씨가 콜로라도 주지사로 최근에 선출되었다.

해설 제시된 elect는 목적보어로 명사를 취하는 5형식 동사로 〈elect+목적어+명사 보어〉 구조로 쓰이는데, 목적어가 주어로 이동했으므로 앞의 was와 수동태를 이루는 (A)가 정답이다.

어휘 hard-line ⓐ 강경 노선의   conservative ⓝ 보수주의자   governor ⓝ 주지사

정답 (A)

120. 언어 교육에 대한 현재 이슈를 다룬 Junee의 논설은 TESOL 저널에 글을 출판하기 위한 기준 형식으로 참고된다.

해설 보기에 제시된 refer(~을 참조하다/참고하다)는 1형식 자동사로 〈refer to+명사〉 구조로 수식어인 전치사구와 함께 나올 수 있는데, 전치사 to 뒤에 전치사의 목적어인 명사가 없기 때문에 수동형인 (B)가 정답이 된다.

어휘 article ⓝ 논설, 기사   standard ⓝ 기준   publish ⓥ 출판하다

정답 (B)

| PART 6 |

(121-124) 다음 공지를 참조하세요.

> **Chapel Hill 주민 자치 센터**
> **규칙과 규정**
>
> Chapel Hill 주민 자치 센터 수영장은 오전 6시부터 오후 9시까지 주 7일 시민들에게 개방합니다. 방문객들은 반드시 다음의 규정을 준수하도록 요구 받습니다.
>
> - 월요일부터 금요일 오후 1시 30분과 3시 30분 사이에는 높은 곳에 있는 다이빙대에서 다이빙 할 수 없습니다.
> - 언제든지, 풀장에서 물장구나 심한 장난을 칠 수 없습니다.
> - 풀장 구역에서 외부 신발을 신을 수 없습니다.
> - 수영모를 반드시 착용해 주세요.
>
> 풀장 깊은 곳은 10대부터 성인까지 모두에게 개방됩니다. 그럼에도 불구하고, 근무 중인 안전 요원이 따로 있지 않기 때문에, 부모나 보호자분들은 그곳에서 수영하는 아이들을 면밀히 지켜 보셔야 합니다.
> 이 규칙들은 모든 사용자들의 안전을 위해 시행됩니다.
> 위 규칙을 어기는 분들은 풀장 입장이 금지됩니다. 경우에 따라, 우리는 그들이 센터에 입장하는 것을 금지시킬 수도 있습니다.

어휘 community center ⓝ 주민 자치 센터   splash ⓝ 물을 튀기다   rough ⓐ 거친, 심한   guardian ⓝ 보호자   closely ⓐⓓⓥ 면밀히   lifeguard ⓝ 안전요원   on duty ⓐ 근무 중인   prohibit ⓥ 금지하다

121. 동사

해설 be required 뒤에 to부정사의 to가 나와 있으므로 동사원형인 (A)가 정답이다.

정답 (A)

122. 접속부사

해설 (A) 유사하게 (B) 예로 (C) 그럼에도 불구하고 (D) 예외적으로의 부사 중에서 앞에 나온, "누구에게나 개방되지만 잘 지켜봐야 한다", 반전의 의미를 이루는 (C)가 정답이다.

정답 (C)

123. 수동태

해설 빈칸 뒤에 목적어 없이 수식어만 나와 있으므로 수동태인 [be + 타Ved] 구조로 (C)가 정답이다.

정답 (C)

124. 문장 넣기

(A) 정규 과정을 등록하기 위해 고객센터 (711) 652-1241로 연락 주세요.
(B) 경우에 따라, 우리는 그들이 센터에 입장하는 것을 금지시킬 수도 있습니다.
(C) 공사 동안 이러한 불편함을 이해해 주셔서 감사 드립니다.
(D) 우리 시설은 적절한 신분증 양식을 갖고 계신 분에 한해 회원으로 승인해 드립니다.

해설 앞 문장에서 규칙을 어길 때 받을 수 있는 불이익에 대한 설명의 연장으로 (B)가 정답이다.

정답 (B)

DAY 7 동사의 시제와 가정법

SPARTA Check-UP   p.167

1. (B)   2. (B)   3. (A)   4. (B)

1. 신임 CEO 임명 때문에 최근 주주총회를 위해 이사회가 모였다.

   해설 부사 recently(최근에)는 과거와 현재완료에 쓰일 수 있는데, 빈칸 뒤에 수식어만 있으므로, 수동형이면서 과거 시제인 (B)가 적절하다.

   어휘 stockholder ⓝ 주주   appointment ⓝ 임명

   정답 (B)

2. 그녀가 주지사로 선출된 이래로, Cohen 씨는 잘 조직된 복지 정책을 도입하고 있다.

   해설 [Since + 주어 + 과거 동사, 주어 + 현재완료] 구조로 과거 시제인 (B)가 적절하다.

   어휘 institute ⓥ 제정하다   welfare ⓝ 복지

   정답 (B)

3. 건물의 안전 점검이 끝나자마자, 여러분은 다른 지시가 없어도 원래 업무를 다시 하면 됩니다.

   해설 "~하자마자"의 의미인 시간부사절의 동사를 묻는 문제이다. 시간/조건 부사절은 미래 시제 사용이 불가능하므로 (C)는 오답이고, 주절의 시제가 미래(will)이니 현재형인 (A)와 (B) 중에 수동태를 이루는 (A)가 적절하다.

   어휘 inspect ⓥ 점검하다   directions ⓝ 지시

   정답 (A)

4. 마케팅팀이 더 많은 고객을 끌어들이기 위해 혁신적인 전략을 제안한다면, 우리 CEO가 마음을 바꿀 텐데요.

   해설 주절에 [would/could/might+V(동사원형)]이 왔으므로 if절은 과거 시제 (B)가 적절하다.

   어휘 mind ⓝ 마음   attract ⓥ (사람을) 끌어모으다

   정답 (B)

SPARTA Practice Test   p.171

101. (B)	102. (C)	103. (C)	104. (C)	105. (D)
106. (D)	107. (A)	108. (C)	109. (D)	110. (B)
111. (A)	112. (A)	113. (D)	114. (D)	115. (B)
116. (C)	117. (D)	118. (D)	119. (A)	120. (B)
121. (B)	122. (A)	123. (D)	124. (A)

| PART 5 |

101. Schneider 씨는 맨체스터에서 그가 지난 주에 참석했던 컨퍼런스에 대한 구체적인 내용을 설명해줄 것이다.

   해설 설명은 미래에 하지만(will explain), 이미 지난 주에 컨퍼런스에 참석했으므로 과거 시제인 (B)가 적절하다.

   어휘 specific ⓐ 구체적인   content ⓝ 내용

   정답 (B)

102. Reina 씨는 회사의 신사옥 건설을 계획했고, 내년에 완공될 때 그녀가 유지 보수 팀을 관리하게 될 것입니다.

   해설 when 이후에 next year라는 미래 시점이 있고, 그때 맡게 될 일을 언급하는 것이기 때문에 미래 시제인 (C)가 정답이다.

   어휘 headquarters ⓝ 본사   maintenance ⓝ 유지, 보수

   정답 (C)

103. 다음주 금요일 오후 8시에 건물 2층 Grand Ballroom에서 Serena 씨의 퇴임을 축하하는 자리가 마련될 것이다.

   해설 next Friday라는 미래 시점 표현과, 빈칸 뒤 수식어에 목적어가 없으므로 수동형인 (C)가 적절하다.

   어휘 retirement ⓝ 퇴임   celebrate ⓥ 축하하다

   정답 (C)

104. 지난 몇 년 동안, Maxon 사는 그들의 사업을 IT 산업으로 확장하기 위해 인수합병 전문가들을 채용하고 있다.

   해설 목적어가 있는 능동태 문장에서 [over + 기간]의 수식어가 있으므로 완료 시제인 (C)가 가장 적절하다.

   어휘 M&A(= Mergers and Acquisitions) ⓝ 인수합병

   정답 (C)

105. 마감기한 이후에 접수된 지원 서류는 고려되지 않는다는 점을 명심하세요.

   해설 빈칸 뒤에 목적어가 없으므로 수동태 (D)가 정답이다.

   어휘 keep in mind ⓥ 명심하다

   정답 (D)

106. 그 직책에 우리가 고려했던 4명의 후보자 중에서, Dan 씨가 마케팅 전략에 관해 가장 잘 아는 것처럼 보인다.

해설 시간을 나타내는 수식어가 없고, 부사절(시간/조건)도 없으므로 현재 시제인 (D)가 적절하다.

어휘 strategy n 전략

정답 (D)

107. T-Bone & Gourmet Food 사의 작년 순수익이 운영진의 예측을 초월했다.

해설 빈칸은 본동사 자리로, (A)가 정답이다.

어휘 net profit n 순수익   surpass v 능가하다, 초월하다

정답 (A)

108. Julian 씨는 다음주에 재무이사 직에서 퇴임할 Nakata 씨의 자리를 대체합니다.

해설 next week라는 미래 시점 부사가 있으므로 (C)가 정답이다.

어휘 substitute for v ~을 대체하다

정답 (C)

109. Liao 씨가 영문학 분야의 석사 과정을 마치면, 그녀는 시카고 대학의 박사 학위 프로그램을 지원할 것이다.

해설 시간 부사절 접속사 when절의 시제가 현재이므로 주절에는 현재, 미래 모두 가능한데 주어는 단수이고 apply는 자동사이므로 (D)가 가장 적절하다.

어휘 doctorate program n 박사 학위 프로그램

정답 (D)

110. Ace Food Service 사는 2010년 사업을 시작한 이래, 다양한 행사에 최고 품질의 케이터링 서비스를 제공하고 있습니다.

해설 [주어 + 현재완료 since + 주어 + 과거동사] 구조로 (B)가 정답이다.

어휘 catering n 음식 공급

정답 (B)

111. 당신이 문의가 있을 때, 우리 고객 서비스 센터 직원들은 언제든지 빠르게 응답해 줄 것입니다.

해설 시간 부사절 접속사 when절의 시제가 현재여야 주절의 시제가 미래(will)가 올 수 있으므로 (A)가 정답이다.

어휘 anytime adv 언제든지

정답 (A)

112. 2015년도에, 세계적으로 유명한 가수 Buncheon 씨는 음악계에서 은퇴해 대학에서 학생들을 가르칠 계획이라고 발표했다.

해설 빈칸 뒤에 명사절(that)이 있으므로 능동태 동사 자리인데, 2015년은 과거이므로 (A)가 적절하다.

어휘 retire from v ~로부터 은퇴하다

정답 (A)

113. Gomez 씨가 임원으로 승진될 쯤이면, 그는 회사에서 30년 일하게 되는 것이다.

해설 By the time(~할 때쯤)은 시간차를 나타내는 시간 부사절 접속사로 주절에 완료시제가 나오는데, 접속사절의 시제가 현재이므로 주절은 미래완료인 (D)가 정답이다.

어휘 promote v 승진시키다   executive n 임원

정답 (D)

114. 그 문서가 신중히 검토되자마자, 연방 시상 위원회는 올해의 주 수상자를 선택할 것이다.

해설 시간/조건 부사절의 시제가 현재이므로 주절에는 현재, 미래가 올 수 있는데, 주어가 단수이므로 (D)가 정답이다.

어휘 winner n 수상자

정답 (D)

115. Lillian 씨가 우리 팀에 합류한 이래로, 지난 2년 동안 혁신적인 마케팅 아이디어를 발전시켜 왔다.

해설 [주어 + 현재완료, for/over/in + 과거 시간] 구조로 (B)가 정답이다.

어휘 innovative a 혁신적인   join v 합류하다

정답 (B)

116. 다음 달까지, 우리 미디어 부서는 충분한 공간을 지닌 상암 미디어 지역의 새로운 사무실 건물로 이전할 것이다.

해설 미래시점의 next month가 있으므로 미래시제 (C)가 정답이다.

어휘 division n 부서   ample a 충분한

정답 (C)

117. 이번 홍보의 성공 덕분에, 판매 수치가 우리가 예상했던 것보다 상당히 증가했다.

해설 주절의 시제가 과거(increased)로, 그보다 전에 예상했으므로 과거완료 시제인 (D)가 알맞다.

어휘 promotion n 홍보   considerably adv 상당히   anticipate v 예상하다

정답 (D)

118. 몇몇 분들이 식단상 제약이 있다는 사실을 저희 직원이 알았더라면, 육류 없는 음식을 대접했을 텐데요.

해설 if절은 가정법 과거 완료로, 주절은 [would/could/might + have Ved] 구조의 (D)가 정답이다.

어휘 fact ⓝ 사실   dietary ⓐ 식단상의   dish ⓝ 음식

정답 (D)

119. 컨퍼런스 일정에 대한 추가적인 정보가 필요하시면, 저에게 요청 이메일을 보내주세요.

해설 가정법 도치 문장으로, 원문이 If you should need ~에서 if가 생략되고 조동사인 should가 도치된 구조로 (A)가 정답이다.

어휘 further ⓐ 더욱   request ⓝ 요청; ⓥ 요청하다

정답 (A)

120. 이번 분기 판매 수익이 증가했더라면, 우리는 더 혁신적인 제품을 개발할 자금을 확보할 수 있었을 것이다.

해설 가정법 if의 대용 접속사 provided that의 시제를 물어보는 문제이다. 주절이 [might + have Ved]이므로 if절은 had V-ed 구조의 (B)가 정답이다.

어휘 profit ⓝ 수익   fund ⓝ 자금   secure ⓥ 확보하다

정답 (B)

| PART 6 |

(121–124) 다음 이메일을 참조하세요.

수신: info@cismobileelec.net
발신: grizman@commonmail.com
날짜: 10월 10일
제목: 주문: GX-Pro 태블릿 PC

관계자님께,
저는 제가 구매한 제품에 관해 이메일을 작성하고 있습니다. 제가 제품을 받았을 때 엄청난 손상이 있었습니다. 예를 들어 표면에 긁힌 자국들이 있었고, 화면은 깨져 있었습니다. 이런 상태로, 이것은 현재 사용이 불가능합니다. 물론 이 제품은 반드시 반품되어야 합니다. 하지만 저는 이것을 반품하는 가장 좋은 방법을 잘 모르겠습니다. 제가 이것을 되돌려 보내야 하는지, 귀사 매장 중 한 곳으로 들고 가야 하는지 저에게 이메일로 알려주세요. 저는 제가 취해야 하는 다음 단계에 관한 정보를 좀 얻고 싶습니다.

어휘 scratch ⓝ 긁힘, 자국   crack ⓥ 깨지다   surface ⓝ 표면

121. 시제 / 수 일치

해설 시간 부사절 접속사 when절의 동사가 과거이므로 주절인 빈칸의 시제는 과거이고, there는 동사 뒤가 주어이므로 단수 형태인 (B)가 정답이다.

정답 (B)

122. 부사

해설 (A) '현재에'는 현재 시제, (B) '이전에'는 과거 시제, (C) '곧'은 미래 시제, (D) '즉시/바로'는 시간 표현 또는 대상이 함께 나와야 하는 부사이므로 현재 시제인 is와 함께 쓰일 수 있는 것은 (A)이다.

정답 (A)

123. 시제

해설 반품이 필요한 상황으로 아직 반품되지 않았으므로 미래 시점이 되어야 한다. 과거와 관련된 시제는 전부 오답이 되므로 (D)가 적절하다. 참고로 조동사 can/may/must/should는 모두 앞으로 해야 하는 미래 시점을 나타낼 수 있다.

정답 (D)

124. 문장 넣기

(A) 저는 제가 취해야 하는 다음 단계에 관한 정보를 좀 얻고 싶습니다.
(B) 저는 당신이 이 문제에 대한 제 요청을 거절한 것에 매우 실망스럽습니다.
(C) 제가 원하는 제품과 서비스를 제공해 주셔서 감사합니다.
(D) 귀사에서 누가 최고의 기술자인지 알려 주세요.

해설 반품 정보를 잘 모르기 때문에 알려달라는 문맥이 이어져야 자연스러우므로 (A)가 적절하다.

정답 (A)

DAY 8 to부정사와 동명사

SPARTA Check-UP   p.175

1. (C)   2. (C)   3. (C)   4. (C)

1. 고객 서비스를 개선하기 위한 우리의 노력에도 불구하고, 고객의 대부분이 노후화된 온라인 주문 시스템 때문에 우리를 점점 떠나고 있다.

해설 명사 뒤 수식어 자리로, effort(노력)은 to부정사로부터 수식 받는 명사이므로 (C)가 정답이다.

어휘 effort ⓝ 노력   increasingly ⓐdv 점점   outdated ⓐ 구식의, 노후화된

정답 (C)

2. 새로운 언어에 능숙해지는 것은 목표 언어로 반복적으로 말하는 연습을 필요로 합니다.

해설 주어 자리에 알맞은 형태로 동명사인 (C)가 적절하다.

어휘 target language ⓝ (학습) 목표 언어

정답 (C)

3. 운영진은 이번 크리스마스 휴일 준비로 너무 바빠지기 전에 신규 직원을 고용할 것을 강하게 제안했다.

해설 타동사 뒤 목적어 자리에는 to부정사와 동명사가 올 수 있는데, suggest는 동명사를 목적어로 취하므로 (C)가 정답이다.

어휘 management ⓝ 운영(진)   in preparation for prep ~을 준비하여

정답 (C)

4. 여러분의 아낌없는 기부와 지지 덕분에, 우리는 이번 자선 행사 준비를 성공시킬 수 있었습니다.

해설 전치사의 목적어인 명사 자리이면서, 뒤따라오는 명사구(this charitable event)를 목적어로 취할 수 있는 동명사 (C)가 정답이다.

어휘 support ⓝ 지지   succeed in ⓥ ~에 성공하다   charitable ⓐ 자선의

정답 (C)

SPARTA Practice Test   p.179

101. (B)   102. (D)   103. (C)   104. (D)   105. (B)
106. (C)   107. (B)   108. (B)   109. (C)   110. (C)
111. (B)   112. (C)   113. (A)   114. (A)   115. (C)
116. (A)   117. (A)   118. (C)   119. (C)   120. (C)
121. (D)   122. (B)   123. (C)   124. (A)

| PART 5 |

101. 기억에 남을 만한 광고를 대중에게 보여주는 것은 우리 마케팅 전략 중 하나입니다.

해설 명사 주어 자리로, 빈칸 뒤에 명사 목적어가 있으므로 동명사인 (B)가 적절하다.

어휘 memorable ⓐ 기억에 남을 만한   commercial film ⓝ 광고   public ⓝ 대중

정답 (B)

102. 지난 분기 원자재 가격이 상당히 낮아졌음에도 불구하고, Fannenca Expressway 사는 순익을 내는 데 실패했다.

해설 fail은 to부정사를 목적어로 취해야 하므로 (D)가 정답이다.

어휘 raw material ⓝ 원자재   lower ⓥ 낮추다   net profit ⓝ 순익

정답 (D)

103. 그들이 보안 소프트웨어의 구식 버전을 사용하는 것은 전자 바이러스를 확산시킴으로써 회사 컴퓨터에 심각한 오류를 초래할 수 있다.

해설 빈칸은 주어 자리로 뒤에 명사 목적어가 있으므로, 동명사인 (C)가 정답이다.

어휘 cause ⓥ 초래하다   spread ⓥ 확산시키다

정답 (C)

104. 다음달 "전국 교사 포럼"은 학교에서 학생들 사이의 따돌림에 관한 이슈를 처리하는 효과적인 방법에 집중할 것이다.

해설 명사(ways)를 수식하는 자리이므로 준동사 to부정사인 (D)가 정답이다.

어휘 effective ⓐ 효과적인   bullying ⓝ 따돌림

정답 (D)

105. 노스캐롤라이나의 Lafayette 대학은 당뇨 환자에 대한 현존하는 치료를 개선하는 데 오랫동안 헌신해오고 있다.

해설 commitment (헌신/기여) 뒤에 나온 to는 전치사 to이므로 동명사인 (B)가 정답이다.

어휘 treatment ⓝ 치료   diabetic ⓐ 당뇨병의

정답 (B)

106. 우리 직원들 대부분이, 분기 회계 감사 준비로 전직원이 정말 바쁘기 때문에 다음달까지 컨퍼런스를 연기해야 한다고 주장한다.

해설 '~하느라 바쁘다'의 [be + busy + -ing]로 (C)가 정답이다.

어휘 insist ⓥ 주장하다 postpone ⓥ 연기하다 quarterly ⓐ 분기의 audit ⓝ 회계감사

정답 (C)

107. 긴급 상황에 즉각적으로 대응한 덕분에, 많은 사람들이 터널 안 차량 사고 순간의 심각한 손해를 피했다.

해설 전치사와 동명사 사이 빈칸에는 동명사를 수식하는 부사인 (B)가 정답이다.

어휘 respond to ⓥ 대응하다

정답 (B)

108. 이번 연간 포럼에 참석 예정인 사람들은 이번 행사의 일정과 내용에 관한 제공된 소책자를 참고하도록 요구 받는다.

해설 require는 '요구하다'는 의미로 [5형식 동사 + 목적어 + to부정사] 구조로 to부정사를 목적보어로 취하므로 (B)가 정답이다.

어휘 brochure ⓝ 소책자

정답 (B)

109. 온라인 설문조사에 참여함으로써, 누구든 모바일 앱을 통해 우리 모든 매장에서 일반 사이즈 음료용 무료 쿠폰을 얻을 수 있습니다.

해설 전치사 뒤 명사 자리로, 명사 (B)와 (C) 중, (B)의 '참석자'라는 사람 명사는 관사나 복수 어미가 붙어야 답이 될 수 있으므로, 동명사인 (C)가 적절하다.

어휘 regular-sized ⓐ 보통 사이즈의 participate in ⓥ 참석하다

정답 (C)

110. 당신이 무리하게 다른 대륙으로 지점을 확장하려고 한다면 파산할지도 모르고 자금을 복구할 방법이 없을지도 모릅니다.

해설 전치사 뒤에서 명사 목적어를 취할 수 있는 동명사 (C)가 정답이다.

어휘 continent ⓝ 대륙 by constraint ⓐⓓⓥ 억지로, 무리하게 recover ⓥ 복구하다

정답 (C)

111. 건물에 들어오는 사람들의 사원증을 확인하기 위해 새 보안팀이 정문에 배치되었다.

해설 빈칸 뒤 동사원형 check를 연결할 수 있는 것은 목적을 나타내는 [in order to + 동사원형]으로 (B)가 정답이다.

어휘 post ⓥ 배치시키다

정답 (B)

112. Tao 씨의 퇴임식을 위한 이벤트 홀을 예약하기 전에 우리는 그에게 가능한 날짜와 시간을 물어봐야 합니다.

해설 전치사와 관사 사이에는 명사의 속성을 지니면서 뒤의 명사를 목적어로 취할 수 있는 동명사 (C)가 가장 적절하다.

어휘 retirement ceremony ⓝ 퇴임식

정답 (C)

113. 회계팀 부장은 전 직원들에게 새로운 급여 체계 계획이 여전히 변경될 수 있음을 알려주었다.

해설 [be subject to 명사/동명사] (~에 영향 받기 쉽다) 구조로 명사, 동명사가 위치할 수 있는데 빈칸 뒤에는 목적어가 없으므로 명사 (A) change가 정답이다.

어휘 remind ⓥ 알려주다

정답 (A)

114. 누구든지 유럽 외부 지역에서 주문하고자 하신다면, 우리 웹사이트로 접속하셔서 국제 배송 섹션을 클릭해 주세요.

해설 would like (원하다)는 to부정사를 목적어로 취하는 대표적인 동사이므로 (A)가 정답이다.

어휘 outside ⓟⓡⓔⓟ 밖에서 section ⓝ 부분

정답 (A)

115. 기호를 사용하는 것은 세부 설명이 없는 지도 한 장에 많은 양의 정보를 입력할 수 있게 해준다.

해설 [make + it(가목적어) + 목적보어 + to부정사(진목적어)]로, 목적어가 너무 길어 뒤로 보내고 가목적어 it을 넣은 5형식 구조로 to부정사인 (C)가 정답이다.

어휘 symbol ⓝ 표상, 기호 map ⓝ 지도

정답 (C)

116. 본사 신사옥 건설에 대한 당장의 계획은 없지만, 경영진은 계획을 세울지 말지 조만간 고려할 것입니다.

해설 plans 뒤에 to부정사를 이루는 (A)가 적절하다.

어휘 immediate ⓐ 당장의, 즉각적인 whether ⓒⓞⓝⓙ ~인지 아닌지

정답 (A)

117. 지난 회의에서 우리가 언급한 것과 같이, 건물 보수가 5월 1일에 시작해서 5월 30일에 끝날 예정이다.

해설 be scheduled to부정사(~할 예정이다)로, (A)가 정답이다.

어휘 mention ⓥ 언급하다 renovation ⓝ (건물) 보수, 개조

정답 (A)

118. 편집자가 필수적인 수정을 하기 위해, 모든 기사문은 출판일 일주일 전에 제출되어야 합니다.

해설 [in order to ~(~하기 위해) 구문으로, to부정사 앞의 'for + 명사'는 의미상 주어 역할을 한다. 따라서 (C)가 적절하다.

어휘 make a revision ⓥ 수정하다 article ⓝ 기사문

정답 (C)

119. 인건비 절감 때문에, 이사회는 애리조나 주에 조립 라인 공장을 건설하기로 결정했다.

해설 전치사 뒤에서 명사구를 목적어로 취할 수 있는 동명사 (C)가 적절하다.

어휘 labor cost ⓝ 노동비 construct ⓥ 건설하다

정답 (C)

120. 스마트폰 이용자들은 대부분의 제품이 빠르게 구식이 되기 때문에 일 년에 한 번씩 교체하는 것을 고려하는 경향이 있다.

해설 consider는 동명사를 목적어로 취하는 동사로 (C)가 정답이다.

어휘 outdated ⓐ 구식의

정답 (C)

| PART 6 |

(121–124) 다음 이메일을 참조하세요.

수신: Chris Brown 〈c.brown@t-mail.com〉
발신: Joshua Debora, Advance Realty 〈j.debora@advancerealty.net〉
날짜: 3월 20일
제목: Commonwealth 거리 매물 건

Brown 씨에게,
저는 Commonwealth 가에 있는 비어 있는 공간에 대해 어제 당신이 문의하신 것에 관해 글을 씁니다. 당신을 만나게 되어 진심으로 기쁘고, 빈 매장이 당신의 요구조건에 딱 맞아떨어진다는 이야기를 듣게 되어 너무 기쁩니다.
임대 협상의 가능성에 관한 당신의 질문에 답하기 위해, 제 경험상 그 매물의 주인은 세입자가 1년치 임대료를 미리 지불한다면 줄어든 임대료를 수락해 줄 것 같습니다. 그래서 주인과 연락하기 전에, 이것이 가능하시면 저에게 알려주세요. 소매상들이 마주한 현재의 어려운 상황에서, 저는 당신의 새로운 사업에 이익을 줄 수 있는 합의에 도달할 수 있을 것이라고 확신합니다. 저는 당신에게 곧 이야기를 듣기를 기대합니다. <u>게다가, 그 계약과 관련된 법률 서비스도 제공될 것입니다.</u> 관심이 있으시다면, Advance Realty는 또한 상업 공간의 보수를 도와줄 수 있는 훌륭한 건물 개발업자들에 대한 선별된 리스트도 가지고 있습니다.

진심으로,
Joshua Debora
매니저, Advance Realty

어휘 inquiry ⓝ 문의 boulevard ⓝ 거리, 가 vacant ⓐ 비어 있는 requirement ⓝ 요구조건 challenging ⓐ 어려운 confident ⓐ 확신하는 agreement ⓥ 합의 select ⓐ 선별한

121. to부정사

해설 '~할 것 같다'라는 뜻의 be likely to ~구문으로, (D)가 적절하다.

정답 (D)

122. 동명사

해설 look forward to ~ 구문으로, 여기서 to는 전치사로 정답은 (B)이다.

정답 (B)

123. 문장 넣기
(A) 기입 날짜가 4월 10일이라는 것을 유의하세요.
(B) 집주인에게 5월 1일 전에 알려 주세요.
(C) 게다가, 계약과 관련된 법률 서비스도 제공될 것입니다.
(D) 이것 이후, 우리는 그 건물을 다른 사람들과 계약할 수도 있습니다.

해설 뒤 문장에서 선별된 건물 개발업자 리스트도 있다고 하고 있으므로, (C)가 문맥상 적절하다.

정답 (C)

124. 관계대명사

해설 빈칸 뒤에 동사가 있으므로 접속사 기능을 하면서 주어 역할까지 할 수 있는 관계대명사 중에서, 빈칸 앞 선행사가 사람이므로 (A) who가 적절하다.

정답 (A)

DAY 9 분사

SPARTA Check-UP p.183

1. (C) 2. (D) 3. (C) 4. (D)

1. 우리는 동남아 지점의 새롭게 만들어진 관리직에 고용될 자격을 갖춘 직원을 찾고 있다.

해설 명사 앞 형용사를 대신해서 분사가 위치하는데 "직책"이라는 사물 명사에는 "만들다"라는 create의 수동형 (C)가 가장 적절하다.

어휘 seek ⓥ 찾다   qualified ⓐ 자격을 갖춘   managerial ⓐ 관리직의

정답 (C)

2. 이사회에 의해 제안되면서, 그 구조조정 계획은 회사의 일 처리 절차를 전보다 더 효율적으로 만드는 것을 도울 수 있다.

해설 빈칸 뒤에 목적어가 없고 수식어가 있으므로 수동형 분사인 (D)가 정답이다.

어휘 restructure ⓥ 구조조정하다

정답 (D)

3. 추수감사절 휴가가 다가오면서, 우리 전 지점들에 선물용 제품 판매가 압도적이 되고 있다.

해설 보기의 overwhelm(압도하다)은 감정 동사로, 주어가 사물이므로 능동형 -ing인 (C)가 가장 적절하다.

어휘 thanksgiving ⓝ 추수감사절   approach ⓥ 다가오다

정답 (C)

4. 복사기가 고장 나서, 우리는 총무과에 가능한 한 빨리 숙련된 기술자를 불러 달라고 부탁했다.

해설 사람 명사(technician)를 수식하는 분사형 형용사로 '숙련한'이라는 뜻의 (D)가 정답이다.

어휘 out of order ⓐ 고장 난

정답 (D)

SPARTA Practice Test p.187

101. (B) 102. (B) 103. (C) 104. (C) 105. (A)
106. (B) 107. (A) 108. (C) 109. (A) 110. (B)
111. (A) 112. (B) 113. (A) 114. (D) 115. (B)
116. (C) 117. (C) 118. (B) 119. (B) 120. (D)
121. (D) 122. (C) 123. (B) 124. (D)

| PART 5 |

101. 제안된 연구의 주요 목적은 새로 시행되는 정책들에 관한 구체적인 정보를 획득하는 것이다.

해설 명사 앞 형용사 자리의 분사를 위치시키고자 할 때, 뒤 명사 (research)는 보기에 제시된 동작(propose)을 당하는 대상이므로 수동형 과거분사 (B)가 정답이다.

어휘 primary ⓐ 주요한, 우선의   acquire ⓥ 획득하다

정답 (B)

102. 제안서를 마무리하기 위한 제한된 시간 때문에, 전 직원들은 초과근무를 하고 각 부서 간에 협력적으로 의사소통을 해야 한다.

해설 명사 앞 형용사 자리의 분사로, time(시간)은 limit(제한하다)라는 동작을 당하는 대상이므로 수동형 과거분사 (B)가 정답이다.

어휘 finalize ⓥ 마무리하다   cooperatively adv 협력하여

정답 (B)

103. 당신의 지원서가 제출되면, 그 일자리에 대한 당신의 지원 상태를 확정하는 자동 이메일을 받게 될 겁니다.

해설 콤마(,) 뒤가 수식어 자리이므로 보기 중에서 분사인 (B), (C)가 올 수 있는데, 명사 앞 수식어(형용사 자리)가 아니기 때문에, 능동형 현재분사인 (C)가 정답이다.

어휘 once conj 일단 ~하면   status ⓝ 상태

정답 (C)

104. 전자주식 거래를 시작하는 방법에 관한 세미나에 관심이 있으신 분들은 사전에 온라인으로 신청해야 합니다.

해설 보기의 interest(흥미를 주다)는 감정동사로, 감정동사의 분사는 사람은 수동형 Ved, 사물은 능동형 Ving로 변형시킨다. 선행사 those who가 '~하는 사람들'이라는 의미로 수동형 분사형인 (C)가 정답이다.

어휘 E-trade ⓝ 전자주식 거래   electronically adv 온라인으로   in advance adv 사전에, 미리

정답 (C)

105. 우리 대학의 교육 과정은 아이들을 위한 실용적인 교수 방법에 초점을 맞춰, 미국 내에서 인지도가 매우 높다.

해설 콤마 앞이 분사구문으로, 빈칸 뒤에 목적어가 없고 수식어인 전치사구가 있으므로 수동형인 과거분사 (A)가 정답이다.

어휘 practical ⓐ 실용적인   curriculum ⓝ 교육 과정

정답 (A)

106. 낮은 수익성 때문에, 이사회는 사우스 캐롤라이나 지역의 현존하는 공장들을 폐쇄하기로 결정했다.

해설 명사 앞 형용사 자리에 분사를 위치시키는데, exist (현존하다)는 자동사이므로 수동형 분사가 불가능하다. 그러므로 능동형 현재분사인 (B)가 정답이다.

어휘 profitability ⓝ 수익성

정답 (B)

107. 작가로부터 받은 그 기사문을 수정할 때 빨간 펜으로 문장이나 단어에 표시를 해줘야 함을 명심하세요.

해설 시간/조건 부사절 접속사는 [주어+동사] 절 외에, [분사/ 형용사/전치사구]를 연결할 수 있는데, 능동형 분사 -ing는 목적어와, 수동형 분사 -ed는 생략 가능한 수식어와 함께 온다. 빈칸 뒤의 명사 목적어로 보아 능동형 (A)가 적절하다.

어휘 mark ⓥ 표시하다   revise ⓥ 수정하다

정답 (A)

108. 지난 분기의 수익 통계 수치와 비교했을 때, 이번 분기의 판매 수치는 우리가 이번 달 초에 예상했던 것보다 훨씬 낮다.

해설 콤마 앞 부사 자리에 위치하는 분사구문이 필요하다. 능동형 [타Ving + O], 수동형 [타Ved (수식어)] 중에서 빈칸 뒤에 수식어인 전치사구가 있으므로 수동형인 (C)가 정답이다.

어휘 statistics ⓝ 통계수치   profit ⓝ 수익

정답 (C)

109. 다음주에 우리 팀에 합류하는 새로운 회계사는 기업금융 회계 감사 분야에 광범위한 지식과 경험을 가지고 있다.

해설 명사 뒤에서 수식하는 분사 자리인데, 빈칸 뒤에 명사 목적어가 존재하므로 능동형 현재분사 (A)가 정답이다.

어휘 extensive ⓐ 광범위한   audit ⓥ (회계)감사하다   corporate financing ⓝ 기업금융

정답 (A)

110. 대부분의 고객들은 배송 지연으로 인한 불편함에 대해 그 매장이 전혀 사과하지 않았기 때문에 매우 실망스러워했다.

해설 빈칸 앞에 사람 주어(customers)가 왔으므로, 보어로 수동형 분사인 (B)가 적절하다.

어휘 inconvenience ⓝ 불편함

정답 (B)

111. 노란색 선들로 표시된 그 주차 구역은 우리 매장을 방문하는 장애인들을 위해 지정되어 있다.

해설 빈칸 뒤에 수식어가 있으므로 수동형 분사 (A)가 적절하다.

어휘 designate ⓥ 지정하다   handicapped ⓐ 장애가 있는

정답 (A)

112. 베트남이 뜨면서, 베트남어를 배우고자 하는 수요가 전세계적으로 점점 증가하고 있다.

해설 정관사 the 뒤의 명사 자리로, (B) 수요, (C) 요구자가 명사인데, 증가하는 것은 '수요'이므로 (B)가 적절하다. (A) demanding은 형용사로 '까다로운'이라는 뜻이다.

어휘 emerge ⓥ 떠오르다   gradually ⓐⓓⓥ 점점

정답 (B)

113. 내일부터, 모든 지원자는 일주일 동안 다양한 종류의 연이은 면접을 위해 12개의 그룹으로 나뉘어질 것입니다.

해설 be동사 뒤 보어 자리인데, 빈칸 뒤에 수식어인 전치사구가 위치해 있으므로 수동형 분사 (A)가 정답이다.

어휘 as of ⓟⓡⓔⓟ ~부터   successive ⓐ 연속의

정답 (A)

114. INNOBIZ 사는 법률사무장 직책에 자격을 갖춘 지원자를 찾는 구인 공고를 올렸다.

해설 명사 앞 형용사 자리로, 분사인 (D)가 정답이다.

어휘 job opening ⓝ 일자리   qualified ⓐ 자격을 갖춘   legal assistant ⓝ 법률사무소 사무장

정답 (D)

115. 8월 20일에 퇴임하는 Krisha 씨를 예우하는 연회를 위한 행사 공지문이 전직원에게 이메일로 발송될 것입니다.

해설 명사(banquet) 뒤에 수식어로 분사가 올 수 있는데, 빈칸 뒤에 명사 목적어가 있으므로 능동형인 (B)가 정답이다.

어휘 honor ⓥ 예우하다   retire ⓥ 사임하다

정답 (B)

116. Lingua 언어 연구소는 혁신적이고 창의적인 언어 이론들을 확립한 Kramsch 씨를 채용하게 되어 기쁩니다.

해설 delight(기쁘게 하다)는 감정동사로, 주어가 감정을 느끼는 대상으로서 수동형 분사 (C)가 적절하다.

어휘 establish ⓥ 확립하다   theory ⓝ 이론

정답 (C)

117. 새로 건설된 백화점의 늘어나는 인기에 대응하여, 임원진들은 별관으로 매장을 확장하기로 결정했다.

해설 명사(popularity) 앞에서 수식하는 자리로, 능동형 현재분사인 (C)가 적절하다.

어휘 wing n 별관

정답 (C)

118. 저렴한 자동차보다 고급 세단을 선택한 소비자의 수에 분석가들은 놀랐다.

해설 보기에 제시된 startle(놀라게 하다)는 감정동사로, 사람 주어인 분석가들은 감정을 느끼는 대상이므로 (B)가 가장 적절하다.

어휘 the number of ~의 수 luxury a 고급 sedan n 세단형 자동차

정답 (B)

119. 회사는 우리의 재무 구조를 체계화시키는 것에 헌신할 재정 전문가를 채용할 계획이다.

해설 선행사가 사람(expert)이므로 '헌신하는'이라는 뜻의 수동형 분사 (B)가 적절하다.

어휘 systemize v 체계화하다 financial structure n 재무 구조

정답 (B)

120. 특정 상품의 수량이 제한적이라는 것을 고려하면, 많은 사람들이 블랙프라이데이에 그것들을 사기 위해 길게 줄을 서서 기다릴 거라는 것을 예상할 수 있다.

해설 빈칸 뒤 that과 함께 쓰여 하나의 접속사 역할을 하는 분사형 접속사는 [considering (that) + 주어 + 동사](~을 고려하면) 구조이므로 (D)가 정답이다.

어휘 wait in a long line v 길게 줄을 서서 기다리다

정답 (D)

PART 6

(121–124) 다음 이메일을 참조하세요.

> 수신: Emma Watson 씨 〈e.watson0605@nixonenergy.net〉
> 발신: Business Month Magazine 〈customerservice@businessmonth.org.us〉
> 날짜: 7월 30일
> 제목: Business Month
>
> Watson 씨에게,
> 저희는 〈Business Month〉 잡지에 대한 당신의 연간 구독에 관한 이른 갱신 공지에 관해 글을 쓰고 있습니다. 지연 지불 프로그램 하에서 12개월을 추가로 구독 연장을 등록하셨기 때문에,
> 귀하의 첫 할부 납부금은 9월 1일이 기한일 것입니다. 물론, 할부 날짜 전에 언제든 지불하실 수 있습니다.
> 저희는 귀하에게 보통 100달러 상당인 저희 잡지 온라인 판을 무료 이용하실 수 있음을 알려드리게 되어 기쁩니다. 이 사이트를 이용하시는 구독자분들은 추가 비용이 부과되지 않을 것입니다. 지금 바로 www.buisnessmonth.org.us로 접속하실 수 있습니다.
> 〈Business Month〉를 읽어 주셔서 다시 한번 감사 드립니다.
>
> 진심으로,
> Anne Isaiah
> 구독 부장

어휘 subscription n 구독 register for v 등록하다 installment n 할부 ordinarily adv 일반적으로 charge v 부과하다

121. 명사 어휘

해설 명사 (A) 환불, (B) 교환, (C) 백분율, (D) 갱신 중에서 '구독'은 '갱신'과 관련되어 있으므로 (D)가 정답이다.

정답 (D)

122. 접속 부사

해설 접속부사 (A) ~에도 불구하고, (B) 예를 들어, (C) 물론, (D) 한편으로 중에서, 앞에서는 지불 기한을 이야기하고 뒤에서는 그 전에 언제든지 가능하다고 했으므로 (C)가 의미상 적절하다.

정답 (C)

123. 분사

해설 명사 뒤 수식어로 분사가 필요한데, 빈칸 뒤에 목적어인 명사(this site)가 있으므로 능동형 현재분사 (B)가 가장 적절하다.

정답 (B)

124. 문장 넣기

(A) 사실, 지불은 지금 편하실 때 온라인으로 하실 수 있습니다.
(B) 당신은 온라인 설문조사 양식을 통해 피드백을 보낼 수 있습니다.
(C) 다음 호는 9월 20일에 배송될 것입니다.
(D) 지금 바로 www.buisnessmonth.org.us로 접속하실 수 있습니다.

해설 앞 문장에서 "무료 이용 가능 사이트"를 설명하고 있으므로 (D)가 가장 적절하다.

정답 (D)

DAY 10 명사절과 형용사절

SPARTA Check-UP   p.191

1. (B)   **2.** (B)   **3.** (A)   **4.** (D)

1. 자문위원은 신입사원들이 효율적으로 업무에 적응하도록 회사가 그들에게 상세한 업무 편람을 만들어줄 것을 권했다.

해설 빈칸 뒤는 완전한 문장으로, 추천/권고하는 사항은 명백한 사실이므로 (B)가 적절하다.

어휘 consultant [n] 자문위원, 상담사 recruit [n] 신입사원 adapt [v] 적응하다

정답 (B)

2. 펜실베이니아의 각 시의회 의원들은 전국 스포츠 선수권 대회를 어느 도시가 개최할지 결정하기 위해 협상 중이다.

해설 동사 determine의 목적어 역할을 하는 명사절을 연결할 명사절 접속사 자리로, 빈칸 뒤의 주어가 없는 불완전한 문장을 연결할 수 있는 것은 (B) which이다.

어휘 council [n] 의회 under negotiation [phr] 협상 중 determine [v] 결정하다 host [v] 개최하다

정답 (B)

3. 이번 현장 실습 교육을 완수한 신입직원들은 각 팀의 일원으로 업무를 받게 됩니다.

해설 선행사가 사람(employees)이고 빈칸 뒤에 동사부터 등장하므로 주격 관계대명사 (A)가 정답이다.

어휘 on-the-job training [n] 현장 실습교육(OJT)

정답 (A)

4. 유명한 학자들에 의해 출간되고 논평된 기사들은 큰 회사가 주식에 투자하기를 주저하는 가장 흔한 이유를 설명한다.

해설 빈칸 뒤는 완전한 문장이고, 선행사가 the reason(이유)이라는 명사이므로 관계부사 (D)가 적절하다.

어휘 prestigious [n] 유명한 hesitate to [v] ~하기를 주저하다

정답 (D)

SPARTA Practice Test   p.195

101. (C)   **102.** (A)   **103.** (A)   **104.** (B)   **105.** (C)
106. (C)   **107.** (B)   **108.** (A)   **109.** (B)   **110.** (C)
111. (D)   **112.** (B)   **113.** (B)   **114.** (A)   **115.** (B)
116. (A)   **117.** (C)   **118.** (B)   **119.** (C)   **120.** (D)
121. (B)   **122.** (C)   **123.** (B)   **124.** (B)

| PART 5 |

101. 저희에게 세부 정보를 주시지 않으면, 문의하신 저희 전자제품 중에서 어떤 제품이 귀하의 집에 최선인지 확신할 수 없습니다.

해설 product(제품)은 셀 수 있는 명사로 한정사가 필요하므로 해당 역할을 할 수 있는 의문대명사 (C)가 정답이다.

어휘 home appliance [n] 가전제품 detailed [a] 세부적인

정답 (C)

102. 갑작스러운 기름 가격 변동에 관한 속보를 들었을 때, 우리는 원자재 가격이 상당히 증가할까 봐 염려되었다.

해설 형용사 afraid는 뒤에 나온 완전한 문장의 "사실"에 대한 내용이므로 명사절 접속사 중에서 (A) that이 적절하다.

어휘 breaking news [n] 속보 sudden [a] 갑작스러운 raw material [n] 원자재 considerably [adv] 상당히

정답 (A)

103. 매장 직원들을 지원하기 위해 이번 성수기 동안 초과근무를 해야 한다고 매니저가 우리에게 말했다.

해설 [notify + 사람 목적어 + 사물 목적어] 구조에서 notify는 사실을 "알려주는" 의미이므로 명사절 접속사 (A) that이 정답이다.

어휘 overtime [adv] 초과로 peak [n] 정점 clerk [n] 점원

정답 (A)

104. Broad & Speed Network 사가 우리 사업 제안을 승인할지 말지는 한동안 두고 봐야 할 것이다.

해설 주어인 명사 자리의 절을 이끄는 접속사가 필요한데, 빈칸 뒤에 or not이 있으므로 (B) whether가 정답이다.

어휘 remain to be seen [v] 앞으로 두고 볼 일이다

정답 (B)

105. 크리스마스 2주 전후는 선물 구매 때문에 판매 수치가 급격히 증가하는 시기이다.

해설 be동사 뒤 보어 자리로, 명사 역할은 주어와 동격을 이루어야 하는데, 주어가 "시간" 표현이므로 보어인 명사절 접속사도 시간을 나타내는 (C)가 알맞다.

어휘 rapidly [adv] 급격히

정답 (C)

106. 이번 회의에서, 기획부서는 우리의 향후 사업을 위한 전략을 세울 방법을 논의해야 합니다.

해설 빈칸 뒤 to부정사를 연결하면서 명사 역할을 할 수 있는 의문사가 필요한데, to부정사 뒤의 구조가 완전하므로 (C)가 정답이다.

어휘 division n 부서   strategy n 전략

정답 (C)

107. 저희는 대만 대표단이 7월 20일에 한국에서 열리는 정상회담에 참석 가능한지 여부를 알고 싶습니다.

해설 know라는 타동사 뒤의 목적어 자리에 명사절을 이끌 수 있는 접속사가 필요하다. if가 명사절 접속사로 타동사 뒤에서 "～인지 아닌지"의 의미이므로, (B)가 정답이다.

어휘 delegation n 대표단   summit talk n 정상회담

정답 (B)

108. Cowa 산업은 늘 안정적인 주식을 매입한다는 점에서, 그들이 그 주식에 투자했다는 것은 매우 놀랍다.

해설 빈칸 뒤에 〈주어+동사〉가 나오고, invest in은 자동사로 완전한 구조의 문장이다. 따라서 (A) That이나 (D) When 중 하나가 정답인데, '주식 투자를 한 사실'을 이야기하는 것이므로 (A)가 정답이다.

어휘 invest in v ～에 투자하다   stable a 안정적인   stock n 주식

정답 (A)

109. 회사가 어떻게 그들의 직원들에게 업무 능력을 보여줄 동등한 기회를 주는지가 중요하다.

해설 빈칸 뒤에 〈주어 + 동사〉 구조가 있으므로 접속사가 필요한데, 보기 중에서 명사절에 사용되는 '방법'의 접속사 (B) how가 정답이다.

어휘 essential a 필수적인   opportunity n 기회

정답 (B)

110. 우리 팀원들은 분기 야유회를 위해 무엇이 준비되어야 하는지를 결정하고, 참석자 수를 확인할 것입니다.

해설 명사절 접속사 자리로, 빈칸 뒤에 주어가 없는 불완전한 문장이므로 (C) what이 알맞다.

어휘 quarterly a 분기의   outing n 야유회   attendee n 참가자

정답 (C)

111. 제품 보증을 갱신하고 싶은 사용자들은 적어도 만료일 40일 전에 각 서비스센터로 알려 주세요.

해설 빈칸 앞 선행사가 사람(Users)이고 빈칸 뒤에 주어가 따로 없으므로 사람 주격 관계대명사 (D) who가 정답이다.

어휘 warranty n 보증(서)   notify v 알려 주다

정답 (D)

112. 임원진들은 다음주에 미국 텍사스 주 오스틴에서 열릴 연례 컨퍼런스에 참석할 예정이다.

해설 빈칸 앞은 사물 선행사(conference)로, 빈칸 뒤에 주어가 따로 없으므로 사물 주격 관계대명사 (B) which가 정답이다.

어휘 be planning to v ～할 예정이다

정답 (B)

113. 교체가 필요한 모든 오래된 회사 컴퓨터는 점검되고 총무부에 보고되어야 합니다.

해설 보기의 공통점은 대명사인데, 동사가 2개(need/should be)이므로 접속사 기능이 필요하다. 보기 중 접속사로 가능한 것은 (B) that이다.

어휘 general affairs division n 총무과

정답 (B)

114. 호텔 운영진은 새해에 오픈할 예정인 신규 행사장 건설에 대한 계획을 논의했다.

해설 빈칸 앞 선행사가 사물(event hall), 빈칸 뒤에 주어가 따로 없으므로 사물 주격 관계대명사인 (A) which가 정답이다. 참고로, 콤마(,) 뒤는 앞 문장 전체를 추가 설명하는 경우가 많고, 주로 which가 답이 된다.

정답 (A)

115. 일류 대학을 졸업한 대부분의 대학원생들은 다양한 학문 분야에서 훌륭한 성과를 보여주고 있다.

해설 [수량 + of whom/which ～] 구문으로, 선행사가 콤마(,) 앞에 있다. 동사가 2개이므로 사람 선행사를 수식하는 관계대명사 (B)가 정답이다.

어휘 prestigious a 일류의

정답 (B)

116. Anan Cove 사에 1천만 주 이상을 소유한 현재의 투자자들은 세무조사 때문에 그들의 돈을 잃을지 모른다.

해설 빈칸 앞에 선행사가 있고 뒤에도 명사와 문장이 나왔다. 문장이 완전한 구조이므로 소유격 관계대명사 (A)가 정답이다.

어휘 tax investigation n 세무조사

정답 (A)

117. Well-Done 문구는 오른편에 Innobiz 센터가 위치한 Penn 교차로를 약간 지나서 위치해 있다.

해설 빈칸 뒤에 [주어 + 수동태]의 완전한 문장이 있으므로 (C)가 정답이다.

어휘 stationery ⓝ 문구 intersection ⓝ 교차로

정답 (C)

118. Papago 전자는 식당 운영자들을 위해 에너지 절약에 가장 효율적인 새로 개발된 냉장고를 출시할 예정이다.

해설 빈칸 앞 명사는 복수이고, 빈칸 뒤 동사가 단수 is이다. 선행사가 refrigerator라는 사물 명사이므로 (B)가 정답이다.

어휘 unveil ⓥ 출시하다 efficient ⓐ 효율적인

정답 (B)

119. 중고물품을 기부하고자 하는 사람이라면 누구든지 금요일까지 시 커뮤니티 센터에 물품 목록을 알려야 한다.

해설 문장에 동사가 need to ~뿐이므로 접속사는 불가, 따라서 (A) anyone이 정답이다.

어휘 used item ⓝ 중고물품

정답 (A)

120. 각 관리자에 의해 발표된 그 보고서들은 시장조사에 기반하여 그것의 통계 수치가 신뢰할 만해야 합니다.

해설 which의 선행사 자리인데, 주격 관계대명사의 경우 선행사와 수 일치하므로 which 뒤의 are를 통해 복수 주어 (D)가 정답임을 알 수 있다.

어휘 statistics ⓝ 통계 수치

정답 (D)

| PART 6 |

(121-124) 다음 리뷰를 참조하세요.

Little Pythagoras

Joe Clein 씀

최신 가을 블록버스터는 〈Little Pythagoras〉입니다. 이것은 Michael Straus가 쓰고 감독했습니다. 이것은 수학에 천재성을 보이고, 모든 수학적 문제들에 막힘 없이 답하는 Amatheus라고 불리는 어린 소년에 대한 이야기입니다.
그는 용감하고, 결단력 있으며 영리하고, 확실히 10대들에게 긍정적인 롤 모델입니다. 미성년자 자녀를 둔 모든 부모들은 그의 모험이 흥미롭다고 여길 것입니다.
이 영화의 유일한 단점은 복잡한 줄거리가 내용을 혼란스럽게 하다는 것인데, 이것은 특히, 10세 미만의 어린이들에게 문제가 될 것 같습니다. 또한, 저는 거의 2시간의 상영 시간이 다소 그들에게 길 수도 있을 것이라 생각됩니다.

그러나 전반적인 이야기들은 매우 환상적이고 흥미로워서, 저는 모든 사람들에게 강력하게 추천하고자 합니다.

어휘 named ⓐ 이름 붙여진 sign ⓝ 조짐 genius ⓝ 천재 hesitate to ⓥ ~할 것을 망설이다 brave ⓐ 용감한 decisive ⓐ 결단력 있는 underaged ⓐ 미성년의 fault ⓝ 오점 complicated ⓐ 복잡한 confusing ⓐ 혼란스럽게 하는 running time ⓝ 상영 시간 somewhat ⓐⓓⓥ 다소

121. 문장 넣기
(A) 이것은 Mesopotamia에 관한 소설에서 처음 발견됐습니다.
(B) 이것은 Michael Straus가 쓰고 감독했습니다.
(C) 이 공식은 우리 일상생활에 매우 유용합니다.
(D) 아마도 여러분은 표를 구하는 데 어려움을 겪을 것입니다.

해설 해당 영화에 대한 설명을 이어가는 (B)가 문맥상 가장 적절하다.

정답 (B)

122. 관계대명사

해설 빈칸 앞 선행사가 사람(Amatheus)이고 빈칸 뒤에 동사가 이어지므로 주격 관계대명사가 필요. 따라서 (C)가 정답이다.

정답 (C)

123. 분사

해설 consider가 5형식 동사로 쓰이면, 목적보어로 형용사/분사 등이 올 수 있다. 목적어가 사물(adventures)이므로 능동형 분사인 (B)가 정답이다.

정답 (B)

124. 관계대명사

해설 빈칸 뒤에 동사 is가 나왔으므로 불완전한 문장을 이끄는 형용사절 접속사 who와 which 중에, 콤마 뒤에서 앞에 나온 문장 전체를 받는 역할을 하는 (B) which가 정답이다.

정답 (B)

RC PART 7 | 독해

DAY 11 주제/목적 찾기 유형

SPARTA Check-UP   p.206

1. (B)   2. (C)

1. 다음 이메일을 참조하세요.

> 수신: Jean Ryan 씨 〈jryan@speedmail.com〉
> 발신: Billy Business 사 〈customerservice@billybiz.net〉
> 날짜: 9월 18일
> 제목: Business Fortune 지
>
> Ryan 씨에게,
> 우리는 당신의 〈Business Fortune〉 잡지 연간 구독에 관한 이전의 갱신에 관하여 이메일을 쓰고 있습니다. 당신께서 우리 지불 프로그램 하에 추가 12개월을 구독 연장하기로 선택하셨기 때문에, 첫 분할 납입은 10월 15일이 되어야 할 것입니다. 물론, 이 날짜 전에 언제든지 지불하실 수도 있습니다.
> 우리는 당신이 우리 잡지의 50달러 상당의 온라인 판 3개월 무료 이용 권한을 받게 됨을 알려드리게 되어 기쁩니다. 이 사이트를 이용하시는 독자 분들은 그 어떤 추가 구독료도 부과되지 않으실 겁니다. 지금 www.billybiz.net으로 접속하실 수 있을 것입니다.
> 다시 한번 〈Business Fortune〉을 구독해 주셔서 감사 드립니다.
>
> 진심을 다해,
> Gilbert F. Amelio
> 구독 관리자

어휘 renewal n 갱신 subscription n 구독 extend v 연장하다 payment n 지불 installment n 분할 납입금 due a 지불되어야 할 edition n 개정판, 호, 권 charge v 부과하다; n 부과금/책임 access v 접근하다

Q1. 이 이메일의 목적은 무엇인가?
(A) 고객들의 새로운 등록을 축하하기 위해
(B) 고객에게 업데이트된 정보를 알려주기 위해
(C) 현재 서비스에 대한 불만을 제기하기 위해
(D) 고객에게 새로운 재정적 팁을 주기 위해

해설 발신자 "From: Billy Business Co. 〈customerservice@billybiz.net〉" 부분 정보를 통해 고객서비스 관련 부서에서 이메일을 보냈음을 알 수 있고, 첫 번째 문장, We are writing about the previous renewal of your annual subscription to Business Fortune magazine.에서 고객에게 갱신된(updated) 정보를 알려주기 위해서임을 알 수 있다. 그러므로 정답은 (B)이다.

2. 다음 공지문을 참조하세요.

> **밀너스빌 대학교**
> 오리엔테이션
>
> 오전 11시 – 오후 4시
> 8월 25일
>
> 밀너스빌 대학교는 9월 1일부터 시작할 새학기에 합류하는 학생들을 환영하는 연례 오리엔테이션을 알리게 되어 기쁩니다. 이것은 신입생들이 저희가 제공하는 이용가능한 강좌들, 수업 시간, 수업료, 그리고 실용적인 자격증들에 관하여 더 알아볼 수 있는 완벽한 기회입니다.
> 또한, 이것은 웨비나(우리의 온라인 수업 시스템)을 포함한 세미나에 합류할 기회를 제공하기도 할 것입니다. 게다가, 이것은 특별한 교육을 하는데, 이는 학교 생활 적응에 도움이 필요한 근로 학생을 위한 것이기도 합니다. 여러분은 또한 각 학과 코디네이터들, 교수들, 그리고 행정 담당자들을 만날 수 있는 기회를 갖게 됩니다. 그 날 내내 우리의 스낵바에서 무료 다과들이 제공될 것입니다. 우리 거기서 봐요!
> 오리엔테이션 참석은 학생들로 제한됩니다. 학부모님과 친구들은 매 여름 학기에 진행되는 오픈 하우스 데이에 와 주시기를 요청하는 바입니다.

어휘 delight v 기쁘게 하다 semester n 학기 lecture n 강좌 tuition n 학비 practical a 실용적인 certification n 인증서, 자격증 including prep 포함하여 session n 교육 complimentary a 무료의 refreshment n 다과(가벼운 스낵류 음식)

Q2. 공지문의 주된 목적은 무엇인가?
(A) 예비 학생들에게 그들의 입학 허가를 알려주기 위해
(B) 특정 수업에 대한 이용 가능성을 논의하기 위해
(C) 신입생들을 위한 행사를 알리기 위해
(D) 교직원들에게 새로운 정보를 알려주기 위해

해설 글의 첫 번째 문단, 첫 문장에 "to announce its annual Orientation Day to welcome students joining us for the new semester,"을 통해 신입생을 위한 오리엔테이션을 알리기 위한 것이므로 (C)가 정답이다.

SPARTA Practice Test   p.208

1. (C)   2. (B)   3. (A)   4. (A)   5. (B)
6. (C)   7. (A)   8. (B)   9. (D)   10. (C)
11. (A)   12. (D)

[1-3] 다음 이메일을 참조하세요.

수신: Daniel Joseph ⟨daniel.joseph@bettyzoo.net⟩
발신: Esther Jasmin, Judith Travel ⟨e.jasmin@judithtravel.com⟩
날짜: 5월 10일
제목: 출장

Joseph 씨에게,
당신은 계획된 것보다 이틀 일찍 베이징으로 출발할 예정입니다. 이것은 당신이 돌아온 다음날 있을 이사회 회의에 참석할 시간을 당신에게 주게 될 것입니다. 저는 고급 Cancoon 모델의 렌터카가 Northern China 공항에서 당신을 기다리게 될 것을 확정하게 되어 기쁩니다. 당신은 또한 Travel VIP 카드를 소지하고 계시기 때문에, Holiday Lodge 모든 객실에 5% 할인 받을 수 있는 자격이 된다는 사실을 아는 것에 관심을 갖고 계실 것입니다. 게다가, 할인 받기 위해 24시간 전 미리 예약을 하실 필요도 없습니다. 일정을 바꾸시려면 www.judithtravel.com/customers/itinerary로 접속하셔서 예약번호를 입력하시는 것이 가장 좋은 방법입니다. 그렇지 않으면, 제 자리 804-211-0445로 직접 연락하시거나 804-211-0553으로 팩스를 주시면 됩니다. 항공사의 누군가와 직접 이야기하실 수 있지만, 처리가 느릴 수 있으니 유념하세요.
당신의 출장에 행운을 빕니다.

그럼 이만,

Esther Jasmin
국제 매니저, Judith Travel

어휘 be scheduled to ⓥ ~할 예정이다   confirm ⓝ 확정하다
be entitled to ⓥ ~할 자격이 있다   cardholder ⓝ 카드 소지자   in advance adv 미리   itinerary ⓝ 여정
otherwise adv 그렇지 않으면   in person adv 직접

1. 이메일은 왜 쓰였는가?
   (A) 회사의 새로운 카드를 광고하기 위해
   (B) 고객에게 웹사이트 가입을 요청하기 위해
   (C) 여행자의 예약을 확정하기 위해
   (D) 직원들에게 출장 일정을 알려주기 위해

   해설 발신자가 Judith Travel이라는 여행사이고, 첫 문장에서 "You are now scheduled to depart for Beijing two days earlier than planned"라고 등장한 것으로 미루어 보아, 예약 상황에 대해 확인한다는 (C)가 정답이다.

2. 이메일에 따르면, Joseph 씨는 어떻게 할인을 받을 수 있는가?
   (A) 그의 렌터카 번호를 줌으로써
   (B) 특정 카드를 갖고 소지함으로써
   (C) 특정 호텔 체인점을 이용함으로써
   (D) 24시간 전에 예약함으로써

   해설 지문 중반에 "you are entitled to a 5% discount ~ since you are a Travel VIP cardholder." 부분을 보면 Travel VIP 카드를 소지하고 있기 때문에 할인 받을 자격이 있다고 했으므로 (B)가 정답이다.

3. Joseph 씨가 여정을 변경하는 최선의 방법은 무엇인가?
   (A) 인터넷을 이용함으로써
   (B) Jasmin 씨에게 연락함으로써
   (C) 항공사에 연락함으로써
   (D) 여행사에 방문함으로써

   해설 지문 후반에 "If you need to make a change to your itinerary, the best way to do this is to go to www.judithtravel.com/customers/itinerary and enter your reservation number."을 통해, 인터넷 웹사이트가 가장 최선의 방법이라는 것을 확인할 수 있다. 그러므로 정답은 (A)이다.

[4-7] 다음 이메일을 참조하세요.

수신: Colin Hunter, 회원 부서
발신: Dixie Amanda, 총괄 매니저, X-Fit Gym Center
날짜: 4월 1일, 월요일
제목: 신분 확인

Hunter 씨께,
저는 새로운 회원 멤버쉽의 수가 지속적으로 증가하는 것을 보게 되어 기쁩니다. 명확하게, 이것은 우리의 전체 수익을 늘리는 데 도움이 될 수 있습니다. 한편으로, 저는 일부 중요한 일들이 때때로 간과되고 있음을 파악했습니다. 구체적으로, 우리 회사 정책상 멤버쉽을 신청하는 사람들이 운전면허증이나, 여권 또는 그와 유사한 정부 발행 문서 같은 것들의 인증된 신분증을 사진과 함께, 적어도 2개의 양식으로 제시되어야 합니다.
그것들의 사본은 반드시 문서 파일의 형태로 저장되어 있어야 하고, 각 지점 매니저와 본사 매니저에게로 보내져야 합니다. 게다가, 이것들은 우리 고객 데이터 베이스 서버와 저장소에 입력되어야 합니다. 그러나 일부 직원들이 이것을 하지 않고 있습니다. 직원들은 이러한 신분증명서 없이는 새로운 멤버쉽을 처리하면 안 됩니다. 직원들은 또한 멤버쉽 생성도 할 수 없고, 신규회원들이 적절한 신분 증명을 가지고 다시 돌아올 때까지 기다려야 합니다. 이러한 과정은 그들이 적절한 신분증을 가지고 와서 신청할 때 완료되어야 합니다. 일부 인원들은 이것이 사소하고 실용적이지 못한 이슈에 불과하다고 생각할 수도 있을 것입니다. 하지만, 그것이 체계화된 작업 효율성을 증대시킨다는 점에서 직원분들이 생각하시는 것보다 더 중요합니다. 직원들은 또한 향후의 신규 회원들에게 모든 개인 정보가 완전히 비밀로 유지되고 있다는 확신을 주어야 합니다. 이러한 이슈들에 대한 세부적인 정보는 우리 웹사이트와 소책자에 있습니다. 또는 프런트 데스크 직원이 나중에라도 그들이 원하는 질문이 있을 경우를 대비하여 그들의 명함을 나눠 드릴 것입니다. 다시 한번, 저는 각 매니저분들께 이러한 규정에 초점을 맞춰 직원들을 위해 특별 워크숍을 열 것을 요구하는 바입니다. 이것은 지원 절차의 부분에서 절대 무시되어서는 안 된다는 것을 확신시키기 위해서입니다. 워크숍은 이번 주 금요일까지 마쳐야 합니다. 해당 세션이 완료된 후 저에게 이메일 보고서를 보내십시오.

감사합니다.
Dixie Amanda

어휘 definitely adv 명확히 overall a 전반적인 revenue n 수익 overlook v 간과하다 specifically adv 구체적으로 certified a 인증된 identification n 신분(증) proof n 증명 appropriate a 적절한 minor a 사소한 impractical a 비실용적인 systemized a 체계화된 assure v 확신시켜주다 prospective a 앞으로의 confidential a 기밀의 brochure n 소책자 business card n 명함 ignore v 무시하다

4. 이메일의 목적은 무엇인가?
(A) Hunter 씨에게 적절한 절차를 알려주기 위해
(B) 멤버쉽 정보를 요청하기 위해
(C) 고객 피드백을 얻기 위해
(D) 정책 변경사항들을 광고하기 위해

해설 지문 초반에 Meanwhile, I noticed that some important tasks are sometimes overlooked. 부분에서 뭔가 지켜지지 않은 것이 있고, 다음 문장에서 "Specifically, the policy of our company is that people applying for memberships should present~" 부분을 보면 적절한 절차에 대해 알려주는 것이므로 (A)가 정답이다.

5. 어떤 문제가 발생했는가?
(A) 보안 담당자들이 그 시설을 조사할 예정이다.
(B) 직원들이 일부 등록 절차를 지키지 않고 있다.
(C) 고객들이 서비스에 불만을 가지고 있다.
(D) 개인 데이터베이스가 온라인에서 유출되었다.

해설 지문 초반에, I noticed that some important tasks are sometimes overlooked. 라고 되어 있으므로 업무 처리가 제대로 되지 않고 있다는 (B)가 정답이다.

6. 이메일에 따르면, 멤버쉽 세부사항을 어디서 찾아볼 수 있는가?
(A) 멤버쉽 카드에서
(B) 이메일의 첨부 파일에서
(C) 온라인 페이지를 통해
(D) 매장에 붙은 포스터에서

해설 지문 후반 "Detailed information on this issue is ~ in our brochures."에서 회사 웹사이트나 소책자를 참고하라고 했으므로 (C)가 정답이다.

7. 교육은 언제까지 열려야 하는가?
(A) 4월 5일
(B) 4월 6일
(C) 4월 7일
(D) 4월 8일

해설 이메일 작성 날짜가 4월 1일 월요일이고, 지문 후반에서 "The workshop should be done by this Friday."을 보면 금요일까지 해야 한다고 했으므로 (A)가 정답이다.

[8-12] 다음 이메일과 공지문을 참조하세요.

수신: Alan Schwartz ⟨aschwartz@qualcomcore.net⟩
발신: Punit Renjen ⟨prenjen@qualcomcore.net⟩
날짜: 11월 20일
제목: 회의 이슈
첨부: 수정.docx

Alan에게,
목요일 부서장 회의에서 당신을 만나게 되어 기뻤습니다. 당신께서 Buffalo 지사로 옮긴 이래로, 우리는 서로 이야기할 기회가 거의 없었습니다. 그 회의에서, 우리는 새로운 본사 건물에 대한 청사진에 대한 몇 가지 이슈를 논의했습니다. 영업부장으로서 저는 우리 부서에만 관련되는 것이 아닌 몇 가지 제안을 하고자 합니다.
지붕의 북쪽 측면이 태양열 판넬에 적합하지 않습니다. 발코니에 커버나 천막이 없기 때문에 비가 올 때 매우 불편할 수 있습니다. 전시와 쇼룸 층이 메인 거리에서 잘 안보입니다. 거리에 광고판을 두기 위해 더 작은 창문들을 설치할 필요가 있습니다. 저는 이러한 이슈들을 반영하기 위해 디자인을 좀 바꿔 봤습니다. 이메일과 함께 있는 첨부 파일에 디자인 수정 사항을 포함시켰습니다. 저는 전문 건축가가 아니기 때문에, 단지 손으로 그린 매우 비전문적인 수준임을 이해해 주세요.
저는 내일부터 휴무입니다만, 당신이 편할 때 연락 주세요.

Renjen

수신: Punit Renjen ⟨prenjen@qualcomcore.net⟩
발신: Alan Schwartz ⟨aschwartz@qualcomcore.net⟩
날짜: 11월 21일
제목: 회신: 회의 이슈

Punit에게,
그 계획들에 대한 귀하의 관심에 진심으로 감사 드립니다. 저는 회사의 성공이 주로 이 새로운 본사 건설에 달렸다고 강하게 믿고 있고, 우리 회사를 위해 이러한 디자인 고려사항들을 주셔서 기쁩니다.
저희 팀의 관점으로, 우리는 광고판 부분에 관한 것을 제외하고 당신의 모든 제안사항에 동의합니다. 우리는 해당 이슈에 대한 또 다른 해결책을 갖고 있습니다. 불행히도, 첨부해주신 문서가 열리지 않아서 제가 그것에 이야기를 할 수가 없어요. 괜찮으시다면 이메일로 다시 보내주시거나 서류 사본으로 팩스를 보내주시겠어요?
우리가 공사 완료를 위한 4월 30일 마감기한을 맞춰야 한다면, 우리는 임원진들과 이 이슈에 대해 검토한 후, 가능한 한 빨리 건축가에게 그것을 제출해야 합니다.

그럼 이만,
Alan Schwartz

공지

날짜: 5월 10일

전직원 주목:
신사옥 건설이 5월 30일에 완료될 것입니다. 불행히도, 우리는 그때 사무실 이사를 하느라 매우 바쁠 것입니다. 6월 2일 이사 업체가 와서 사무실 가구와 장비들을 신사옥으로 옮길 것입니다. 여러분들의 구역은 5월 30일 저녁까지 작은 물건들과 우선 순위 문서들을 싸고 포장하면서 이사를 완전히 준비해야 함을 명심하세요. 상자는 각 층의 창고에서 가져가시면 됩니다.

어휘 blueprint ⓝ 청사진 headquarters ⓝ 본사 opposite ⓐ 반대의 awning ⓝ 천막 invisible ⓐ 안 보이는 attachment ⓝ 첨부(물) reflect ⓥ 반영하다 revision ⓝ 수정사항 architect ⓝ 건축가 handwritten ⓐ 손으로 쓴 moving company ⓝ 이사업체 wrap ⓥ 포장하다 first-priority ⓝ 최우선 순위

8. Renjen의 이메일의 목적은 무엇인가?
  (A) 다른 사람들에게 회의록을 전달하기 위해
  (B) 건물 계획에 수정사항들을 추천하기 위해
  (C) 적절한 본사 위치를 제안하기 위해
  (D) 그 계획에 대한 고객 반응을 제안하기 위해

해설 Renjen의 이메일은 첫 번째 글이다. 첫 문단 마지막 문장의 "As the head of sales, I have some suggestions, which are not just related to our department."를 통해 건물 건축에 관한 몇 가지 제안을 한다고 했으므로 (B)가 적절하다.

9. Renjen 씨에 대해 알 수 있는 것이 아닌 것은?
  (A) 곧 휴가를 간다.
  (B) 부서장이다.
  (C) Schwartz와 다른 곳에서 일한다.
  (D) 회사에서 퇴직할 예정이다.

해설 (A)는 첫 번째 이메일 마지막 줄 "I am going to be on vacation as of tomorrow"에, (B)는 첫 번째 문장 "I was really pleased to meet you at the meeting of department heads on Thursday"을 통해 알 수 있고 (C)는 두 번째 문장 "Since you moved to the Buffalo office~"를 통해서 알 수 있으나 (D)는 언급되어 있지 않다.

10. Schwartz 씨는 어떤 문제를 가지고 있는가?
  (A) 그는 예산이 부족하다고 생각한다.
  (B) 그는 그 이슈들을 고려할 시간이 없다.
  (C) 그는 Renjen 씨가 보낸 파일을 열 수 없다.
  (D) 그는 Renjen 씨의 제안이 마음에 들지 않는다.

해설 두 번째 이메일 중간에 "Unfortunately, I cannot open the document you attached." 부분을 보면 첨부 파일이 열리지 않는 문제가 있음을 알 수 있으므로 (C)가 정답이다.

11. Renjen 씨의 제안 중에서 Schwartz 씨가 동의하지 않은 것은 무엇인가?
  (A) 창문의 크기를 줄이는 것
  (B) 쇼룸의 위치를 변경하는 것
  (C) 비바람이 들이치지 않는 발코니를 제공하는 것
  (D) 지붕의 디자인을 다시 하는 것

해설 두 번째 이메일 "we agree with all of your suggestions except the one about the section of advertising signs" 부분에서 광고판 부분은 다른 해결책이 있다고 했는데, 이 부분은 첫 번째 이메일의, 제안사항 중 네 번째 "We need to set up smaller windows at the front to put some advertising signs there."에서 이야기한 광고판 때문에 창문을 작게 해야 할 필요가 있다는 부분과 맞아떨어지므로 (A)가 정답이다.

12. 건설 계획에 대해 알 수 있는 것은?
  (A) Renjen의 권장사항이 반영되지 않았다.
  (B) 예상보다 예산이 덜 들었다.
  (C) 가장 자격을 갖춘 건축가를 고용하는 데 실패했다.
  (D) 원래 마감기한을 맞추지 못했다.

해설 연계 지문 문제로, 두 번째 이메일 후반에서 "If we are to meet the April 30 deadline for the completion of construction"에서 공사 완료 시점이 4월 30일인데, 세 번째 지문 초반에서 "Construction of the new headquarters will be completed on May 30."라고 했다. 따라서 마감이 미뤄졌음을 알 수 있으므로 (D)가 답이다.

DAY 12 세부사항 및 추론 유형

SPARTA Check-UP   p.215

1. (D)   2. (C)

1. 다음 기사문을 참조하세요.

이달의 책 선정

글쓴이: Jason Kang

일반 대중에게 있어서, 가장 급변하고 있는 산업 중 하나는 단연 주식 시장이라고 할 수 있다. 지금, 우리는 당신이 개인 투자자로서 온라인을 통해 전문가의 도움을 약간 받으며 어떻게 주식을 사고 팔 수 있는지를 소개하고자 한다. 하지만 명심해야 할 것은, 온라인 상에는 너무 많은 정보들이 있어서, 대부분의 신입 투자자들은 당황하고, 심지어 어디서부터 투자를 시작할지 모를 수 있다. 이러한 투자자들을 위해, 우리는 Charles Hunter라는 미국 주식 시장에서 유명한 분석가의 책인 〈온라인 거래에 접근하고 성공하기 위한 쉬운 단계들〉이라는 가장 도움이 될 만한 책을 추천하고자 한다. 이 책은 온라인 은행 서비스를 고르는 방법과 어디에서 신뢰할 만한 정보를 획득하는지 등의 기본적인 사항을 제공한다. 도입 챕터는 초보 투자자가 반드시 읽어야 할 부분이다. 이 챕터 안에서, Hunter 씨는 사람들이 투자 위험에 너무 신경을 쓰고 인터넷으로부터 쓸데없는 정보를 취득하는 것을 경고한다. 게다가, 그는 초보 투자자들에게 온라인 모의 주식 투자를 함으로써 연습하는 것을 권장하고 있다.

어휘 drastically adv 급격히   stock market n 주식시장   investor n 투자자   private a 개인의   puzzled a 당황한   at a loss a 어쩔 줄 모르는   renowned a 유명한   analyst n 분석가   instructions n 지시사항   trustworthy a 신뢰할 수 있는   warn v 경고하다   attentive a 경청하는   encourage v 독려하다   novice n 초보, 신입   practice v 연습하다   simulated a 모의의

Q1. 온라인으로 투자하는 것에 대해 알 수 있는 것은?
(A) 분석가의 도움이 필요하다.
(B) 전문가에 의해 이루어져야 한다.
(C) 관련 정보를 찾기가 어렵다.
(D) 입문자들에게는 혼란스러울 수 있다.

해설 초반부의 "so most first-time investors are puzzled and even at a loss as to where to start." 부분을 보면, 초보 투자자들은 당황할 수 있다고 했으므로 (D)가 답이다.

2. 다음 송장을 참조하세요.

Fast Laundry Corporation
1930 Kovalchick Center

9월 9일

송부합니다: Tommy Stark
890 Fleming Avenue

Stark 씨께,
우리 서비스에 대한 송장이 아래에 있으니 보세요. 지불 마감일은 위의 날짜이고, 이때까지 다음의 방법으로 결제하실 수 있습니다.
- 현금이나 우편환을 통해(우리 매장에서)
- Fast Laundry Corporation에서 발행된 회사 수표를 제시함으로써
- 신용 또는 직불카드 정보를 719-281-2921로 팩스로 보냄으로써

결제를 위한 우리의 자동 응답 서비스가 현재 업그레이드 중이고, 9월 20일까지 일시적으로 이용 불가능함을 알아 두세요. 저희 웹페이지는 현재 수리 중입니다.

설 명	세부사항	가격
드라이 클리닝과 가정 배송 서비스	셔츠/블라우스 x 8 바지/청바지 x 4 자켓 x 6	220.45 달러
소계		220.45 달러
10% 정규 고객 할인		22.05 달러
10달러 할인 쿠폰		10.00 달러
총합		188.40 달러

* 죄송하지만, 개인 수표는 받지 않습니다. 총 요금은 미국 달러로 지불되어야 합니다.

어휘 invoice n 송장   payment n 지불, 결제   money order n 우편환   issue v 발행하다   debit card n 직불카드   automated a 자동화된   temporarily adv 일시적으로   pick up v 수령하다

Q2. 송장으로부터 추론할 수 있는 것은 무엇인가?
(A) 매장에서 물품을 수령했다.
(B) 일부 바지들이 세탁되지 않았다.
(C) Stark 씨는 할인 혜택을 받았다.
(D) 캐나다 달러도 승인된다.

해설 표의 3~4번째 줄을 보면, Subtotal(소계)에서 금액이 할인되어 $220.45에서 $188.40로 원래 금액보다 적어졌음을 알 수 있다. 따라서 (C)가 적절하다.

SPARTA Practice Test   p.217

1. (B)   2. (D)   3. (C)   4. (C)   5. (C)
6. (D)   7. (A)   8. (B)   9. (B)   10. (C)
11. (B)   12. (A)

[1-2] 다음 광고를 참조하세요.

Green Wood Suite and Villa Resort의 특별 제안

유일한 북쪽 국립공원 지역에 위치한 Green Wood Suite and Villa Resort는 당신이 이곳의 놀라운 서비스와 환대를 경험해 보시기를 권유합니다. 걸어갈 수 있는 거리 내에 환상적인 풍경과 웅장한 산이 있습니다. 그래서, 저희는 손님들께서 가능한 한 최고로 편안한 휴가를 보내시는 것을 보장합니다. 현재, 저희는 각 스위트룸에 할인 요금을 제공합니다. 한시적 제공 상품을 이용하기 위해 지금 예약하세요.

슈페리얼 스위트

2000평방피트의 넓은 스위트룸
열대 정원이 내려다 보임
15마일의 푸른 숲이 내려다 보임
각 스위트룸마다 야외 월풀 욕조 구비
하루에 단도 350달러의 특가

스탠다드 스위트

1,500평방피트의 넓은 스위트룸
열대 정원이 내려다 보임
각 스위트룸마다 개인 온수 욕조 구비
하루에 단도 200달러의 특가

모든 스위트룸과 빌라는 무료 조식, 장비를 모두 갖춘 체육관, 무선 인터넷 접속, 그리고 국립공원과 시내 지역의 다양한 관광 명소로의 셔틀버스 서비스가 포함되어 있습니다.

어휘 exclusive ⓐ 유일한, 독점의 incredible ⓐ 놀라운 hospitality ⓝ 환대 scenery ⓝ 풍경 guarantee ⓥ 보증하다 relaxing ⓐ 편안한 tropical ⓐ 열대의 overlook ⓥ 내려다보다 open-air ⓐ 야외의 complimentary ⓐ 무료의 equipped ⓐ 갖춰진 attraction ⓝ 관광명소

1. Green Wood Suite and Villa Resort에 대해 알 수 있는 것은?
   (A) 모든 객실에서 산이 보인다.
   (B) 다른 유형의 객실이 이용 가능하다.
   (C) 스위트룸은 지역 내에서 최상의 가격으로 제공된다.
   (D) 투숙객은 개인 테라스를 이용할 수 있다.

해설 슈페리얼과 스탠다드 스위트로 나뉘어서 설명된 것으로 보아, 다른 타입(유형)의 방으로 구성된 리조트임을 알 수 있다. 따라서 (B)가 정답이다.

2. 슈페리얼 스위트 손님들에게만 제공되는 것은 무엇인가?
   (A) 열대 정원 풍경
   (B) 충분한 공간
   (C) 무료 조식
   (D) 야외 욕조

해설 슈페리얼 스위트의 "An open-air whirlpool bathtub in each unit."을 보면 (D)가 답임을 알 수 있다.

[3-7] 다음 광고와 이력서를 참조하세요.

구인

Geoplex 물류 사는 캐나다 토론토에 본사를 두고 있는 빠른 성장세의 기업입니다. 당신이 열정과 성실함을 갖고 계시다면, 우리는 다양한 세계적 기회들을 제공합니다. 우리는 동유럽 지역의 물류 창고들을 관리할 전문가를 찾고 있습니다.

이 직책은 폴란드를 기반으로 하지만, 동유럽 여러 국가들, 특히 크로아티아, 슬로베니아, 불가리아, 헝가리 등으로 광범위한 출장을 가게 됩니다. 그 일의 주된 직무는 회사의 동유럽 시장에서의 재고품 상태를 확인하고 물류 전반을 관리하는 것입니다. 영어 또는 기타 유럽언어들에 대한 유창성이 요구됩니다. 합격자는 의사소통 기술과 리더십, 비즈니스 관련 분야에서의 학사 학위, 그리고 관리직 수준의 3년 이상 경력이 있어야 합니다. 능숙한 컴퓨터 기술이 선호됩니다.

추가 정보를 위해, 인사과 직원 Elaine Hellena 씨에게 연락을 주시고, Peter Dixon에게는 이메일 dixon@geoplex.net으로 7월 20일까지 경력사항을 기재한 당신의 이력서를 보내주세요.

Jonathan Erving
390 Fleming Avenue
Indiana, PA 16701
714-9201-1029
erving@calmonlogi.com

목표
신흥 회사와 함께 헌신적인 매니저가 되기 위해

경력
유통 매니저 2016-2017년
Gourmet Dish 출장 음식 유통 센터, Altoona, PA
직무: 대형 물류 창고에서 유통 식품 재고 관리

판매 관리자 2014-2015년
Target Incorporation, Fairfax, VA
직무: 매장 판매사원 고용, 훈련 및 관리

학력
석사, 경영학(2012), West Virginia University, WV, the United States

어휘 logistics ⓝ 물류 fast-growing ⓐ 빠르게 성장하는 based ⓐ 기반으로 하는(본사의) passion ⓝ 열정 diligence ⓝ 성실함 distribution ⓝ 유통, 분배 primary ⓐ 우선적인 inventory ⓝ 재고 status ⓝ 상태 fluency ⓝ (외국어) 유창성 bachelor's degree ⓝ 학사 학위 managerial ⓐ 관리직의 competence ⓝ 능력 preferred ⓐ 선호되는 dedicated ⓐ 헌신하는 emerging ⓐ 신흥의, 떠오르는 responsibility ⓝ 직무 catering ⓝ 음식 제공업 business administration ⓝ 경영학

3. Geoplex 물류회사의 본사는 어디에 있는가?
   (A) 폴란드
   (B) 크로아티아
   (C) 토론토
   (D) 헝가리

   해설 첫 번째 지문 도입부의 "Geoplex Logistics is ~ based in Toronto, Canada."에서 캐나다 토론토에 본사가 있음을 알 수 있으므로 답은 (C)이다.

4. 어떤 일자리가 지원 가능한가?
   (A) 판매 사원
   (B) 인사부장
   (C) 창고 관리자
   (D) 컴퓨터 프로그래머

   해설 첫 번째 지문 초반에 "We are seeking a specialist to manage our distribution warehouses in Eastern Europe."에서 동유럽 지역의 물류 창고를 관리할 사람을 찾는다고 했으므로 (C)가 정답이다.

5. 이 일자리를 위해 필요한 것이 아닌 것은?
   (A) 영어나 유럽 언어를 구사하는 것
   (B) 비즈니스 학사 학위를 소지하는 것
   (C) 컴퓨터 소프트웨어를 다루는 것
   (D) 리더쉽 스킬을 갖는 것

   해설 (A)는 "Fluency in English or other European languages is required"을, (B)는 "a bachelor's degree in a business-related field"을, (D)는 "must have communication and leadership skills."을 통해 확인할 수 있다. (C)는 "Competence in computer skills is preferred"로 언급, 필수가 아닌 선호되는 것이다.

6. 이력서에서, 11번째 줄의 "inventory"와 의미상 가장 유사한 것은?
   (A) 계좌
   (B) 창고
   (C) 발명
   (D) 재고

   해설 "Controlling inventory for catering foods at a large warehouse." 문장에서 inventory는 물건의 '재고'를 의미하므로 (D)가 가장 적절하다.

7. 왜 Erving 씨의 지원서는 거절될 수도 있는가?
   (A) 그는 경력 년수를 충족시키지 못한다.
   (B) 그는 학사 학위가 없다.
   (C) 그의 거주 지역이 너무 멀다.
   (D) 그는 높은 임금을 원한다.

   해설 연계 문제로, 첫 번째 지문에서 "at least three years of sales experience at a managerial level."라고 언급했고, 두 번째 지문을 보면 '판매 매니저'에서는 2014-2015년으로 경력이 2년이므로 (A)가 정답이다.

[8-12] 다음 이메일과 광고를 참조하세요.

수신: Tim Haywood 〈t.haywood@solarrealty.com〉
발신: Jerry Fisherman 〈fisherman@vegaslawfirm.net〉
답신: 임대 - 사무실 공간

Haywood 씨에게,

당신의 웹사이트 www.solarrealty.com을 보았을 때, 저는 피츠버그에 당신이 보유한 많은 임대용 매물을 보았습니다. 저는 3월 5일에 도심지역으로 제 사무실을 이전할 계획이어서, 임대할 공간이 필요합니다. 저는 제 다음 사무실이 Amtrack 피츠버그 역이나 Grey Hound 버스터미널 같은 대중교통에 인접한 위치였으면 합니다. 게다가, 차를 이용하는 고객분들을 위해 주차 공간이 있었으면 합니다. 저는 당신의 회사가 다양한 매물들로 저의 요구를 충족시켜 주실 수 있을 것이라 확신합니다. 저는 곧 필라델피아로 출장을 갈 예정이어서, 이용 가능한 매물들을 둘러보기 위해 당신의 중개인과 약속을 잡고자 합니다. 가능하다면, 평면도가 있는 공간 정보 파일을 저에게 메일로 보내주실 수 있나요?

그럼 이만
Jerry Fisherman
Vegas 법률사무소

임대를 위한 피츠버그 사무 공간

얼마나 큰 공간이 필요하세요?
상업지구에서 얼마나 떨어진 곳을 선호하시나요?
Solar Realty는 사업을 번창하기 위해 피츠버그 도심지역의 매물을 찾고 있는 모든 분들을 진심으로 환영합니다.

Shadyside 매물
위치: 5743 Walnut Street Pittsburgh, PA 15232
(East of Walnut Street 상업지구에서 2블록 떨어짐)
임대료 : $2,100 + 공공요금
주차: 공영주차장 사용 가능
(30분 무료)

Lucernmines 매물
위치: 51 11th Street, Pittsburgh, PA 15221
(Grey Hound 버스터미널 옆 좌측 도로)
임대료: $1,725 (공공요금 포함)
무료 와이파이

Oakland 매물
Location 3360 5th Avenue, Pittsburgh, PA 15213
(역에서 걸어서 5분 이내 거리)
임대료: $2,250 + 공공요금
차량 4-5대를 위한 주차 공간

Filbert Street 매물
Location: 732 Filbert Street, Pittsburgh, PA 15232
(뛰어난 위치! 상업지구의 중심지)
Rent: $2,300 (공공요금 포함)
1대만 주차 가능

어휘 browse ⓥ 둘러보다 property ⓝ 매물 relocate ⓥ 이전하다 in proximity to ⓟⓡⓔⓟ ~에 인접한 public transportation ⓝ 대중교통 arrangement ⓝ 약속 within walking distance 걸어갈 수 있는 거리 내에 business district ⓝ 상업지구

8. Fisherman 씨가 걱정하는 것은 무엇인가?
    (A) 사무실 공간의 크기
    (B) 이용 가능한 주차장
    (C) 공공요금 금액
    (D) 사무실 공간 임대료

    해설 첫 번째 이메일 글에서 "there should be some parking spaces for my clients using their cars." 부분을 보면 주차 공간이 필요함을 알 수 있으므로 (B)가 정답이다.

9. Fisherman 씨는 누구인가?
    (A) 부동산 중개인
    (B) 법률사무소 직원
    (C) 변호사의 비서
    (D) Haywood 씨의 동료

    해설 첫 번째 지문 이메일의 발신자가 Fisherman 씨로, 이메일 도메인을 통해 law firm을 확인할 수 있고, 중간에 my office라고 했으므로 (B)가 적절하다.

10. 어떤 공간이 Vegas 법률사무소에 적합할 것 같은가?
    (A) Shadyside 매물
    (B) Lucenrmines 매물
    (C) Oakland 매물
    (D) Filbert Street 매물

    해설 첫 번째 글에서 발신자가 중요하게 고려하는 사항들이, "to be in proximity to public transportation ~ Bus Terminal" 로 대중교통과의 근접성, 그리고 "some parking spaces for my clients"로 주차 공간이므로 적합한 매물은 (C)이다.

11. Shadyside 매물에 대해 알 수 있는 것은?
    (A) 도심 지역의 버스 터미널 근처에 있다.
    (B) 주차 공간이 따로 없다.
    (C) 주거 지역과 인접해 있다.
    (D) 가장 비싼 매물이다.

    해설 두 번째 지문에서 해당 매물 정보를 보면 "Parking: Using the public parking lot(free for just half an hour)"에서 공영주차장 이용이 명시되어 있으므로 (B)가 정답이다.

12. Solar Realty는 Fisherman 씨에게 정보를 어떻게 전달할 것인가?
    (A) 이메일로
    (B) 직접
    (C) 팩스로
    (D) 우편으로

    해설 첫 번째 지문 마지막에 "If possible, could you e-mail me the space information on file with their floor plans?"에서 매물 정보 파일을 이메일로 보내 달라고 요청했으므로 (A)가 정답이다.

DAY 13 문장 넣기 유형

SPARTA Check-UP p.225

1. (D)   2. (B)

1. 다음 편지를 참조하세요.

Supreme Mart

7월 30일
Cavin Feige 씨
92 Fleming Avenue
Indiana, PA 15701

Feige 씨에게,
축하합니다!
당신의 수필이 Supreme Mart가 후원하는 "Supreme Mart와 나"라는 주제의 일반 범주에서 1등을 수상하게 되었습니다. 우리는 8월 5일 금요일 Eagles Ballroom에서의 시상식에서 당신의 수상을 축하하기를 바랍니다. 우리 매장으로 들어오시자마자, 왼쪽으로 안내데스크를 지나쳐 시상식이 열리게 될 컨퍼런스 층으로 오세요.
수상작들은 Supreme Mart의 뉴스레터에 실릴 것이고, 이는 우리 회원들에게 보내지고 우리 웹사이트에 게시될 것입니다. 추가로, 그것들은 출력되어 모든 Supreme Mart 매장에 전시될 것입니다. 1등 수상자로서, 당신은 12월 31일 전에 모든 Supreme Mart에서 사용하실 수 있는 300달러의 상품 교환권을 받게 되실 것입니다. <u>그것을 시상식에서 수령하시거나, 제출물에 적힌 주소로 보내 드릴 수도 있습니다.</u>
다시 한번, 당신의 훌륭한 수필에 축하 드립니다!

진심으로,
Brad Triana, 매니저
Supreme Mart

어휘 award ⓥ (상을) 주다 prize ⓝ 상 category ⓝ 범주 sponsor ⓥ 후원하다 celebrate ⓥ 축하하다 accomplishment ⓝ 성취, 업적 award ceremony ⓝ 시상식 essay ⓝ 수필, 글 display ⓥ 전시하다, 보여주다 voucher ⓝ 상품권 redeemable ⓐ 상환할 수 있는, 사용 가능한 outstanding ⓐ 뛰어난

Q1. [1], [2], [3] 그리고 [4]로 표시된 곳 중 다음 문장의 위치로 가장 적절한 곳은 어디인가?
"그것을 시상식에서 수령하시거나, 제출물에 적힌 주소로 보내 드릴 수도 있습니다."
(A) [1]
(B) [2]
(C) [3]
(D) [4]

해설 "~ pick it up ~"에서 it은 '수령하는 물건'으로, [4] 앞 문장에서 '300달러상당의 상품 교환권(a 300-dollar gift voucher)을 받게 된다'고 했으므로 (D)가 적절하다.

2. 다음 리뷰를 참조하세요.

더블린에서, "카트리나를 위한 장미"의 리뷰

Nancy Gibbs
팬분들은 Carla Dorothy의 이 미스터리하고 기괴한 이야기를 오랫동안 기다려 왔습니다. 저는 그들이 이 소설이 출시될 것에 매우 기뻐할 것이라는 것을 확신합니다. Dorothy는 작가로 점점 성장하고 있고, 아마 이 책은 그녀가 썼던 책 중에 최고라고 저는 생각합니다. 거기에는 많은 인물들이 등장하고, 줄거리는 잘 짜여 있으며, 독자들을 흥분시키는 여러 요소들이 있습니다. 주요 등장인물들 간의 복잡하게 얽힌 관계들은 매력적이고 독자의 주의를 끕니다. 줄거리 내에서, 이 이야기에서 세 번째로 소개되는 인물인 Harry 씨가 그 미스터리한 이슈의 해결책을 찾습니다. 개선되었으면 하는 한 가지는 바로 결말입니다. 그것은 매우 전형적인 그녀 스타일의 글이고, 이는 많은 팬들이 초반부터 의심의 여지 없이, 결말을 예측할 거라는 점입니다. 그러나, 저는 이 책의 다른 장점들이 이러한 단점을 충분히 상쇄시킨다고 믿습니다. 두말할 여지 없이, 그녀는 계속해서 그녀의 헌신적인 팬들에게 다음 소설을 기다리게 할 것입니다.

어휘 mysterious ⓐ 미스터리한 grotesque ⓐ 기괴한 confident ⓐ 확신하는 gradually ⓐdv 점점 probably ⓐdv 아마도 character ⓝ 인물, 등장인물 plot ⓝ 줄거리 well-organized ⓐ 잘 조직된 complicated ⓐ 복잡한 relationship ⓝ 관계 make up for ⓥ 보상하다 weakness ⓝ 약점, 단점

Q2. 지문에 표시된 [1], [2], [3] 그리고 [4] 중에서 다음의 문장이 들어가기에 가장 좋은 위치는?

"그것은 매우 전형적인 그녀 스타일의 글이고, 이는 많은 팬들이 초반부터 의심의 여지 없이, 결말을 예측할 거라는 점입니다."

(A) [1]
(B) [2]
(C) [3]
(D) [4]

해설 제시 문장의 it은 그녀의 앞 문장에서 언급된 "개선될 필요가 있는 한 가지" one thing을 나타내고, the outcome이라는 것은 앞 문장에 언급된 the ending과 매칭된다. 그리고 뒷 문장에서 However (반전-그러나)를 통해 이러한 단점 (this weakness)을 충분히 상쇄한다고 했으니, [2]에는 단점 또는 약점이 언급되어야 한다. 따라서 해당 문장이 들어갈 적절한 곳은 (B)이다.

SPARTA Practice Test
p.227

1. (D)	2. (B)	3. (C)	4. (A)	5. (D)
6. (B)	7. (A)	8. (D)	9. (D)	10. (A)
11. (B)	12. (C)			

[1-4] 다음 정보를 참조하세요.

건물 세입자들이 이용 가능한 추가 주차 장소

새로운 주차장 건설의 완료로, TF Square Premise는 우리 건물의 세입자들이 이용가능한 새로운 주차 공간이 있음을 알리게 되어 기쁩니다. 아쉽게도, 그 공간들의 제한으로 인해서, 적어도 3년의 임대 계약을 맺은 세입자들에게 우선순위가 돌아가게 됩니다. 3년 미만의 세입자들은 2순위가 될 것입니다.

추가 주차 공간을 신청하기 위해서, 5월 10일까지 건물 관리소로 신청 양식을 작성해서 제출해 주세요. 모든 신청자들은 다음의 자격 요건을 충족시켜야 합니다. 등록비가 위에 명시된 날짜까지 지불되어야 합니다. 차량 소유 증빙 자료로, 공식 차량 등록증 사본이 첨부되어야 합니다. 신청하는 세입자들은 현재 주차 공간이 없어야 합니다. 이미 한 곳 또는 그 이상의 주차 공간을 확보하고 있다면, 더 이상 자격이 없습니다.

5월 말까지 신청서가 검토된 후 6월 첫째 날 주차 공간이 지정될 것입니다. 문의 사항이 있다면, 959-0505로 편하게 연락 주세요.

TF Square Premise
707 Middle Boulevard
Tel. 959-0505
www.tfsquarepremise.com

어휘 slot ⓝ 장소, 위치 completion ⓝ 완성 premises ⓝ 부지 tenant ⓝ 세입자 lease ⓝ 임대 priority ⓝ 우선 순위 administration ⓝ 행정 proof ⓝ 증명(서) eligible ⓐ 자격 있는 designate ⓥ 지정하다

1. TF Square Premise의 새로운 주차공간에 대해 알 수 있는 것은?

(A) 그것들은 다른 세입자들과 공유할 수 있다.
(B) 그것들은 한 달에 한번 지불되어야 한다.
(C) 그것들은 이전보다 비싸다.
(D) 그것들은 주로 장기 계약자들이 이용 가능하다.

해설 첫 번째 문단, 두 번째 줄 "~ tenants who have at least three years of lease agreement will be given priority ~"에서, 적어도 3년 계약을 한 세입자들에게 우선 순위가 간다고 했으므로 (D)가 정답이다.

2. 주차 공간 신청 자격 요건으로 언급되지 않은 것은?
(A) 마감기한까지 관련 서류들이 제출되어야 한다.
(B) 새로운 주차 공간을 위한 비용은 입주 전에 지불되어야 한다.
(C) 각 세입자는 그들의 차량 소유권을 증명해야 한다.
(D) 신청자들은 현재 주차 공간이 없어야 한다.

해설 두번째 문단 첫 줄에서 "~, please fill in and submit an application form to the building administration office by May 10" 5월 10일까지 신청서를 작성해서 제출하고, 세 번째 줄에서 "The registration and parking fees must be paid by the date stated above" 요금을 5월 10일까지 지불하고, 네번째 줄에서 "A copy of an official vehicle registration card needs to be accompanied~" 차량 등록증도 제출하라고 했다. 즉, (A) 관련 서류가 제출되어야 하고, (C) 차량 등록증으로 차량 소유를 증명해야 하며, 다섯 번째 줄 "Tenants applying for this should currently have no parking slots~"을 보면 (D) 현재 주차 공간이 없어야 한다고 했다. 입주 전에 주차 비용을 지불하라는 언급은 없으므로 (B)가 정답이다.

3. 주차 공간 신청 시, 지원자들은 무엇을 제출해야 하는가?
(A) 차량 지불 증명서
(B) 운전 면허증
(C) 차량 등록 문서
(D) 월 명세서

해설 두 번째 문단의 세 번째 줄, "A copy of an official vehicle registration card needs to be accompanied~" 공식 차량 등록증이 동반되어야 한다고 했으므로, 신청서를 제출하면서 차량 등록증이 같이 제출되어야 함을 알 수 있으므로 (C)가 정답이다.

4. 지문에 표시된 [1], [2], [3] 그리고 [4] 중에서 다음의 문장이 들어가기에 가장 좋은 위치는?
"3년 미만의 세입자들은 2순위가 될 것입니다"
(A) [1]   (B) [2]   (C) [3]   (D) [4]

해설 기간에 따른 우선순위를 언급하는 부분이므로 [1]번 앞의 "tenants who have at least three years of lease agreement will be given priority"(적어도 3년의 계약자들이 우선순위를 받을 것이다)와 대비되는 3년 미만의 세입자들의 자격을 언급한 것으로 (A)가 적절하다.

[5-8] 다음 편지를 참조하세요.

6월 5일
Daniel McKenzie 씨
Beoulegit Corporation
450 Oakvalley Street, Podalski
Prague, 230573

귀하께,

저는 제안된 Vltava 강 활성화 건에 대해 반대를 표하고 싶습니다. Vltava 강의 부동산 소유주이자 오랜 주민인 저는, 귀사의 계획이 우리 동네에 미칠지도 모르는 상당한 부정적인 영향이 걱정됩니다. 비록 더 많은 방문객과 수익을 창출하기 때문에 대규모의 쇼핑 단지 건설이 매력적으로 보일지라도, 이것은 도로 혼잡과 강도, 소음 등의 치안과 관련한 동네의 잠재적인 문제점에 대한 심각한 부담도 초래할 수 있습니다. 게다가, 현재 다양한 새, 곤충 그리고 기타 다른 동물의 보호 구역인 근처의 Vltava 시립공원이 그 개발로 인해 부정적인 영향을 받을 수도 있습니다. 저는 우리가 자연을 훼손하기보다 보존해야 한다고 생각합니다. 저는 7월 10일에 Beoulegit Corporation 사에 의해 열리는 주민 회의에서 저의 이러한 우려의 목소리를 공식적으로 낼 계획입니다. 저는 Beoulegit Corporation 사가 그때 이러한 이슈들을 처리할 방법에 관하여 신중하게 고려하기를 희망하는 바입니다.

그럼 이만
Erica Yeshiva

어휘 opposition n 반대   revitalization n 재생   property n 부동산   impact n 효과   community n 공동체, 동네   large-scale a 큰 규모의   complex n 복합단지   congestion n 혼잡, 체증   impose v 부과하다   burden n 부담, 짐   robbery n 강도   insect n 곤충   preserve v 보존하다   voice v 목소리를 내다

5. Yeshiva 씨에 대해서 알 수 있는 것은?
(A) 그녀는 Vltava 강 근처에서 기념품점을 관리한다.
(B) 그녀는 강에서 파티를 즐긴다.
(C) 그녀는 Vltava 지역으로 최근에 전근 왔다.
(D) 그녀는 오랫동안 Vltava 강 지역에 살고 있다.

해설 두 번째 문장의 "As a property owner and long-time resident of Vltava River, ~" 부분에서 오랜 거주자라고 했으므로 (D)가 정답이다.

6. Beoulegit Corporation 사가 하려고 하는 것은?
(A) 고급 호텔을 연다
(B) 쇼핑센터를 건설한다
(C) 야생 동물 보호 구역을 개발한다
(D) 정부 시설을 설치한다

해설 도입부의 "I am concerned about ~ Although the construction of a large-scale shopping complex may seem attractive ~"을 보아, Beoulegit 사가 큰 규모의 쇼핑 단지 건설을 계획하고 있음을 알 수 있으므로 (B)가 정답이다.

7. Yeshiva의 걱정으로 언급되지 않은 것은?
(A) 그 계획이 관광산업을 망칠지도 모른다.
(B) 그 계획이 심각한 교통혼잡을 야기할지도 모른다.
(C) 그 계획이 시민들에게 해를 입힐지도 모른다.
(D) 그 계획이 동물에게 역효과를 미칠지도 모른다.

해설 (B)는 "it may also cause road congestion", (C)는 "the town's potential problems with public security such as robbery, noise, and so on." (D)는 "a variety of birds, insects, and other small animals may be adversely affected by the development" 부분을 통해 알 수 있으나, 관광객이 모이는 것은 추정되는 사실일 뿐, 걱정되는 사안은 아니므로 (A)가 정답이다.

8. 다음 표시된 [1], [2], [3], [4] 중에서 다음의 문장이 들어갈 가장 알맞은 곳은?

    "저는 Beoulegit Corporation 사가 그때 이러한 이슈들을 처리할 방법에 관하여 신중하게 고려하기를 희망하는 바입니다."

    (A) [1]　　　　(B) [2]　　　　(C) [3]　　　　(D) [4]

해설 제시 문장은 개발사인 Beoulegit Corporation 사가 '이러한 이슈(these issues)들을 심사숙고하길 바란다'는 의미로, Yeshiva가 생각하는 문제들에 대한 언급 이후에 등장하게 될 것이다. 그러므로 글의 마지막 부분인 (D)가 가장 적절하다.

[9-12] 다음 이메일을 참조하세요.

수신: Shipping Service(deliver@movieflex.net)
발신: Alyssa Monica(a.monica777@xteam.com)
날짜: 6월 20일, 화요일
제목: 서비스 요금 명세서

Movieflex 사 귀하,

저는 귀사의 IPTV(인터넷 프로토콜 텔레비전)으로부터 지난 3년 동안 많은 영화를 주문했습니다. 제가 시청하는 대부분의 영화들은 대개 찾기 쉽지 않은 독립 영화입니다. 저는 주로 이 서비스에 만족하고 있는데, 제가 구독하고 있는 서비스에 관한 5월 명세서에 최근에 오류가 발생했습니다.

저는 지금 부가세 5달러가 포함된 75달러로 디럭스 서비스를 이용하고 있습니다. 5월 명세표에 100달러가 부과되었는데, 제 생각에 이것은 귀사의 프리미엄 서비스 요금 같습니다. 게다가, 저는 UHD IPTV 서비스를 위한 새로운 셋업 박스를 갑자기 받았습니다. 저는 제 서비스를 업그레이드 한 적이 전혀 없고, 심지어, 현재 서비스에 너무도 만족하고 있습니다. 웹사이트를 통해 제 서비스 상태를 확인했을 때, 여전히 전과 같았습니다.

귀사의 고객 서비스 센터로 연락했을 때, 저는 온라인 데이터 처리에 문제가 있었다고 들었습니다. 귀사의 직원과 그 이슈를 논하면서, 저는 다른 추가적인 불만 없이 제 다음달 명세서에서 차액을 공제하기로 결정했습니다. <u>저는 그 문제가 해결되었다는 답변에 기뻤습니다.</u>

그런데, 저는 그 셋업 박스에 한 가지 추가 문의가 있습니다. 저는 제가 받은 그 박스를 어떻게 돌려보내야 할지 모르겠습니다. 제가 고객 서비스 센터에 연락해서 직원 Lillian Trisha와 이 문제를 이야기했을 때, 그녀는 저에게 반품과 배송 이슈는 당신의 부서에서 처리된다고 알려주었습니다. 거기에, 그녀는 저에게 당신의 메일 주소를 알려주었습니다. 이 물품을 제가 어떻게 돌려보내면 되는지 알려주시겠어요?

가능하면 빨리 답을 주시기를 기다리겠습니다.

감사합니다.
Alyssa Monica

어휘 independent film [n] 독립 영화　subscribe to [v] 구독하다　billing statement [n] 요금 명세서　value-added tax [n] 부가세　charge [v] 부과하다　processing [n] 처리　deduct [v] 공제하다

9. Movieflex 사에 대해 알 수 있는 것은?
    (A) 그들의 모든 고객들은 서비스 업그레이드의 기회를 얻었다.
    (B) 고객들은 영화 장르가 다양하지 않다고 느끼고 있다.
    (C) 고객 불만은 메일을 통해서만 처리한다.
    (D) 그들의 업무는 부서별로 나눠져 있다.

해설 글의 후반부를 살펴보면 "When I called the customer service center and talked an employee there—Lilian Trisha—about this, she said to me that the issues with returns and shipping are dealt with by your department." 부분을 통해, 요금 관련 문제와 배송 관련 문제는 나누어서 처리하고 있음을 알 수 있으므로 (D)가 정답이다.

10. Monica 씨에 대해 알 수 있는 것은?
    (A) 그녀는 업그레이용 장비를 최근에 받았다.
    (B) 그녀는 신규 고객이다.
    (C) 그녀는 현재 서비스가 만족스럽지 못하다.
    (D) 그녀는 추가 부과금을 지불해야 한다.

해설 두 번째 문단의 "In addition, I got a new set-up box suddenly for the UHD IPTV service." 부분을 보면 갑자기 업그레이드용 셋업 박스(장비)를 받았음을 알 수 있으므로 (A)가 정답이다.

11. Trisha 씨가 한 것은 무엇인가?
    (A) 그녀의 상사와 이야기했다
    (B) 실수를 설명했다
    (C) Monica 씨에게 이메일을 보냈다
    (D) 빠른 주문을 처리했다

해설 세 번째 문단 "When I called your customer service line, I was informed that there was a mistake in the electronic data processing."에서 처리상 실수가 있음을 인정하고, 마지막 문단 중 "When I called the customer service center and talked an employee there — Lilian Trisha — about this,"에서 이를 담당한 것이 Trisha 씨라고 했으므로 (B)가 정답이다.

12. 다음 표시된 [1], [2], [3], [4] 중에서 다음 문장이 들어가기에 가장 알맞은 곳은?

    "저는 그 문제가 해결되었다는 답변에 기뻤습니다"

    (A) [1]　　　　(B) [2]　　　　(C) [3]　　　　(D) [4]

해설 해결된 문제는 "실수로 부과된 금액"이므로 문맥상 (C)가 가장 적절하다.

DAY 14 의도 파악 및 유의어 유형

SPARTA Check-UP
p.236

1. (B)　　**2.** (A)

1. 다음 문자 메시지를 참조하세요.

> **Gilbert Amelio** 오후 2:20
> 저는 지금 Terra Tech 사 앞에 있습니다만, 여기 아무도 없는 것 같습니다. 벨을 다섯 번이나 눌렀는데 대답이 없습니다.
>
> **Dixie Lynn** 오후 2:22
> 지금요? 그거 정말 이상한데요. 제가 영업 관리자에게 바로 연락해 보고 상황을 알려줄 테니 어디 가지 마요.
>
> **Gilbert Amelio** 오후 2:23
> 어디 안 갈게요. 버스를 타고 여기 다시 오고 싶지 않아요!
>
> **Dixie Lynn** 오후 2:30
> 네, Amelio. 그들은 지금 위스콘신에서 세미나에 참석하고 있대요. 그들의 우리에게 알리는 것을 잊었다고 사과하네요. 분명히, 관리자가 입구 옆 사무실에 있을 거예요. 그분한테 관련 서류들을 맡기면 돼요.
>
> **Gilbert Amelio** 오후 2:33
> 좋아요. 문제가 없으면 연락하지 않을게요. 나중에 봐요.

어휘 in front of [prep] ~앞에　push [v] 누르다　unusual [a] 일반적이지 않은　immediately [adv] 즉시, 바로　apologize for [v] 사과하다　apparently [adv] 분명히　superintendent [n] 관리인　relevant [a] 관련된

Q1. 오후 2시 23분에, Amelio 씨가 "I won't"라고 쓴 의미는 무엇인가?
(A) 그는 그 사무실에 오지 않을 것이다.
(B) 그는 Lynn의 응답을 기다릴 것이다.
(C) 그는 Lynn의 제안을 수락하지 않을 것이다.
(D) 그는 벨을 다시 울릴 것이다.

해설 바로 앞에서 상황을 알려줄 테니 어디 가지 말라고 했고, 이에 대한 답으로 그러지 않겠다고 한 것은 답을 기다리겠다는 의미이므로 (B)가 정답이다.

2. 다음 기사문을 참조하세요.

> **Serengeti 야생동물 공원**
>
> Mugabe Mbape 씀
>
> 1971년 이래로, 중앙아프리카에 있는 Serengeti 야생동물공원은 퓨마, 사자, 코끼리, 다양한 새의 종들을 포함한 전 대륙의 고아가 되고 부상 당한 동물들의 보호소를 마련해주고 있습니다. 3000에이커 공원이 사적으로 소유되어 있고, 개인들, 회사들, 기관들의 기부금에 매우 의존하고 있습니다. The Kingdom of Universe라는 인기있는 공상과학 영화 감독으로 널리 알려진 Jonathan Splibergh 씨가 1달간의 가족 휴가를 공원 내에 위치한 통나무집에서 보낸 후, 1000만 달러를 Serengeti 야생동물 공원에 기부해 주셨습니다. "저는 공원에 있는 자원봉사자들과 직원들의 노력에 진정으로 감동을 받았고, 그들을 후원해주고 싶었습니다."라고 그가 말했습니다.

어휘 wildlife [n] 야생(동물)　shelter [n] 보호소, 피난처　orphaned [a] 고아가 된　injure [v] 부상을 입히다　continent [n] 대륙　species [n] 종　privately [adv] 개인적으로　heavily [adv] 매우　sci-fi [a] 공상과학의　donate [v] 기부하다　log cabin [n] 오두막집　support [v] 후원하다

Q2. 첫 번째 단락, 첫 번째 줄의 "shelter"와 의미상 가장 가까운 것은?
(A) 안식처
(B) 제품
(C) 기부
(D) 치료

해설 shelter는 '피난처, 보호소'라는 뜻으로, 어떠한 위험이나 재난으로부터 피하는 장소를 의미하는데 보기 중 '안식처'를 뜻하는 (A) sanctuary가 의미상 가장 가깝다.

SPARTA Practice Test
p.238

1. (C)	2. (B)	3. (A)	4. (C)	5. (A)
6. (D)	7. (B)	8. (A)	9. (D)	10. (C)
11. (C)	12. (C)	13. (D)		

[1-3] 다음 온라인 채팅을 참조하세요.

> **Matthew Johns** [오전 10:10]
> 안녕하세요. 이번 주말 박람회 일정을 다들 알고 있는지 확인하려고 해요.
>
> **Reuben Sylvia** [오전 10:12]
> 장소와 건물이 오픈하는 시간은 알지만, 언제 거기로 가야 하는지는 잘 모르겠어요.
>
> **Matthew Johns** [오전 10:15]
> Sylvia 씨, 전시 물품 정리 담당이니까, 오전 8시 30분경에 거기로 오면 돼요. 바로 뒤따라가서 도와줄게요. 아이들을 위한 제품을 낮은 곳에 둬야 하는 것을 잊지 마요.
>
> **Fang Liao** [오전 10:16]
> Min 씨하고 저는 그의 차로 가기로 약속했어요. 10시까지 거기로 가면 되는 거죠?

Matthew Johns [오전 10:17]
맞아요. 판매 설명서를 자세히 봐둬요. 부모들이랑 얘기할 때 우리 제품의 교육적 측면을 강조해 주셨으면 해요.

Fang Liao [오전 10:18]
이미 하고 있어요. 어제 Min 씨가 그 내용을 이메일로 보내 줬어요.

DK Min [오전 10:20]
본 무대에서의 제품 시연 시간은 아직 안 정해졌어요?

Matthew Johns [오전 10:22]
아직요. 근데 점심 이후가 될 것 같아요. 누가 그날 시연할지 정할 수 있어요. 누가 하든 훌륭하게 해낼 거라 확신해요. Sylvia 씨, 취합해야 할 목록을 제가 보내 드렸죠?

Reuben Sylvia [오전 10:23]
네, 맞아요. 모든 게 제대로 있는지 확인하기 위해 창고 층으로 내려갈 거예요. 그리고 내일 제 차로 옮길게요.

Matthew Johns [오전 10:25]
좋아요, Sylvia 씨. 제가 같이 갈게요. 모두 고마워요.

어휘 arrangement n 약속 be responsible for v ~을 책임지다 on display 전시 중인 give a hand v 거들어주다 description n 설명 focus on v ~에 집중하다

1. Johns 씨는 어떤 종류의 회사에서 일하겠는가?
   (A) 컨퍼런스 센터
   (B) 개인 교습소
   (C) 장난감 제조업체
   (D) 아동복 회사

   해설 10시 15분에 Johns 씨가 Just remember to arrange the products at a low-level for children에서 아이들용 제품을 아래쪽에 정리하라고 했고, 10시 17분에 I'd like you to really focus on ~ when talking to the parents.에서 부모들에게 제품의 교육적 측면을 강조해 달라고 했다. 20분에 Min 씨가 Don't we have a confirmed time for the item demonstration ~ yet?에서 제품 시연을 해야 한다고 했으므로, (C) 장난감 제조업체로 유추할 수 있다.

2. 행사장에 처음으로 도착할 사람은 누구인가?
   (A) Johns 씨
   (B) Sylvia 씨
   (C) Liao 씨
   (D) Min 씨

   해설 10시 15분에 Johns 씨가 말한 Ms. Sylvia, because you're responsible for arranging the items on display, you need to get there around 8:30 A.M.에서 Sylvia가 오전 8시 30분에 도착해야 함을 알 수 있다. 나머지는 10시 도착이므로 정답은 (B)이다.

3. 오전 10시 18분에, Liao가 말한 "I'm already on it"은 무엇을 의미하는가?
   (A) 그녀는 내용을 검토하고 있다.
   (B) 그녀는 기꺼이 제품 시연을 할 것이다.
   (C) 그녀는 박람회에 참여하는 부모들 중 한 명이다.
   (D) 그녀는 포럼에서 연설하도록 권유 받았다.

   해설 10시 17분에 Johns 씨가, Be sure you go through the sales descriptions thoroughly. ~ when talking to the parents.라고 한 부분에서, 판매 설명을 잘 확인해 두라고 했고 이에 대한 응답으로 한 긍정적인 말이므로 (A)가 정답이다.

[4-8] 다음 웹페이지와 이메일을 참조하세요.

http://www.nottinghillbook.com

Nottinghill 서점
영국의 가장 특별한 책들의 원천!
Grand Forest Square로부터 잠깐 걸어서 갈 수 있는 곳에서, 당신은 영국의 가장 위대한 문학의 일부 특별판을 마주할 수 있을 것입니다. 저희가 보유한 서적은, 영국, 웨일즈, 아일랜드, 스코틀랜드 출신의 대가들이 쓴 책들이 포함되어 있습니다. 모든 출판물은 원본이며 그들의 원어로 쓰여 있습니다.
저희는 또한 효과적인 복원 서비스와 더불어 책 보관과 보존에 대한 조언도 해드립니다. 이러한 고서 분야에 능숙한 저희 직원과 무료 상담을 받으러 오세요.
저희의 온라인 카탈로그를 클릭해서 보시면, 거기에 매우 합리적인 가격에 책을 주문하고, 댁으로 받아 보실 수도 있습니다.

온라인 카탈로그

수신: Customer Service <notinghill.cs@nottinghillbook.com>
발신: Alex Williams <a.williams@newmexico.edu>
날짜: 3월 10일
제목: 위대한 유산, Charles Dickens 지음

담당자분께,
어제 저는 Portsmouth에 있었고 당신의 훌륭한 서점에 방문할 기회가 있었습니다. 그곳에 Charles Dickens의 <위대한 유산>을 당신이 가지고 있음을 알게 되었습니다. 유감스럽게도, 그때 저는 제 지갑을 호텔방에 두고 왔다는 것을 깨달았습니다. 저는 고전문학 작품들에 대한 연간 학술 심포지움에 참석해야 했고, 제 지갑을 가지고 와서 그 책을 살 시간이 없었습니다. 행사가 끝나고 당신의 가게로 다시 갔을 때, 이미 문을 닫았더군요. 당신 서점의 쇼윈도를 보았을 때 이 이메일 주소를 보았습니다. 저는 미국의 저희 집으로 그 책이 배송 가능한지 여쭙고 싶습니다. 이 포럼이 내년에는 다른 나라에서 개최될 것이기 때문에 가까운 미래에는 런던에 다시 방문할 것 같지 않습니다. 곧 답을 듣기를 희망합니다.

진심으로,
Alex Williams

어휘 source ⓝ 원천 come across ⓥ 마주하다 unique
ⓐ 특별한 literature ⓝ 문학 master ⓝ 장인
preservation ⓝ 보존 restoration ⓝ 복원, 복구
consultation ⓝ 자문, 상담 reasonable ⓐ 합리적인
brilliant ⓐ 훌륭한

4. Nottinghill 서점에 대해 알 수 없는 것은?
(A) 다양한 언어의 책들을 보유하고 있다.
(B) 영국 Portsmouth 지역에 위치하고 있다.
(C) 새로 출판된 책들만 판다.
(D) 고객 주소로 책을 배송해 준다.

해설 (A)는 첫 번째 지문 "~ in their original languages."에서, (B)는 두 번째 지문 "Yesterday I was in Portsmouth and had an opportunity to visit your brilliant store."에서, (D)는 첫 번째 지문 마지막에 "you can order books and even get them delivered to your home ~"를 통해 확인 가능하다. (C)는 언급된 바 없다.

5. 웹페이지에서, 첫 번째 단락, 첫 번째 줄의 "come across"와 의미상 가장 가까운 것은?
(A) 발견하다
(B) 지나치다
(C) 이익을 얻다
(D) 따르다

해설 문맥상 위대한 문학작품을 만나볼 수 있다는 의미로 "발견하다"는 뜻의 (A)가 정답이다.

6. Williams 씨는 어떤 분야에서 일할 것 같은가?
(A) 건설
(B) 책 복원
(C) 회계
(D) 교육

해설 두번째 지문의 "I had to attend the annual scholarship symposium on classical literary works"에서 학술 심포지움에 참여한다는 것으로 보아 교육업계 종사자임을 추측할 수 있으므로 (D)가 정답이다.

7. 이메일의 목적은 무엇인가?
(A) 도서 이용 가능 여부를 문의하기 위해
(B) 매장의 배송 정책을 묻기 위해
(C) 온라인 카탈로그의 오류를 언급하기 위해
(D) 특별 서적의 할인을 요구하기 위해

해설 두번째 지문 중 "I would like to ask whether it would be possible to have the book shipped to my home in the U.S."에서 미국까지 해외 배송이 가능한지를 묻고 있으므로 (B)가 정답이다.

8. Williams 씨에 대해 알 수 있는 것은?
(A) 그는 미국에 살고 있다.
(B) 그는 가족과 관광차 런던에 왔다.
(C) 그는 Nottinghill Bookstore에 세 번 방문했다.
(D) 그는 그 가게에 곧 방문할 예정이다.

해설 두 번째 문단 "to my home in the U.S."에서 볼 수 있듯이, 미국에 거주하고 있음을 알 수 있으므로 (A)가 적절하다.

[9-13] 다음 기사, 일정표, 이메일을 참조하세요.

보스턴 – 보스턴 태생의 David Conte가 겨우 4살이 되었을 때, 그의 부모는 음악, 특히 피아노 연주에 있어서 그의 재능을 인지했습니다. 그가 6살이 되었을 때 그의 부모는 보스톤의 버클리 음대와 제휴된 영재 아이들을 위한 학교 프로그램에 그를 등록시켰습니다. 2년 뒤, 기본 음악 프로그램을 이수한 후, 그는 메사추세츠 음악 축제 무대에 오를 기회를 잡았습니다. 12살까지, Conte는 100편 이상의 다양한 장르의 곡을 작곡했습니다. 이제 겨우 15살인 David Conte는 이미 다양한 음악 시상식에서 전국적, 지역적으로 많은 상을 휩쓸고 있습니다. 요즘 뉴욕에 살고 있는 Conte는 영화를 위한 음악 감독, TV 광고를 위한 작곡, 뮤지컬 공연과의 협업 등 다양한 분야의 음악 활동을 이어가고 있습니다. Conte는 일년에 한 번은 그의 고향에서 정기 공연을 하고 싶어 해서, 저희가 그의 계획을 입수하는 대로 공연 정보를 여러분께 알려드리겠습니다.

XD GARDEN 극장의 11월 행사

Benjamin의 스탠딩 쇼 투어 --- 11월 5일, 오후 6시
동료들과 비평가들이 한결같이 칭찬한, Benjamin은 우리 세대의 가장 강한 희극의 대변자 중 한 명입니다. 전국적으로 유명한 희극인으로서, 그는 대중들에게 건강한 웃음을 선사하고 있습니다.
주의) 휴대전화, 카메라 또는 녹음 장비들은 쇼가 진행되는 동안 허용되지 않습니다.

David Conte --- 11월 12일, 오후 6시
보스턴 땅에서 태어난 가장 위대한 천재 음악가 David Conte는 다양한 곡을 연주할 것입니다. 그가 버클리 음대에서 작곡한 그의 작품 모음이 포함됩니다. 이 10대 신동은 내년까지는 XD GARDEN 극장에 오지 않으므로, 그의 훌륭한 피아노 선율을 들을 기회를 놓치지 마세요!

ELF the Musical --- 11월 19일, 오후 7시
모두가 좋아하는 ELF는 이번 휴가 시즌 XD GARDEN 극장에 〈ELF The Musical〉로 보스턴으로 돌아올 것입니다. 〈ELF The Musical〉은 실수로 산타의 선물 가방으로 기어들어가 북극으로 이동하게 된 어린 고아 Buddy에 대한 유쾌한 이야기입니다.

Rolling Hollywood의 콘서트 --- 11월 26일, 오후 5시
최고의 그리고 최고 판매율을 자랑하는 아티스트 Rolling Hollywood가 특별공연 "환상적인 크리스마스 콘서트"로 XD Garden 극장으로 옵니다. 이 캘리포니아 출신의 락밴드가 미국 전역을 순회하고, 마침내 이곳에 도착하게 되었습니다! 그들은 이번 콘서트가 그들이 신곡 "Rolling Christmas"를 발표했다는 점에서 매우 의미가 있다고 말했습니다.

수신: Information <info@xdgardentheater.org>
발신: Joshua Melisa <j.melisa@bkportal.net>
제목: 장애인을 위한 이용 가능 좌석
날짜: 11월 19일

XD GARDEN 극장에,

저는 지금 휠체어를 타고 있고, 이러한 어려움 때문에 공연을 잘 볼 수 없을 거라고 생각했기 때문에 당신의 극장에 가본 적이 없었습니다. 하지만 저 같은 장애인을 배려하는 당신의 극장에서 최근에 특별한 경험을 했습니다. 제가 Bejamin의 스탠딩 쇼를 즐겼다는 사실이 너무 놀라웠습니다. 저는 앞줄의 제 좌석에서 잘 보고 들을 수 있었고, 중앙 복도에서 다른 사람들과 부대끼는 상황을 겪을 필요도 없었습니다.

저는 마지막 행사를 위한 좌석을 확보할 수 없을 것 같아 걱정됩니다. 저는 가능한 한 표를 얻기 위해 노력하겠지만, 장애인을 위한 좌석이 여전히 이용 가능한지를 문의드리고자 합니다. 곧 소식을 듣기를 바랍니다.

그럼 이만
Joshua Melisa

어휘 be cognizant of ⓥ ~를 인식하다 gift ⓝ 재능
enroll in ⓥ 등록하다 gifted children ⓝ 영재 affiliated ⓐ 제휴된 compose ⓥ 작곡하다 sweep ⓥ 휩쓸다
recital ⓝ 공연 peer ⓝ 동료 critic ⓝ 비평(가)
comedic ⓐ 희극의 generation ⓝ 세대 genius ⓝ 천재
prodigy ⓝ 신동 brilliant ⓐ 훌륭한 hilarious ⓐ 유쾌한
orphan ⓝ 고아 crawl into ⓥ ~에 기어 들어가다
transport ⓥ 이동하다 disabled ⓐ 장애의 secure ⓥ 확보하다

9. Conte 씨에 대해 알 수 있는 것은?
(A) 그는 음대를 졸업했다.
(B) 그는 4세 이후로 공식적으로 음악을 공부했다.
(C) 그는 지금 광고에 등장한다.
(D) 그는 더 이상 보스톤에 살지 않는다.

해설 첫 번째 지문 중 "Nowadays, Conte is living in New York City and ~"에서 현재 뉴욕 시에 살고 있다고 했으므로 (D)가 답이다.

10. 그가 지역 축제에서 연주할 때 Conte 씨는 몇 살이었는가?
(A) 4세
(B) 6세
(C) 8세
(D) 12세

해설 첫 번째 지문에서 "When he reached age 6, his parents enrolled him in a school program for gifted children, ~ in Boston."라고 했고, 다음 문장에서 "Two years later, after completing ~ he had a chance to be on stage at the Massachusetts Music Festival."에서 2년 뒤 음악 축제에서 연주했다고 했으므로 (C)가 정답이다.

11. 이메일에서, 첫 번째 단락, 다섯 번째 줄의 "compete"와 의미상 가장 가까운 것은?
(A) 다투다
(B) 연주하다
(C) 애쓰다
(D) 공격하다

해설 "I could see and hear very well from my seat in the front row, and I didn't need to compete with the crowded situation in the central aisle with others"를 보면, 직접 경쟁한다는 의미보다 관람을 위해 복잡한 상황에서 어렵게 애쓸 필요가 없었다는 의미로 (C)가 정답이다.

12. Melisa 씨가 그의 극장 좌석에 대해 언급한 것이 아닌 것은?
(A) 무대 근처에 편리하게 위치해 있었다.
(B) 가시적으로 장애물이 없었다.
(C) 다리를 뻗을 수 있는 공간이 많았다.
(D) 중앙을 통과할 필요가 없었다.

해설 세 번째 지문을 보면 "I could see and hear very well from my seat in the front row, and I didn't need to compete with the crowded situation in the central aisle with others."에서 (A), (B), (D)를 확인할 수 있으나, 다리를 뻗는 공간에 대한 언급은 없으므로 (C)가 정답이다.

13. Melisa 씨가 다음에 참석하고 싶은 공연은 무엇인가?
(A) Benjamin's Standing Show Tour
(B) David Conte
(C) ELF the Musical
(D) Rolling Hollywood's Concert

해설 이메일에서 "I am concerned that I cannot secure a seat for your final event."라고 한 부분을 보면 마지막 공연을 보고 싶어 한다는 것을 알 수 있고, 두 번째 지문인 일정표에서 마지막 이벤트는 (D)임을 알 수 있다.

DAY 15 다중 지문 유형

SPARTA Check-UP
p.248

1. (D)

1. 다음 소책자, 이메일, 공지문을 참조하세요.

프리미엄 리조트
매년 수천 명을 끌어들이는 도심지 최대 규모의 리조트

수많은 나무, 다양한 야생동물, 그리고 맑고 순수한 계곡물이 시끌벅적한 도시의 삶에서 벗어나 휴식을 취하고 상쾌한 자연을 즐기고 싶은 분들을 환영합니다.

활동과 지역:

Green Valleyside	**Skihut Wood**	**Zulu Fields**
자전거 대여	도보길	농구 코트
스케이트 대여	자전거길	축구장
카누 대여	조깅 길	배드민턴 코트
		배구 코트

Mountain Adventure
지정 피크닉 장소
도시 주변의 뛰어난 경치
새, 꽃 그리고 야생동물 보기(동물에게 먹이를 주지 마세요)

> 모두를 위한 것이 여기 있습니다. 책임감 있게 즐겨 주시고, 우리 지역에서 즐기시는 동안 모든 리조트 규칙을 지켜 주세요.

Nick Hamilton
리조트 총괄 부장

수신: Gary D. Cohn
발신: Melissa Beth
날짜: 5월 2일
Subject: 야유회

Cohn 씨,

내 책상에 프리미엄 리조트 브로슈어를 갖다줘서 고마워요. 그 지정 피크닉 구역을 한두 번 가본 것 같아요. 거기를 가자고 한 당신의 아이디어는 6월 우리 연간 야유회에 딱일 것 같아요. 제 생각에 많은 우리 직원들이 배구와 농구를 즐기기 때문에 이 활동에 참여하는 것을 그들이 좋아할 것 같아요. 게다가, 우리는 강력한 팀워크를 발전시킬 수 있을 거라 믿어요. 서로 그룹을 만들어 경기하는 것도 좋을 것 같아요.
Min-sung, Whitney, Brian이 있는 Iris Stella의 그룹은 모두 광적인 걷기 여행자들이죠. 그들은 숲에서 길을 걷는 좋은 시간을 가질 수 있어요.

저는 이 계획을 마무리하고 발표하려고 해요. Alyssa 씨에게 우리 부서 예산 내에서 견적과 기타 서류 작업을 처리하라고 요청해 주세요.
이것들이 다 끝난 이후, 우리는 5월 12일에 있을 다음 부서 회의에서 야유회 계획을 발표할 거예요.
고마워요.

Melissa Beth
부서 책임자

공지
5월 3일자

프리미엄 리조트
우리는 이 훌륭한 장소에 오신 모든 분을 환영합니다.
최근에 시행된 몇 가지 변경사항을 확인해 주세요.

온라인 결제:
리조트 서비스 또는 활동을 결제하고자 하는 개인 또는 기관들은 우리 웹사이트 또는 휴대폰 앱을 통해서 하시길 권장합니다. 앱을 사용하시는 방문객들은 3% 할인을 받을 수 있습니다.

운동 시설 구역:
Zulu Fields의 모든 공간은 앞으로 5개월 동안 리모델링을 이유로 임시로 폐쇄됩니다. 이런 갑작스런 계획으로 인해 발생된 불편함에 진심으로 사과 드립니다.

계곡을 따라 있는 오솔길:
계곡을 따라 있는 길들은 매우 좁다는 것을 명심하세요. 자전거는 이 길을 달려서는 안 됩니다. 전 지역에 걸쳐 헬멧이나 무릎보호대 그리고 다른 유사 보호 장비들을 반드시 착용하세요.

어휘 countless [a] 셀 수 없이 많은 wildlife [n] 야생동물 pure [a] 순수한 hubbub [n] 소란스러움 feed [v] 먹이를 주다 outing [n] 야유회 favorable [a] 호의적인, 좋은 trek [v] 오래 걷다 trail [n] 길 estimate [n] 견적서 temporarily [adv] 임시로 sudden [a] 갑작스러운 path [n] 오솔길 protective [a] 보호용의 kneepad [n] 무릎 보호대

Q1. Beth 씨가 리조트에서 이미 가본 곳은 어디인가?
(A) Green Valleyside
(B) Skihut Wood
(C) Zulu Fields
(D) Mountain Adventure

해설 첫 번째 지문의 "reserved picnic spots"에 해당하는 곳이 Mountain Adventure라는 것을 알 수 있고 두 번째 지문 중 I've been there only once or twice, at the reserved picnic areas.에서 가봤다고 했으므로 (D)가 답이다.

SPARTA Practice Test p.250

1. (C)	2. (C)	3. (A)	4. (B)	5. (C)
6. (D)	7. (D)	8. (B)	9. (B)	10. (A)
11. (C)	12. (C)	13. (B)	14. (D)	15. (A)

[1-5] 다음 광고와 기사문을 참조하세요.

Greenwich 주식 거래소

Fairfax, Virginia

The Glare Metal 펀드

지금 현재 여러분은 이용 가능한 가장 경쟁력 있는 주식 펀드로부터 뛰어난 재정적 수익을 즐길 수 있습니다; 바로 The Glare Metal 펀드입니다. 그 펀드는 남아공, 케냐, 에디오피아와 아프리카의 다른 국가들에서 본사를 운영하는 가장 크고, 오래되고, 안전한 회사 주식들에 특화되어 있습니다.

그 펀드는 해당 범주의 다른 펀드들을 쉽게 누르고, 지난 3년 동안 20퍼센트의 평균 성장률을 보이고 있습니다. 그 성장이 너무 뛰어나서 〈Top Stock Trade 매거진〉에 언급되었습니다. 이 주식 펀드에 투자하는 것은 누구에게나 쉽습니다. 여러분이 해야 하는 것은 우리 지역 지점이나 온라인으로 등록하는 것입니다. 그 후, 여러분이 지정하는 수량이 여러분의 적립 은행계좌에서 매달 Glare Metal 펀드 계좌로 자동 이체될 것입니다. 게다가, 여러분은 온라인 주식 거래소로부터 쉽게 그 수량을 변경하실 수 있습니다. 또한 언제든지 자동이체를 일시 정지시킬 수 있습니다.

더 많은 정보와 세부사항을 www.greenwichstock.com/glaremetalfund에서 찾아 보세요.

* 계좌를 개설하기 위해 초기 보증금으로 최소 1000달러 또는 US 달러로 이에 상응하는 금액이 요구됩니다.

---

http://www.topstocktrade.com

여러분의 돈이 여러분을 위해 운용되도록 하기

Finance 지 Lynn M. Martin 작가 작성
게시: 10월 1일, 오전 10시 20분

특정 주식 펀드에 투자하는 것은 시간 소비적이고 복잡하곤 합니다. 그러나 이 절차는 오늘날 매우 빠르게 변화하고 있습니다. 신규 고객을 모으고자 하는 투자 회사들이 손쉽게 고객의 계좌에서 주식 펀드로 돈을 이체시킬 수 있는 온라인 거래 시스템을 가지고, 거래 방식을 훨씬 더 유연하게 하고 있습니다. Glare Metal 펀드는 이런 혁신적인 방법의 뛰어난 예입니다.

단 하나의 문제점은 계좌 개설 요건인데, Greenwich 사처럼, 일반적으로 고객들이 대면으로 그것에 동의해야 한다는 것입니다. Greenwich 사가 말하기를, 이러한 절차는 불합리하지 않다고 합니다. 그러나, 이와 대조적으로 저는 각 지점을 방문해야 한다는 불편함과, 이는 온라인 거래 시스템으로서 전적으로 웹을 기반으로 할 수 없다는 생각이 강하게 듭니다.

저의 10월 10일 기사문에, 온라인 방문객들은 이 문제들과 펀드에 대한 전반적인 동향에 대해 해당 펀드의 선임 매니저인 Dorothy Rebecca 씨와 실시간 인터넷 방송 인터뷰를 시청할 기회를 갖게 될 것입니다.

어휘 specialize in ⓥ ~로 특화하다 average ⓥ 평균으로 하다 growth rate ⓝ 성장률 beat ⓥ 이기다 designate ⓥ 지정하다 sign up ⓥ 등록하다 transfer ⓥ 이체하다 deposit ⓝ 보증, 적립 stock exchange ⓝ 주식거래(소) equivalent ⓐ 상응하는 time-consuming ⓐ 시간 소비적인 flexible ⓐ 유연한, 융통성 있는 commonly ⓐdv 일반적으로 inconvenient ⓐ 불편한 real-time ⓝ 실시간

1. 광고에 따르면, Glare Metal Fund는 무엇에 중점을 두고 있는가?
   (A) 작은 회사들
   (B) 신규 회사들
   (C) 국제적 회사들
   (D) 미국 회사들

   해설 첫 번째 지문 중 "The fund specializes in stocks ~ and other countries in Africa."을 보면 아프리카 지역에 본사를 운영하는 해외 회사들의 주식에 특화되어 있다고 했으므로 (C)가 답이다.

2. 왜 〈Top Stock Trade 매거진〉이 언급되는가?
   (A) 새로운 주식 펀드를 발표하기 위해
   (B) 왜 성장률이 악화되었는지 설명하기 위해
   (C) 서비스 장점을 지지하기 위해
   (D) 새로운 투자 규칙을 제안하기 위해

   해설 첫 번째 지문의 "The fund has averaged an impressive 20% growth rate in the past three years, ~ so it was even mentioned in The Magazine of Top Stock Trade."를 보면 이 펀드의 장점을 언급하면서 잡지를 언급했으므로 (C)가 정답이다.

3. Glare Metal Fund에 대한 장점으로 언급되지 않은 것은?
   (A) 전문가들로부터의 조언 입수
   (B) 온라인 시스템 활용
   (C) 월간 수량 선택하기
   (D) 달러나 다른 통화로 적립

   해설 첫 번째 지문 중, (B) "All you have to do is sign up ~ online."과 "our online stock exchange"에서 온라인 시스템 이용이 가능하다는 점, (C) "the amount you designate will be automatically transferred ~ every month" 매월 수량을 지정할 수 있다는 점, (D) "A minimum of $1,000 or the equivalent amount in U.S. dollars" 미국 달러와 그에 상응하는 화폐도 가능하다는 했으나, (A)는 언급되지 않았다.

4. Martin 씨가 동의하지 않은 Glare Metal Fund의 특징은 무엇인가?
   (A) 이체의 어려운 점
   (B) 오프라인으로 인증 절차가 필요함
   (C) 성장률에 대한 데이터 부족
   (D) 거래 시작 절차의 지연

   해설 Martin 씨는 두 번째 지문인 기사의 작성자로, 두 번째 문단에서 "The only problem is that ~ to agree with it in person."과 "I strongly think that it is a little inconvenient in terms of visiting each branch,"를 보면 지점을 직접 방문해야 하는 불편함이 있다고 했으므로 (B)가 정답이다.

5. 10월 10일에는 무슨 일이 있을 것인가?
   (A) 성장률 관련 차트가 업로드될 것이다.
   (B) 웹 서버가 보안 부분에 있어 업데이트될 것이다.
   (C) 작가는 펀드 담당자와 이야기를 나눌 것이다.
   (D) 거래를 위한 모든 비밀번호는 변경될 것이다.

   해설 두 번째 지문 마지막 부분에 "In my October 10 article, online visitors will have a chance to watch my real-time webcast interview with ~"라며 펀드 담당자와 실시간 인터뷰가 있을 거라고 했으므로 (C)가 적절하다.

[6-10] 다음 회람과 이메일을 참조하세요.

수신: 전 직원
발신: 인사부장
답신: 지원 절차

각 부서의 누구든지 이번 승진 신청에 지원하고자 한다면, 다음 문서를 다음 주인 5월 1일까지 제출해 주세요.
- 사진이 첨부된 신분증 사본과 공식 지원서 양식
- 이전 또는 현재 관리자로부터 3장의 추천서와 추천인 연락처 정보

승인 위원회는 당신의 지원 서류를 철저히 검토할 것이며, 각 부서에서 3명만 본인의 업무 능력과 앞으로의 기획 능력에 관해 5월 20일에 5분 발표를 할 기회를 얻게 될 것입니다. 이사회가 어떤 후보자가 승진에 적합한지 결정하기 전에 여러 번의 면접이 이어질 것입니다. 최종 결정 이후, 승진 예정자는 6월 초까지 메일을 통해 통지 받을 것입니다. 문의가 있으시다면, timberton@dreamculture.org로 저에게 메일 보내주시고, 가능하면 빨리 답을 드리도록 하겠습니다. 여러분의 관심에 감사 드립니다.

그럼 이만
Ganette Timberton
인사과

수신: Ganette Timberton ⟨timberton@dreamculture.org⟩
발신: Jacy Swift ⟨j.swift@dreamculture.org⟩
제목: 승진 지원

지원 서류와 함께 제출해야 하는 추천서에 관해 몇 가지 문의가 있어서 이메일을 씁니다. 저는 여기 Dream Culture 사에서 딱 1년 정도 일했고, 불행히도, 제 상사 세 명 중 한 명인 Daven 씨는 6개월 전에 퇴사하셔서, 두 분만 여기서 일합니다. 지금 그와 연락할 방법도 없을 뿐만 아니라, 그는 저와 몇 개월만 같이 일했기 때문에 제 업무 능력에 대해 잘 모릅니다. 다른 상사인 Rebecca 씨와 Steven 씨는 추천서를 써주기로 동의했습니다.
그래도 지원을 위해 추가로 한 장의 추천서를 제출해야 하나요? Daven 씨에게 퇴사했음에도 불구하고 저를 위해 추천서를 써 달라고 요구해야 하나요? 그와 연락이 닿기까지 제 예상보다 시간이 더 걸릴지도 모르니, 가능한 한 빨리 알려주시기 바랍니다.

진심으로,
Jacy Swift
마케팅 부서 (내선번호: 7810)

어휘 promotion n 승진 following a 다음의 identification n 신분 reference n 추천(인) committee n 위원회 work capacity n 직무 능력 planning ability n 기획력 successful candidate n 합격자

6. 다음 중 5월 말 전까지 예정된 것이 아닌 것은?
   (A) 면접
   (B) 발표
   (C) 양식 제출
   (D) 승진 공지

   해설 첫 번째 지문 후반부 "After the final decision, the successful candidates will be notified via e-mail by the beginning of June."에서 6월 초에 승진 예정자에게 알려준다고 했으므로 정답은 (D)이다.

7. Jacy Swift가 걱정하고 있는 것은?
   (A) 그녀의 사진 신분증
   (B) 그녀의 이전 경력
   (C) 그녀의 의사소통 기술
   (D) 그녀의 추천인들

   해설 상관 중 한 명이 퇴직한 상황으로, "one of my three bosses, Mr. Daven, resigned from his position six months ago, so just two bosses remain."라며 추천인 1명이 부족함을 걱정하고 있으므로 (D)가 답이다.

8. Jacy Swift에 대해 추론할 수 있는 것은?
   (A) 그녀는 훌륭한 직무 능력을 보여주고 있다.
   (B) 그녀는 상사와의 연락을 시도할지도 모른다.
   (C) 그녀는 현재 다른 지점에서 일하고 있다.
   (D) 그녀의 상관이 그녀의 요청을 거절했다.

   해설 두 번째 지문 후반부의 "Do I still have to submit one more letter to apply for the promotion?" 이하 내용을 보면, 추가로 추천서가 필요할 경우 사임한 상사에게 연락을 취할 것임을 유추할 수 있으므로 (B)가 정답이다.

9. Rebecca 씨는 누구인가?
   (A) 인사과 부장
   (B) 마케팅 부서의 직원
   (C) 판매부서의 부장
   (D) 승인 위원회의 일원

   해설 두 번째 지문 "My other current bosses, Ms. Rebecca and ~ write a letter of recommendation."을 통해 추천서를 써주기로 한 사람이 현재의 상사임을 알 수 있고 발신자 정보에서 Jacy Swift는 "Marketing Division(Extension: 7810)"에서 마케팅 부서 소속임을 알 수 있으므로 Rebecca 씨 역시 마케팅부서의 일원임을 알 수 있다. 따라서 (B)가 정답이다.

10. 이 이메일은 언제 쓰였을 것 같은가?
    (A) 4월
    (B) 5월
    (C) 6월
    (D) 7월

    해설 첫 번째 지문 도입부에서 "If anyone wants to apply for a promotion in their department, please submit the following documents by next week, May 1st"라고 했다. 다음주 5월 1일이라고 했고 제출 서류와 관련하여 문의하는 이메일로 보아 제출일 전인 4월 중 쓰였음을 알 수 있으므로 (A)가 정답이다.

[11-15] 다음 메뉴, 주문서 그리고 이메일을 참조하세요.

Gourmet Catering 사 메뉴

76 Lunger Drive #80, Bloomsburg, PA 17815, USA

런치 – 1인당 25달러, 11:00 A.M. – 2:00 P.M.
두 개의 파스타 음식
(파스타 메뉴를 보세요)

버거 바이츠 – 1인당 15달러
10:00 A.M. – 1:30 P.M.
주방장이 제공하는 다양한 버거
8월 30일까지 이용 가능

간편한 디너 – 1인당 25달러
5:00 P.M. – 6:00 P.M.
두 개의 파스타 음식
(파스타 메뉴를 보세요)

디럭스 디너 – 1인당 30달러
6:00 P.M. – 8:00 P.M.
두 개의 파스타 음식과 샐러드
(파스타 메뉴를 보세요)

슈페리얼 디너 – 1인당 50달러
5:00 P.M. – 9:00 P.M.
음료 및 디저트뿐 아니라, 두 개의 메인 음식과 디럭스 메뉴에서 두 접시 포함

오리엔탈 음식 – 1인당 32달러
5:00 P.M. – 8:00 P.M.
다양한 동남아 음식이 포함.
금요일과 토요일 저녁만 이용 가능

유의:
모든 주문은 배송 시간 최소 이틀 전에 이루어져야 합니다. 펜실베니아 Bloomsburg 이내 30명 이상 주문 건에 대해 무료 배송. 50명 이하인 경우, Bloomsburg 교외 20마일 이상 떨어진 지역 배송에는 5% 추가 금액이 있습니다.

Gourmet Catering 사 (GCC) 온라인 주문 확정서

'완료' 버튼을 클릭하기 전에 다음 주문 정보를 신중히 확인하세요. 구매 증명으로 이 페이지를 출력해 두세요.

주문 번호: AU2019921
배송지: Randall Seedorff (Angel Power Energy)
배송 날짜와 시간: 8월 20일 금요일 오전 11:30(런치), 오후 6:30(디너)
주소: 32 Ideal Park Road, Catawissa, PA 17820
전화: 570-799-5006
이메일: r.seedorff@angelpowerenergy.net

주문 날짜/시간: 8월 17일, 오후 2:35
계산서 청구: Angel Power Energy
주소: 145 Brooklyn Avenue, Brooklyn, NY, 111213
전화: 718-735-4400

품목	수량	인당 가격	총합
런치	48명	25달러	1,200달러
슈페리얼 디너	45명	50달러	2,250달러
		배송 5%	172.50달러
		판매 세금 7%	241.50달러
		총합	3,864달러

유의: 해당 시간에 제가 없을 때 배송지에 도착했다면, 저에게 710-2083-1923으로 문자 넣어 주세요.

| 주문 처리자 | Scott Fitzgerald |

수신: GCC Orders <orders@gourmentcatering.com>
발신: Randall Seedorff <r.seedorff@angelpowerengery.net>
제목: 주문번호 AU2019921
날짜: 8월 19일

관계자분께,

저는 8월 17일자 주문을 변경하고자 합니다. 저희는 런치 서비스 세트에 추가 방문객들이 있을 것 같아서, 48명에서 55명으로 주문을 바꾸고자 합니다. 게다가, 12시 30분에 제공되는 버거 바이츠에 15명을 추가하고 싶습니다. 송장을 다시 계산하셔서 가능한 한 빨리 저에게 다시 보내주시면 감사하겠습니다.

그럼 이만,

Randall Seedorff
매니저, 인사과
Angel Power Energy

어휘 per [prep] ~당, 마다 dish [n] 음식, 요리 plate [n] 음식 cuisine [n] 요리 proof [n] 증빙, 증명 appreciate [v] 감사하다 recalculate [v] 다시 계산하다 invoice [n] 송장

11. 8월 20일에 배송되지 않는 음식은 무엇인가?
    (A) 파스타
    (B) 샐러드
    (C) 아시아 음식
    (D) 음료

해설 두 번째 지문을 보면 Lunch와 Superior Dinner가 주문되어 있다. 첫 번째 지문에서, Lunch에 (A) Pasta가, Superior Dinner에 (D) Beverage(drinks)가 있고, 여기에는 Deluxe가 포함된다고 했으므로 (B) Salad까지 포함된다. (C) Asian dish는 해당되지 않는다.

12. Seedorff 씨의 주문에 대해 알 수 있는 것은?
(A) 100명 이상의 단체 주문이다.
(B) 무료 후식과 배송을 받을 수 있다.
(C) Bloomsburg로부터 20마일 이상 떨어진 곳으로 배송을 요청한다.
(D) 전화로 배송 이틀 전에 주문이 이루어졌다.

해설 두 번째 지문에 Delivery 5%가 붙어 있고, 첫 번째 지문 하단 "For orders for under 50 people, there is a 5% surcharge ~ Bloomsburg."을 통해 50명 미만, Bloomsburg로부터 20마일 이상 떨어진 지역에 있다는 것을 알 수 있으므로 (C)가 정답이다.

13. 이메일의 목적은 무엇인가?
(A) 회사를 축하하기 위해
(B) 주문을 업데이트하기 위해
(C) 행사를 위한 최상의 메뉴를 물어보기 위해
(D) 할인을 요구하기 위해

해설 세 번째 지문의 도입부 "I would like to change my order submitted on August 17"에서 주문을 변경하고 싶다고 했으므로 (B)가 정답이다.

14. Scott Fitzgerald는 누구일 것 같은가?
(A) Seedorff 씨의 방문객
(B) Angel Power Energy 사의 인사과 매니저
(C) 배송 담당자
(D) 음식 공급업체 직원

해설 두 번째 지문 맨 아래 order processed by(주문 처리자)로 Scott Fitzerald 씨가 언급되었으므로 Angel Power Energy 사의 음식 배송 서비스 주문을 받은 Scott 씨는 Gourmet Catering 사 즉, 음식 공급업체의 직원으로 볼 수 있으므로 (D)가 정답이다.

15. Seedorff 씨의 품목 추가 요청은 왜 거절될 것 같은가?
(A) Gourmet Catering 사는 이틀 전 공지를 요구한다.
(B) 임시 품절 상태이다.
(C) 제한된 기간에만 이용 가능하다.
(D) 배달 제한을 넘은 곳에 위치한다.

해설 첫 번째 지문의 유의사항 "All orders must be made at least two days before the delivery time."에서 변경 요청은 배송 이틀 전에 해야 한다고 했고, 두 번째 지문에서 배송일이 8월 20일인데 세 번째 지문에서 추가 요청을 한 날짜가 8월 19일로 배송 하루 전이기 때문에 (A)가 답임을 알 수 있다.

실전 모의고사 정답

1. (C)	2. (D)	3. (A)	4. (B)	5. (C)
6. (A)	7. (C)	8. (C)	9. (B)	10. (A)
11. (A)	12. (C)	13. (B)	14. (C)	15. (B)
16. (C)	17. (C)	18. (B)	19. (B)	20. (C)
21. (C)	22. (C)	23. (B)	24. (C)	25. (C)
26. (A)	27. (C)	28. (A)	29. (B)	30. (C)
31. (B)	32. (B)	33. (B)	34. (C)	35. (A)
36. (B)	37. (A)	38. (A)	39. (B)	40. (D)
41. (B)	42. (D)	43. (C)	44. (D)	45. (A)
46. (C)	47. (B)	48. (C)	49. (A)	50. (B)
51. (C)	52. (C)	53. (A)	54. (C)	55. (C)
56. (C)	57. (B)	58. (D)	59. (A)	60. (B)
61. (C)	62. (A)	63. (C)	64. (D)	65. (D)
66. (B)	67. (A)	68. (A)	69. (A)	70. (B)
71. (C)	72. (B)	73. (D)	74. (B)	75. (B)
76. (C)	77. (B)	78. (C)	79. (C)	80. (D)
81. (A)	82. (B)	83. (C)	84. (B)	85. (B)
86. (C)	87. (D)	88. (A)	89. (C)	90. (B)
91. (D)	92. (C)	93. (C)	94. (B)	95. (A)
96. (B)	97. (A)	98. (A)	99. (C)	100. (A)
101. (B)	102. (A)	103. (A)	104. (B)	105. (D)
106. (A)	107. (D)	108. (C)	109. (A)	110. (A)
111. (A)	112. (A)	113. (B)	114. (C)	115. (A)
116. (B)	117. (C)	118. (A)	119. (B)	120. (B)
121. (A)	122. (D)	123. (C)	124. (A)	125. (C)
126. (B)	127. (C)	128. (C)	129. (C)	130. (A)
131. (C)	132. (C)	133. (B)	134. (C)	135. (C)
136. (A)	137. (C)	138. (C)	139. (D)	140. (C)
141. (C)	142. (C)	143. (A)	144. (B)	145. (D)
146. (C)	147. (C)	148. (C)	149. (C)	150. (B)
151. (D)	152. (D)	153. (B)	154. (C)	155. (B)
156. (B)	157. (A)	158. (C)	159. (C)	160. (A)
161. (D)	162. (D)	163. (C)	164. (A)	165. (C)
166. (B)	167. (B)	168. (B)	169. (B)	170. (C)
171. (B)	172. (B)	173. (B)	174. (A)	175. (A)
176. (B)	177. (B)	178. (D)	179. (A)	180. (B)
181. (C)	182. (A)	183. (B)	184. (C)	185. (B)
186. (B)	187. (D)	188. (D)	189. (A)	190. (C)
191. (B)	192. (D)	193. (C)	194. (B)	195. (D)
196. (D)	197. (C)	198. (A)	199. (C)	200. (B)